DRAMA
for Students

Advisors

Jayne M. Burton is a teacher of secondary English and an adjunct professor for Northwest Vista College in San Antonio, TX.

Klaudia Janek is the school librarian at the International Academy in Bloomfield Hills, Michigan. She holds an MLIS degree from Wayne State University, a teaching degree from Rio Salado College, and a bachelor of arts degree in international relations from Saint Joseph's College. She is the IB Extended Essay Coordinator and NCA AdvancEd co-chair at her school. She is an IB workshop leader for International Baccalaureate North America, leading teacher training for IB school librarians and extended essay coordinators. She has been happy to serve the Michigan Association for Media in Education as a board member and past president at the regional level, advocating for libraries in Michigan schools.

Greg Bartley is an English teacher in Virginia. He holds an M.A.Ed. in English Education from Wake Forest University and a B.S. in Integrated Language Arts Education from Miami University.

Sarah Clancy teaches IB English at the International Academy in Bloomfield Hills, Michigan. She is a member of the National Council of Teachers of English and Michigan Speech Coaches, Inc. Sarah earned her undergraduate degree from Kalamazoo College and her Master's of Education from Florida Southern College. She coaches the high-ranking forensics team and is the staff adviser of the school newspaper, *Overachiever*.

Karen Dobson is a teen/adult librarian at Plymouth District Library in Plymouth, Michigan. She holds a Bachelor of Science degree from Oakland University and an MLIS from Wayne State University and has served on many committees through the Michigan Library Association.

Tom Shilts is the youth librarian at the Okemos branch of Capital Area District Library in Okemos, Michigan. He holds an MSLS degree from Clarion University of Pennsylvania and an MA in U.S. History from the University of North Dakota.

DRAMA
for Students

**Presenting Analysis, Context, and Criticism
on Commonly Studied Dramas**

VOLUME 33

Sara Constantakis, Project Editor

Foreword by Carole L. Hamilton

GALE
CENGAGE Learning·

Farmington Hills, Mich • San Francisco • New York • Waterville, Maine
Meriden, Conn • Mason, Ohio • Chicago

GALE
CENGAGE Learning·

Drama for Students, Volume 33

Project Editor: Sara Constantakis

Rights Acquisition and Management: Ashley Maynard, Carissa Poweleit

Composition: Evi Abou-El-Seoud

Manufacturing: Rhonda Dover

Imaging: John Watkins

For product information and technology assistance, contact us at
Gale Customer Support, 1-800-877-4253.
For permission to use material from this text or product,
submit all requests online at **www.cengage.com/permissions.**
Further permissions questions can be emailed to
permissionrequest@cengage.com

While every effort has been made to ensure the reliability of the information presented in this publication, Gale, a part of Cengage Learning, does not guarantee the accuracy of the data contained herein. Gale accepts no payment for listing; and inclusion in the publication of any organization, agency, institution, publication, service, or individual does not imply endorsement of the editors or publisher. Errors brought to the attention of the publisher and verified to the satisfaction of the publisher will be corrected in future editions.

Gale
27500 Drake Rd.
Farmington Hills, MI, 48331-3535

ISBN-13: 978-1-4103-1300-3
ISSN 1094-9232

This title is also available as an e-book.
ISBN-13: 978-1-4103-1301-0
Contact your Gale, a part of Cengage Learning sales representative for ordering information.

Printed in Mexico
1 2 3 4 5 6 7 20 19 18 17 16

Table of Contents

The Study of Drama

We study drama in order to learn what meaning others have made of life, to comprehend what it takes to produce a work of art, and to glean some understanding of ourselves. Drama produces in a separate, aesthetic world, a moment of being for the audience to experience, while maintaining the detachment of a reflective observer.

Drama is a representational art, a visible and audible narrative presenting virtual, fictional characters within a virtual, fictional universe. Dramatic realizations may pretend to approximate reality or else stubbornly defy, distort, and deform reality into an artistic statement. From this separate universe that is obviously not "real life" we expect a valid reflection upon reality, yet drama never is mistaken for reality—the methods of theater are integral to its form and meaning. Theater is art, and art's appeal lies in its ability both to approximate life and to depart from it. For in intruding its distorted version of life into our consciousness, art gives us a new perspective and appreciation of life and reality. Although all aesthetic experiences perform this service, theater does it most effectively by creating a separate, cohesive universe that freely acknowledges its status as an art form.

And what is the purpose of the aesthetic universe of drama? The potential answers to such a question are nearly as many and varied as there are plays written, performed, and enjoyed. Dramatic texts can be problems posed, answers asserted, or moments portrayed. Dramas (tragedies as well as comedies) may serve strictly "to ease the anguish of a torturing hour" (as stated in William Shakespeare's *A Midsummer Night's Dream*)—to divert and entertain—or aspire to move the viewer to action with social issues. Whether to entertain or to instruct, affirm or influence, pacify or shock, dramatic art wraps us in the spell of its imaginary world for the length of the work and then dispenses us back to the real world, entertained, purged, as Aristotle said, of pity and fear, and edified—or at least weary enough to sleep peacefully.

It is commonly thought that theater, being an art of performance, must be experienced—seen—in order to be appreciated fully. However, to view a production of a dramatic text is to be limited to a single interpretation of that text—all other interpretations are for the moment closed off, inaccessible. In the process of producing a play, the director, stage designer, and performers interpret and transform the script into a work of art that always departs in some measure from the author's original conception. Novelist and critic Umberto Eco, in his *The Role of the Reader: Explorations in the Semiotics of Texts* (Indiana University Press, 1979), explained, "In short, we can say that every performance offers us a complete and satisfying version of the work, but at the same time makes it incomplete for us, because it cannot simultaneously give all the other artistic solutions which the work may admit."

Thus Laurence Olivier's coldly formal and neurotic film presentation of Shakespeare's *Hamlet* (in which he played the title character as well as directed) shows marked differences from subsequent adaptations. While Olivier's Hamlet is clearly entangled in a Freudian relationship with his mother Gertrude, he would be incapable of shushing her with the impassioned kiss that Mel Gibson's mercurial Hamlet (in director Franco Zeffirelli's 1990 film) does. Although each of performances rings true to Shakespeare's text, each is also a mutually exclusive work of art. Also important to consider are the time periods in which each of these films was produced: Olivier made his film in 1948, a time in which overt references to sexuality (especially incest) were frowned upon. Gibson and Zeffirelli made their film in a culture more relaxed and comfortable with these issues. Just as actors and directors can influence the presentation of drama, so too can the time period of the production affect what the audience will see.

A play script is an open text from which an infinity of specific realizations may be derived. Dramatic scripts that are more open to interpretive creativity (such as those of Ntozake Shange and Tomson Highway) actually require the creative improvisation of the production troupe in order to complete the text. Even the most prescriptive scripts (those of Neil Simon, Lillian Hellman, and Robert Bolt, for example), can never fully control the actualization of live performance, and circumstantial events, including the attitude and receptivity of the audience, make every performance a unique event. Thus, while it is important to view a production of a dramatic piece, if one wants to understand a drama fully it is equally important to read the original dramatic text.

The reader of a dramatic text or script is not limited by either the specific interpretation of a given production or by the unstoppable action of a moving spectacle. The reader of a dramatic text may discover the nuances of the play's language, structure, and events at their own pace. Yet studied alone, the author's blueprint for artistic production does not tell the whole story of a play's life and significance. One also needs to assess the play's critical reviews to discover how it resonated to cultural themes at the time of its debut and how the shifting tides of cultural interest have revised its interpretation and impact on audiences. And to do this, one needs to know a little about the culture of the times which produced the play as well as the author who penned it.

Drama for Students supplies this material in a useful compendium for the student of dramatic theater. Covering a range of dramatic works that span from 442 BCE to the 1990s, this book focuses on significant theatrical works whose themes and form transcend the uncertainty of dramatic fads. These are plays that have proven to be both memorable and teachable. *Drama for Students* seeks to enhance appreciation of these dramatic texts by providing scholarly materials written with the secondary and college/university student in mind. It provides for each play a concise summary of the plot and characters as well as a detailed explanation of its themes. In addition, background material on the historical context of the play, its critical reception, and the author's life help the student to understand the work's position in the chronicle of dramatic history. For each play entry a new work of scholarly criticism is also included, as well as segments of other significant critical works for handy reference. A thorough bibliography provides a starting point for further research.

This series offers comprehensive educational resources for students of drama. *Drama for Students* is a vital book for dramatic interpretation and a valuable addition to any reference library.

Sources

Eco, Umberto, *The Role of the Reader: Explorations in the Semiotics of Texts*, Indiana University Press, 1979.

Carole L. Hamilton
Author and Instructor of English at Cary Academy, Cary, North Carolina

Introduction

Purpose of the Book

The purpose of *Drama for Students* (*DfS*) is to provide readers with a guide to understanding, enjoying, and studying dramas by giving them easy access to information about the work. Part of Gale's "For Students" literature line, *DfS* is specifically designed to meet the curricular needs of high school and undergraduate college students and their teachers, as well as the interests of general readers and researchers considering specific plays. While each volume contains entries on "classic" dramas frequently studied in classrooms, there are also entries containing hard-to-find information on contemporary plays, including works by multicultural, international, and women playwrights. Entries profiling film versions of plays not only diversify the study of drama but support alternate learning styles, media literacy, and film studies curricula as well.

The information covered in each entry includes an introduction to the play and the work's author; a plot summary, to help readers unravel and understand the events in a drama; descriptions of important characters, including explanation of a given character's role in the drama as well as discussion about that character's relationship to other characters in the play; analysis of important themes in the drama; and an explanation of important literary techniques and movements as they are demonstrated in the play.

In addition to this material, which helps the readers analyze the play itself, students are also provided with important information on the literary and historical background informing each work. This includes a historical context essay, a box comparing the time or place the drama was written to modern Western culture, a critical essay, and excerpts from critical essays on the play. A unique feature of *DfS* is a specially commissioned critical essay on each drama, targeted toward the student reader.

The "literature to film" entries on plays vary slightly in form, providing background on film technique and comparison to the original, literary version of the work. These entries open with an introduction to the film, which leads directly into the plot summary. The summary highlights plot changes from the play, key cinematic moments, and/or examples of key film techniques. As in standard entries, there are character profiles (noting omissions or additions, and identifying the actors), analysis of themes and how they are illustrated in the film, and an explanation of the cinematic style and structure of the film. A cultural context section notes any time period or setting differences from that of the original work, as well as cultural differences between the time in which the original work was written and the time in which the film adaptation was made. A film entry concludes with a critical overview and critical essays on the film.

To further help today's student in studying and enjoying each play or film, information on audiobooks and other media adaptations is provided (if available), as well as suggestions for works of fiction, nonfiction, or film on similar themes and topics. Classroom aids include ideas for research papers and lists of critical and reference sources that provide additional material on each drama. Film entries also highlight signature film techniques demonstrated, as well as suggesting media literacy activities and prompts to use during or after viewing a film.

Selection Criteria

The titles for each volume of *DfS* are selected by surveying numerous sources on notable literary works and analyzing course curricula for various schools, school districts, and states. Some of the sources surveyed include: high school and undergraduate literature anthologies and textbooks; lists of award-winners, and recommended titles, including the Young Adult Library Services Association (YALSA) list of best books for young adults. Films are selected both for the literary importance of the original work and the merits of the adaptation (including official awards and widespread public recognition).

Input solicited from our expert advisory board—consisting of educators and librarians—guides us to maintain a mix of "classic" and contemporary literary works, a mix of challenging and engaging works (including genre titles that are commonly studied) appropriate for different age levels, and a mix of international, multicultural and women authors. These advisors also consult on each volume's entry list, advising on which titles are most studied, most appropriate, and meet the broadest interests across secondary (grades 7–12) curricula and undergraduate literature studies.

How Each Entry Is Organized

Each entry, or chapter, in *DfS* focuses on one play. Each entry heading lists the full name of the play, the author's name, and the date of the play's publication. The following elements are contained in each entry:

Introduction: a brief overview of the drama which provides information about its first appearance, its literary standing, any controversies surrounding the work, and major conflicts or themes within the work. Film entries identify the original play and provide understanding of the film's reception and reputation, along with that of the director.

Author Biography: in play entries, this section includes basic facts about the author's life, and focuses on events and times in the author's life that inspired the drama in question.

Plot Summary: a description of the major events in the play. Subheads demarcate the play's various acts or scenes. Plot summaries of films are used to uncover plot differences from the original play, and to note the use of certain film angles or techniques.

Characters: an alphabetical listing of major characters in the play. Each character name is followed by a brief to an extensive description of the character's role in the play, as well as discussion of the character's actions, relationships, and possible motivation. In film entries, omissions or changes to the cast of characters of the film adaptation are mentioned here, and the actors' names—and any awards they may have received—are also included.

Characters are listed alphabetically by last name. If a character is unnamed—for instance, the Stage Manager in *Our Town*—the character is listed as "The Stage Manager" and alphabetized as "Stage Manager." If a character's first name is the only one given, the name will appear alphabetically by the first name. Variant names are also included for each character. Thus, the nickname "Babe" would head the listing for a character in *Crimes of the Heart,* but below that listing would be her less-mentioned married name "Rebecca Botrelle."

Themes: a thorough overview of how the major topics, themes, and issues are addressed within the play. Each theme discussed appears in a separate subhead. While the key themes often remain the same or similar when a play is adapted into a film, film entries demonstrate how the themes are conveyed cinematically, along with any changes in the portrayal of the themes.

Style: this section addresses important style elements of the drama, such as setting, point of view, and narration; important literary devices used, such as imagery, foreshadowing, symbolism; and, if applicable, genres to which the work might have belonged, such as Gothicism or Romanticism. Literary terms are explained within the entry, but can also be found in the Glossary. Film entries cover how the director conveyed the meaning, message, and mood of the work using film in comparison to the author's use of language, literary device, etc., in the original work.

Historical Context: in play entries, this section outlines the social, political, and cultural climate in which the author lived and the play was created. This section may include descriptions of related historical events, pertinent aspects of daily life in the culture, and the artistic and literary sensibilities of the time in which the work was written. If the play is a historical work, information regarding the time in which the play is set is also included. Each section is broken down with helpful subheads. Film entries contain a similar Cultural Context section, because the film adaptation might explore an entirely different time period or culture than the original work, and may also be influenced by the traditions and views of a time period much different than that of the original author.

Critical Overview: this section provides background on the critical reputation of the play or film, including bannings or any other public controversies surrounding the work. For older plays, this section includes a history of how the drama or film was first received and how perceptions of it may have changed over the years; for more recent plays, direct quotes from early reviews may also be included.

Criticism: an essay commissioned by *DfS* which specifically deals with the play or film and is written specifically for the student audience, as well as excerpts from previously published criticism on the work (if available).

Sources: an alphabetical list of critical material used in compiling the entry, with full bibliographical information.

Further Reading: an alphabetical list of other critical sources which may prove useful for the student. It includes full bibliographical information and a brief annotation.

Suggested Search Terms: a list of search terms and phrases to jumpstart students' further information seeking. Terms include not just titles and author names but also terms and topics related to the historical and literary context of the works.

In addition, each entry contains the following highlighted sections, set apart from the main text as sidebars:

Media Adaptations: if available, a list of audiobooks and important film and television adaptations of the play, including source information. The list may also include such variations on the work as musical adaptations and other stage interpretations.

Topics for Further Study: a list of potential study questions or research topics dealing with the play. This section includes questions related to other disciplines the student may be studying, such as American history, world history, science, math, government, business, geography, economics, psychology, etc.

Compare and Contrast: an "at-a-glance" comparison of the cultural and historical differences between the author's time and culture and late twentieth century or early twenty-first century Western culture. This box includes pertinent parallels between the major scientific, political, and cultural movements of the time or place the drama was written, the time or place the play was set (if a historical work), and modern Western culture. Works written after 1990 may not have this box.

What Do I Read Next?: a list of works that might give a reader points of entry into a classic work (e.g., YA or multicultural titles) and/or complement the featured play or serve as a contrast to it. This includes works by the same author and others, works from various genres, YA works, and works from various cultures and eras.

The film entries provide sidebars more targeted to the study of film, including:

Film Technique: a listing and explanation of four to six key techniques used in the film, including shot styles, use of transitions, lighting, sound or music, etc.

Read, Watch, Write: media literacy prompts and/or suggestions for viewing log prompts.

What Do I See Next?: a list of films based on the same or similar works or of films similar in directing style, technique, etc.

Other Features

DfS includes "The Study of Drama," a foreword by Carole Hamilton, an educator and author who specializes in dramatic works. This essay examines the basis for drama in societies and what drives people to study such work. The essay also discusses how *DfS* can help teachers show students how to enrich their own reading/viewing experiences.

A Cumulative Author/Title Index lists the authors and titles covered in each volume of the *DfS* series.

A Cumulative Nationality/Ethnicity Index breaks down the authors and titles covered in each volume of the *DfS* series by nationality and ethnicity.

A Subject/Theme Index, specific to each volume, provides easy reference for users who may be studying a particular subject or theme rather than a single work. Significant subjects from events to broad themes are included.

Each entry may include illustrations, including photo of the author, stills from stage productions, and stills from film adaptations, if available.

Citing Drama for Students

When writing papers, students who quote directly from any volume of *DfS* may use the following general forms. These examples are based on MLA style; teachers may request that students adhere to a different style, so the following examples may be adapted as needed.

When citing text from *DfS* that is not attributed to a particular author (i.e., the Themes, Style, Historical Context sections, etc.), the following format should be used in the bibliography section:

> "Candida." *Drama for Students*. Ed. Sara Constantakis. Vol. 30. Detroit: Gale, Cengage Learning, 2013. 1–27. Print.

When quoting the specially commissioned essay from *DfS* (usually the first piece under the "Criticism" subhead), the following format should be used:

> O'Neal, Michael J. Critical Essay on *Candida*. *Drama for Students*. Ed. Sara Constantakis. Vol. 30. Detroit: Gale, Cengage Learning, 2013. 12–15. Print.

When quoting a journal or newspaper essay that is reprinted in a volume of *DfS*, the following form may be used:

> Lazenby, Walter. "Love and 'Vitality' in *Candida*." *Modern Drama* 20.1 (1977): 1–19. Rpt. in *Drama for Students*. Ed. Sara Constantakis. Vol. 30. Detroit: Gale, Cengage Learning, 2013. 18–22. Print.

When quoting material reprinted from a book that appears in a volume of *DfS*, the following form may be used:

> Phelps, William Lyon. "George Bernard Shaw." *Essays on Modern Dramatists*. New York: Macmillan, 1921. 67–98. Rpt. in *Drama for Students*. Ed. Sara Constantakis. Vol. 30. Detroit: Gale, Cengage Learning, 2013. 26. Print.

We Welcome Your Suggestions

The editorial staff of *Drama for Students* welcomes your comments and ideas. Readers who wish to suggest dramas to appear in future volumes, or who have other suggestions, are cordially invited to contact the editor. You may contact the editor via e-mail at: **ForStudentsEditors@cengage.com.** Or write to the editor at:

Editor, *Drama for Students*

Gale

27500 Drake Road

Farmington Hills, MI 48331-3535

Literary Chronology

1564: William Shakespeare is baptized on April 26 in Stratford-upon-Avon, England.

1603 or 1604: William Shakespeare's *Othello* is performed.

1616: William Shakespeare dies of unknown causes on April 23 in Stratford-upon-Avon, England.

1888: Eugene O'Neill is born on October 16 in New York, New York.

1920: Eugene O'Neill is awarded the Pulitzer Prize for Drama for *Beyond the Horizon*.

1922: Eugene O'Neill is awarded the Pulitzer Prize for Drama for *Anna Christie*.

1928: Eugene O'Neill is awarded the Pulitzer Prize for Drama for *Strange Interlude*.

1933: Eugene O'Neill's *Ah, Wilderness!* is produced.

1936: Marge Piercy is born on March 31 in Detroit, Michigan.

1936: Eugene O'Neill is awarded the Nobel Prize for Literature.

1938: John Guare is born in New York, New York.

1940: Frank Chin is born on February 4 in Berkeley, California.

1943: Michael Bennett is born on April 8 in Buffalo, New York.

1950: Ira Wood is born on April 9 in New York, New York.

1950: Howard Ashman is born on May 17 in Baltimore, Maryland.

1953: Eugene O'Neill dies of cerebellar atrophy on November 27 in Boston, Massachusetts.

1957: Eugene O'Neill is awarded the Pulitzer Prize for Drama for *Long Day's Journey into Night*.

1962: Rita Dove is born on August 28 in Akron, Ohio.

1965: Tracy Letts is born on July 4 in Tulsa, Oklahoma.

1969: Josefina López is born on March 19 in San Luis Potosi, Mexico.

1970: Ayad Akhtar is born on October 28 in Staten Island, New York.

1972: Frank Chin's *The Chickencoop Chinaman* is produced.

1975: Michael Bennett's *A Chorus Line* is produced.

1976: Michael Bennett is awarded Tony awards for Best Direction of a Musical and Best Choreographer.

1977: Quiara Alegría Hudes is born in Philadelphia, Pennsylvania.

1980: Marge Piercy and Ira Wood's *The Last White Class* is produced.

1982: Howard Ashman's *Little Shop of Horrors* is produced.

1987: Michael Bennett dies of lymphoma on July 2 in Tucson, Arizona.

1987: Rita Dove is awarded the Pulitzer Prize for Poetry for *Thomas and Beulah.*

1990: John Guare's *Six Degrees of Separation* is produced.

1991: Howard Ashman dies of complications related to AIDS on March 14 in New York, New York.

1992: The play *Real Women Have Curves* is produced.

1993: The film *Six Degrees of Separation* is released.

1994: Rita Dove's *The Darker Face of the Earth* is produced.

1995: The film *Othello* is released.

2007: The play *August: Osage County* is produced.

2008: Quiara Alegría Hudes is awarded the Tony Award for Best Musical for *In The Heights.*

2008: Tracy Letts is awarded the Pulitzer Prize for Drama for *August: Osage County.*

2008: Tracy Letts is awarded the Tony Award for Best Original Play for *August: Osage County.*

2011: The play *Water by the Spoonful* is produced.

2012: The play *Disgraced* is produced.

2012: Quiara Alegría Hudes is awarded the Pulitzer Prize for Drama for *Water by the Spoonful.*

2013: Ayad Akhtar is awarded the Pulitzer Prize for Drama for *Disgraced.*

Acknowledgements

The editors wish to thank the copyright holders of the excerpted criticism included in this volume and the permissions managers of many book and magazine publishing companies for assisting us in securing reproduction rights. We are also grateful to the staffs of the Detroit Public Library, the Library of Congress, the University of Detroit Mercy Library, Wayne State University Purdy/ Kresge Library Complex, and the University of Michigan Libraries for making their resources available to us. Following is a list of the copyright holders who have granted us permission to reproduce material in this volume of DfS. Every effort has been made to trace copyright, but if omissions have been made, please let us know.

COPYRIGHTED EXCERPTS IN _DfS_, VOLUME 33, WERE REPRODUCED FROM THE FOLLOWING PERIODICALS:

African American Review, Vol. 34, Issue 1, 2000, pp. 143-145. Copyright © 2000 Theodora Carlile.—_American Theatre_, Vol. 31, Issue 3, March 2014, p. 23. Copyright © 2014 Theatre Communications Group, Inc.—_Asian Theatre Journal_, Volume 2, Issue 2, Autumn 1985, pp. 240-243. Copyright © 1985 University of Hawaii Press.—_Back Stage West_, Vol. 9, Issue 42, October 17, 2002, p. 7. Copyright © 2002 _Backstage_.—_Backstage_, Volume 53, Issue 30, July 26, 2012, p. 11. Copyright © 2012 _Backstage_.—_Backstage_, Vol. 54, Issue 2, January 10, 2013, p. 61. Copyright © 2013 The Nielsen Company.—_Backstage_, Volume 54, Issue 51, December 19, 2013, p. 22. Copyright © 2013 _Backstage_.—_Backstage_, Vol. 56, Issue 6, February 6, 2014, p. 56. Copyright © 2014 The Nielsen Company.—_Brooklyn Rail_, July-August 2012, p. 109. Copyright © 2012 _The Brooklyn Rail_.—First published as the article "'Feed Me!': Power Struggles and the Portrayal of Race in 'Little Shop of Horrors'", by Marc Jensen, in _Cinema Journal_ Volume 48 Issue 1, pp. 51-67. Copyright © 2008 by the University of Texas Press. All rights reserved.—_Comparative American Studies_, Vol. 10, Issue 1, March 2012, pp. 63-77. Copyright © 2012 W.S. Maney & Sons Ltd.—_Hollywood Reporter_, Vol. 385, Issue 24, September 1, 2004, p. 12. Copyright © 2004 Prometheus Global Media.—_New Statesman_, January 19, 2010. Copyright © 2010 New Statesman.—_The Rumpus_, June 2, 2015. Copyright © 2015 Dara Barnat.—_State Magazine_, Vol. 596, January 2015, p. 12. Copyright © 2015 U.S. Department of State.—_Variety_, October 29, 2012. Credit: Marilyn Stasio/_Variety_ © Variety Media, LLC.—_Variety_, January 22, 2002. David Rodney/_Variety_ © Variety Media, LLC.—_Variety_, January 14, 2013. Credit: Marilyn Stasio/_Variety_ © Variety Media, LLC.—_Variety_, September 17, 2013. Scott Foundas/_Variety_ © Variety Media, LLC.—_Variety_, October 28, 2014. Credit: Marilyn Stasio/_Variety_ © Variety Media, LLC.—_Washington Post_, December, 29, 1995. Copyright © 1995 _Washington Post_.

COPYRIGHTED EXCERPTS IN *DfS*, **VOLUME 33, WERE REPRODUCED FROM THE FOLLOWING BOOKS:**

From *Gender Meets Genre in Postwar Cinemas*. Copyright 2012 by the Board of Trustees of the University of Illinois. Used with permission of the University of Illinois Press.—Kimbel, Ellen. From *Critical Essays on Eugene O'Neill*. Boston, MA: G.K. Hall 1984, pp. 137-141 Copyright © 1984 G.K. Hall.—Piercy, Marge and Ira Wood. From *So You Want to Write: How to Master the Craft of Writing Fiction and Memoir*. Wellfleet, MA: Leapfrog Press, 2005, pp. 17-21. Copyright © 2005 Leapfrog Press.—Plunka, Gene A. From *The Black Comedy of John Guare*. Newark, DE: University of Delaware Press, 2002, pp. 197-202. Copyright © 2002 University of Delaware Press.—Wollman, Elizabeth L. From *The Theater Will Rock: A History of the Rock Musical, from "Hair" to "Hedwig"*. Ann Arbor, MI: The University of Michigan Press, 2006, pp. 130-133. Copyright © 2006 The University of Michigan Press.

COPYRIGHTED EXCERPTS IN *DfS*, **VOLUME 33, WERE REPRODUCED FROM THE FOLLOWING WEBSITES:**

RogerEbert.com, December 20, 1985. © 1995 The Ebert Company. Dist. by UNIVERSAL UCLICK. Reprinted with permission. All rights reserved.—*RogerEbert.com*, December 19, 1986. © 1995 The Ebert Company. Dist. by UNIVERSAL UCLICK. Reprinted with permission. All rights reserved.

Contributors

Bryan Aubrey: Aubrey holds a PhD in English. Entry on *A Chorus Line*. Original essay on *A Chorus Line*.

Rita M. Brown: Brown is an English professor. Entry on *Othello*. Original essay on *Othello*.

Klay Dyer: Dyer is a freelance writer specializing in topics relating to literature, popular culture, and the relationship between creativity and technology. Entry on *Six Degrees of Separation*. Original essay on *Six Degrees of Separation*.

Kristen Sarlin Greenberg: Greenberg is a freelance writer and editor with a background in literature and philosophy. Entry on *Real Women Have Curves*. Original essay on *Real Women Have Curves*.

David Kelly: Kelly is a writer and an instructor of literature and creative writing. Entry on *Little Shop of Horrors*. Original essay on *Little Shop of Horrors*.

Amy L. Miller: Miller is a graduate of the University of Cincinnati, and she currently resides in New Orleans, Louisiana. Entries on *Disgraced* and *Water by the Spoonful*. Original essays on *Disgraced* and *Water by the Spoonful*.

Jeffrey Eugene Palmer: Palmer is a high school English teacher, scholar, and freelance writer. Entry on *Ah, Wilderness!*. Original essay on *Ah, Wilderness!*.

April Paris: Paris is a freelance writer with a degree in classical literature and a background in academic writing. Entry on *The Chickencoop Chinaman*. Original essay on *The Chickencoop Chinaman*.

Kathy Wilson Peacock: Wilson Peacock is an editor and writer on literary topics. Entry on *August: Osage County*. Original essay on *August: Osage County*.

Laura B. Pryor: Pryor has a master's degree in English and over thirty years of experience as a professional writer. Entry on *The Last White Class*. Original essay on *The Last White Class*.

Bradley A. Skeen: Skeen is a classicist. Entry on *The Darker Face of the Earth*. Original essay on *The Darker Face of the Earth*.

Ah, Wilderness!

EUGENE O'NEILL

1933

First performed on Broadway in 1933, *Ah, Wilderness!* remains the only comedic work of the great American playwright Eugene O'Neill. As a distinct departure from his usual blend of contemporary and classic themes of tragedy, the play is set instead right after the turn of the twentieth century, before the outbreak of World War I and during the period of the playwright's own boyhood. The play was an immediate success among American audiences and managed to draw unprecedented attendance despite the crushing poverty of the Great Depression (1929–1939), an era in which many citizens could scarcely afford their daily bread, let alone theater tickets.

A requiem for youth and the innocence of a bygone age, *Ah, Wilderness!* remains a monument to American perseverance in otherwise dark times. O'Neill himself described it as an "evocation of the mood of emotion of a past time" and a comedy that made him weep. The outwardly lighthearted play touches upon a number of sobering themes: the plight of wayward youth and the corrupting influence of alcohol and unchecked physical desire, even foreshadowing the gradual disappearance of the hallowed American nuclear family unit. The play's lasting message, however, is ultimately optimistic and represents O'Neill's hugely successful revival, ushering in a period of unparalleled productivity and professional achievement for the playwright.

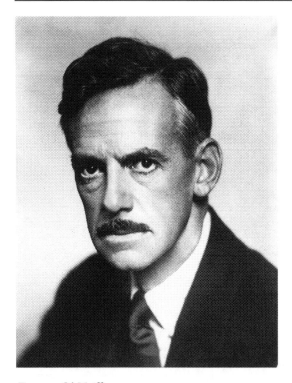

Eugene O' Neill (© *General Photographic Agency | Getty Images*)

AUTHOR BIOGRAPHY

Eugene Gladstone O'Neill is hailed as the father of American tragedy and a visionary of the modern and postmodern stage. His personal life was as complex, and at times as squalid, as the story lines for which he would become immortalized. He was born on October 16, 1888, in a New York City hotel room. He was the second son of a famous actor of melodramas, James O'Neill, and his wife, Mary Ellen Quinlan. The transient circumstances and setting of his birth would prove emblematic of O'Neill's young life, as he spent much of his childhood deprived of the comfort of a permanent home, touring the nation in accordance with his father's successful acting career.

As a young teenager, his eyes were opened prematurely to some of life's harsher realities. O'Neill first encountered alcohol with his wayward older brother, Jamie; drinking would cause irreparable harm to both brothers over the course of their lives. This newfound dependency on drink contributed, less than half a decade later, to O'Neill's expulsion from Princeton University after just one semester of failing grades. His

second attempt at higher education in the form of tutoring by a well-regarded Harvard professor of drama, George Pierce Baker, proved no longer lived than the first.

With the financial backing of his father, O'Neill was able to put his intuitive, largely untrained gift for the literary craft into practice and publish a portfolio of plays. His first big break came in the late summer and early autumn of 1916 when the Provincetown Players, a group of subversive and visionary artists, expressed a willingness to stage O'Neill's first production, *Bound East for Cardiff*, and a subsequent string of his shorter plays. The support of his newfound friends soon catapulted O'Neill's career to dizzying heights and established him as the most prolific, insightful, and revolutionary playwright of his age. By the end of his career in the late 1940s, O'Neill had published nearly two dozen plays of often unparalleled length and complexity. He received the coveted Pulitzer Prize for Drama four times, for *Beyond the Horizon, Anna Christie, Strange Interlude*, and *Long Day's Journey into Night*. This last play, considered a masterpiece, also earned O'Neill the distinction of becoming the only American dramatist to hold a Nobel Prize in Literature. Although O'Neill is best known for his tragic plays, his one comedy, *Ah, Wilderness!*, proved to be just as successful. He wrote it in 1933, a time when the nation was in dire need of a laugh during the Great Depression.

Although he was much loved by millions of Americans as an embodiment of dauntless national spirit, O'Neill demonstrated deep flaws as a family man. His tendency toward drinking and philandering, his virtual abandonment of two of his wives and all three of his children, and his aloof regard for those friends and family most supportive of his achievements revealed in O'Neill a devastatingly self-defeating character. He died in 1953 at the age of sixty-five, a victim of pneumonia, after a period of worsening depression and writer's block. His life ended, much as it had begun, in the bed of a sparsely populated hotel room.

PLOT SUMMARY

Act 1
Ah, Wilderness! opens in the dappled sunlight of the beautiful morning of July 4, 1906, in the household of the Millers, a well-to-do Connecticut family of solid respectability and upper-middle-class

MEDIA ADAPTATIONS

- The first film adaptation of O'Neill's *Ah, Wilderness!* is a 1935 production of the same name directed by Clarence Brown and adapted for the screen by Frances Goodrich and Albert Hackett. Released little more than a year after the debut of the actual play on Broadway, this production speaks to the tremendous contemporary popularity of *Ah, Wilderness!* It stars the well-known actors of the day Lionel Barrymore, Wallace Beery, and Aline MacMahon.

- Adapted for television in 1959 by Robert Hartung, Robert Mulligan's homage to the play stars Norman Fell, Betty Field, and Helen Hayes.

values. The interior of the home is spacious and tastefully modern, but in a way that rejects individuality and reveals a certain flatness of character. Into this highly conventional space comes eleven-year-old Tommy, the youngest member of the Miller household, eager to escape his parents and join his neighborhood friends in setting off firecrackers outside. Following Tommy's boyish banging of the screen door emerge two older Miller children, Arthur and Mildred, and their parents, Nat and Essie. Accompanying the gathering members of the nuclear family are Sid, Essie's brother, and Lily, Nat's sister. While Arthur and Mildred exchange playful banter, Nat and Sid announce, somewhat bashfully, that they are expected to attend a picnic in recognition of the Fourth of July holiday. The reason for their guilty manner becomes evident when Essie insists that the two men be careful about how much they drink and return home, unlike previous times, in an appropriate state to enjoy the family meal.

Essie's concerns over the two grown men blend into concern over her son Richard, who seems mysteriously absent from the scene. She encourages her husband to summon the boy to join the rest of the family and to lecture him

on his habits of reading books that are overly scholarly, and quite possibly unwholesome and subversive. Richard emerges from the den, sheepishly, and is subjected to mingled concern and mockery from his family members in regard to his reading habits and, in particular, his liking for love poetry. Mildred, always sharp and mischievous, links this phenomenon to Richard's growing attachment to a neighborhood girl, Muriel McComber.

As if on cue, Muriel's father, David McComber, approaches the Miller residence and asks to speak with Nat about the inappropriate nature of Richard's relationship with his daughter. As evidence of this misbehavior, McComber presents letters between the two that he found in Muriel's underwear drawer. Before being forced to leave by Nat, the unwelcome guest leaves a letter addressed to Richard from Muriel, which, while quite possibly written under duress, declares the romance to be over. Angered by the contents of the letter and what he is convinced is Muriel's cowardice, Richard gives way to an outburst of childish passion and strides furiously from his family home.

Act 2

It is now the evening of the same day, and there is a bustle of activity in the Miller kitchen and dining room. The lady of the house is assisting a servant, an Irish girl by the name of Norah, in the final preparations for the family gathering, and Lily joins them. The men have not yet returned from the day's festivities, but they are expected home at any minute. While they are gone, Lily voices a concern that her ongoing presence burdens the Millers with an additional expense, a concern that Essie gracefully and decisively puts to rest. This conversation moves to Lily's former engagement to Sid and his habits of drunkenness, which contributed to their breakup.

Richard returns to the house then and, after exchanging a few tense words with his mother and pretending to be indifferent about his newly realized heartbreak, again stomps out seeking solitude. On his way out, Richard encounters Wint Selby, a college friend of his older brother, Arthur, who also attends Yale. Hearing that Arthur is out, Wint proposes to Richard that they join him and some women at a local hotel bar for drinks and some carefree carousing later that night. Richard agrees, a decision perhaps fueled by his compromised state of mind and his desire to appear worldly and mature in the presence of his brother's friend. As Wint goes out, Tommy announces that his father and uncle are about to return.

The pair emerge flushed, jovial, and, despite their best attempts at maintaining composure, quite obviously intoxicated. Sid is by far the worse off of the two and moves very carefully to the dinner table, guiltily avoiding the eyes of his former fiancée. The dinner conversation soon degenerates into drunken banter, and the entire family, much to the initial chagrin of Lily and Essie, joins in the exchange. The mealtime ends when the effects of Sid's drinking begin to catch up with him and he is forced to remove himself from the table, proposing once more to Lily and being refused in turn, before retreating to the sleeping quarters prepared for him. Watching the parting exchange between his aunt and uncle, Richard remarks that Lily is to blame for Sid's broken condition and his dependence upon drink. This unfair assessment sparks a general uproar among the family and results in Richard's storming out of the house for the second time that day.

Act 3

SCENE 1

A far cry from the wholesome and sheltering backdrop of the Miller residence, the hotel bar in which Richard now finds himself is dank, lightless, and largely empty. Having long since been abandoned by Wint, Richard broods awkwardly over a flat, half-empty pint of beer, attempting to feign confident conversation with Belle, a newly recruited prostitute. Observing the young man's inept manner, the bartender shames and bullies Richard into buying another, more potent drink that pushes Richard over the edge of tipsiness. Taking advantage of Richard's increasing state of intoxication, Belle urges her underage client to procure a room upstairs. Richard almost agrees, but through the haze of alcohol he recalls his lingering affection for Muriel and stalls, instead, by buying another round of drinks. A salesman at the bar, sensing an opportunity to get rid of Richard and employ Belle himself, joins their table and inserts himself into the conversation. Richard, made bold by liquor, becomes angry at the stranger's blatant and ungentlemanly attempt to hire Belle and creates such an uproar that the bartender takes note. The salesman suggests that Richard is underage,

and, fearing for his job, the bartender forcefully muscles the young man off the premises in a convincing display of justified indignation.

SCENE 2

The concern back at the Miller household is now much greater as the fireworks cease and midnight approaches without any sign of Richard's return. The family members are all present and awake, except for Sid, who is recuperating, and Arthur, who is out with friends. They all pretend to be preoccupied with chores and distractions to conceal their growing unease. Unable to contain her worries any longer, Essie expresses her fears in an outburst to her assembled family and is comforted, but with lessening conviction, by each member in turn. Arthur returns, looking rather pleased with himself, and is initially mistaken by his mother for Richard. Sid contributes to the mounting unease of the room by stumbling out of bed, full of shame and remorse, to beg forgiveness of a stone-faced Lily Miller. Faced with her rejection, Sid gives in to a fit of tears that succeeds in moving his lost love to forgiveness but does nothing to lessen the now-considerable anxiety of Essie over her missing son.

Just as Nat agrees to take the car in search of his son, Richard stumbles back into the Miller house, looking considerably worse for the wear, dirtied and swaying uneasily on the threshold. Fittingly, a now cheerful Sid is the first member of the family to accurately gauge Richard's condition, a revelation that results in a general uproar. Nat Miller moves to strike his son, but an understandably sympathetic Sid stops him. Richard, emboldened by his alcoholic stupor and somewhat enjoying having caused such a stir, begins baiting his assembled family with provocative literary quotes. Before they can rise to the challenge, however, Richard's condition takes a predictable turn, and he promptly becomes sick. He is escorted upstairs by his uncle while Nat attempts to calm his upset wife, and the rest of the Miller children are left looking on in shocked, somewhat envious disbelief.

Act 4

SCENE 1

Although it is already past noon, Richard has yet to emerge from his room following the previous night's events, and the entire family is united by a guilty thrill of anticipation. Essie browbeats Nat into taking the afternoon off work to perform his fatherly duty and discipline his son, a task to which he responds with deep ambivalence and even nervousness. Unbeknownst to his wife, Nat had, earlier that morning, received an anonymous note detailing the exact events of the night before and the complicity of the bartender in Richard's near corruption. Nat is reminded of an important meeting that requires his attendance, and he leaves the house, determined to speak to his son upon his return later that night. Richard emerges from the bedroom immediately after his father's departure and is reprimanded by his mother for his behavior of the previous night. He responds, although unapologetically, that he has no love of alcohol and will never repeat the transgression. Somewhat saddened by Richard's youthful earnestness, Sid begins to reflect on the mistakes of his own life and how they might have been avoided had he been possessed of Richard's good sense. Muriel interrupts the melancholy exchange to present Richard with a new letter from Muriel, begging reconciliation and proposing a secret meeting later that night on the beach. Richard is overjoyed, but he also begins to experience a dawning sensation of guilt over the kisses he lavished on Belle less than a day ago and his near willingness to sleep with a stranger.

SCENE 2

In the only scene of the play that takes place outdoors, the audience is transported to a darkening, peaceful beach, waves lapping gently at the prow of a small rowboat half adrift and half in the sand. Richard is seated in the boat. He is whistling and pretending to be casual, though in reality he is torn by conflicting feelings of excitement, nervousness, and no small degree of guilt. Muriel approaches out of the twilight, cautiously and somewhat apologetically, and hails her young sweetheart. Richard pretends to be surprised and no more than vaguely pleased at her sudden presence. After apologies are exchanged and Muriel admits that she wrote the letter under pressure from her father, the pair reconcile and set the rowboat adrift so that they can talk in peace. After remarking on Muriel's otherworldly beauty, Richard attempts to kiss her, an attempt that she resists shyly but firmly. Somewhat ruffled by this rejection, Richard decides to take a self-righteous approach and begins to tell the story of the previous night, with highly embellished details, in light of the overwhelming sense of rejection he experienced after reading Muriel's

letter. His account stumbles slightly with the mention of Belle, and Muriel immediately demands to know if Richard kissed her or took any similar liberties. At first, Richard denies the charge, but then he qualifies his answer by placing the blame solely on Belle. After an initial outburst from Muriel of horror and indignation, the couple once again pledge their undying love for each other and begin to speak of marriage. Richard and Muriel kiss then, for the first time, under the light of the moon.

SCENE 3

The play ends, much as it begins, in the Miller's cozy if tastelessly furnished sitting room. Nat and Essie wait up together, she sewing and he chuckling over the books he confiscated from Richard's collection. Essie expresses her disapproval of this, a comment that blends into a discussion of the proper disciplinary measures to be inflicted upon their son upon his return. Essie is of the opinion that, having pledged himself to sobriety and been forced to sleep through the lion's share of the day, Richard should be excused from any further punishment. Her husband disagrees. The spat only serves to bring the couple closer together, however, and soon all talk of discipline is forgotten as they begin to reminisce on their own youth, the contentment of the present, and the changes to come in the future. Richard comes home, and his father assumes an air of gravity appropriate to their imminent talk while Essie, in acknowledgment of the bond between father and son, prepares to leave the room.

Richard enters in a dreamy daze, this not time not from liquor but love-induced, and hails his parents with a detached goodwill. Having satisfied herself that Richard is not, in fact, intoxicated, Essie leaves the two alone together. Nat begins his lecture with an intense but brief outburst regarding his son's drunkenness of the previous night, at which Richard seems appropriately ashamed. It soon becomes clear, however, that the real topic under discussion is Richard's relationship with Belle. The young man is astonished that his father knows about this part of his experience but honestly denies the charge of having had sexual relations with the prostitute. Awkwardly, but determinedly, Nat imparts to his son hard-won wisdom regarding the distinction between carnal desire and true and reputable love, and the ideal state of their overlap in a relationship. Richard seems to take this advice to heart, swearing his devotion to Muriel on both fronts, and the genuine nature of the response seems to please Nat.

Essie returns then, and both father and mother reconcile fully with Richard before wishing the boy a good night and preparing for bed themselves. In a scene that evokes a more mature version of the exchange between Richard and Muriel on the beach, Nat and his wife linger for a moment in the moonlight, reflecting on the beauty of the seasons of life and exchanging soft phrases of their enduring affection over the years. The two of them disappear into the dimness as a serene silence falls on the Miller household, signaling the end of the play.

CHARACTERS

Bartender

An unsavory character in an unsavory establishment, the unnamed bartender who serves the underage Richard is characterized by a cruel grin and a pushy manner. He cunningly observes the exchange between Richard and Belle and pressures the young man into buying another, stronger drink, which pushes him over the edge into true intoxication. When officially alerted to the underage nature of his customer, the bartender takes matters into his own hands and forcefully expels Richard into the street.

Belle

A "recently recruited" prostitute, Belle's youthful appearance and playful demeanor contribute an additional tragic element to her newfound profession. Behind her excessive makeup and bold professional facade, the young woman seems gnawed by a lingering doubt and reluctance. She tries, unsuccessfully, to secure Richard as a customer over drinks at the hotel bar.

Sid Davis

Beloved Uncle Sid is simultaneously the most endearing and the most pathetic character of the play. Although he is short, fat, and bald, Sid more than compensates for his lack of physical glamour with an unmatched charm and wit and a warm if somewhat undisciplined heart. He is equally inclined to outbreaks of mirth and of sorrow, a volatility that is in no way lessened by his weakness for alcohol. He flirts shamelessly with his former fiancée, Lily, throughout the play and it becomes clear that he still holds deep feelings for her.

David McComber

"Old Man McComber" is one of the few unpleasant characters within the play and represents the first disturbance within the otherwise idyllic Miller home. The father of Richard's young love interest, Muriel, David is utterly without a sense of humor or grace and is also something of a bully. His physical features mirror his personality in that he appears prematurely aged and joyless, his pinched features and slit of a mouth betraying no mirth. Nat and David are natural antagonists and almost come to blows in discussing the behavior of the love-struck Richard toward Muriel.

Muriel McComber

The character of Muriel McComber, a soft-featured and dimpled innocent, stands in stark opposition to that of her sweetheart, Richard. While he is sullen and jaded, she is lively and naïve. His inborn rebelliousness and disdain is tempered by her sweet and open demeanor and her overdeveloped regard for authority. He is brazen, and she is timid. In the end, however, Muriel defies the will of her father to sneak from her home and join Richard on the beach to resume their engagement.

Old Man McComber

See David McComber

Arthur Miller

Arthur is the oldest of the Miller children who appears in the play. His air of hard-earned wisdom and respectability is tempered somewhat by an unmistakable hint of condescension toward his younger siblings. He is robust and classically handsome in accordance with the blond-haired, blue-eyed stereotype of the day and is described as "solemnly collegiate" in his appearance. Arthur is almost twenty years of age and a student at nearby Yale University.

Essie Miller

A doting mother and dutiful housewife of the period, Essie Miller is described as having reached a state of plump and pleasant middle age, the prettiness of her youth subsiding into a wholesome attractiveness. Her primary concerns are for the safety of her children and the integrity of the household, and she is confident in expressing her opinion when it coincides with either of these goals.

Lily Miller

The white lily flower represents purity and innocence, and in keeping with her name, Nat's sister
was in her youth a paragon of purity. In her
advancing age, however, she has come to be
regarded even by those close to her as an unfortunate spinster without any marriage prospects
or opportunities for individuality outside her
family. She was once engaged to Sid, for whom
she still feels affection, but long ago broke off the
arrangement out of concern over his wayward
tendencies and love of strong drink. Her gentle,
tragic eyes and soft, sensuous voice are at odds
with her spidery build and unassuming, almost
intentionally unattractive manner of dress.

Mildred Miller

Mildred is the equal of her brother, Arthur, in
every respect. Although she is described by
O'Neill as having inherited her father's graceless-
ness of figure and feature, the only girl of the
Miller household is considered quite good-looking
by those who know her because of her sparkling
wit, expressive gray eyes, and disarming smile.
Already at fifteen, Mildred shows signs of developing into a lively and self-aware young woman.

Nat Miller

A prominent and respected man in his community as the owner of the local newspaper, Nat is
also the head of the Miller household and husband to Essie, brother to Lily, and father of the
four children mentioned in the play. Physically,
Nat is unassuming, and the weight of the world
seems to further stoop the shoulders of his lean
and leggy frame. His stylized and awkward
clothing suggests that he is only pretending to
understand the outward signs of prosperity and
their relation to their quiet but more meaningful
integrity he expresses throughout the play.

Richard Miller

The next-to-youngest son of the Miller household, Richard is the black sheep of the family in
such details as his sullen temperament, inborn
rebelliousness, and misunderstood literary leanings. He is the moral heart of the play and the
character around whom most of the action and
humor revolves. Physically, he seems plain and
average, a perfect and unassuming blend of the
less noteworthy traits of both his parents.
Richard has something of the artist about him,
and he shows a detached sensitivity toward those
family members who would seek to understand

his ways. He is courting Muriel, and the two are
secretly engaged.

Tommy Miller

Tommy, the youngest member of the Miller
household, is on the verge of adolescence. He
embodies American friendliness and innocence in
every detail of his being. From his unruly blond
hair to his flushed face, perpetual milk mustache,
and childish patterns of speech, his sole purpose in
the play is to act as a contrast to the dawning
adulthood of his older brother, Richard.

Norah

The Millers' treatment of their household servant
girl, who is straight off the boat from Ireland, is
perhaps less than gracious. Although she is
described as friendly, warmhearted, and eager to
please, the family members consider Norah clumsy
and endearingly empty-headed; they treat her as an
awkward, though necessary, appendage of the
household.

Salesman

The unnamed salesman who makes his one and
only appearance at the hotel bar plays a brief
and somewhat sinister role in the play. He first
seeks to undermine Richard in an attempt to
gain access to Belle, then succeeds in having the
young man ejected from the bar, and finally
leaves with the implicit threat of alerting Nat
Miller to the incident and thereby costing the
bartender his livelihood.

Wint Selby

Although he is not a particularly well-developed
character, Wint Selby is instrumental in the
initial exchange that threatens to lead young
Richard astray. Wint is a friend of Arthur's at
Yale, fond of liquor and easy companionship.
His unscrupulous character clashes with his
handsome, presentable facade and easy manner.

THEMES

Bohemianism

In 1906, bohemianism—a culture of free spirits,
mostly made up of artistically inclined and anti-
materialist young people—was just beginning to
take root and gain widespread cultural recognition
in America. Aspects of Richard's character are
modeled, intentionally or not, on these emerging

TOPICS FOR FURTHER STUDY

- *Ah, Wilderness!* centers on a stereotypical middle-class American household at the beginning of the twentieth century, inspiring among audiences of 1933 a nostalgia for the perceived simplicity of their childhood. Does this image of the Miller family still speak to us as modern readers? In what ways has the changing fabric of American society altered these perceptions? Using Internet image searches, magazine or newspaper clippings, or personal photos, assemble a collage of images from the period of your childhood that evoke, for you, a comparable nostalgia. Accompany this collage with a brief write-up detailing the significance of the pictures you chose for comparison with those assembled by other members of your group.

- Debuting in the depths of the Great Depression, the popularity of *Ah, Wilderness!* demonstrated a deep national need, despite the shortage of money for performance tickets at the time, for the release of laughter. What events of the early new millennium, almost a century after the writing of the play, parallel the deprivations of that time? Do we also seek laughter as a form of release from our more modern concerns? Select a more modern comedic stage production or film that brought you the solace of humor in your own lifetime. Using a Venn diagram, show the similarities and differences it holds with O'Neill's timeless play.

- O'Neill was an Irish American playwright who lived through the greatest period of immigration in this nation's history. His work deals with emerging American identity and the survival of this country's working class, both foreign and domestic, in a land of limited opportunity and sometimes outright hostility. In light of O'Neill's own ethnic heritage and his insistence upon portraying the everyman as well as the elite, what do you make of the relative snobbery of the Millers toward their immigrant maid, Norah, and the precarious position of the Irish bartender, and his livelihood, in a traditionally Anglo-oriented society? Write a dramatic monologue from the perspective of one of these characters, detailing his or her reactions to the present circumstances in this "new land of opportunity" and their treatment by the natives.

- *Ah, Wilderness!* both revels in youth and emphasizes its fragility. Uncle Sid is unable to rise above his childish lack of discipline to achieve true adulthood, and his former fiancée, Lily, is frozen in a state of perpetual innocence and dependence upon her family, How does the existence of these characters cast doubt on the otherwise optimistic picture of Richard's future? Assume the persona of a reporter employed by the Miller-run *Globe* newspaper several decades after the time of this play. Write an honest and unapologetic obituary for the recently deceased Richard Miller. Include details of his standing within the community, family life, academic and professional achievements, and any other specifics that you feel are relevant to the unveiling of his character. Who do you think he became after that important evening of July 4, 1906?

- Do you consider the play to be a true comedy, or is it tinged, as many critics believe, with a bittersweet quality, as if it is a memorial for a lost time? Compose a list of the details of the work consistent with the opposing genres of comedy and tragedy to weigh your final evaluation. Read the comparably ambiguous work of young-adult fiction, *The Catcher in the Rye*, by J. D. Salinger, and apply the same guidelines to it in a brief essay comparing parallel themes in these two classic coming-of-age stories.

freethinkers. This is evident in details of his manner, such as his rejection of the societal convention of Independence Day, his pointed consumption of controversial literary works, and his prickly, and perhaps overly righteous, sense of personal decency. This comparison is supported by O'Neill's own involvement in the bohemian scene throughout his career.

In particular, Richard's voracious appetite for edgy literature of the day speaks to his self-styled identity as a man of the world. This mindset, especially in combination with his youth and inexperience, serves as a comic vehicle by which to reinforce his delusions of intellectual grandeur. This surface interpretation is challenged, however, by his close relationship with his soft-hearted, if somewhat seedy, Uncle Sid. The older man also spouts poetry throughout the play, much to the mingled joy and consternation of the Miller household. Uncle Sid seems to be the individual most closely aligned with Richard's sensibilities.

The insinuation that what passes for free-thinking in youth leads to moral decrepitude in old age places bohemianism and the artistic awareness it elevates at the intersection of worldliness and corrupting influence. Especially with its emphasis on notoriously loose continental visionaries, the bohemian movement promises both the explosion of the American art scene and the erosion of idyllic family values in decent, middle-class households like the Miller's.

Substance Abuse

The abuse of alcohol is a recurrent theme throughout the play and a looming menace threatening the cozy conception of the idyllic American family. Prohibition, the American ban on the sale and manufacture of alcoholic beverages between the years 1920 and 1933, is not yet in effect by the setting of the play and is newly abolished by the time of its production. Even in 1906, however, anti-alcohol sentiments are already prevalent among many respectable, middle-class citizens like the Millers. This is represented in the play by Essie's fierce disapproval of the intoxication of her son and husband, the seedy portrayal of the hotel bar, and the pathetic rendering of Uncle Sid—unable to rein in even the most basic emotions and rise to respectability—and Lily's unyielding rejection of all drinking men upon which her near spinsterhood is premised. The play's final stance on

alcohol seems tinged with ambiguity, however, as many of the sentiments against it are voiced by hypocritical characters and Richard falls short of completely condemning his actions, stating only that drink does not agree with his natural temperament.

O'Neill composes *Ah, Wilderness!* not only from the perspective of an alcoholic but in light of the recently failed experiment of Prohibition. This historical context suggests a certain hardened realism in his treatment of the controversial topic and contributes additional significance to the decision of his protagonist to choose drunkenness or sobriety. American society, as exemplified by the respectable Miller household in the play, is ultimately powerless to exert control over the will of the individual.

Youth

Perhaps the most central theme of *Ah, Wilderness!*, youth—and sometimes its absence—influences almost every exchange of the play. The most obvious embodiment of this theme can be found in Richard and his siblings, who range in age from eleven to nineteen and display various striking developmental characteristics. Their parents, too, often reminisce on the bygone days of their youth, as does Lily, who, though just barely middle-aged, has already resigned herself to a life of spinsterhood. Themes of youth even pervade interactions with lesser characters, such as Belle, whose relative youth serves to compound the misfortune of her fallen profession. Age is both the morbid obsession of the play and its greatest wellspring of humor and charm, unifying even the most different of characters along a continuum of worldly experience.

In the context of the play, youth, and in particular adolescence, is portrayed as both a peril and a blessing to characters like Richard and his sweetheart, Muriel. Childish innocence is checked by a growing desire for experience and a naïveté of the crueler realities of life. Torn between his desire for pampered dependence on his parents and his craving for adult self-sufficiency, Richard is a complex and delicate character. His dalliance with drinking and the dangers of sex raise moral issues which potentially affect the trajectory of his mature life. His willingness to deceive Muriel, a young lady raised on ironclad ideals of chastity and proper courtship, casts doubt not only upon Richard's character but the sanctity

Ah, Wilderness! takes place in a small town in Connecticut on the Fourth of July. (© artcphotos, 2010 | Used under license from Shutterstock.com)

of their engagement and future as a married couple as well.

These same concerns of advancing adulthood are echoed in graver moments throughout the play, not only in the insinuated vices of Richard's college-going brother, Arthur, and his close friendship with the unsavory Wint but also by the words of outwardly respectable Nat Miller himself. His dubious fatherly advice to Richard suggesting prostitution as an alternative to the sexual frustrations of monogamy suggest that the true distinction between youth and adulthood resides in discretion rather than integrity.

STYLE

Allusion

Ah, Wilderness! is a comedic play composed of seven scenes in four acts. The cast of the play is fairly small, which contributes to the intimate and domestic nature of the plot. The playwright goes to great lengths to establish the setting as representative of small-town America, and he uses dialogue that reflects the laid-back, somewhat provincial speech of the turn of the century. Richard and Uncle Sid are two notable exceptions to this trend, both demonstrating a degree of education and comfort with flowery language that makes their fellow characters feel ill at ease and occasionally somewhat ruffled. Richard, in particular, makes many literary allusions, ranging from the *Rubaiyat* of Omar Khayyam, from which the play takes its title, to the works of English and Irish poets and playwrights Algernon Charles Swinburne, Oscar Wilde, George Bernard Shaw, and countless others.

American Modernism

Richard, with his dual regard for the past and commitment to the present, is in many ways the embodiment of the central ideas of American modernism, a literary movement that came into prominence between the first and second world wars and that endures in a changed form to the present day. Although they fully acknowledged their rich cultural and literary heritage, writers of this genre sought to emphasize the ability of the individual to break from the bonds of tradition and societal expectations to make their own way in life. The main emotions associated with American modernism are undaunted empowerment and optimism, sentiments more consistent with *Ah, Wilderness!* than O'Neill's other, darker plays.

Character Foil

O'Neill makes ample use of character foils—intentionally opposed characters who serve to offset each other's differences—to help emphasize conflicting beliefs and give hints of upcoming plot developments. This is shown by the comparisons between more minor characters such as the sparkling Mildred and her rather dull brother Arthur, the happily married Essie and the dejected spinster Lily, and the corrupted Belle and the chaste Muriel. Most striking, though, is the contrast between Richard and Uncle Sid. Through the depth of their literary connection and what seems to be an intuitive understanding born of open-mindedness, Sid is the first to recognize Richard's drunken condition, acting as his caretaker and furnishing the young man with sound (though hypocritical) advice the next morning.

Foreshadowing

The use of character foils has the additional benefit of preparing the audience for events both on and off the stage that throw dissimilar personalities into even sharper contrast. This is one form of foreshadow, a literary device used by the playwright to hint at future developments and preempt the narrative flow of events. While the intoxication of Sid earlier in the day foreshadows the later intoxication of his nephew, for instance, the two differ fundamentally in their reaction to the experience. Richard rejects the vice, while Sid embraces it, unable to control his dependence on alcohol despite the fact that drinking cost him Lily's love and the respect of his family. By placing his central character, Richard, at the troubled intersection of childhood and adulthood, O'Neill further allows his audience to speculate on the outcome of the young man's future success and happiness.

HISTORICAL CONTEXT

Though *Ah, Wilderness!* is set in 1906, O'Neill wrote it in the mid-1930s, in the depths of the Great Depression and at the height of unemployment and national despair. In the years leading up to the debut of the play on Broadway, and the corresponding apex of O'Neill's career, fundamental shifts in creative sentiment and social vision had begun to take root in the form of bohemianism, a movement dedicated, among other things, to the reimagining of the stylized, traditional artistic contributions of the past Victorian age.

According to Jeff Kennedy in "Playwright of the Modern World: Eugene O'Neill in Context," bohemian playwrights and novelists were influenced by such important events as the famed 1911 Armory Show of modern art in New York City and the Paterson Strike Pageant in New Jersey, a theatrical protest that further convinced O'Neill of the untapped power of his craft. These artists sought to depict ordinary Americans in their struggle for survival and fulfillment. This meant voicing themes hitherto considered inappropriate for the stage, which posed a challenge to the adoption of high ideas by many affluent Americans in the years preceding and immediately following World War I. These cultural mores of empathy and authentic depiction among the elite corresponded with the immigration of thousands of displaced and destitute persons from Europe, resulting in the unprecedented swelling of city centers and the industrial machine, as well as advancements in labor rights and unionization. O'Neill himself became deeply involved in the bohemian scene—which spread from an isolated literary community in Chicago to far greater renown on the East Coast—in his frequenting of bars and meetings in such places as Greenwich Village in Manhattan and Provincetown at the far tip of Cape Cod.

Yvonne Shafer, in the essay "Filtering America's Past through Sunlight: Eugene O'Neill's *Ah, Wilderness!*," contends that although 1933, when *Ah, Wilderness!* debuted, was a period of rare contentment and familial engagement for O'Neill, the same year represented a decidedly low point for millions of his fellow Americans. In the four years following the start of the Great Depression in 1929, the country's industry and production had slowed to a crawl, crippling the market and resulting in the unemployment and dispossession of countless workers. While O'Neill was planning an impressive estate on the beaches of Georgia, massive tracts of land in other

COMPARE
&
CONTRAST

- **1906:** Both O'Neill and his fictional counterpart, Richard, come of age during a period of unmatched immigration in the history of the United States. In 1906, the year in which *Ah, Wilderness!* takes place, President Theodore Roosevelt signs the Naturalization Act of 1906. It is a revision of an 1870 immigration bill, the first of many, requiring immigrants to demonstrate proficiency in English before applying to become naturalized citizens.

- **1930s:** The high unemployment rate of native-born American citizens during the Great Depression prompts disgruntled workers to scapegoat the growing population of Mexican American immigrants in California and several southwestern states. These immigrants are subjected to harassment, intimidation, and even forceful repatriation (being returned to their home country). The US government attempts to counter this aggression, with some small degree of success, by establishing migrant worker camps with aid from the newly established Farm Security Administration.

  Today: Debates over the regulation and rights of immigrants glow hotter than ever. In early 2015, the Immigration Rule of Law Act is presented in Congress. If passed, this law would threaten to deprive the progressive immigration reforms of the Obama administration of any monetary support.

- **1906:** A large portion of San Francisco is laid to waste by a devastating earthquake that results in widespread loss of life and property damage; roughly a quarter million Americans are made homeless. This natural disaster results in a plummet of stock prices, which President Theodore Roosevelt fights to remedy during his second term in office.

- **1930s:** O'Neill writes his only comedic work in the depths of the greatest depression in American history, spanning a full decade from 1929 to 1939. Stemming from a devastating stock market crash, the calamity results in the unemployment of a full quarter of American workers, and other countries worldwide suffer even more.

  Today: Although it does not approach the severity of the Great Depression, the economic recession of the early twenty-first century lasts nineteen months, from 2007 to 2009, and has serious implications for the global economy. In 2015, the US economy is still recovering from the economic devastation.

- **1906:** The Pure Food and Drug Act is passed in this year. It is the first of several laws aimed at protecting American consumers from blatant misinformation and unscrupulous advertising. Among other pressing concerns, the law addresses the addition of dangerous and addictive substances such as alcohol and narcotics to household medicines, demanding stricter standards of regulation.

- **1930s:** Born of misguided but well-intentioned idealism, Prohibition—when alcohol was made illegal in the United States—is ended when the Twenty-First Amendment to the US Constitution is passed in 1933. Although initially enforced in the hope of bettering society, the movement inadvertently contributes to the rise of organized crime and the broadening of alcohol consumption across all segments of American society. Alcohol is widely available through "speakeasies," unregulated and illegal bars.

  Today: The union of modern innovation and the age-old allure of vice gives birth to "powdered alcohol" that can be mixed with water to create liquor (outwardly marketed to campers, picnickers, and other individuals in need of lightweight provisioning). Concerns over misuse of the product continue to spark anxiety and fierce debate among lawmakers on a local and national scale.

Richard's mother is concerned about his choice of reading material. (© file404 | Shutterstock.com)

Southern states became virtually untenanted, auctioned off to those few still wealthy enough to seek economic opportunity in the midst of nationwide destitution. The decade from 1929 to 1939 was not one for frivolities and expensive entertainment among Americans. Countless theaters closed their doors for lack of attendance, resulting in the mass cancellation of productions and a lull in the theatrical creativity that had begun to take hold in the prior decade. It is all the more remarkable, then, that *Ah, Wilderness!* created such a splash among American audiences. Whether this play was born of O'Neill's own present circumstances or his understanding of a growing need for comic relief in dark times, O'Neill's only comedic work out of more than two dozen tragedies could not have come at a better time.

CRITICAL OVERVIEW

Much critical speculation has been devoted to the reason for O'Neill's departure from his traditional genre of tragedy in the play *Ah, Wilderness!*

and its comparison to what is widely considered, according to Trevor M. Wise, to be his most autobiographical work, *Long Day's Journey into Night.* While the tremendous extent of his contribution to the American stage is beyond question, critics differ on the exact nature of O'Neill's contribution and whether it represents, as Kennedy asserts, a decisive victory of dramatic realism over the melodrama that had held sway over previous generations, an affirmation of emerging modernist sentiment, or the foundation for what has come to be known as postmodernism.

In what she terms O'Neill's "comic valedictory," scholar Eleanor Heginbotham acknowledges both the leavening spirit of the play's humor and its poignant portrayal of a bygone age of American innocence. Through her comparison of *Ah, Wilderness!* with novelist William Faulkner's comparable venture into comedy in his novel *The Reivers*, she asserts that O'Neill transcends the distinction between the comic and the tragic to forge a uniquely instructive romance. According to Heginbotham, novel and play are rich in homely details . . . but both also follow patterns of romance, a higher world than that of ordinary experience. . . . In their descent, ascent, and hard-won wisdom, Richard and Lucius lead us to accept Grandfather's advice: to embrace the necessity and joy of living with embarrassment and moving into the unknown with hope.

Although Shafer rejects the assertion that *Ah, Wilderness!* is as much an autobiographical piece as *Long Day's Journey into Night*, she echoes this understanding of the play as emblematic of hope and optimism that is based on an admittedly embellished past. Shafer writes:

> The vision of life constructed by O'Neill has continued to appeal to audiences as a hopeful representation of past reality during the vicissitudes of World War II, the Cold War, and Vietnam. In recent times it has charmed audiences with depictions of a past which O'Neill, himself, did not experience and which, in the wake of recent tragedies and the contemporary ironic view of life, seems paradoxically to be both real and imaginary.

Other critics, like John V. Antush, writing in the scholarly article "O'Neill: Modern and Postmodern," comment primarily on O'Neill's unparalleled productivity during the "modern" period of American artistic innovation in the twentieth century, from the 1920s to the mid-1950s. In this view, O'Neill was dedicated in attacking the era's superficial depictions of human behavior, using complex characters like Sid and Richard in *Ah, Wilderness!* to lay the groundwork for the more unaffected style of later postmodern playwrights. Scholars like Kennedy, on the other hand, shift the focus to what they believe is the most singular contribution of O'Neill to the American stage: his willingness to delve into the psyche of his characters and explore their conflicting motivations for often misguided, self-defeating behavior. In so doing, Kennedy argues, O'Neill and his company extended an enduring mirror to the face of national identity. As Kennedy claims,

> In the process, they changed the definition of dramatic realism from simply depicting realistic settings to creating authentic and powerful drama that revealed psychological motivations for behavior in American life. The Players' desire to create an American identity on stage, with O'Neill as their most accomplished playwright, paved the way for future American playwrights . . . to further explore the American psyche and to present the dichotomies that make America both great and sometimes deeply conflicted.

IT IS THE IDEALISM INHERENT TO POETRY, NOT PRACTICALITY, THAT ACTS AS THE YOUNG MAN'S MORAL COMPASS IN BOTH OF THESE INSTANCES."

CRITICISM

Jeffrey Eugene Palmer
Palmer is a high school English teacher, scholar, and freelance writer. In the following essay, he examines the literary lens favored by O'Neill in writing Ah, Wilderness!

The reimagining of classical themes of tragedy in a contemporary context is but one of many dramatic hallmarks of the great American playwright O'Neill. His one break with this tragic tradition, his widely praised 1933 comedy *Ah, Wilderness!*, seems to escape the serious tone of antiquity in its earnest all-American account of a well-adjusted middle-class family living in Connecticut right after the turn of the twentieth century. The many domestic details included within the play, the endearingly folksy vernacular of many of its characters, and even the alignment of the action with Independence Day all work to furnish the impression that this is an America secure in its simplicity and modernity and untouched by the troubled shadows of a darker age.

The initial mood established by the introduction of the Millers and their tranquil household is soon undermined, however, by the persistent presence of literary allusion in the form of their second-youngest son, Richard. Routinely quoting such literary (and notably un-American) greats as Wilde, Swinburne, and Charles Baudelaire, the self-proclaimed black sheep of the family often falls laughably short of his attempts to impress and shock those around him. Although he succeeds in worrying his doting mother, Essie, with his wayward European-influenced notions, the other characters of the play regard the young man's attempts at showing off his education as opportunities for mirth or even dull disdain. Such amusing details as the aspiring scholar's ignorance of the archaic spelling of "jail," which prompts him to mispronounce Wilde's *Ballad of*

WHAT DO I READ NEXT?

- Friedrich Nietzsche's *Thus Spake Zarathustra*, apart from being one of the most influential philosophical works of the modern age, was O'Neill's favorite book and the inspiration behind the unique "perspectivism" and haunting implications of many of his most celebrated plays. The book was published between 1883 and 1891.

- *Bless Me, Ultima* (1972), by Rudolfo Anaya, is one of the most academically recognized and widely beloved examples of Chicano literature in this country. Set in rural New Mexico in roughly the same era that O'Neill wrote *Ah, Wilderness!*, the classic details the coming of age of another young man, Antonio Márez y Luna, in language that alternates fluidly between English and Spanish and is rich with the unique cultural motifs of the American Southwest.

- Betty Smith's 1943 perennial American classic, *A Tree Grows in Brooklyn*, is the semi-autobiographical account of a girl who comes of age in an impoverished household in an immigrant neighborhood in Brooklyn, New York, just after the turn of the century, grappling with young love, loss, and the trauma of her childhood.

- *The Glass Menagerie* (1944) elevated playwright Tennessee Williams to instant fame and cemented his status alongside O'Neill and Arthur Miller as one of the foremost American visionaries of his age. A simple but poignant tale about the loneliness of a young woman who finds solace not in human companionship but in a collection of glass animal figurines, the bittersweet account of Laura Wingfield in many ways mirrors the perceived plight of Lily in *Ah, Wilderness!*

- *Death of a Salesman* (1949) is one of the most widely read and analyzed works of the great playwright Arthur Miller. Committed to portraying the often devastating abyss separating illusion and reality, self-perception and self-actualization, Miller creates in the character of aging salesman Willy Loman a tragic foil for the endearing, albeit pitiable Uncle Sid.

- *The Ballad of Reading Gaol* was written by renowned Irish novelist, personality, poet, and playwright Oscar Wilde during the period of his imprisonment on charges of indecent behavior with a young man, a member of the English nobility. Often quoted by Richard throughout the course of *Ah, Wilderness!* the despairing, serious tone of this poem strikes a marked contrast with the childish, largely inconsequential woes afflicting the young man. The poem was published in 1898.

- *Long Day's Journey into Night*, the play that won O'Neill one of four Pulitzer Prizes and helped garner him a Nobel Prize in Literature, is widely considered to be his most autobiographical work. As such, it not only provides a tragic comparison to the comedic *Ah, Wilderness!* but also is representative of O'Neill's most polished prose and the secret life of the man behind the masterpiece. The play was published in 1956.

Reading Gaol, allow the audience to dismiss the pervasive presence of literature in the play with little more than a chuckle. On the surface, then, Richard's definite if perhaps underdeveloped literary pretensions seem to serve no deeper purpose than to set him apart from the rest of his family and pave the way for subsequent acts of rebellion.

In his scholarly article "Bohemians on the Bookcase: Quotations in *Long Day's Journey into Night* and *Ah, Wilderness!*," Robert Combs suggests another dimension to the playwright's inclusion of so many literary allusions. While O'Neill goes to great lengths to limit the threatening implications of these references to a contemporary

---

audience, Comb argues, their very existence indicates concealed but ever-present divisions in an otherwise seamless society.

> *Ah, Wilderness* contains quotations also, from the same or similar nineteenth-century authors, but they are not so troubling because there are fewer of them, they are briefer, and their purpose is clear and less threatening to the audience. They are the reading material of Richard Miller, the adolescent son of a prominent small-town family, who uses them to express his angst and to impress his girlfriend Muriel with his worldly wisdom.... The quotations in *Ah, Wilderness!* serve another purpose, to point up a difference between two kinds of early twentieth-century middle-class characters: the Millers, especially Richard's father, Nat, who are sophisticated and conversant with the darker side of life, and the McCombers, especially Muriel's father, David, who are unsophisticated and live in denial of it.

The play equates being well-read with being sophisticated and presentable, implying sharp divisions in social class and thus casting a shadow over an otherwise lighthearted play. More interesting still, however, is a contradictory correlation that seems to exist between the potential for moral corruption that comes along with European romanticism and the salvation offered by American "good sense." Endowed with the natural temperament of a poet, susceptible to the lofty ideals contained in his favored reading material, Richard nevertheless allows this idealism, perceived as a laughable weakness by those around him, to guide him toward decisions of decency. Although he gets drunk and nearly goes to bed with a prostitute, Richard actually conducts himself quite admirably. Not only does he, out of loyalty to Muriel, refuse to engage Belle's services, he pays her money to take the night off and protects her honor, albeit unnecessarily and unsuccessfully, against the advances of another prospective customer. Although he refuses to express regret over his drunken state, Richard later rejects the vice with the conviction of a man who knows himself and wishes to live his life with dignity until the end. It is the idealism inherent to poetry, not practicality, that acts as the young man's moral compass in both of these instances.

In contrast to the decency and self-mastery displayed by Richard, both his father and uncle give him advice that, while undeniably well intentioned, falls decidedly short of any degree of romantic sentiment. Sid shakes his head with a sad and world-weary knowingness at his nephew's condemnation of drink, believing Richard's firm stance on the matter to be little more than the folly of youth. His own experience, lacking any lingering remnants of romanticism, has taught him that while the spirit is willing, the flesh is weak and that resolutions of sobriety are as fleeting as hangovers.

More distasteful still, Nat imparts to his son the hard-boiled "facts of life" about the relations between men and women. Candidates for marriage and for intercourse, he contends, are rarely one and the same, a horrifying proclamation against which Richard's poetic temperament rebels. Tempered by an endearing awkwardness and a genuine regard for his son's happiness in life, Nat's words are nevertheless deeply revealing of his poisoned outlook on life.

> Well, you're a fully developed man, in a way, and it's only natural for you to have certain desires of the flesh, to put it that way—I mean, pertaining to the opposite sex—certain natural feelings and temptations that'll want to be gratified—and you'll want to gratify them. Hmm—well, human society being organized as it is, there's only one outlet for.... Well, there are a certain class of women—always have been and always will be as long as human nature is what it is. It's wrong, maybe, but what can you do about it?... But that doesn't mean to ever get mixed up with them seriously! You just have what you want and pay 'em and forget it. I know that sounds hard and unfeeling but we're talking facts.

Both Nat and Sid talk with the authority of adult experience out of a genuine desire to instruct the adolescent Richard and initiate him into the harsh realities of life. Although Richard respectfully acknowledges their opinions, it seems just as likely, especially given the optimistic ending of the play, that he will instead follow the poetic convictions of some of his favorite authors.

On another level, the almost obsessive presence of literary allusion in *Ah, Wilderness!* contributes to what Combs calls an "impasse of identity": an inability to reconcile the role of a flawed past in creating a good present. This is shown by such seemingly incidental details of the play as its title, a line taken from the *Rubaiyat* of Omar Khayyam, a poem that sheds doubt upon the sanctity of tradition, and Richard's inability to write his own modern compositions despite his love of the poets of an earlier age. The fear of the subversive power of the antiquated poetry of

Richard and Muriel meet to talk on the beach, where they kiss for the first time. *(© Lisa A | Shutterstock.com)*

which Richard is so fond is strikingly ironic within the context of a play that celebrates both modernity and the blissful illusions of a bygone age. By setting a play so obsessively disturbed by the past *in* the past, O'Neill suggests that while the face of the future is ever-changing, the sentiments that underlie that change, as represented by the many literary allusions voiced by Richard, exist as the only comfortable constants in an otherwise changeable world.

Whatever O'Neill's true intention in providing the audience of *Ah, Wilderness!* with such a wealth of literary allusions, literature and the classics are tremendously important in his work overall. Combs asserts that each of the great playwrights of the twentieth century made use of a unique "lens" through which they scrutinized contemporary American society in an attempt to usher in their respective reforms of modernity. Tennessee Williams focused upon the psychological self-made prisons of his characters, and Arthur Miller focused upon the role of uncontrollable influence and corresponding regret in perpetuating the human condition. O'Neill's lens, Combs suggests, is largely literary. In allowing so

graceful and yet evocative a fusion of past and present references as well as modern and classical themes in his works, O'Neill achieved what even the most accomplished of his contemporaries could not, simultaneously bridging the gap between modes of ancient, Victorian, and modernist creativity while laying the foundation for the dawning postmodern age. This incredible achievement is embodied in the unlikely character of Richard, a boy who feels equally comfortable in the wisdom of the past and the urgency of the present and will not be discouraged, even by the reluctant and fearful society of which he is a part, to dream of a future that is not bound by stifling social conventions.

Source: Jeffrey Eugene Palmer, Critical Essay on *Ah, Wilderness!*, in *Drama for Students*, Gale, Cengage Learning, 2016.

Ellen Kimbel

In the following excerpt, Kimbel explains how Ah, Wilderness! *is different from O'Neill's other work.*

It is exactly half a century since the first production of Eugene O'Neill's only major

INDEED, IT SEEMS THAT THE NUMBER OF PRODUCTIONS OF *AH, WILDERNESS!* ACCELERATES EVEN AS THE TIME AND SPIRIT IT RECREATES RECEDE INTO THE EVER MORE DISTANT PAST."

comedy, *Ah, Wilderness!* and an appropriate time for a reassessment. Although it is one of O'Neill's most performed plays, its critical history has been odd, to say the least. It has been variously: dismissed as too false and sentimental to be worthy of serious consideration; judged as having substance only insofar as it is the sunny counterpart of *A Long Day's Journey into Night*, that is, as wish fulfillment fantasy; assessed as a nostalgic family comedy whose true meanings exist in the currents of evil and despair beneath its bright and sparkling surface. While these approaches to *Ah, Wilderness!* differ from one another, it is interesting to note that they share a certain common assumption: that is, they suggest that the play's real value, when there at all, is found in its subtle evocation of the tragic vision expressed in the rest of the O'Neill canon. In short, critics of O'Neill's work have not known quite what to make of this unprecedented and atypical sampling of good cheer.

The dramatist was himself aware of the play's anomalous [sic] relationship to the rest of his work. He referred to it as a "dream walking" and admitted it was "out of [his] previous line." And, he had this to say about the work's focus:

> My purpose was to write a play true to the spirit of the American large small town at the turn-of-the-century. Its quality depended upon atmosphere, sentiment, an exact evocation of the mood of a dead past. To me, the America which was (and is) the real America found its unique expression in such middle-class families as the Millers, among whom so many of my own generation passed from adolescence into manhood.

This statement shows O'Neill to be the most cogent of the play's commentators, most of whom, eager to avoid committing the intentional fallacy, have paid scant attention to O'Neill's view of the play and have insisted on its correspondence to *Long Day's Journey*. Such interpretations, while

illuminating the dramatist's psychological development and/or his personal history, do not take sufficiently into account the play's final effect, both as read and performed. And that effect, particularly from the perspective of the nineteen-eighties, is one of affirmation tinged with nostalgia for a time of innocence, simplicity, and safety—a time long gone but summoned up and revitalized with great poignancy in *Ah, Wilderness!*

That it has always been a hugely popular work is in itself revealing. It had a long run on Broadway in 1933, its first production; it has been filmed twice (once with music as *Summer Holiday*); it was made into a Broadway musical as *Take Me Along*; it has been adapted for television; and even at this writing it is playing in New York. Indeed, it seems that the number of productions of *Ah, Wilderness!* accelerates even as the time and spirit it recreates recede into the ever more distant past. It should be obvious that its ongoing success is due not to its reworking of the intricate O'Neill family relationships or to its place in the dramatist's technical or thematic evolution but rather to its clear and convincing presentation of the cultural milieu of middle-class small town America at the turn of the century, in fact, to what O'Neill had all along claimed for it.

There are a number of ways in which the work is firmly anchored to the period which is its setting. First, the conventions and beliefs of the Miller family are to a great extent characteristic of that large, increasingly powerful business and professional group that was to become the mainstream of American culture and it is these attitudes, genteel and conservative, that shape the broad plot outline of the play. Further, the details of O'Neill's stage directions (painstakingly accurate here as in all his plays), recreate the look and feel of the period, contributing to the authenticity. The Miller home, for example, is furnished in the "medium-priced tastelessness" of the period: there are sliding doors and portières, a front parlor, a back parlor, a piazza, and an open front porch. The hotel bar has at least two items that have since disappeared from view: a "family entrance" and a brass cuspidor. There are several references to the popular ballads of the day: in the bar, the player piano grinds out "Bedelia," Arthur Miller sings "Then You'll Remember Me," "Dearie," and "Waiting at the Church" and Sid refers to performances at Hammerstein's Victoria theater in New York.

There are, too, a number of contemporary colloquialisms; and if O'Neill's critics have judged the language of his plays to be less than felicitous (the dramatist himself frequently complained that he had no ear for dialogue), here, the use of long forgotten phrases is less clumsy than essential to the play's periodicity. Thus, Sid, when funny is "a caution," Waterbury is a "nifty old town," a spanking is a "good hiding," and a prostitute is a "tart" or a "swift baby." The play then, is rather remarkable in its capacity to catch and hold for a few brief hours a whole constellation of manners and morals redolent of a bygone age.

This should not be construed as a reductive view of *Ah, Wilderness!* Clearly, the play by the very nature of its genre—nostalgic family comedy—lacks the philosophical, mythic, and poetic suggestiveness of the tortured dramas for which O'Neill is justifiably famous. However, it does have some interesting things to say about adolescence and the nature of the family unit early in the century, and in so doing, it acts as a reflecting lens for these same areas of experience in the high-tech, media-saturated, coolly cynical present.

The values by which the Miller family is defined, the old traditional ones of home and family, respectability and success have been judged by some readers to suggest a Philistine view, one embracing all that O'Neill's major works reject as patently false and hollow. But this is either an objection to the form itself (compare, for example, the beliefs, behavior, and goals of the families in *Our Town, Life With Father, I Remember Mama*, or the Andy Hardy movies), or is a response to the known facts of the author's own very different life. Neither of these is a valid basis for judging *Ah, Wilderness!*, which is either a success or a failure entirely on its own terms.

The values dramatized and implicitly endorsed by the play are those of affirmation: there is, in the main, approval, even admiration of the Millers and the patterns of experience they represent, and of the kind of adulthood toward which Richard moves at the work's conclusion. When there is irony, it is gentle and it is directed toward the follies of adolescence—the theatrical posturing, the self-aggrandizement, the tendency to see the world in extremes of black and white. And when there is psychological probing—as there is in Sid's obdurate need to fail, in Lily's

prim self-righteousness, and in Nat's painfully inhibited approach to sex in his "man to man" talk with Richard—it is accomplished with a most delicate and compassionate scalpel. These are—these men and women in a "large small town" in Connecticut early in the century—good and decent people who are regarded by their creator with tenderness and not a little wistfulness.

The play's fundamental optimism is in evidence from the beginning. It is suggested by the description of the set—a bright sitting-room, cheerful in the morning sunlight, comfortable rockers and armchairs around a table, and books everywhere (books, the stage directions assure us, "the family really have read") and it is enhanced by the animated buzz of conversation from an unseen dining room; and then by the appearance of a blond, sunburnt boy who is "bursting with bottled up energy." The day is July Fourth, the year is 1906, a period of time when Americans still believed in the promise and the dream and when that holiday gave the signal to families all over the country to join in celebration—on picnics, on day-long journeys to a relative for the annual barbecue, and of course for the ubiquitous fireworks.

In *Ah, Wilderness!*, the day is of more than usual significance, for it symbolizes Richard's own personal, if short-lived revolution. That which he rebels against is to some extent that which his parents represent: this, of course, makes him not only typical, but healthy. But since his parent's values are those espoused by the work as a whole and since, by implication, they become his own, they must be given particular scrutiny.

Nat and Essie Miller are neither idealized nor flat and predictable. Their weaknesses—Nat's tolerance of Sid's drinking, his insensitivity to his sister's unhappiness, his occasional boorishness; Essie's needless prolonging of the bluefish joke, her snappishness under stress—make them credible, convincing. Their great strengths, and it is these that the play emphasizes, is in their essential relationship to one another, and in their attitude toward their children. They function in their attributes as that against which other relationships are measured—throwing into bolder relief, for example, the loneliness of Sid and Lily, becoming the normative pattern for Richard to emulate. And, tangentially, but not insignificantly, they provide a perspective on turn-of-the-century middle class mores.

It was customary in that period of our history for men to be alternately protective and patronizing of their women. That we now regard such behavior as a ritual of deference and *politesse* masking a very real, if unconscious oppression, is both beside the point and after the fact. It is historically accurate and the play catches this attitude perfectly in the relationship of Nat to his wife. Thus, the contents of the books Richard is now reading (Swinburne, Ibsen, Carlyle, Shaw, Wilde, *The Rubaiyat*) remain secreted from Essie; she is expected not to be present during the "birds and bees" dialogue; and it is presumed she will not mind when her husband, in full view of the family, "slaps her jovially on her fat buttocks." Her retaliation (like that of millions of women like her) is subtle but effective: the perpetuation of the bluefish joke; her own cherished belief that "men are weak" and her unblinking announcement to Nat that her mother had never thought him "overbright."

But that which most often distinguishes Nat and Essie Miller in their relationship to one another is their capacity for loving. During much of the play, they manifest real awareness of and concern for each other's feelings. For example, Nat, sensing his wife's distress over Richard's absence, tries to keep her mind off the lateness of the hour and encourages Mildred and Arthur to provide some distracting entertainment. And when Sid taunts Nat about his annual retelling of a story of his youthful heroism, Essie comes to her husband's defense. That they are still romantically involved is demonstrated in the famous last scene, a moment at least quietly suggestive of the mood of lovers:

> Mrs. Miller: . . . I'm going to turn out the light. All ready?
> Miller: Yep. Let her go, Gallagher. (She turns out the lamp. In the ensuing darkness the faint moonlight shines full in through the screen door. Walking together toward the front parlor they stand full in it for a moment, looking out. Miller puts his arm around her. He says in slow voice)—There he is—like a statue of Love's Young Dream. (Then he sighs and speaks with a gentle nostalgic melancholy) What's it that *Rubaiyat* says
> "Yet Ah, that Spring should vanish with the Rose! That youth's sweet-scented manuscript should close!"
> (Then throwing off his melancholy, with a loving smile at her) Well, Spring isn't everything, is it

Essie? There's a lot to be said for Autumn. That's got beauty, too. And Winter—if you're together.
> Mrs. Miller (simply): Yes, Nat. (She kisses him and they move quietly out of the moonlight, into the darkness of the front parlor.)

And there is the sense throughout of a genuine and tender comradeship, particularly in evidence in their unified response to their children. . . .

Source: Ellen Kimbel, "Eugene O'Neill as Social Historian: Manners and Morals in *Ah, Wilderness!*," in *Critical Essays on Eugene O'Neill*, edited by James J. Martine, G. K. Hall, 1984, pp. 137–41.

SOURCES

Antush, John V., "O'Neill: Modern and Postmodern," in *Eugene O'Neill Review*, Vol. 13, No. 1, Spring 1989, pp. 14–26.

"The Barack Obama Administration," in *Encyclopædia Britannica*, http://www.britannica.com/place/United-States/History#ref1074326 (accessed October 21, 2015).

Bever, Lindsey, "Just Add Water: Here Comes Powdered Alcohol," in *Washington Post*, March 12, 2015, http://www.washingtonpost.com/news/morning-mix/wp/2015/03/12/just-add-water-here-comes-powdered-alcohol/ (accessed October 21, 2015).

Combs, Robert, "Bohemians on the Bookcase: Quotations in *Long Day's Journey into Night* and *Ah, Wilderness!*," in *Eugene O'Neill Review*, Vol. 33, No. 1, 2012, pp. 1–13.

"Eugene O'Neill: American Dramatist," in *Encyclopædia Britannica*, http://www.britannica.com/biography/Eugene-ONeill (accessed August 1, 2015).

Heginbotham, Eleanor, "Living with It: The Comic Valedictories of Faulkner and O'Neill, *Ah, Wilderness!* and *The Reivers*," in *Studies in American Fiction*, Vol. 28, No. 1, Spring 2000, pp. 101–12.

Hurd, Mary G., "Great Depression," Immigration to the United States website, http://immigrationtounitedstates.org/527-great-depression.html (accessed October 21, 2015).

Kennedy, Jeff, "Playwright of the Modern World: Eugene O'Neill in Context," in *Critical Insights: Eugene O'Neill*, edited by Steven F. Bloom, Salem, 2012, pp. 29–43.

O'Neill, Eugene, *Ah, Wilderness!*, Random House, 1933.

Pells, Richard H., "Great Depression," in *Encyclopædia Britannica*, http://www.britannica.com/event/Great-Depression (accessed October 21, 2015).

"Prohibition: United States History 1920–1933," in *Encyclopædia Britannica*, http://www.britannica.com/event/Prohibition-United-States-history-1920-1933 (accessed October 21, 2015).

"S. 534, Immigration Rule of Law Act of 2015," in *Congress.gov*, 2015, https://www.congress.gov/bill/114th-congress/senate-bill/534 (accessed October 21, 2015).

"San Francisco Earthquake of 1906," in *Encyclopædia Britannica*, http://www.britannica.com/event/San-Francisco-earthquake-of-1906 (accessed October 21, 2015).

Shafer, Yvonne, "Filtering America's Past through Sunlight: Eugene O'Neill's *Ah, Wilderness!*," in *Laconics*, Vol. 1, 2006, http://eoneill.com/library/laconics/1/1a.htm (accessed August 14, 2015).

Smith, Marian L., "Race, Nationality, and Reality: INS Administration of Racial Provisions in U.S. Immigration and Nationality Law Since 1898, Part 1," in *Prologue*, Vol. 34, No. 2, Summer 2002, http://www.archives.gov/publications/prologue/2002/summer/immigration-law-1.html (accessed October 21, 2015).

Wise, Trevor M., "Biography of Eugene O'Neill," in *Critical Insights: Eugene O'Neill*, edited by Steven F. Bloom, Salem, 2012, pp. 20–26.

"The 1906 Food and Drug Act and Its Enforcement," FDA website, http://www.fda.gov/AboutFDA/WhatWeDo/History/Origin/ucm054819.htm (accessed October 21, 2015).

FURTHER READING

Black, Stephen A., *Eugene O'Neill: Beyond Mourning and Tragedy*, Yale University Press, 1999.
> Using O'Neill's personal correspondences, diary entries, and evaluations of his own work, Black masterfully establishes a link between the playwright's own tragic life and the immortal, haunting characters he brought to the American stage.

Damon, Duane, *Headin' for Better Times: The Arts of the Great Depression*, Lerner Publications, 2002.
> An accessible but comprehensive overview of the unique role of the arts in one of the darkest decades of American history, Duane's examination details the contributions of painters, designers, musicians, novelists, playwrights, and visionaries of all types in the years between 1929 and 1939.

Dowling, Robert M., *Eugene O'Neill: A Life in Four Acts*, Yale University Press, 2014.
> A holistic view of O'Neill's life and his contributions to modern American theater, this major biography of the great playwright represents the most comprehensive and up-to-date resource of its kind.

Egan, Leona Rust, *Provincetown as a Stage: Provincetown, the Provincetown Players, and the Discovery of Eugene O'Neill*, Parnassus Imprints, 1994.
> In this work on the once-sleepy New England beach community that would become the birthplace of a new age of modern American theater, Egan examines the formative influence of the bohemians on the work of O'Neill and his lifelong relationship with the famed Provincetown Players.

SUGGESTED SEARCH TERMS

Eugene O'Neill

great American playwrights

bohemianism

Greenwich Village

Provincetown Players

Ah, Wilderness!

O'Neill AND Ah, Wilderness!

early modern theater

Irish American playwrights

August: Osage County

TRACY LETTS

2007

August: Osage County, a three-act play by Tracy Letts, debuted in June 2007 at the Steppenwolf Theatre in Chicago. The drama premiered on Broadway at the Imperial Theatre in December 2007 with the original Steppenwolf cast. *August* tells the story of the dysfunctional Weston family as they gather in their dilapidated farmhouse in rural Oklahoma after Beverly Weston, the family patriarch, goes missing. His wife, Violet, is a manipulative, spiteful, and drug-addicted woman who psychologically torments her three daughters, each of whom is going through her own crises. *August: Osage County* received rave reviews and won the Pulitzer Prize for drama and five Tony Awards in 2008, including one for best play. The drama is considered a dark comedy for Letts's liberal use of humor, although bad language, vindictive behavior, drug abuse, and sexual themes figure just as prominently. It is also notable for its length—three and a half hours—and its large cast of thirteen characters.

When Barbara, Ivy, and Karen Weston gather at their parents' house in Osage County in the sweltering summer heat, Violet, who is suffering from cancer of the mouth, takes apparent delight in dwelling on their insecurities even as she sinks deeper into her addiction to painkillers. These conflicts ricochet outward to include Barbara's husband and teenage daughter; Violet's sister, Mattie Fae; and her husband and son. Letts based Violet Weston on his maternal grandmother, who herself descended into drug abuse

Tracy Letts *(© Matt Carr / Getty Images)*

and alcoholism after her husband committed suicide by drowning, as Beverly does in the play. Many critics favorably compared the play to Eugene O'Neill's 1956 masterpiece *Long Day's Journey into Night*, which is also about a dysfunctional family torn apart by a drug-addicted mother.

Letts is a successful Chicago-based playwright and actor who previously wrote the well-regarded play *Man from Nebraska* (2003), which garnered him a Pulitzer Prize nomination for best drama in 2004, but *August: Osage County* catapulted him into the top echelon of living playwrights for his ability to create a family drama in the same vein as twentieth-century masters Edward Albee and Tennessee Williams. The play also had a successful run in London and toured nationally in the United States. Letts adapted *August: Osage County* as a screenplay that was produced in 2013, starring Meryl Streep as Violet Weston and Julia Roberts as her eldest daughter, Barbara. Both actors received Oscar nominations for their work.

AUTHOR BIOGRAPHY

Letts was born on July 4, 1965, in Tulsa, Oklahoma, and grew up in Durant, Oklahoma; his parents were both college instructors. His father, Dennis Letts, later in life became an actor and played Beverly Weston in the Chicago and Broadway premieres of *August: Osage County*, though he passed away just two months after the New York opening. Letts's mother, Billie, later in life became a best-selling author, penning the award-winning 1995 novel *Where the Heart Is*, about a pregnant teenager who is abandoned by her boyfriend and gives birth in an Oklahoma Wal-Mart.

A couple of years after graduating from high school, Letts's desire for a career in the arts led him to Chicago, where he began his long association with the Steppenwolf Theatre Company as both an actor and playwright. His first play produced at Steppenwolf was 1993's *Killer Joe*, the story of a hit man hired to kill a woman so that her son would receive the insurance money. While some critics considered the play's characters stereotypical, many also commended its sharp wit. Letts's next work, *The Man from Nebraska*, was produced on Broadway in 2007 and earned the playwright a Pulitzer nomination. The story concerns a long-married, devoutly religious couple in crisis. When the husband takes off by himself for an extended, soul-searching stay in England and has an affair, his long-suffering wife patiently awaits his return even as their daughter turns against him.

August: Osage County, Letts's fourth play, was an instant hit in Chicago and in New York, earning Tony Awards for best play, best director, best leading actress, best featured actress, and best set design. This success led Letts to write the screenplay for the film version, which was directed by John Wells. Previously, Letts had also adapted his plays *Bug* (1996) and *Killer Joe* (1993) for film.

In addition to the Tony Award he won for best play for *August: Osage County*, Letts also received a Tony Award for best actor in 2013 for his portrayal of George in a revival of Edward Albee's seminal *Who's Afraid of Virginia Woolf?*, another play about the twisted relationship of a married couple anchored by resentment and alcoholism. Letts followed up *August: Osage County* with *Superior Donuts*. The play is about an aging hippie who runs a small café in Chicago and his young African American employee's plans to modernize it. While critics appreciated the play, most noted that it lacked the dramatic heft of *August*.

Over the years Letts has also acted in a number of plays, independent films, and television series, including the critically acclaimed Showtime series *Homeland*. He married fellow film and stage actor Carrie Coon in 2013, with whom he starred in *Who's Afraid of Virginia Woolf?* Coons herself was nominated for a Tony in that production. The couple have no children and live in Chicago.

PLOT SUMMARY

Prologue

Beverly Weston is in his study in his ramshackle country house in rural Oklahoma interviewing Johnna Monevata for a job as a live-in housekeeper. Beverly reveals to her that he is an unrepentant alcoholic and that his wife is addicted to pills. "My wife takes pills and I drink. That's the bargain we've struck," he says. He is hiring a housekeeper because neither he nor his wife has the energy to take care of the house anymore. Beverly, a former poet and college professor, mulls over T. S. Eliot's quote "life is very long" from the poem "The Hollow Men" and lends Johnna a volume of Eliot's work. Violet, Beverly's wife, can be heard offstage, swearing. Johnna explains that although her father was named Youngbird, she has changed her name to Monevata, the Cheyenne translation of the word.

Beverly quotes poet John Berryman's "The Curse" as Violet disturbs his meeting with Johnna. Violet enters, slurs her words, and addresses Johnna rudely, asking what kind of an Indian she is. Johnna, despite Violet's drug-induced bad manners, states that she desperately needs this job. Beverly mentions that Violet has cancer of the mouth. The scene ends with Beverly once again quoting "The Hollow Men."

Act 1, Scene 1

Beverly is missing. Violet's sister and brother-in-law, Mattie Fae and Charlie, have arrived to help Violet through this difficult time. Ivy, the Westons' middle daughter, who lives nearby, believes Beverly is gone for good; Mattie believes he'll come back. Mattie is discussing her son, Little Charles, with others and describes him as lazy, uncomplicated, and unemployed. Charlie and Mattie Fae's relationship becomes clear; she

MEDIA ADAPTATIONS

- Letts adapted *August: Osage County* for film in 2013. Meryl Streep and Julia Roberts were nominated for Academy Awards for their roles as Violet and Barbara, respectively. Sam Shepard, Ewan McGregor, and Benedict Cumberbatch also star. The film was produced by Smokehouse Pictures, directed by John Wells, and released by the Weinstein Company.

- A live production of *August: Osage County* featuring the original cast is available on CD and as a digital download from L.A. Theatre Works.

criticizes him for drinking beer at a time like this, even though she's drinking whiskey. Charlie is kind and soft-spoken, and Mattie Fae is domineering. She demands that he feel her sweaty back, which is the result of Violet's not believing in air conditioning, "as if it is a thing to be disbelieved," as Beverly told Johnna in the prologue.

Violet says the police have not found Beverly at any hospital but that his boat is missing. Ivy says Barbara, the oldest Weston daughter, and her husband, Bill, are coming in from Colorado. Violet gets upset because she thinks Ivy is withholding information about their arrival. Violet then rips into her for being forty-four years old and unmarried.

Bill, Barbara, and their fourteen-year-old daughter, Jean, arrive. Outside the house they talk about the stifling heat, the relentlessly oppressive climate of Oklahoma, and their displeasure with Jean's smoking habit. Violet is happy to see them, Barb tells everyone that she's in charge now, and everyone is momentarily nice.

Act 1, Scene 2

Violet, who is loopy from her painkillers, recounts Beverly's disappearance to Barb. She tells Barbara about a safe deposit box that Beverly told her to open if anything happened to him. This suggests that Violet knows he has committed suicide. The arguments begin in earnest: Barbara is upset about the safe deposit box, and Violet accuses Barbara of breaking her father's heart when she moved to Colorado. Violet has a malevolent edge in her voice, which she blames on her mouth cancer and chemotherapy, but Barbara knows that her mother has relapsed into her painkiller addiction. Violet complains that there is an "Indian" in her house and launches into a petty argument with Barbara, who says they like to be called "Native Americans" now.

Upstairs in the attic bedroom, Jean smokes marijuana and talks with Johnna about her parents' separation, brought about by her father's affair with a much younger student. Jean compliments Johnna's necklace, a turtle containing her dried umbilical cord, a Cheyenne tradition.

Act 1, Scene 3

Bill and Barbara are settling in for the night on the hide-a-bed in the living room. Bill pages through a copy of Beverly's award-winning and only book of poems, *Meadowlark*, and Barbara criticizes his interest in it. It is clear that Barbara is upset about Bill's affair; they are simply presenting a united front for Violet and the family, who do not yet know about their separation. They begin arguing over their relationship, and Bill wants to table the discussion until after Beverly returns. Barbara tells him, despite not yet having proof, that her father is dead.

Act 1, Scene 4

Police lights flash through the living room; the sheriff is at the door. It is 5:00 a.m. Barbara wakes up Violet, whose slurred words indicate that she is quite drugged. Sheriff Gilbeau, who went to school with Barbara, informs the family that Beverly's body was found washed up on a sandbar not too far from his boat. She asks whether his death is an accident or suicide, and the sheriff suggests that it is suicide. Barbara volunteers to identify the body at the beach.

Violet appears, slurring her words, and plays an Eric Clapton record on the stereo. Her actions and words are inappropriate to the situation. She repeats "and then you're here" nonsensically as the lights go out.

Act 2

The extended Weston family gathers at the house following Beverly's funeral. Violet is alone in Beverly's study, well-dressed and sober. She briefly quotes Emily Dickinson before taking a pill. She is bitter about Beverly's leaving her, calling it his choice, not hers.

Elsewhere, Karen, the youngest Weston daughter, is engaged in a one-sided, self-absorbed conversation with Barbara about how true love has eluded her and that she has always envied Barbara and Bill's relationship. Finally, she gets around to talking about Steve, her new boyfriend, who has accompanied her on this trip. She's over-the-moon in love, unrealistically believing that he is at long last going to fulfill all her romantic childhood fantasies. Karen is so besotted with Steve that she does not appear to be grieving her father at all. She desperately wants her big sister to approve of Steve, but the two have barely met. Barbara says they need to discuss what to do about their mother, but Karen continues her manic monologue about her newfound happiness and wanting to develop a closer relationship with Barbara and Ivy.

Upstairs, Violet and Ivy argue about clothes. Violet wants Ivy, who is wearing a black pantsuit, to try on a dress. Ivy refuses, wanting her mother to accept her as she is. Violet says Ivy looks like "a magician's assistant." Ivy accuses her mother of insulting her, and Violet accuses Ivy of being too sensitive. Mattie Fae mentions that Little Charles is thinking of moving to New York and says he would not last a day there. She is still upset that her son overslept and missed the funeral. Mattie Fae criticizes her husband for coddling Little Charles by picking him up at the bus station. The conversation descends into two mothers, Violet and Mattie Fae, criticizing their children.

Violet, continuing in her characteristically negative tone, mentions that older women are fat and ugly. Ivy and Mattie Fae disagree, but Violet stands firm. Ivy becomes increasingly indignant at her mother's insistence that she wear a dress to attract a man. She finally blurts out that she has a man, but she refuses to divulge any details even as Violet and Mattie Fae demand to know more.

Downstairs, Steve and Bill arrive back from the store, talking about Steve's business, which sounds somewhat sketchy. Jean is excitedly watching the 1925 *Phantom of the Opera* on television, but Barbara criticizes her for prioritizing it over her grandfather's funeral. Steve is interested in the movie and strikes up a conversation with Jean. He immediately recognizes the smell of marijuana on her and starts flirting. He promises to hook her up with some good dope. Karen walks in as they are talking, oblivious to their revealing body language. Steve has forgotten to buy cigarettes at the store, but Jean offers Karen some of hers.

On the porch, Charles and Little Charles arrive. Little Charles is extremely apologetic about missing the funeral. Charles accepts his apology and is not angry. Little Charles's low self-esteem and sensitivity permeate the scene. He is quite aware that he is the butt of family jokes, but he and his father proclaim their love for each other.

Back in the dining room, Bill and Barbara argue over Bill's parenting skills. He believes that Jean is mature enough to handle their separation in stride. Barbara disagrees, but her colorful language indicates that perhaps she is not the role model she believes herself to be. Barbara is very clear: she cannot handle the stress that the separation is causing her, on top of her father's death and her daughter's behavior. Bill's assessment of Barbara as a "good, decent, funny, wonderful woman" who is "a pain in the ass" seems on the mark.

During preparations for dinner, simultaneous conversations take place in various parts of the house. Topics of conversation include Little Charles's apologizing for his tardiness to his mother, Ivy's irritation at her mother's probing questions about her love life, Mattie Fae's inedible casserole, and who will sit with Jean at the children's table.

At the front door, Little Charles, having fetched his mom's casserole from the car, has a brief conversation with Ivy in which it is revealed that he, in fact, is Ivy's new boyfriend. Entering the dining room, Little Charles drops his mother's casserole. He apologizes, but his mother takes it personally, believing that it is an unconscious attack on her. Attention is deflected from the incident only when Jean announces that she is a vegetarian. Several members of the family react as if they have never heard of something so preposterous.

Violet arrives and admonishes the men for taking their suit jackets off in the stifling heat. During grace Steve's phone rings, and he excuses himself from the room to take the call. Abruptly, Violet asks Barbara if she wants the dining room sideboard; she explains that she wants to downsize. A chorus of approval for the food is met with Violet's curt response that the paid servant made it. Her speech grows more confrontational and inappropriate. She steers the conversation to an awkward place by screeching, "Where's the meat?"

Talk turns to the funeral service. Violet is critical; she would have preferred an open casket. Bill and Steve try to stay positive while Violet recalls unseemly incidents from her husband's past. Finally, Violet asks who Steve is; she seems not to know that Karen is engaged. Karen says they are getting married on New Year's Eve in Miami, and Violet rudely says she will not be there. Violet drills Steve on how many times he has been married previously and continues an inhospitable conversation about him.

Charles has disrespected his daughter by making fun of her vegetarianism; Violet castigates Jean for talking back to him. Tempers become heated. Violet announces that even though Beverly's will says otherwise, Beverly intended to leave everything to her. Violet announces to everyone that she knows Bill and Barbara are separated. She tells Barbara that there is no way Barbara could hope to compete with a younger woman. When questioned about her increasing aggression, Violet says that "the day calls for it" and that she is "just truth-telling." Her voice becomes louder and louder, her language more and more vulgar. Violet recounts an incident from her childhood in which one of her mother's boyfriends attacked her with a claw hammer and Mattie Fae had to save her.

According to Violet, no one has had a harder life than she and Beverly, who lived in a car with his parents during his impoverished childhood. "We sacrificed everything and we did it all for you," she tells her daughters. "You never had real problems so you got to make all your problems yourselves." Finally, Violet admits, with prodding from Barbara, that she is a drug addict. Barbara tries to grab Violet's bottle of pills from her, and the two end up in a vicious brawl. After they are separated by Charles and Bill, Barbara asserts her power. She orders others to search the house for pills and for someone to call the doctor. Barbara yells at Violet, "I'M RUNNING THINGS NOW!"

Act 3, Scene 1

The sisters are in their father's study discussing whether or not Violet needs to be institutionalized, as she has been before. They realize that Violet has threatened a number of doctors with malpractice lawsuits in order to obtain prescriptions to further her habit.

Barbara asks if something is going on between Ivy and Little Charles, who are first cousins. Ivy admits that Little Charles is her new boyfriend. Barbara and Ivy discuss their rather distant relationship, but Karen maintains that she feels close to them now more than ever. Barbara is unconvinced, and Ivy says, "I can't perpetuate these myths of family or sisterhood anymore. We're all just people, some of us accidentally connected by genetics, a random selection of cells. Nothing more." Ivy conveys that she feels abandoned by her sisters, both of whom moved away from Oklahoma and left her to deal with their parents. They argue over who was their father's favorite and whether or not he had a moral right to kill himself. Barbara believes that he "had a responsibility to something greater than himself." Ivy, tired of dealing with her parents, says she and Charles are leaving for New York and that Barbara can handle Violet herself.

A sober Violet enters, feeling slightly sentimental. She tells a horrible story from her childhood and comments on how mean her own mother was. Violet denies needing any help, especially from Barbara, to get over her pill addiction. Downstairs, Mattie Fae criticizes Little Charles for watching too much television. Charles stands up for his son, telling his wife,

> I don't understand this meanness. I look at you and your sister and the way you talk to people and I don't understand it. I just can't understand why folks can't be respectful of one another. I don't think there's any excuse for it. My family didn't treat each other that way.

In a conversation with Barbara, Mattie Fae, who suspects something is going on between Ivy and Little Charles, insists that Barbara must intervene and end the relationship. They are not first cousins; they are half-siblings. Little Charles is Beverly's son, the result of an affair he had with Mattie Fae. Mattie Fae assumes her husband knows, but they have never discussed it. Mattie Fae leaves it up to Barbara to end their relationship because "you said you were running things."

Act 3, Scene 2

Late that night Jean and Steve are smoking marijuana in the dining room while flirting and engaging in inappropriate physical contact. Jean tells Steve that she is fifteen, but he is undeterred by her age. Ultimately, Jean rejects his advances, worried that he is going to get them in trouble. He replies, "I'm white and over thirty. I don't get in trouble." Just then Johnna flips on the light; she's brandishing a frying pan and hits him over the head with it. Others come running at the sound of the commotion.

Karen is horrified that Steve has been injured. Barbara wants to know what happened. Johnna says, "He was messing with Jean. So I tuned him up." Barbara attacks Steve, threatening to murder him. Steve proclaims his innocence, and Jean just wants the commotion to stop. Karen and Steve begin packing their bags. Jean implores her parents to stop freaking out and accuses them of not caring about her. She yells, "I hate you!" to her mother, and Barbara replies, "I hate you too, you little freak." Karen tells Barbara that she knows Steve is not perfect but that Jean was complicit in his behavior. Bill decides to leave with Jean. Barbara's response is "I fail. As a sister, as a mother, as a wife. I fail." She realizes that Bill is never coming back to her, and as he leaves she calls out, "I love you."

Act 3, Scene 3

Barbara and Johnna are in the study. Barbara has assumed her father's role, sitting at his desk and drinking whiskey. Johnna wants to know if she is being fired and relates how much Beverly loved his daughters. Barbara assures Johnna that she still has a job, because she knows how to lie.

Act 3, Scene 4

The window blinds are open for the first time, making the house light and airy. Barbara and Sheriff Gilbeau converse in the living room. She calls Jean a nymphomaniac and enumerates many regrets. Barbara tells the sheriff that she has "the Plains." He asks her out to lunch and mentions that he has received a phone call from a motel manager who saw Beverly just before his suicide. Barbara seems uninterested in the news. Instead, she kisses him, but he pulls away.

Act 3, Scene 5

Barbara tells Ivy that their mother, if not drug free, is "moderately clean." Ivy has come to tell her mother than she and Little Charles are leaving for New York in the morning. Barbara has not yet revealed that Ivy and Charles are brother and sister. Instead, she is hostile to Ivy's declaration that she is in love with Little Charles and says she is too old to go to New York. Ivy declares that she has a right to her own happiness. Johnna serves dinner, but Violet refuses to eat. Violet and Barbara have settled into an unhealthy, symbiotic relationship.

Barbara insists that Violet eat her catfish, and soon they are hurling obscenities at each other. Ivy simply cannot get their attention, so she throws her dinner plate against the wall. Barbara responds by grabbing a vase and smashing it on the floor. Violet joins in. Barbara becomes truly unhinged as Ivy tries to yell above the din that she and Little Charles—who she insists on calling Charles—are in love. Barbara counters by calling him "Little Charles." Finally, Violet declares that she knows Ivy and Little Charles are brother and sister. Ivy is shocked and devastated. She calls both of them "monsters" and insists they are still going to New York. Violet believes Ivy will stay in Oklahoma because she is weak. Violet admits that she has always known about Mattie Fae's affair with Beverly and that Beverly knew that she knew—although they never talked about it.

Then Violet mentions that maybe she would have talked to Beverly about Little Charles at the motel. It turns out that Violet knew his whereabouts before his suicide. Instead of stopping him, she went to the bank and got the safe deposit box, as per their arrangement. When Barbara mentions that Violet could have prevented Beverly's death, Violet calls Barbara a "smug little ingrate" and tells her that "there is at least one reason Beverly killed himself and that's *you*. . . . His blood is just as much on your hands as it is on mine." Violet believes that Beverly never recovered from Barbara's move to Colorado. Ultimately, Violet says that her husband's suicide was simply a tactic "to weaken me, just to make me prove my character." This is the last straw for Barbara, and she leaves.

Violet is alone, calling after Ivy and Barbara and, finally, Johnna. Violet, desperate, climbs up the stairs into Johnna's room and crawls into her lap. Johnna sings quietly to Violet as Violet repeats over and over, "and then you're gone."

CHARACTERS

Charles Aiken

Charles, also known as Charlie, is Violet's brother-in-law, having been married to Mattie Fae for many years. Charles is a peacemaker who is stunned that his wife's family is so cruel to one another. Charles probably knows that Little Charles is not his son, but he has always treated him kindly and taken his role as father seriously, even though Mattie Fae has a low opinion of Little Charles.

Little Charles Aiken

Little Charles is the son of Charles and Mattie Fae Aiken, although unbeknownst to him his real father is Beverly Weston. He has recently fallen in love with Ivy Weston, whom he believes is his cousin, and is planning to move to New York with her. Little Charles, like Ivy, is the black sheep of his family. He does not drive, and he has no career to speak of (he was fired from a shoe store). His mother regards him as a failure owing to his laziness and lack of direction in life. Many of his actions appear to be instances of passive-aggressiveness against his mother. For instance, he insists that he missed his uncle's funeral because he overslept, although it seems likely that he purposely failed to set his alarm. Little Charles also commits the Freudian slip of dropping his mother's casserole onto the floor during dinner. This gesture is a passive-aggressive way of retaliating against her cruel remarks. He knows it will infuriate her, and yet he can claim it is an accident, just like oversleeping.

Mattie Fae Aiken

Mattie Fae is Violet's older sister, supposedly their mother's favorite. She once saved Violet from one of their mother's boyfriends, who attempted to beat Violet with a claw hammer. Mattie Fae is just as cruel to her own child, Little Charles, as Violet is to her three daughters. Even though he is an adult, she refuses to call him anything other than "Little Charles," and she constantly calls him lazy, untalented, and a failure. She knows he is really Beverly's son from their long-ago affair. She has never discussed this fact with anyone, not even her husband or Violet, although she suspects that they both know. Mattie Fae is nearly as self-centered as her sister. She is oblivious to the fact that no one likes her casserole. She is also mean to Charles, her husband, who she believes makes excuses for Little Charles.

Barbara Fordham

Barbara is Beverly and Violet Weston's eldest and favorite daughter. Her arrival from Colorado with her husband and daughter to deal with her father's disappearance is what kicks off the main action of the play. When it becomes obvious that Violet is impaired by drugs, Barbara announces that she is in charge. Barbara intends to keep her separation from Bill Fordham under wraps for the duration of their stay, so she does not have to admit she has failed as a wife. However, it is obvious that Barbara is deeply hurt by her husband's affair. During this stressful time, Barbara is just as cruel to her own daughter, Jean, as Violet is to her. She berates Jean's interest in movies and calls her a nymphomaniac. Barbara is tasked by Mattie Fae with ending Ivy and Little Charles's relationship owing to its incestuous nature. Ultimately, Barbara assumes her father's role in the household and conversely with Johnna in his study. Ultimately, Barbara abandons her mother when she learns that Violet could have prevented Beverly's suicide.

Bill Fordham

Bill Fordham is Barbara's husband and a college professor. Even though they are separated, he dutifully travels with her and Jean, his daughter, to Oklahoma from Colorado in order to keep up appearances. Bill admits to still loving Barbara and calls her a "good" and "decent" person, but he is tired of her relentlessly controlling demeanor. Thus, he is having an affair with a much younger student. Bill, unlike Barbara, believes that Jean is resilient enough to survive her parents' divorce. He leaves with Jean after a compromising episode with Steve, but he is still kind to Barbara in her worst moments as a mother.

Jean Fordham

Jean Fordham is fourteen years old, interested in old movies, and smoking marijuana. She seems unaffected by her parents' separation and is not particularly close to any of her relatives. In fact, she has extended conversations only with Johnna and Steve, her aunt's fiancé. She is a typical teenager, somewhat distant and moody. Her anger at her parents surfaces only in the aftermath of the incident with Steve, who was acting inappropriately toward her. She claims his behavior is no big deal and that everyone is overreacting. She

vilifies her mother and refuses to take responsibility for her actions or even comprehend their seriousness.

Sheriff Deon Gilbeau

Sheriff Deon Gilbeau informs the family that Beverly's body has been found. Later, he tells Barbara that a local motel manager recalls seeing him in the days before his suicide. Barbara and Deon Gilbeau knew each other in high school and attended the prom together. He appears to have a soft spot for her still and asks her out to lunch. However, he is taken aback when she suddenly and inappropriately kisses him. Sheriff Gilbeau's father was a convict, but unlike the Westons, he overcame his troubled childhood to be a successful, well-adjusted member of the community.

Steve Heidebrecht

Steve is Karen Weston's fiancé. He appears to be an easygoing guy. However, it becomes clear from his conversation with Bill that he is taking part in shady business deals involving mercenaries in the Middle East. Steve immediately takes an inappropriate liking to Jean, encouraging her to smoke marijuana with him. He flirts with her and is obviously trying to have his way with her, using as his excuse that he is "white and over thirty," so he will not get in trouble. He is unconcerned with the fact that Jean is underage or that his fiancée is in the same house. Johnna whacks him over the head with a frying pan when she catches him in a compromising position with Jean. He defends himself dishonorably by claiming that he did not do anything.

Johnna Monevata

Johnna is the Westons' live-in housekeeper. She is a member of the Cheyenne Nation and has recently lost her parents. She desperately needs the job Beverly offers her. For the duration of the play she serves as a point of stability in the vortex of action. She cooks, cleans, and ignores cruel comments from Violet. The only significant conversation she has is with Jean, who seems genuinely interested in her. Johnna has embraced her ethnic heritage, changing her last name from the Anglicized Youngbird to the Cheyenne-language equivalent, Monevata. She wears a turtle amulet around her neck that contains her dried umbilical cord, a Cheyenne tradition that imbues her with power. She saves Jean by whacking Steve with a frying pan when his behavior becomes predatory. Ultimately, she is the only person remaining in the house after Violet has alienated her entire family.

Beverly Weston

Beverly Weston is the patriarch of the Weston family of Osage County, Oklahoma. He is a retired college professor who once published an award-winning collection of poems called *Meadowlark* and never published anything again. It is his disappearance and suicide that prompt the unraveling of his entire family as they gather first in concern and then in grief. He appears during the prologue when he is interviewing Johnna. The fact that Beverly is hiring Johnna as a live-in housekeeper hints that he is preparing to commit suicide. He is at peace with his alcoholism and his wife's drug addiction, telling Johnna that that is the deal they have struck with each other. He quotes the poets T. S. Eliot and John Berryman, each quote indicating that he is tired of life's hassles but not willing to confront his mistakes. He does not acknowledge that Little Charles is his son. He puts into motion a previously agreed-upon plan that gives Violet an opportunity to save him, but she does nothing.

Ivy Weston

Ivy Weston is the Westons' middle daughter. She has never been married and still lives in Oklahoma. She is a tomboy and protests her mother's attempts to change her appearance so she can attract a man. Ivy seems happy with who she is but is unable to convince her mother of that fact. To get her mother to leave her alone, she says that she has a boyfriend but refuses to give details when pressed. She is coy because her boyfriend is her cousin, Little Charles. She sticks up for him every chance she can by insisting that he be called Charles. She intends to start a new life with him in New York. Her feelings and wishes are constantly steamrolled by her mother and sister. When her mother finally blurts out the truth—that Charles is actually her half-brother—she is horrified and calls Barbara and Violet monsters.

Karen Weston

Karen Weston is Violet and Beverly's youngest daughter, who has traveled to Oklahoma from Miami. She is bubbling with newfound love and excited to introduce Steve, her fiancé, to her family. She is too consumed with euphoria over having found the "perfect" man to be concerned with her father's disappearance and death. She is blind to Steve's faults and unrealistic about her happiness. She claims to want to forge closer ties to her sisters, but they do not want the same closeness in return. She bores Barbara with a long-winded monologue about her childhood fantasies of love and how they have finally come true. She claims that Steve is a business genius, but she is clearly overlooking the fact that he is actually engaged in shading business dealings. When Steve is found in a compromising position with Jean, Karen suspects that Jean is at least partly culpable.

Violet Weston

Violet Weston is the matriarch of the highly dysfunctional Weston family. She has once before been treated for her painkiller addiction, but she is once again taking the drugs. Violet projects her own unhappiness onto her three daughters, taking a perverse pleasure in highlighting their insecurities and revealing their darkest secrets in a sadistic effort to control them. Her outbursts most likely come from a place of deep resentment and insecurity, especially over her husband's suicide. Violet meets every bit of news with scorn and insists that she, above all others, has led a difficult and tragic life and that her daughters should be grateful for all she has given them. She considers her vindictive behavior as mere "truth-telling" and attacks each of her daughters in turn. She tells Barbara, her oldest, that she was her father's favorite and that he was devastated when she left Oklahoma for Colorado. In fact, this is the reason why her father killed himself. Violet also rudely brings up the fact that she has figured out that Barbara and Bill are separated.

Violet's middle daughter is Ivy. She is appalled that Ivy has no interest in appearing feminine or finding a suitable man. She continually calls Ivy's previous boyfriend a "loser" and disregards Ivy's current declaration of happiness. Violet's final cruelty toward Ivy is casually blurting out the long-suppressed truth—that Ivy and Little Charles are half-siblings, not cousins. With this simple statement she ruins two lives but retains her power over both of them.

Violet demeans her youngest daughter, Karen, by telling her how rude it is to bring a date to a funeral. She seems not to know or care that her daughter is engaged to Steve; she sees him only as an interloper at their dinner table. When Karen asks if her mother will be at their

New Year's Eve wedding, Violet responds patronizingly, "I don't really see that happening."

Violet's dysfunction reaches its zenith when she tells Barbara that she knew how to reach Beverly during his disappearance but failed to do so only out of spite. Thus, her inaction resulted in her husband's death. Violet, having already chased Ivy and Karen away, now prompts Barbara to leave. Violet's physical and emotional self-destruction leads to her mental destruction as she climbs into Johnna's lap and cries about having been abandoned.

THEMES

Dysfunctional Families

August: Osage County is about the dysfunctional Weston family and how their dysfunction is passed down from one generation to the next. The focus of the drama is on Violet Weston, an overbearing, manipulative, pill-popping wife, mother, and grandmother. The way her daughters relate to her reveals how they have either become like her or rejected her. The ultimate dysfunction belongs to Beverly, the Weston patriarch, who, having descended into his own addiction, commits suicide rather than deal with his family in a mature and constructive way.

Both Beverly and Violet's dysfunction has roots in their families of origin. Beverly grew up poor and lived in a car during his childhood, and Violet was nearly beaten with a hammer by one of her mother's boyfriends. Violet tells her children, "we lived too hard, then rose too high," perhaps overestimating her middle-class existence and definitely holding it against her children, who she believes are not sufficiently grateful for her hard work.

As for Violet's sister, Mattie Fae, her only child, Little Charles, is the result of her affair with Beverly. Both women and their milquetoast husbands know about his illegitimacy, but none has ever acknowledged it. This is highly dysfunctional. Even Little Charles's name is dysfunctional. He is neither little nor Charles's son, and yet the extended family insists on infantilizing him with the moniker *little*, which has become a kind of self-fulfilling prophecy. Little Charles cannot hold a job, drive a car, or be honest with his mother.

Violet demonstrates dysfunctional jealousy when she tells her children,

> You girls, given a college education, taken for granted no doubt, and where'd you wind up?.... Jesus, you worked as hard as us, you'd all be president. You never had real problems so you got to make all your problems yourselves.

Her bitterness and air of superiority is the opposite of how functional parents treat their children, which is with pride and love. Barbara, Violet's oldest daughter, has internalized this vindictiveness and now demonstrates it toward her own daughter, Jean, when she calls her a "nymphomaniac" and criticizes her interest in movies.

Violet is even mean to Mattie Fae, calling her "as sexy as a wet cardboard box." When it comes to family dysfunction, Letts seems to imply that women lead the way. The most conciliatory characters in the play are the men, notably Charles Aiken, who consistently tries to calm Mattie Fae, and Bill Fordham, who, despite his infidelity, has agreed to accompany Barbara from Colorado to deal with her family. Both men always stick up for their children when their wives criticize them, revealing that the Weston family is the source of the dysfunction.

The Weston family's dysfunction is highlighted when Charles tells Mattie Fae,

> I look at you and your sister and the way you talk to people and I don't understand it. I just can't understand why folks can't be respectful of one another. I don't think there's any excuse for it. My family didn't treat each other that way.

Johnna and Sheriff Gilbeau also serve to highlight the Westons' dysfunction. Johnna becomes a part of the Weston household because she needs a job. She is insulted by Violet and has conversations with only two people—Beverly and Jean. Johnna explains her love for her parents and her sadness that they are gone. Sheriff Deon Gilbeau grew up in a dysfunctional family; his father spent time in jail for killing a dog. Deon and Barbara made the best of their senior prom night when his father got drunk, stole his son's car, and drove to Mexico. Despite this background, Deon has become a respected member of the community, which illustrates that children can transcend their parents' dysfunction. To be in the Westons' sealed-off farmhouse is to enter into an environment of unhealthy self-absorption into which no light shines.

TOPICS FOR FURTHER STUDY

- Johnna wears a beaded pouch in the shape of a turtle around her neck. According to Cheyenne tradition, it contains her dried umbilical cord and will prevent her soul from becoming lost. Research and choose ten Cheyenne symbols. Create a poster with illustrations of these symbols, either drawn yourself or pictures you find. Label each symbol and explain its significance in one or two sentences.

- Research narcissistic personality disorder (NPD). Decide if you think Violet Weston meets the criteria for the disorder. Write a short essay discussing whether or not Violet meets the criteria. Use examples from the play to support your position. Also mention if you think anyone else in the play suffers from the condition and why or why not.

- Paul Zindel's 1964 young-adult play *The Effect of Gamma Rays on Man-in-the-Moon Marigolds* is about a dysfunctional family consisting of an abusive, drug-addicted mother and two adolescent daughters, Tillie and Ruth. Read the play (which was made into a film in 1972) and write a paper that compares and contrasts the mother, Beatrice, with Violet Weston. Write an introduction, a conclusion, and three supporting paragraphs that give examples of how she is both like and different from Violet. Use examples from both works in your paper.

- Beverly Weston was a poet, and during the prologue he quotes T. S. Eliot's "Hollow Men" and John Berryman's "The Curse." Both of these works hint at his dissatisfaction with life and may serve to foreshadow his suicide. Read these poems, and then write your own poem about the Weston family, adhering to Eliot's or Berryman's style as much as possible. Your work should be at least twenty lines long, and it does not have to rhyme. Choose descriptive words and similar themes.

- One of the most visceral scenes in *August: Osage County* is the dinner scene following Beverly's funeral. The scene has been praised for its realistic dialogue and conflict. Videotape a dinner scene or similar gathering at your home. Then transcribe up to 750 words of it on paper. Write an introduction to your scene that briefly describes all the characters, the setting, and the overall tone of the piece.

Parent-Child Relationships

The theme of family dysfunction is illustrated through the mother-child relationship. This includes Violet's relationships with Barbara, Ivy, and Karen; Mattie Fae's relationship with Little Charles; and Barbara's relationship with Jean. All three mothers undermine rather than support their children.

Violet is harsh on all her children, but she saves the worst for Barbara, who is most like herself. Violet calls her eldest daughter "a smug little ingrate" and says that Beverly killed himself because Barbara abandoned them after "wasted lifetimes devoted to your care and comfort." In fact, Barbara moved to Colorado for her husband's career, and in the prologue Beverly gives no inkling that his children are the reason for his unhappiness. Furthermore, Violet tells Barbara, "You couldn't come home when I got cancer but as soon as Beverly disappeared you rushed back." These outbursts illustrate that Violet feels abandoned by and resents Barbara.

Barbara, in turn, has internalized this dynamic and is now acting it out with her own teenage daughter. She criticizes Jean's behavior, from smoking to watching old movies, and she believes her husband's infidelity is responsible for Jean's bad behavior. When Jean lashes out in anger at her mother after the incident with Steve, Barbara responds very childishly. Jean says, "I hate you!," and Barbara retaliates with "I hate you too, you little freak!"

Violet refuses to accept her children as they are. She is on a mission to get Ivy, an independent, forty-four-year-old adult, to wear a dress against her will. Violet says that Ivy's black pantsuit makes her look like a "magician's assistant." Her only concern is that Ivy find the right kind of man to settle down with, whether or not that is what Ivy herself wants.

Violet is dismissive of her youngest daughter, Karen. She remarks that it is "peculiar . . . to bring a date to your father's funeral," after Karen has explained that Steve is, in fact, her fiancé. Violet cruelly quashes Karen's excitement over her upcoming wedding by stating dismissively, when asked if she will travel to Miami for the nuptials, "I don't really see that happening, do you?" Violet is unable to be happy for Karen, further driving a wedge into their relationship.

Mattie Fae, the other mother in the story, constantly disrespects her son, beginning with insisting on calling him "Little Charlie," despite the fact that he is thirty-seven years old. She believes that he is lazy and stupid, that his brain is rotting from watching television, and that New York City will eat him alive. Like her sister, Violet, Mattie Fae seems to want her son to fail and offers him no encouragement. She even tells her husband to stop coddling him.

When Violet's daughters and Little Charles try to assert themselves, they are never heard. Ivy tries relentlessly to ask why people keep calling Charles "Little Charles" but is always cut off. When she asks her mother to stop insulting the way she dresses, Violet tells her to "stop being so sensitive."

The father-child relationships in the play are much more supportive. For example, Charles is protective of Little Charles, which is all the more remarkable because he is most likely aware that he is not his father. He calls Little Charles "an observer" while Mattie Fae calls him stupid and unemployed. Charlie tells his son to "stop apologizing" for missing his grandfather's funeral and comforts him when he starts to cry. Bill believes that Jean is resilient enough to survive her parents' separation and that she is more "sophisticated" than Barbara gives her credit for. As for Beverly's relationship with his three children, he never once mentions them in the prologue.

The play begins and ends with Johnna, the young Cheyenne woman whom Beverly hired as housekeeper. (© arek_malang | Shutterstock.com)

Addiction

While it is primarily about dysfunctional families, *August: Osage County* also plays out against a backdrop of addiction. This is apparent from the prologue, when Beverly admits that his addiction is alcohol and his wife's is pills. In fact, Violet has once before attended a rehabilitation clinic, but having cancer has given her an excuse to resume taking painkillers. Beverly clearly sees the damage that addiction has caused in his life and hires Johnna to take care of the aspects of housekeeping that he and Violet no longer care to undertake.

Violet's current addiction is obvious from her slurred speech and nonsensical outbursts, yet she refuses to believe that she has a problem—a sure sign she is an addict. "I'm not hooked on anything," she tells Barbara, even though she has admitted to taking a muscle relaxer. Later, Violet, who is enjoying antagonizing everyone at the dinner table, changes her tune. "I am a drug addict.... Try to get [my pills] away from me and I'll eat you alive." This outburst leads to a physical confrontation that ends with a makeshift intervention spearheaded by Barbara.

Alcohol, cigarettes, and marijuana flow freely throughout the play, indicating that substance abuse is how many members of the family cope with stress. The youngest member of the Weston clan, Jean, who is only fourteen, has picked up this behavior—from her father, according to Barbara—and continues it into the next generation.

STYLE

Realism

August: Osage County is a work of realism. It is intended to represent people and events realistically, with no magical, supernatural, or science fictional elements. In a work of literary realism, the setting is familiar or historically accurate, and the characters' motivations and actions serve to highlight the universal truths of human nature. Many works of realism focus on the ways in which people are cruel to one another.

The leading playwrights to develop realism for the stage include Henrik Ibsen (1828–1906) and Anton Chekhov (1860–1904), and Letts is often compared to both of them. Realism is embedded into Letts's play through the setting, a ramshackle old house in a rural area of middle America that many audience members would find familiar. The discord of the middle-class Weston family, in which the father worked and the mother stayed home, would also be familiar to many playgoers. Divorce, infidelity, alcoholism, and family squabbles are common, if unhappy, elements of modern society that have touched many people's lives. In a work of realism, endings are often neither happy nor cut-and-dried. Realist endings often convey the sense that life simply goes on and that certain patterns of behavior will continue. In *August: Osage County*, it seems likely that none of the characters will change all that much. The Weston sisters retreat to their separate lives, and Violet fails to appreciate her daughters or truly understand why they have abandoned her.

Symbolism

A symbol is something that stands for something other than itself. In *August: Osage County*, one of the most obvious symbols is the Weston's dilapidated, dark, and hot farmhouse. This rural location, sixty miles northwest of Tulsa, Oklahoma, symbolizes Beverly and Violet's isolation, not only from the rest of their family but also from each other. Their children have physically abandoned them to move to Colorado, Florida, and soon New York City, as much as they have psychologically abandoned them.

The windows of the unkempt and unwelcoming structure are covered with cheap plastic shades sealed on all sides with duct tape. This symbolizes the family's inward focus and willful blindness to the outside world. This unhealthy environment feeds their addictions; they literally cannot see beyond themselves. Furthermore, the updates to the house, as the stage directions read, end in 1972. This coincides with their children's youth and Beverly's zenith as a poet, possibly the last year the Westons functioned constructively as a family. The house's lack of air conditioning is symbolic of the family's hot-house nature. They are literally and figuratively steaming as the result of Violet's refusal to be comfortable by installing air conditioning; she, in fact, wants to be uncomfortable. Beverly acknowledges this symbolism when he tells Johnna that "my wife is cold-blooded and not just in the metaphorical sense."

Another symbol in the play is Violet's cancer of the mouth. Her physical illness is a symbol of her psychological illness, which manifests itself in her filthy and coarse language. Her words are a figural cancer, eating away at her own sanity as the cancer is eating away her mouth. Even Violet's name is a tongue-in-cheek ironic symbol. Rather than being a typical "shrinking violet," a term for a shy, meek person, Violet Westin is foul-mouthed, strong-willed, and filled with hate. Nothing about her is delicate or flower-like.

Prologue

A prologue, literally "before word," is a self-contained introduction to the people, setting, and events of a literary work. The prologue in *August: Osage County* is integral to the story. Beverly speaks for himself, allowing the audience to gauge his personality firsthand rather than having to rely on what his family says about him after his death. Beverly's conversation as he interviews Johnna for the position of live-in maid reveals that he has given up on life and on his wife in particular. At no time does he blame his daughters or even mention them. Thus, the prologue gives the audience insight into Beverly's mindset. Violet's later proclamations about her husband reveal how little she knows about him or about her attempts to make her children feel guilty by lying to them. The prologue allows the audience to sympathize with Beverly and sets Violet up to be the villain of the story.

The prologue is one of the oldest devices in drama, having been an essential part of Greek plays in ancient times. Throughout the centuries, various playwrights have continued this tradition. In Shakespeare's *Romeo and Juliet*, for example, a short prologue delivered by a narrator tells the audience that they are about to see a story about a pair of "star-cross'd lovers" who take their own lives. Letts's prologue is different, in that he allows Beverly to function as his own narrator, with Johnna serving as a stand-in for the audience.

Like dramatists of the Elizabethan era, Beverly resorts to prose in his prologue. As a poet by profession, he quotes poems about discontentment by T. S. Eliot and John Berryman to foreshadow the play's action. In speaking to Johnna, Beverly serves the same function as ancient prologues—he tells the audience what they're in for. "Rather than once more assume the mantle of guilt . . . vow abstinence with my fingers crossed in the queasy hope of righting our ship, I've chosen to turn my life over to a Higher Power," Beverly says, hinting at his impending suicide.

HISTORICAL CONTEXT

Osage County

Osage County, Oklahoma, is a rural area that lies along the northern border of the state and at the eastern edge of the Great Plains. Violet and Beverly Weston live in Pawhuska; with a population of 3,500 as of 2010, it is the largest town in the county. Pawhuska was founded in 1872 and serves as both the county seat and the capital of the Osage Nation, a Native American tribe that has lived in the region since the mid-eighteenth century. Native Americans, in fact, make up over 25 percent of Pawhuska's population. A small portion of Tulsa—Oklahoma's largest city, with a population of over four hundred thousand people—seeps into Osage County as well. In the early twentieth century, the county is home to an oil refinery and mining operations for asphalt, limestone, sand, and gravel. The location of the Weston's house in one of the most rural counties in a rural state exemplifies the family's isolation from civilization. The median income of both Osage County and Pawhuska is below the US average. Few colleges and universities are in the area. Tulsa, about fifty-seven miles away, is home to Oklahoma State University, Tulsa Community College, and Oral Roberts University.

Johnna Monevata is a member of the Cheyenne Tribe, which is based in Concho, Oklahoma, southwest of Osage County in the middle of the state. Many Native American tribes play a crucial role in Oklahoma's history. In fact, before Oklahoma became a state in 1906 it was known as Indian Territory. Violet's unfamiliarity with the term *Native American* demonstrates how out of touch she is with the modern world.

The American Family in the Twenty-First Century

Many of the issues that seem to be driving a wedge between the members of the Weston family are quite common in early-twenty-first-century family life. Alcohol abuse affects 7 percent of all adults over the age of eighteen, and about 10 percent of children in the United States live with a parent who has an alcohol problem. Divorce is common. The US divorce rate reached its peak in 1981 and has been falling slowly since. Although reliable statistics are hard to come by, most experts believe that between 40 and 50 percent of all marriages end in divorce. Thus, the troubles between Bill and Barbara Fordham are hardly unique. In fact, more children in the United States grow up in a one-parent household than not, suggesting that, as Bill believes, Jean will survive her parents' split without severe repercussions. Additionally, the fact that Ivy, who is forty-four, has never been married—a fact that greatly upsets her mother—is not that unusual in the twenty-first century. In 1960, when Violet was a young woman, only 9 percent of adults over the age of twenty-five had never been married. By 2012 that figure had risen to 20 percent.

About forty thousand people in the United States commit suicide each year, making it the tenth leading cause of death among Americans. Furthermore, the highest suicide rate is for people between the ages of forty-five and sixty-four,

Violet's smoking habit has resulted in mouth cancer, which serves as an exaggerated reflection of the toxic things she says to her family. (© Saravut Biacharas / Shutterstock.com)

the upper limit roughly corresponding with Beverly's age. Men historically have always had a higher rate of suicide than women—about four times as high—and white people commit suicide more often than any minority. About half of all suicide deaths are the result of guns; drowning is quite rare, accounting for less than 2 percent of all suicide deaths.

While it is by no means as widespread as divorce or alcohol abuse, drug use is far from rare in contemporary US society and, by most accounts, is still rising in the twenty-first century. About 9.4 percent of the US population reported using an illegal substance in 2013, with marijuana the most commonly used drug. In 2007, the year *August: Osage County* ran on Broadway, about 14.5 million people in the United States admitted to using marijuana. In 2013, 6.5 million Americans admitted to abusing prescription drugs. Painkillers, to which Violet is addicted, are the most common form of abused prescription drug. The only point at which Violet does not mirror US drug statistics is in her age. Illicit drug use by older Americans is

uncommon. Most illicit drugs are used by those between the ages of sixteen and thirty-four. This puts Jean, who smokes marijuana, at the low end and her father and Steve, who also smoke pot, at the upper end of the statistic.

CRITICAL OVERVIEW

August: Osage County was an immediate hit with critics when it debuted at Chicago's Steppenwolf Theatre in June 2007 and again several months later at its Broadway premiere with the same cast. *New York Times* drama critic Charles Isherwood calls it "a fraught, densely plotted saga of an Oklahoma clan in a state of near-apocalyptic meltdown" that is "flat-out, no asterisks and without qualifications, the most exciting new American play Broadway has seen in years." Mollie Wilson O'Reilly summarizes the play in *Commonweal* as "a comedy without manners" that is "an emotional workout." It is "ferociously entertaining," writes David Rooney in *Variety*, "laced with corrosive humor so darkly delicious and ghastly that you're squirming in your seat even as you're doubled over laughing."

Many critics compare *August: Osage County* favorably to classic American dramas and Letts to several esteemed playwrights. Kate Kellaway, in a review for the London *Observer*, calls Letts "a natural heir (or, perhaps, wayward stepchild) to Tennessee Williams, Edward Albee and Eugene O'Neill." Brooke Allen, writing in the *New Criterion*, considers the play's similarity to O'Neill's *Long Day's Journey into Night*, another work about a dysfunctional family with a drug-addicted mother, saying that

> Letts has taken O'Neill's material, personalized it, and added the badly needed laughter. The story of Letts's Westons, like that of O'Neill's Tyrones, is harrowing—but you howl with laughter while you feel their pain and rage.

Elizabeth Fifer, writing in the *Eugene O'Neill Review*, agrees that the plays share striking similarities, but she thinks that Letts's work is more than an updated version of the O'Neill's story. Fifer notes that Letts's

> borrowings create the shiver of recognition: a family reunited, the exposing of hidden secrets and truths about characters, contrasts between the aspirations of one generation and the failure to realize them in the next, a doomed matriarch, a tragic patriarch.

The character of Violet Weston has received much critical attention. Fifer calls her "unrepentant" and says that she "does not accept her loss of power or any guilt, either for the suicide of her husband—whose last telephone call she did not take—or for her attempts to escape reality through drugs." Isherwood, conversely, has a perverse admiration for her. Violet, he writes,

> possesses a spirit of aggression that a pro linebacker would envy, and a sixth sense for finding and exploiting the sore spots and secret hurts of everyone around her.... The results are as harrowing as they are hilarious.

Allen deems Violet a "vicious creature" who is "proof that when someone devotes every ounce of energy to willful intransigence, no distracted and responsible adult can ever win." O'Reilly takes note of the "astonishing...cruelty" with which Violet "eviscerates her children." In praising Deanna Dunagan's performance as Violet, Rooney applauds the way the actress exposes "just enough of the fragile cracks in [Violet's] dragon-lady persona to make her a human monster."

New Yorker critic Hilton Als appreciates Letts's previous works for creating "drama by pitting violence against our banal sense of decency," but he is one of the few to assess *August: Osage County* in less-than-glowing terms. "The family's secrets feel as contrived as the play's regionalism," Als writes, concluding that it tastes like "a corny mint julep laced with Valium." Ultimately, Als feels, Letts "parodies his roots, rather than revealing them." Nevertheless, the critical reception was reinforced when the play won the Pulitzer Prize for drama and the Tony Award for best play in 2008. Deanna Dunagan, who originated the role of Violet Weston, and Rondi Reed who played Mattie Fae also won Tony Awards for their work.

CRITICISM

Kathy Wilson Peacock

Wilson Peacock is an editor and writer on literary topics. In the following essay, she examines the similarities between Letts's August: Osage County *and O'Neill's* Long Day's Journey into Night *as well as several other literary works.*

One of the most famous opening lines in all of literature belongs to *Anna Karenina*. Leo Tolstoy begins the story of his tragic heroine with the oft-repeated, seldom analyzed statement that all happy families are alike; each unhappy family is unhappy in its own way. Is Tolstoy's proclamation actually true? Given the long history of the dysfunctional family in literature, Russian and otherwise, the curious reader has numerous great works to consider in examining the issue. One of the most esteemed dramas of recent years, Letts's 2007 play *August: Osage County* has been compared to several canonical works, including Eugene O'Neill's *Long Day's Journey into Night* and Edward Albee's *Who's Afraid of Virginia Woolf?*, both of which feature some of the most dysfunctional families to ever hit the stage. A close look at each play reveals, however, that unhappy families actually have quite a bit in common. The Westons of Letts's work are not as unique as they, or perhaps even Tolstoy (were he alive today), would like to believe.

The similarities between the three dramas are stunning, right down to the awards they have won, which, at the very least, proves how much critics love a dysfunctional family. *Long Day's Journey into Night* won the 1957 Pulitzer Prize for drama, *Who's Afraid of Virginia Woolf?*

WHAT DO I READ NEXT?

- *Man from Nebraska* (2003) is a play by Letts that, like *August: Osage County*, concerns a long-married, religious Midwestern couple, Ken and Nancy, who are having marital troubles. The fractures in their relationship are healed only after the death of Ken's mother and an extended soul-searching trip to England.

- *Who's Afraid of Virginia Woolf?* (1962) is a play by Edward Albee that showcases the disintegration of the marriage of George and Martha, a middle-aged couple who invite a younger couple from George's university to dinner. The play won the Tony Award for best play in 1963, and Letts won the Tony Award for best actor in 2013 for his portrayal of George in a Broadway revival of the play.

- *Long Day's Journey into Night* (1956), by Eugene O'Neill, takes place during one day at the Tyrone family's shabby summer cottage in Connecticut. James Tyrone is a washed-up, alcoholic actor and his wife, Mary, is a morphine addict. Long-festering resentments surface as each member of the family, which includes the couple's two adult sons, descend into their respective addictions.

- *The Glass Castle: A Memoir* (2005), by Jeannette Walls, recounts the author's truly dysfunctional childhood during the 1960s and 1970s, being raised by an alcoholic father and an irresponsible mother. Walls overcomes the poverty and psychological torment of her upbringing to flourish as an adult.

- *The Corrections* (2001), by Jonathan Franzen, is a sprawling, award-winning novel about the twilight years of Enid and Alfred Lambert, whose three adult children return home for Christmas as their parents' marriage begins to fracture and as Alfred suffers from worsening dementia and Parkinson's disease. No one in the Lambert family is living the life he or she envisioned, with infidelity, divorce, anxiety, depression, and failed careers all part of the mix.

- Sherman Alexie's *The Absolutely True Diary of a Part-Time Indian* (2007) is the story of Junior, a Native American, who moves from the impoverished Spokane Indian Reservation, where alcoholism is rampant, to a wealthy rural high school, where he represents the only minority.

- *Mommie Dearest* (1978), by Christina Crawford, is a memoir that recounts the twisted relationship between the Hollywood legend Joan Crawford and her daughter Christina. Crawford was the mother of four and an alcoholic who subjected her children to various forms of physical and psychological abuse.

- *This Is How I Find Her* (2013), by Sara Polsky, is a young-adult novel about sixteen-year-old Sophie, who must deal with her mother's drug abuse and bipolar disorder. After her mom's suicide attempt, Sophie goes to stay with her aunt and uncle, neither of whom want to face the truth about Sophie's mother.

---

won the Tony Award for best play in 1963 (and would have won the Pulitzer, but the judges withheld the award owing to the play's profanity), and *August: Osage County* won both awards in 2008. All three dramas have been adapted as critically acclaimed films starring the most iconic actresses of their day: Katharine Hepburn in *Long Day's Journey into Night*, Elizabeth Taylor in *Who's Afraid of Virginia Woolf?*, and Meryl Streep in *August: Osage County*. All three women were nominated for Academy Awards for their roles, though only Taylor won. The first ingredient for an unhappy family, according to these examples, is an angry, resentful wife.

AUGUST: OSAGE COUNTY EXPLORES THE AFTERMATH OF BEVERLY WESTON'S SUICIDE AS HIS EXTENDED FAMILY STEWS IN THE SUMMER HEAT AND HIS WIDOW, VIOLET, VERBALLY EVISCERATES THEM WHILE WAITING FOR HER PAINKILLERS TO KICK IN."

While the plays share major similarities, each is an original work with a unique plot. *Long Day's Journey into Night*, written by O'Neill in the late 1930s and not performed until after his death in the 1950s, concerns James and Mary Tyrone, an alcoholic and a morphine addict, respectively, and their maladjusted adult sons, all of whom are getting on one another's nerves as they while away the summer in their dilapidated home. *Who's Afraid of Virginia Woolf?*, first performed in 1962, features George and Martha, a middle-aged couple whose alcohol-fueled sparring is the centerpiece to the most uncomfortable double date in theater history. *August: Osage County* explores the aftermath of Beverly Weston's suicide as his extended family stews in the summer heat and his widow, Violet, verbally eviscerates them while waiting for her painkillers to kick in.

Alcoholism and drug abuse mixed with marital discord are the foundation of all three plays. The central characters are all middle-aged or older and have not attained the life they envisioned for themselves. Beverly Weston published a well-received book of poetry early in his academic career but failed to maintain his momentum. Instead, he sequesters himself in his study with a bottle and hires a live-in housekeeper so that nothing will interrupt his drinking. Violet lashes out at anything that moves, believing she deserves a prize simply for living an adequate life. No one has had it as hard as she has. "Jesus, you worked as hard as us, you'd all be president," she tells her fairly successful children.

In *Long Day's Journey into Night*, James Tyrone is a once-successful actor known for a signature role who never achieved the world renown he believes he deserves. Mary believes that being an actor's wife is beneath her social station. Both of their sons are disappointments. "Ingratitude, the vilest weed that grows," Tyrone says of his eldest son, Jamie. Mary, like Violet Weston many decades later, tells her son to "stop sneering at your father! . . . Thanks to him, [you] have never had to work hard in your life." Like Violet, Mary has once conquered her drug addiction but has since fallen back into her old habit. Mary claims the arthritic pain in her hands requires medication, just as Violet claims that her mouth cancer requires painkillers. In both cases, physical ailments are outward manifestations of mental anguish.

As Mary's mental state deteriorates through the long day of the play, her husband and sons begin to drink, just as the Westons do to get through a dinner after Beverly's funeral. Both families live in isolation in a neglected house. The Westons' rural farmhouse has blacked-out windows and has not been updated in decades. The Tyrones' house, according to Mary, "was wrong from the start. Everything was done in the cheapest way. . . . It's just as well we haven't any friends here. I'd be ashamed to have them step in the door." Both families suffer because of their isolation, although for both families it seems that substance abuse and isolation go hand in hand.

In *Who's Afraid of Virginia Woolf?*, the twisted family dynamic is not so straightforward. Certainly, Martha and George are both alcoholics. George's career at the university has stalled; Martha has not been able to become a mother. They have coped with these disappointments by constructing a life of illusion for themselves. They have fashioned an imaginary child whom George kills off during the course of the play just to spite his wife. Martha calls her mythical son "beautiful; wise; perfect" and later says that he "could not tolerate the shabby failure his father had become." Though earlier in the evening she has said that George is the only man she ever loved, she later criticizes "the sewer of this marriage." The Tyrones and the Westons also share this paper-thin veneer of marital harmony, telling their children not to criticize them but then turning right around and doing just that to each other.

The characters in all three plays are alike in that their conversations, no matter how initially innocuous, invariably descend into argument. Husbands and wives believe they are due more than they have achieved, siblings resent each other, and everyone self-medicates to dull their psychological pain. An unhappy family, it seems, is composed of members who take even the most innocent statements as a personal attack. In *August*, Barbara and Bill cannot even agree on her father's legacy. "This book was a big deal," Bill says. "It wasn't that big a deal," she replies. "In those circles it was," he says. "Those are small circles," she says. George says, "There are easier things than being married to the daughter of the president of that university." Martha responds, "For *some* men it would be the chance of a lifetime!" They practically come to blows over the color of their imaginary son's eyes.

The parents' disgruntlement is passed down to the children. Mary complains endlessly that her husband is a cheapskate. The children become jealous of one another. Jamie tells Edmund that he was "always jealous of you. Mama's baby, Papa's pet. . . . And it was your being born that started Mama on dope. . . . I can't help hating your guts." Ivy, after a disastrous attempt by Barbara and Karen to maintain a veneer of sibling camaraderie, says that "I can't perpetuate these myths of family or sisterhood anymore. We're all just people, some of us accidently connected by genetics, a random selection of cells. Nothing more."

These unhappy families, apart from their inability to be civil to one another, cannot even exhibit common courtesy to others, a further indication of their own low self-esteem. In *August*, Violet complains that her house has been overtaken by an "Indian" and that she doesn't "know what to say to an Indian." She criticizes the sheriff's father and her daughter's fiancé. In *Long Day's Journey into Night*, Mary calls the maid "stupid" and the cook "lazy" and "sly." She says that she has "always hated this town and everyone in it." Jamie calls the family doctor "a cheap old quack." In *Virginia Woolf*, both George and Martha make a game of insulting their guests, Nick and Honey, to their faces, making fun of their youth and inexperience with the ways of the world.

Violet and Beverly, despite their respective addictions, seem to have had a fairly successful marriage. They are not divorced, and though they may have had quarrels, neither blames the other for their unhappiness. However, this belies their true dysfunction. When Beverly disappears, Violet could have contacted him. The fact that she doesn't until it's too late represents a deadly bluff on Beverly's part. At the heart of

Virginia Woolf is another deadly bluff. George warns Martha not to talk about their son. Her punishment for going against this warning is that George kills him. In both cases, the wife's intransigence leads to a death.

These families' similarities are deep and multilayered. Their differences are only skin deep. Mary is a passive woman, a product of her generation. She grew up in the 1920s and 1930s and would have expected her husband to take care of her. Violet and Martha, a generation or two younger, are much more physically and emotionally aggressive than Mary, but ultimately they both rely solely on their husbands for their self-worth and societal prestige. James Tyrone was an actor and Beverly and George primarily academics, but they all devote a good portion of their dialogue to quoting literature. Beverly quotes T. S. Eliot, James quotes Shakespeare, and George quotes the Latin Mass. By contrast the women appear uneducated, or at the very least uninterested in a life of the mind. One could blame the feminine mystique for Mary and Martha's unhappiness, given their prefeminist upbringings, but Violet should know better.

These three plays, written in three different decades, prove that the more things change, the more they stay the same. While Tolstoy's declaration that each unhappy family is unhappy in its own way imparts a sense of truthiness, it does not hold up to scrutiny. The unhappy families of *August: Osage County, Long Day's Journey into Night*, and *Who's Afraid of Virginia Woolf?* are anchored by once-promising marriages that have suffered from failed expectations. The pain of these failed expectations have been dulled by substance abuse and a disturbing lack of self-awareness. The characters' resulting mental anguish escapes in volleys of quick-witted dialogue and blame. The audience, watching from the safety of the darkened theater, can then either choose to identify with the characters' struggles and the pitfalls of the human condition or gaze upon the staged train wreck smugly and thank the heavens they fall into the "all happy families are alike" category.

Source: Kathy Wilson Peacock, Critical Essay on *August: Osage County*, in *Drama for Students*, Gale, Cengage Learning, 2016.

Scott Foundas

In the following review, Foundas describes the film as a faithful adaptation of the play.

There are no surprises—just lots of good, old-fashioned scenery chewing—in *August: Osage*

After Beverly's funeral, Violet is angry at him for leaving her. *(© Kzenon | Shutterstock.com)*

County director John Wells' splendid film version of playwright Tracy Letts' acid-tongued Broadway triumph about three generations in a large and highly dysfunctional Oklahoma family. Arriving onscreen shorn of some girth (the stage version ran more than three hours, with two intermissions) but keeping most of its scalding intensity, this two-ton prestige pic won't win the hearts of highbrow critics or those averse to door-slamming, plate-smashing, top-of-the-lungs histrionics, but as a faithful filmed record of Letts' play, one could have scarcely hoped for better. With deserved awards heat and a heavy marketing blitz from the Weinstein Co., this Christmas release should click with upscale adult auds who will have just survived their own heated holiday family gatherings.

Onstage, confined to a creaking, cavernous old house that seemed variously a womb, a prison and a sarcophagus for those who passed through it *August* consciously aligned itself with a particular strain of Great American Plays set in just such environs (including multiple works by Edward Albee, Eugene O'Neill, Arthur Miller and Tennessee Williams). Onscreen, gently opened up to include the big skies and infinite horizons of the real Osage County (where the pic was lensed), it suggests a more barbed, astringent *Terms of Endearment* for the Prozac era, with fewer tears and far more recriminations.

Once again, we are introduced to the Weston clan by way of patriarch Beverly, a melancholic poet (played here by an excellent Sam Shepard, in a role originated by Letts' own late father, Dennis) who quotes T.S. Eliot's immortal maxim that "life is very long" just before taking matters into his own hands: first by mysteriously disappearing, then by turning up drowned in a local lake. The ensuing funeral serves as a de facto family reunion, the previously empty house filling to the rafters with Beverly's three grown daughters, their significant others and assorted relations. All have come to pay their last respects. None will leave without incurring the wrath of the widow Weston, Violet (Meryl Streep), a cancer-stricken, pill-popping martinet whose idol was Liz Taylor and who could be Albee's Martha a few decades—and many rounds of marital prizefights—on from *Who's Afraid of Virginia Woolf?*

From all points they converge: Barbara (Julia Roberts), the eldest, with her estranged husband Bill (Ewan McGregor) and moody teen daughter Jean (Abigail Breslin) in tow; Karen (Juliette Lewis), the youngest, who shows up on the arm of her supposed fiance (Dermot Mulroney), a sleazy Florida hustler with unsavory business connections; and middle child Ivy (Julianne Nicholson), whose big secret is that she's sweet on her first cousin "Little" Charles (Benedict Cumberbatch)—a secret, it turns out, much bigger than even Ivy knows.

Whatever else one may think of *August* in Violet, Letts (who adapted *August* for the screen) has created one of the great, showstopping female roles in recent American theater—his Mother Courage, Mama Rose and Mary Tyrone, all rolled into one—and Streep plays it to the hilt, in and out of a black fright wig (to hide the character's chemo-stricken hair) and oversized sunglasses, cursing like a longshoreman and whittling everyone down to size. Nothing slips by her, she says repeatedly. You'd better believe it. It's a "big" performance, but it's just what the part calls for, since Vi is something of an actress herself, craving the attention that comes with turning a solemn family gathering into an occasion for high theater. This may be Beverly's funeral, but it's Vi's chance to shine.

Shine she does, especially during the long funeral dinner at the end of Act Two that is, as it was onstage, Letts' piece de resistance. Streep is electrifying to watch here, goosing, prodding, meting out punishment and laying family secrets bare, surprisingly gentle one moment, demonic the next. And Roberts, who hasn't had a big, meaty part like this in years, possesses just the right hardened beauty to play an aging woman let down by life, terrified at the thought of becoming her mother.

Wells, who is best known for having produced such smallscreen phenoms as *ER* and *The West Wing* does an impressive job shooting and cutting among 10 major characters, all of whom get their chance to engage Vi in verbal tango. He isn't a natural film director per se, but he understands what *August* needs in order to work onscreen, how to preserve its inherent claustrophobia without rendering it completely stagebound, and the result is far more successful than any more stylized "cinematic" treatment probably would have been.

If Streep and Roberts have the roman-candle roles here, the entire cast is commendable, with Letts and Wells giving even the most seemingly incidental character (like the fine Native American actress Misty Upham as Vi's live-in caretaker) a grace note or two. Lewis is a particular hoot as the daughter hanging on to her carefree youth with all fingernails firmly dug in, while Cumberbatch is touching as the clumsy, unemployed young man whose diminutive name is one of Letts' few overtly symbolic touches.

Shooting in widescreen—a practical necessity with this many characters to squeeze into a frame—Adriano Goldman (*Jane Eyre*, *The Company You Keep*) beautifully captures the hazy half-light of a house whose permanently drawn window shades are mentioned in the dialogue. Indeed, it is a place where we can never be sure whether we are traveling a long day's journey into night, or a long night's journey into day.

Source: Scott Foundas, "Feisty *Osage* Hits Mark," in *Variety*, Vol. 321, No. 11, September 17, 2013, p. 119.

Suzy Evans

In the following review, Evans praises the ensemble cast of a film adaptation of August: Osage County.

One of the most memorable moments of *August: Osage County* is the dinner scene, which comes at the movie's halfway point. The meal ends with eldest daughter Barbara (played by Julia Roberts) launching across the table to strangle her caustic, pill-popping mother Violet (Meryl Streep), and shouting one of the piece's most famous lines: "I'm running things now!" After three-and-a-half days of filming the 20-minute scene, which remains word-for-word in director John Wells' film version of Tracy Letts' Pulitzer Prize-winning play, Wells says the cast could have performed it on any stage, anywhere. And while the play's move to the screen wasn't a wrestling match, per se, Letts did have to relinquish some control to Wells, who is now, as they say, running things.

"The plays are the plays and they're my plays, and I'll answer for those. But ultimately I viewed my job on *August: Osage County* as the job of helping John Wells make the best John Wells film he could make," Letts says. "Who the hell would I think I am to say, let me tell you guys how to make the best movie!"

Wells wanted the film to retain the essence of the play, and he and Letts collaborated for

18 months on cutting the three-and-a-half-hour drama down to two hours. Though the play's language reads as deceptively simple on the page, on the stage it attains a heightened theatrical power that Letts worked to tone down for the film.

The onstage action takes place entirely in the Westons' three-story house, but the movie steps out into the sprawling, sunbaked landscape of Osage County, which helps to avoid the "filmed play" trap into which many adaptations fall. Also helping the film's naturalism was the cast's extracurricular work. Living next door to each other in condos while filming in Oklahoma, the actors gathered at Streep's house to rehearse the next day's work—even finalizing the blocking of the dinner scene over a meal of their own.

"Tracy doesn't make it easy to get all this information across," explains Roberts, adding that Streep was the first one to offer to run lines. "And we were all very devoted to having it really down. Because once emotions start flying, you have to really have it in your hand to not throw everybody off."

Finding actors who could handle that language was key to the film's success. Streep and Roberts came on to the project at the same time Wells joined, and the team wanted to build a family around them. Wells, who trained in theater at Carnegie Mellon, knew that creating a familial atmosphere between the cast would be crucial.

"I asked the actors to spend time studying each other," says Wells. "They picked up things, motions, movements, of Meryl's and of each other's. You can take people who don't look exactly alike and make them seem very similar simply by having them do things the same way."

And Margo Martindale, who plays Violet's sister, is convinced that Streep imitated her. "I noticed at one point that we laughed alike," recalls Martindale. "And I thought, 'But that is the way I laugh. I never noticed that Meryl laughed like that.'"

The two-week rehearsal process also allowed the actors time to get to know each other and their characters. With some input from Letts—who was only on set for the first day—Wells created backstories for each character. However, the most powerful experiences the actors used in their processes were personal ones.

"I had a son who had severe disabilities and was told by the medical establishment, 'Don't invest too much in this boy. He'll never be intellectually normal.'" says Chris Cooper, who plays Charles Aiken, Violet's brother-in-law who must consistently stand up for his son due to what others see as his shortcomings. "He proved to be intellectually superior but he always had to prove himself to others. So naturally my wife and I coming to his defense was a way of life for us. He passed away in '05. So I thought the time was appropriate. It's OK to touch on those emotions and bring them to my work."

Even though the cast and creative team try to keep some of the feeling of the stage version, they had the luxury of multiple takes. The cast members who saw the show on Broadway are still impressed by the stamina of the original team.

"I remember leaving the theater and feeling exhausted and just wrung out, and that's really how we felt at the end of every day," remembers Roberts. "I don't know how they did it as a play. It seems like the acting Olympics, really, eight shows a week. I don't know how they would have survived that."

Source: Suzy Evans, "Family Files: How *August: Osage County* Built Its Tight-Knit Acting Ensemble," in *Back Stage*, Vol. 54, No. 51, December 19, 2013, p. 22.

Back Stage

In the following essay, Letts explains how he balances working as both an actor and a playwright.

His first play, *Killer Joe*, was written in 1991 and won top honors at the 1994 Edinburgh Festival Fringe in Scotland, followed by London and New York runs, and then countless remounts all over the world—at last count, it had been performed in 15 countries. This week the film adaptation, directed by Oscar winner William Friedkin, hits screens. "Frankly, when I wrote it, I thought, 'Well, this is my first play, and it's going to run for four weeks at this little theater in Chicago and that'll be that,'" Letts says. "The fact that it's had such a life and gone on for 20 years now to this point that the movie's coming out is still shocking to me."

Letts didn't quit his day job—he'll debut on Broadway this fall as George in *Who's Afraid of Virginia Woolf?*—but his writing career has also flourished. After penning *Bug* (which Friedkin adapted for the screen in 2006), Letts went on to write *Man From Nebraska* and *August: Osage County*, which won the 2008 Pulitzer Prize for drama. A film version with Meryl Streep and Julia Roberts is due in 2013. He followed that with 2008's *Superior Donuts*, and his adaptation of Chekov's *Three Sisters* is running through Aug. 26 at Steppenwolf Theatre Company, of which he is a longtime member.

Letts says that balancing two successful careers has forced him to make tough decisions when jobs conflict. But the variety is good for him. "My friend Amy Morton, an actor and director, and skilled at both, refers to this as 'crop rotation,'" Letts says. "It's very good for the soil to do one and then do another." Because of the massive success of *August*, followed by *Superior Donuts*, Letts estimates he was offstage for nearly two and a half years, his longest hiatus since he began acting at 15. "I was very eager to get back onstage. Not only because it exercises some public part of my personality, but it's nice not to have all the responsibility of a writer," he says. "An actor is mainly responsible for their own track, with an eye to the larger production overall. As a writer, you're responsible for so much more than that, and sometimes it's nice to be able to walk away from a rehearsal saying, 'Someone else gets to deal with that.'"

Writing has also "changed the game" for Letts as an actor, allowing him to be pickier in the parts he chooses. He jokes that he doesn't need "a day on *Law and Order* with Vincent D'Onofrio throwing you up against a fence in Queens for 500 bucks." He auditioned for the role of a government official in *Contagion*, the 2011 Steven Soderbergh flick. "Nothing fancy, but it was a guy with a name and he wore a suit and he had a nice little scene," he says. "They called me a week later and said, 'We want to cast you as Paramedic #2.' I said I'm not going to do that. I don't need to do that because I don't need the money from it and I've done that gig before, and I don't have to do it anymore."

Source: "The Man behind the 'Killer': Tracy Letts Was a Working Actor When He Tried His Hand at Writing," in *Back Stage*, Vol. 53, No. 30, July 26, 2012, p. 11.

SOURCES

Albee, Edward, *Who's Afraid of Virginia Woolf?: A Play*, Atheneum, 1963.

"Alcohol Facts and Statistics," National Institute on Alcohol Abuse and Alcoholism website, http://www.niaaa.nih.gov/alcohol-health/overview-alcohol-consumption/alcohol-facts-and-statistics (accessed July 14, 2015).

Allen, Brooke, "Never the Twain," in *Contemporary Literary Criticism*, Vol. 208, edited by Jeffrey W. Hunter, Gale, Cengage Learning, 2010; originally published in *New Criterion*, Vol. 26, No. 3, February 2008, pp. 39–43.

Als, Hilton, "Family Planning," in *New Yorker*, December 24, 2007, p. 132.

"DrugFacts: Nationwide Trends," National Institute on Drug Abuse website, June 2015, http://www.drugabuse.gov/publications/drugfacts/nationwide-trends (accessed July 14, 2015).

"Facts and Figures," American Foundation for Suicide Prevention website, https://www.afsp.org/understanding-suicide/facts-and-figures (accessed July 14, 2015).

Fifer, Elizabeth, "Memory and Guilt: Parenting in Tracy Letts's *August: Osage County* and Eugene O'Neill's *Long Day's Journey into Night*," in *Eugene O'Neill Review*, Vol. 34, No. 2, Fall 2013, p. 183.

Isherwood, Charles, "Mama Doesn't Feel Well, but Everyone Else Will Feel Much Worse," in *New York Times*, December 5, 2007, http://www.nytimes.com/2007/12/05/theater/reviews/05august.html?pagewanted=all&_r=0 (accessed July 15, 2015).

Kellaway, Kate, "The First Great American Play of the 21st Century," in *Observer* (London), November 23, 2008, p. 4, http://www.theguardian.com/stage/2008/nov/23/theatre-tracy-letts-august-osage-county (accessed July 15, 2015).

Letts, Tracy, *August: Osage County*, Dramatists Play Service, 2009.

"Marriages and Divorces," Centers for Disease Control and Prevention website, February 20, 2015, http://www.cdc.gov/nchs/mardiv.htm#state_tables (accessed July 14, 2015).

May, Jon D., "Osage County," in *Encyclopedia of Oklahoma History and Culture*, http://www.okhistory.org/publications/enc/entry.php?entry=OS004 (accessed July 14, 2015).

O'Neill, Eugene, *Long Day's Journey into Night*, Yale University Press, 1955.

O'Reilly, Mollie Wilson, "Domestic Disputes: 'God of Carnage' & 'August: Osage County'," in *Commonweal*, Vol. 136, No. 11, 2009 p. 22.

Rooney, David, "A Blistering 'August'," in *Variety*, Vol. 409, No. 4, December 10, 2007, p. 68.

Tolstoy, Leo, *Anna Karenina: A Novel in Eight Parts*, translated by Richard Pevear and Larissa Volokhonsky, Penguin, 2002.

Wang, Wendy, and Kim Parker, "Record Share of Americans Have Never Been Married," Pew Research Center, September 24, 2014, http://www.pewsocialtrends.org/2014/09/24/record-share-of-americans-have-never-married/ (accessed July 14, 2015).

FURTHER READING

Letts, Tracy, "The Immutable Radish: An Interview (Via E-mail) with the Playwright," in *American Theatre*, Vol. 30, No. 4, April 2013, p. 59.

> In this tongue-in-cheek piece written as Letts was acting in Will Eno's play *The Realistic Joneses*, the playwright interviews himself about the nature of his plays. His nonsensical answers provide a glimpse into his writing process and his feelings about the theater world.

Nance, Kevin, "Tracy Letts: No Place Like Home," in *American Theatre*, Vol. 24, No. 6, July–August 2007, pp. 42–45.

> Nance traces Letts's career from his promising beginnings as the author of *Bug* and *Killer Joe* to his flourishing as the author of *August: Osage County*. Letts speaks of growing up in Oklahoma and the importance of his involvement with the Steppenwolf Theatre in his career and how the artistic environment of Chicago helped him develop as an artist.

"'Osage' Hits Close to Home for Writer Tracy Letts," in *Weekend Edition Saturday*, NPR, January 11, 2014.

> In this National Public Radio interview with Scott Simon, Letts talks about the genesis of *August: Osage County* being his own family but how the character of Beverly, which his own father originated, was mostly fiction.

Shapiro, Anna D., "The Discipline of Directing," in *TriQuarterly*, Vol. 134, 2009, p. 123.

> Shapiro directed the original Steppenwolf production of *August: Osage County*. In this lengthy piece, she ruminates on the theme of family in Letts's play, particularly in its account of the demise of the patriarchy.

Skrebneski, Victor, *Steppenwolf at 25: A Photographic Celebration of an Actor's Theater*, Sourcebooks, 2000.

> This large-format book provides an overview of Chicago's most famous theater, which has launched the careers of many famous actors and playwrights alike, including Letts, Gary Sinese, and John Malkovich. Photographs are accompanied by short essays from some of the theater and literary world's most renowned writers, including Don DeLillo and Sam Shepard.

Witchel, Alex, "'Well, Dad, These Events Haunted Me My Whole Life'," in *New York Times Magazine*, March 23, 2014, p. 16.

> In this lengthy interview, Witchel discusses with Letts his father's role in *August: Osage County* and how his death before Letts won the Pulitzer and the Tony Award affected the enjoyment of his success. They also discuss Letts's television work and his relationship with his mother.

SUGGESTED SEARCH TERMS

Tracy Letts

August: Osage County

Tracy Letts AND August: Osage County

realism AND drama

black comedy

dysfunctional family

Osage County, Oklahoma

family drama OR dysfunctional family drama

suicide AND dysfunctional family

alcoholism OR drug abuse AND drama

The Chickencoop Chinaman

FRANK CHIN

1981

Chin's *The Chickencoop Chinaman* is the first play by an Asian American ever produced in New York. Like Chin's other works, the play utilizes wit and humor to explore the devastating effects of racism and assimilation. The surreal play with its angry monologues generated controversy when it first opened, but it is a groundbreaking work that helped paved the way for future Asian American playwrights and artists. Although it was written in 1971 and first performed in 1972, the themes of racial stereotypes, family, and individual identity are still relevant today. *The Chickencoop Chinaman* is included in *The Chickencoop Chinaman and The Year of the Dragon: Two Plays by Frank Chin*, published by University of Washington Press in 1981.

AUTHOR BIOGRAPHY

Frank Chin was born on February 4, 1940, in Berkeley, California. Unable to care for him, Chin's parents placed him in a foundling home when he was an infant. For the first six years of his life, Chin lived with an elderly white couple in Placerville, California. After his parents claimed him, Chin lived in Oakland, California, with his family before moving to San Francisco.

Chin attended the University of California at Berkeley in 1958, and in 1961 he earned a scholarship to the Writer's Workshop at the

University of Iowa. In 1963, however, he took a job with the Southern Pacific Railroad. He "was the first Chinese-American brakeman" for the company, according to his interview with *News of the American Place Theater*, which is quoted by Dorothy Ritsuko McDonald in her introduction to *The Chickencoop Chinaman and The Year of the Dragon: Two Plays by Frank Chin*. He completed his degree at the University of California at Santa Barbara in 1965 and then was employed at a television station in Seattle before teaching Asian Studies at San Francisco State University and the University of California.

In 1971, Chin submitted *The Chickencoop Chinaman* to the East West Players' playwriting contest and shared the first prize. The play opened in New York the next year, and it was the first play by an Asian American performed in New York. Chin helped found the Asian American Theater Workshop in 1973. In 1974, his second play, *The Year of the Dragon*, debuted. Chin worked collaboratively with other editors on the first major anthology of Asian American literature, *Aiiieeeee! An Anthology of Asian-American Writers*, published in 1974. Chin's strict interpretation of authentic Asian American literature resulted in harsh criticism of other Asian American playwrights, such as David Henry Hwang. Chin finally chose to abandon playwriting and focus on other literary goals.

Chin's short stories were collected into the volume *The Chinaman Pacific & Frisco R.R. Co.* in 1988. The author's first novel, *Donald Duk*, was published in 1991, and his second, *Gunga Din Highway*, followed in 1994. His collection of essays, *Bulletproof Buddhists and Other Essays*, was published in 1998, and a history text, *Born in the U.S.A.: A Story of Japanese America, 1889–1947*, was published in 2002. The novel that continues the story of the main character in *The Chickencoop Chinaman, Confessions of a Number One Son*, was published in 2015. Over the years, Chin has crafted numerous teleplays, literary essays, and comics. As of 2015, Chin lives in Los Angeles, California.

PLOT SUMMARY

Act 1

SCENE 1

The play begins with a surreal scene. In the background, a female voice instructs the passengers on a plane to prepare for landing in Pittsburgh in the 1960s. Tam, alone on the stage, tells the audience that Hong Kong Dream Girl asked him if he could tell she was born in Hong Kong. She enters wearing an American drill team costume. Tam tells her that he knows she is from Hong Kong. She is disappointed but continues the conversation. She asks him where he was born, and he tells her, "Chinamen are made, not born." *Chinaman* is a racial slur that Chin reclaims as his identity. Tam continues his description of what makes a Chinaman, shifting between dialects and locations. He identifies himself as the Chickencoop Chinaman and Chinatown as the chicken coop. At the end of his story, Tam attempts to kiss Hong Kong Dream Girl. She runs away before they kiss. The scene returns to the flight attendant, who is finishing the instructions for landing.

SCENE 2

The scene takes place in Oakland, which Chin describes as the predominantly African American neighborhood in Pittsburgh where Tam and his friend Kenji grew up. They are in Kenji's apartment, where the two speak in an African American dialect. Kenji is a dentist who has chosen to stay in Oakland. As they talk about the past, Lee, who lives with Kenji, calls to him from the bedroom. Kenji speaks with her, and he imitates Helen Keller (a blind and mute woman who overcame her disabilities) when he returns. As he imitates Keller, he and Tam connect her to the concept of the model minority with a mock sermon.

Robbie, Lee's son, has entered from the kitchen during the commotion. Kenji and Tam give Robbie high fives, and he and Kenji play-fight. Lee takes Robbie away from Kenji in anger. She becomes annoyed when Tam asks her how many children she has. Lee tells him that she is pregnant and moving to Africa; she also says that the baby is not Kenji's. Lee insists that Tam shake hands with Robbie, and she prevents Tam from giving Robbie five. She tells Tam and Robbie to stop making fun of African Americans because her ex-husband is African American. She is angry over the act of giving five because it originated in African American culture.

Tam talks about the documentary he is making of the prizefighter Ovaltine Jack Dancer. He is in town to interview Ovaltine's father and trainer, Charley Popcorn. He is excited about the movie and what it will do for his career. Kenji tells him to get some sleep first, but Tam insists on seeing Charley Popcorn that night. Lee clearly dislikes Tam and the effect he has on Kenji.

Lee scolds Tam and Kenji for making a mess in the apartment after Tam gets cake crumbs on the floor. She complains about the noise outside, and Tam tells her that a railroad is under construction. Lee responds that he believes it is a railroad only because he is Chinese. Tam is enraged but decides not to comment. Kenji tells Tam to take a shower while he speaks with Lee alone. Robbie escorts Tam to the bathroom and promises to cut Tam a piece of cake.

Kenji tells Lee to respect his friend or be quiet. In the bathroom, Robbie continues talking to Tam. Robbie is sure that Tam likes children. Tam asks Robbie if Kenji is his father and why he speaks like an adult. Still angry over Lee's comment about the railroad, Tam tells Robbie that he knew the sounds of the railroad because he worked on one. Robbie reveals that Kenji is not his father and asks Tam why he wears swim trunks in the shower. Tam explains that he developed the habit because an old dishwasher he knew wore trunks while showering to keep white women from seeing him naked. When he was a child, Tam guided the old man to boxing matches. He also translated for him and helped wash his back. The old man died in the bathtub after a boxing match one day.

Robbie leaves to get the some cake for Tam, and Lee asks what the he has been talking about with Tam. She asks Tam why he hates being Chinese. Kenji attempts to silence her, but she asks again. Robbie returns to Tam with some cake and tells him that his favorite father was Chinese; he had a white father and African American father as well. Lee, however, said his favorite father "wasn't a man." Tam asks Robbie if he is a racist and tells him to stop talking.

Lee asks Kenji about Tam, and he tells her that Tam is making a documentary about Ovaltine Jack Dancer. She accuses Tam of making money off African American culture. Kenji explains that they grew up in Oakland and African American culture was part of their world. They idolized Ovaltine and met him once when they were in college. When they met Ovaltine, Tam told him one of Kenji's anecdotes, passing it off as his own. Lee calls Tam a fraud, and he enters the room.

Tam tells Lee that Robbie's hovering in the bathroom while he showers is odd. He goes on to say that people might consider it "funny," meaning "gay." She insinuates that he knows this only because he is gay. Kenji rages at Lee for being rude to his friend. He also tells her to stop redecorating his apartment in a Japanese style because he is not Japanese.

Lee tells Kenji that her Chinese American ex-husband, Tom, is coming to see her. He wants to be a father to her baby. Tom is a writer who is working on the book *Soul on Rice*. They all laugh at the name. Tam asks if the baby is Tom's, and she says no. Kenji insists that the child is not his. Tam tells Lee that he reminds her of her ex-husband and makes the comment, "Chinamans do make lousy fathers. I know. I have one." He tells her to keep the door locked if she does not want to see Tom while he and Kenji go visit Charley Popcorn.

Lee accuses Tam of being cruel and tells him that having children would make him more compassionate. He tells her that he has two children. When he confirms her suspicion that his wife was white, she attacks him and other Chinese American men for manipulating white women because Chinese American women will not have them. She then attacks his use of different dialects and accents. Tam tells her that he adjusts his dialects because he was tired of people correcting his pronunciation. People even told him that his name was Tom, a reference to her former husband. He concludes his explanation by telling Lee that he knows she is part Chinese, not white.

Lee asks Tam about his children. He tells her that his wife took them and married a white writer. He wants his children to forget him because they will be better off without a Chinese American father. He asks who in her family is Chinese. She refuses to answer but says that she misses the children who are not with her.

Tam recalls trying to act white as a child and the pride that his parents took in him when the white people commented on how well he spoke English. Tam continues talking about positive Chinese stereotypes and the racism entrenched in them. He states that the lack of juvenile delinquency in Chinese Americans is due to immigration laws restricting Chinese women from entering the country and limiting Chinese men from marrying and creating families. He says that he gave his parents white grandchildren who are better without him. He also claims his mother insinuated that he was "no good."

Lee tells Tam that he would be a good father, and she says that she will keep her baby and not let Tom's mother have it. Tam tells Kenji that he is taking Lee away from him.

Both Kenji and Lee insist that there is nothing romantic between them. Kenji says that he would never want a white girlfriend unless she were the stereotypical blonde sex symbol. He admits that he is too cowardly or chicken. The trio begins making jokes about being chicken along with chicken sounds. Robbie enters and says that dinner is ready.

Act 2

SCENE 1

This surreal scene occurs with Kenji seated before a large radio while Tam begins his monologue. He says that the Lone Ranger, a hero of the West, is not Chinese. As a boy, Tam searched for a Chinese role model on the radio, which shaped his worldview. Meanwhile, his grandmother's view of the world came from her experience with the railroad. She talked about the Iron Moon Hunter, a fictional locomotive that carried away the souls of the Chinese workers killed on the railroad.

Tam decided that the Lone Ranger was Chinese because he wore a mask and had black hair. He believed the mask was to hide his Chinese eyes. An aged Lone Ranger and Tonto, his Native American sidekick, appear on the stage. The Lone Ranger shoots Tam in the hand. Tam goes to Kenji and continues speaking. Tonto aims his bow at Kenji and asks the famous question from the television program, "Who was that masked man?" He tells them to answer and shoots at them when Tam does not speak the line.

Tonto asks if they saw the Lone Ranger's horse, Silver, and his silver bullets. Kenji is excited that the Lone Ranger shot Tam. Kenji finishes the line and says thank you after Tonto's prompt. The Lone Ranger exits saying the classic line: "Hi yo Silver, Awayyy!"

The Lone Ranger returns to the stage with difficulty, and Tonto injects him with a hypodermic needle. Tonto loses the stereotyped Native American accent, which makes the Lone Ranger think he is not Tonto. Tonto fakes the accent again, making Tam jeer. Kenji shakes the radio when the Lone Ranger fails to complete his lines. The Lone Ranger talks about Tam and Kenji preserving their culture and says that he wants light starch in his shirts. This is a reference to Chinese laundries. He asks them if they hear hoofbeats and sits on Tam when he and Kenji bend over to listen for the sound.

The Lone Ranger reminisces about a time when he did not want to ride off because he was in love with a woman who was blind, deaf, and mute, Helen Keller. He compares her with the three monkeys from the Japanese proverb who "Hear no Evil, See no Evil, Speak no Evil."

A train whistle blows, and Tam says that it is the Iron Moon Hunter. Refusing to acknowledge the train, the Lone Ranger tells him they do not hear anything, and he curses Tam as "honorary white." He invokes Helen Keller, the author Pearl S. Buck, and Charlie Chan, a Chinese caricature from the movies. The Lone Ranger tells Tam that he speaks English well, and Tam thanks him before leaving with Tonto.

SCENE 2

Tam and Kenji arrive at the adult movie theater Charley Popcorn owns. When Charley Popcorn sees them, he assumes that they are a couple. Tam introduces himself, reminding Charley Popcorn of their conversation on the phone. Charley Popcorn is surprised that Tam is Chinese American. He does not trust Tam and makes racist jokes before calling Ovaltine. Tam is insulted, but Kenji tries to calm him. Tam says that Kenji hates himself and berates him for his relationship with the disrespectful Lee. Kenji tells Tam that he is simply tired.

Charley Popcorn returns, ready to do business with Tam after speaking with Ovaltine. He tells Tam about an elderly Chinese man who would come watch Ovaltine fight and did not speak English. Tam is convinced that he is talking about the old dishwasher he would guide to the fights.

Charley Popcorn describes the first time he saw Ovaltine fight, and Tam is outraged to discover that Charley Popcorn is not Ovaltine's father. He begs Charley Popcorn to acknowledge Ovaltine as his son. He picks a fight with Charley Popcorn but falls over without hitting the man.

SCENE 3

This surreal scene takes place on an empty stage. Tam is on Charley Popcorn's back saying words in his parent's language and translating them. He says that he speaks his wife's language now, but she still left him. She left him on his birthday and took the children. His mother was proud of him for taking it so well and not fighting for her.

SCENE 4

Back in Kenji's apartment, Lee is moving posters, and the radio is playing in the background. Groceries and Japanese cooking utensils are in view. Tom is in the apartment, carefully avoiding any physical contact with Lee.

Robbie enters and tells Lee that Tam and Kenji are back. Tom tries to give Robbie five and reminds him that Robbie once called him dad. Lee instructs Robbie to open the door, and Tam walks in carrying Charley Popcorn. He notices Tom before dropping Charley Popcorn on the sofa. Tom assumes that Tam is Kenji. Tam does not identify himself and offers Tom some gum, saying that he knew Lee would let Tom inside the apartment. Tam comments that Tom is an English name and asks about the book that Tom is writing. Charley Popcorn says that he has never heard of an Asian American writing a book, and Tam jokes that it is a cookbook.

Kenji enters and asks Lee what she is doing. She replies that she is tired of living out of trunks. Kenji asks her if she is still going to Africa. Lee responds that she might go, but she never knows what Kenji wants her to do because he will not talk to her. Tom introduces himself to Kenji and tells him to continue the conversation with Lee. When Kenji says that he is "the strong silent type," she replies that someone said the same thing about Tom. Tam says that it was Tom's mother, which Tom confirms. Tam says that he knows because he is the ghost of Christmas past.

Tam asks about Tom's book, and Lee tells him not to bring up the subject. Tom explains that the book is about Chinese American identity. Kenji tries to get Tam to go to bed, but Tam refuses and promises to be quiet. Tom wants to know who Tam is, but Tam simply gives him a gum wrapper and says that the silver bullet will identify him. Everyone but Robbie laughs because he is not old enough to know who the Lone Ranger is.

Kenji does not want Robbie to hear their conversation and sends him to bed. Robbie ignores him and talks to Tam, promising to make blueberry pancakes in the morning. Tom interjects, and Robbie replies that he is not talking to Tom. Lee tells them both to leave Robbie alone and that she is not pregnant. Tam tries to interject, but Kenji tells him to be quiet in his house. Kenji orders Robbie to bed and stares at him until he goes.

Tom asks Tam who he is, and Tam asks Kenji for permission to respond. Tom tells Tam that Lee is manipulating him and that they have to stand against her because she is white and they are Chinese Americans. Tam replies that he is not interested in Lee. The two of them argue about what it means to be Chinese when Tom accuses him of being prejudiced against Chinese Americans. Tom also informs Tam that he is small and should immerse himself in Chinese culture to avoid people assuming he is gay. Tam tells Tom that he gave away his baby just to be acceptable. Tom justifies his actions by telling Tam that his mother took the baby because Lee is white. He refuses to believe Tam when he says that Lee is part Chinese. Kenji intervenes and takes Tam aside, but Lee follows.

Kenji tells Tam that is vicious, not funny or brave like he used to believe. Tam jokes around, making Lee laugh. Tom interjects, asking if they can be friends. Tam replies that he does not want to be friends. The statement is directed toward Tom and Kenji. Kenji realizes that their relationship is at an end.

Charley Popcorn becomes uncomfortable with the situation and says that he has never been around so many Chinese people. Lee asks him who he is. Charley Popcorn introduces himself, making a point of saying that he is not Ovaltine's father. Tam asks him if he will say he is Ovaltine's father for the camera. He decides that he will not mock Ovaltine in the movie by revealing the lie about Charley Popcorn just to make a name for himself. Tam decides to leave the subject of Ovaltine's father out of the film.

Tam goes to the kitchen to cook, and he promises to leave in the morning. He comments that Kenji will need a larger home, and Kenji tells him that he is going to be a father. Tom is surprised but does not fight for Lee. Charley Popcorn says that he is having a great time, and Lee asks Kenji to talk to her. He agrees to sing and makes up a song about riding with the Chickencoop Chinaman. The scene freezes, and Tam continues the song in a monologue where he returns to his grandmother's story of the Iron Moon Hunter.

CHARACTERS

Charley Popcorn

Charley Popcorn was Ovaltine Jack Dancer's trainer. He now owns an adult theater in Pittsburgh. He does not trust Asian Americans, and he is very uncomfortable in Kenji's apartment.

Hong Kong Dream Girl

Hong Kong Dream Girl is a fantasy Tam talks to in the first scene. She desires to be seen as an American and wears a drill team costume.

Kenji

Kenji is a Japanese American who grew up with Tam. He is a dentist in the Oakland district of Pittsburgh. Lee and Robbie live with Kenji, but he denies being the father of the baby Lee claims to be carrying. Tam's best friend in childhood, he is uncomfortable with Tam's anger as an adult. The two end their friendship by the end of the play.

Lee

Lee appears white, but she really is Eurasian or part Chinese. She has been married at least three times to men of different ethnicities, and she has many children she no longer sees. In the play, she says she is pregnant and lives in Kenji's apartment with the only child she parents, Robbie. She questions Tam's masculinity and the masculinity of all Chinese American men.

Lone Ranger

The Lone Ranger is a character from a radio program. When Tam was a child he assumed that the Lone Ranger was Chinese but discovers that he is a racist cowboy when he shoots Tam in the hand.

Old Dishwasher

The old dishwasher is unnamed and never appears in the play. Tam took him to the fights, and Charley Popcorn knew and respected him. He died in the bathtub when Tam was a child and may have known Charley Popcorn.

Ovaltine

Ovaltine Jack Dancer is a retired boxer idolized by Tam and Kenji. Although he does not appear in the play, his claim that Charley Popcorn is his father influences the actions of different characters.

Robbie

Robbie is Lee's son. He explains that he has had a lot of different father figures because of Lee's multiple marriages. Robbie is curious about Tam and talks to him a lot.

Tam Lum

Tam is a Chinese American writer who travels to Pittsburgh to work on a movie about his childhood hero, boxer Ovaltine Jack Dancer. He stays with his childhood friend, Kenji, while he is in town. He hopes that the film will be a legacy for his two children, but he refuses to remain part of their lives. Tam's plans for the film and his life change when he discovers the truth about Ovaltine's story. He rages against the model minority stereotype throughout the play.

Tom

Tom is a writer and Lee's ex-husband. He is passive and praises the success of Chinese Americans. Tam considers Tom assimilated, and the two fight over their identities as Chinese Americans.

Tonto

Tonto is the Lone Ranger's sidekick. He is Native American and speaks with a stereotypical accent to please the Lone Ranger, who becomes confused when Tonto speaks in an American accent.

THEMES

Stereotypes

Cultural and ethnic stereotypes pervade *The Chickencoop Chinaman*. Dialect and accent develop the stereotypes that Chin showcases in the play. For example, Lee accuses Tam and Kenji of mocking African Americans because they speak using the same African American accent and dialect of the community they lived in as children. Additionally, Charley Popcorn is surprised that Tam is not African American when they meet in person. Both Lee and Charley Popcorn assume that a Chinese American would have a stereotypical Chinese accent.

Lee and Charlie Popcorn also embrace the stereotype that Chinese American men are weak and effeminate. Each one assumes that Tam is gay upon meeting him. Charley Popcorn, for example, believes Tam and Kenji are a couple when he first sees them. Lee makes sweeping and accusatory generalizations when she says, "not a man in all your males." Tom, another Chinese American, who should reject the false narrative of stereotypes, advises Tam to connect with his Chinese culture as a way to prove that he is straight. Tam rejects this idea and mocks Tom for his desire to "be 'accepted' by whites."

TOPICS FOR FURTHER STUDY

- Read *American Born Chinese* by Gene Luen Yang. This young-adult graphic novel explores themes of identity and racial stereotypes. Create your own comic that includes at least one character from the play and one from the graphic novel. How do the characters explore their personal and cultural identities? The comic may be hand drawn, or you can use a computer program.

- Research Asian American literature, including the work of Frank Chin. Create a web page that provides an overview of significant authors and their works. Be sure to include information about the debate between Chin and other artists on your web page.

- Read the young-adult novel *The Absolutely True Diary of a Part-Time Indian*, by Sherman Alexie, and compare the trials of Arnold and Tam. Work with a partner, and develop a one-act play that stars the two characters. How would they relate to each other? What ideas and feelings do they share, and how are they different? Act out the play with your partner, and upload it to the Internet using EDpuzzle.

- Research the history of Asian Americans and civil rights. Be sure to include the transcontinental railroad, student protests, and Frank Chin in your work. Create a graphic to display this information using easl.ly, and present your findings to the class.

- Research popular culture references in the play, such as the Lone Ranger or Charlie Chan. How do these characters represent Asian Americans and other minorities? Share your findings and thoughts in a blog post. Include links, music, video clips, and images that are relevant to the topic.

Family

Family is an important theme in Chin's work, particularly the familial relationship between fathers and their children. Both Tam and his hero, Ovaltine Jack Dancer, lack strong father figures in their lives. Ovaltine compensates for the void by lying to the world and claiming his trainer, Charley Popcorn, as his father. When Tam learns that his male role model and hero is a liar, he is devastated and must face his own illusions.

Early in the play, Tam tells Lee, "Chinamans do make lousy fathers. I know. I have one." The relationship with his father causes Tam to question his ability to be a father, and he gives up his children to his ex-wife and her new husband without a fight. Tam convinces himself that they are better off being raised by their white stepfather than they would be with him in their lives. He does desire to do something that they can be proud of by making the documentary about Ovaltine. Tam tells Lee, "I should leave them something.... I should have done some THING." Tam's desire to leave behind something great for his children, however, is ruined once he learns the truth about Ovaltine.

Kenji also faces his personal issues with fatherhood. Throughout most of the play, he refuses to take responsibility for Lee's son, Robbie, or the baby she says she is carrying. Robbie has called other men in Lee's life dad, but he repeatedly says Kenji is not his father. Kenji's refusal to take parental responsibility forces Lee to make alternative arrangements to care for her family. In a desperate attempt to find a father for her children, Lee meets with her ex-husband Tom. Tom desires to be a father to please his mother, but he does not personally take the responsibility for raising his children. His mother already took one child he had with Lee. In the end, Kenji chooses to claim Lee's baby as his own. This decision is a step towards building a family. It is not clear, however, if this family unit will survive.

Identity

Many of characters in *The Chickencoop Chinaman* are exploring their personal and cultural identities. Lee, for example, has a history of trying to assimilate into other cultures by marrying men of different ethnicities. Although Lee appears white, she is part Chinese. She resents all Chinese American men because of her history with Tom, whom she describes as "not a real man." Her instant dislike of Tam reveals an internal prejudice against herself, which Tam recognizes. He tells her that his half-white children

The play's protagonist, Tam Lum, is a young Chinese American filmmaker making a documentary. (© Zush / Shutterstock.com)

should stay away from him because "they'd grow up to be like you."

Tom is the example of assimilation in Tam's eyes. He accepts his status as a member of the ideal minority. Tom does not express anger at injustice, be it personal attacks or racial stereotypes. He finds his way in the world by immersing himself in his Chinese heritage for the purpose of earning the acceptance of American society. He advises Tam to do the same so that people will not assume he is gay.

Before the play begins, Tam tried to find acceptance with his family and American society in his marriage and mastery of the English language. With the failure of his marriage and his film, Tam finds himself. Tam finds his identity in the injustices Chinese Americans have suffered, his family history, and in his anger by the end of the play. As he tells Kenji, "I have hard feelings. And I like 'em, they're mine! Thank you."

STYLE

Monologue

Chin uses monologues extensively throughout *The Chickencoop Chinaman*. A monologue is "the discourse of one speaker," according to William Harmon and Hugh Holman's *A Handbook to Literature*. For example, in the final scene of the play, the cast freezes, and the set

fades to black during Kenji's song about the Chickencoop Chinaman. The light focuses on Tam, who concludes the song alone, speaking to the audience and not other characters in the play. Here, he returns the audience's focus to the stories of his grandmother and the history of Chinese Americans in the American West.

Surrealism

The play includes three fantastic or surreal scenes that serve to make the author's point through humor. According to M. H. Abrams's *A Glossary of Literary Terms*, surrealism's influences on literature include: "free association, a broken syntax, nonlogical and nonchronological order, dreamlike and nightmarish sequences, and the juxtaposition of bizarre, shocking, or seemingly unrelated images." The first scene in act 1 with Hong Kong Dream Girl is a dream sequence where Tam flirts with the woman from Hong Kong, who is attempting to be an American. Surrealism appears again in act 2, scene 1, in which Tam and Kenji meet the Lone Ranger and Tonto. The hero of the American West reinforces racism when he shoots Tam in the hand and curses him to be "honorary white." The final surreal scene is act 2, scene 3. Here Tam rides on Charley Popcorn on an empty stage in limbo. During the nonsensical action, he talks about adopting his white wife's language and the subsequent loss of his family.

HISTORICAL CONTEXT

Asian Americans and Civil Rights

The American civil rights movement began in the 1960s. Malcolm X and other African American leaders inspired Asian Americans to take pride in their heritage, according to Monique Avakian in *Atlas of Asian-American History*. A major aspect of Asian American participation in the struggle for civil rights developed in the student movement. In 1968, Asian American students united with African American students to strike for the inclusion of an ethnic studies program at San Francisco State University. Another strike occurred at Berkeley the following year.

Students also worked to expose the conditions of people living in Chinatowns and bring improvement. With the Immigration and Nationality Act of 1965, immigrants from Asian nations were no longer barred from

COMPARE
&
CONTRAST

- **1860s:** Chinese men are sought out to work building the Transcontinental Railroad. The men are paid less and given more dangerous work than other employees.

- **1960s:** Asian Americans are considered the model minority. Statistics, however, show that large percentages of the Asian American population are working low-paying jobs such as cook or dishwasher.

  Today: According to the 2000 census, Asian Americans have a high college education rate, and many work in highly skilled occupations. The median personal income for Asian Americans is still lower than the median personal income of white Americans.

- **1860s:** Most Chinese Americans are not legal citizens of the United States. The Chinese Exclusion Act of 1882 would limit immigration from China and legally remove the opportunity for Asian Americans to become naturalized citizens.

- **1960s:** The Immigration and Nationality Act of 1965 ends the system of national origin–regulated immigration in favor of family reunification. The number of immigrants from Asian countries increases dramatically.

  Today: The Immigration and Nationality Act still caps the number of immigrants from each country. Many immigrants wait years to be reunited with their family members.

- **1860s:** Asian Americans are legally and socially marginalized. Unflattering stereotypes develop, including the idea that Asian American men lack strength and masculinity.

- **1960s:** Asian American students join with other students from other minorities and organize strikes at San Francisco State and Berkeley to include ethnic studies courses. The students hope to develop pride and understanding in the cultures at a time when unflattering stereotypes still abound.

  Today: Asian American stereotypes persist in American society and media. Many of them are positive stereotypes, such as being self-disciplined and intelligent. Unfortunately, even positive stereotypes minimize the struggles that Asian Americans face.

---

entering the country solely based on their national origin. This increase in immigration led to overcrowding in America's Chinatowns. Avakian explains that activists worked, "establishing community centers that provided assistance" to people in their communities.

The difficulties that the Asian American population faced in the 1960s flew in the face of the model minority stereotype. Sucheng Chan notes in *Asian Americans: An Interpretive History*, "25 percent of all gainfully employed Chinese men in the United States were cooks, waiters, busboys, dishwashers, and janitors" in 1970. The data support the stereotypes of Chinese Americans that appear throughout *The Chickencoop Chinaman*.

Asian Americans and the Chinese Exclusion Act

Tam refers to the building of the Transcontinental Railroad throughout *The Chickencoop Chinaman*. Men from China traveled to California during the Gold Rush of 1849. Over the years, railroad companies began hiring Chinese employees and paying them less than white employees. The employees from China cost less and worked hard. Soon, railway organizations such as the San Francisco and the San Jose "arranged with labor contractors to recruit large numbers of workers directly from China," according to Stanford University's "Chinese Railroad Workers in North America."

No one is sure how many men came from China to build the railroad. Some experts place

Tam Lum's documentary focuses on boxer Ovaltine Jack Dancer. (© *Alan Bailey / Shutterstock.com*)

the number of Chinese laborers at fifteen thousand. Chinese workers were given the most dangerous jobs, and there is no accurate account of how many died completing the construction of the railroad because their deaths were not recorded. The death toll is estimated to be twelve hundred based on the report that twenty thousand pounds of bones were discovered.

Despite the contributions of Chinese laborers, anti-Chinese sentiment grew in the late nineteenth century. After the railroad was complete, the men who built it were dismissed without warning. While some returned to China, others turned to agriculture and domestic service. Again, they were paid lower wages. Economic hardship in the 1870s and 1880s led to a government-sanctioned anti-Chinese movement. Many Americans saw Chinese men as a threat, "stealing jobs away from the 'true Americans,'" as Avakian explains.

The prejudice against Chinese Americans culminated in the Chinese Exclusion Act of 1882. The act strictly limited immigration from China to the United States. Additionally, no courts, at either the state or the federal level, were allowed to grant citizenship to Chinese individuals already in the country. The Geary Act of 1902 made Chinese exclusion permanent. It also demanded that anyone of Chinese heritage "register and obtain a certificate of residence. Without a certificate, she or he faced deportation," according to the Our Documents website. Few Chinese women were allowed in the country during this time. Additionally, wives legally shared their husbands' nationality with a 1907 act of Congress. Any woman who married a man of Chinese ancestry would share the same limits on citizenship. The Chinese Exclusion Act was not repealed until 1943, and immigration continued to be tightly controlled until the Immigration and Nationality Act of 1965.

CRITICAL OVERVIEW

Chin has been an influential yet controversial literary figure. When *The Chickencoop Chinaman* first ran in 1972, for example, the reviews were mixed. Jack Kroll's *Newsweek* review, as quoted by Ritsuko McDonald, praises the production. He says that there is "real vitality, humor and pain on Chin's stage." Michael Feingold of the *Village Voice*, also quoted by Ritsuko McDonald, describes the monologues as "hot air, disguised as Poetry." Ritsuko McDonald goes on to note that the reviews for his next play, *The Year of the Dragon*, are mainly positive. The play was so admired that *The Year of the Dragon* aired on PBS in 1975 with George Takei as the lead.

In 1974, *Aiiieeeee!: An Anthology of Asian-American Writers*, the first major anthology of Asian American authors, was published by Chin, Jeffery Paul Chan, Lawson Fusao Inada, and Shawn Wong. The anthology included only authors who fit Chin's definition of true Asian American artists. He criticized writers such as Maxine Kingston, Amy Tan, and David Henry Hwang, excluding their work from the original anthology as well as the 1991 update to the collection, *The Big Aiiieeeee!: An Anthology of Chinese American and Japanese American Literature*. The *Publishers Weekly* review of the updated anthology calls the book "remarkably diverse, ranging from haiku to autobiography," and explains that the selections "present a subtler, often poignant picture of Chinese and

Japanese immigrants and their American-born children." Despite the feud between Chin and other Asian American writers, the anthologies have been crucial texts for the study of Asian American literature.

Along with his plays, Chin has been the author of essays, novels, and short stories. His first novel, *Donald Duk*, was not published until 1991, but it earned great acclaim. Janet Ingraham says in her review for the *Library Journal*, "Chin spices his first novel with a flip, clipped, present-tense narrative voice, slapstick dialogue, and kinetic dreamscapes." *Gunga Din Highway* followed in 1994, and Wen-ching Ho calls it "an ambitious novel of satire and protest" in his *Amerasia* review, as quoted in *Asian American Novelists: A Bio-Bibliographical Critical Sourcebook*. Chin's latest novel, *The Confessions of a Number One Son*, was published in 2015 and is described as "the author's funniest, most powerful, and most poignant work to date" by the University of Hawai'i Press catalog.

CRITICISM

April Paris

Paris is a freelance writer with a degree in classical literature and a background in academic writing. In the following essay, she examines how the loss of Tam's illusions in Frank Chin's The Chickencoop Chinaman *provides him with the opportunity to find his true identity.*

Masculinity and fatherhood are important subjects in *The Chickencoop Chinaman*. They haunt Tam as he journeys to find his identity. He is tied to three men in this play: Ovaltine, the Lone Ranger, and Tom, and each one shows him the dangers of lies and illusions. The Lone Ranger and Ovaltine are the masculine role models of his youth. In them, Tam creates an ideal. They provide Tam with a way to escape from "white racism's feminization of black and Asian men by foregrounding fantasies of an aggressive masculinity," which Ryan Schneider describes in his review for *American Literature*. The ideals these characters represent contrast with Tom, who is weak and unable to stand up for himself. As Tam learns the truth about each one of these men, he is forced to discard illusions about them and about himself. In facing reality, Tam begins to find his way back to his roots, where he has the opportunity to find himself.

WHAT DO I READ NEXT?

- Published in 1991, *Donald Duk* is Chin's first published novel. It tells the story of eleven-year-old Donald Duk, who is torn between his desire to be American and his Chinese heritage. The book is an excellent example of Chin's fiction.

- *The Chinese in America: A Narrative History*, by Iris Chang, provides a history of Chinese Americans from the nineteenth century to the twenty-first century. Published in 2003, the book has a narrative style that makes this nonfiction text as engaging as it is insightful.

- Maxine Hong Kingston is a contemporary author whose work Chin considers a false representation of Chinese American culture. Her book *The Woman Warrior: Memoirs of a Girlhood among Ghosts* by was first published in 1976. Kingston blends Chinese folktales into her life story and shows the contrast between Chin's and Kingston's styles and their definitions of Asian American identity.

- Matt de la Peña's young-adult novel *Mexican White Boy* (2010) tells the story of Danny, a boy who searches for his own identity in the two cultures of his parents.

- *The American Dream in African American, Asian American, and Hispanic American Drama: August Wilson, Frank Chin, and Luis Valdez* (2009), by Tsui-fen Jiang, examines how the American dream influences minority cultures. Jiang specifically analyzes *The Chickencoop Chinaman* alongside plays by Luis Valdez and August Wilson to show the writers' common themes and experiences.

- Published in 2009, *Untold Civil Rights Stories: Asian Americans Speak Out for Justice*, by Stewart Kwoh, explains how Asian Americans have worked toward civil rights in America. The stories of ordinary individuals included in the book provide a deeper understanding of history.

> AS TAM LEARNS THE TRUTH ABOUT EACH ONE OF THESE MEN, HE IS FORCED TO DISCARD ILLUSIONS ABOUT THEM AND ABOUT HIMSELF. IN FACING REALITY, TAM BEGINS TO FIND HIS WAY BACK TO HIS ROOTS, WHERE HE HAS THE OPPORTUNITY TO FIND HIMSELF."

Tam has a very poor opinion of Chinese American fathers, which he shares in act 1, scene 2. In act 2, scene 1, he reveals that he could find no Asian American role models on the radio as a child. To compensate for this masculine void in his life, Tam decides to imagine the Lone Ranger as Chinese. He is certain that the Lone Ranger wears the mask to hide his Chinese identity. He sees the Lone Ranger as "Chinaman vengeance on the West." The illusion he created, however, shatters when he and Kenji meet the Lone Ranger in the first scene of act 2. The Lone Ranger is an elderly drug addict who shoots Tam in the hand for no reason. To add insult to injury, he demands that Tam thank him for the inexplicable deed.

When he is not saying his classic radio lines, the hero of the American West reveals himself to be a racist who insults Tam and Kenji's strength and masculinity. At one point, the Lone Ranger complains to Tam about the starch in his shirts. This reference to the Chinese laundry is a reminder that anti-Chinese sentiment in the nineteenth century limited the number of jobs Chinese men could take. Laundry and kitchen work were considered feminine jobs that most men avoided, but they were some of the few options left to Chinese men who were denied work simply for being Chinese. As Michael Park explains in "Asian American Masculinity Eclipsed: A Legal and Historical Perspective of Emasculation through U.S. Immigration Practices," "the Chinese laundry 'phenomenon' represented a retreat into self-employment in a restricted labor market, to perform a traditional role assigned to women." In addition to insulting Tam's masculinity, the Lone Ranger curses him as an "honorary white." This insult is a reference to the model minority stereotype and assumes that Tam is fully assimilated into the dominant white culture.

He believes that Tam and Kenji are cast with him, and he expects them to play their parts in American society. He sees Tam's refusal to thank him after being shot as a refusal to play his part in the American dream.

The Chickencoop Chinaman consistently connects Tam with the Lone Ranger. For example, Kenji calls him "Masked Man" in act 1, scene 2. This is the name that Tonto calls the Lone Ranger in the radio program. Tonto is the Native American sidekick of the masked hero in the radio program, and Kenji's reference reveals him to be Tam's sidekick. Even after Tam's disastrous encounter with the Lone Ranger, the link between them continues throughout the play. Like the Lone Ranger, Tam is always leaving people behind. In the final scene, Tam tells Kenji, "You were my silent pardner. We used to run together." Like Tonto for the Lone Ranger, Kenji has always been by his side. Their close partnership, however, dissolves by the end of the play. Tam is left friendless and alone. His life reflects the warning from the Lone Ranger "you'll be like me, spendin your whole lifetime ridin outa your life into everybody's distance." In this loneliness, however, Tam find the ability to focus, which allows him to return to the stories of his grandmother and the American West. It is in this state of loneliness that Tam is able to honestly consider his identity as an Asian American without the distractions of Western influences, like the Lone Ranger, whom he finally recognizes, "deafened my ear for trains all my boyhood long."

Tam's determination to find a strong, masculine role model in his youth moved beyond the realm of fiction. As boys, he and Kenji idolized the African American prizefighter Ovaltine Jack Dancer. This idolatry helped to create an illusion that continued in Tam's adult life. It is an illusion he hopes to share and celebrate in his documentary about the fighter's life. While Ovaltine's strength and masculinity make him an excellent role model in Tam's eyes, the appeal goes even further. Tam finds a hope for family and fatherhood in the relationship between Ovaltine and his father and coach, Charley Popcorn. In their relationship, Tam sees the relationship that he missed with his own father and with his children. The ideal father-son relationship, however, is an illusion that does not last for long. A. D. Huan points out in his review for *Bulletin of Concerned Asian Scholars*, "Charley Popcorn, the trainer, rejects the stories that he is the father of the prize fighter and forces Tam to realize the falseness of his illusions about ideal father-son relationships." The loss of the second illusion shatters Tam, causing him to lash out at Charley Popcorn. In a final attempt to salvage his dream, Tam asks Charley Popcorn to lie before he summons the courage to face the truth about his hero and himself.

The sad truth about Tam's search for masculine role models outside Asian American society is that he fails to see the positive role models who were available to him. One such example is the old dishwasher Tam took to the fights as a child. The physically frail man earned the respect of Charley Popcorn because of his strength of character. Charley Popcorn describes the old man as "fierce" when he refused Charley's offer to watch a fight for free. He insisted on paying his own way. In this encounter, Charley Popcorn recognizes and admires the man's pride. He tells Tam, "I could see his whole life, you understand?" Tam realizes that he failed to see the example of strength before him while he was chasing after illusions. Tam states, "I've failed all the old men that ever trusted me." Seeing the truth of his illusion torments Tam, but it also allows him to face the world honestly. As Huan says, "Now that the fragile, protective shell of his dreams has been shattered, he must pull back to reexamine his perceptions and fashion a legitimate mechanism for dealing with the outside world." He chooses to create art that is honest rather than lie and sell illusions to make a name for himself. Tam's resolve to project honesty, even if it makes him unpopular, stands in stark contrast to Tom.

Unlike Ovaltine and the Lone Ranger, Tom is not a role model to Tam. He represents the existence that Tam will have if he fails to learn from the past and continues in his attempts to earn approval from others. In a telling reveal, Chin has the same actor play both Tonto and Tom. Both are characters who have "come to terms with the dominant white society," according to Haun. Tom is the embodiment of the assimilated, model minority, which Tam rejects. Tom tells Tam, "We're accepted. We worked hard for it. I've made my peace." Tam finds Tom repulsive because of their similarities. In Tom, Tam sees the worst of himself. Like Tom, Tam allowed his children to be taken from him without a fight. Additionally, both characters had white wives who left them for other men. Tam's connection with Tom is further complicated by their names. Tam informs Lee that he alters his accent because people correct the way he speaks. Some people have even told him that the correct pronunciation of his name is *Tom*.

The significant difference between Tom and Tam lies in Tam's ability to express anger. Tam attempted assimilating to earn the respect of his parents and other people, but he lost his family and any illusions that once comforted him. All he has left is his anger, and he lashes out at the people around him. In the final scene, Tam tells Kenji, "I have hard feelings. And I like 'em, they're mine." As Tam's anger separates him from the other characters, it also helps him make his first step toward self-discovery. Tam's future, however, is uncertain. Dorothy Ritsuko McDonald points out in her Introduction to *The Chickencoop Chinaman and The Year of the Dragon: Two Plays by Frank Chin* that Tam is "isolated and wounded." She argues that Chin's characters are "articulate but incapable of the action necessary to fulfill the hope and promise of the past." If Tam is willing to pay the price of telling the truth, however, it may be possible for him to discover and accept his personal and cultural identity.

Source: April Paris, Critical Essay on *The Chickencoop Chinaman*, in *Drama for Students*, Gale, Cengage Learning, 2016.

Ashis Sengupta

In the following excerpt, Sengupta explains how Chin ties together the concepts of masculinity and race in The Chickencoop Chinaman.

... Frank Chin's theatre protests against institutional as well as internalized racism and attempts to reclaim the cultural legacy of a people. He calls his theatre "real" and "authentic," as did the leaders of the Black Revolutionary Theatre who had considerably influenced him. Chin refused to be called a cultural nationalist, but he certainly is a product of the cultural nationalism of the 1960s and 1970s (Lee, 2006: 54–55). The word "Chinaman" smacks of a long history of white racism. Yet Chin (1993) would prefer "Chinaman" to "Chinese American" because he believes that the former, despite all its racist baggage, reminds us of the valour and masculinity of Chinese immigrants as compared with the "sold-out," "assimilated," and "endangered" Chinese American of the present. But Chin (1993) must have had in his unconscious the ancient image of the Chinese martial warrior, which, as the Chinese masculine ideal, was partly replaced by the image of the dainty scholar by

Tam Lum imitates the speech of African Americans, though he is of Chinese descent and grew up in Chinatown. *(© Andrey Bayda / Shutterstock.com)*

the end of the Tang dynasty. In fact, thereafter, ideal Chinese masculinity came to mean, as Kam Louie (2002) would have it, the dyad of wu and wen in a single man.

Yet the prioritization of wen (intelligence, self-control, and discipline) over wu (physical strength, martial valour, and leadership) with the adaptation of Confucianism in dynastic government policies since the Han period, and its long-term impact on the perception of Chinese masculinity, might be seen ultimately to have resulted—during the latter half of the Qing dynasty—in a preference for delicate, hypersensitive men with no hypermasculine features. Finally, as Zhou says, "the May Fourth generation condemned the old Chinese masculine image even more virulently than the most critical Western intellectuals of the 19th century," and the Chinese masculine image has changed drastically ever since. This might have contributed somewhat to the Western perception of immigrant Chinese men as less masculine, although that gaze had more to do with white America's racist construction of them as sexless. Chin

(1993) alludes to the ancient periods of Chinese history, particularly the Spring, Autumn, and Warring States Period, and the Qin dynasty, and ignores later Chinese constructions of masculinity in order to vie with the old American model of rugged masculinity that consists of relentlessly repudiating the feminine, acquiring power, success, and status, exuding an aura of manly daring and aggression, and being sexually desirable to women (Harris). This appears further complicated when we consider his conscious attempt to hypermasculinize his protagonist whose senses of "ideal" masculinity are self-contradictory and inconsistent.

To answer why Chin should hypermasculinize his hero is to understand historically the position that a large section of Chinese men had held in American society until the early half of the last century. In the mid-1850s, the Chinese started immigrating to the US in search of jobs to support their families back in China. American labour recruiters also hired them on short-term contracts and wanted them to return to their homeland eventually. Many Chinese labourers—mainly

> "EVIDENTLY, TAM IS NOT A SPOKESPERSON WHO ADVOCATES CHIN'S GENDER/SEX AGENDA BUT AN EMOTIONALLY DAMAGED CHARACTER WHO EMBODIES THE CHINESE AMERICAN MAN'S PSYCHOSEXUAL CRISIS WHICH NEVER FAILED TO ELICIT CHIN'S ANGRY REACTION."

mine workers, launderers, dishwashers, and railroad workers—could not return home because of a lack of money or having been refused return permits as many of them were not legally-admitted aliens, while others chose to stay on to earn more. The Chinese Exclusion Act was passed in 1882. In 1924, alien Chinese were declared ineligible for naturalization. The anti-Chinese movement was on the rise, resulting in the segregation/ghettoization of Chinese populations and denial of employment and other social benefits to them. The Chinese male, above all, was forbidden to bring his China-born wife to the US or to marry an American woman. The denial of rights to become an American and have a normal sex and family life emasculated them psychosexually and put them into a state of deep despair. Chinese American family life began only after 1949, six years after new legislation was passed to allow entry to China-born wives and children. This had not only given rise to a society of "forced" and "married" bachelors but to a life of gambling, prostitution, and other "perversions." They felt socially castrated *vis-à-vis* US Americans who had most of what they lacked and who also "protested the employment of Chinese in factories," on farms, in teaching, and dentistry (Kim, 1982: 98). Elaine H. Kim notes that, by 1950, "the majority of Chinese [men] in America were concentrated in half a dozen occupations, laundry work being seventy-four times as numerous as any other occupation" because it was clearly considered "menial work for a despised people" (Kim, 1982: 99) and not at all fit for white Americans. Most of the immigrants who gained employment in "women's work" as cooks, launderers, and servants were perceived as docile and "effeminate." No wonder they internalized this perception so rapidly.

But why, then, was a section of the same people at once viewed as Yellow Peril invaders, hired killers, and abductors? Little of early Chinese life in the US was private, away from the prying eyes of freelancers, authors, and tour operators. The tourist interest about the Chinese in America lay mainly in the image of Chinatown as a den of criminals and "opium-sodden yellow slaves" (Kim, 1982: 93). Anglo-American literary portrayals of Chinatown equally reinforced the popular prejudices against the Chinese in America, although such images of Chinese people had little connection with Chinatown life. The crime rate among Chinese youth was not greatly disproportionate to that among black and white youth in urban areas (Kim, 1982: 93) and therefore not enough to establish its connection to old Chinese tong wars or any plot to occupy large territories of the US (as imagined by racist Americans). The ambivalent American attitude towards Chinese immigrants, partly due to ignorance of an alien culture, reflected a sense of threat the host society perceived, marking the Chinese male body as predatory and hypersexual and needing to be monitored and policed. The result was again a desexualized, feminized group that felt emasculated, and more so following the notorious exclusion laws. By the end of World War II, and after Chinese American family life began officially in 1949, the successful middle-class Chinese population in the US came to be considered as a community of law-abiding, educated people that made good use of all opportunities available to them and thus qualified as "a model minority." This image of Chinese Americans bolstered itself especially with the 1965 Immigration and Nationality Act that let in more educated Chinese from China. The quasi-official American admiration for a considerable section of Chinese Americans might have been a product of what Frank Chin and Jeffrey Paul Chan called "racist love" that aimed to discredit by contrast the "bad" blacks and Mexicans (Kim, 1982: 178). Yet, the upwardly mobile Chinese who tended to comply with the norms of mainstream society and avoid confrontation for individual success were simultaneously (re)marked as docile Chinese Americans. The generation of forced bachelors in the late nineteenth and early twentieth century Chinatown with their low self-esteem was thus succeeded in a different social context by a second or third generation of Chinese males who, as Chin and Chan write, were "praised" by male white America as men without "sinful manhood" and "essentially feminine in character" (Quoted in Kim, 1982: 178). So Chin would view Chinese American history, writes Esther H. Kim, as "a wholesale and systematic attempt to emasculate the Chinese American male" (1982: 179). Interestingly, long after the repeal of exclusion laws, most Chinese women continued to treat Chinese men as effeminate, even "homosexual" at times, and would prefer to marry a white American man.

Seeking to reverse the "trend," Chin (1993) reconstructed the image of the Chinese American male by hypermasculinizing him and thus also recasting him unwittingly in the image of hegemonic American manhood, although his "hero" frequently finds himself inadequate according to the Western matrix of masculinity. Evidently, Tam is not a spokesperson who advocates Chin's gender/sex agenda but an emotionally damaged character who embodies the Chinese American man's psychosexual crisis which never failed to elicit Chin's angry reaction. The figure of the Lone Ranger stands for protagonist Tam Lum's boyhood desire to equal a white American man by being like him. One argument could be that Tam is attracted to the Lone Ranger as a child because he imagines him as Asian, not as white (which is made possible by the Lone Ranger's mask which obscures his racial features). But I would argue that Tam might have also transformed the white figure in his imagination into an Asian image and kept mystifying it until he was jolted out of his secret idealization of white masculinity by the "arrows" of disillusionment.

The Chinese male is again anxious to have his maleness endorsed by a white woman, and the failure to do so would result not only in self-loathing but in misogyny. His self-loathing and misogyny have a common source in his awareness of his social unacceptability on the grounds that he is considered inferior to a white American man. Such anxiety about maleness, however, occasionally projects itself through comedy in *The Chickencoop Chinaman*. Tam Lum is described by the editors of *Aiiieeeee!* as "the comic embodiment of Asian American manhood, rooted in neither Asia nor white America" (quoted in McDonald, 1993: xv). The "comic" basically lies in the Chinaman's overplaying of masculinity to get over his castration anxiety, which also explains his hatred towards his own women and his mixed feelings of fear and attraction towards white females. While telling Chinese sons of their ancestors, Tam narrates the history of perceived emasculation

suffered by early Chinese immigrants, in the US, and he himself is also seen struggling to escape the threat of "castration." Tam's encounter with Lee, the Eurasian wife of his childhood friend Kenji, brings out the ignominious layers of the Chinaman's life. Lee describes all Chinese men as "mama's boys and crybabies" who, rejected by Chinese women, take advantage of some stupid white girl (Chin, 1993: 24). Tam also married a white woman, but Barbara has left him for a white husband and taken his children away. The assimilated Chinese American has been praised for "no juvenile delinquency," whereas the actual reason was that there were no children as the laws "didn't let our women in [...] and our women lost their citizenship if they married a man from China" (Chin, 1993: 26). That an American woman marrying a resident Asian man later could bestow citizenship on him is an interesting development in Asian American history. Barbara and Lee are white/-looking women whom Asian/Chinese men in the US look to as sexually active, domineering subjects who, at the same time, are scary, emasculating figures due to those men's own fear of being found wanting. The anxiety of lack, transferred from the female on to the male, is not ungrounded as those women—who can not only affirm their manhood but help them earn their US citizenship—are positioned to change their husbands, as both Barbara and Lee have done. And Lee directly taunts Tam with effeminacy: "All afraid of the pretty girls? But oh so anxious to do the right thing—avoid trouble—save face" (Chin, 1993: 13). Tam's symbolic castration is attended by his gnawing sense of "thwarted fatherhood" (Lee, 1997: 67). In the story of the effeminate, emasculated Chinese, gender is thus racialized. Tam's angry rhetoric and action issue from his predominantly male anxieties in a racist and gendered society, although it has subjected Chin to charges of misogyny....

Source: Ashis Sengupta, "Different Strokes: The Chinese Male Subject in *The Chickencoop Chinaman* and *M. Butterfly*," in *Comparative American Studies*, Vol. 10, No. 1, March 2012, pp. 64–67.

Carol Fisher Sorgenfrei
In the following review, Sorgenfrei points out that Chin does not allow his characters to become stereotypes.

Rich, varied, and unpredictable, the plays in these three volumes are like the mirrored scales on the tip of some fantastic dragon's tail. Resting peacefully, they reflect the outer world; flailing about in fury or in playfulness, they suggest unimagined creatures shrouded in mist. Reflecting, distorting, recreating the Asian-American experience, these tantalizing samples compel us to seek more work by Asian-American playwrights.

What immediately impresses is the wide variation in both form and content. The plays of Frank Chin, vigorous and hallucinatory in their desperate search for an authentic Chinese-American identity, veer madly between the jazzy rhythms of the Chinatown ghetto, the tinny clang of American pop culture, and the shrill cacophony of displaced souls. *The Chickencoop Chinaman* follows a young Chinese-American named Tam on an odyssey of self-discovery. Alternating between surreal dream sequences and the "reality" of life in Pittsburgh's surreal black ghetto, the play overflows with linguistic bravado and breathless pace. Defying convention, Chin refuses to let himself, his plays, or his characters be stereotyped. Speaking to the Hong Kong Dream Girl, Tam says:

> Chinamen are made, not born, my dear. Out of junk-imports, lies, railroad scrap iron, dirty jokes, broken bottles, cigar smoke, Cosquilla Indian blood, wino spit, and lots of milk of magnesia. . . . I am the natural born ragmouth speaking the motherless bloody tongue. No real language of my own to make sense with, so out comes everybody else's trash that don't conceive. But the second truth is that I AM THE NOTORIOUS ONE AND ONLY CHICKENCOOP CHINAMAN HIMSELF that talks in the dark heavy Midnight, the secret Chinatown Buck Buck Bagaw. I am the result of a pile of pork chop suey thrown up to the chickencoop in the dead of night and the riot of dark birds, night cocks and insomniac nympho hens running after strange food that followed.

Apparently more "realistic" in construction, *The Year of the Dragon* is equally devastating in its manic account of the last days of a Chinatown patriarch. Bitterly sardonic, the patriarch's oldest son Fred Eng is consumed by self-loathing; as a tourist guide in San Francisco's Chinatown, he is forced to play the fawning Asian to gawking white visitors. His sister has "married out white," his kid brother is involved with gang crime, his mother is incessantly frantic in her Mission Christianity. On the eve of Chinese New Year, the dying Pa Eng has sent for China Mama—his first wife from China, and Freddie's true mother. Frustration, anger, bitterness, confusion, and

comedy pervade this work. Chin again steeps his play in a rich linguistic stew, this time spicing Chinatown pidgin, university English, Cantonese, Mandarin, and the stereotypical jargon of Charlie Chan or of Flower Drum Song, with a dash of obscenity and a shake of poetry. It is powerful, raw, insistent, potent language from a unique and talented writer.

Equally talented yet stylistically Chin's polar opposite is David Henry Hwang. The four plays comprising *Broken Promises* are carefully structured in the traditional Western sense. Each is a gleaming gem of startling perception.

FOB confronts the complacency of totally Americanized Chinese university students with a challenge from their own cultural mythology. A Chinese student in Los Angeles, fresh off the boat (FOB), reveals himself to be Gwan Gung, legendary god of warriors, writers, and prostitutes. This revelation—or fantastic obsession?—gradually leads a first-generation Chinese girl to question her identity as a Chinese and as an American. Slipping under the stranger's spell, she is transformed into Fa Mu Lan, the Woman Warrior. The term FOB ceases to have a derogatory connotation, indicating instead glorification of the girl's Chinese heritage.

Gwan Gung reappears as forceful cultural icon in the remarkable one-act *The Dance and the Railroad*. A tour de force for two male actor-dancers, *The Dance and the Railroad* is a lyrical, heart-rending, vigorous battle between the abandoned culture of China and the false promises of Gold Mountain. It is 1867, and the Chinese builders of America's transcontinental railroad have gone on strike. A wide-eyed newcomer seeks out the aloof Lone as he practices the disciplines of Cantonese opera dance. The heroic spirit of Gwan Gung, protagonist of the opera Lone is rehearsing, is embodied in the tale of these long-dead "ChinaMen." This is a deeply felt and memorable work demanding exquisite acting and choreography.

Radically different is *Family Devotions*, a black comedy of manners set in affluent Bel Air, California. A fanatically Christian, economically successful family of first- and second-generation Chinese is visited by a devoutly Marxist mainland relative. What follows is a bizarre ritual exorcism in which truth is revealed and twisted, and salvation is only achieved through denial and death.

The final play in the volume is *The House of Sleeping Beauties*, a haunting and evocative work based on Yasunari Kawabata's short story. Hwang deftly imagines the writer's last days, incorporating Kawabata's unexplained suicide with the incidents of his much earlier fictional tale. Love, fear, beauty, youth, fragility, art, and death swirl like a delicate mist around the refined brothel and its mystified guest. This play alone of the four confronts issues other than Chinese-American identity. Like its companion plays, it reveals a writer of skill and talent, equally at home in a variety of styles.

While Hwang and Chin command our attention as important and authentic young playwrights, the eight authors represented in *Kumu Kahua Plays* are interesting chiefly because they reveal a culture with which most Americans are unfamiliar. The multiethnic life of Hawaii permeates these plays. Enlivening many of them is the wonderful color of Hawaiian pidgin. With two exceptions, the playwrights represented here are still learning their craft; seven of the eight authors were students or recent graduates of the University of Hawaii when their plays were first produced. While the honesty, enthusiasm, and sheer youthful vitality of these varied works are evident, so too is the inexperience of most of the writers.

The exceptions therefore seem to soar majestically above the others. Edward Sakamoto's *In The Alley* is a visceral one-act of racial violence. Set in a sleazy side alley behind the inner-city tenements of Honolulu, the drama reflects the frustration of the native Hawaiian unable to enter the longed-for world of the Haole (Caucasian). The insidious lure of the unattainable combines with fear and hatred of dominating outsiders, resulting in teenagers caught up in an escalation of tensions. These child-men indulging in beer and machismo reveal the dark and secret underbelly of what most mainland Americans imagine to be a languid paradise. Frightening, powerful, and believable, *In The Alley* is a play deserving attention.

Equally noteworthy is James Grant Benton's joyous and freewheeling Hawaiian pidgin adaptation of Shakespeare's *Twelfth Night*, entitled *Twelf Nite O Wateva!* Here Illyria is transformed into the Hawaiian islands, and the characters to charmingly anachronistic members of the old island nobility. In the original production, devised and directed by Terence Knapp, the setting combined tapa mats and potted plants, with costuming reminiscent of the nineteenth century, cleverly invigorated by such contemporary elements as blue jeans, bicycles, Lahaina pearls, and orange lava-lavas. The flavor of this wonderful theatrical melange can only be hinted at. Orsino's famous first speech, here spoken by his Hawaiian counterpart Prince Amalu, is rendered as follows:

> If music going be da food of love, go play on,
> gimme mo den extra, so dat appetite going get
> sick and go make. Oooh, dat vamp again. It
> had one dying beat, and wen come ova my ear
> like da sweet sound dat breathes on one bank
> of pakalana, stealing and giving odor. Nuff,
> pau already. Da baga not as sweet as was
> befo. Ho, spirit of love, you so alive and fresh
> dat if you was da frolicking Pacific, I would
> drink you all. Auwe! So full of different forms
> is love dat, by himself, he is one unending
> purple dream.

While an excellent glossary of Hawaiian pidgin is included in *Kumu Kahua Plays*, the liveliness of the dialogue in this and the other plays using pidgin generally creates a clarity by its context.

These three anthologies demonstrate the vitality and variety of Asian-American playwriting. Far from a comprehensive survey, this review can only hint at the many other Asian-American authors who demand serious attention. A few of these are Philip Kan Gotanda, Momoko Ito, Winston Tong, R. A. Shiomi, and Wakako Yamauchi. It is time to see what wonders lie beyond the tip of the dragon's tail.

Source: Carol Fisher Sorgenfrei, Review of *The Chickencoop Chinaman*, in *Asian Theatre Journal*, Vol. 2, No. 2, Autumn 1985, pp. 240–43.

SOURCES

Abrams, M. H., "Surrealism," in *A Glossary of Literary Terms*, 7th ed., Heinle & Heinle, 1999, p. 311.

Avakian, Monique, *Atlas of Asian-American History*, Checkmark Books, 2002, pp. 43, 166–67.

Chan, Sucheng, *Asian Americans: An Interpretive History*, Twayne Publishers, 1991, p. 168.

Chin, Frank, "Back Talk," in Introduction to *The Chickencoop Chinaman and The Year of the Dragon: Two Plays by Frank Chin*, by Dorothy Ritsuko McDonald, University of Washington Press, 1981, p. ix; originally published in *News of the American Place Theater*, Vol. 4, No. 4, May 1972, pp. 1–2.

———, *The Chickencoop Chinaman and The Year of the Dragon: Two Plays by Frank Chin*, University of Washington Press, 1981.

"Chinese Exclusion Act (1882)," Our Documents website, http://www.ourdocuments.gov/doc.php?flash = true&doc = 47 (accessed August 2, 2015).

"Chinese Railroad Workers in North America," Stanford University website, http://web.stanford.edu/group/chineserailroad/cgi-bin/wordpress/faqs/ (accessed August 2, 2015).

Feingold, Michael, "Portnoy's Chinese Complaint," in Introduction to *The Chickencoop Chinaman and The Year of the Dragon: Two Plays by Frank Chin*, by Dorothy Ritsuko McDonald, University of Washington Press, 1981, p. xv; originally published in *Village Voice*, June 15, 1972, p. 56.

"Frank Chin Biography," Asian American Theater website, January 31, 2011, http://aatheatre.web.unc.edu/2011/01/31/frank-chin-biography/ (accessed August 2, 2015).

Harmon, William, and Hugh Holman, "Monologue," in *A Handbook to Literature*, 9th ed., Prentice Hall, 2003, p. 320.

Ho, Wen-ching, Review of *Gunga Din Highway*, in *Asian American Novelists: A Bio-Bibliographical Critical Sourcebook*, edited by Emmanuel S. Nelson, Greenwood Press, 2000, p. 54; originally published in *Amerasia Journal*, Vol. 22, No. 2, 1996, pp. 158–61.

Huan, A. D., Review of *The Chickencoop Chinaman and The Year of the Dragon: Two Plays by Frank Chin*, in *Bulletin of Concerned Asian Scholars*, Vol. 16, No. 1, January–March 1984, pp. 69–71.

Ingraham, Janet, Review of *Donald Duk*, in *Library Journal*, February 15, 1991, p. 220.

Kroll, Jack, "Primary Color," in Introduction to *The Chickencoop Chinaman and The Year of the Dragon: Two Plays by Frank Chin*, by Dorothy Ritsuko McDonald, University of Washington Press, 1981, p. xv; originally published in *Newsweek*, June 19, 1972, p. 55.

Park, Michael, "Asian American Masculinity Eclipsed: A Legal and Historical Perspective of Emasculation through U.S. Immigration Practices," in *Modern American*, Vol. 8, No. 1, 2013, pp. 5–17.

Review of *The Big Aiiieeeee!*, in *Publishers Weekly*, January 1, 2007, http://www.publishersweekly.com/978-0-452-01076-5 (accessed August 2, 2015).

Review of *The Confessions of a Number One Son*, University of Hawai'i Press catalog, Spring 2015, p. 9, https://uhpress.files.wordpress.com/2008/12/2015spring-web.pdf (accessed December 17, 2015).

Ritsuko McDonald, Dorothy, Introduction to *The Chickencoop Chinaman and The Year of the Dragon: Two Plays by Frank Chin*, University of Washington Press, 1981, pp. xiv, xx.

Schneider, Ryan, Review of *Writing Manhood in Black and Yellow: Ralph Ellison, Frank Chin, and the Literary Politics of Identity*, in *American Literature*, Vol. 78. No. 4, December, 2006, pp. 894–97.

Zhang, Aiping, "Frank Chin," in *Asian American Short Story Writers: An A-to-Z Guide*, edited by Guiyou Huang, Greenwood Press, 2003, p. 51.

FURTHER READING

Ancheta, Angelo N., *Race, Rights, and the Asian American Experience*, Rutgers University Press, 2006.
> Ancheta carefully examines the history of oppression and civil rights in the United States. The text is perfect for anyone who wants a detailed understanding of Asian American civil rights.

Chin, Frank, and Calvin McMillin, *The Confessions of a Number One Son*, University of Hawaii Press, 2015.
> *The Confessions of a Number One Son* continues the story of Tam Lum from *The Chickencoop Chinaman*. Although Chin wrote the book in the 1970s, the novel was lost until McMillin found the drafts in his research and restored the work with Chin's permission.

Chan, Jeffery, Frank Chin, Lawson Fusao Inada, and Shawn Wong, eds., *The Big Aiiieeeee!: An Anthology of Chinese American and Japanese American Literature*, Plume, 1991.
> This anthology provides an overview of the literature from Chinese and Japanese Americans. Students will find the text includes stories and poems not found in other collections.

Kim, Daniel, *Writing Manhood in Black and Yellow: Ralph Ellison, Frank Chin, and the Literary Politics of Identity*, Stanford University Press, 2005.
> Kim examines the emasculating stereotypes of Asian Americans and African Americans in the United States. He highlights the work of Frank Chin and his construction of masculinity.

Takaki, Ronald, *Strangers from a Different Shore*, Little, Brown, 1998.
> This nonfiction text provides an overview of Asian American history. The blend of facts with narrative and personal testimony makes the information accessible to anyone interested in the topic.

SUGGESTED SEARCH TERMS

Frank Chin

Frank Chin AND biography

Frank Chin AND The Chickencoop Chinaman

Asian American civil rights movement

Chinese Exclusion Act

Frank Chin AND criticism

Chinese immigration

Asian American literature AND Frank Chin

A Chorus Line

MICHAEL BENNETT

1975

A Chorus Line was a long-running Broadway musical that was first presented by the New York Shakespeare Festival at the Newman Theater, New York City, on April 16, 1975. It ran there for 101 performances. It then transferred to the Sam S. Shubert Theatre, New York City, where it played 6,137 performances before closing in late April 1990. The original show was choreographed and directed by Michael Bennett, with music by Marvin Hamlisch, lyrics by Edward Kleban, and the book (the nonmusical parts of the story) by James Kirkwood and Nicholas Dante.

A Chorus Line is based on real Broadway dancers' stories, as told to Bennett at a meeting he had with twenty-four dancers (known on Broadway as "gypsies" because they move around from show to show) in January 1974, in which they discussed the rewards and frustrations of their jobs. The conversation was tape-recorded, and the material was then developed in two five-week workshops. The resulting show takes place on a bare stage at a generic Broadway theater in 1975, where a group of dancers are auditioning for a place in the chorus of an upcoming musical. There is almost no plot, the story consisting for the most part of the stories the dancers tell about their lives. An immediate hit with critics and public alike, the show won nine Tony Awards, including best musical, best choreography, best book, and

best score. The show also won the Pulitzer Prize for Drama and the New York Drama Critics Circle Award.

AUTHOR BIOGRAPHY

Theater director and choreographer Michael Bennett was born on April 8, 1943, in Buffalo, New York. He started taking dance lessons at the age of three and by the age of twelve was well schooled in a variety of dances, including tap, ballet, modern, and folk dancing. At the age of sixteen, he dropped out of high school and joined a touring company of *West Side Story*, which took him to Europe as well as many locations in the United States. In the early 1960s, he danced in choruses for several Broadway shows, and by the late 1960s he had emerged as a choreographer, winning Tony nominations for the musicals *Henry, Sweet Henry* in 1967; Neil Simon's *Promises, Promises*, which ran from 1968 to 1971; André Previn and Alan Jay Lerner's *Coco*, which ran for three hundred performances beginning in 1969; and Stephen Sondheim and George Furth's *Company*, which opened in 1970. In 1971, Bennett won his first Tony Awards, as choreographer and codirector, with Harold Prince, of Sondheim and James Goldman's *Follies*, which opened in April 1971. His third Tony Award was for choreographing the musical *Seesaw*, which opened in 1973. Bennett's greatest success came in 1975, when he created *A Chorus Line*, for which he won two Tony Awards, for Best Director of a Musical and Best Choreography, in 1976. Bennett's next musical, *Ballroom* (1978), also won him a Tony Award, although it was not a commercial success. *Dreamgirls* (1981), which he directed and co-choreographed with Michael Peters, won for him his seventh Tony Award. The show ran for over three years. Bennett died of lymphoma, a cancer that resulted from AIDS, at the age of forty-four on July 2, 1987, in Tucson, Arizona.

Composer Marvin Hamlisch was born in Manhattan, New York City, on June 2, 1944. Hamlisch graduated from the Juilliard School of Music and also earned a bachelor of arts degree from Queens College in 1967. He wrote the music for the Broadway shows *A Chorus Line*, *They're Playing Our Song* (1978), *The Goodbye Girl* (1993), and *Sweet Smell of Success* (2002), among others. He also composed more than forty film scores, including *The Way We Were* (1973), for which he won an Oscar for both score and title song. Hamlisch adapted Scott Joplin's music for *The Sting* (1973), for which he received another Oscar. His film scores included original compositions or musical adaptations or both for *The Swimmer* (1968), *Ice Castles* (1978), *Take the Money and Run* (1969), *Bananas* (1971), *Save the Tiger* (1973), *Ordinary People* (1980), *Sophie's Choice* (1982), *Three Men and a Baby* (1987), and *The Informant!* (2009). All told, Hamlisch won three Oscars, four Grammy Awards, four Emmy Awards, a Tony Award, and three Golden Globe awards for his music. He also held the position of principal "pops" (popular songs) conductor for a number of orchestras, including the Pittsburgh Symphony Orchestra, Dallas Symphony Orchestra, San Diego Symphony, and the National Symphony Orchestra in Washington, DC. Hamlisch died on August 6, 2012, in Los Angeles.

Lyricist Edward Kleban (1939–1987) was born in the Bronx, New York, and graduated from Columbia University. He wrote the lyrics for *A Chorus Line*, for which he and Hamlisch won the Tony Award in 1976 for Best Original Score. After Kleban's death, *A Class Act*, a musical based on his life, was produced at the Ambassador Theatre on Broadway in 2001. The musical contained songs Kleban wrote for several musicals that had never been produced. The show won for Kleban a posthumous Tony Award nomination for Best Original Score and Drama Desk nominations for Outstanding Music and Outstanding Lyrics.

Nicolas Dante (1941–1991) was a dancer and writer who cowrote the book of *A Chorus Line*, for which he won the 1976 Tony Award for Best Book and Drama Desk Award for Outstanding Book of a Musical.

James Kirkwood, Jr. (1924–1989), was a playwright, novelist, and actor. Along with Dante, he won the 1976 Tony Award for Best Book and Drama Desk Award for Outstanding Book of a Musical for *A Chorus Line*.

PLOT SUMMARY

The musical opens on a bare stage where three lines of dancers in rehearsal clothes are being taught a dance routine by Zach, the director and choreographer. Zach is assisted by Larry,

MEDIA ADAPTATIONS

- *A Chorus Line* was made into a movie in 1985, directed by Richard Attenborough and starring Michael Douglas as Zach. The film was produced by Cy Feuer (Embassy Film Associates). Running time is 113 minutes.

to a piano accompaniment. All the dancers are desperate to be chosen for the show, as the song "I Hope I Get It" reveals. They wonder how many dancers are needed. The rehearsal continues, with Zach asking a few questions of some of the dancers, such as whether they have ever been in a Broadway show. He also tries to correct some of the dancers' errors, which makes them feel insecure, as if they have blown their chances. After a few minutes, Zach eliminates some of the dancers, leaving just seventeen, eight men and nine women, whom he refers to as boys and girls. Larry collects their pictures and résumés.

Zach says he wants to know each person's stage name, his or her real name (if it is different), and where and when he or she was born. Starting with Don, each dancer steps forward and gives the basic biographical information requested. They come from all over the country and have a variety of ethnic backgrounds. The only one who does not give any information is Cassie, who tells Zach that she wants to speak to him in private.

Zach then says that he wants a strong set of dancers who look good together and function cohesively as a group. He needs to know a little more about them than what is on their résumés. He wants to know what their personalities are like and says he is going to ask each of them a few questions so that they can talk about themselves. He tells them to treat this as an interview. In response to a question from Sheila, Zach says he needs eight dancers for the show—four men and four women.

The first dancer to speak is Mike, who says that he comes from a large Italian family and

began dancing after watching his older sister taking lessons and thinking that he could do that too. He elaborates in the song, "I Can Do That." Next up is Bobby, who tells of the unusual antics he would get up to as he grew up in a conventional upper-middle-class home. Interspersed with his story, Richie, Val, Judy, and others sing the song "And..." as they wonder about what they are going to say when their turns come. Sheila is next. She has been dancing since she was five. As she reveals in the song "At the Ballet," her family was not a happy one, but she was happy whenever her mother took her to the ballet. As the song continues, first Bebe and then Maggie join with Sheila in singing about their own family backgrounds.

Kristine then steps up and tells her story. She always wanted to be a dancer and a movie star, but as she sings, with the help of her husband, Al, the song "Sing!" she reveals that she cannot carry a tune and her voice is terrible. As she sings, she frequently goes off-key. Next comes Mark, who talks about using a medical textbook to diagnose acute appendicitis at the age of eleven. Along with Val, Richie, Maggie, Al, Bebe, Diana, Mike, Paul, Judy, and the rest of the company, he sings in the montage sequence "Hello Twelve, Hello Thirteen, Hello Love" about the physical and emotional changes that take place in early adolescence and the experimentation that kids get up to.

The next dancer to tell her story is Connie. She laments the fact that she is short, at four feet ten inches, and spent her childhood waiting in vain to grow taller. Then Diana tells of the improv (improvisational) acting classes she took in high school. They had to imagine they were on a bobsled during a snowstorm and really feel what it would be like. But Diana, as she explains in the song "Nothing," was unable to feel anything, which displeased her teacher. She got no better at other, more advanced improvisations, but then she found another teacher and fulfilled her dream of becoming an actress. Diana is followed by Don, who tells of how at the age of fifteen he found a job in a strip club and became friendly with one of the strippers.

Members of the company sing more lines from the song "Hello Twelve, Hello Thirteen, Hello Love," during which Judy steps forward and sings about how her father lost his job and they had to move from El Paso to St. Louis. As a teenager she developed the desire to perform.

She also remembers noticing boys for the first time and also practicing kissing with her best friend, Leslie. Next, Greg, Mike, and Bobby sing or speak of feeling awkward and sometimes embarrassed by the fact that they were frequently sexually aroused for no apparent reason. When Greg elaborates on his story, it is revealed that he is gay. When he first realized this, he got depressed about it. After that, members of the company resume the montage "Hello Twelve, Hello Thirteen, Hello Love," with the emphasis on the later period of adolescence, including romance, sex, and conflict with parents.

After a dance in which the entire company participates, Richie sings about his success in high school, his winning of a college scholarship, and his fear later about what he was going to do with his life. Then Val steps forward and tells her story about going to New York City at the age of eighteen, wanting to become a Rockette. (The Rockettes are a famous dance company.) But in spite of excellent training and preparation, she failed. She concluded that her looks were the problem, as she sings the song "Dance: Ten, Looks: Three"—a reference to how she was once scored on a dance card at an audition. She solved the problem with plastic surgery, and then she began to have success in her career. Next is Paul, who is something of an introvert and does not want to reveal much about his family background, although he does say that he started dancing when he was sixteen.

Zach then calls for a break, during which he and Cassie talk. It turns out that they used to be in a relationship together. Zach wonders why Cassie is there, thinking she is too good to be in a chorus. Cassie replies that she needs a job. Zach, who had thought her career was moving along well, tries to encourage her, but she insists that she is not a good actress and has not worked for two years. Zach offers to give her some money, but Cassie says that what she needs is a job. In the song "The Music and the Mirror" (which includes a dance routine) she pleads for a job as a dancer. Zach tells her she is not suited to being in the chorus, but then he relents and tells her to learn the lyrics.

Paul returns, and Zach draws him out, getting him to talk about his past. When he was a boy, his father took him to movies in New York City, and Paul found that he loved musicals. He grew up wanting to be actor. He also realized at the age of fourteen that he was gay. At high school, he was afraid of being laughed at, and his grades were poor. On the advice of a school psychologist, he quit school at the age of fifteen. A year later, he got a job as a dancer in a drag show. After a while he left because the job lacked dignity, but without an education he could not get a decent job, so he returned to the drag show, doing four shows a day at the Apollo Theater. The show was about to go to Chicago, and at the last performance his parents came to say goodbye. His father told the producer to look after him, referring to Paul as his son, which he had never done before. Paul breaks down as he recalls this, and Zach comes down the aisle and puts his arm around his shoulder.

The rehearsal continues. The company puts on hats and performs the flashy song-and-dance number "One," which demands that they dance in unison. Zach gives instructions, and Larry demonstrates. They then perform the song in four different groups. One group sings the refrain while another counts the beat and the other two groups speak out the instructions about the dance steps.

Zach asks the girls to perform again, with the boys upstage; as they do, he gives instructions and critiques their performances. He finds particular fault with Cassie. Then it is the men's turn, and they come forward to perform. Zach tells Cassie to do it again, too, but he again finds fault with her and tells her to dance like everyone else. Then everyone, male and female, gets into a single line and sings.

While they are doing so, Zach pulls Cassie out of the line and tells her she cannot do it. They argue. Zach still thinks she is too good to be in a chorus. Zach abruptly asks her why she left him, referring to the romantic relationship they formerly had, in which they lived together. Cassie counters that, in effect, he had left her weeks before she left him, because he was so involved in directing his first play that it was all he had time for. She felt she was no longer part of his life and that she could not keep up with him in the way he expected her to. She says he is a workaholic who still feels he has something to prove. For her part, though, she is just doing what she wants to do. She wants to dance. Then she apologizes for judging him and asks that he treat her just as he does everybody else. Zach asks if being in the chorus is really what she wants to do, and she says she would be proud to be in it if he selects her.

The company then performs a tap-dancing routine. Individual members speak single lines expressing their feelings. Larry gives instructions and critiques their performances. Paul falls and hurts his knee, aggravating an old injury. The company gathers round in concern. Larry calls a doctor, and Paul is helped off the stage; he will be taken by cab to the hospital.

Zach asks everyone what they would do if they were unable to dance anymore. Their answers reveal the insecurity they feel about their chosen career. They may end up unemployed at any time. They also talk about their ambitions. Judy says that she wants to be a star. Mark's ambitions are more limited; he just wants to get into a chorus. Zach asks the question again. Val replies that she does not care whether she ever dances another step. She has dreams of succeeding in Hollywood as an actress. Mike says the dancers are no better off than athletes, because their bodies will not stay young forever. Val talks again about pursuing acting, trying to persuade the others, but Al is not convinced. Greg says he just takes one day at a time. Don tells Zach that since he is married with children, he needs a regular paycheck. He is thinking of going into stage management or directing. The others chime in with their own thoughts. Diana says she is determined to go on as a dancer as long as she can. Sheila says she is thinking of opening a dance studio.

After more prodding from Zach, Diana and the company sing "What I Did for Love," a song that anticipates the time when they will no longer be able to dance and expresses satisfaction and positive feelings about what they have done with their lives. Then Zach announces the eight dancers he has chosen to be in the show: Cassie, Val, Diana, Judy, Mike, Richie, Mark, and Bobby. He tells them rehearsals begin in September and will be for six weeks. He explains their contracts. The entire company then sings in full costume the spectacular finale, which is a reprise of the song "One."

CHARACTERS

Mark Anthony

Mark Anthony is from Tempe, Arizona. At twenty years old, he is the youngest of the auditioning dancers. He tells of how at the age of eleven he immersed himself in a medical textbook and diagnosed his own case of acute appendicitis. He also thought he had a venereal disease, until a priest told him that since he had not had sex with anyone, this was impossible. Mark excels as a dancer, and Zach chooses him at the end of the audition as one of the eight who will be given a contract to appear in the upcoming show.

Sidney Kenneth Beckenstein
See Greg Gardner

Bebe Benzenheimer

Bebe Benzenheimer is from Boston. She is twenty-six years old. When she was a child, her mother told her she would be attractive when she grew up. Bebe took that to mean she was not considered attractive as she was, and she hated her mother for, in effect, saying it. Now, as an adult, she does not think of herself as beautiful or even pretty. She is deeply committed to her career as a dancer. When Zach asks the company what they would do if they could not dance, Bebe says she would kill herself.

Sheila Bryant

Sheila Bryant is from Colorado Springs, Colorado. She is nearly thirty years old. Her mother was a ballerina, but when she married, her husband made her give it up. To compensate for the sacrifice, Sheila's mother was determined that Sheila would be able to follow in her footsteps and become a dancer. Sheila did not get along with her father, and her parents' marriage was not a good one. However, Sheila has been dancing since the age of five. She is confident and sassy, even insolent, and thinks of herself as a strong person. She makes witty comments.

Val Clark

Val Clark is from Arlington, Vermont. She is twenty-five years old. As a child, she studied tap dancing and acrobatics for seven years. When she was eighteen, she left home for New York City, wanting to become a member of the Rockettes, a famous dance company. She had to wait six months for an audition, which she failed. She then auditioned for Broadway but failed again. She concluded that she was unattractive and not well enough developed physically to get any parts. She solved the problem by having plastic surgery, and after that she was successful. She and Sheila see themselves as rivals. Val is one of the final eight dancers chosen at the end of the audition.

Mike Costa

Mike Costa is from Trenton, New Jersey. He is the youngest of twelve children in an Italian family. His interest in dancing began when he was only four years old, when his mother took him along to watch his sister Rosalie at her dance lesson. He soon realized that he could do that too, and one morning, when Rosalie did not go to her class, he ran seven blocks and took her place. He has been dancing ever since, even though his parents did not encourage him in this career, pointing out the fact that his brother was going to medical school. He is one of the final eight dancers chosen at the end of the audition.

Al DeLuca

Al DeLuca comes from the Bronx, New York. He is thirty years old and is married to Kristine Ulrich. They are affectionate with each other on stage, and when the nervous Kristine tells Zach about herself, Al helps her, sometimes finishing her sentences for her. Al had plenty of girlfriends before Kristine, and a friend of his, Eddie, was killed in a car accident.

Cassie Ferguson

Cassie Ferguson is a dancer who was formerly in a romantic relationship with Zach. The couple lived together for a while, but Cassie became frustrated and ended the relationship because Zach was too obsessed with his work. Cassie went to Los Angeles with high hopes of establishing a career as a movie actress, but she did not succeed. She returned to New York and is seeking a role in the chorus because she needs the job. Zach is reluctant to select her because he thinks she can do better than being in a chorus, since before she left New York she was successfully performing solo roles as a dancer. In the end, he relents, and Cassie is chosen as one of the final eight.

Greg Gardner

Greg Gardner is a stage name; the young man's real name is Sidney Kenneth Beckenstein. He is Jewish, and his Jewish name is Rochmel Lev Ben Yokov Meyer Beckenstein. A dancer from New York City's East Side, he is very much at home there. He is thirty-two years old. Greg is gay, which depressed him when he first realized it as a teenager, but he later accepted his sexuality wholeheartedly.

Don Kerr

Don Kerr is from Kansas City, Missouri, and is twenty-six years old. At the age of fifteen he worked in a strip club and became friendly with a stripper who drove a pink Cadillac convertible. He pretended to his friends that he was having a romance with her. Don now has a wife and two children, with an ambition to become a stage manager or director when his dancing days are over.

Larry

Larry is Zach's assistant. He helps to guide the dancers through their routines.

Bobby Mills

Twenty-five-year-old Bobby Mills comes from upstate New York, near Buffalo. He was raised in a wealthy, upper-middle-class family, but he was bored with the upbringing he received, and he cultivated a more unusual persona for himself. He used to give strange music recitals in the garage, in one of which he spray-painted a boy with silver from head to toe, which led to the boy's hospitalization. Later, Bobby developed the habit of going to an intersection near his home and directing the traffic; he also used to break into people's homes, not to steal but to rearrange the furniture. At school, he hated sports and was bullied. He is obviously a good dancer, since Zach selects him as one of the eight successful ones at the end of the audition.

Diana Morales

Diana Morales was born in the Bronx, New York. She is twenty-seven years old and is Puerto Rican. She took acting classes in high school but did not impress her teacher, who told her she would never be an actress. Undiscouraged, she found another teacher and managed to fulfill her ambition. She is one of the eight dancers selected by Zach at the end of the audition.

Paul San Marco

Paul San Marco is from Spanish Harlem, New York City. He is Puerto Rican, but he changed his name to make it sound Italian; he did not much like being Puerto Rican. Paul is twenty-eight years old and shy. As a child he developed a love of musicals after his father regularly took him to the movies. At the age of fourteen, he realized he was gay, which made him very uncomfortable at his high school. He left school at fifteen and started dancing a year later, getting work with a drag show. He hid all his gear, such as makeup and earrings, from his parents. Later, they came to see him perform before the show moved to Chicago, and when he saw them at the stage door—he was in full drag regalia—they spoke to him in a very accepting way, telling him to be sure to write and take care of himself. Paul does not have the opportunity to be one of the eight chosen dancers because during the audition he falls and injures his knee.

Judy Turner

Twenty-eight-year-old Judy Turner is originally from El Paso, Texas, but the family had to move to St. Louis, Missouri, after her father lost his job. Her father used to enjoy watching her dance around the living room, although she did not get along so well with her mother and younger sister. At the age of fifteen, she nearly committed suicide after missing an audition for the Ted Mack Amateur Hour. Judy has a lively sense of humor and is one of the eight dancers selected by Zach at the end of the audition.

Kristine Ulrich

Kristine Ulrich is from St. Louis, Missouri. She is married to Al DeLuca. She has wanted to be a dancer since she was a child, and her mother paid for her to have dance lessons. Kristine loved the movies and wanted to be like Doris Day, except that she could not sing. During the audition she is nervous.

Richie Walters

Richie Walters is from Herculaneum, Missouri. He is a twenty-seven-year-old African American. In high school he was good at sports, and he won a scholarship to college. He was at first going to be a kindergarten teacher but changed his mind and then felt insecure about his future because he did not know what course he wanted to take in life. Richie is one of the eight dancers selected by Zach at the end of the audition.

Maggie Winslow

Maggie Winslow is from San Mateo, California. Her parents were not happy together, and in fact only had a child in an attempt to save their marriage. The tactic failed, and her father left home. Now twenty-five years old, Maggie had an active fantasy life as a child; she used to dance around the living room pretending she was an Indian chief and that her father was dancing

with her. She can think of nothing she would rather do than dance and has in mind a time line for herself. She hopes to meet her career goals by the time she is a certain age, although she does not say what her target age is.

Connie Wong

Connie Wong is from Chinatown, New York City, on the Lower East Side. She does not at first give her age, saying only that she was born in the year 4642, according to the Chinese calendar. As a child she wanted to be a ballerina. She was short, standing four feet ten inches and could not even be a cheerleader because of her lack of height. She just waited during childhood to grow, but it never happened. At the age of thirty-two, she played a fourteen-year-old on stage. Despite this handicap, however, Connie has never had a problem finding work.

Zach

Zach is the director and choreographer of the show the dancers are rehearsing. He knows exactly what he wants from them in terms of their performance, and he asks them questions that will encourage them to speak about their personal lives. Some years earlier, Zach was in a relationship with Cassie, but they split up partly because Zach was very committed to his work and did not seem to have time for Cassie. He is a hard-driving man who seeks excellence in all his endeavors, but he shows a softer side when he comforts Paul after the young man recounts an upsetting incident from his past.

THEMES

Ambition

The theme of ambition, both fulfilled and not, recurs in many of the characters' stories. The best example is probably Cassie. Before she left New York, she was performing well in solo roles, and she went to California with the ambition of becoming a movie actress. This did not work out, so now she is auditioning for a chorus line because she needs a job, although she also loves to dance. Nevertheless, she has been thwarted in her larger ambition to make a name for herself as a solo performer. Zach is also an ambitious person, and the eagerness with which he pursued his career was one of the reasons that his relationship with Cassie did not succeed. Unlike her, he

TOPICS FOR FURTHER STUDY

- The cast of *13*, a Broadway musical that ran from 2008 to 2009, consisted entirely of teenagers. Consult *13: The Complete Book and Lyrics of the Broadway Musical*, by Dan Elish, Robert Horn, and Jason Robert Brown (2011), and also listen to an audio CD of the show, which as of 2015 is being made into a movie by CBS films. Write an essay in which you discuss the themes of the musical and how they are presented. Is the musical comic or serious? Is it true to life? How would you compare its themes to the montage sequence "Hello Twelve, Hello Thirteen, Hello Love" in *A Chorus Line*?

- Research how a musical is developed and produced. What stages does it go through, and how is it financed? Are musicals driven by the need to make a profit or are artistic concerns more important? How did *A Chorus Line* break the mold for how a Broadway musical is conceived and developed? Consult John Kenrick's article "How Broadway Musicals Are Made," at http://www.musicals101 .com/makemusi.htm, and then give a class presentation in which you discuss your findings.

- Compare *A Chorus Line* to Sondheim and Prince's *Company* as a "concept musical." What do the two musicals have in common that makes them fit that definition? How do they differ? Write an essay in which you present your research.

- With three classmates, imagine that you are being asked by Zach (or someone else) to talk briefly about yourself, for the purpose of giving an insight into your personality and who you are and where you have come from. Prepare a one- or two-minute speech, as the dancers do in *A Chorus Line*, and then present it to your class.

- Go to http://www.easel.ly/ and create an infographic for *A Chorus Line*. Try to present all the most important factual information about the musical in a way that is easy to comprehend and visually pleasing.

---

appears to be realizing his ambitions, as director and choreographer of a Broadway show.

Many of the other dancers show similar ambition. Diana wanted to become a "serious actress" when she was in her teens and remains ambitious now, as do Sheila and Maggie, both of whom have their own time lines in mind by which they will judge their success in achieving their ambitions. Judy and Val also have ambitions to be more than dancers in a chorus line. Many of the dancers, such as Mike and Maggie, have been dancing since they were young children. Don entered show business in a drag show at the age of sixteen. Val pursued dancing single-mindedly, even getting cosmetic surgery to enhance her physical appeal and improve her job prospects. Some of the dancers have been performing professionally for many years—Richie and Connie,

for example, to name just two. These dancers are determined, competent people who want to make their mark. Dancing in a chorus line may not be the summit of their ambitions, but they are doing what they love. Sometimes they may need reminding of what they have achieved. For example, when Diana doubted her chosen career, someone said to her, "Wow, you dance on Broadway! How fabulous! You got somewhere. You're something," which reminded her of how far she had come. For Mark, the youngest of the dancers, just landing a part in a chorus line would be a breakthrough, a step up the chosen career ladder. When Judy asks him whether he wants to do more than dance in a chorus, he says "I just want to get in one."

The career they have chosen is a difficult one, however. Dreams do not always get fulfilled, and

A Chorus Line *opened on Broadway in 1975.* (© *Fer Gregory* / *Shutterstock.com*)

ambition comes up against the realities of business. Dancing in a chorus line is not a secure occupation; they can find themselves out of work at any time and possibly for long periods. Cassie says she has been out of work for two years, for example. Some need the job just to pay the rent, never mind their higher ambitions. Richie, although he has had fun in the business for eight years, wonders about the future. He does not feel he has gotten anywhere, or that he could in the future—"There's no promotion and no advancement." Another downside is that a dancer's career is a short one, like that of an athlete, because of the physical demands it makes on the body. There is also the possibility of injury interrupting a career, as is shown dramatically on stage when Paul injures his knee.

Adolescence

Adolescence emerges as a theme in many of the stories the dancers tell about the earlier part of their lives. It is particularly apparent in the song ""Hello Twelve, Hello Thirteen, Hello Love," which takes up about fifteen minutes of the show. The dancers reveal some of the thoughts

and feelings that emerged during that time. Prominent is a developing curiosity about sex, awareness of the opposite sex, experiments with the same sex (Judy, Kristine, and Sheila all admit to kissing a girlfriend), and the discovery of sexual identity: Greg and Paul realize they are gay. Richie, who is heterosexual, recalls difficulties in getting a girlfriend, while Al recalls enjoying great success in that area. Discovering racy literature may also be a part of adolescence: Mark spends time in the bathroom reading *Peyton Place*, a novel published in 1965 and notorious for its sexual content.

The dancers also remember adolescence as a time to question things and to strike out on their own individual path in life but also as a time of uncertainty. For at least two of the girls, there was some self-consciousness about their bodies and a desire for them to be different. Connie desperately waits to get taller, while Val waits anxiously, and in vain, for her body to acquire some womanly curves.

As adolescents gradually discover a sense of self-identity, they may come into conflict with their parents, who may have different ideas about how their offspring should behave and what career they should choose. Mike's parents are appalled that he wants to pursue a career in show business, comparing his choice to that of his brother, who is going to medical school. Cassie's parents nag her about doing her homework before she goes to the movies, and Paul has to deal with implied threats of punishment ("Wait until your father gets home"). Connie's parents tell her she may not leave home until she is twenty-one, and Sheila's parents make critical and dismissive remarks about her friends.

Adolescence may also be a time of immature emotional ups and downs, and reactions that seem out of proportion to the situation. Unhappy at home and school. Bobby keeps thinking of ways to commit suicide, and Judy at the age of fifteen tries to walk in front of a moving streetcar because she did not hear about an audition for the Ted Mack Amateur Hour until after the audition had taken place.

STYLE

Musical

A musical is a dramatic stage work that features songs (or "numbers"), dance, and spoken dialogue, although some musicals are described as "through-composed," which means that the entire play is set to music. In *A Chorus Line*, the musical numbers are composed in a number of different styles, including elements of jazz, rock, ballad, funk, and contemporary pop. Dance provides spectacle and communicates dramatic meaning as the dancers learn and rehearse the various steps required of them under the watchful eyes of Zach and Larry.

For a musical to be created, there must be a director, who "maintains creative control of the show," according to Raymond Knapp in *The American Musical and the Formation of National Identity*. Knapp identifies three other elements that must also be in place for a musical to be created. First, the book, which is "a highly specialized artifact that resembles a normal play in most respects, but will lead up to a somewhat larger number of internal climaxes . . . which will be embodied musically." A composer and lyricist are also needed. Sometimes one person may be both composer and lyricist, and the lyricist may also sometimes be the author of the book.

(In *A Chorus Line*, book author, composer, and lyricist were separate.) Also needed is a choreographer, "who stages the musical numbers." Knapp also notes that the importance of the choreographer varies according to the type of show, but "the importance of this function has grown over time, in part because significant creative personalities have emerged in this realm." (Michael Bennett, director and choreographer of *A Chorus Line*, would be in that category.) The musical also needs a musical director to rehearse the numbers and a conductor to lead the orchestra during the performance. Sometimes one person will fulfill both these roles.

Sometimes musicals are classified as either "book musicals" or "concept musicals." A book musical tells a well-made, unified story, integrating the songs, choruses, and dances into the plot. Every element—plot, character, music, dance—contributes to the overall effect of the show. *Oklahoma!* (1943) and *Les Misérables* (1985) are examples of book musicals, a form that dominated American musical theater in the mid-twentieth century. In concept musicals, however, there is often no linear plot. The emphasis instead, as John Kenrick writes in *Musical Theatre: A History*, is on "a central issue, event, or theme." Such musicals, which include Stephen Sondheim's *Company* (1970), as well as *A Chorus Line*,

> went beyond traditional narrative, breaking the limitations of time, place, and action to simultaneously examine numerous individuals and relationships. Every character has a story to tell, and all of them can comment on and/or illustrate different aspects of the concept.

Frame Story

As noted by Joseph P. Swain in *The Broadway Musical: A Critical and Musical Survey*, *A Chorus Line* has the structure of a frame story, in which many individual stories are told within one larger story, or "frame." In this show, the frame is the audition and the fact that Zach has to select eight dancers; the stories within that frame are those of the individual dancers. The frame story has often been used in English literature, the most famous example being Geoffrey Chaucer's *The Canterbury Tales*. According to Swain, the stories of the individual characters "are neither episodes of a high-level plot nor subplots, which abound in more traditional musicals." These stories could be rearranged, altered, or replaced without any effect on the overall show. The frame story

COMPARE
&
CONTRAST

- **1975:** It is not common to see sympathetic portrayals of gay people in Broadway musicals. However, *Applause* (1970) and *Seesaw* (1973) each has a gay character presented in a favorable light, and *A Chorus Line* has two.

  Today: Gay characters and situations involving gays and lesbians occur in Broadway musicals with some regularity and are not considered especially worthy of comment. In 2015, the successful Broadway shows *It Shoulda Been You, Kinky Boots,* and *Fun Home* all include gay characters and examine issues concerning the gay community.

- **1975:** New York City goes through a financial crisis and only just avoids declaring bankruptcy. Financial troubles coupled with high crime rates and falling population suggest a city in serious decline. The Theater District is rundown and unsavory, spoiled by the presence of strip clubs, illegal drugs, and prostitution.

  Today: New York City has a flourishing economy, and the crime rate has been falling for more than two decades. The Theatre District has long since been cleaned up and flourishes as a safe and vibrant place for tourists and theatergoers alike to visit.

- **1975:** Attendance at Broadway shows drops during the mid-1970s, down to 7.3 million in 1975–1976, but improves by the end of the decade. The success of *A Chorus Line* helps to bring about the revival.

  Today: Broadway is thriving. In 2014, thirteen million people attend shows at Broadway's forty theaters, a 13 percent increase over the previous year. Successful musicals in the mid-2010s include *Aladdin, Beautiful—the Carole King Musical,* and *The Book of Mormon.*

emphasizes the low-level events, that is, the individual stories, at the expense of overall plot. The frame story sacrifices high-level tension and resolution, and puts in its place a series of small dramas, little waves of tension and resolution.

HISTORICAL CONTEXT

Broadway in the 1970s

Toward the end of the show, some of the dancers in *A Chorus Line* make negative comments about the decline of Broadway at the time. "There's no work anymore," says Richie, and all the members of the group agree with him. When Bebe complains that she does not want to hear that "Broadway's dying," since she only just got there, Connie says, "They're not doing big musicals like they used to." The characters, speaking in 1975, reflect a contraction that did indeed take place during the 1970s, when there was a decrease in the number of shows produced on Broadway. According to John Kenrick in "Theater in NYC: History—Part IV,"

> By the 1970s, Times Square was one of the grungiest and most dangerous neighborhoods in New York. The last quarter of the 20th Century saw the demolition of dozens of old Broadway theaters, and the construction of only four new ones. The once glamorous theaters along 42nd Street . . . were all in varying states of disrepair. Some showed pornography or kung fu films, while others were crudely converted into retail space. Many felt the decline of Times Square was irreversible.

In spite of this, Kenrick writes in *Musical Theatre: A History,* Broadway "remained a hotbed of creativity" in the 1970s. According to Kenrick, three different types of musical fought for dominance: the rock musical, the concept musical, and the more traditional book musical. Rock musicals included *Hair,* which opened in

The show's challenging choreography requires skilled dancers. (© Rus S / Shutterstock.com)

1968 and ran until 1972; *Two Gentlemen of Verona* (1971), an adaptation of Shakespeare's play of that name; *Godspell* (1971), which was based mostly on the Gospel of Matthew and ran for 2,645 performances; and *Jesus Christ, Superstar* (1971), the first rock musical by British composer Andrew Lloyd Webber and Tim Rice. The most popular rock musical of the 1970s was *Grease* (1972), which ran for 3,388 performances.

Concept musicals included *Company* (1970) and *Follies* (1971), both of which were collaborations between composer and lyricist Stephen Sondheim and producer-director Harold Prince. *Follies* won seven Tony Awards. Sondheim and Prince went on to create *A Little Night Music* (1973) and *Pacific Overtures* (1976). Other concept musicals, in addition to *A Chorus Line*, were *Chicago* (1975) and *Dancin'* (1978), both notable for the work of director Bob Fosse.

Many of the book musicals that flourished during the decade were revivals. These included *No, No, Nanette* (1971), *My Fair Lady* (1976), *Hello, Dolly!* (1976), *Fiddler on the Roof* (1976), *The King and I* (1977), and *Oklahoma!* (1979).

The most successful of these was *The King and I*, which ran for 807 performances. Of new book musicals, several ran for more than a thousand performances. These included *Shenandoah* (1975); *The Best Little Whorehouse in Texas* (1978), which was the longest-running of this group, with 1,703 performances; *Ain't Misbehavin'* (1978); *They're Playing Our Song* (1979); and *Sugar Babies* (1979).

CRITICAL OVERVIEW

The success of *A Chorus Line* is obvious from its fifteen-year run on Broadway, the many awards the show won, and its national and international tours. It was highly praised by critics as well as the theatergoing public. According to Samuel G. Freedman, in his preface to *A Chorus Line: The Book of the Musical*, it was greeted by "universal raves." In the introduction to the same volume, Frank Rich writes that New York audiences were "electrified" when *A Chorus Line* first appeared. The show "was and is the touchstone that defines the glittering promise, more often realized in legend than in reality, of the Broadway theater." When the show closed in April 1990, Mervyn Rothstein commented in the *New York Times*:

> Many theater people believe that *A Chorus Line* revolutionized the way musicals are staged, produced and written, that it expanded the conception of what a musical was, freeing it from telling a story in a specific way, from having to go from one event to another.

Rothstein notes that the workshop process, which up to then had been used only by experimental theater groups, had been instrumental in the development of the show. This showed that such a process could be used to successfully create a Broadway musical.

In the decades that have passed since the show ended on Broadway, historians of musical theater have also weighed in on the topic. For example, in his essay "Choreographers, Directors and the Fully Integrated Musical," Paul R. Laird comments,

> Those who saw *A Chorus Line* during its original run will not easily forget it. The plot was minimal and somewhat artificial, but the characters were engrossing. We recognised types of people that we knew and with each part of their stories our fascination grew.

Laird also notes that Michael Bennett had "the vision to forge an unconventional show" and that the using the device of the audition "gave the audience the feeling of peeking backstage, even though the device was essentially unrealistic." Commenting on the legacy of the show, Laird notes that it "pav[ed] the way for the megamusicals of the 1980s and 1990s, but without the huge stage effects that mark many of those shows."

CRITICISM

Bryan Aubrey

Aubrey holds a PhD in English. In the following essay, he discusses the theme of individuality versus conformity in A Chorus Line.

The dazzling finale of *A Chorus Line*, in which the whole company in full costume performs a reprise of the song "One," has sent audiences home happy and exhilarated for decades, wherever the show has been performed. It is as if the whole show has been leading up to these final minutes of joyous synchronized movement, in

IT MAY CARRY A COLLECTIVE RATHER THAN INDIVIDUAL REWARD, BUT FLAWLESS ENSEMBLE WORK IS SURELY TO BE ADMIRED JUST AS MUCH AS INDIVIDUAL EXCELLENCE."

which the dancers move as one. Lovers of *A Chorus Line* might therefore be surprised if they were to stumble across the comment once made by its creator, director, and choreographer, Michael Bennett, as quoted in *Unfinished Business: Broadway Musicals as Works-in-Progress*, by Bruce Kirle:

> You're going to get to know all these dancers as individuals and care about each one. Then, at the very end of the play, they're all going to come out in tuxedos and top hats, and you're not going to be able to tell one from another. They're going to blend. They're going to do everything you've ever seen anyone in a chorus line do. It's going to be the most horrifying moment you will ever experience in a theatre.... If I do this right, you will never see another chorus line in a theatre.

It seems unlikely that many in the audience would describe their experience of the finale as "horrifying"; indeed, Bennett himself seemed to have worked hard to make such a reaction on the part of the audience almost impossible, since he used, as Kenrick writes in *Musical Theatre: A History*, "every eye-popping trick in the Broadway chorus repertory. His smiling ensemble danced in a circle, a pyramid, and wound up in a prolonged kick line." Be that as it may, what exactly did Bennett mean by his comment, and what underlying issues and themes does it raise about the show?

At issue is the question of individuality versus conformity, personal self-expression versus the demands and needs of the group. When the show begins, the dancers are all anonymous. They are bodies on the move, not yet known as individuals. When Zach, the fictional director, wants to direct them either upstage or downstage, he calls out their number and refers to them collectively (and rather condescendingly) as boys and girls. At one point, as Zach watches and instructs as they learn the dance routine, Richie leaps out of formation in front of Paul.

WHAT DO I READ NEXT?

- *Broadway Musicals: The 101 Greatest Shows of All Time*, by Ken Bloom and Frank Vlastnik (revised and updated edition, 2010), is a book that any fan of the Broadway musical will likely enjoy: an illustrated survey of a selection of the stage's most popular shows, including *A Chorus Line*. The book includes commentary, plot synopses, cast and song lists, production details, and anecdotes.

- *Great Songs from Musicals for Teens* (2001) compiled by Louise Lerch, is a collection of music from a wide variety of well-known musicals. The book comes with a CD of recordings by young singers and an accompaniment track. There is a Young Men's edition and a Young Women's edition.

- In 1975, the same year that *A Chorus Line* opened, *The Wiz*, a musical by African American composer Charlie Smalls, had a successful Broadway run of 1,672 performances. In *Black Musical Theatre: From Coontown to Dreamgirls* (1989), Allen L. Woll gives an account of African American musical theater from the end of the nineteenth century until the 1980s, discussing many performers and shows.

- In *On the Line: The Creation of "A Chorus Line"* (2006), by Robert Viagus, Baayork Lee, and Thommie Walsh, nineteen members of the original cast of the show recall their roles in it—how they got involved, the months of workshops they participated in, and how the show affected their lives and careers.

- *What They Did for Love: The Untold Story Behind the Making of "A Chorus Line"* (1989), by Denny Martin Flinn, who was a member of the original cast, tells the stories of many people in the original cast who contributed to the success of the show. Flinn himself was a dancer and choreographer who took part in one of the national tours of *A Chorus Line*, playing both Greg and Zach.

- *"A Chorus Line" and the Musicals of Michael Bennett* (1989), by Ken Mandelbaum, examines the career of director-choreographer Michael Bennett, with particular emphasis on *A Chorus Line*, Bennett's greatest success. Mandelbaum discusses the workshops during which the show was developed and Bennett's distinctive style of directing.

Seeing this, Zach says to him, "Listen, that's really great, but stay in the formation and tone it down," a remark that raises the issue of individual flair and improvisation against the collective need of a chorus, which must perform in unison. A short while later, after Zach has winnowed the number of dancers down to seventeen, he has them all stand in a line holding their glossy promotional photos up in front of their faces. What the audience sees is a line of publicity shots rather than people, and such carefully produced images, aimed at advancing a person's career, reveal little about the actual individual behind them. As Paul sings tellingly at this point, "Who am I anyway? / Am I my résumé? That is a picture of a person I don't know."

This raises the issue of self-identity. Who are these people and how do they see themselves? What drives them? What has brought them to this point in their lives, where they are auditioning for a Broadway chorus line? Fortunately—if somewhat artificially, since no real-life director would have time or interest in such things—Zach is about to give all of them a chance to explain exactly who they are. This allows them to emerge as individuals, each with a unique life story. What transpires as they step forward and tell their compelling vignettes is that they have put a great deal of effort and commitment into understanding and accepting who they are and what their distinctive path in life is. They have all been through a process of becoming unique individuals; they have not just gone with the crowd and done what was expected of them. They have discovered, sometimes by accident, where their talents lie, and in many cases have shown considerable courage and persistence in pursuing their individual goals for self-expression, even when their families did not approve and the way forward did not appear clear.

Numerous examples will occur to those familiar with the show: Mike discovered as a child that he loved to dance after watching his older sister take lessons ("I Can Do That"); he soon found out that dance was his life's calling, and he stuck to it in spite of being teased and facing the disapproval of his parents. Bobby was an unusual boy who did not fit in, either in his upper-middle-class family or at school; he admits, "I was the strange one." A disappointment to his father, he had to find his own way. Several of the dancers, including Sheila and Maggie, overcame difficult family backgrounds. Connie used to think that at four feet ten inches she was too short, and she suffered some setbacks because of it, but it did not deter her from dancing and landing roles on the stage—even if in her most recent one, at the age of thirty-two, she played a fourteen-year-old—and she has just continued to do what she knows she has to do. "'Whatever I am / I am," she sings in "Nothing." Once again, the note of self-knowledge and acceptance is sounded: the dancer has been through the process of individuation and is happy to express who she is as a unique person. This applies to Diana, too. "They called me hopeless," she sings of her high school acting class, but she learned as a result of prayer to follow the "voice" that came "from down at the bottom of [her] soul" that said she could fulfill her dream and become an actress. Greg and Paul discovered that they were gay, and they accepted it as part of their distinctive individual makeup.

It has, then, been a long and personal road for these dancers, yet now, in the audition, they are being asked to collapse all that developed individuality and become an anonymous member of a chorus line in which everyone looks exactly the same and moves in exactly the same way. Zach keeps telling Cassie that she is not suitable for the chorus simply because she has too much individual talent: "You don't fit in. You don't dance like anybody else." As Zach

tells the company just before they perform "One" together, "I want to see *Unison Dancing*. Every head, arm body angle, *exactly the same*. You must blend." There is no room here for individual expression. One member of a chorus must not stand out against any other member. There is to be no individual glory, no personal quirks on view. It is as if the waves of an ocean are being asked to sink back into the ocean, losing their identity in the larger whole. It is this phenomenon that Bennett was referring to in his comment quoted earlier, saying that it would horrify the audience.

This issue of individual creativity versus conformity in *A Chorus Line* has been taken up in the context of American culture by Kirle in *Unfinished Business*. Kirle writes that the show "tried to reconcile the 1970s 'me' generation with the need for conformity," but such a reconciliation was hard to accomplish: *A Chorus Line* "glorifies the cog in the American wheel. Its conflict is that of insider . . . versus outsider (the individual)." The dancers' loss of identity "is not an egalitarian ideal but a demand for mediocrity"; the characters "fight for assimilation into insider status by ultimately losing their identities." Cassie, for example, who has genuine individual talent, must suppress it in order to get the job. The dancers, in Kirle's view, accept compromise in order to be able to do what they love but pay a high price for it.

Audiences, however, have always tended to see the finale differently, as the climax of the dancers' hard work and dedication, something they can be proud of. After all, the skill that enables a dancer to become a seamless part of the whole is also an individual achievement in its own right. It may carry a collective rather than individual reward, but flawless ensemble work is surely to be admired just as much as individual excellence. As Kenrick puts it in *Musical Theatre: A History*: "Glorifying the individual fulfillment that can be found in ensemble efforts, *A Chorus Line . . .* was a triumph on all levels."

Source: Bryan Aubrey, Critical Essay on *A Chorus Line*, in *Drama for Students*, Gale, Cengage Learning, 2016.

Roger Ebert
In the following review, Ebert gives a film adaptation of the play praise, but faults the ending.

Show business is the only business that reminds us there is no business like it. And it never tires of that message. If there were as

The play's premise of a big audition pushes the characters to talk about themselves.

(© bikeriderlondon | Shutterstock.com)

many books about books as there are musicals about musicals, there wouldn't be room on the shelf for books about anything else.

A Chorus Line is the quintessential back-stage musical, a celebration of the lives and hard times of the gypsy dancers who turn up by the hundreds to audition for a handful of jobs on Broadway. It takes years of brutal hard work to become a good-enough dancer to dare to go to an audition, and then the reward usually is a brusque "thank you" and a sweaty ride home on the subway. In order to succeed as a Broadway dancer, applicants need a limitless capacity to absorb rejection, and *A Chorus Line* celebrates that masochism in song and dance.

A Chorus Line is now in its 11th year on stages all over the world; its story is by now well-known. A choreographer is casting eight dancers for a new musical he hopes to stage, and during one long and truthful day he auditions dozens of dancers before he makes his final

selection. Richard Attenborough's film treatment of this story sticks to the outlines of the stage version, by and large, although he leaves the stage to fill in the details of the choreographer's old romance, and he leaves out some of the original songs to make room for some new ones.

The result may not please purists who want a film record of what they saw on stage, but this is one of the most intelligent and compelling movie musicals in a long time—and the most grown up, since it isn't limited, as so many contemporary musicals are, to the celebration of the survival qualities of geriatric actresses.

Most of the scenes take place inside a theater. Zach (Michael Douglas), the choreographer, sits behind a writing platform somewhere out there in the darkness. Occasionally he lights a cigarette, and the ash glows as he takes the measure of the dancers on the stage. He can see them. They can't see him. He communicates by microphone. They step hesitantly to the edge of the stage, blinded by the spotlight, and talk into the void. Well, if that isn't the life they wanted, why did they volunteer for it?

Platoons of dancers are brought on stage, winnowed, dismissed. Finally there are 16 left, and Zach asks each one of them to talk on a personal level—talk about when they were born, and where, and what their lives have been like, and what their dreams are. Many of the dancers have the most extraordinary difficulties in doing this, and one of them is frank: "Give me the lines, and I can play anybody. Just don't ask me to talk about myself."

Meanwhile, a backstage drama is taking shape. An unexpected dancer has appeared for the auditions—Sheila (Vicki Frederick). Zach's former girlfriend. They met in the theater, courted in the theater, broke up because Zach's job left no time for a personal life. Sheila was a star, but now she simply needs a job.

Unlike the play, the movie opens up by going offstage for flashbacks to their affair, but the flash-backs are notable mostly for the way they focus on the theatrical lives of this couple—the way their private lives seem valid only to the degree that they reflect acceptance from the audience.

The underlying tension in the movie circles around Zach's eventual decision: Will his heart or his profession make the eventual decision about Sheila? Douglas plays Zach on a staccato, harsh note; this is a workaholic who walks around with a lot of anger. That makes it all the more effective when he occasionally relents and gives one of the dancers a break; softening momentarily before putting on his mask again.

I thought Zach's most revealing moment came when he made the cut from 16 dancers to eight, reading out eight names and then, when the eight were assembled downstage with smiles on their faces, thanking them and dismissing them; he had chosen the eight he did not name. Was this a misguided attempt to tell the rejected eight that they were also winners? Or was it simply cruelty? We are left to answer for ourselves. Such questions are intercut with song and dance, with virtuoso solo numbers (my favorite was Charles McGowan's "I Can Do That!") and ensemble production numbers, leading up to a big and splashy finale, in which all of the dancers who originally auditioned are back on stage, together once again. That leads to my one major difference with Attenborough's approach.

Since *A Chorus Line* is a musical about itself, and since the whole hard, bitter, romantic truth of the story is that many are called but few are chosen, the roll call at the end strikes a false note of triumph. Better, perhaps, to have eight dancers on stage, and then cut to the others putting on their street clothes, waiting at bus stops, explaining to friends how they didn't get the job, or going to their dance classes yet once again. I think the message of the play is that you don't get called back for a grand finale; you simply go to another audition.

Source: Roger Ebert, Review of *A Chorus Line*, in *RogerEbert.com*, December 20, 1985.

SOURCES

"Best Broadway Shows: Musicals, Plays and Revivals to Be Seen Now," in *Time Out*, 2015, http://www.timeout.com/newyork/theater/broadways-best-shows-broadway (accessed July 15, 2015).

"Biography," Marvin Hamlisch website, http://marvinhamlisch.us/biography/ (accessed July 13, 2015).

"Broadway's Box Offices Say Goodbye to Record-Setting 2014," in *Crain's New York Business*, January 5, 2015, http://www.crainsnewyork.com/article/20150105/ARTS/150109971/broadways-box-offices-say-goodbye-to-record-setting-2014 (accessed July 18, 2015).

Freedman, Samuel G., "Broadway Economic Season Is Called Worst in a Decade," in *New York Times*, May 20, 1985, http://www.nytimes.com/1985/05/20/theater/broadway-economic-season-is-called-worst-in-a-decade.html (accessed July 15, 2015).

———, Preface to *A Chorus Line: The Book of the Musical*, Applause, 1995, p. v.

Gerard, Jeremy, "Michael Bennett, Theater Innovator, Dies at 44," in *New York Times*, July 3, 1987, http://www.nytimes.com/1987/07/03/obituaries/michael-bennett-theater-innovator-dies-at-44.html (accessed July 13, 2015).

Goodman, J. David, "New York Crime Keeps Falling, de Blasio Says; Cites Years of 'Momentum,'" in *New York Times*, December 2, 2014, http://www.nytimes.com/2014/12/03/nyregion/violent-crime-in-new-york-has-dropped-to-historic-low-mayor-de-blasio-says.html (accessed July 18, 2015).

Kenrick, John, *Musical Theatre: A History*, Continuum, 2008, pp. 319, 325, 332.

———, "Stonewall and After," in *Musicals101.com*, 2008, http://www.musicals101.com/gay7.htm (accessed July 13, 2015).

———, "Theater in NYC: History—Part IV," *Musicals101.com*, 2003, http://www.musicals101.com/bwaythhist4.htm (accessed July 13, 2015).

———, "What Is a Musical?," in *Musicals101.com*, 2003, http://www.musicals101.com/musical.htm (accessed July 13, 2015).

Kirkwood, James, and Nicholas Dante, *A Chorus Line, the Book of the Musical*, conceived, choreographed, and directed by Michael Bennett, Applause, 1995.

Kirle, Bruce, *Unfinished Business: Broadway Musicals as Works-in-Progress*, Southern Illinois University Press, 2005, pp. 150–52.

Knapp, Raymond, *The American Musical and the Formation of National Identity*, Princeton University Press, 2005, p. 286.

Laird, Paul R., "Choreographers, Directors and the Fully Integrated Musical," in *The Cambridge Companion to the Musical*, 2nd ed., edited by William A. Everett and Paul R. Laird, Cambridge University Press, 2008, pp. 220, 232.

"Michael Bennett," in *Broadway: The American Musical*, PBS website, http://www.pbs.org/wnet/broadway/stars/michael-bennett/ (accessed July 13, 2015).

Quinn, Dave, "Broadway and Off-Broadway Shows Featuring Prominent GLBT Characters," NBC 4 NY, June 30, 2015, http://www.nbcnewyork.com/entertainment/the-scene/8-Broadway-and-Off-Broadway-Shows-Featuring-Prominent-LGBTQ-Characters—310585061.html (accessed July 18, 2015).

Rich, Frank, Introduction to *A Chorus Line: The Book of the Musical*, Applause, 1995, p. xi.

Rothstein, Mervyn, "After 15 Years (15!), 'A Chorus Line' Ends," in *New York Times*, April 30, 1990, http://www.nytimes.com/1990/04/30/theater/after-15-years-15-a-chorus-line-ends.html (accessed July 18, 2015).

Swain, Joseph P., *The Broadway Musical: A Critical and Musical Survey*, 2nd ed., Scarecrow Press, 2002, p. 336.

FURTHER READING

Kelly, Kevin, *One Singular Sensation: The Michael Bennett Story*, Doubleday, 1989,

This is a biography of the famed choreographer-director.

Mordden, Ethan, *Anything Goes: A History of American Musical Theatre*, Oxford University Press, 2013.

Mordden examines Broadway musicals from the 1920s to the present day, including a discussion of *A Chorus Line*.

Stempel, Larry, *Showtime: A History of the Broadway Musical Theater*, W. W. Norton, 2010.

This comprehensive scholarly history has been highly praised by reviewers. It includes more than a hundred photographs and has generous sections on concept musicals, including *A Chorus Line*.

Stevens, Gary, *The Longest Line: Broadway's Most Singular Sensation: A Chorus Line*, Applause, 2000.

This oral history of the show contains three hundred photographs as well as reminiscences by cast and crew members.

SUGGESTED SEARCH TERMS

A Chorus Line

Michael Bennett AND director

Broadway musical

Broadway musicals AND 1970s

concept musical

Marvin Hamlisch

Edward Kleban

individuality versus conformity

Broadway AND gypsies

The Darker Face of the Earth

Literature must constantly renew itself at the source of tradition. In her play, *The Darker Face of the Earth* (published in 1994, first produced in 1996), the Pulitzer Prize–winning poet laureate Rita Dove revisits Sophocles's ancient Greek Drama *Oedipus Tyrannus*. The original story of a man who unknowingly kills his father and marries his mother and is destroyed when he discovers the truth has a deep psychological resonance. It is echoed again and again in Western literature, not least in Shakespeare's *Hamlet*. Dove retells the story at an antebellum plantation on the verge of a slave revolt led by a mulatto (mixed race) slave who is the unknown son of the plantation's owner. In her appropriation of the myth, Dove links the original sin of incest with miscegenation, the mixing of the races, and creates a symbolic drama exposing slavery and racism as the fatal flaws inherent in the founding of the United States.

RITA DOVE

1996

AUTHOR BIOGRAPHY

Dove was born in Akron, Ohio, on August 28, 1952. She was raised in a middle-class household in Akron, where her father worked as an industrial chemist. Dove studied at the University of Miami of Ohio and at the University of Tübingen, Germany, on a Fulbright scholarship, before attending the Iowa Writers' Workshop,

Rita Dove (© *Barbara Zanon* / *Getty Images*)

where she earned a master of fine arts degree. In Iowa, she met her German-born husband, the writer Fred Viebahn. She taught creative writing at the University of Arizona beginning in 1981. She won the Pulitzer Prize in 1987 for her poetry collection *Thomas and Beulah*, sonnets based on the lives of her maternal grandparents. Since 1989, Dove has held an endowed chair at the University of Virginia at Charlottesville.

Dove originally published her play, *The Darker Face of The Earth*, in 1994 and, after working with several theater companies to prepare it for performance, brought out a heavily revised second edition in 1996. The world premiere performance of the play was at the Oregon Shakespeare Festival in 1996. The Broadway premiere later that same year was not successful. The European premiere was at the Royal National Theatre in London in 1999. Since then, the play has been performed regularly by both university and professional theater groups.

Dove has published collections of lyric poems, including *Mother Love* (1995), inspired by *The Homeric Hymn to Demeter*, and *On the*

Bus with Rosa Parks (1999). Dove published another substantial book of poetry, *Sonata Mulattica* in 2009. This work is a large narrative poem based on the true story of a mixed-race violinist, George Augustus Polgreen Bridgetower, who played for Beethoven and who was the original dedicatee of the Kreutzer Sonata before the two men fell out upon becoming romantic rivals.

In 2011, Dove edited *The Penguin Anthology of Twentieth-Century American Poetry*, which involved her in a public controversy with the prominent critic Helen Vendler, who suggested that race seemed to have been a more important criterion for inclusion in the anthology than artistic merit. Dove has published a collection of short stories, *Fifth Sunday* (1985), and a novel, *Through the Ivory Gate* (1992). The gate of ivory is, according to the ancient Greek poet Homer, the portal through which the gods send false dreams to mortals.

Dove served as poet laureate of the United States from 1993 to 1995, the first African American and the youngest person ever to do so. In addition to the Pulitzer Prize and numerous other awards, Dove has received the National Humanities Medal (1996), the Fulbright Lifetime Achievement Medal (2009), and the National Medal of Arts (2011). She and her husband are competitive ballroom dancers, and videos of their performances are widely available on the Internet.

PLOT SUMMARY

The Darker Face of the Earth was originally published in 1994. It was republished in a substantially revised version in 1996, having been rewritten for its first production, at the Oregon Shakespeare Festival. References to the play are to the 1996 text unless otherwise specified.

Directions

The directions establish that the play takes place on a plantation in antebellum South Carolina. They also specify performance practices reminiscent of Greek drama.

Prologue

Amalia, the wife of the plantation owner, Louis, is giving birth in her own bed, attended by the family doctor. These were the usual conditions of birth in the early nineteenth century. What is not usual—what is unnatural—is that the son the aristocratic white woman bears is obviously of mixed race. When Louis sees the child, he suggests that his wife must have been raped by one of the slaves, but Amalia quite openly tells him that she betrayed him to take revenge for his frequent practice of raping the female slaves. Louis is completely dominated by his wife, so there is no question of his punishing her, but the couple and the doctor agree (Amalia reluctantly) that the child must be done away with. Louis is too cowardly to kill the infant himself, and the doctor refuses, but he suggests selling him to another plantation and offers to make the arrangements. This is done, but when the baby is carried out in Amalia's sewing basket, Louis slips in a pair of spurs, hoping the baby will die accidentally. The slaves, including the real father, Hector, gathered on the front porch to hear news of the birth are told that the child, whom they heard cry, died moments after birth.

Act 1, Scene 1

Twenty or so years later, discussion among the slaves at work in a field reveal that Scylla is a sort of shaman, inspiring the slave community with her prophecies that the others receive with the call and response typical of traditional black church services. She also enforces her authority over the other slaves with threats based on her power to control spirits. She orders her fellow slave Phebe to visit her after dark. Amalia comes upon them and refuses medical treatment and rest to the young slave Diana, who is overcome by the strenuous work in the heat, and orders the overseer, Jones, to come and see her that night.

Act 1, Scene 2

Meeting with Jones in her parlor in the big house, Amalia reveals that she has bought a new slave, Augustus Newcastle. Jones is so taken aback that he argues against bringing this slave to the plantation because he is a well-known troublemaker. Jones explains that Augustus is dangerous because he has been the slave of an English sea captain, who took him around the world and allowed him to become educated, particularly to learn how to read. Jones can think of nothing so subversive to the slave system as an educated black man and points out that Augustus has famously been flogged twenty-two times for rebelliousness. Amalia seems to consider dominating so intelligent and insubordinate a slave a challenge. She mocks Jones by saying that Augustus may make a better overseer, suggesting that the black man may be smarter than the white man who is supposed to be his superior.

Act 1, Scene 3

On Sunday, the Christian Sabbath, the only day the slaves are allowed to rest, Augustus is introduced to his fellow slaves, having spent the previous night shackled in the barn. Despite his own Roman name, the slave Scipio has never heard the name Augustus before. When Scipio asks about it, Augustus replies that it is "the name of a king."

It is also a declaration that Augustus has no intention of remaining a slave. Phebe takes charge of introducing Augustus to the other slaves. He demonstrates his knowledge of Greek mythology, commenting that Scylla was a monster who attacked the sailors in *The Odyssey* and that Phebe and Diana are the sun and moon together.

Act 1, Scene 4

Phebe visits Scylla at night in her cabin, and the conjure woman carries out a divinatory ritual, telling the girl to act and speak cautiously. Leaving, Phebe meets Augustus (hobbled with chains), in whom she is obviously developing a romantic interest. He seems oblivious of this. Noting that the slaves in the distance are singing a gospel song, Augustus finds it incredible that slaves could embrace the same religion as their masters, the same religion whose doctrines their masters use to justify the practice of slavery. Phebe asks him whether he is not afraid of the whites, afraid because of the number of times he has been whipped. He is not afraid, he says, because he has "a purpose. Something bigger than anything they can do to you."

He means his desire to end slavery, or at least strike a blow against it. Augustus is equally contemptuous of the religion of the conjure woman. He tells Phebe precisely what Scylla has told her, because, he explains, the whole system is just predictable nonsense. He has been cursed by voodoo chiefs in Haiti to no ill effect. He further tells Phebe that many people have tried to kill him, starting at birth, an attack that left him unable to walk until he was three years old.

Act 1, Scene 5

While working in the fields the next day, Scylla denounces Augustus's influence on the slaves and calls him uppity for telling stories of his life aboard a merchant ship. He says she seems to be the only one who objects and attacks the emptiness of her magical practice, daring her to curse him. Scylla says he does not need to be cursed; he already has been, and the evil inside of him will humble him.

Act 1, Scene 6

The scene begins with Hector out in the swamp at night, hunting snakes. He perceives that others are nearby and hides himself. Augustus meets with conspirators working to foment a slave revolt. The scene is surreal. (The stage directions suggest conveying it through pantomime or ballet.) Augustus agrees to join the rebellion, swearing to kill white men and women. The conspirators perform an ersatz Christian ritual, citing fake Bible quotes to denounce the practice of slavery and—like witches at a Sabbath—signing their names in a book that they call the book of life.

Act 1, Scene 7

During the lunch break in the cotton fields, Augustus tells the other slaves about the revolt in Haiti, in which the slaves murdered their masters and became a nation of free black men. Amalia overhears this without being seen and then dramatically reveals herself, ordering Augustus to come and see her that evening.

Act 1, Scene 8

Throughout this scene, Louis is busy on the upper story of the house attempting, but never succeeding, to observe some obscure astronomical phenomenon.

In her parlor, Amalia questions Augustus about his education. He says he has read the Bible, John Milton, and Greek mythology. She tells him no slave could be as smart as he seems without seeming not to be. Amalia complains to Augustus about the limitations imposed on her life, particularly her education, as a woman in a patriarchal society. She mentions that Louis's family came to Charleston fleeing the Haitian slave revolt. She tells him about the *Amistad*, noting that the case has recently been reported in the newspaper (dating the setting of the play to around 1841).

The *Amistad* was a Spanish slave ship transporting Africans from Havana to their final destination in a smaller port in Cuba. The slaves were kidnapped in Africa after the international slave trade had been outlawed by treaty. The slaves managed to revolt and take control of the ship, sparing only the navigator, whom they ordered to take them back to Africa. He instead guided them to the United States, where the *Amistad* was captured by a naval vessel. This resulted in a well-publicized court case to decide the fate of the Africans: whose property they might be, whether they should be treated as mutineers, and whether they were free men. Amalia tells Augustus that the blacks were executed, but actually the Supreme Court ruled that they should be set free.

Augustus narrates what he imagines must be the story of his own conception. Using highly poetic language—the title of the play, *The Darker Face of the Earth*, is a line in this section—he describes an imagined slave master raping his imagined slave mother. After this rather strange courtship, the scene ends with Augustus and Amalia making love.

Act 2, Scene 1

In a passage described in the stage directions as a dream sequence, Amalia and Augustus profess their love for each other, while the slaves act as a chorus and sing the Gospel song "Sometimes I Feel like a Motherless Child." Louis meanwhile correctly states that the astronomical phenomenon of the precession of the equinoxes means that natal horoscopes are based on relative positions of stars that they occupied thousands of years ago, meaning that modern horoscopes would be invalid, but he suggests that this requires only a new system of astrological prediction.

Act 2, Scene 2

Phebe stops Augustus on his way to the big house to visit Amalia. She tells him that her mother, who was a house servant, died of fever when Phebe was five. She contracted the illness while giving food to sick field hands Amalia's father had ordered her to be starved rather than risk spreading the illness. When the master found out, he made it clear that Phebe's mother would have been terribly punished if she had survived the illness. Augustus asks her if she wants to take revenge—sounding her out as a possible recruit to the conspiracy.

Act 2, Scene 3

While storing the harvested cotton, the slaves gossip about Augustus, who they are well aware spends all night every night at the big house. Some hint at the truth, but others believe their mistress is merely trying another way to control him because violence has obviously failed to do so. Scylla is especially critical of Augustus. To defend Augustus, Phebe denies Scylla's power as a conjure woman. She openly asks that if Scylla she has the power to curse and kill through magic, why does she not kill their mistress? Scylla cryptically hints that there is something poisonous inside Augustus that will destroy him and any other slave who follows him.

Act 2, Scene 4

Hector is again in the swamp, killing snakes. He again hides from Augustus, who has come to meet with the conspirator Benjamin Skeene. They go on discussing the plot as if nothing has changed, but after Skeene leaves, Augustus reveals in a soliloquy that loving Amalia has healed him of the psychic wounds imposed on him by a lifetime of enslavement.

Hector confronts Augustus and speaks incoherently but reveals that he has taken to the swamp to keep the curse he feels himself to be under as far as possible from Amalia. He perceives that Augustus is plotting a revolt and insists that he will not let Augustus harm Amalia. Hector begins shouting. To keep him quiet and avoid alerting the whole plantation, Augustus begins to choke the old man and kills him without meaning to. He laments that he intended to save all black men but now finds himself in the position of having killed one.

Act 2, Scene 5

In a soliloquy, Amalia tells her life story through an allegorical fairy tale. When Augustus comes to her, they discuss the impossibility of their position but see no way to change it, so they must derive what private happiness they can.

Act 2, Scene 6

The slaves are gathered at Hector's funeral. Phebe found him, as she tells Augustus, when she answered the call to go to the swamp to tell the conspirators that Augustus could not come that night. She has joined the conspiracy.

Act 2, Scene 7

The moment to launch the revolt has come. Augustus and Phebe are waiting for the other conspirators, and she says she is more concerned about him than the revolution. If his life had not been so consumed by hatred, he might have been able to love her. Overcome with regret, she runs off. The other conspirators arrive. They are aware of Augustus's affair with Amalia and take him to headquarters.

Act 2, Scene 8

Augustus returns, charged to prove his loyalty to the cause by killing both Louis and Amalia. It was simple for him before, hating and being hated, but now he must choose between love and freedom.

Augustus enters Louis's study but finds Louis prepared with a pistol. While he delays firing, Louis muses that long ago he should have strangled the baby in the sewing basket. On hearing this, Augustus manages to knock the gun away. Augustus holds a knife to Louis's throat and demands that he describe the basket. Louis does and mentions the spurs. Augustus recognizes the story and the description of the basket in which he was brought to his childhood home. Augustus seizes on the idea that Louis must be his father, but Louis realizes the truth. Augustus kills him.

Augustus can hear the other conspirators outside raising the plantation in revolt. He goes to Amalia's bedroom and tells her the slaves are rising, that Jones the overseer must already be dead. Augustus demands to know what happened to his mother. He believes Louis is his father and that Amalia made Louis get rid of the child who was evidence of his infidelity. He imagines Amalia must have punished his mother. He describes his foundling basket as proof. Hearing this, Amalia realizes that Augustus is her son. She tells him, and Phebe too, who has rushed in to say the conspirators are coming. Realizing what she has done, Amalia kills herself. Overwhelmed, Augustus sees around him the ghosts of murdered slaves. The other slaves rush in, overjoyed to see their masters dead. They carry Augustus out on their shoulders in triumph.

CHARACTERS

Alexander

In the play, as in history, many slaves were given names derived from classical mythology or history. In this case, Alexander is probably meant to recall Alexander the Great, the king of Macedon who conquered the Persian Empire in the fourth century BCE and was recognized as representative of the highest ideals of Greek society. Alexander wants to maintain peace and order among the black community, hoping in this way to avoid provoking the owners.

Henry Blake

Henry is an ordinary slave who originally wants no part of the revolt, but its leader persuades him (in an event reenacted through a sort of pantomime on stage) that he has received a spiritual call to revolution.

Chorus of Slaves

The chorus of slaves is constantly on stage, even if in the background, usually singing or chanting. The other slaves emerge and then vanish back into the chorus. A female member of the chorus often emerges as a narrator at the beginning or end of the acts to make a moralizing comment on the action.

Diana

Diana is the Roman name of the Greek goddess Artemis, the sister of Apollo, who was associated with the moon and who was in charge of hunting and rural life. On the plantation, Diana is a young girl born after Augustus. She is too young and frail for the hard work of picking cotton, but this does not excuse her.

Doctor

The family doctor who has attended Amalia since her own birth helps to deliver her baby (Augustus) at the beginning of the play. He refuses to kill the infant, claiming it is against medical ethics. Because he disposes of the mixed-race child by selling him, the doctor corresponds to the slave in the Oedipus story who was charged with exposing the infant but who out of pity instead gives him to a Corinthian shepherd. The doctor, however, is not needed back on stage to confirm the identity of the adult Augustus.

Hector

Hector is named after the prince of Troy, who is one of the principal characters of *The Iliad*: "Hector, mighty warrior, abandoned by the gods," as Augustus tells him at their introduction. Hector is identified in the dramatis personae as an African, that is, he was born in Africa, kidnapped into slavery, and made the Atlantic crossing to be sold in America. He is the same age as Amalia and was raised with her as her companion. He is the one Amalia chooses to be the father of her child when she desires to take revenge on her husband for his adultery with the female slaves. Hector is devastated by the loss of his son (like the other slaves, he believes that Augustus dies immediately after birth) and retreats into the swamp, where his anguish is displaced into his fanatical killing of snakes. Hector also retreats into African culture, and unexpectedly, as he does so, he also becomes less human, less engaged with his community because of his obsession.

Jones

Jones is the white overseer of the plantation, who spends his days directly supervising the slaves at their work. He is an alcoholic, slipping off to drink whenever he has the chance, a habit played for comic relief.

Amalia Jennings Lafarge

Although Amalia's name may at first seem as classical as her slaves' (suggesting the Latin Aemilia), it is in fact a Germanic name (though given a Latinate ending) and refers to fertility. Amalia is the daughter of a plantation owner, whose property, in her patriarchal society, has passed to the control of her husband, Louis. Amalia sets the plot of the play in motion when she takes the step, unthinkable in her culture, of bearing the child of a black man. She is forthright in asserting that her motive was to take revenge on her husband for sleeping with their female slaves.

Paradoxically, Amalia is the dominant figure in the marriage, because her personality is much more forceful than her husband's. In parallel to the traditional power arrangement of master over slave, the American culture of the nineteenth century was patriarchal. Women did not have the same rights as men, lacking not only the right to vote but also the right to control their own property within marriage. Like slavery, patriarchy was justified by the false assertion that women were inherently inferior to men and fit only to be controlled by their fathers and then their husbands. Amalia's marriage makes it clear that this is not the case, but it was another fiction that had to be maintained at all costs, lest the exposure of the truth collapse the structure of traditional society.

Through conceiving Augustus with the African slave Hector, Amalia exposes the lie that slavery is built on with the contradiction of giving birth to a child who is simultaneously white and black in a way that cannot be so simply denied. She also exposes the lie that patriarchy is built on by the contradiction of asserting her own sexual agency, especially by choosing a forbidden partner. Amalia's reaction to losing her son is to take on the role of her father, the ruthless and cruel plantation master. Unexpectedly, however, she becomes more sympathetic as the play progresses. She makes a journey from love, bridging the races with Hector, toward cruelty, then back again to love and racial harmony with Augustus. Although Augustus is ready to deny it to justify her murder, Amalia has been genuinely changed by her experiences.

Louis Lafarge

Louis is descended from a family of white planters who fled the slave uprising in Haiti. Amalia has accepted him for marriage more or less as a symbol of masculinity and feels betrayed when he begins pursuing the slave women on the plantation. After the birth of Augustus, Louis withdraws from his role as master of the plantation, devoting himself to stargazing. Louis, like Hector, is derived from Laius in the Oedipus myth. As master of the plantation, Louis is a king symbol, whereas Hector, somewhat more desperately, declares himself king of the wild, mad world he inhabits in the swamp. Perhaps the lesson Dove intends is that kingship is possible only by withdrawal from the community, which must function cooperatively to sustain its true character. Louis's astronomical concerns, his quest for visual knowledge, also mark him as a descendant of Tiresias the seer. Louis's confusion of astronomy and astrology marks him as mentally unbalanced.

Leader

Augustus meets the leader of the impending slave revolt once in the swamp at night. The leader is the least realistic and least human of the play's characters.

Augustus Newcastle

Augustus was the name of the first Roman emperor and was later used as an imperial title. Augustus is the protagonist of the play. He is born in the prologue and later returns unknowingly to his home, where he breeds revolution, kills his father, and has sex with his mother. Augustus takes on a curious range of identities. He is the savior of the slave community—or at least they accept him as such, as Scylla accuses, "you think he's the Savior!"—just as Oedipus is hailed as savior by the Thebans whom he delivers from the Sphinx. Augustus Newcastle is not Jesus—whose enemy was the Roman emperor Augustus—but Moses. Like Moses, Augustus is carried away in a wicker basket after his birth and returns to lead his people, in Augustus's case, to the promised land of freedom in Haiti. But he fails. Like Jesus, however, he is pierced in the side. Oedipus's intellectual feat of solving the Sphinx's riddle has its counterpart in Augustus's literacy and education. But just as Oedipus is ignorant of his origins as a Theban, Augustus is ignorant of his origins as an African. He belittles Scylla's Africanized religion in favor of his own European learning.

Phebe

Phebe is an authentic nineteenth-century spelling of the name that both before and after would be more typically spelled Phoebe. The original Greek could be transliterated into modern English as *Phoibe*; the vowel in the first syllable was originally pronounced as the vowel in the English word *toy*. The characters depicted in the play would probably have pronounced the first syllable *fee*. In the play, Augustus associates the name Phebe with the sun, on the basis of his limited reading in Greek mythology. He would have encountered the masculine epithet Phebus in association with the Greek sun god Apollo. The word itself does refer to light (compare the English word *photon*). However, Phebe is an epithet of Artemis (Latin Diana) because she is Apollo's sister, not because she is a solar deity. Artemis is also a lunar divinity.

Phebe in the play, though seemingly not much younger than Amalia (she is among the group of slaves awaiting the birth on the porch of the big house), is presented as Augustus's natural love interest, had he not been fated for his disastrous relationship with Amalia. Phebe takes up the revolutionary cause, seemingly as much out of devotion to Augustus as for any other reason, and becomes his second in command.

Psyche

The Greek word *psyche* means "soul" and is the name of the mortal lover of the god Cupid in Apuleius's Latin novel *The Metamorphoses*. In the play, she is among the group of slaves on the porch of the big house awaiting Augustus's birth.

Scipio

Scipio was the name of one of the most distinguished families of the Roman Republic. Its members over several generations were largely responsible for the defeat and conquest of Rome's greatest enemy, Carthage, and its army led by Hannibal. In the play, Scipio is the natural storyteller and singer among the slaves.

Scylla

In the Greek epic poem, *The Odyssey*, Scylla is the name of the seven-headed monster that preys on Odysseus's crew when they attempt to return to their home in Ithaca. In the play, Scylla is a shaman, or conjure woman, a priestess of traditional African religion whose contact with the spirits makes her both a prophet and a healer. She experiences the shamanic call, the first contact with the spirits, at the same moment Augustus is born. (Such calls are commonplace in traditional African American culture, often leading to careers as Christian preachers, as Augustus describes to Amalia in the story of the preacher Isaac.) Scylla is Dove's stand-in for the blind seer Tiresias in Sophocles's play. As Tiresias did Oedipus, Scylla holds contempt for Augustus because she knows what he is fated to do.

Benjamin Skeene

A common alternative to classical names for slaves in the American South were biblical names. In the Hebrew Bible, Benjamin was one of the sons of Jacob and had a tribe of Israel named for him. In the play, Benjamin is a conspirator who, because he is a skilled carpenter, has more freedom to move around the city of Charleston. If Augustus's biography is based on Denmark Vesey's early life, Benjamin reflects Vesey's life in Charleston.

Ticey

Ticey is a servant in the big house.

THEMES

African Culture

One of the oldest traditions of human society is the ability of certain individuals to contact a different reality that is interpreted as a spiritual world by those who experience it but which scientists studying the phenomenon interpret as an interior psychological reality. In modern Western culture, people who pursue this kind of practice are generally called shamans because of the historical accident that the phenomenon was first studied by Western scholars among the tribal peoples of Siberia, where that term originated. (The slaves in the play use the term *conjure woman*.) The practice of shamanism goes back tens of thousands of years, leaving its mark on the Paleolithic cave art in Chauvet and other caves in France and in younger examples of rock art from around the world.

Shamans are generally believed to be in contact with a spiritual world from which they derive the authority and power to perform miracles of prophecy and healing for their

TOPICS FOR FURTHER STUDY

- Shamanism is practiced in cultures all over the world, and the phenomenon has been widely documented by anthropologists. One Mexican shaman, María Sabina, has been extensively studied. Several monographs have been devoted to her, including *Maria Sabina: Her Life and Chants* (1981), by Álvaro Estrada, and *Maria Sabina and Her Mazatec Mushroom Velada* (1974), by George Wasson. These volumes record extensive interviews with her and her repertoire of songs and prayers. Write a paper comparing María Sabina's shamanistic practice with Scylla's in *The Darker Face of the Earth*.

- Scylla represents the religious tradition of Santería, which arose in the culture of slaves in the Americas and was based on fragments of the religious traditions of the Yoruba in Africa. (Vodun, or voodoo, is similar but derives from Ewe religion.) Santería has at least twenty thousand followers in the United States. Websites such as orishanet.org and santeriachurch.org help to organize the individual communities of the religion. Using these websites and related social media as a guide, make a presentation to your class giving an overview of the current practice of Santería in the United States.

- *Escape to Freedom* (1976), by Ossie Davis, is a play for young adults about Frederick Douglass, a black leader whose view of liberation and abolition was very different from Denmark Vesey's. Write a paper comparing this play to *The Darker Face of the Earth*.

- The black arts movement of the 1960s and 1970s represents the cultural orthodoxy that Dove encountered as a black literature student and young poet. Its goal was to produce authentic black art separate from white culture. Although she is often associated with this movement, Dove draws on European, even classical, sources of inspiration, such as Sophocles in the case of *The Darker Side of the Earth*. Discuss in a paper how Dove's theme of the mulatto, particularly its embodiment in the character of Augustus, seems to express a revolt against this cultural orthodoxy. How does that relate to the theme of revolution in the play?

---

communities. Shamans experience the other world through the result of ascetic practices, including self-denial and repetitive prayer or chanting. Sometimes considered a precursor of the more formal religions of later civilizations, shamanic practices persist in the life of religious visionaries even in urban cultures, such as Pythagoras or Saint Paul in Mediterranean antiquity.

In *The Darker Face of the Earth*, Scylla is clearly a shaman. As sometimes happens, the spirits come and take her against her will, showing her a vision of a curse on the plantation: "The veil was snatched from my eyes—and over the hill I saw bad times a-coming. Bad times coming over the hill on mighty horses." This happens on the night Augustus is born. Since then, Scylla has tended to her fellow slaves as a healer. She claims through her control of the spirits to be able to strike dead anyone who disobeys her. Like Phebe, one wonders why Scylla does not use her powers to kill Amalia and the other whites. For Dove, however, the supernatural is at most a metaphor for the miraculous power of revolution, the revolt planned by Augustus that would free the slaves. Nevertheless, Scylla, and to a lesser degree Hector, represents a connection to the pre-Christian African religion of the Yoruba people.

Slaves in the new world were required to convert to Christianity, but they also preserved their own traditions in secret, giving rise to syncretistic religions like vodun and Santería that mixed the two together. The Yoruba religion that lies behind Santería embraced hundreds of deities that were all seen as manifestation of a single divine principle. The entities became orishas in the Americas, taking on the outward form of Christian saints and holy figures while secretly maintaining their Yoruban names. The phrase "Eshu Elewa ogo gbogbo!" often repeated in *The Darker Face of the Earth* is an invocation of the orisha Eshu, a trickster who mediates between the worlds of the living and the dead.

Race Relations

The slave plantation was an economic structure developed in North Africa by the Carthaginians before the third century BCE. It was taken over by the Romans, later by Arab culture, and finally by Spain as the basis of economic development in its New World colonies. It was embraced there by other colonial powers, including France and Britain and ultimately the United States. To maintain a slave economy, violence and the threat of violence must be constantly applied to the slaves. Just as important, however, the slave owners must convince themselves that their slaves are somehow completely inhuman and therefore not deserving of the basic human dignity that every person is entitled to. Otherwise they could not justify the cycle of hard manual labor and punishment that often resulted in the death of slaves after only a few years of captivity. The brutality of slavery does strip away the human dignity of the slave, but it also strips away the human dignity of the masters compelled to act with inhuman cruelty to maintain their position, as Amalia admits in *The Darker Face of the Earth*: "Don't you think I see the suffering? Don't you think I know I'm the cause? But a master cannot allow himself the privilege of sorrow. A master must rule or die."

The idea that slaves are naturally inferior goes back to Greek philosophy, an origin that exposes its falsity. Even in a Greek world, where slavery was a relatively minor part of the economy, Aristotle argued that slaves were slaves by nature, that there was something inherently inferior about them that justified keeping them as slaves. He made this argument even at a time when, as a result of wars between city-states, Greeks who had lived their whole lives as free men were regularly captured and enslaved by other Greeks, some even being sold to plantation slavery in Carthage. Aristotle himself could have easily succumbed to this fate, except for the vagaries of chance. It is amazing that Aristotle could assert a proposition that was obviously falsified by everyday events.

The ideology of slavery involves a staggering degree of denial, the ability to maintain, for personal or financial interests, that something is true, even when it is self-evidently not true, in this case the ability to look at a human beings and claim that they are no different in their talents and dignity from animals. This hypocrisy is the main weakness in the ideology of slavery. It nevertheless permeated American society so that even otherwise enlightened thinkers like Thomas Jefferson and Abraham Lincoln reflexively believed that African Americans, if not deserving of slavery, were nevertheless inferior to whites. Even after the abolition of slavery, the hypocritical belief persisted as the basis of American racism, during the period of legal discrimination against blacks, and continues to a degree into the twenty-first century.

In *The Darker Face of the Earth*, Dove attacks racism at its weak spot. A slave owner has to come to terms with the fact that her own child is a slave, something not quite human. This was not a hypothetical concern. Male slave owners routinely raped their female slaves and had children by them. The practice was well known in the antebellum South but at the same time could never be admitted. Attempts to deny that Thomas Jefferson had children by his slave Sally Hemings persist. It was a common but not universal practice for such children to be sold away quickly so that the slave owner's wife would not have to see the mixed-race children who would be constant reminders of the husband's infidelity. (Augustus imagines this is what happened to him.) Dove has Amalia expose this hidden truth in the taunting of her husband, adding a humiliating insult that must reflect her own deep sense of humiliation upon discovering the truth for herself: "So it's all right for you to stroll out by the cabins any fine night you please? Ha—The Big White Hunter with his scrawny whip."

The entire edifice of slavery depended on a series of lies that nevertheless had to be believed. This is shown in Dove's play by the doctor's concern in the prologue that the slaves not discover the truth. He means the truth that Amalia has

The story is set on a southern plantation. *(© David P. Smith | Shutterstock.com)*

transgressed the ideology of the antebellum south, but more generally the truth that they are not slaves by nature.

STYLE

Dramaturgy

Dove is principally a lyric poet and in her early career had little experience with longer narrative forms such as drama. *The Darker Face of the Earth* was written during the 1970s, while Dove was in graduate school, but she saw little hope of developing it or publishing it and set it aside for many years. Finally, her husband convinced her that it was worth publishing. Even then, Dove doubted the drama would ever be performed. In an interview with Robert McDowell, Dove recalled how, to her surprise, soon after the first edition of the play was published, she was contacted by several theater groups interested in performing it. After meeting and reading through the play with the staff and actors of the Oregon Shakespeare Festival, in particular, she became convinced that the play needed major revision to be viable for the stage. Under this influence, Dove reformulated her play into a structure of much tighter discrete scenes with traditional verse structures. She took seriously

the forms and restrictions of the classical drama that had inspired the play. This version rewritten for the stage premiered in Oregon in 1996 and has had several performances since then. The revised text was republished as the second edition of the play.

Intertextuality

If a modern writer writes "to be or not to be," the reader will recognize this as a direct quotation of the text of *Hamlet*. But not all literary references take so simple a form. More subtle is an inter-textual reference in which the text of the work being referred to is not directly quoted and not even named but is nevertheless inevitably evoked in the mind of the reader, as if the author and reader are having a conversation in which they can refer to the intertext as something they both know and therefore need not name.

The most prominent of Dove's intertextual conversations is with Sophocles' drama *Oedipus Tyrannus*, of which *The Darker Face of the Earth* is an adaptation. This might be called inspiration rather than intertextuality, but the difference is one of scale rather than mechanism. One way to look at any work of literature is as a rearrange-ment of elements drawn from the author's whole lifetime of reading. Carrying on in this same way, perhaps, Dove invokes elements of other works of literature in her play. The plot in which

Augustus engages in the play is not derived from the ancient Greek drama but was inspired by a historical event, the Charleston slave conspiracy led by Denmark Vesey in 1822. Dove does not follow the historical events and character of that conspiracy with any particular fidelity. Rather, the conspiracy in *The Darker Face of the Earth* reminds the reader of the conspiracy that is central to the plot of the nineteenth-century Russian novelist Fyodor Dostoevsky's novel *The Possessed* (sometimes called in English *The Demons* or *The Devils*). The mysterious and elliptical way that the conspirators appear in the novel, their meetings in the wild, their godlike knowledge all recall Dostoevsky's conspirators.

Another work that stands behind *The Darker Face of the Earth* is Kyle Onstott's 1957 novel, *Mandingo*. This novel, set on an antebellum plantation, created a public sensation when it was published because it insisted on the historical facts that the white supremacist ideology of that era would sooner deny, namely, that female slaves were routinely used by their masters for sex. Although much of its impact was lost after its author sold the rights to a publisher who produced a series of sensationalistic sequels, in recent years scholarly interest in the novel has revived. It also resurfaces in popular culture, such as a source of inspiration for Quentin Tarantino's 2012 film, *Django Unchained*).

In *Mandingo*, a plantation owner's new bride grows angry that she is neglected in favor of her husband's slave mistress and takes revenge by having relations herself with one of his slaves, resulting in the birth of a mixed-race child. The event is so far beyond the pale of slave-owning culture that the husband, along with his father and the attending physician, takes it for granted that the wife, child, and slave all must be destroyed. This theme is repeated in *The Darker Face of the Earth*. In the play, however, Amalia's husband lacks the force of will to even consider reprisals against his wife, and the doctor, on the ground of professional ethics, insists that the child only be sold into slavery on a different plantation. Dove equates the unnatural birth of the racially mixed child to a white mother with the unnatural birth of Oedipus, destined to murder his father and marry his mother, whose uncleanness is the cause of a plague that ravages his country. The reader is left to ponder the institutional racism and whether Augustus's birth is part of a plague ravaging America.

HISTORICAL CONTEXT

The Charleston Slave Conspiracy of 1822

The Darker Face of the Earth has a definite historical setting in the antebellum South. Dove chose that setting because she wanted to find a rigidly hierarchical society that paralleled archaic Greece to support a retelling of the Oedipus myth. The new setting also allowed the introduction of the original American sin of miscegenation. Just as the play is not a precise retelling of the Oedipus myth, it is not strictly historical, but it does draw on specific historical events for its American setting and elements. Therese Steffen, in *Crossing Color*, related the play to a black conspiracy in Charleston, South Carolina, in 1822. Although the event is not referenced in detail, it is, Steffen argued, implicitly present in the play. At the most obvious level of detail, the chronology, the play does not match up with history (because Augustus is born around 1820, and the slave revolt takes place twenty years later), but the idea of a revolt in the plantations around Charleston parallels the historical plot, and Augustus's character is to a large extent modeled on Denmark Vesey, the black freedman who was leader of the conspiracy. Steffen observes:

> Denmark Vesey, like Augustus Newcastle, demonstrated a certainty and sophistication not thought possible for a black person at that time. Denmark is reported to have proved a most faithful slave and to have traveled all over the world with his master, learning to speak various languages.

Vesey was eventually tried, convicted, and executed by a special court that met in secret (a violation of the US Constitution. Although the white supremacist bias of the court means that anything produced by it must be treated with caution, its proceedings are the main source of knowledge of Vesey. Some of the evidence it heard was published later, in 1822, by the judges Lionel H. Kennedy and Thomas Parker in *An Official Report of the Trials of Sundry Negroes, Charged with an Attempt to Raise an Insurrection in the State of South-Carolina*.

Vesey was reportedly born on the Caribbean island of Saint Thomas in 1767 and was bought at the age of fourteen by a slave ship captain, Joseph Vesey. The boy so impressed Vesey and the other crewmen with his quick-wittedness that they adopted him as a sort of mascot, which he probably considered preferable to being kept in

COMPARE
&
CONTRAST

- **Nineteenth Century:** Slavery is a legal institution in the United States, and most blacks, several million people, are enslaved.

  Today: Although slavery ends after the Civil War and Reconstruction era amendments to the U.S. Constitution, legal racism persists until the civil rights movement of the 1950s and 1960s. The black community continues to face a large measure of institutional racism.

- **Nineteenth Century:** A slave revolt takes place in South Carolina in 1822. The leader is Denmark Vesey, who is also a founder of the Emanuel African Methodist Episcopal Church in Charleston, the first black church in the United States, which is burned down by a white supremacist mob in retaliation for the revolt.

  Today: In 2015, the same Emanuel African Methodist Episcopal Church is attacked by the white supremacist Dylann Storm Roof,

who shoots the pastor and eight other congregants during a prayer meeting and reportedly announces during the shooting that he is retaliating for miscegenation and intends to start a war of whites against blacks.

- **Nineteenth Century:** Although abolitionists argue against slavery because it is against Christian principles, many of the political arguments supporting slavery are based on Christian scripture and theology.

  Today: Christian religious arguments and rhetoric are common in the defense of legal racial segregation, such as those made against interracial marriage in the *Loving v. Virginia* Supreme Court case (1967), and continue to be used against extensions of personal freedom, as in the *Obergefell v. Hodges* case (2015), which legalizes same-sex marriage.

---

the ship's hold. He was named Telemaque (the French version of Telemachus, the son of Odysseus in Greek mythology), which was soon corrupted to Denmark. Vesey was sold in Haiti before the slave revolt there, but the planter who purchased him returned him to Captain Vesey, claiming he had epilepsy.

Joseph Vesey took his slave on several more voyages until Denmark won a lottery with a ticket he had bought with the small allowance he was given to take care of his personal needs. His master allowed him to exchange the money for his freedom. Vesey took his master's surname, as was usual for freedmen. Thereafter he lived in Charleston, working as a carpenter. He became a founding member of the Emanuel African Episcopal Church, the first black church in the United States, seeing a promise of freedom in the message of the Gospel.

Shortly before 1822, Vesey supposedly launched a conspiracy of free and enslaved blacks in Charleston to take over the city, massacre the slave owners on the surrounding plantations, and seize merchant ships to take the entire black population of the area to the black-ruled nation of Haiti. It is not clear to what extent Vesey was the head of a real conspiracy or whether Kennedy and Parker and other whites fabricated the affair as an excuse to suppress the free black community in Charleston. In any case, the accusations worked against the black community. Thirty-one of its leading citizens were deported, and thirty-five were lynched. Although they were ostensibly executed, there was no legal authority for the death sentences because their trials would have been illegal by federal standards. Laws more strictly controlling free and enslaved blacks alike were passed, and the Emanuel African Episcopal

Although Dove's story was inspired by an ancient play by Sophocles, it explores the American institution of slavery and its consequences, which continue to this day. (© Anton Watman | Shutterstock.com)

Church was burned down by a white mob, though its congregation remained intact, meeting in secret for a time. Augustus's life story is based in large part on Vesey's biography, and he possesses some of Vesey's qualities, such as his affinity for languages.

CRITICAL OVERVIEW

Owing to Dove's position as U.S. poet laureate, *The Darker Side of the Earth* has been extensively discussed in the critical literature. Therese Steffen, in *Crossing Color* (2001), related the play to its historical source material in the supposed slave rising planned by Denmark Vesey and to its literary model *Oedipus Tyrannus*, by Sophocles. Malin Pereira, in *Rita Dove's Cosmopolitanism* (2003), interpreted the play as a repressed account (given its twenty-year-long gestation) of the primal scene of the African American community. In this Freudian reading, according to Pereira, "the trope of sexual miscegenation articulates an African American primal scene of cultural amalgamation." Pereira meant that the theme of incest, which occurs in *The Darker Face of the Earth* and much of Dove's early work, and the theme of the mulatto, the individual of mixed race, are used to cover the reality of Dove's intellectual background, unacceptable to the ideology of the black arts movement, that her own work mixes themes and materials from both white and black cultures.

The very existence of *The Darker Face of the Earth*, based on a play by the Greek dramatist Sophocles, is a testament to this repressed fact. In a 2003 article in *Critical Voicings of Black Liberation: Resistance and Representations in the Americas*, Valerie Bada concentrated on Dove's play's modeling on Greek drama. Bada found the tragic flaw of *The Darker Face of the Earth* in Louis's attempt to murder the young Augustus by putting spurs in the sewing basket that doubled as his crib (a recollection of the pins put through Oedipus's ankles to make him easier to carry). Kevin J. Westmore (*Black Dionysus*, 2003) argued that the tragic flaw lies in the decision to sell the newborn Augustus, supposedly free because he was born to a free mother (though probably no law was meant to cover the situation). He also covers the significant differences in the plot between the first and second editions of the play. Westmore discussed the practice of giving slaves Greco-Roman names, evidence not only of the reading habits of the slave owners but also of a conscious attempt to justify the practice by linking slavery to classical precedents.

In *Crossroads in the Black Aegean* (2007), Barbara Goff and Michael Simpson saw the incest and parricide of Dove's play as symbols of the colonized social relations imposed on American blacks. Those critics saw Dove's emphasis on miscegenation as referring to the interior colonization of the black American identity. Emily Wilson's "Black Oedipus," in *A Companion to Sophocles* (2012), concentrated on comparisons between Dove's play and its Sophoclean source material but also delved into some obscure points that may have been beyond Dove's interest (for example, trying to find significance for the play in the fact that Octavian, once he had gained control of the Roman world though civil war, never used the title *king* but latched on to substitute titles such as *emperor* and *Augustus* to preserve an illusion of personal and political liberty in the state).

CRITICISM

Bradley A. Skeen

Skeen is a classicist. In the following essay, he analyzes The Darker Face of the Earth *in comparison with its source material in Sophocles's* Oedipus Tyrannus.

During her first private interview with Augustus, Amalia offers him a book to read, mockingly asking him if he could do better reading it in the original Greek. She snatches it away when he says: "I've read that one already. In my opinion, the Greeks were a bit too predictable." It is often supposed that the unnamed book is a translation of Sophocles's fifth-century play *Oedipus Tyrannus*. Because *The Darker Face of the Earth* is meant to be an adaptation of that play, this otherwise difficult scene would, in that case, become a sort of postmodern in-joke: the characters of the play already know what is going to happen to them ("a bit too predictable")

because they've read the book. They would be no better off—or no worse off—than Sophocles's original audience, who would have known, in at least general terms, the story of Oedipus, though Dove, who makes significant changes in her story, is blessed—or cursed—with an audience who may not know at the beginning how it will end.

The name *Oedipus* is best known from the Oedipus complex described by the pioneering psychoanalyst Sigmund Freud. Freud hypothesized that the human ability to form affective (close and stable) relationships, particularly adult romantic relationships, is built on the model relationship that first attaches an infant to its mother. Accompanied by the jealous desire to eliminate the father as a rival, the first growth of a child's personality comes when these desires are repressed and brought under control so that the psychic energy invested in them can be used for the work of maturing. In Sophocles's drama of Oedipus, Freud thought, the origins of the repressed desires are laid bare by showing an adult acting out these infantile feelings. The story is powerful because it is universal to the human experience of growing up. For Dove, the story of Oedipus becomes one of gaining freedom at the cost of unconditional maternal love.

The story of Oedipus is an old one in Greek culture, but one that grew over time. As Homer knew it, Oedipus was a king of the city of Thebes long before the Trojan War. His tragedy was that his sons killed each other in civil war. Almost a century before Sophocles, the poet Pindar knew of the oracle that Oedipus fulfilled by murdering his father, Laius. Many fifth century playwrights besides Sophocles adapted the Oedipus myth into drama, but their plays do not survive. But it is known that Euripides added the detail that Laius incurred his punishment by disobeying Apollo's order not to father a son. The play by Sophocles does survive and has become the canonical version of the story in

WHAT DO I READ NEXT?

- *The Poet's World* (1995) is a collection of literary essays Dove wrote during her tenure as poet laureate.

- Laurent Dubois and John D. Garrigus's *Slave Revolution in the Caribbean, 1789–1804: A Brief History with Documents* (2006) is now a standard account of the Haitian slave uprising.

- *I Heard God Talking to Me: William Edmondson and His Stone Carvings* (2009), by Elizabeth Spires, tells the story of Edmondson, who during the Depression was working as a janitor with no artistic training or background when he was suddenly inspired to become a sculptor. This call follows a pattern well known in the African community and reflected in Scylla's sudden call to shamanism. Edmondson was the first black artist to exhibit at the Museum of Modern Art in New York City. Spires describes Edmondson's work for a young-adult audience in a series of twenty-eight poems.

- *The Invention of Wings* (2014) is a historical novel by Sue Monk Kidd that is based on the life of Sarah Grimké, a southern belle from Charleston who eventually became a leading abolitionist. Denmark Vesey is a character in the novel.

- The Nigerian poet Ola Rotimi made a modern adaptation of the Oedipus story in 1968 called *The Gods Are Not to Blame* (published in book form in 1974). This version is much closer to Sophocles's than to Dove's version and transposes the story to an ancient Yoruba kingdom. Rotimi also novelized the material of the play, but this treatment is less widely available.

- Alejo Carpentier's novel *The Kingdom of This World* (English translation, 2006) is set during the corrupt and tyrannical black regime that governed Haiti in the first days of its independence.

- Dove's *Selected Poems* (1993) collects some of the best work of her early period.

Western culture, the one that Dove had in mind as she wrote *The Darker Face of the Earth*.

Dove's imitation of Sophocles starts with the basic conditions of performance. Greek drama was different from modern dramatic theater. A play was acted by only three actors, each playing many different roles as the individual scenes dictated, and all three were men, even if they portrayed female characters. For this reason, in her dramatis personae, Dove suggests how the roles of her play can be divided with various actors portraying several characters each. A Greek drama had a chorus, a group of actors who would both interact with the other characters and stop the action between acts to comment on its development, singing their lines and dancing. This is the model for the chorus and narrator (*choragus*, or chorus leader) and the extravagant amount of song and dance in Dove's play. Ancient Greek drama may well have been closer to opera than to a conventional play with only spoken dialogue. (Opera was devised in the seventeenth century with the purpose of imitating Greek drama.)

Greek drama preserved what are known as the dramatic unities, meaning that the action dramatized took place at a single location that could be depicted on stage without changing backdrops or similar devices and that it occurred in the amount of time required to act it. Dove abandoned this convention because it would have required long messenger speeches, reporting all action that cannot take place in the square in front of Oedipus's palace. If the play had to begin only a few hours before its ending (in medias res), it would also mean that events in the past could only be recalled by characters on stage. That kind of staging would mean that the events of the prologue would all have to be narrated, probably by Louis, who is the only one who witnessed everything. But as she often does in the play, Dove preferred cinematic models to dramatic ones and so showed everything directly, with long passages of time between scenes. Because Dove's audience knows everything Louis knows, they must realize the truth no later than Louis does and long before Augustus does, so Augustus's recognition cannot be the audience's and is anticlimactic.

Because of the different time lines of the two plays, *Oedipus Tyrannus* and *The Darker Face of the Earth* cannot be directly compared scene by scene. But Dove reproduces much of Sophocles's material. Oedipus is trying to find out the cause of the plague that is devastating Thebes. The oracle of Apollo at Delphi tells him it is because Thebes is harboring the murderer of Laius, who must be found and cast out. So Oedipus starts an investigation to find the killer. *Oedipus Tyrannus* is structured like a detective story or courtroom drama, in which Oedipus questions one witness after another and gets closer and closer to the truth until he knows. In Dove's play, the cause of Augustus's people's suffering is all too clear.

Just as Oedipus does, Augustus murders his father and has sex with his mother. Oedipus is made king and formally married to the queen after he saves the land of Thebes from the ravages of the monstrous Sphinx by solving her riddle, and the old king, Laius, is killed, as it seems, by robbers on the road. Augustus's role as king and savior is at most hinted at as he becomes a revolutionary leader. The newborn Oedipus is turned out by his parents to die in the wilderness because they had received a prophecy from Apollo (his life is saved by the pity of the shepherd entrusted with carrying out the exposure). Augustus, however, is condemned by his very nature. The physical damage the infant Augustus suffers leaves him unable to walk until he is three years old. Oedipus's ankles are pierced with a pin so that he can be carried like an animal carcass. The wound gives him his name, which means *swollen foot*. This is recalled also by the spurs (worn about the ankles) that Louis uses to wound Augustus.

The figure of Augustus's father is split in two as his supposed father, Louis, and his actual father, Hector. Augustus kills Louis intentionally, believing him to be his father and avenging his own abandonment and injury and the rape of his mother. Hector he kills unwillingly; he wants to save him but wants more to save the revolution. Oedipus kills Laius in a fight when they meet on a road and argue about which one should step aside so the other can pass.

Augustus's mother, Amalia, corresponds to Oedipus's mother and wife, Jocasta, but the two characters can hardly be more different. Amalia chafes under the yoke of patriarchy as much as Augustus does under the yoke of slavery and is transgressive and subversive, whereas Jocasta is hardly developed beyond being an ideal wife.

The third of Dove's characters who is directly comparable to one in Sophocles is Scylla, who stands in for Tiresias. Tiresias is a blind seer whom Oedipus consults in the hope that his supernatural powers can reveal who has killed Laius. It may at first seem strange to make the character into a woman, but as the Oedipus mythos developed in postclassical works, his role was more and more taken over by his daughter Manto, as in Seneca's *Oedipus*. Another consideration is that before he became a seer, Tiresias was cursed by Hera after he struck two copulating snakes (compare Hector's obsession with the evil in snakes) with a staff and was turned into a woman. When he is returned to his original gender, it is at the cost of his sight but also with the gift of prophetic powers. So there is ample justification for turning Tiresias into a woman in a modern version. However, Dove also intends Louis, with his constant peering into the universe through his telescope, to be a type of Tiresias. So she has separated the single Sophoclean character into two, as she does with Laius. Tiresias knows exactly who murders Laius but does not want to tell Oedipus. He instead tells Oedipus, as Scylla does Augustus, that there is an unclean poison seething inside him of which he is ignorant but that has doomed him. When Oedipus finally drags the truth out of Tiresias, he is taken aback, because he left his home in Corinth after he received a prophecy that he would kill his father and marry his mother. He decides to run as far away from them as possible. But because Oedipus is positive that his parents are safe in Corinth, he concludes that Tiresias is lying as part of some political plot and discounts his prophetic powers. This is echoed in Augustus's skepticism of Scylla.

Dove's purpose is not to translate or in a strict sense adapt *Oedipus Tyrannus*. Instead, she invokes the universal power of its incestuous myth, using it to call out the original sin of American history: slavery. America too was doomed to a bloody civil war by this flaw, just as Oedipus and Jocasta's sons, Polynices and Etecoles, killed each other on the battlefield of a civil war.

Source: Bradley A. Skeen, Critical Essay on *The Darker Face of the Earth*, in *Drama for Students*, Gale, Cengage Learning, 2016.

Theodora Carlisle

In the following excerpt, Carlisle explains how the character of Scylla reflects an African belief system.

Toussaint L'Ouverture, an influential leader in the Haitian slave revolution, inspires Augustus and the other slaves on the Jennings plantation.

(© Everett Historical / Shutterstock.com)

Scylla's vision is associated in the drama, and resonates with, three deep strengths: the earth, the feminine, and the spiritual values of an African belief system. Her conjurations are clearly earth-centered. She places earth objects—bones, twisted roots, a branch, a round white stone—on a makeshift altar and proceeds to invoke the spirits with words pointing to a physical reality: "The body moves through the world. / The mind rests in the body." And in her admonishments Scylla's message and warning are to value the earth and the body, especially as the conduit to the soul or spirit. She indicts Phebe with having "tried to make the earth / give up her dead." And she cautions her to "guard your footsteps; / they are your mark on the Earth." Later in confronting Augustus she attempts to reconnect him with the physical, saying, "You are in your skin wherever you go."

THE PROMINENCE OF THE YORUBA INVOCATION IN THE FUNERAL SCENE IS CRITICAL. WHEN SUCH WORDS HAVE BEEN SPOKEN BEFORE, THEY WERE HEARD AGAINST A NON-AFRICAN BACKGROUND, IN BROKEN AND DEBASED CIRCUMSTANCES."

In a like manner, Scylla is aligned with feminine forces. Augustus's birth has brought a curse "over the land." Scylla, able to feel the living baby's kick in her own womb, is one of those stricken directly. Later she explains that, as her womb "dried up," she gained her "powers," second-sight to fathom the curse. Indeed the power that "churned" in her at the time of the birth, and continues to churn in her, is a supplanted maternal power. Though Scylla is bent, harsh, and angry, the source of her rage is not vindictive. In laying charges against Augustus she locates that source, not in envy of him or in a will to dominate, but in her care for her people:

What will
these people do with your hate
after you free them—as you promise?

Thus Scylla exhibits two aspects. She is both frightening and irrational, gentle and protective. In this she may seem to reproduce a well-worn binary stereotype of maternal or feminine nature: the two sides of feminine power represented, for example, by the Furies/Eumenides of Aeschylus's *Oresteia*. Their unleashed maternal rage must be contained and soothed by law before civil society can thrive. Once the Furies have been tamed to become Eumenides, their gentle beneficence is recovered to protect and nurture the community. In *The Darker Face of the Earth* a related but nonetheless very different pattern of interaction is at work. Maternal fury will not be separated off and quieted for use. Compassion and rage are inseparable. Compassion is not a weakened, pale version of rage but the source and wellspring of both maternal fury and the prospering community.

The third element allied to Scylla is one closely related to the other two. By attempting to recreate the rites and rituals of the Yoruba spiritual tradition, Scylla provides a link for the slaves to their African roots. While Scylla herself has no command of an African language, she regularly threads Yoruba words and phrases into her incantations and laments. Her only direct tie to Africa is through Hector, who was captured and brought as a child from Africa. And although Hector himself has only a distant memory of the original homeland, he provides Scylla with an authentic connection to it. Fittingly, then, it is in Hector's funeral scene where Scylla's authority becomes most clearly manifest and, moreover, where the power of an Africanist vision and sensibility is revealed most clearly.

The scene begins with a procession of slaves, carrying the body of Hector, singing a version of an early African American Spiritual. The song itself is among those in the Spiritual tradition for which scholars have established links to African musical roots:

> Oh Deat' him is a little man,
> And him goes from do' to do',
> Him kill some souls and him cripple up,
> And him lef' some souls to pray.
> Do Lord, remember me,
> Do Lord, remember me
> I cry to the Lord as de year roll aroun',
> Lord, remember me.

Hector is mourned for his individual suffering and loss, especially since he has "no children, and his kinfolk / scattered around this world." But the scene as a whole is structured around the funeral ritual of "passing," in which "the youngest child of the deceased is passed under and over the coffin to signify the continuity of life." This ritual illustrates an "Afocentric orientation [which] conceptualizes time in a cyclic fashion...assum[ing] that the appearance of [a] phenomenon always changes, but that the underlying essence of [the] phenomenon remains basically unchanged" (Harris 157). In the funeral portrayed here, a larger sense of time with its cycles of birth and death does indeed enfold and absorb the pains of life. In this particular instance, the distinctly non-European customs and musical elements both emphasize and honor the community's African roots.

During the funeral the slaves join together to support and encourage each other, putting aside their differences in the harmony of community. Hector's bizarre life and apparent incoherence are reinterpreted and reclaimed in compassion:

> All those years folks thought
> he was crazy...
> when he was just sick at heart.

Augustus's entrance threatens to disrupt this communal harmony. Though one member of the group, Scipio, attempts to forgive his lack of participation and solidarity ("Each soul grieves in its own way"), a hostile encounter appears about to erupt. Scylla challenges Augustus with, "You believe you can cure the spirit / just by riling it." However, Augustus, sick at heart, refuses to rise to her challenge. And Scylla, seeming to sense the depth of his pain, moves from a spirit of bitterness to one of compassion. Thus, even in this potentially belligerent exchange, the harmony and unity of the funeral spirit mute their ordinary pitched animosity, and the two come closer to a meeting of the minds than at any other point in the drama. Scylla's next words lament the inevitability of Augustus's errors as much as they blame him:

> But do you know what's inside
> you, Augustus Newcastle?
> The seeds of the future; they'll have their way.

As the focus shifts back to the funeral, Scylla begins to weave Yoruba expressions into the lamentations:

> Who can I talk to about his journey?
> He stood tall, so they bent his back.
> He found love, so they ate his heart.
> Eshu Elewa ogo gbogbo! ...
> Eshu Elewa ogo gbogbo!
> Where are the old words now?
> Scattered by the wind.

Hearing these expressions the audience is, as it were, invited to read the scene informed by an Africanist perspective. In the 1994 version of the play, Yoruba phrases occur only in Scylla's conjuration scenes. By adding them to Hector's vocabulary, to Augustus's increasingly conflicted internal monologues, to the chanting choral motif of the "Dream Sequence" which begins Act II, and especially to the funeral scene, Dove reveals and validates an African context. This context was underscored in the OSF production by African elements referenced in Richard L. Hay's stage design and by a dancer in African-style mask woven into much of the action, variously suggesting the spirit world of the ancestors, a prophetic impulse, and the sense of holistic community. In addition, and most emphatically, the key positioning and the ongoing percussive pulse of the accompanying drummers proclaimed the African context.

The prominence of the Yoruba invocation in the funeral scene is critical. When such words have been spoken before, they were heard against a non-African background, in broken and debased circumstances. Scylla's rituals were scorned as mere "mumble jumble" and Hector's allusive, running train of consciousness was misunderstood as insanity. The funeral, on the other hand, gives the African words the dignity of context. This evocative context allows a "reader" to hear in them the African cultural values and strengths of the slave community, to see the beauty of the sensibilities and the originality of African culture in its own terms, and not to judge it against a European template of values. . . .

Source: Theodora Carlisle, "Reading the Scars: Rita Dove's *The Darker Face of the Earth*," in *African American Review*, Vol. 34, No. 1, 2000, pp. 143–45.

SOURCES

Bada, Valerie, "'Dramatising the Verse' or Versifying the Drama: Rita Dove's *The Darker Face of the Earth: A Verse Play*," in *Critical Voicings of Black Liberation: Resistance and Representations in the Americas*, edited by Kimberley L. Phlilips, LIT Verlag, 2003, pp. 93–104.

Dove, Rita, *The Darker Face of the Earth: A Verse Play in Fourteen Scenes*, Story Line Press, 1994.

———, *The Darker Face of the Earth: Completely Revised Second Edition*, Story Line Press, 1996.

Goff, Barbara, and Michael Simpson, *Crossroads in the Black Aegean: Oedipus, Antigone, and Dramas of the African Diaspora*, Oxford University Press, 2007, pp. 135–77.

Kennedy, Lionel H., and Thomas Parker, *An Official Report of the Trials of Sundry Negroes, Charged with an Attempt to Raise an Insurrection in the State of South-Carolina: Preceded by an Introduction and Narrative; and in an Appendix, a Report of the Trials of Four White Persons, on Indictments for Attempting to Excite the Slaves to Insurrection*, James R. Schenck, 1822, pp. 42–43, http://memory.loc.gov/cgi-bin/query/h?ammem/ llstbib:@field%28NUMBER + @band%28rbcmisc + lst01 01%29%29 (accessed June 20, 2015).

McDowell, Robert, "Language Is Not Enough," in *Conversations with Rita Dove*, edited by Earl G. Ingersoll, University Press of Mississippi, 2003, pp. 174–79.

Pereira, Malin, "Going Up Is a Place of Great Loneliness," in *Conversations with Rita Dove*, edited by Earl G. Ingersoll, University Press of Mississippi, 2003, pp. 148–73.

———, *Rita Dove's Cosmopolitanism*, University of Illinois Press, 2003, pp. 31–51.

Sophocles, *Oedipus the King*, translated by Anthony Burgess, University of Minnesota Press, 1978, pp. 1–100.

Steffen, Therese, *Crossing Color: Transcultural Space and Place in Rita's Dove's Poetry, Fiction, and Drama*, Oxford University Press, 2001, pp. 122–39.

Vendler, Helen, "Are These Poems to Remember?," in *New York Times Review of Books*, November 24, 2011, http://www.nybooks.com/articles/archives/2011/nov/24/ are-these-poems-remember/ (accessed August 4, 2015).

Westmore, Kevin J., *Black Dionysus: Greek Tragedy and African American Theater*, McFarland, 2003, pp. 120–31.

Wilson, Emily, "Black Oedipus," in *A Companion to Sophocles*, edited by Kirk Ormand, Blackwell, 2012, pp. 572–85.

FURTHER READING

Dove Rita, *Through the Ivory Gate*, Pantheon, 1992.
This semiautobiographical work is Dove's only novel. Its main character finds that as a black woman, she has little hope of advancing in the careers she has trained for as a cellist and actress and so returns to her hometown of Akron, where she takes a job as an artist in residence in the public school system, teaching puppetry. Much of the novel is devoted to recollection of her family life and history.

Egerton, Douglas R., *He Shall Go Out Free: The Lives of Denmark Vesey*, Rowman and Littlefield, 2004.
Egerton reconstructs the life of Vesey as a charismatic leader of the Charleston black community who found hope of freedom in Christian spirituality. But this assessment is balanced by a careful consideration of the evidence taken by Charleston authorities from black witnesses. The earliest phases of the investigation revealed what may have been an actual conspiracy based on testimony from blacks who spoke voluntarily, but Vesey was connected to the plot only later in the investigation and only by witnesses who were probably coerced by torture, a technique in which those being questioned agree with their interrogators' preconceptions rather than reveal the truth.

Jones, Ernest, *Hamlet and Oedipus*, Doubleday, 1949.
Jones presents the most developed form of an interpretation of *Hamlet* that originated in the earliest days of the psychoanalytical movement and that he explored in a series of previous publications. Its main idea is that although Shakespeare had no conscious intention of retelling the ancient Oedipus plays of Sophocles or Seneca, he is nevertheless telling

the same story, which derives from the universal experience of the Oedipus complex. *Hamlet* is explained as retelling the story of Oedipus in a more disguised form, in which Hamlet kills only his stepfather and denounces his mother for her sexual impurity in betraying his father. The anxiety occasioned by the repression is also offered as an explanation for Hamlet's hesitation in killing Claudius.

Seneca, *Oedipus*, edited and translated by A. J. Boyle, Oxford University Press, 2011.

Sophocles' *Oedipus Tyrannus* is often considered the authoritative dramatic version of the Oedipus myth, but many other dramas based on the story were written and performed in antiquity. Of these, the only other version to survive intact is by the Roman dramatist Seneca, active in the middle of the first century (and an important politician during the reign of the emperor Nero). Seneca's version could be described as baroque or gothic compared with Sophocles's, dwelling on the horrible and especially on the supernatural. Boyle's commentary is exceptionally full and thorough and is useful for every level of reader.

SUGGESTED SEARCH TERMS

Rita Dove

The Darker Face of the Earth AND Dove

Greek drama

Oedipus

Sophocles

shaman

plantation slavery

Denmark Vesey

Disgraced

AYAD AKHTAR

2013

In Ayad Akhtar's Pulitzer Prize–winning play *Disgraced*, a dinner party involving four successful New Yorkers becomes a tangled nightmare of deceit and anger. The four characters exemplify the harsh reality of the American dream: Amir, a powerful corporate lawyer who keeps his true identity as a Pakistani American a secret from his Jewish bosses; Emily, an idealistic artist whose naiveté is tied to her privilege as an attractive, white woman from a wealthy background; Isaac, a Jewish art curator who manipulates Amir's inner conflict to his own gain with Emily; and Jory, an African American lawyer who raised herself from poverty to become a partner at a law firm through an uncompromising belief in order over emotion. Before the end of the meal, the characters are engaged in a brutal debate that ends in catastrophe. *Disgraced* won the 2013 Pulitzer Prize for Drama and was nominated for the 2015 Tony Award for Best Play.

AUTHOR BIOGRAPHY

Ayad Akhtar, a Pakistani American, was born on October 28, 1970, on Staten Island, New York, and was raised in Milwaukee, Wisconsin. He studied theater at Brown University in Rhode Island before earning his master of arts degree in directing from the Graduate Film

Ayad Akhtar (© *Walter McBride / Getty Images*)

Program at Columbia University in New York City. An actor as well as a playwright, Akhtar studied acting under Jerzy Grotowski while living in Italy after the completion of his undergraduate degree. Akhtar cowrote and starred in the 2005 film *A War Within*, for which he was nominated for a 2006 Independent Spirit Award for best screenplay. He played Neel Kashkari in HBO's *Too Big to Fail* in 2011.

Disgraced, Akhtar's first major play, premiered at the American Theater Company in Chicago on January 30, 2012. The play went on to open in New York City at the Lincoln Center Theater/LCT3 on October 22, 2012. On May 22, 2013, *Disgraced* made its international premier at London's Bush Theatre. *Disgraced* was awarded the 2013 Pulitzer Prize for Drama and the 2013 Obie Award for playwriting.

Akhtar's second play, *The Invisible Hand* (2012), was awarded the 2015 Outer Critic's Circle Award. His third play, *The Who and the What*, premiered at La Jolla Playhouse in 2014. In addition to his plays, Akhtar has written a novel, *American Dervish*, published in 2012. *Kirkus Reviews*, *O Magazine*, *Shelf-Awareness*, and *Globe and Mail* each awarded *American*

Dervish the 2012 Best Book of the Year. The novel has been published in more than twenty languages.

PLOT SUMMARY

Scene 1

Disgraced is set in a beautiful apartment on New York's affluent Upper East Side. The year is 2011. Inside the apartment is a large marble fireplace, with a statue of Siva, one of the principal gods of Hinduism, displayed on the mantle. Emily, an attractive white woman in her early thirties, sits at the end of the dining room table, sketching a portrait of her husband. Her husband, Amir, is forty years old, of Pakistani heritage. He poses for his wife, wearing an expensive Italian suit jacket, a crisp button-up shirt, and his boxers. He asks if he should put pants on for the portrait.

Emily holds up the painting on which she is basing her portrait—Diego Velázquez's *Portrait of Juan de Pareja*—to remind him she is drawing him only from the waist up. Amir still finds it strange that she has chosen to represent him in the style of a painting of Velázquez's slave.

He was Velázquez's assistant, Emily says; Velázquez had freed Juan de Pareja from slavery. Emily is drawing in this style because she sees a connection—which Amir does not—between the story behind this painting and an incident that they had experienced at a restaurant the night before. A waiter had been rude to Amir; worse, in Emily's view, he ignored Amir, making assumptions about him because of his race. Amir lets the casual racism of the incident roll off him.

Emily explains that the incident reminded her of Velázquez's painting. Those who first saw it must have thought they were just looking at a portrait of an assistant (Amir interjects a reminder that Juan de Pareja was a slave), when in fact the portrait is one of Velázquez's most complex—more so than his portraits of European kings and queens.

She asks Amir to relax and says that no one will see this portrait, but Amir thinks she has gained ground in the New York art scene after her last show and that it is likely to gain some attention. His phone rings—a client calling. He answers. On the phone, he is harsh, forceful, and brutally honest. He tells the client he is not his therapist. Another call comes in, and Amir chastises the paralegal for missing a change in the contract that could have cost his client 850,000 dollars. He hangs up, drifting from his seat to look at the progress of Emily's sketch. Emily likes this ruthless way Amir has of handling business. They kiss.

Amir calls his boss, Mort, to update him on the situation. Emily and Amir fantasize about Amir's making partner at the firm. Emily asks whether Mort thinks Amir is Hindu, because of the statue of Siva he gave him. Amir avoids the question.

Abe, Amir's young nephew, stops by the apartment. Amir calls him by his birth name, Hussein. Abe, exasperated, explains how much easier his life has been since he changed it. When Amir tries to argue, Abe points out that Amir changed his last name to hide his Muslim heritage as well.

Abe wants Amir's legal help defending his friend, Imam Fareed, who was wrongfully jailed while collecting money for a mosque. Amir tells him that he is not a Muslim, and in any case, he is a corporate lawyer, not a public defender.

Abe tells him his grandmother and mother say that Amir is going through a phase of self-denial. Amir tells him the story of his first crush: a girl named Rivkah. Amir, who had been raised with values of anti-Semitism (prejudice against Jews), did not realize that Rivkah was a Jewish name. When Amir's mother discovered he was trading notes with a Jewish girl, she spat in Amir's face. The next day at school, when Rivkah confirmed to Amir that she was Jewish, he spat in her face in turn.

After Abe leaves, Emily reminds him that Imam Fareed only wants his own people around him after four months in jail. Amir tells her he does not want to talk about this, and Emily replies that they never do talk about it.

Scene 2

Two weeks later, Emily sits over her morning coffee, reading the newspaper aloud to Amir. Amir is quoted, speaking in support of Imam Fareed's case. He is panicked at the thought that the article implies he is representing Fareed. The paper even mentions the law firm at which he works. Emily does not see the problem. She is proud of the stand Amir took for Fareed's rights. They argue.

As Amir is leaving, Isaac arrives at the apartment to meet with Emily. Isaac is an art curator at the Whitney Museum. He is an attractive Jewish man of Amir's age. The tension between Amir and Emily runs high as he leaves. Isaac jokes that Amir will still get to the firm before his wife, who works as a lawyer there as well.

Left alone with Emily, Isaac admits that he was wrong about his first impression of Emily's work. At first, he had told her she had no right to use Islamic forms as a white woman. He now sees the merit of her work, though he tells her to be prepared for backlash. Some will accuse her of Orientalism—a fetishistic appropriation of Eastern culture—especially considering she is married to Amir. Emily defends her art forcefully, saying it is ludicrous to ignore the influence of the Islamic tradition while embracing the Greeks and Romans. Isaac is impressed.

Scene 3

Three months later, in the fall, Amir stands on the terrace, drinking. Suddenly he smashes the glass on the ground. Still agitated, he goes inside to make himself another drink. Emily arrives, her arms full of groceries. She was getting supplies for that night; Amir had forgotten they are hosting a dinner party, with Isaac and his wife, Jory, as their guests.

Amir apologizes for forgetting, telling her that two of the partners at the law firm walked into his office today and asked where his father was born. They found out that he had misrepresented himself as Indian when in fact his father was born in Pakistan. They also discovered that his last name was Abdullah before he had it changed to Kapoor. Mort is no longer answering his phone calls.

Jory and Isaac arrive much earlier than expected. Emily rushes to the bedroom to get dressed, leaving Amir to greet them. Jory is an African American woman in her late thirties. Jory and Amir talk about work companionably over their drinks, and Amir suggests they break away from the firm and start their own.

Isaac tells Emily that her work will be featured in his newest show at the Whitney: *Impossible Heroes*. Emily is overjoyed. Everyone gives their congratulations. Isaac mentions he is considering using Emily's portrait of Amir. Amir, uncomfortable, says he prefers Emily's landscapes.

Emily says that Amir likes her landscapes best because they have nothing to do with Islam. Isaac defends her work: "A young Western painter drawing on Islamic representation? Not *ironically*? But in *service*? It's an unusual and remarkable statement." They toast to her career.

Jory asks where in India the last name "Kapoor" originates. Amir tells her that the partners asked him the same question today. Emily helps recover from the awkward silence that follows by suggesting the name is Punjabi in origin. Isaac says he is on his way to India in a few days for a studio visit. He mentions he is terrified of flying, and the conversation settles on heightened airport security. Jory asks Amir what it is like for him at the airport. After another awkward pause, Amir admits he volunteers himself to be searched, since he will be racially profiled anyway. Emily finds this behavior extremely passive-aggressive, but Jory admires him for it.

Amir says the next terrorist attack will come from a guy who looks like him. Emily says the next attack will come from a white man with a gun. "And pointing it at a guy that looks like me," Amir adds.

Isaac suggests that the act of giving oneself up to security would seem to justify others' suspicions. Amir asks whether he is suspicious about Middle Easterners. Isaac hesitates, and Amir says he does not blame him. Isaac is bewildered by this stance.

Emily gets a phone call from Abe. Amir admits he had ignored earlier calls from Abe. Emily ignores his call as well. She and Jory go into the kitchen, as dinner is almost ready.

Isaac tries to apologize to Amir, but Amir tells him it is fine. Everyone knows that he and his wife do not agree on the subject of Islam. He does not think art has much to do with the religion. In fact, the Quran states that angels will not enter a house where there are pictures. Emily and Jory return with the salads and join the debate in progress. Amir believes that because it was a religion founded in the desert, Islam is about accepting suffering as a way of life. Isaac points out that the Jewish faith was founded in the desert as well but does not have that attitude. Amir counters that Jewish people used reason and negotiation in order to find a better way to survive in the desert, while Muslims simply submitted. The definition of the world *Islam* is "submission."

Isaac says the problem is not with Islam but with Islamo-facism. The women interrupt, insisting they sit down and eat. Amir says Isaac cannot have an opinion of Islam if he has not read the Quran.

They all dig in to the salad. Isaac compliments the salad, and Emily answers that she found the recipe in Spain. All four at the table have been to Barcelona. Isaac says he does not understand why Amir believes Muslims are so different when he is so similar to Isaac—he would have never known Amir was a Muslim without that article about Fareed's trial.

Amir says he is not a Muslim, he is an apostate—one who has renounced his religion. He says that, according to the Quran, he could be put to death for that offense. Emily says he has not read that part closely enough, proving him wrong. Amir says that wife beating is encouraged. Emily says the translation is unclear. Jory says when given the choice between justice and order, she chooses order. Emily says she would choose justice every time.

After Isaac claims to know many intelligent Muslim women who choose to wear the veil for modesty, Amir says Isaac does not understand the nuances of Islam because he was not raised in the religion. Isaac says he understands that Amir is full of self-loathing toward his Muslim heritage.

Jory shoots him a glare. Amir ignores the barb, continuing to explain that the Taliban are attempting to re-create the world in the Quran's image. Emily attempts to end the conversation, but Amir does not stop. He explains that to be Muslim is to feel pride in the purity of emotion in those willing to act out those beliefs.

Isaac asks whether Amir felt pride on learning of the terrorist attacks of September 11, 2001. Amir, after hesitating, says yes. The table is in an uproar. Emily says he does not mean that. Jory asks what about the attacks, exactly, made Amir proud.

"That we were finally winning," Amir says and admits he forgot which "we" he belonged to at the time. He says it was a tribal feeling, a result of his upbringing. Emily has had enough; she disappears into the kitchen.

After a long, uncomfortable silence at the dining room table, Amir attempts to make amends by comparing his emotions to those Isaac must feel toward Israel as a Jewish man.

Isaac says he does not support Israel. Amir asks how he feels when he hears threats against Israel. Isaac says he is outraged by the violence in the Middle East, like most people. Amir says that some people like hearing those threats; upon prompting by Isaac, Amir admits that he sometimes is one of those people.

Desperate to change the subject, Emily reminds Amir that they are supposed to be celebrating. Amir ignores her. He says that the feeling he gets, the blush of pride, is wrong, and it comes from being raised Muslim.

Isaac says the pride comes from Amir alone, that Islam does not own fundamentalism any more than any other religion in the world and that the generalizations Amir makes so easily are frightening.

Jory tells Isaac to stop arguing, and he does. Amir calls him naïve. Emily tells him to come with her into the kitchen. Left alone at the table, Jory asks why Isaac keeps picking fights with Amir. Isaac calls Amir a closet jihadist. Jory says Amir is not acting like himself, and wonders if he knows her secret. She decides she needs to tell him, that he deserves to hear it from her.

Amir bursts from the kitchen door, grabbing his coat in preparation to leave. He says he is going out to get champagne, so that they can celebrate Emily's involvement in the art show. Jory grabs her coat to go with him to the store.

As soon as they leave, Emily turns on Isaac, and they argue: it becomes clear that they had been romantically involved. Isaac suspects her of sleeping with him only to get into the art show, and she retorts that if that is the reason she got in, she does not want to be included. Twice he tries to touch her; she pulls away quickly the first time, but more slowly the next time.

Isaac asks whether Amir knows about Jory's promotion to partner. Emily is shocked. Isaac says Amir was passed over because of his association with Fareed, which Isaac considers a foolish decision. Emily says he did it for her sake.

Isaac tells her he is in love with her and leans in to kiss her. Emily holds still. Jory enters. She takes in the scene in front of her and demands an explanation. Amir enters behind her in a rage, hurt that Jory took so long to tell him about her promotion. Jory, ignoring him, asks Emily bluntly if she is having an affair with Isaac.

Isaac and Emily both deny it, but Jory tells Amir she saw them kissing.

Amir accuses Jory of trying to destroy his marriage as well as his career, and he spits in Isaac's face and tells Jory to get out. She leaves, but not before telling Amir that Mort does not trust him.

Alone, Amir asks Emily if she is sleeping with Isaac. She admits it happened once, but she is disgusted by her behavior. He hits her in the face, multiple times, viciously, just as someone starts to knock at the front door. When the knocking goes unanswered, the door opens slowly to reveal Abe, who takes in the scene in front of him in shock.

Scene 4

Six months later, in the spring of 2012, the apartment is nearly empty except for moving boxes. Emily's paintings are absent, except for a small, covered canvas leaning against the wall. Amir, alone, is packing. He answers a knock at the door to find Emily and Abe, who is now dressed in muted, conservative colors and a Muslim skullcap. Abe cannot meet Amir's eyes. Emily explains to Amir that Abe was stopped by the FBI after a friend he was with made a scene, telling a waitress who asked if they were Muslims that the Americans created al-Qaeda. His friend Tariq lost his patience with her questions and told her that America deserved what happened. The police arrived and took Abe and Tariq to the station, where two men from the FBI were waiting.

Emily attempts to leave, but Abe begs her to stay. Reluctantly, she agrees, though she goes to the kitchen rather than remain in the room. Amir tells Abe that he needs to remember that the world is not neutral toward him. Abe suggests that Amir should spend more time with his own people, but Amir says he will get deported if he remains so careless. Abe reveals that he knows Amir was fired, and he knows what Amir did to Emily. He says Amir has forgotten who he is. Amir, disbelieving, reminds Abe that he has changed his name to Abe Jensen to blend in to American society. Abe says he changed his name back, but Amir is unimpressed.

Abe says Amir will always turn on his own people and that those outside his community do not respect him more for it. They think that he hates himself, and Abe thinks they are right. Abe gains steam, saying that it is pointless to try to live by society's rules. He believes Muslims who attempt to assimilate with non-Muslim cultures have disgraced Islam and that it is the destiny of Muslims to take the world back. Emily enters the room, and Abe, realizing that she has been listening, leaves abruptly.

Amir asks Emily whether she has read his letters. He got the painting from her. Emily says she did not want to throw it out. Amir says he wants Emily to get their apartment in the divorce, but Emily does not want it. Amir says he finally understands her art, but Emily says her art was naïve. Emily says she played a role in what happened between them, that she was selfish. Amir says no; he wants Emily to be proud of him and to be proud that she was with him. Emily asks him to stop writing to her. She leaves. Amir uncovers the painting—Emily's portrait of him—and stares searchingly at the canvas.

CHARACTERS

Jory Brathwaite

Jory, an African American woman in her late thirties, is the newest partner at Leibowitz, Bernstein, and Harris. She is Isaac's wife. She and Amir get along well at the office, though she does not tell Amir about her promotion right away because she knows he had also wanted the job. Jory attributes her success to her ability to value order over justice. She is straightforward with her opinions and emotions. When she discovers her husband kissing Emily, she confronts them both immediately. She leaves the dinner party after telling Amir that no one trusts him at the office. Their friendship is ruined by the revelation that she has gotten the promotion instead of him.

Imam Fareed

Fareed is a friend of Abe's who is wrongfully in jail awaiting trial for collecting money for a terrorist organization. In fact, Fareed was collecting money for a mosque. Abe begs Amir to appear in court in support of Fareed. It is Amir's first instinct to avoid association with a suspected terrorist, but Emily encourages him to support Fareed. He appears at his trial and is quoted by the newspaper making a passionate argument in Fareed's defense. This leads to his falling out at the law firm where he works.

Emily Hughes-Kapoor

Emily is a painter who incorporates Islamic tile patterns and architectural elements into her work. She is married to Amir, with whom she disagrees on the nature of the Muslim religion. Emily and Isaac have an affair in London while attending an art fair. She is very excited and happy to learn that she will be included in Isaac's upcoming show at a prominent art gallery, though she is upset by Isaac's argumentative behavior toward her husband during their dinner party. After Jory catches Isaac and Emily embracing, Emily admits her infidelity to Amir. He beats her and is caught in the act by Abe. Emily does not press charges against Amir, though they do divorce. Emily does not want the apartment and gives the portrait she painted of Amir to him rather than throw it out.

Isaac

Isaac is a forty-year-old art curator at the Whitney Museum. He is an attractive Jewish man who is perplexed by Emily's art. He feels at first that she has no place as a white woman in using Islamic forms, but she convinces him that Islamic art is like Greek or Roman art in that it is ancient and part of humanity's shared history. Isaac is married to Jory. He cheats on his wife with Emily and then adds Emily to his art show at the Whitney. At the dinner party, Isaac provokes Amir by drawing him into arguments throughout the night. When he is left alone with Emily he tells her he loves her and tries to kiss her. Jory catches them, revealing the affair.

Abe Jensen

Abe Jensen is Amir's twenty-two-year-old nephew, the son of his sister. Abe is a practicing Muslim, like the rest of Amir's family. He turns to Amir for help after his friend, Imam Fareed, is wrongfully imprisoned. When Abe first appears, he is dressed in the modern fashion of a young American and has recently changed his name from Hussein to Abe to escape discrimination. He is idealistic and indefatigable, calling Emily when Amir ignores his calls. He witnesses the aftermath of the disastrous dinner party, walking in the apartment to find Emily bleeding after Amir has beaten her. The next time Abe appears, he has changed his name back to Hussein and dresses in a Muslim skullcap and muted colors. The FBI interrogates him after he and a friend cause a scene at a Starbucks. He is at risk for deportation.

However, Abe no longer wants Amir's help and has trouble looking him in the eye.

José

José is Emily's ex-boyfriend, a black Spanish man who speaks little English.

Amir Kapoor

Amir is a successful corporate lawyer at Leibowitz, Bernstein, and Harris. He is married to Emily. He changed his last name from Abdullah to Kapoor in order to avoid discrimination against Arab Americans. At the office, he pretends to be an Indian American. He was brought up in a strict Muslim household but has renounced his religion. Amir is deeply troubled by his Muslim heritage and is quick to make negative generalizations about the religion and its practitioners. Both Isaac and Abe accuse him of hating himself. Once Amir is quoted in defense of Imam Fareed, the partners at the law firm begin to realize he has lied about his background. He is eventually fired after bursting out in tears during a meeting. Amir struggles with his own aggressive nature but attributes it to his Muslim upbringing. At the dinner party, already on edge because of the discovery of his heritage at work, Amir argues with Isaac over what it means to be Muslim and the nature of Islam, as well as his own rejection of the religion. Amir beats Emily after she admits to her affair, acting out one of the passages he finds most offensive in the Quran. After the dinner party, Amir has lost Jory as a friend, Abe's respect, and Emily. He is left staring at Emily's portrait of him, lost as to his own identity.

Hussein Malik

See Abe Jensen

Mort

Mort is Amir's boss, who gave Amir a Siva statue as a present, thinking he was Hindu. Mort and Amir are close until the newspaper article about Fareed is published. Mort stops taking Amir's calls afterward. Jory reveals that Mort is retiring and Jory will be taking on his caseload, not Amir.

Rivkah

Rivkah is Amir's first love. She is a pretty classmate from sixth grade with whom he shared his first kiss. Amir's mother discovers a love note Rivkah has written to Amir and tells her son she will not allow him to become involved with a Jewish girl. Amir does not fully understand why his mother disapproves of Jewish people, so he simply tries to deny that she is Jewish. His mother spits in his face. The next day at school, when Rivkah approaches to give Amir another note, Amir tells her she has a Jewish name. When Rivkah states that she is Jewish, Amir spits in her face.

Steven

Steven is a partner at the law firm where Jory and Amir work. Jory tells Amir that Steven, not Mort, holds the real power at the firm. Steven asks Amir about his heritage on the day of the dinner party, revealing that the firm has discovered Amir's deception.

Tariq

Tariq is Abe's friend. After an argument with a waitress, he shouts inside a Starbucks that the United States deserved what it got in the terrorist attacks, and it deserved what it would get in the future. As a result, he and Abe are arrested and taken to the police station, where two FBI agents are waiting to interrogate them.

THEMES

Anger

Ten years after the 9/11 terrorist attacks, Amir is still aware of the target on his back as a Pakistani American and former Muslim. In the play's opening scene, Amir and Emily have just had an encounter with a racist waiter, Emily is painting a portrait of Amir based on a slave, and Amir's family—Emily and Abe—are begging him to represent in court a man accused of fund raising for an Islamic extremist organization. Amir feels safer falsifying his identity than admitting his background at work, despite his professionalism, his years of hard work, and his good standing with the firm. Amir, an American success story, is associated every day with 9/11, terrorism, and radical Islam. The constant pressure of living in an Islamophobic society has turned Amir sour, passive-aggressive, and angry. His anger is internalized, taking the form of self-hatred, for most of the play. Viewed with suspicion by the world around him ("duplicitous," as Jory describes him), he knows that acting out his anger will only prove

TOPICS FOR FURTHER STUDY

- Research Islamic art and architecture online. Create a blog featuring five works of Islamic art or architecture that you admire. Include photos, background information about the work, and where it can be found. Also choose an artistic or architectural term relevant to each of the works to define (for example, *arabesque*, *symmetry*, or *minaret*). Free blog space is available at http://www.blogspot.com.

- Read Marina Budhos's young-adult novel *Ask Me No Questions* (2007) about a teen-aged Muslim girl living in New York City as an undocumented alien. Compare and contrast Nadra's life and Amir's. How does some Americans' fear or hatred of Muslim people following the terrorist attacks of September 11, 2001, affect their lives? What struggles are unique to their individual situations? Organize your thoughts into a comparative essay.

- In a small group, perform a two- to five-minute selection from *Disgraced*, with one member of the group acting as director.

Film and edit the video as a group, using the tools found on http://www.edpuzzle.com.

- Write an additional scene for *Disgraced* that takes place in the months between scene 3 and scene 4, illustrating one of the results of the dinner party. For example, you could chose to write a scene showing Emily's decision to move out, Amir's last day at the law office, Abe's changing personal style, or a scene involving Isaac and Jory's relationship. Use your imagination and remember to include stage directions as well as dialogue.

- Choose a character other than Amir who plays a role in the climactic dinner party to examine more closely. What is that person's attitude at the beginning of the scene? What topics of conversation are of the most interest? How does this person react to the growing tension, and does he or she encourage the tension or discourage it? What has changed for this person by the end of the scene? Summarize your observations in a brief essay.

---

those who judge him right. Instead, he gives in to the outside pressures—posing as a peaceful Hindu, giving himself up to airport security—while allowing the anger he represses to eat away at him from the inside out. As a powerful American man, he believes he should be enjoying a well-earned life of luxury without dragging the weight of his cultural identity behind him. But in a climate of suspicion and fear, he is not free. He cannot take on a charity case for his nephew without being thought to be a terrorist sympathizer, just as Fareed cannot collect money for a mosque without being jailed for four months on vague charges, just as Tariq cannot throw a fit in a Starbucks without being interrogated afterward by the FBI. The Muslim characters of *Disgraced* are chained to their religious identity in

the eyes of society, but any anger that they express is harshly punished.

Identity

Amir's struggle with identity drives the play from its first moments to the final curtain. Born in Pakistan and raised in a proud Muslim family, Amir lives an affluent American lifestyle as a vocal critic of Islam. Yet he remembers the lessons his mother taught him, such as the story of his first crush on a Jewish girl named Rivkah. As a child, he spit in the girl's face, parroting his mother's hatred. As an adult, he pretends to be an Indian at work to avoid upsetting the Jewish partners with the truth of his heritage. There is no balance to Amir's identity. His childhood instruction tugs him in one

The action takes place in an apartment in New York's Upper East Side. *(© Marco Rubino | Shutterstock.com)*

direction, and his fierce adult determination tugs him in another direction, creating a tangle of confused emotions: anger, shame, pride, and pain. This war within Amir is no secret. His family, his wife, even his coworkers and acquaintances share their opinions of who he is and how he should act. To Emily, Amir is a Muslim "in a way that's unique." Amir rejects this assessment at once. Amir's mother claims that his rejection of Islam is a phase, a theory of Amir's behavior that she passed on to Amir's sister, who in turn teaches it to Abe. To Isaac, Amir is a "closet jihadist," implying he is potentially violent, an extremist.

Abe tells Amir, in the final scene: "You'll always turn on your own people. You think it makes these people like you more when you do that? They don't. They just think you hate yourself. And they're right!" Though Amir begins the play a confident, powerful lawyer with the apartment to match, trouble takes the form of the portrait Emily makes of him, based on Veláz-quez's freed slave, Juan de Pareja. Amir finds the connection that Emily sees between himself and the slave disturbing, just as he later changes the

subject when she attempts to discuss his Muslim background. Amir wants to be seen as a successful American man, not a Muslim, not an underdog, and not a victim. He has achieved the American dream, an immigrant who has risen to the top of his field, but the political environment after 9/11 conspires to keep his Middle Eastern and Islamic heritage front and center, a red hot issue preventing anyone—but especially Amir himself—from forgetting the past that he so disdains. While the other characters have complex views of Islam, none are as full of contradictions, memories, and bewildered emotions as Amir's, so much so that Islam is tied directly to Amir's identity. The repression of that identity leads directly to his collapse.

STYLE

Climax

The climax of a work of literature is the point of highest tension or a decisive moment, and it occurs at the peak of the rising action, usually near the end of a story. For example, the climax of *Disgraced* is the argument at the conclusion of the dinner party that ends in Amir's beating Emily. The climax is the result of the building tensions throughout the night: Amir's fear of losing his job over falsifying his background, Jory's secret promotion, and Isaac and Emily's affair. The climax brings all secrets into the open and reveals what the characters truly think of one another. Akhtar engineers the especially shocking climax of *Disgraced* through the progressively antagonistic dinner conversation between Amir and Isaac, building tension as both Emily and Jory try and fail to end the discussion. The party separates in an attempt to cool hot heads, but Jory's discovery of the affair between Emily and Isaac brings the climax crashing down to disastrous conclusion.

Denouement

Denouement is a French term literally meaning "untying." In a work of literature, the denouement is the resolution or conclusion of a story in which the results of the climax are described, plots are resolved, and characters are shown to have changed for the better or worse. Scene 4 makes up the denouement of *Disgraced*. Taking place six months after the dinner party, the scene shows the results of the actions of the four characters that night. The denouement mainly concerns the dissolution of Amir and Emily's relationship, leaving Amir staring at the portrait that began the play as if questioning his identity. In this way, the denouement finalizes the plot, while placing an emphasis on the ways in which the characters have changed as a result of the climax.

HISTORICAL CONTEXT

September Eleventh

In the heat of their argument at the dinner party, Isaac asks Amir if he felt pride on September 11. *Disgraced* deals both directly and indirectly with the experience of Middle Eastern Americans in the post-9/11 environment. On the morning of September 11, 2001, nineteen members of the Islamic extremist group al-Qaeda carried out terrorist attacks on the World Trade Center in downtown Manhattan and the Pentagon in Arlington, Virginia, killing more than three thousand people. The attacks, referred to simply as 9/11 or September 11, involved four airliners, three of which the terrorists hijacked and crashed into their targets: the north and south Twin Towers, which collapsed from the resulting damage, and the Pentagon. Though the fourth airliner was similarly hijacked and turned off course toward an unknown target on the Eastern Seaboard, the passengers successfully revolted, crashing the plane into a field in Pennsylvania.

Fifteen of the terrorists were from Saudi Arabia, two from the United Arab Emirates, and one each from Lebanon and Egypt. They carried knives and box cutters through airport security and then used these weapons to take over the planes. The attack was symbolic, as the World Trade Center, with its massive twin skyscrapers, represented the height of American global power. As a result of the attack, the "war on terror" was launched, seeking to wipe out terrorist cells in the Middle East, as well as a manhunt for al-Qaeda's leader, Osama bin Laden. A defining moment in the history of the United States, September 11 changed the country both drastically and instantaneously. Martin Kettle writes in the British newspaper *Guardian*, "I covered American politics for the *Guardian* for four years from 1997. I moved back to Britain towards the end of August 2001. Three weeks later, the country I had lived in ceased to exist."

Islam and Islamophobia Post-9/11

No group felt the changes following the September 11 terrorist attacks more keenly than Middle Eastern Americans. Muslims and people who were perceived as being Muslim fell victim to suspicion, prejudice, and violence simply as a result of their superficial resemblance to the members of al-Qaeda. In reality, Islam is the second-largest religion in the world, with more than a billion followers. Based on the teachings of the prophet Muhammad, passed down in the Quran (alternately spelled Qur'an or Koran), the religion is monotheistic, with the worship of God as its centerpiece. Like Christianity and Hinduism, Islam is divided into denominations, and those denominations are further divided. Islamic extremists make up a small percentage of the much larger Muslim population.

Islamophobia, an irrational fear and hatred of Muslims, spread across the United States overnight following the attacks. In 2001, hate crimes against Muslims increased 1,700 percent from the previous year. Fueled by their

Lawyer Amir has become involved in a case surrounding an imam accused of financing terrorist groups.
(© paul prescott | Shutterstock.com)

ignorance concerning the differences between the religion of Islam and Islamic extremism, Islamophobic individuals tend to view all Muslims as dangerous and anti-American. Islamophobia appears throughout *Disgraced*, from the wrongful imprisonment of Imam Fareed, whose collections for a new mosque are mistaken for collections for a terrorist organization, to Amir's experience with heightened airport security.

CRITICAL OVERVIEW

Disgraced won the 2013 Pulitzer Prize for Drama, and the Broadway production was nominated in 2015 for the Tony Award for Best Play. *Disgraced* has been widely praised by critics since its debut in 2012. Stefanie Cohen, in her interview of Akhtar for the *Wall Street Journal*, calls him "the de facto voice of the American Muslim in theater."

Critics have been particularly enamored of the contrast between the sophisticated dinner party setting and the brutal behavior of those seated at the table. The *New Yorker* calls *Disgraced* a "smart, sharp-edged play . . . cocktail hour gone bananas." In his interview of Akhtar for *PBS NewsHour*, Jeffrey Brown praises the play's emotional range, which keeps the audience uncomfortable but engaged: "There's plenty of humor in *Disgraced*, but quite a bit more pain, as Amir's world and identity comes undone." Stephen Moss characterizes Amir's battle in his interview with Akhtar for the *Guardian*: "American v. Asian, Muslim v. secularist, passive observer of injustice v. activist."

Charles Isherwood, in a review for the *New York Times*, "Beware Dinner Talk on Identity and Islam," admires the social depth of the play's themes. He calls it "a continuously engaging, vitally engaged play about thorny questions of identity and religion in the contemporary world . . . [and] the incendiary topic of how radical Islam and the terrorism it inspires have affected the public discourse."

The play has seen successful runs in Chicago, New York, and London. In a time when issues of terrorism and Islamic extremism are consistently in the news, *Disgraced* vividly illustrates the effects of fear, anger, and discrimination. Writing for *Variety*, Marilyn Stasio describes *Disgraced* as "an intellectually engaging play on a politically provocative topic."

CRITICISM

Amy L. Miller

Miller is a graduate of the University of Cincinnati, and she currently resides in New Orleans, Louisiana. In the following essay, she examines how the four participants in the catastrophic dinner party of Ayad Akhtar's Disgraced *represent the American social landscape at both its best and its worst.*

Akhtar's *Disgraced* breaks the cardinal rule of polite conversation. As Isherwood reminds us: "Everyone has been told that politics and religion are two subjects that should be off limits at social gatherings." The play, with its brutal conclusion, illustrates why this rule was put into place but not before expertly challenging stereotypes, prejudices, and phobias, as well as working diligently to prod uncomfortable subjects from out of the shadows of our collective consciousness and into the light. As the pressure mounts when conversation turns from the inappropriate to the taboo and finally to the inexcusable, the explosive climax should come as no surprise, but it is still shocking. The sheer magnitude of the violence, betrayal, and hatred exposed between Amir, Emily, Jory, and Isaac is as frightening as it is representative of the larger social climate in America. The table of four people represents the twenty-first-century American dream in all its promise: magnificent opportunity blind to race, to gender, to religion, to class. This is not the American dream of the twentieth century—that one can come from nothing and achieve stability and safety through a bootstraps existence—but the American dream of the twenty-first—that one can make the leap from nothingness to outlandish success (exemplified in the national folklore by professional athletes from humble backgrounds, movie stars with difficult childhoods, or pop music icons from small towns). They are each—white, black, brown, Muslim, Jew, atheist, male, and

> THE SHEER MAGNITUDE OF THE VIOLENCE, BETRAYAL, AND HATRED EXPOSED BETWEEN AMIR, EMILY, JORY, AND ISAAC IS AS FRIGHTENING AS IT IS REPRESENTATIVE OF THE LARGER SOCIAL CLIMATE IN AMERICA."

female—brilliantly successful people. Well read, impeccably dressed, skilled conversationalists with sophisticated palates for fennel, Spanish wine, and liver mousse, yet their collapse is as vicious as any shown on a daytime talk show. Stasio writes that *Disgraced* "is constructed like a house of cards, its highly civilized human relationships in perfect harmony until someone breaks out of character and throws them all off balance." Though each character brings a dangerous imbalance to the table, it is Amir who brings the house down.

Unlike the others, Amir's version of the American dream has been tainted by a part of his identity that he actively fights. As a counterexample, Jory is an African American from an impoverished neighborhood. While she cannot hide her race, she could hide her roots in the ghetto, but instead she chooses to draw strength and wisdom from the adversity she has overcome. Amir, who is Pakistani American, hides in plain sight as an Indian American to avoid discrimination at work. Though he was raised Muslim, he accepts a statue of the Hindu god Siva from his boss. Appropriately, Siva is also known as "the destroyer," and he watches over the play's action from the living room mantelpiece. In every way that Jory is grounded in her identity, Amir struggles. Her self-reliant attitude coupled with her devotion to order over the more humanistic and thus much messier ideal of justice is rewarded with a promotion to partner, while Amir's cover-up of his identity coupled with his support of Imam Fareed leads the partners at the law firm to lose faith in him. His waffling between shame and pride at both his American lifestyle and his Muslim upbringing is sometimes mystifying, such as his description of himself as "one of those lapsed Muslims . . . alongside your beautiful white

WHAT DO I READ NEXT?

- Banned in Saudi Arabia, Abdelrahman Munif's *Cities of Salt* (1987) describes the disastrous results following America's discovery of oil in a small village in an unnamed country in the Middle East.

- In *American Dervish* (2012), Akhtar's first novel, the life of Hayat Shah, a typical American teenager, is changed forever when he falls for Mina, his mother's friend from Pakistan. Mina teaches Hayat about Islam, opening up a brilliant new world for him where before there had been only video games and school. But when Mina begins to date a new man, Hayat acts out on his heartbreak, with a disastrous result.

- In Mohsin Hamid's novel *The Reluctant Fundamentalist* (2007), Changez is living a charmed life in America, a Princeton graduate with a high-status job at a firm in Manhattan. But as he watches the Twin Towers collapsing on September 11, he is surprised to find himself smiling. His life overturned, Changez returns home to Pakistan to discover who he is and what he has become.

- *American Islam: The Struggle for the Soul of a Religion*, by Paul M. Barrett (2007), dispels the myths and assumptions surrounding the six million Muslims living in the United States by giving an intimate, journalistic account of seven American Muslim lives.

- *Brick Lane*, by Monica Ali (2003), tells the story of Nazneen, a Bangladeshi child bride brought by her new husband to live in London. Nazneen finds her own voice so many miles from the familiarity of home amidst the chaos following the September 11 terrorist attacks and their wide-reaching effects in England.

- In Michael Muhammad Knight's *The Taqwacores* (2004) a group of young Muslims in Buffalo, New York, merge Islam and punk rock in their run-down apartment. Taking their name from the Arabic word for a "consciousness of the divine," *taqwa*, the Taqwacores fuse riotous parties with earnest worship.

- Rajaa Alsanea's novel *Girls of Riyadh* (2005) features four wealthy Saudi Arabian women who must navigate the treacherous gap between their modern lives and the harsh restrictions on women in their society.

- *Does My Head Look Big in This?*, by Randa Abdel-Fattah (2005), is a young-adult novel about sixteen-year-old Amal's decision to wear the hijab and the way her life changes as a result of her devotion to her religion.

- *Qur'an and Woman: Rereading the Sacred Text from a Woman's Perspective*, by Amina Wadud (1999), provides the first published interpretation of the Qur'an written by a woman, with a specific focus on those passages that have been used to dictate what is proper feminine behavior under Islamic laws.

- *The Good Muslim*, by Tahmima Anam (2011), features an irreconcilable feud between a brother and sister over religious fundamentalism, set in the decade following a civil war in Bangladesh.

American wife... seeing folks in the Middle East dying for values you were taught were purer— and stricter... you can't help but feel just a little bit of pride." But this conflicted dual identity is meant to mystify those outside it, a method

Akhtar uses to help his audience understand just how complex the Middle Eastern American identity became following 9/11. Akhtar described his own experience in an interview with Moss: "Post-9/11, folks who looked like me became very visible.... Life changed.... Like Amir, the fact of being Muslim, whether religious or cultural, became a significant fact that could not be avoided." Amir is an ex-Muslim working to forget his mother's harsh lessons, and his Muslim heritage is exactly what he would like to avoid most, yet the insidious Islamophobia of American culture after 9/11 reminds him daily that he cannot sever his connection to Islam any more than Jory can stop being identified as African American.

Feeling the sting of exclusion following his coworkers' discovery that he is not Indian but Pakistani, Amir enters the dinner party in an emotionally unstable state. He is not the only character whose dishonesty will be revealed. Isherwood writes that the dinner scene "feels at times like observing a hotly contested game of Twister.... Someone is going to lose his or her balance and take a hard fall. You're just not sure who it's going to be."

Emily, who is concealing her affair with Isaac, has been protected by her wealth and beauty from the harsher realities of the world. Intelligent enough to know this, she makes an effort to understand where Amir is coming from with his rejection of Islam. But, born surrounded by beauty, she instinctively seeks beauty, and she finds it in the stunning geometry of Islamic art. Her privilege as a white woman is revealed in small details. She drinks port—a desert wine— before dinner, explaining herself with a charming, "I know I'm strange. I just love it so much...." This is a casual flouting of the social rules that someone born into less privilege (Jory, for example) would have had to learn while climbing society's ladder. It is no surprise, then, that it is Jory who questions Emily's drink of choice, indirectly illustrating the flaws inherent in the American dream. Some are born directly into it, some must work for it, and for some it is forever unattainable.

Isaac's involvement in the party carries immense cultural overtones, as his long argument with Amir adds to a centuries-long tradition of Arab–Jewish conflict. Though the topic of Israel and Palestine has a place in the increasingly uncomfortable conversations throughout the night, it is a much more ancient conflict— that between two men over a woman—that is the secret inspiration behind Isaac's impulse to argue against an increasingly frustrated Amir. In a surreal moment—in the midst of a heated argument over Muslim women's right to wear the veil—the men realize they both go to the same gym for personal training. Isherwood reflects that much of the foursome's lives are perfectly in agreement: "What they cannot agree on ... is who they really are and what they stand for, once the veneer of civilized achievement has been scraped away to reveal more atavistic urges." Both men give in to these primal urges by the end of the night: Isaac with an adulterous kiss and Amir with his fists.

Jory, too, arrives at the apartment with a secret. Not only has she been promoted over Amir but also she knows the details about office politics that Amir has only guessed. She knows that Mort will not take Amir's calls, that she will be taking on Mort's caseload, and that Steven is the true dominant force in the office. She knows that the partners do not trust Amir, and she knows about his deception. But she and Amir are friends, and she wants to tell him the bad news herself. What she is not prepared for is her husband's puzzling, aggressive behavior or the revelation of his affair. She destroys Amir's professional dreams moments before his marriage comes crashing down, leaving Amir without a job, a wife, or an identity.

The pressures of the night see Amir admitting pride in the events of September 11, though the aftermath of that day has caused the slow buildup of anger and self-hatred inside him: "We were finally winning ... Yeah ... I guess I forgot ... which *we* I was." In a play of shocking moments, it is one of the most disturbing—so at odds with the Amir who gives himself up to airport security as passive aggressive acknowledgment of institutionalized Islamophobia, the Amir who works passionately alongside Jews and defends the rights of women. But the careful barrier he has constructed to block out his strict Muslim upbringing falls when he lacks the emotional energy to keep it in place. Suddenly, Amir is revealed as very much a member of the religion he claims to hate. Not only that, but a harsh practitioner—finding pride in extremist acts and beating his wife in a fit of rage. Isherwood writes that Akhtar "puts contemporary attitudes toward religion under a microscope, revealing how tenuous self-image can be for people born into one way of being who have embraced another." Amir would gladly forget his Muslim heritage, but no one around him will allow it. His identity is under constant debate,

Amir's case sparks a discussion about religious persecution and racial stereotyping, leading the cordial dinner party into controversy. (© bikeriderlondon | Shutterstock.com)

from Emily's portrait in the opening scene to Abe's condemnation of Amir as a Middle Eastern Uncle Tom in the final moments. In itself, identity as a Muslim or a member of any other group does not imply that one is good or bad, compassionate or cruel. But self-hatred will become hatred for others, which can be expressed in one's actions, just as Amir turns on Jory—who reveals her promotion only out of respect for him—and on Emily, whose adultery does not warrant physical abuse in any modern society.

The complexity of *Disgraced* sees four of the best and brightest Americans, successful in the arts and in business, representing the melting pot, the American dream, equality, and freedom, come together for a meal and fall apart before the entrée is served. All the potential for good in the world can be squandered by ignorance, pettiness, and hatred. When Amir attempts the impossible task of pleasing others before learning the simple trick of loving himself, he loses his identity.

Source: Amy L. Miller, Critical Essay on *Disgraced*, in *Drama for Students*, Gale, Cengage Learning, 2016.

Eliza Bent and Ayad Akhtar

In the following interview, Akhtar explains that his inspiration sometimes comes from unlikely sources.

For Pulitzer-winning playwright Ayad Akhtar, the spark for his latest show, *The Who & The What*, running at La Jolla Playhouse through March 9, came in an unlikely location—a New York City taxicab.

"I saw an ad for *Kiss Me, Kate* and I thought, 'Why are people so obsessed with this play? This doesn't make any sense. It's not truthful to gender politics or to the way they have evolved,'" says Akhtar, adding that his ideas are never real ideas until three or four thoughts come together into one. In the case of his latest show, a funny and quirky narrator a la *Annie Hall*, coupled with *The Taming of the Shrew* and Akhtar's reflections on his own friends' lives and experiences, resulted in the script for *The Who & The What*.

In the play, Zarina is the proverbial willful daughter at odds with her father, and it's her book about women and Islam that threatens to tear the family apart. "It's both a departure and a continuity of some of my other work, which takes on different points of view about Muslim life in America," says Akhtar. "There's a warmth to *The Who & The What* that's different in tone compared to *Disgraced*. There's a respectful but very uncompromising questioning of how the Prophet operates in the psyche of the community."

It wasn't always like that for Akhtar, who describes his early writing as attempts at Continental European modernism. "I was trying to write in spare settings that were muted of specificity—Beckettesque, or God-awful Adrienne Kennedy wannabe plays," he recalls with a laugh. It wasn't until he came to terms with his own roots as a Pakistani-American that he began to write with a specificity that has found universal appeal.

"In developing *The Who & The What*, audiences are always surprised at how familiar the characters feel," Akhtar observes. Indeed, if you've ever had an overbearing sister, or a protective father with slightly old-fashioned Republican values, you'll recognize Zarina and her well-intentioned father, Afzal.

Source: Eliza Bent and Ayad Akhtar, "You Know How," in *American Theatre*, Vol. 31, No. 3, March 2014, p. 23.

Marilyn Stasio

In the following review, Stasio describes Disgraced as "engaging."

It always makes Broadway look good to have a Pulitzer Prize-winning drama on the boards. *Disgraced* won the 2013 prize for scribe Ayad Akhtar, and fits the bill as an intellectually engaging play on a politically provocative topic. The sordid subject matter—the unconscious prejudices of liberal New Yorkers—flares during a dinner party given by an ambitious (Muslim) corporate lawyer and his (WASP) artist wife for another power couple, an (African-American) litigator and her husband, an influential (Jewish) museum curator. Helmer Kimberly Senior directed a more intimate version of this play at LCT3 in 2012.

Issue-driven plays are thought to be relatively impervious to production vagaries. That's generally true of Akhtar's perhaps overly schematic work here, which is constructed like a house of cards, its highly civilized human relationships in perfect harmony until someone breaks out of character and throws them all off balance.

The person who acts against his own principles is Amir (Hari Dhillon), a brilliant Muslim lawyer on track to make partner in a Jewish law firm. That ambition is dashed when he foolishly lets his politically liberal wife, Emily (Gretchen Mol, stuck in a vapid role), talk him into privately counseling the legal team for a radical Muslim imam on trial for sedition.

But word gets out, and virtually overnight, the thoroughly Americanized Amir is suspected of being an Islamic extremist, leaving him politically, professionally and sexually wounded, and forcing him to reassess the heritage he's long denied.

Some of the production alterations are purely cosmetic. John Lee Beatty's set design of a stylish Manhattan apartment (a terrace!) and Jennifer Von Mayrhauser's fashionable costumes put more emphasis on the elegant lifestyle of the characters. The new cast, including Josh Radnor as the curator, is perfectly satisfactory. (The only returning member is Karen Pittman, reprising her smart work as Jory, the cutthroat lawyer.)

Replacing Aasif Mandvi (busy on his upcoming HBO series, *The Brink*) as Amir with Dhillon, the American thesp who played the role to much acclaim in London, does put a new perspective on the central character. There's not a whiff of insecurity about Dhillon, who is tall, confident and strikingly handsome, a man who would stare down his enemies and turn them into lead. It's a more classical approach, a study of a powerful man destroyed by hubris. The kind of tragic hero you don't often see nowadays.

Source: Marilyn Stasio, "A Risky Riff on Racial Rifts," in *Variety*, Vol. 325, No. 12, October 28, 2014, p. 121.

Marilyn Stasio

In the following review, Stasio calls Disgraced a "blistering social drama."

Playwright Ayad Akhtar really sticks it to upper-class liberals in *Disgraced*, his blistering social drama about the racial prejudices that secretly persist in progressive cultural circles. When the Muslim heritage of a successful corporate lawyer is revealed, his friends and colleagues claim to think nothing of it. But all it takes is one intimate dinner party for that disingenuous claim to go up in flames. Dynamically staged by helmer Kimberly Senior and earnestly acted by a cast topped by Aasif Mandvi (*The Daily Show*), this play has *Transfer me!* written all over its face.

The restrained luxury of Lauren Helpern's Upper East Side apartment setting and the tasteful elegance of Dane Laffrey's costumes tell us a lot about Amir, the highflying lawyer played by Mandvi, and his white wife, Emily (Heidi Armbruster), an up-and-coming artist.

Life is good, maybe even perfect, for this loving couple. But all that changes when Emily, who has developed an obsessive interest in Islamic art and culture, urges her thoroughly Americanized husband to take on the cause of an imprisoned cleric. Amir is a corporate animal, but because his beloved Emily is a nag, he eventually gives in and offers his professional advice to the cleric's legal counsel.

Unfortunately, Amir's name gets into the newspaper, and the senior partners in his law firm suspect he has Islamic sympathies. Suspicion leads to investigation, and it eventually comes out that Amir has been less than truthful about his background.

The repercussions of this subterfuge are felt at a dinner party that Amir and Emily give for Isaac (a nice performance from Erik Jensen), who has invited Emily to show her paintings at his art gallery, and his African-American wife, Jory (the commanding Karen Pittman), a tough cookie and a topflight litigator in Amir's law firm.

Scribe Akhtar knows how to build a scene and maintain suspense, so there's a sense of inevitability about the damage that's done over the course of the evening. But because of the artful construction, it still comes as a shock when the two couples go into attack mode. Racial tensions are exposed, religious prejudices are aired, and the liberal principles these people supposedly live by are totally trashed.

Among this enlightened company, Amir is the only one with the courage to admit his true feelings about racial politics—and he's doomed by his own honesty. Mandvi, who has been a good soldier throughout the play, grows in strength and stature at the end, earning our respect for Amir as a man willing to accept the public disgrace that comes from telling the truth.

Source: Marilyn Stasio, Review of *Disgraced*, in *Variety*, Vol. 428, No. 12, October 29, 2012, p. 100.

SOURCES

Akhtar, Ayad, *Disgraced*, Back Bay Books, 2013.

Brown, Jeffrey, "*Disgraced* Interrogates Definitions of Identity and Islam in America," PBS website, October 30, 2014, http://www.pbs.org/newshour/bb/disgraced-interrogates-definitions-identity-islam-america/ (accessed June 29, 2015).

Cohen, Stefanie, "*Disgraced* Playwright: 'I'm Writing about the American Experience,'" in *Wall Street Journal*, November 7, 2014, http://www.wsj.com/articles/disgraced-playwright-ayad-akhtar-im-writing-about-the-american-experience-1415365558 (accessed June 29, 2015).

"FAQ about 9/11," National September 11 Memorial and Museum website, http://www.911memorial.org/faq-about-911 (accessed July 10, 2015).

Isherwood, Charles, "Beware Dinner Talk on Identity and Islam," in *New York Times*, October 22, 2012, http://www.nytimes.com/2012/10/23/theater/reviews/disgraced-by-ayad-akhtar-with-aasif-mandvi.html (accessed June 9, 2015).

"Islamophobia: Understanding Anti-Muslim Sentiment in the West," Gallup.com, 2015, http://www.gallup.com/poll/157082/islamophobia-understanding-anti-muslim-sentiment-west.aspx (accessed July 10, 2015).

Kamp, David, "Rethinking the American Dream," in *Vanity Fair*, April 2009, http://www.vanityfair.com/culture/2009/04/american-dream200904 (accessed October 21, 2015).

Kettle, Martin, "What Impact Did 9/11 Have on America?," in *Guardian*, September 6, 2011, http://www.theguardian.com/commentisfree/cifamerica/2011/sep/06/impact-9-11-america (accessed July 10, 2015).

Khan, Muqtedar, "American Muslims Should Fight Islamophobia in 2016 Elections," *Al Jazeera America* website, April 18, 2015, http://america.aljazeera.com/opinions/2015/4/american-muslims-should-fight-islamophobia-in-2016-elections.html (accessed July 10, 2015).

Moss, Stephen, "Pulitzer Playwright Ayad Akhtar: 'I Was in Denial,'" in *Guardian*, May 7, 2013, http://www.theguardian.com/stage/2013/may/07/pulitzer-playwright-ayad-akhtar (accessed June 29, 2015).

"9/11 Attacks: Facts & Summary," in *History.com*, 2010, http://www.history.com/topics/9-11-attacks (accessed July 10, 2015).

Review of *Disgraced* in *New Yorker*, http://www.newyorker.com/goings-on-about-town/theatre/disgraced-2 (accessed June 29, 2015).

Rose, Steve, "Since 9/11, Racism and Islamophobia Remain Intertwined," in *Huffington Post*, December 9, 2013, http://www.huffingtonpost.co.uk/steve-rose/911-racism-islamophobia_b_3908411.html (accessed July 12, 2015).

Stasio, Marilyn, "Broadway Review: *Disgraced*," in *Variety*, October 23, 2014, http://variety.com/2014/legit/reviews/broadway-review-disgraced-josh-radnor-1201337499 (accessed June 9, 2015).

FURTHER READING

Akhtar, Ayad, *The Who and the What*, Back Bay Books, 2014.

> In Akhtar's 2014 play, Zarina, daughter of a strict Muslim family living in Atlanta, Georgia, writes a daring novel about wearing the veil that threatens to tear her conservative family apart.-

Cottee, Simon, *The Apostates: When Muslims Leave Islam*, Hurst, 2015.

> Cottee looks into the lives of Muslims in the West who have given up their faith, a controversial topic in Islam and one whose consequences in the West are rarely explored.

Gray, Richard, *After the Fall: American Literature since 9/11*, Wiley-Blackwell, 2011.

> Gray's work focuses on the changes in American culture and literature following the September 11, 2001, terrorist attacks, with a particular interest in those literary voices that have resisted the temptation to simplify the world after 9/11 as a war between "us" and "them."

Green, Todd H., *The Fear of Islam: An Introduction to Islamophobia in the West*, Fortress Press, 2015.

> Green traces the origins of Islamophobia throughout history to learn more about Western society's struggles with prejudice against Muslims today, emphasizing the role of the conflict between Israel and Palestine in stifling discussions that should be open and honest.

SUGGESTED SEARCH TERMS

Ayad Akhtar

Ayad Akhtar AND Disgraced

Disgraced AND Pulitzer Prize for Drama

Ayad Akhtar AND Disgraced AND Islam

Amir AND Emily AND Disgraced

Ayad Akhtar AND Disgraced AND 9/11

Disgraced AND drama AND 2013

Disgraced AND Akhtar AND Islamophobia

The Last White Class

MARGE PIERCY
IRA WOOD

1980

The Last White Class was published in 1980. It grew from an earlier, shorter play titled *It's Not the Bus*, written by Ira Wood, Gene Bruskin, and Susan Eisenberg and first performed in 1976. When this shorter play was abandoned after a short run, Ira Wood and Marge Piercy decided to write a longer play about busing and racism in Boston. The play follows three families in the same Boston neighborhood: the Burkes, a white family headed by an unemployed father; the Douglases, an African American family held together by widow Rosetta Douglas; and the Caseys, a younger family in a slightly higher income bracket. All three families are affected in different ways by the busing controversy, which aggravates the racism already present in the neighborhood. Piercy and Wood explore themes of racism and women's rights as the action of the play moves toward a violent climax in which the characters must choose sides and take a stand for what they believe is right. The play includes some profanity, as well as offensive racial slurs.

AUTHOR BIOGRAPHY

Piercy was born in Detroit, Michigan, on March 31, 1936. Her parents, Robert and Bert Piercy, were originally from Pennsylvania and came to Detroit not long before their daughter's birth.

Marge Piercy (© *AP Photo* / *David Pickoff*)

Her father worked installing and repairing heavy industrial machinery; her mother stayed home and cared for Piercy. Like many families during the Depression era, the Piercys were poor. They lived in a working class, biracial neighborhood, where Piercy observed racism, poverty, and oppression firsthand.

While still in grade school, Piercy was stricken first with German measles and then with rheumatic fever, which left her debilitated and sickly. While recovering, she spent a great deal of time reading. She was nursed back to health by her beloved grandmother, Hannah. Though Piercy's father was Welsh, her mother and grandmother were Jewish, and she was raised in the Jewish faith.

As she grew older, Piercy felt her parents were disappointed by her bookish nature and disinterested in her education; she reacted with rebellious behavior, such as shoplifting and promiscuity. Through it all, however, her grades remained high, and she won a scholarship to the University of Michigan, becoming the first in her family to attend college.

Piercy excelled at Michigan, winning two of the university's prestigious Hopwood Awards for writing. It was during her college years that Piercy was first exposed to radical political groups; she would become more involved with them in the 1960s. After graduating from Michigan, Piercy briefly lived in France and married French particle physicist Michel Schiff in 1958. The marriage did not last long (they divorced in 1959), and Piercy moved back to the United States. She lived in Chicago, supporting herself by doing odd jobs while pursuing her writing career. These were lean years, as Piercy wrote several novels but was unable to find a publisher for them.

In 1962, Piercy married computer scientist Robert Shapiro. They moved to the East Coast, but as she became more and more concerned about the Vietnam War, Piercy began making frequent trips to Ann Arbor to take part in antiwar activities. She was an early organizer of the group that would eventually become Students for a Democratic Society (SDS). During the latter half of the 1960s, Piercy's main focus was political activity, though she continued writing in what other time she had available. However, she still managed to publish two volumes of poetry and her first novel, *Going Down Fast* (1969), during this time.

In 1971, Piercy and her husband moved to Cape Cod. Piercy was in poor health and was also discouraged by warring factions within the antiwar movement. She began to focus more of her activism on the growing women's movement. She flourished in Cape Cod; her health improved, and she became more productive as a writer. This same year her novel *Dance the Eagle to Sleep* was published; in this novel, Piercy used her experience in the antiwar movement to write about a group of political protesters who attempt to establish their own utopian society.

By the mid-1970s, Piercy's marriage had disintegrated, though she and Shapiro remained legally married until 1980. She met her third husband, Wood, with whom she wrote *The Last White Class*, in 1976. It was also in 1976 that one of Piercy's best-known novels, *Woman on the Edge of Time*, was published. It features a main character who travels into a utopian future.

Wood and Piercy were married in 1982. A prolific writer, Piercy published five novels and several volumes of poetry during the 1980s alone. In the 1990s, five more of her novels were published, including *Storm Tide* (1998), written in collaboration with her husband. The couple founded their own publishing company, Leapfrog Press, in 1997. One of Piercy's more well-known works, an instructional book on writing titled *So You Want to Write: How to Master the Craft of Writing Fiction and the Personal Narrative*, was released by Leapfrog Press in 2001. Piercy also published a memoir titled *Sleeping with Cats* in 2002 and two more novels in 2003 and 2005. Her most recent release is a volume of poetry titled *Made in Detroit*, published in 2015. Her work has been included in over a hundred anthologies. As of 2015, Piercy lives in Wellfleet, Massachusetts, with her husband and collaborator, Ira Wood.

Wood was born on April 9, 1950, in New York, New York. His father, Marvin, worked as a dress manufacturer, and his mother, Lucille, was a nurse. Wood attended the State University of New York and graduated in 1971. Throughout the 1970s, Wood worked in theater as a writer, director, and actor. When he met Piercy in 1976, she was fourteen years his senior and still married to Shapiro. With fellow writers Gene Bruskin and Susan Eisenberg, Wood created a short play about racism and busing in Boston titled *It's Not the Bus*. It was performed three times in 1976 and then abandoned; Piercy and Wood decided to write a new play together on the same subject matter, which became *The Last White Class*. Wood wrote two other plays: *The Escape of Ellen Craft* (1980) and an adaptation of Bram Stoker's *Dracula* (1981).

Wood and Piercy were married in 1982. Throughout his career, Wood has written in a wide variety of forms; for instance, he has written several interactive computer stories for children, short fiction for literary journals, plays, and novels. His first novel, *The Kitchen Man* (1985), tells the humorous story of a struggling playwright working as a waiter, and his second, *Going Public* (1991), chronicles the romantic entanglements of the founder of a successful computer software company during the dot-com boom. He collaborated with Piercy on a third novel, *Storm Tide*, in 1998. Along with Piercy, he co-founded Leapfrog Press in 1997 and worked as a book editor until they sold the company in 2007. He has also been a book critic on a Boston NPR radio station and a literary TV talk show host.

Wood is very active politically in the small fishing village, Wellfleet, Massachusetts, where he lives with his wife. He has served several terms as a selectman in the town's government. He currently hosts a weekly radio interview program on WOMR-FM in Massachusetts.

PLOT SUMMARY

Act 1, Scene 1
Act 1 opens on a racially integrated working class neighborhood in Boston in 1975. Peter Thibault is in his bachelor apartment; his eighteen-year-old brother, Michael, arrives to visit him. Michael's jacket is stained with red spray paint, because he has just vandalized the home of the Douglases, an African American family in the neighborhood, on Peter's orders. Peter encourages Michael to recruit friends to help campaign for Iris Mayo Teague, a candidate for city councilor who plans to stop integration and "clean up" the neighborhood. Part of Peter's campaign plan is more hate activities aimed at black families in the neighborhood.

Act 1, Scene 2
Michael is pasting up campaign posters when his friend Terry Burke comes by. Terry is skipping school; he wants to drop out and get a job. Michael boasts that Peter is paying him for his work and that he gets girls for him as well (a lie). He tells Terry the neighborhood has fallen apart since black kids have started going to their school and that Peter and he are forming an organization to take back the neighborhood. Terry asks if Peter can get him a job; Michael implies that if he joins the organization, Peter might do him a favor. As they talk, sixteen-year-old Suzanne Douglas walks by on her way home from school. Michael blocks her way, makes sexual comments, and then grabs her arm. Suzanne hits him in the stomach with her books and runs away. Michael chases after her, yelling racial slurs, but Terry holds him back.

Act 1, Scene 3
Suzanne arrives home after escaping Michael to find that the family's laundry, which was hung out to dry in the yard, has been ruined by red spray paint. Her favorite blouse, a gift from her late father, now has the words "N——rs Suck" painted across it. Her big brother, Franklin, tells

her "two punks" did it but ran away when Franklin opened the door. Suzanne tells Franklin about the incident with Michael.

Their mother, Rosetta Douglas, shows up with her new boyfriend, Curtis. Rosetta shows him around the house, proud of the work she has done to fix it up. Franklin tells his mother about the painted laundry, and Rosetta calls the police, despite everyone's objections that the police are not interested in helping blacks. While she calls, Curtis and Franklin come up with a plan to go find the vandals themselves. When Rosetta gets off the phone, they tell her the plan, but Rosetta insists the police should handle it. After a brief argument, they decide to forget it for now and have dinner.

Act 1, Scene 4

Scene 4 takes place in the Burke home. Terry's mother, Eileen, arrives home from work and sits down to talk to Terry. She has brought home some cake left over from a farewell party at work; one of the other women in the secretarial pool has been laid off, which worries Eileen. Her husband, Joe, has been out of work for a year, and the family desperately needs the income from Eileen's job.

Eileen confronts Terry about a call she got from school; Terry has been skipping school. Terry complains that school is boring and says he wants to drop out and get a job. He also complains about having to go to school with "n——rs." Eileen scolds him for the racial slur, telling him that her best friends at work are black. Terry tells her that Peter Thibault is going to get him a job, but Eileen knows Peter Thibault and has no high opinion of his character,

Joe Burke arrives home in a good mood after a day out fishing but then senses the tense mood between Terry and Eileen. He asks what is going on, and Terry says he wants to quit school and get a job. Joe, hypersensitive about being unemployed, attacks them both, accusing Eileen of telling Terry to get a job because he cannot support them and laying into Terry for thinking it will be easy to find work. Terry storms out.

As the argument is coming to an end, Gina arrives at the door. Gina is married to Joe's cousin Keith Casey, an accountant. Gina reminds Eileen that there is a meeting of neighborhood parents that evening, parents concerned with the trouble Iris Mayo Teague is stirring up in the neighborhood.

Act 1, Scene 5

In this scene, Joe is at the Jack of Diamonds, where Peter Thibault tends bar. Joe tells Peter he hears he has connections and asks if Peter can get him a job. Just as he asks this, Joe's cousin Keith enters the bar. Peter laughs at Joe, denying he has any connections, and ridicules him in front of Keith. Keith asks Joe why he will not take the job he offered him with his family's hardware store, a job as a janitor. Joe says it is no job for a man of his experience.

Keith is in a suit, having just come from the bank, where he was trying to get a loan to renovate homes on their block. Peter tells him the bank will not invest money in the neighborhood if there are too many black families living there and tries to persuade Keith to get behind Iris Teague's campaign to "keep this neighborhood white." He criticizes Keith's wife, Gina, for trying to promote unity between black and white families.

Act 1, Scene 6

Scene 6 takes place in the Burke household; Gina has come over to cut Eileen's hair, and they are discussing their marital and family problems. Gina says Keith is a different man since he started working in the family business, and now nothing about her is good enough for him. Rosetta Douglas is one of her best friends, and Keith disapproves of that as well. Eileen talks about Terry's insistence on dropping out of school to get a job and about Joe's difficulty finding work. The two women also discuss a rumor that the kids at the neighborhood school may be bused across town to a school in Roxbury, a predominantly black neighborhood of Boston, the next year.

Act 1, Scene 7

Terry is at Michael Thibault's house, and they are making prank phone calls; Michael's is an obscene call to Gina Casey, making sexual suggestions about her affinity for black men. Michael says they should call "the n——rs" and threaten them; he tells Terry to do it. Terry hesitates; Michael tells him Peter might be able to get him a job reading meters with the city. They call the Douglas home, but the line is busy. Michael tells Terry the name of their new organization: WHIP, White Homeowners in Patriotism. He paints a picture for Terry of how they will be heroes, ridding the neighborhood of the undesirable African American families. He gives Terry five dollars and tells him to buy four cans of spray paint and meet him the next morning.

Act 1, Scene 8

The Douglas family is waiting for Franklin to cook a special duck dinner for Rosetta's birthday, but it is taking a long time. Throughout the scene, Suzanne keeps yelling into the kitchen about how she is starving to death.

Rosetta asks Suzanne repeatedly to try on the dress Rosetta is making her for the school awards ceremony, where Suzanne will receive an academic award. Suzanne is waiting to find out if she has gotten a scholarship for college. She is not as enthusiastic as her mother about the award, calling it "just a piece of pasteboard with a sticker."

Franklin complains about the white kids in the neighborhood, who chase him down the block calling him "big n——r." Rosetta tells him not to fight them, that it will only make things worse. Curtis calls while they are waiting for dinner and makes a date with Rosetta for Friday. Finally, Franklin emerges with the duck, and they all sit down to eat. The phone rings; thinking it will be Curtis again, Rosetta picks it up, but it is not Curtis. It is a threatening phone call from Michael Thibault.

Act 2, Scene 1

Keith and Gina Casey are in their kitchen, getting ready to leave for work. Gina works as a dental assistant. Keith is poring over mortgage papers for the renovation project. Another bank has rejected his proposal. Irritable, he criticizes Gina's long black hair, saying she looks like a hippie. Then he demands to know why Suzanne Douglas has been babysitting their kids. Gina tells him she does a good job and that if she leaves the kids with Keith's mother, she gives them too much sugar and lets them watch television all day. Gina urges him to come to the Parent Council meeting; Keith refuses and demands that she stop taking the kids to Suzanne's for babysitting. She ignores him, and he asks angrily, "Are you going to stop?" Gina shouts, "NO!" and leaves the house.

Act 2, Scene 2

Terry Burke is sneaking out of the house the next morning, skipping school to meet Michael with the cans of spray paint. Joe, asleep on the couch, wakes up and talks to him, asking him to come fishing with him. Terry says he has to

meet Michael. They reminisce together about a fishing trip they went on when Terry was younger. Then Terry insists he needs to leave to meet Michael. Joe tries to give him a dollar to take with him; Terry tries to refuse, but Joe, getting angry, insists he take the money.

Act 2, Scene 3

Terry meets Michael outside the Jack of Diamonds; Michael is sporting a new jacket with the initials "WHIP" on the front. Michael says that Peter wants him to gather a group of boys to be marshals for Teague's campaign rally; they will get jackets, too. Terry volunteers.

Act 2, Scene 4

Rosetta and Curtis are at Curtis's apartment, in the morning; Rosetta has spent the night. Curtis is still in bed, but Rosetta is dressed and ready to leave. Curtis is irritable because she set the alarm clock, and it woke him up. Curtis tries to get her to stay, but she is on a mission: she is going to Little City Hall to complain about how her family is being harassed. Curtis tells her they will not do anything to help her and also complains that she is trying to tie him down. Rosetta has no time for Curtis's complaints. She leaves for Little City Hall.

Act 2, Scene 5

Mrs. Ross, the director of Little City Hall, is on the phone in her office when Peter Thibault arrives to tell her that he has arranged for a former pro basketball player to speak at Teague's rally. She is unimpressed. She gives him more leaflets for the boys to pass out and tells Peter to keep an eye on his "hoodlums," because they are causing too much trouble in the neighborhood. Peter says their tactics are getting results—there used to be four black families in the neighborhood; now there are only three.

Peter takes the leaflets and leaves; Eileen Burke enters. She asks Mrs. Ross if it is true that students will be bused to Roxbury the next school year. After a few moments of conversation, Rosetta Douglas arrives.

Rosetta complains to Mrs. Ross about the persecution of her family and asks if she could get the Department of Public works to fix the streetlight near their house; without the light, it is easier for troublemakers to harass the family without being seen. Mrs. Ross says there is nothing she can do and that if a white family moved into Roxbury they would get the same treatment, because "people like to be with their own kind." Rosetta gets angry and shows Mrs. Ross the blouse with the words "N——rs Suck" painted on it; she tells her to put it on, that it suits her. Mrs. Ross throws her out, threatening to call the police.

Act 2, Scene 6

Michael is putting up more campaign posters when Franklin and Suzanne Douglas spot him on the street. Suzanne recognizes him, and Franklin tells Michael that if he ever messes with Suzanne again, calls their house, or vandalizes their property, he will beat him "purple as a grape." Michael, terrified, runs away. Afterward, Franklin tells Suzanne he is tired of having to fight all the time, just to have a normal life.

Act 2, Scene 7

Keith Casey and Peter Thibault are talking at the Jack of Diamonds; Joe Burke is playing darts nearby. Keith tells Peter that he went to the Douglas house while Suzanne was babysitting his kids and demanded they come home with him, threatening to charge her with kidnapping if he ever sees her with them again. Peter tells him what happened at Little City Hall with Rosetta Douglas and Mrs. Ross, only in Peter's version, Rosetta is ranting maniacally and threatening to have Mrs. Ross's daughter beaten by thugs from Roxbury. Keith complains about Gina and her activities with the Parent Council; Peter shows him a flyer from the parent group that urges black and white parents to work together to improve the quality of the schools, which is declining. Keith says he is tired of Gina making trouble for him and that he is going to leave her. Joe, overhearing this, urges him to reconsider, telling him that all marriages have difficult times. Peter ridicules him and tells him to leave Keith alone.

Michael Thibault shows up and speaks with Peter off to one side of the stage. After their conversation, Peter announces that they have been challenged and that a "bunch of n——rs led by Franklin Douglas just cornered my brother." Michael has embellished his confrontation with Franklin to make it seem as if he has declared war on every white man in the neighborhood. Joe continues in vain to talk Keith out of leaving

his wife, but Keith, drunk, begins throwing darts at Joe's feet. Joe, disgusted, leaves the bar.

Act 2, Scene 8

The Burke family is celebrating Eileen's birthday. Gina brought over a dish of lasagna for the family, and Joe and Terry have given Eileen gifts. However, as soon as dinner is over, Terry gets ready to leave, saying he is going to the movies with Michael. He puts on his new WHIP jacket and heads out. Eileen tells Joe they are losing him; neither Eileen nor Joe is pleased with his relationship with Michael. Eileen wonders if the boys are going to an X-rated film; Joe tells her he thinks there is going to be trouble in the neighborhood, and Terry and Michael are going to be mixed up in it. He tells her what he heard at the bar about Rosetta Douglas. Eileen tells him what really happened. Concerned, Eileen tries to call Rosetta, but the line is busy. Eileen puts on her coat, saying she is going to go warn Rosetta in person. Joe tells her not to get involved. Eileen says she has to do it and asks Joe to come with her. Joe refuses, and Eileen leaves.

Act 2, Scene 9

At the Douglas house, Rosetta and Curtis are dressed up to go out to dinner, but Rosetta has just gotten a call from Gina, warning her of the impending trouble. Rosetta is reluctant to leave Suzanne alone. Then Eileen shows up at the door. At first, Rosetta and her family are wary of her, but she warns them about the lie Peter is spreading about Rosetta's visit to Little City Hall. Suzanne tells Rosetta that Terry was one of the boys who harassed her on her way home from school; Eileen is horrified.

Gina shows up; she has been crying. She says Keith came home drunk, ranting about how "all the guys from WHIP" were going to war. She also tells Rosetta of a rumor that a gang of blacks beat up Michael Thibault. Suzanne tells her it was only her and Franklin, and they did not hurt him. Now Rosetta is worried that Franklin is going to be ambushed on his way home from work. She asks Curtis to go pick him up. Gina says she will stay with Rosetta; after some hesitation, Eileen decides to stay too.

Curtis leaves to pick up Franklin. Eileen asks Rosetta why they stay in the neighborhood, with all the trouble; Rosetta tells her it is their home, just as Eileen's house is her home.

Eileen apologizes for never having visited Rosetta before. As the women come to an understanding, they begin to hear crowd noises outside. Voices are shouting racial slurs, telling Rosetta and her family to get out. They step out onto the porch, and Eileen is saddened to see Terry in the crowd. Goaded by Michael, Terry picks up a megaphone and begins reading a speech about how much better the neighborhood was before black families moved in. Meanwhile, Joe arrives but stands to one side of the stage, watching silently.

Eileen yells at Terry to stop and tries to tell the mob what really happened that morning at Little City Hall. Terry falters, but Michael eggs him on. Terry begins to chant, "We want them out!," and the crowd joins in. When Suzanne steps forward to tell what happened with Franklin and Michael, someone throws a rock at her head, and she collapses. Furious, Eileen yells at the crowd, calling Michael a coward. Michael climbs onto the porch and pushes her; Joe rushes to her defense. Franklin grabs the megaphone from Terry, and some members of the crowd grab Franklin. Michael begins beating Franklin, but Rosetta comes at him, swinging a baseball bat. Joe tells the crowd to go home, that the Douglases have done nothing to hurt them. He says he will be at the Douglas house every night to fight them off if he has to. Peter and Michael ridicule him from the crowd, but Joe stands firm.

Michael tells the crowd it is time to leave. Peter gestures to Terry to come with them, but Joe tells him to come home. Terry seems torn for a moment but then calls Joe a "loser." Eileen grabs his arm; Terry curses at her and leaves with Peter and Michael. Peter yells, "We'll be back!" Both Rosetta and Joe answer that they will be there, waiting.

CHARACTERS

Eileen Burke

Eileen is a housewife who recently entered the workforce when her husband, Joe, lost his job as a truck driver. She is trying to hold the family together through this difficult time, and it is taking a toll on her. Eileen is a peacemaker, sacrificing her own needs to keep her family happy. Disliking conflict, she is at first reluctant to get involved with the racial strife in the neighborhood, but her sense of fairness and morality

eventually overcome this reluctance. Eileen makes decisions based on her own observation, not on the influence of others; her direct experience working with African Americans at her job has proved them to be much like herself. As she tells Gina, "Audrey and Lucille got kids, they got money problems, they got troubles with their husband no different than me." Eileen's main priority is her family.

Joe Burke

Joe Burke is aptly named; he is the play's regular Joe, a basically good, hardworking man who has fallen on hard times. He is not sophisticated or intellectual. Much of his self-worth is based on his ability to provide for his family, and now that he is unemployed, he is struggling with feelings of inadequacy. This makes him hypersensitive to innocent comments Eileen or Terry make about jobs or money, even though they are not talking about him. Wrapped up in his own misery, he pays less attention to Terry's declining performance at school and his disturbing friendship with Michael Thibault than his wife does.

Joe is prejudiced; for most of the play, he echoes the racist sentiments of the other white male characters. At one point he calls the janitorial position offered to him by Keith a "n—r job" that is beneath him. He warns Eileen not to get involved in the Douglases' problems, because the Burkes already have enough problems of their own. However, when he observes the mob chanting outside the Douglas home and threatening violence, he can no longer deny that this persecution of the neighborhood's black families is wrong. His decision to stand up against the mob seems to strengthen him, to wake him up from up from his former depressed, apathetic state.

Terry Burke

Terry, who is seventeen, is upset about the changes at school and at home and is looking for a scapegoat. Michael Thibault offers him one: the black families in the neighborhood. Terry is naive and easily persuaded by Michael's lies and boasts. Terry has also experienced discrimination, because of his family's working-class status; when Eileen wonders aloud why he did not get put into the more advanced college preparatory courses at school, Terry says, "They don't put kids like me in there." Terry is impressed with Peter because he is good-looking, has a lot of girlfriends, has a job, and fought in the Vietnam War. To Terry, Peter seems a more exciting figure than his morose, unemployed father. Being a part of the WHIP group makes Terry feel important, and as though he has some control over the circumstances of his life for the first time.

Gina Casey

Gina is the young wife of Keith Casey, Joe's cousin. She works as a dental assistant and has two young children. From an Italian family, Gina is a disappointment to her mother-in-law, who criticizes her constantly. Marrying an Italian was a rebellious act for Keith, who used to find his family's attitudes narrow and old-fashioned. Gina is outspoken and proactive, attending Parent Council meetings and speaking out for the rights of black families. Eileen Burke and Rosetta Douglas are her best friends.

Keith Casey

Keith Casey is Joe Burke's cousin, on his mother's side. The Caseys own a hardware store where Keith works as the store's accountant. Though Keith and Joe come from similar backgrounds, Keith is more successful and condescends to Joe. Keith is married to Gina, whom he married in spite of his family's disapproval. Keith is the first Casey to marry "out of the neighborhood"; Gina is from an Italian family. According to Gina, Keith used to think his family was narrow-minded, but since he lost his job at a company called Liquitronics and joined the family business, "His father's next to the Pope." He has delusions of grandeur, imagining himself a mogul in the making. He has a real estate development scheme he is trying to get funding for, but no bank is interested in helping him. Now that he has these ambitions, he sees Gina's outspoken, free-spirited nature as an embarrassing liability.

Curtis

Curtis is Rosetta Douglas's boyfriend. He is not encouraging when Rosetta decides to go to Little City Hall to complain about the harassment her family has been experiencing, but when there is trouble in the neighborhood, he is willing to pick up Franklin at work to help keep him safe.

Franklin Douglas

Franklin is nineteen. He attends cooking school during the week and buses tables at a local restaurant on weekends. Described as "a large black man, the tallest person in the play," he has sophisticated tastes (for his mother's birthday

he creates Duck Bigaraude) and dreams of someday being a chef in a luxury hotel. Franklin is frustrated by the constant harassment his family has to face, just to live in the neighborhood. He is protective of his mother and sister and threatens Michael with violence only in their defense. He would like to move out of the neighborhood, but his pride will not let him; he tells his sister, "I wouldn't give them the satisfaction."

Rosetta Douglas

Rosetta is a widow raising her two teenagers alone in a predominantly white neighborhood. She works in a fabric store. Most of her spare time is devoted to her family and her home. Though she is growing weary of fighting the racism her family faces on a daily basis, Rosetta is at heart an optimist. She is proud of her children's accomplishments and has high hopes for their future. When her home is vandalized, she insists on calling the police, even though her boyfriend and her children all feel that it is futile. When calling the police results in little action, she goes to the city offices to ask for help. Unlike Peter and Michael Thibault, Rosetta tries to accomplish her goals by following legal, established procedures, but she has little success.

Rosetta is determined, persistent, and not easily intimidated. Even when an angry racist mob comes to her house and threatens her, she does not back down; instead, she first calls the police, gets a baseball bat, and threatens to use it on anyone who tries to hurt her family.

Suzanne Douglas

Rosetta's daughter, Suzanne, is sixteen. She is bright and artistic and does well at school. Like Franklin, Suzanne is tired of having to fight every day just to live a normal life and would like to move out of the neighborhood. Like her mother, she is not easily intimidated and stands up for herself when harassed by Michael Thibault. However, she does not share her mother's optimism that the police will help them or that life will improve for them in the neighborhood.

Suzanne has a wry sense of humor, which provides some comic relief throughout the play. For instance, when her mother asks her if she minded having Curtis over for dinner, Suzanne quips, "Sure, no account. You bring men home every forty years or so, it's a regular thing like

Haley's Comet." When Franklin is taking too long making dinner, Suzanne yells into the kitchen, "Franklin, was that duck dead when you started?"

Pauline Ross

Pauline Ross (Mrs. Ross) works as the Director of Little City Hall (the neighborhood adjunct office for the larger City Hall in downtown Boston). Unlike the more unapologetically racist characters in the play (such as Peter and Michael Thibault), Mrs. Ross affects an air of being impartial and reasonable, while being just as inherently racist. She refuses to help Rosetta, saying she has no authority to do so, though Rosetta knows she has intervened for white homeowners in the same way. When Rosetta gets angry, Mrs. Ross exclaims, "Is that how you people think you can get what you want?"

Iris Mayo Teague

Iris Mayo Teague is the candidate for city council that Peter is supporting. She does not appear in the play, but her campaign to "keep this neighborhood white" adds to the hateful atmosphere.

Michael Thibault

Michael is eighteen and the younger brother of Peter Thibault. Michael has little going for him—he is not particularly bright, he is overweight, and he is unemployed. To boost his own self-image, he has aligned himself with his better-looking, more popular brother, Peter, who works as a bartender at the local bar. Throughout the play, Michael lies and exaggerates about all the things Peter does for him, when in reality Peter treats him rather poorly (at one point Peter tells him he is "fat as a pig"). Peter bullies Michael, and Michael in turn bullies Terry and the Douglases. Like most bullies, Michael is ultimately a coward; when Franklin confronts him about harassing Suzanne, Michael cowers and runs away.

Peter Thibault

Peter Thibault is a bartender at the Jack of Diamonds, the bar portion of a popular steak house restaurant in the neighborhood owned by Jack Sculley. Though we never see Jack Sculley, he operates through Peter, giving him the authority to deal with his business contacts. This and Peter's popularity with women give Peter an exaggerated sense of his importance in the neighborhood. The men in the neighborhood

accord him respect because of his success with women, his military service, and his ability to serve them liquor.

Peter, on the other hand, has little respect for anyone. He values people only for their usefulness to him. He ridicules and belittles Joe, who is unemployed and asks him for help. Because Joe has no connections, he is of no use to Peter. Peter treats Keith with more respect because Keith's family has more money and owns a successful business. Women get the least respect of all. When Keith says his wife would not sleep with him for a year if she heard him talking with Peter about getting rid of the black families in the neighborhood, Peter casually suggests that he sleep with someone else. In one phone call, he speaks disrespectfully of City Council candidate Iris Teague, even though he works for her campaign. Not surprisingly, the women in the play have a much lower opinion of Peter than the men do.

THEMES

Racism

The main theme of *The Last White Class* is racism. Through the spectrum of characters, who exhibit racism to varying degrees, Piercy and Wood demonstrate the sources of racism: ignorance, misinformation, and fear. The white characters who have actually spent time with African Americans (such as Eileen Burke and Gina Casey) are less prejudiced toward them, because their firsthand reality does not match the stereotypes that people like Peter Thibault believe in. When characters have little firsthand experience, they are more likely to believe misinformation, such as the lies Peter and Michael spread about Rosetta and Franklin. The element of fear is heightened in this story because of the drastic changes in the Boston area. People fear change, especially change they have no part in instigating. School busing was a court-ordered mandate, but many white Bostonians blamed the situation on the city's black population.

Another factor that aggravated the conflict and heightened racism was the class status of the neighborhoods where the busing occurred. Busing occurred mainly in working-class, lower-income urban neighborhoods, neighborhoods where many were already struggling with their normal, everyday lives. The busing situation, for many, was the last straw. People who feel

TOPICS FOR FURTHER STUDY

- Currently, black people in America constitute about 14 percent of the population, with Mississippi having the largest proportion at 38 percent. What percentage of students in your school are black? Is it more or less than 14 percent? If the percentage is much more or less, why do you think this is so? Put your findings together in a chart and write a paragraph explaining your theory.

- One of the most enduring images of the effort to racially integrate American schools was six-year-old Ruby Bridges of New Orleans being escorted by four federal marshals into her new elementary school, where she would be the only black student and the very first African American child to attend a formerly all-white public elementary school in the South. Watch the biographical made-for-TV movie *Ruby Bridges* (1995) (available at Amazon). Write a paper comparing the struggle of the Douglas family in *The Last White Class* to the ordeal that Ruby experienced.

- When the play ends, Piercy and Wood leave the outcome of the conflict uncertain, and Peter Thibault promises as he leaves, "We'll be back." What do you think will happen will happen when Peter and his gang return? Do you think the Douglases will stay in the neighborhood or move out? Write the scene of Peter's return, including stage directions and dialogue. Perform the scene with some of your classmates.

- The action of the play takes place in the 1970s, when women had less of a voice in their marriages, in their communities, and in politics. Choose one incident in the play that you think would have turned out differently today, now that women have more of a say in these areas. Write the scene the way it would take place in today's society.

- Though the women in the play have jobs, they are the kind of lower-level jobs historically associated with women: Eileen is part of a secretarial pool, Gina is a dental hygienist, and Rosetta works in a fabric store. Do some research online about women in the workforce. Find statistics like the number of women in the US workforce, the average salary of a woman compared to that of a man, and so on, and plot the data on a graph, according to the decades. Display your graph in a multimedia presentation and explain it to your classmates.

- Read the young-adult novel *My Mother the Cheerleader* (2009), by Robert Sharenow. The main character, Louise, attends the school in New Orleans where Ruby Bridges becomes the first black student. Louise's mother, Pauline, becomes a "cheerleader"—one of the protestors who arrives day after day to taunt and jeer at Ruby. Compare Pauline to some of the characters in *The Last White Class*. Which one is she most like? How do Louise and Pauline's views change during the course of the novel? Pick one character from the play and one from the novel and write a comparison of the two.

---

powerless often seek someone else to dominate or oppress, just to feel some measure of control. Piercy and Wood demonstrate this with the characters of Peter, Michael, Terry, and Joe. Peter bullies and demeans Michael; Michael, in turn, bullies Terry and the Douglases; and Terry, after wavering, finally chooses to bully both the Douglases and his own family. Joe is in a similar dilemma. He too feels powerless, unable to find work to support his family and being bullied by Peter and Keith Casey. Fortunately, Joe ultimately chooses more wisely than Terry.

The story takes place in Boston in the 1970s. *(© Zack Frank | Shutterstock.com)*

Women's Rights

Piercy's writing frequently features feminist themes, and she and Wood weave parallels between racism and the oppression of women throughout the play. For instance, the play's most heinous character, Peter Thibault, is a womanizer and chauvinist as well as a racist. He treats women as dismissively as he does the black characters in the play. He suggests to Keith that he should cheat on his wife and gives him the name of a divorce lawyer, saying that when he gets through with Gina, "she'll be lucky to walk out with the clothes on her back." The audience also learns that Peter got a girl pregnant in high school and then used this same lawyer to evade any responsibility for the child.

More subtle feminist themes are included as well. In one scene, Joe is feeling particularly vulnerable about being unemployed and accuses Terry and Eileen of "ganging up" on him. Eileen calms him down with a shoulder massage and soothing words about his skill as a truck driver and the unfairness of his unemployment. Eileen herself is exhausted from a full day's work (while Joe spent the day fishing). The stage directions read, "*Our last image of EILEEN is of a woman completely drained—as if a transfer of her energy has occurred before our eyes and it is now he who is moving and she who is wan and transfixed.*" Eileen has literally given her power over to Joe.

The strongest characters in the play are women. Rosetta Douglas is a strong, independent woman; she is cautious in her relationship with Curtis, unwilling to make a man the center of her life. As she tells him, "You not my problem, Curtis. You just a little honey on my burnt toast." Eileen, though less sure of herself, becomes more independent as the play progresses. Gina Casey stands up to her husband, Keith, and his disapproving family, while he kowtows to them and abandons his earlier convictions to gain their approval. Joe is the only white male character to step forward and stand up for what is right, and it takes him until the last scene of the play to do it. Because they too have been oppressed and stereotyped, the women characters feel more of a kinship with the Douglases.

STYLE

Drama

The Last White Class is a drama; while there is occasional levity (such as when Suzanne ribs her brother about his duck dinner), the main theme of the play is serious. In some ways, the play borders on melodrama. Elements of a melodrama include heightened emotions, sensational subjects, and stock characters (individuals who are wholly evil or virtuous). Typical characters in a melodrama include a villain (Peter), the villain's less effectual accomplice (Michael), a hero, and a heroine. The hero and heroine in this play are less identifiable; Eileen and Joe end up playing somewhat heroic roles, but so do the Douglases. The play also differs from a melodrama in that the ending is inconclusive; the villain is not vanquished or punished but continues on, likely to menace the heroes again in the future.

Political Theater

The Last White Class falls in the genre of political theater. Political plays strive to make commentary on social issues; in this play, Piercy and Wood examine the effects of racism. The play also brings up the issue of busing for the purpose of racially desegregating schools, a controversial practice in the 1960s and 1970s, but while Piercy and Wood's play takes a clear stand against racism, it takes no definite position on busing. The play uses an actual historical event—busing in Boston, which began in 1974—to make a statement on racism. Some characters are based on real individuals involved in the controversy. However, in order to make a stronger political statement, the behavior of the characters is more polarized. Peter Thibault is a villain with few redeeming characteristics, as is his brother, Michael, and at the other end of the spectrum, the Douglas family is long-suffering, virtuous, and hardworking. Only the Burke family represents the middle ground, people still trying to make sense of the controversy and decide how they feel about it.

Realism

The Last White Class is a realistic play, seeking to portray a real period in history, in an actual city. In a realistic play, the staging and dialogue of the play are designed to involve the audience and encourage them to identify with the characters as real human beings, to make them forget, in a sense, that they are watching a play. In contrast, some other forms of theater consciously alert the audience to the dramatic form—characters speak directly to the audience, actors pay multiple roles, characters burst into song, and so on.

Two-Act Play

Like many modern plays, *The Last White Class* has two acts. Typically, in a two-act play, the first act establishes the characters, their relationships, and the problems and conflicts they face. In the second act, these conflicts rise to a dramatic climax and are resolved in one way or another. Over time, historically, the number of acts in dramatic plays has decreased. Until the eighteenth century, five-act plays were the norm (such as those by Shakespeare). Today, one-act plays are becoming more common (such as Yasmina Reza's *God of Carnage* or James Lapine's appropriately titled *Act One*).

HISTORICAL CONTEXT

Busing in Boston

In the case of *Morgan v. Hennigan* in 1974, US District Judge Arthur Garrity ruled that the segregation of schools in the Boston area discriminated against African American children. To begin integrating the Boston school system, Garrity ordered the busing of groups of black students to predominantly white schools and white students to mostly black schools. This program of forced busing was vehemently protested by white neighborhoods, most notably the Irish-Catholic neighborhood of South Boston. On the first day of busing in September 1974, many families kept their children at home, some in protest and some in fear of potential violence.

One particularly vocal opponent of busing in Boston was Louise Day Hicks, city councilwoman and head of the Boston School Committee (likely the model for the play's character Iris Mayo Teague). A lawyer who had narrowly lost the mayoral election in Boston in 1967, Hicks became the central figure of a group called ROAR (Restore Our Alienated Rights). Unlike the WHIP organization in *The Last White Class*, the stated philosophy of ROAR was to use the tactics of the civil rights movement—civil disobedience and nonviolent protest—to demonstrate

COMPARE
&
CONTRAST

- **Mid-1970s:** The US economy is in a major recession; inflation is high, and economic growth is sluggish, leading to double-digit inflation rates and unemployment as high as 9 percent.

  Today: The US economy is still recovering from a recession that lasted from 2007 to 2009. The unemployment rate is about 5 percent.

- **Mid-1970s:** Though race riots such as those in the mid- to late 1960s are less common now, racial tensions are still high in many areas of the United States, as evidenced by the violent protests of school busing in Boston and other urban areas.

  Today: While race relations between ordinary citizens have greatly improved since the 1970s, multiple incidents of police brutality toward African Americans have recently been in the spotlight.

- **Mid-1970s:** Women are entering the workforce in larger numbers than in previous decades but still make just sixty cents for every dollar a man makes.

  Today: Women are rising to higher and higher positions in corporations across America. The CEO of PepsiCo, one of the largest companies in the world, is a woman, as are the current CEOs of computer giants Hewlett-Packard and IBM. However, pay for women is still stalled at less than eighty cents for every dollar a man makes.

---

their opposition to busing. However, violence did become a part of the protest on many occasions. Some protestors threw eggs, bottles, and even bricks at buses carrying black children to school.

After an incident in which a black student stabbed a white student in a fight, an angry mob gathered outside the school, refusing to allow the rest of the school's black students to go home to Roxbury (a predominantly black neighborhood of Boston). Hicks used a bullhorn to plead with the crowd to go home, but it took four hours to clear the protesters away. Decoy buses had to be sent out so that the black students could be taken home using an alternate route. In another protest, photographer Stanley Forman of the Boston Herald American shot a now-famous photo of a white protestor with a large American flag, seemingly about to stab civil rights activist Ted Landsmark with the flagpole. (The photo is titled *The Soiling of Old Glory*.) Despite the initial uproar over busing in Boston, the policy stayed in effect until 1999, when the Boston School Committee voted to end school assignment based on race.

Women's Liberation Movement

The Women's liberation movement, which began in the 1960s, gained momentum in the 1970s. The formation of the National Organization for Women (NOW) in 1966 was followed in the 1970s by the founding of more women's organizations, including the National Women's Political Caucus (1971), the Coalition of Labor Union Women (1973), and the Equal Rights Amendment Ratification Council (1973). This last organization was formed to advocate for the states' ratification of the Equal Rights Amendment, which would make equality for women a part of the US Constitution. The ERA was approved by both the House of Representatives (in 1971) and the Senate (in 1972) but failed to gain enough states' approval for ratification before the deadline in 1982. ROAR, the conservative women's group that was originally formed to fight busing in Boston, also opposed the passage of the Equal Rights Amendment. A conference titled "A Revolutionary Moment: Women's Liberation in the Late 1960s and Early 1970s" was held at Boston

Being the only African American family in a white neighborhood during turbulent times takes its toll.
(© wavebreakmedia | Shutterstock.com)

University in March 2014. Piercy delivered the invocation at the event, reading several of her poems with feminist themes.

CRITICAL OVERVIEW

Piercy and Wood have collaborated on three writing projects: *The Last White Class, Storm Tide,* and the instructional book *So You Want to Write*. Their novel *Storm Tide,* released in 1998, was a political thriller that received mixed reviews. The two authors wrote separate chapters and then combined them into the finished novel; Brad Hooper in *Booklist* and Andrea Lee Shuey in *Library Journal* praised the novel, both saying it was "seamlessly" written. A reviewer in *Publishers Weekly,* however, described it as "clunky." Critical reception of Piercy and Wood's writing guide, *So You Want to Write,* was more consistently positive. In a review in *Booklist,* David Pitt told readers to

"put this on the shelf right beside Strunk and White."

Though Wood has written two well-reviewed novels and a book of essays, he is more well known as a publisher. Piercy has been the more prolific and critically acclaimed author. Praised as both a poet and novelist, she has written a dozen novels and more than a dozen poetry collections, as well as a memoir and a collection of essays. While reviewers consistently praise Piercy's talent as a writer, some find her work too didactic and political, preaching the views she has practiced as an activist for so many years. Others find that her strident feminism colors her portrayal of men in her work; her novel *Small Changes,* for example, featured few positive male characters. Similarly, some feel that Piercy's experience as an antiwar activist prevents her from giving a balanced portrayal of war and politics in her novels.

However, not all critics feel this way about Piercy's writing; Joyce Ladenson, in a collection of essays on Piercy's work, writes, "If

Piercy is accused of being preachy, it is because her characters are struck by pain which they need to explain and about which they are enraged once they examine its social sources." In some works, Piercy moves away from overtly political themes and focuses more on relationships. In a review of her 1989 novel, *Summer People*, Ron Grossman writes that he "knows no other writer with Piercy's gifts for tracing the emotional route that two people take to a double bed, and the mental games and gambits each transacts there."

CRITICISM

Laura B. Pryor

Pryor has a master's degree in English and over thirty years of experience as a professional writer. In the following essay, she examines the identity crises experienced by the male characters in Piercy and Wood's The Last White Class *and how this affects the play's outcome.*

Piercy is known as a feminist political writer whose work often focuses on the problems of women living and working in a patriarchal society. In fact, some critics have suggested that her political opinions sometimes overwhelm other factors in her writing. Critic Elayne Rapping is a fan of Piercy's work, calling her novels *Woman on the Edge of Time* and *The Longings of Women* "classics of feminist fiction," but even she admits that in Piercy's lesser works, she can become "prosaic and preachy." The main female characters in *The Last White Class* are strong women with minds of their own: African American widow Rosetta Douglas, keeping her family moving forward on her own, without a husband; Eileen Burke, a _former housewife who has stepped up to support her family during her husband's unemployment; and Gina Casey, an outspoken Italian woman who refuses to abandon her principles to please her husband. Indeed, the women in Piercy and Wood's play are so exemplary that in order to find real inner conflict and change, we must turn to the male characters. In these characters, we find a shared crisis of male identity, as the economy, the busing situation, and their evolving female partners leave them struggling to define what it means to be a man.

The play's male characters represent a spectrum of emotional evolution, from the most

> IN A PATRIARCHAL SOCIETY, WEALTH
> FLOWS FROM MEN, A LESSON BROUGHT HOME FOR
> JOE WHEN HE IS GIVEN NO PART OF THE CASEY FAMILY
> BUSINESS, BECAUSE HE IS RELATED TO THEM ON HIS
> MOTHER'S SIDE."

brutish and primitive (Peter) to the more sensitive and adaptable (Joe). Peter's reputation and self-worth stem from the most basic male motivations: competition and sex. Early man was motivated to mate with as many women as possible to increase the chances of propagating the species in a time when infant mortality rates were extremely high. Male animals are very territorial as well. We can see all these primitive tendencies in Peter, in his womanizing behavior, his marking of territory (such as sending Michael out to spray the Douglases' laundry with paint and dressing his gang in matching jackets), and his need to belittle the other men (such as Joe, whom he repeatedly calls "Two-Beer Burke") so that he comes out on top. Peter excels at activities traditionally seen as "macho": drinking, flexing his muscles, dominating others, sexual conquest, and warfare (Peter is a veteran of the Vietnam War). Peter's military service could be construed as a positive quality, but given the political leanings of the authors (Piercy was a vehement protestor against the Vietnam War and one of the early founders of the Students for a Democratic Society, an antiwar group), it is unlikely that it was intended to be a virtue.

On the other end of the spectrum is Franklin Douglas. Piercy and Wood have endowed Franklin with many traditionally feminine qualities. Franklin attends cooking school and cooks for the family, a traditionally female task (especially when this play was first performed, in the late 1970s). It is Franklin who brings in the laundry after Michael vandalizes it. (In contrast, in the opening scene of the play, Michael brings Peter his clean laundry, which his mother still does for him.) Franklin avoids fighting but is protective of his sister and mother. Because of his large size, he is always being encouraged to participate in sports: "Look at that big black

WHAT DO I READ NEXT?

- In the young-adult novel *The Lions of Little Rock* (2012), author Kristin Levine tells the story of Marlee, a junior high school girl who never speaks except at home with her family, until she meets Liz. The novel is set in 1958 during the battle over school integration in Little Rock, Arkansas. Liz is removed from Marlee's school when it is discovered that she is a light-skinned black girl passing for white. Marlee's refusal to abandon their friendship means she must risk disapproval and even danger.

- The classic play *A Raisin in the Sun* (1959), written by African American playwright Lorraine Hansberry, tells the story of the Youngers, a black family living in Chicago who are set in conflict with each other when the matriarch of the family finally receives life insurance benefits from her late husband. Each character has his or her own dreams of how the money should be used; as they attempt to realize these dreams, racism and other hardships stand in their way. *A Raisin in the Sun* was the first play written by a black woman to be produced on Broadway.

- *Farewell to Manzanar* (1973) is the true autobiographical account of Jeanne Wakatsuki Houston's childhood experiences in a Japanese internment camp in California. Ten thousand Japanese Americans were uprooted from their homes and sent to Manzanar during World War II, suspected of being potential traitors and spies, though many (like Houston) were born in the United States, and most were US citizens.

- In *The Watsons Go to Birmingham—1963* (1995), a black family living in Flint, Michigan, in the early 1960s, decide to move

south to Alabama to live with Grandma to get the troubled oldest boy away from the bad influences of the city. Narrated by nine-year-old Kenny Watson, the story takes a grave turn when his grandmother's church is bombed with four little girls inside (an actual historical incident that occurred at Birmingham's Sixteenth Street Baptist Church). The novel is written by Newbery Award–winning author Christopher Paul Curtis.

- *Common Ground: A Turbulent Decade in the Lives of Three American Families* (1985), written by former *New York Times* journalist J. Anthony Lukas, tells the story of the Boston busing controversy from the viewpoint of three different Boston families: a white, working-class family headed by an Irish American widow, a working-class black family, and a middle-class white family. The book won a Pulitzer Prize in 1986.

- Piercy and Wood collaborated on one novel, *Storm Tide* (1998), a political thriller with romantic entanglements. Main character David Greene's sports ambitions and his marriage have both failed, and he returns home to Cape Cod and becomes involved in politics as well as an affair with a married woman.

- The Pulitzer Prize–winning play *Driving Miss Daisy* (1987), written by Alfred Uhry, tells the story of an unlikely friendship between an elderly Jewish woman and her African American chauffeur. Daisy, who is initially prejudiced against Hoke and resentful that she can no longer drive, eventually comes to trust and rely upon him, as well as defend him from the prejudice of others.

boy, he ought to play football." However, Franklin prefers "a job where I please people, make them mellow." In the scene where Franklin

cooks the family dinner and they all complain about how long it is taking, Franklin scolds them from the kitchen like an exasperated housewife,

"Did you set the table yet, did you even set the table? Tuna fish for you."

Between these two poles of narcissistic caveman and nurturing earth mother lie the other male characters of the play. Two of the remaining adult male characters, Joe Burke and Keith Casey, have recently experienced job loss; Keith now has a job with the family hardware store, while Joe, a truck driver, has been unemployed for over a year. Stripped of his role as the breadwinner of the family, Joe is now insecure and defensive. His manhood is in question. According to Amy Finnegan of the Center for Child and Family Policy, workers who remain unemployed for more than six months often find it harder to re-enter the job market; such individuals may then take a lesser job for which they are overqualified (such as the janitorial position Keith offers Joe). This can lead to loss of self-worth for the overqualified worker. The emasculation Joe experiences from losing his job is exacerbated by the fact that his wife, Eileen, is able to find employment as a secretary. A 2013 study published in the *Journal of Personality and Social Psychology* found that men whose wives or girlfriends succeed in any endeavor experience a dip in their self-esteem, even if the success is unrelated to any pursuit in which the men themselves are involved.

Joe's loss of income correlates to a loss of self-esteem and masculinity. In a patriarchal society, wealth flows from men, a lesson brought home for Joe when he is given no part of the Casey family business, because he is related to them on his mother's side. Every Casey sibling except Joe's mother received some portion of the family business. Joe is cut off from this inheritance just as his mother was, and he cannot find good-paying work to generate income; he is essentially experiencing life as a woman, from an economic standpoint.

Keith, on the other hand, has fallen back on the family business and is supported by the patriarchy of the Casey family. The family money comes at a price; Keith has sacrificed his individuality and freedom and now must think and act like his family. In the end, this means he sacrifices his marriage as well. We see this transition take place gradually over the course of the play. In the first act, Keith resists Peter's attempts to interfere in his relationship with Gina, telling him, "You mind the bar. My wife is my own business." By the second act, he is planning to leave Gina, and Peter is giving him recommendations for a divorce lawyer.

Both Keith and Joe have similar dilemmas; their wives are defying them, making decisions based on their own values and principles, without deferring to their husbands. Keith asks his wife to stop taking their kids to the Douglas home; she refuses. Joe tells his wife not to get involved in the Douglases' problems; she insists on helping them. At the same crossroads, the two men take different directions. Joe, with little to lose but his wife's respect (and his own self-respect), chooses to follow his conscience. Keith, on the other hand, seems to have a less defined sense of self to begin with. His original choice of Gina as his wife was based in large part on defying his family, in an attempt to define himself as an independent adult. Now that it is more profitable to conform to his family's expectations, Keith shifts his identity and discards Gina. Unlike Joe, who has temporarily lost connection with his true self in his depression, Keith never had a true self in the first place, or at least not one strong enough to survive unemployment and family pressure. When Joe tries to counsel Keith on the merits of enduring rough spots in a marriage, Keith is too drunk to listen, and the bartender, of course, is Peter. Peter has served up both alcohol and an easy way out: if everything is Gina's fault, then discarding her will solve everything. Joe, on the other hand, is careful not to swallow too much of Peter's philosophy; he never drinks more than two beers at Peter's bar.

Like Keith, Joe's son, Terry, has not defined himself; even when he makes his choice and speaks out in support of WHIP, he has to read his speech off a piece of paper. He is reading a script, playing the role of a racist to win Peter's approval and separate himself from his "loser" father, much the way Keith married Gina to defy his own family. Rather than define themselves positively according to what they believe in, they define themselves negatively, as what they do not want to be. Similarly, the male characters who define what it means to be a man as simply "not woman" are doomed to uncertainty, because women's roles are in constant flux throughout this revolutionary time for gender roles in society.

Source: Laura B. Pryor, Critical Essay on *The Last White Class*, in *Drama for Students*, Gale, Cengage Learning, 2016.

The court-ordered practice of busing students to enforce desegregation of schools caused controversy.
(© Frank11 / Shutterstock.com)

Marge Piercy

In the following excerpt, Piercy gives advice to aspiring writers.

I believe the barriers to creativity are both inner and outer. The distinction between madness and sanity is one made by those around us: they honor us or they commit us. An act that brings admiration in one society will get you locked up in another. Seeing visions was a prerequisite for adulthood in Plains Indian societies, and quite dangerous today. Societies also differ in how they regard the artist, how integrated into the ordinary work of the community she or he is thought to be, how nearly the society regards artistic production as real production, as a reasonable adult activity—a job, in other words.

Working in any of the arts in this society is a self-elected activity. Although parents may applaud their children's performances in school plays, I have never heard of a parent who did not try to discourage a child who decided to become a professional actor. Even the occasional bit of back-slapping advice you get from peers is usually based on the misapprehension that writing is much easier than it is and that it is infinitely more well paid than is the case. If you tell a friend one week that you are trying to start a novel, likely they will ask you what you are doing the next month, be astonished that you are still writing the same novel, and so on; and when you have finished, they will ask whether you have sold it yet, as if selling a novel were easy.

Basically there is little support in our culture for apprenticeship. Even in a relatively sophisticated movie such as *Amadeus*, the proof of Mozart's genius is that he doesn't correct, doesn't hesitate, but the music gushes out of him almost too fast for him to write it down.

In writing there is always more to read, study, learn, try out, master. The more you as a writer are open to understanding the United States and the world in which we live as richly and variously cultured, the more there is to learn, the more different strands of language and crafts to which you will apprentice yourself. It is not nearly sufficient to know and know thoroughly British and American

"

THE MORE YOU AS A WRITER ARE OPEN TO
UNDERSTANDING THE UNITED STATES AND THE
WORLD IN WHICH WE LIVE AS RICHLY AND VARIOUSLY
CULTURED, THE MORE THERE IS TO LEARN, THE MORE
DIFFERENT STRANDS OF LANGUAGE AND CRAFTS TO
WHICH YOU WILL APPRENTICE YOURSELF."

literature, even if you throw in, as we increasingly must, Canadian and Australian authors. Who would strive to understand contemporary literature without Atwood, Munro, Keneally, White? But lacking a knowledge of Japanese literature, of French, Italian, Spanish, South American and Mexican literature, of Russian, Scandinavian, Greek, or contemporary African writing, all makes us stupider than we can afford to be if we mean to write. Most foreign literatures you will read in translation, although being in command of at least one foreign language helps a writer immensely in understanding her own.

If you want to write a memoir, read memoirs. If you want to write science fiction, read science fiction. Often in workshops, participants will ask us to recommend a "how to write" book—like this one. But the truth is, the best books you can read on how to write are books that are in the genre in which you want to write. What we hope to teach you, in part, is to read like a writer: to read noticing craft. The books you don't think work well may teach you as much as the ones that wring admiration from you. Whatever the author is doing, you want to ask how and look at the choices made.

All of this notion of apprenticeship is at odds with the model of success in the arts so many young people bring to bear, mostly from the careers of rock musicians. You can make it as a rock musician with three or four chords and a gimmick, at least for one record, but you can also be a has-been at twenty-two. There are equivalents among writers, but not many. Basically you may publish an occasional poem or short story in college, usually in the college literary magazine, but few serious writers reach visibility before thirty to thirty-five.

Giant conglomerates control the big media and own the New York publishing houses. They are run the same way as other large conglomerates, and in spite of the wishes of many dedicated editors, they would like to put out generic products like brands of toothpaste or breakfast cereal with an assured cut of a guaranteed market. As one delighted publishing CEO gushed in his company's year-end report, "Fewer titles have translated into more attention for each book, greater publishing success and higher revenues." Books, real books, are risky. Better financial projections can be obtained on the *All Chocolate Eat Yourself Skinny Diet Book* and thrillers that, like the movies *Halloween 16* and *Die Hard 56*, offer exactly the same product in a slightly jazzier package—the romance, the success story. It no longer shocks people to hear that chain and the large on-line booksellers rent space to publishers the same way that supermarkets sell the most ideal shelves for corn chips and pretzels. Publishers can pay to have their titles stacked at the front table, or positioned face-out at the checkout counter and at the ends of aisles. Large publishers, of course, can better afford the thousands of dollars it may cost for a fifty-copy display or a large window sign. But of course they expect a return on their investment and the best chance of getting that return is with a product—or author—that got one before: one with name recognition. It's not some evil plan, just a business plan. But these marketing strategies work against all writers just starting out or those who want to do original work.

The inner and outer barriers interact because we tend to internalize rejection and lack of recognition, and because we are programmed by the media and our peers to believe that writers who are "successful" produce better work.

Work in the arts requires your best energy. That means figuring out how, in the course of a life that usually includes another full-time job whether paid or unpaid, you can organize your time so that you write with your best energy, not your slackest. That may require getting up before everyone else in your house or your close circle; it may mean working after everyone else is in bed. It certainly means having time that is devoted to work, when you pull the phone out of its jack and do not answer the door. If you have children and thus cannot quite cut yourself off from interruption, you can attempt to make it clear that only an emergency is suitable for interrupting you. You may feel guilty setting boundaries, but what kind of adults will grow from never having learned that other people have boundaries that must not be crossed? Should they not rather learn what I hope you have realized, that work is precious and concentration is to be valued, to be sharpened, to be refined? We look more carefully at organizing time in the chapter "Work and Other Habits."

What I will return to again and again is the ability to use your mind mindfully and purposefully. To know when to go with the flow and when to turn on the cold critical eye. To know when to loose your imagination and when to keep it under control. Concentration is learned by practicing it, just as is any other form of exercise or excellence. Even when the focus of the concentration is something in the past of the writer or some nuance of feeling or precise tremor of the emotions, the writer at work is not the emotion. Work has its own exhilaration. You can be happy as a clam—precisely because you are not self-regarding at all, but doing your own tidal work—when you are writing a poem about how somebody was cruel and nasty to you. You can even have fun writing a story imagining your own suicide. You can experience joy writing a story about total nuclear destruction, because in that clear high place where concentration is fully engaged, there is no feeling of self. Learning to reach that state and prolong it is another apprenticeship we all undergo. You have to find the work more interesting than you find yourself, even if the work is created out of your own guts and what you are writing about is your own life.

In the ancient and very modern approach to spiritual energy and experience, the Kabbalah, which is my discipline, we speak of developing the adult mind. For a writer that is particularly important. The adult mind can decide not to fuss like an adolescent because our work and our persons have experienced rejection. The adult mind can put victories or defeats into perspective. The adult mind can choose not to allow interference from the worries of the day, not to give way to irrelevant fantasies when trying to craft a meaningful fantasy. The adult mind has learned to focus and to retain focus for a much longer period of time. We can all have bad days and we can all be distracted; it is a matter of degree and how often we can combat our idiotic and self-regarding tendencies.

Beside my computer is a window and on the ledge of the window are twelve rocks. They have accumulated over the years. Each represents some place I found sacred or meaningful. When I need to focus and center my mind, I pick up the rocks and weigh them in my hands. Eventually 1 will settle upon a particular rock to contemplate: maybe the rock I picked up after I climbed the Acrocorinth from the ruins of the temple of Aphrodite there. Maybe one from the Oregon coast from a dawn when I experienced a strong vision. It does not really matter which stone I select. What matters is that to me these are meaningful and radiant objects that I can focus on to get rid of clutter and distraction. It is a matter of closing down the noise of the ego, of worry, of casual boredom, of gossip, of concern with what people may think, thoughts of who has not been sufficiently appreciative of my great virtues lately. It does not matter what particular pattern you use to bring yourself into sharp focus on what you are about to write. It is only necessary that you do so. For some people, their screen saver works in the same way—or a piece of meditative music. Whatever works for you, use it. . . .

Source: Marge Piercy and Ira Wood, "Sharpening Your Innate Skills," in *So You Want to Write: How to Master the Craft of Writing Fiction and Memoir*, 2nd ed. Leapfrog Press, 2005, pp. 17–21.

SOURCES

"About Ira Wood," Ira Wood website, http://irawood. com/about/ (accessed July 27, 2015).

"About Marge," Marge Piercy website, http://margepiercy. com/portfolio-items/about-marge/ (accessed July 27, 2015).

"African American Population by State," in *Black Demographics*, http://blackdemographics.com/population/ black-state-population/ (accessed August 3, 2015).

"America's Act II: Will the Economy Come Back?," CNN website, August 2, 2015, http://money.cnn.com/ 2015/08/02/investing/stocks-market-lookahead-america-comeback/ (accessed August 3, 2015).

"A Brief History of Women's Rights Movements," Scholastic website, http://www.scholastic.com/teachers/article/ brief-history-womens-rights-movements (accessed August 3, 2015).

Cihlar, Lisa J., Review of *So You Want to Write*, in *Library Journal*, Vol. 126, No. 12, July 2001, p. 103.

Cronin, Brenda, "Male-Female Pay Gap Hasn't Moved Much in Years," in *Wall Street Journal*, September 17, 2013, http://blogs.wsj.com/economics/2013/09/17/male-female-pay-gap-hasnt-moved-much-in-years/ (accessed August 3, 2015).

Finnegan, Amy, "Unemployment: How it Effects Family Behavioral Health," https://www.purdue.edu/hhs/hdfs/fii/wp-content/uploads/2015/07/s_ncfis08c03.pdf (accessed August 3, 2015).

Grossman, Ron, Review of *Summer People*, in *Chicago Tribune Books*, July 5, 1989, p. 3.

"Historical Unemployment Rates in the United States Since 1948," in *DaveManuel.com*, http://www.davemanuel.com/historical-unemployment-rates-in-the-united-states.php (accessed August 3, 2015)

Hooper, Brad, Review of *Storm Tide*, in *Booklist*, Vol. 94, No. 16, April 15, 1998, p. 1357.

Ladenson, Joyce R., "Political Themes and Personal Preoccupations in Marge Piercy's Novels," in *Ways of Knowing: Essays on Marge Piercy*, edited by Sue Walker and Eugenie Hamner, Negative Capability, 1991, pp. 111–19.

Nutter, Kathleen Banks, "'Militant Mothers': Boston, Busing and the Bicentennial of 1976," in *Historical Journal of Massachusetts*, Vol. 38, No. 2, Fall 2010, pp. 52–75.

Piercy, Marge, and Ira Wood, *The Last White Class*, Crossing Press, 1980.

Pitt, David, Review of *So You Want to Write*, in *Booklist*, Vol. 97, Nos. 19/20, June 1, 2001, p. 1825.

Rapping, Elayne, Review of *City of Darkness, City of Light*, in *Women's Review of Books*, Vol. 14, No. 5, February 1997, pp. 5–6.

Review of *Storm Tide*, in *Publishers Weekly*, http://www.publishersweekly.com/978-0-449-00166-0 (accessed October 5, 2015).

Shuey, Andrea Lee, Review of *Storm Tide*, in *Library Journal*, Vol. 123, No. 9, May 15, 1998, p. 117.

Thompson, Dennis, "In Showdowns Between Sexes, Male Ego Bruises Easily," in *HealthDay*, August 30, 2013, http://consumer.healthday.com/mental-health-information-25/behavior-health-news-56/in-showdowns-between-sexes-male-ego-bruises-easily-679725.html (accessed August 3, 2015).

"The Top 10 Highest-Paid Female CEOs," CBS News, http://www.cbsnews.com/media/the-top-10-highest-paid-female-ceos/ (accessed August 3, 2015).

"2014 Census Black Population Estimates," in *Black Demographics*, http://blackdemographics.com/population/ (accessed August 3, 2015).

FURTHER READING

Formisano, Ronald P., *Boston against Busing: Race, Class, and Ethnicity in the 1960s and 1970s*, University of North Carolina Press, 2004.

    In this book, Formisano examines the diverse motivations of those who protested busing in Boston, positing that racism was not the only factor in their discontent. He also looks at the varying reactions of different Boston neighborhoods to the court-ordered busing program.

Frankenberg, Erica, and Gary Orfield, eds., *Lessons in Integration: Realizing the Promise of Racial Diversity in American Schools*, University of Virginia Press, 2007.

    With desegregation policies originally instituted in the 1970s now coming to an end, American schools are once again becoming increasingly segregated racially. This collection of essays explains the social benefits of racial diversity in schools and describes changes that must be made in our educational system to take advantage of these benefits.

Giardina, Carol, *Freedom for Women: Forging the Women's Liberation Movement, 1953–1970*, University Press of Florida, 2010.

    Scholar and activist Giardina wrote this history of the origins of the women's liberation movement, using her firsthand experience as one of the founders of the movement, as well as extensive research. She shows how experience with other movements, including the black freedom movement, served as the catalyst for women's liberation.

Sokol, Jason, *All Eyes Are upon Us: Race and Politics from Boston to Brooklyn*, Basic Books, 2014.

    When we think of racism in the United States, we think first of the South, whereas the northeastern part of the country has a better reputation for championing equality and civil rights. In this book, however, Sokol examines the reality of racial politics in the Northeast and finds that this reputation is not completely accurate (the uproar over busing in Boston being one example).

SUGGESTED SEARCH TERMS

Marge Piercy

Ira Wood

The Last White Class AND Piercy AND Wood

The Last White Class AND drama

Marge Piercy AND feminism

Marge Piercy AND politics

Ira Wood AND politics

The Last White Class AND Marge Piercy

The Last White Class AND Ira Wood

The Last White Class AND busing

The Last White Class AND desegregation

The Last White Class AND Boston

Little Shop of Horrors

HOWARD ASHMAN

1982

In 1960, the B-movie producer Roger Corman—B-movies being low-budget movies originally made to accompany the main films in double features—took advantage of access to some street sets and had the screenwriter Charles Griffith put together a quick script. In two days, they filmed a parody of horror movies called *The Little Shop of Horrors*, about a plant that grows by consuming human blood. The film was cheap and funny, making it a natural for Howard Ashman, a young actor, writer, and producer, to adapt for his small theater company twenty-two years later. With memorable songs by Alan Menken and book and lyrics by Ashman, *Little Shop of Horrors* became an audience favorite and went on to a five-year off-Broadway run. The musical was adapted to a 1986 film with Rick Moranis; Steve Martin; Ellen Greene, who achieved national fame from her role in the play; and Levi Stubbs, the lead singer of the Temptations, as the voice of the plant.

The story tells of Seymour, a timid young assistant in a bankrupt flower shop who finds that business picks up when people come in to see a strange new plant he has brought to the shop. His boss is happy, and Audrey, the coworker Seymour secretly loves, is happy. The only one not happy is the plant, which soon starts talking, first begging for and then demanding human blood. As Audrey's boyfriend, a motorcycle-riding dentist with a sadistic streak,

becomes increasingly abusive, it becomes easier and easier for Seymour to see who should supply blood to satisfy the plant's thirst. The plant is not satisfied with just one victim, though, and insists on more and more. The plant's popularity ensures that bloodthirsty offshoots will be spread across the globe.

Like the carnivorous plant, Ashman and Menken's musical spread. Even before a successful 2003 Broadway revival, it was a standard of school and community theater companies. It has yielded songs considered classics of modern musical theater, including "Downtown (Skid Row)," "Somewhere That's Green," and "Suddenly Seymour." Its awards included the New York Drama Critics' Circle award for Best Musical of 1982–83; Drama Desk Awards for Outstanding Musical, Outstanding Lyrics, and Outstanding Special Effects; and Outer Critics Circle Awards for Best Off-Broadway Musical and Best Score.

AUTHOR BIOGRAPHY

Ashman was born in Baltimore, Maryland, in 1950. His father, Raymond, was a salesman, and his mother, Shirley, was a full-time homemaker. Ashman was interested in theater at a young age and acted in the Baltimore's Children's Theater Association as a child. He attended several colleges, including Boston University, Tufts University, and Goddard College, from which he received his bachelor's degree. He went on to earn his master of fine arts degree from Indiana University in 1974.

After graduate school, Ashman moved to New York City with Stuart White, his longtime companion. He worked by day in the editing department at Grosset & Dunlap publishers while trying to break into musical theater. He and White were founders of the WPA Theater, an off-off-Broadway company. One of Ashman's first projects for WPA was an adaptation of the Kurt Vonnegut novel *God Bless You, Mr. Rosewater*. Ashman wrote the book and the lyrics. To write the music, he enlisted Alan Menken, who would be his collaborator for the rest of his life.

After their successful collaboration on *Little Shop of Horrors* in 1982, Ashman and Menken were recruited, at the suggestion of David Geffen, the famed musical producer who produced the film adaptation of the play in 1986, to work for Disney studios. Their songs for Disney's *The Little Mermaid* in 1989 have been credited with reviving the studio's legendary animation department, which had become a shadow of its formal self. They went on to write the music for Disney's *Beauty and the Beast* (1991) and *Aladdin* (1992). Ashman also wrote and directed the Broadway musical *Smile*, featuring the music of Marvin Hamlisch, in 1986. Though it did not do well at the time, *Smile* continued in constant revival into the twenty-first century.

In 1988, Ashman discovered that he had symptoms of AIDS. At the time, the disease was new and mysterious and associated with homosexuality. Ashman kept his condition a secret from his working associates because of the stigma that was attached to being gay at that time. He died of AIDS in New York City on March 14, 1991, before *Aladdin* was released and before he could see *Beauty and the Beast* become the first animated film ever nominated for an Academy Award for Best Picture. He won a posthumous Academy Award for Best Song for the title song from *Beauty and the Beast*.

PLOT SUMMARY

Prologue

The prologue of *Little Shop of Horrors* establishes the setting. A voice-over narrator, whose godlike voice is deep and resonating, explains that the events being conveyed concern a serious threat to the human race. A placard with the play's title, surrounded by fog, raises to reveal three street characters—Crystal, Ronnette, and Chiffon. They function as a Greek chorus, commenting on and explaining the action to the audience.

At the end of the prologue, a screen rises to reveal the interior of Mushnik's Skid Row Florist, where most of the action takes place.

Act 1, Scene 1

The lights rise in the flower shop, where Mr. Mushnik is working at a table when he hears his employee, Seymour, break something in a room offstage. The onstage clock moves through the hours, passing eleven, twelve, and one o'clock. At the stroke of two, Mushnik's other employee,

MEDIA ADAPTATIONS

- The success of *Little Shop of Horrors* led to a Hollywood adaptation in 1986, produced by the Geffen Company. The film was directed by Frank Oz, one of the original Muppets puppeteers. The film starred Rick Moranis as Seymour and Ellen Greene, from the off-Broadway and London productions, as Audrey. It also featured a standout performance by the comic Steve Martin as Orin Scrivello, the sadistic dentist. It is available on DVD and Blu-ray from Warner Home Video and for download from various sources.

Audrey, enters. She has a black eye, which Mushnik suspects is from her boyfriend, Orin. Seymour enters, trips, and breaks a tray of flowers, earning him verbal abuse from Mushnik.

Mushnik tries to chase away the three singers, and they sing "Downtown (Skid Row)" about the impoverished inner-city, or skid row, area of town they live in. When Seymour joins in the singing, he explains that he has lived a difficult life of poverty and neglect. He and Audrey finish the song with a duet about their dreams of escaping from their oppressed lives.

After the song, the flower shop employees think they hear a customer, but it is just a derelict standing outside their window. They have not had a customer all day. Mushnik talks about closing the store, but Seymour brings out from the back room a new plant he has been working on, which he names Audrey II. Seymour and Audrey suggest that a strange and interesting plant like this may bring curious, paying customers into the shop.

As if by amazing coincidence, a customer enters the shop. He asks where this plant has come from, and Crystal, Ronnette, and Chiffon sing "Da-Doo" as Seymour explains finding it in the shop of an old Chinese man just as there was a total eclipse of the sun. When they finish, the customer asks to buy fifty dollars' worth of roses. Mushnik is not able to give him change for a one hundred dollar bill, so the customer doubles the order.

Thrilled at such a big sale, Mushnik offers to take his employees to dinner, but Audrey says she must leave for a date. Mushnik leaves Seymour at the shop to care for the plant, which is wilting.

While singing "Grow for Me" about the many ways he has tried to encourage Audrey II to grow, Seymour cuts his finger. The plant opens and closes to catch and swallow Seymour's blood. Quickly, Seymour realizes that his blood is nourishing the plant. He continues the song as he squeezes more and more blood into Audrey II.

Act 1, Scene 2

In front of the flower shop, the chorus and Mushnik listen as Seymour is interviewed on the radio about his amazing new plant. They sing "Ya Never Know" about Mushnik's surprise at how the plant has made his store suddenly popular and profitable and how Seymour, who joins them onstage during the song, has gone from being a pathetic loser to being a celebrity.

At the end of the song, Seymour leaves, and Audrey enters. She explains that she is late because she has been handcuffed, and the girls warn her once more about her abusive boyfriend. They encourage her to leave him, but Audrey says she is afraid to. The chorus encourages Audrey to consider Seymour as a new boyfriend. Audrey sings "Somewhere That's Green," expressing her dream to leave the hectic urban life and move away to a place that is natural and wholesome, just as she would like to get out of her twisted relationship and be in a quiet relationship with Seymour.

Act 1, Scene 3

As Seymour empties trash into a can on the curb, Mushnik sings into the phone the song "Closed for Renovation," explaining to a customer how the business has expanded since Seymour and Audrey II brought it fame. The lights come up to show that the interior of the shop has been renovated with new paint and decorations. Audrey and Seymour join the song. She has on a clean new apron, and he has bandages on all of his fingers. Audrey comments on his injuries, but he attributes them to his new pruning shears.

At the end of the song, Audrey II is revealed. The plant is much larger than it was before and is covered with spikes.

Mushnik criticizes Seymour for forgetting a funeral flower order from Mrs. Shiva, their most important account (shivah is a period of mourning in Judaism). Audrey tells Seymour that he should not put up with the boss's verbal abuse. She offers to help him pick out new clothes that will reflect his newfound fame. She is impressed with him, and he is smitten with her.

When Audrey steps offstage, her boyfriend, Orin, enters. He wears a black leather motorcycle jacket and has a smug, self-important attitude. The chorus singers know that he is the one who has been abusing Audrey, and they try to send him away. Orin tries to explain that he is not vicious but that being a dentist has given him a fascination with pain and suffering. He sings "Dentist" about torturing small animals when he was young, which led him to his profession.

At the end of the song, Seymour enters the room. Orin is friendly to him while at the same time being intimidating. He suggests that Seymour use the new plant and his new fame to move up to a better plant store, but Seymour stays loyal to Mushnik. When Audrey enters, Orin is rude to her and insists that whenever she talks to him she address him as doctor. They leave on his motorcycle, Orin reminding her to bring the handcuffs he will use on her.

After they leave, Mushnik and Seymour sing "Mushnik and Son," in which Mushnik expresses his gratitude to Seymour. He offers to adopt Seymour, who was raised in an orphanage. Seymour is hesitant, but Mushnik insists until Seymour accepts the offer.

When Mushnik leaves, the plant talks to Seymour for the first time. It sings "Git It" about its need for more blood. It offers Seymour anything he might desire if he provides enough human blood for it to feast on. At first Seymour is skeptical, but Audrey II points out the good fortune that has already come to him, including his fame and his prospective adoption. Just as Seymour, trying to hold back, points out that he cannot think of anyone who deserves to be chopped up and fed to a plant, Orin and Audrey return.

Orin is furious with Audrey, shouting at her because she let him forget his sweater when they were there before. He slaps her. When they leave, Audrey II continues the song, urging Seymour to consider feeding Orin to the plant.

Act 1, Scene 4
This scene takes place at Orin's dentist office. The mood is eerie, like that of a horror movie.

Seymour enters and pulls a gun from a paper bag. Orin, who does not take him seriously, thinks that the gun is there because Seymour, like many people, is afraid of the dentist. He pushes Seymour into the examination chair and begins poking at his teeth and gums, inflicting pain with a rusty drill. Orin inhales nitrous oxide—the anesthetic commonly called laughing gas—but does not give any to his patient. Seymour sings "Now (It's Just the Gas)" to gather his courage to kill Orin. He puts the gun down, but the gas mask is stuck on Orin's head. Unable to remove the mask, Orin calls out to Seymour, who sits and watches him suffocate.

Act 1, Coda
While the chorus revives the play's opening song outside the flower shop, Seymour, inside, enters, carrying a bloody bucket. He takes Orin's severed hand out and feeds it to Audrey II. He then feeds a string of intestines to the plant, which laughs maniacally.

Act 2, Scene 1
At the start of act 2, Audrey II is huge, taking up a third of the stage space. The flower shop is now named Mushnik and Son and is alive with business. Mushnik and Audrey and the three chorus members are writing up orders for thousands of dollars' worth of flowers.

After a few minutes of busy chaos, everyone leaves the stage except Seymour and Audrey. While answering the phones, they sing "Call Back in the Morning" about how successful the business is. In the middle of the song, though, Audrey expresses her lonely depression. At six o'clock sharp, they stop answering phones and focus on each other.

On Audrey's advice, Seymour has been shopping for new clothes and has bought a leather jacket, like the one Orin wore, because he assumes it is the kind of thing she likes. The sight of the jacket saddens Audrey because Orin has disappeared. She feels guilty because she wished that something would happen to him, and what she has wished for has apparently come true. When Seymour holds out his hand to her, making the offer to be by her side, they sing the duet "Suddenly Seymour" about their close friendship.

As Audrey leaves, Mushnik enters. He says that he was taken in to the police station for questioning because they found a bag from the flower shop at Orin's dental office while investigating his disappearance. It is the bag Seymour carried his gun in when he went to confront Orin. Mushnik draws Seymour's attention to the red spots that dot the shop floor and then takes him to the garbage can at the curb, where Seymour has disposed of the dentist's uniform.

As Mushnik explains why he thinks Seymour has killed Orin and threatens to tell the police all he knows, Audrey II sings "Suppertime," urging Seymour to feed him Mushnik. Seymour starts for the police station with Mushnik but then stops. He makes up a story about the day's receipts being hidden in the plant. Mushnik is suspicious, but Seymour tells him to lean far into the plant's opening. This gives Audrey II the chance to eat Mushnik.

Act 2, Scene 2

Seymour is now a guilty man, having killed someone who, unlike Orin, did not deserve a gruesome fate. He is also poised to be a wealthy, famous man. Crystal, Ronnette, and Chiffon sing "The Meek Shall Inherit" about the fame that is coming to Seymour. A television executive named Bernstein wants him to do a weekly gardening show. Mrs. Luce, the wife of the editor of *Life*, wants him to be on the cover of the magazine. Skip Snip, a booking agent, wants to arrange a lecture tour for him. At the end of the song, Seymour mulls over the offers set before him and whether he would be able to keep Audrey interested in him if he were no longer famous. He signs with Snip.

Act 2, Scene 3

Some time has passed. The plant is now enormous. A memorial picture of Mushnik on the wall indicates that the flower shop is now in Seymour's hands.

When Audrey II begs for food, Seymour refuses. He leaves the shop to get some roast beef to satisfy the plant for a while. While he is gone Audrey enters. She has been bothered by uneasy feelings about Seymour and has taken a sleeping pill, which she relates in "Sominex/Suppertime II" (Sominex is the brand name of an over-the-counter sleep aid). The plant calls out to her. At first, Audrey is amazed that the plant can talk, but when it asks her to bring it a drink of water, she complies. As Audrey pours water into Audrey II's open trap, the plant pulls her in and eats her.

Seymour, returning to the store, tries to rescue Audrey, only to find that she wants to be eaten by the plant. She sees that Audrey II's growth, which comes from eating people, is the reason for Seymour's success, and she feels that giving her life to the plant is the one gift that she can give Seymour. As the plant devours her, she sings a reprise of "Somewhere That's Green." This time, though, the lyrics refer not to a suburban existence but to the inside of the plant. As Audrey dies, Seymour holds her in his arms and then puts her inside the plant.

Patrick Martin, a representative of a plant distributor, shows up. He wants to get Seymour to agree to distribute leaf cuttings from Audrey II around the world. Seymour immediately understands what this means: that the plant, with its appetite for human flesh, would conquer the world. He tries shooting Audrey II, and when that does not work, he tries pouring rat poison into its mouth. Then he climbs inside the plant to attack it from the inside.

Crystal, Ronnette, and Chiffon sing to the audience the news of what happens next. The plants spreads across the country, then the world, feeding on unsuspecting owners. The last item on their list of places taken over by Audrey II plants is the theater in which the audience is seated at the moment. As the chorus sings, the biggest Audrey II of all is revealed. It has four flowers on it, and in those flowers are the faces of Orin, Mushnik, Audrey, and Seymour, who join the cast in singing a warning song—"Finale (Don't Feed the Plants)"—about the plant that is coming to destroy the world. Stems of the plant fall down on the audience as the play comes to an end.

CHARACTERS

Audrey

Audrey, the play's female lead, is a more complex character than she seems at first. As a worker at the flower shop, she seems to be a shy, vulnerable girl who has fallen into an abusive relationship and dreams of a calm life in the suburbs, where people are kind and peaceful and plants grow abundantly (as characterized by the song "Somewhere That's Green"). The more that people show how obvious it is that her boyfriend, Orin, abuses her, the more defensive of him she becomes, which indicates that she feels she deserves to be treated badly.

Later in the play, Audrey reveals that she has a history in society's underside. When she met Orin, she was working at a nightclub called The Gutter, wearing clothes that she describes as cheap and tasteless, contrasting them to the nice ones that she wears to work at the flower shop. She is clearly ashamed of her past, and that is what makes her feel she deserves to be abused.

Audrey finds out Seymour's secret at the end of the play. She understands that the plant can survive only by eating human flesh, so she sacrifices herself. She climbs into the plant so that it can grow and make Seymour even more rich and successful. She has such low self-esteem that she does not see that he loves her, that his only reason for wanting fame is to impress her. With her death, his fame is meaningless.

Audrey II

Throughout the play, the personality of Audrey II, the plant, changes as it reveals its true intentions. At first, it is small and dependent on Seymour for nutrition, begging him for food. It behaves as if it were his child. As it becomes more powerful, though, the plant becomes more self-reliant. Instead of asking, it demands more and more from Seymour.

When Seymour threatens to destroy the plant after it has devoured Mushnik, it laughs at him and taunts him, daring him to stand up to it. At the end of the play, viewers can see that Audrey II, which is begging for food when it first appears, has been working all along toward its plan for world domination.

Bernstein

Bernstein is an executive with the NBC network who comes to the flower shop at the height of Seymour's fame to try to persuade him to do a weekly television show, *Seymour Krelborn's Gardening Tips*.

Chiffon

Chiffon is one of the three street urchins who stand outside the flower shop and comment on the action. Like Crystal and Ronnette, her name comes from that of a 1960s singing group, known as a girl group, who sang in the style used for this play's music. The Chiffons are known for songs such as "He's So Fine" and "One Fine Day."

Crystal

Crystal is one of the three street urchins who loiter outside the flower shop and comment on the action, fulfilling the function of a Greek chorus. Like the others in the chorus, her name comes from the name of a doo-wop singing group in the 1960s. The Crystals' most famous hits, "Da Doo Ron Ron," "He Hit Me (and It Felt like a Kiss)," and "And Then He Kissed Me," exemplify the girl group sound of the chorus of urchins in this play.

Customer

In act 1, scene 1, as Seymour explains to Mr. Mushnik how having an exotic plant like Audrey II in the window may make more customers come in out of curiosity and buy things, a customer enters, expresses his curiosity about the strange plant, and leaves after buying one hundred dollars' worth of roses.

The Derelict
See Wino #1

Seymour Krelborn

Seymour is the protagonist of the play. The playwright's notes describe him as being in his mid-twenties and possibly balding, a way to illustrate his nervous insecurity. The notes also advise against playing Seymour as too broad a comic nerd. He is an honest, hard-working little man without much success to show for his work, but he is not meant to be a ridiculous caricature.

Seymour's main objective is to impress Audrey, the coworker he loves. This is shown early on when he names the new plant species he has discovered Audrey II in homage to the woman he desires. Seeing her abusive relationship with her boyfriend ignites mixed emotions in Seymour. On the one hand, he sees for the first time that she is vulnerable and ready for a different boyfriend, but he also knows that he has to impress her if he wants to steal her away from Orin. Audrey mentions Seymour's growing celebrity, and he knows that he has to nurture Audrey II to increase his celebrity status, even if it means harming himself to provide the plant with blood.

When the blood he can give is not enough, Seymour is driven to murder. Seymour's moral decline is gradual. Killing Orin and feeding him to the plant is almost a moral act, because it stops Orin from his physical and emotional abuse of Audrey. When he kills his boss and mentor, Mushnik, Seymour is clearly crossing a moral line. At that moment, Mushnik is a danger to Seymour, threatening to turn him in, but he has also adopted Seymour and made the young man his heir. Later, when Audrey agrees to sacrifice herself to the plant for his sake, Seymour allows it. He soon realizes the problem with what he has done. Without Audrey, there is no reason to support the plant's growth, and he dies trying to undo her sacrifice.

Mrs. Luce

Mrs. Luce introduces herself as the editor's wife and offers to put Seymour's picture on the cover of *Life* magazine. She is clearly inspired by Clare Boothe Luce, an American playwright (*The Women*) and diplomat who was married to Henry Luce, the publisher of several magazines, including *Life*, *Time*, *Fortune*, and *Sports Illustrated*.

Patrick Martin

Martin shows up in the last scene. He is a representative of the licensing and marketing division of World Botanical Enterprises, the company that is going to reproduce the Audrey II plant and distribute cuttings all over the world. It is Martin's involvement in Audrey II's popularity that makes Seymour realize that he is not just dealing with one hungry plant; he is dealing with a plant that has plans for world domination.

Gravis Mushnik

Gravis Mushnik is the owner of a flower shop on skid row, the poor part of town. The shop does little business, and Mushnik is on the verge of closing it when Seymour's discovery, Audrey II, starts bringing in business. Mushnik cares only about his business. When it is failing, he orders Seymour around and mocks him, but when he sees Seymour as a source of wealth, he becomes warmer toward him. Eventually, he offers to adopt Seymour, even though Seymour is much too old to need a legal guardian. It is not clear whether Mushnik wants to adopt Seymour as a ploy to keep him from taking his business-generating plant with him or if being financially comfortable for the first time has actually made him feel affection for his employee, but either interpretation points to the same conclusion: Mushnik's understanding of the world is colored by his thirst for money.

In act 2, Mushnik puts morality over greed, and it costs him his life. When he discovers that Seymour is responsible for Orin's death, Mushnik declares his intention to take this information to the police. He knows that Seymour is the cause of his business's success and that turning Seymour in puts him at risk of failure once more. He also knows, however that it would be wrong to leave a murder unpunished, even though Orin was clearly a person who deserved punishment.

Narrator

The narrator is an unseen voice-over role. He has a booming, authoritative voice.

Ronnette

One of the three street urchins who serve as a chorus in this play, Ronnette stands around near the flower shop with her friends and comments on the action. Like the other two urchins, Crystal and Chiffon, she is named after a 1960s singing group, the Ronettes. The lead singer was Ronnie Spector, wife of Phil Spector, the record producer associated with the distinctive 1960s girl group sound. The group spelled its name with one *n*, a difference from the character in the play.

Orin Scrivello

Orin Scrivello is Audrey's boyfriend. He is an unusual combination of archetypes. He is a professional man, a dentist, but he is also a leather-jacketed motorcyclist. The play binds these two distinct character types together humorously by stating that they are both traits of a sadistic personality.

Orin is openly cruel toward Audrey. His cruelty comes so naturally to him that he does not even realize that there is anything wrong with it. He makes her carry handcuffs with her so that he can bind her, and he corrects her if she talks to him without addressing him as doctor. Audrey puts up with his abuse because she has low self-esteem and feels that she deserves it.

Being a dentist gives Orin a chance to exercise his cruel nature toward someone other than his girlfriend. When Seymour goes to confront him, Orin sings "It's Just the Gas" about how much he enjoys inflicting pain on his patients. He augments his excitement by inhaling nitrous oxide, a gas that was once used as a dental anesthetic, heightening the natural high he gets from inflicting pain.

Skip Snip

Snip is an agent who comes to the shop to persuade Seymour to go on a lecture tour of colleges to talk about Audrey II for profit.

Wino #1

The character referred to in the production notes as the derelict is known in the play itself as Wino #1. He does not interact with the other characters but stands around to add to the mood of the inner-city skid row setting of the play.

THEMES

Social Class

From the opening song on, much is made in *Little Shop of Horrors* about the location of Mushnik's flower shop, referred to as skid row. The name skid row was used, mostly in the first half of the twentieth century, to describe the poorest section of many cities, inhabited by vagrants, criminals, and failed businesses. Though the play is clearly patterned on New York City, where the similar section has been known for generations as the Bowery, the most famous skid row is in Los Angeles. Mixing elements of different cities is useful for making this a story that happens in no definite, real city in particular.

In "Downtown (Skid Row)," the chorus and main characters sing about living in poverty. The secondary characters, who help to establish the tone of the play, are known by such underclass identifiers as urchins and the derelict. That the play's characters are from the lower class makes them underdogs, struggling against the existing social system, fighting to rise up, as Seymour is able to do, to positions of social power and respectability.

The class differences in this play become most evident at the beginning of act 2 with the song "Call Back in the Morning." The failing

flower shop is so popular by this point that the staff can turn away customers and accept business only from those of the highest social positions. It has crossed over, owing to interest in the unusual plant, from lower class to upper class.

Middle-Class Values

Seymour is a poor, inept assistant in a failing business. Audrey is a woman with low self-esteem mired in an abusive relationship. In the duet "Somewhere That's Green" they describe their simple, unambitious aspirations. They do not want fortune or fame. The best they both can dream of is the kind of solid, somewhat boring life that is associated with the middle class of the postwar 1950s: verdant suburban lawns, nice furniture with plastic slipcovers, television, children. To a great many people, this would have simply been the place they lived out their lives with nothing remarkable about it. To the people living lives of poverty and desperation, represented by characters in this play, the calm middle-class lifestyle holds the promise of an ideal existence.

Parent-Child Relationships

It is not surprising that upon discovering a new plant species, Seymour wistfully decides to treat the plant as if it is his and Audrey's daughter. He names it after her, as people often do to affirm the family lineage. He finds out later, however, once the plant starts talking, that a masculine name would have been more appropriate.

At first, Seymour is awkward about assuming a nurturing parental role toward Audrey II. Like a new parent, he is uncertain about what to feed it. When he finds out that it wants blood, he accepts his responsibility to feed it the blood from his own veins, like a parent who is called on to make sacrifices for his child. As the plant grows more independent, Seymour tries to hide its blood thirst from the world with the same protectiveness that the parent of a criminal child might feel. It is only after Audrey II has killed Audrey, the love of his life, that Seymour realizes he can no longer protect the plant. He stops looking at it as his child and sees it as the invasive foreign species that it really is.

At the same time that he is learning the responsibilities of fatherhood, Seymour, an adult orphan, learns what it is like to be a son. Mushnik adopts him, even though Seymour is too old to need a legal guardian. It is clear that

TOPICS FOR FURTHER STUDY

- Choose a common, nonthreatening object that you use every day that you can characterize as a man-eating killer. Create a puppet version of it. Make your puppet big enough to devour a human being but small enough so that two puppeteers can manipulate it. After showing it off, explain to your class its inner workings.

- *Urinetown*, like *Little Shop of Horrors*, started off Broadway and went on to a successful Broadway run before becoming a standard of community theaters. It is also a musical that pokes fun at conventions of musical theater (starry-eyed lovers, greedy corporate henchmen, sonorous narrators). Read the libretto for *Urinetown*, published by Faber & Faber, and create a chart that compares its effectiveness as a social satire with that of *Little Shop of Horrors*. Be sure to clearly define the standards you think a musical social satire should have.

- Many of Menken's songs for *Little Shop of Horrors* are patterned after the Motown sound. In the 1960s, Motown, a record company started in Detroit, was instrumental in crossing the color barrier and making the music of dozens of African American recording artists familiar to white Americans. Read about Motown in Nelson George's book *Where Did Our Love Go? The Rise and Fall of the Motown Sound*. After reading about the history of this particular genre of music,

write an essay about the things you think Menken got right about the Motown sound and what things he, an outsider to the culture that it sprang from, might have misinterpreted.

- Using the graphic novel format, write a sequel to *Little Shop of Horrors*, showing the story of some particular individuals once the world has become invaded by offshoots of Audrey II.

- *Beauty and the Beast* is a story that has been told many times, in many formats, but the book and music that Ashman and Menken wrote for the 1991 Disney movie have an enduring effect on young adults. In the years since it became a modern classic, the film has been adapted to the stage, like *Little Shop of Horrors*, also with Ashman and Menken's music and lyrics. Watch *Beauty and the Beast* and take notes on the story line and the lyrics. Write an essay explaining whether or not you think Ashman and Menken were better writing for young adults than for adults. Use examples from each work to illustrate your ideas.

- Find a little-known movie from the 1940s or 1950s and write songs for particular scenes. Present your songs to your class with clips from the movie, so they can judge how well you captured the meaning of the scene while changing its tone to that of a musical comedy.

Seymour wants to become part of a family, to establish some sense of normalcy in his life. The adoption is not necessarily based on parental feelings. Mushnik is a father figure to his workers from the start but a bad parent. He berates and belittles Seymour until Seymour becomes a financial asset to the flower shop. Even though Mushnik's reason for adopting Seymour is unclear, Seymour is desperate to have a family—until Mushnik threatens to turn him in

to the police for Orin's murder. His willingness to send Seymour to jail shows that Mushnik is not that interested in Seymour after all, that he is not willing to protect his son in the way that Seymour has been taking risks to protect Audrey II.

Sadomasochism

This play makes light of Orin's abusive tendencies by linking them to his profession as a dentist. The joke is that dentists were traditionally

Sheridan Smith in a 2007 performance of Little Shop Of Horrors *at the Duke of York's Theatre in London, England. (© MJ Kim / Getty Images)*

known, before modern anesthesia, to cause pain while working on their patients. Ashman follows the creators of the original 1960 *The Little Shop of Horrors* film, Charles B. Griffith and Roger Corman, in assuming that a profession that inflicts pain may attract someone who actually likes inflicting pain. Orin's fondness for causing pain has the sexual element often associated with sadism. The woman he hits, binds with handcuffs, and abuses verbally is the woman he is dating.

Sadists like Orin need masochistic partners who want pain inflicted on them. Audrey has low self-esteem and feels she deserves to be abused and demeaned. She comes from a sexually shady background, having once danced in demeaning clothes (which she herself calls cheap and tasteless) in a place called The Gutter. Although the rest of the cast can see the bruises Orin leaves on her, and they cringe at the way he orders her around, Audrey looks on Orin as her savior, someone to whom she owes a debt. He has lifted her up out of her former life, which makes her feel he is entitled to demean her in any way he wants.

Success

Little Shop of Horrors takes a sarcastic view of social success. Seymour may be well-meaning, but he is not particularly intelligent. He does not create Audrey II through careful horticulture; he just finds it—to be more accurate, it finds him. He is able to cultivate the plant only by pouring out his own life force. Despite his limitations, Seymour ends up being a national celebrity with offers for speaking engagements, a national television show, and a cover story in *Life* magazine.

Success in the world of this work comes from having something interesting to offer. One day, Mushnik's flower shop is on the brink of failure, but in an instant—the instant the customer wanders in to look at Audrey II and buys one hundred dollars' worth of roses—the shop becomes a success.

The negative side of success is that it makes Seymour indebted to Audrey II, who tells him that success is something that the plant can give him only if he will cooperate. He must continue to provide the flower with human blood to stay successful. In this sense, success in the play reflects the careers of hundreds of minor celebrities with marginal talent or familial connections who become popular for one thing and end up desperately struggling to prolong fame that they never deserve.

STYLE

Parody

As the title suggests, *Little Shop of Horrors* is a parody of horror and science fiction films of the 1950s and 1960s. It captures the paranoia of 1950s science fiction, in which strange visitors from other planets are viewed as possible hostile invaders in films such as *The Day the Earth Stood Still* (1951), *The Thing from Another World* (1951), *Invasion of the Body Snatchers* (1956), and *The Blob* (1958). Several of the films in this genre speculated that contact with other worlds would prove to be disastrous for humanity if the inhabitants of those planets were to come to Earth pretending to be friendly while hiding malicious intent, as Audrey II is doing in this play.

The other strain of movies parodied in *Little Shop of Horrors* is the nature attacks genre. These films resemble the films that imagine invasions from space, except that whether by alien influence or ecological catastrophe, animals and plants mutate and attack humanity. In one of the earliest examples, *Them!* (1954), ants affected by nuclear tests in Nevada grow to the size of automobiles and attack. Other notable examples are *The Day of the Triffids* (1962), about plants that manage to walk and attack; *The Fly* (1958), about a botched laboratory experiment that makes a scientist half human, half fly; and *Food of the Gods* (1976), loosely based on an H. G. Wells novel. Other films about attacking frogs, moths, snakes, and more have been a staple of low-budget horror movies.

It is the low-budget production values that make these films funny and endearing to camp film fans and that made them ripe for parody in the original 1960 movie of *Little Shop of Horrors* and in the stage musical based on it.

Homage

Whereas a parody exaggerates aspects of its target to make fun of it, sometimes with affection, an homage aims to reproduce the best parts of another person's work as a tribute to the work.

The musical score that Menken wrote in turning *Little Shop of Horrors* into a stage musical centers on homage to the girl group sound of the late 1950s and early 1960s—popularized by songwriters such as Carole King and Gerry Goffin, the producer Phil Spector, and Motown Records. In the first half of the 1960s, groups like the Marvelettes, the Dixie Cups, the Shangri-Las, and the namesakes of the street singers in this play—the Ronettes, the Crystals, and the Chiffons—were regulars on the pop music charts. Because of the confluence of the times and the heavy influence of the Spector studio, the hundreds of girl groups are remembered for a distinct, memorable sound, to which Menken pays homage with his songs. The girl group sound was a memory when *Little Shop of Horrors* was first produced in 1982 and is even more distant for modern audiences, but patterning the music after the girl group sound has given it a distinct identity.

Adaptation

The writers of *Little Shop of Horrors* had few of the troubles that usually come with adapting a work from another medium. The 1960 Roger Corman film was cheaply made and, though it was a cult classic, was not widely familiar, so they did not have to worry about fans who would be angered with changes to the original plot or characters. The story was established in the shape of a play. Unlike writers adapting a novel or television show, they did not have to choose large segments to leave out. Like the play, the film was a comic parody of science fiction conventions of its time and had already established the lighthearted, tongue-in-cheek mood that suits musical theater. In an unusual twist, the Broadway run of the play, and even the original off-Broadway run, had a better budget for realizing the plant's growth than the movie had. Whereas stage adaptations like Disney's *The Lion King, Aladdin,* and *Spider-Man: Turn Off the Dark* are faced with trying to translate a reality that was imagined for drawings into a world of tangible objects, *Little Shop of Horrors* was bound to be more visually impressive than its source.

HISTORICAL CONTEXT

Cold War Horror Films

Roger Corman's 1960 film *The Little Shop of Horrors,* which provided the inspiration for this

COMPARE & CONTRAST

- **1982:** Roger Corman's B-movie *The Little Shop of Horrors* is a mostly forgotten relic. It is best remembered by fans of camp movies who like to laugh at cheap production values and who appreciate Corman's subversive comic vision and by fans of Jack Nicholson who appreciate his early, pre-fame performance.

  Today: *Little Shop of Horrors* is defined by the stage musical and the 1986 film adaptation.

- **1982:** Broadway's fame has faded. The theater district of New York is associated with crime and decay.

  Today: Broadway is as popular and financially stable as it has ever been, thanks in part to the kind of musical adaptations of familiar stories that *Little Shop of Horrors* represents.

- **1982:** Ashman and Menken are basically unknown outside New York, having worked together on only one off-Broadway production together: their adaptation of Kurt Vonnegut's *God Bless You, Mr. Rosewater*.

  Today: Ashman and Menken are one of film's legendary partnerships. Their work on *The Little Mermaid, Beauty and the Beast*, and *Aladdin* for the Walt Disney studio establish a tone that helps the studio establish itself once again as the top animation producer in the world.

- **1982:** People who grew up in the 1950s emulate the biker culture of leather jackets and greased hair that the character Orin adopts as his style.

  Today: More than sixty years after Marlon Brando brought biker culture to the screen in *The Wild One*, there are few bikers who were active in the 1950s. What people remember is nostalgic reproductions, like Danny from the play *Grease* and Fonzie from the television program *Happy Days*.

- **1982:** The idea of a mutant plant developing both the ability to talk and a taste for human flesh is a subject of science fiction and fantasy.

  Today: Horticulturists emphasize how the use of genetically modified organisms (GMOs) can help create stronger, bigger, more resilient plants to feed a growing world population, but many people fear that food with modified genes can actually produce horrible mutations like Audrey II.

play, was a cheap, quick production made in two days. What it lacked in budget and production values it more than made up for in comic conceits and theoretical speculation, most of which reflected the political spirit of its time, giving a particular sense of paranoid hysteria to Ashman and Menken's 1982 musical.

After the Second World War ended with the detonation of nuclear devices over Hiroshima and Nagasaki, the world was awakened to the unimaginable power of nuclear energy. Two cities had been flattened by a single bomb each. A nuclear war, in which multiple nuclear devices might be exploded in back-and-forth retaliation, could theoretically create enough force to destroy the planet. And if that were not terrifying enough, another fearsome aspect that came from the nuclear bomb detonations was the concept of genetic mutations caused by exposure to radiation.

The new awareness of the awesome powers of nuclear radiation coincided with the postwar rivalry between the United States, with its allies in the North Atlantic Treaty Organization, or NATO, and the Soviet Union and its Warsaw Pact allies. In the late 1940s, the House Un-American Activities Committee of the U.S. Congress brought to national attention the threat that communism posed. Americans were warned daily that their opponents in what came to be called the Cold War wanted to take over the world. The war was called cold because it was thought of as being fought not with weapons but with stealth. People believed that enemies would infiltrate American society disguised as normal citizens to attack from within. The newfound power of atomic energy and threat of attack, whether overt or covert, provided filmmakers of the 1950s and 1960s ample material for science fiction stories.

One of the first and most influential of these horror movies was *Godzilla*, a film made in Japan in 1953 and re-released in the United States in 1954 with additional footage that included American actors. The premise of the film—a dinosaur-like creature mutates by nuclear power to a gigantic size—would be reflected in later films such as *The Amazing Colossal Man* (1957) and *The Attack of the 50-Foot Woman* (1958) and films about creatures that grow well beyond their normal sizes because of radiation, such as *Earth vs. the Spider* (1958) and *Them!*, a 1954 film about irradiated giant ants. In these and dozens of other movies made on low budgets and mostly forgotten, spurious scientific explanations were given to explain mutations that were brought to life with simple special effects.

Other films speculated on what would happen if invaders from space tried to take over the world in the same way that communist countries were reportedly trying to do. In *This Island Earth* (1955), for instance, scientists from around the world are recruited by inhabitants of the planet Metaluna and told that they are going to help that planet avert an ecological disaster when they are actually being used to create weaponry that will be used in attacking Earth. *The Day the Earth Stood Still* is a respected, full-budget studio production about an alien who arrives with a message of peace and cooperation but is faced with suspicion and attacked. *Plan 9 from Outer Space* (1959) is often cited as the epitome of cheap alien invasion movies with laughably rubbery special effects and continuity problems.

The politically paranoid strain of 1950s sci-fi and the unnatural mutation strain come together in *Invasion of the Body Snatchers* (1956), in which people are replaced by a plant life-form from another world that grows pod people—duplicates of the people who touch the pods—who answer to the master plant's agenda.

Corman's *The Little Shop of Horrors* took elements from all of these Cold War horror films and, in the course of two days' filming, created a parody that made fun of them all. Ashman's script for *Little Shop of Horrors* retains much of what Corman mocked and, with a few decades' hindsight, also made a loving tribute to the films of the 1950s and 1960s.

Adapted Musicals

It is common to see musical theater that has been adapted from other, nonmusical sources, such as *La Cage aux Folles*, *Sunset Boulevard*, *Young Frankenstein*, and *Catch Me If You Can*. Much of this can be attributed to the financial stakes in the Broadway musical, which have risen dramatically since *Little Shop of Horrors* was first performed off-Broadway in the 1980s.

By the 1970s, Broadway, which had been synonymous with New York theater since before the turn of the century, had fallen into disrepair. The Times Square area had deteriorated. Famed theaters had been divided up into stores or converted to movie houses showing cut-rate films or had simply been demolished. Forty-Second Street, the area known worldwide as the theater district, had gained a reputation as a haven for prostitution and drug sales. Though a revitalization of Broadway seemed unlikely if not impossible, corporations invested in large, high-return plays. In the early 1980s the big plays in town were *Les Misérables* (adapted from the novel by Victor Hugo) and *Cats* (adapted from a book of poems by T. S. Eliot). Soon the Disney corporation invested heavily in the Times Square area to present adaptations of its musical films, particularly films from the most recent surge of Disney animation: *Beauty and the Beast*, *The Little Mermaid*, and *Aladdin*, each of which contained work by the *Little Shop of Horrors* writers Ashman and Menken.

Broadway rebounded and became an entertainment center once again because of the new focus on family-friendly entertainment. The new focus was financially successful, drawing more and more corporate support, but at a price: investors are interested in vehicles that offer the highest return for the lowest risk. Traditionally, that has meant offering audiences the comfort of stories that have already proved popular in

Seymour works at a florist when he acquires the odd plant. (© Pressmaster | Shutterstock.com)

books, theater, television, and movies, but with the excitement of memorable music and increasingly awe-inspiring sets. That is why Corman's low-budget film was able to yield a successful off-Broadway production when Ashman and Menken's music was added. The 2003 Broadway revival included a large, complex Audrey II that was greater than anything offered in the B-movie original and the small-theater production. It rivaled the big-budget special effects of the 1986 Hollywood film.

CRITICAL OVERVIEW

When it debuted at the WPA Theater in 1982, *Little Shop of Horrors* was a certified hit. It soon moved to the Orpheum Theatre, where it ran for years with an impressive 2,209 performances, was adapted to a star-studded Hollywood movie, became one of the most popular plays for high school theater ever, and reemerged in New York, this time in a Broadway production, in 2003.

The original production, with Ellen Greene as Audrey and Lee Wilkof as Seymour, was hailed by critics, including Mel Gussow in the *New York Times*, who calls it "as entertaining as it is exotic. It is a show for horticulturists, horror-cultists, sci-fi fans and anyone with a taste for the outrageous." In the second edition of his book *Broadway Musicals: Show by Show*, Stanley Green writes that the play, although still in its initial run, "would seem far riskier than the usual theatrical enterprise, but *Little Shop of Horrors* won over a majority of the critics with its offbeat humor."

The play's Broadway revival, directed by Jerry Zaks and starring Hunter Foster and Kerry Butler, also met with critical acclaim. The small musical combo (Menken leading on the piano) was replaced with a house band, and the puppeteering for Audrey II was given a larger budget, but, as Don Shewey puts it in his review for the *Advocate* in November 2003, this "smashing new revival...isn't just a cynical Xerox of a presold product but a first-class remounting." He credits the show not only for having nonstop entertainment but also for having political implications: "We don't have to look any further than tabloid TV and the murky war-making machinery in Washington to supply our own contemporary parallels" to the show's grand audience-attacking finale.

Not all critics were enchanted with the 2003 revival, which seemed to draw more cynical attention than the initial off-Broadway run. Elysa Gardner, in *USA Today*, for example, praised Zaks's direction and Foster and Butler in the leads but believed that their talents were not enough. "Unfortunately," Gardner writes, "these appealing young performers can't sustain the show on their own, and the comic support from actors cast in darker, more flamboyant roles is disappointingly flimsy." She is lukewarm toward Rob Bartlett's portrayal of Mushnik, who "to his credit, manages to lend some credibility to the caricature." She was unimpressed, however, with the comedic talents of Douglas Sills, who played the roles of Orin and several walk-on characters late in the play, performances that Gardner finds "vaguely amusing at best."

CRITICISM

David Kelly

Kelly is a writer and an instructor of literature and creative writing. In the following essay, he makes the case that Orin is a dangerous character for a musical comedy—a sexual abuser—and examines the steps taken in Little Shop of Horrors *to make Orin acceptable for the play's message.*

The 1960 Roger Corman film *The Little Shop of Horrors* did not have much going for it. It was quickly thrown together; was a science fiction film with zero budget for sets, props, or special effects; had no movie star actors (though one of the actors, Jack Nicholson, did later go on to be one of the biggest names in movies from the 1970s through the 2000s); and was not particularly well written, seeming as if the writing has been rushed. Corman and the screenwriter Charles Griffith were able to make their slapdash work memorable because they went for the one thing that can be done best on a low budget— humor, especially macabre black humor, laughing at the triumph of evil in the eternal battle between good and bad. Like many dark comedies, though, the film passes through the triumph of evil and ends up affirming the

> THERE WILL ALWAYS BE PEOPLE WHO COMPLAIN THAT IT SHOULD BE ACCEPTABLE BECAUSE, THIS IS, AFTER ALL, JUST A COMEDY. SOME PEOPLE WILL ALWAYS ASSERT THAT ANYTHING DONE WITH HUMOROUS INTENT MUST BE ALLOWABLE AS THEY MOAN, 'DOES EVERYTHING HAVE TO BE POLITICALLY CORRECT?'"

traditional sense that good is better. The dark world of *The Little Shop of Horrors* goes one step beyond mean-spiritedness. The good characters win but not because they are good. They win in spite of their own goodness: they bungle along with simple-mindedness, showing the nastier characters to be too clever to succeed.

Adapting this story to the stage in the 1980s, taking the time in crafting it that the original could not afford, Ashman and Menken added another element. Just starting their legendary career together at the time, they fitted the movie's story into the stage musical tradition. This tradition emphasizes joy. Looking at the world as a place where song and dance can break out at any moment is quite the opposite of a world with no music, no dance, no joy.

It would be a mistake to think that the musical version takes audiences to a completely cheerful world. Even with the stage spectacle, with the hummable tunes and impressive special effects featuring trained puppeteers bringing the killer plant to life, *Little Shop of Horrors* is still a black comedy. The good characters are too bland to deserve their good fortune, and the nasty characters cause their own undoing. The stage musical was so dark in its vision that the ending had to be lightened for the Hollywood film: in the film of the musical, the good, sympathetic humans, Seymour and Audrey, survive and kill the destructive plant, Audrey II.

As is usual with a comedy, expectations are reversed. The nice people, Seymour and Audrey, are depicted as being nice because they lack intelligence. The smart people—the all-seeing chorus of Chiffon, Crystal, and Ronnette—are

WHAT DO I READ NEXT?

- The first musical that Ashman and Menken collaborated on was also an adaptation: in 1980 they brought Kurt Vonnegut's novel *God Bless You, Mr. Rosewater* (1965) to the stage. The story involves a man from a wealthy family who decides to use his inheritance to help people—and the people who try to stop him.

- *Little Shop of Horrors* is mentioned briefly in Thomas S. Hischak's study *Through the Screen Door: What Happened to the Broadway Musical When It Went to Hollywood.* This brief mention helps put Ashman and Menken's play into perspective in a discussion of adapting musicals to film. Readers who have seen the 1986 Frank Oz film and are studying the play would be interested in finding out the tradition of making films from musicals. Hischak's book was published in 2004.

- Of the many books written about science fiction movies of the postwar era, Barry Atkinson's *Atomic Age Cinema: The Offbeat, the Classic and the Obscure* (2014) captures the mood of *Little Shop of Horrors* best. Like Ashman, Atkinson has a keen eye for the kind of camp sensibilities in films that were awful but fun to watch, somewhat sincere and exploitative at the same time. Published in 2014, this book covers the paranoia of a time that did not understand science well.

- The most revolutionary musical of recent years is Matt Stone and Trey Parker's 2011 instant classic, *The Book of Mormon*, winner of several major awards, including Tony Awards for Best Musical, Best Book of a Musical, and Best Original Score and a Grammy for Best Musical Theater Album. Whereas Ashman and Menken safely skewered cheap movies from decades earlier, Stone and Parker took a chance on insulting the Church of Jesus Christ of Latter-day Saints, whose official response was congenial, appreciative of the play's good-natured parody. The book of the play, *The Book of Mormon Script Book: The Complete Book and Lyrics of the Broadway Musical*, was published in 2011.

- *Little Shop of Horrors* is so often adapted for school theaters that it is mentioned in Victor V. Bobetsky's book *The Magic of Middle School Musicals*. Bobetsky's text takes a broad view of which plays work best on a school budget with a school cast and crew. Published in 2009, it gives readers a background for school productions.

- The sense of nostalgia that imbues *Little Shop of Horrors* is directly reflective of one of the longest-running musicals in Broadway history, *Grease*, by Jim Jacobs, Warren Casey, and John Farrar. The play, a community theater favorite, was first staged in 1971 and offered an idealized version of high-school life in 1959. Although twelve years seems soon for invoking nostalgia, the intervening decade was the turbulent 1960s, a time when music, youth, and all of society experienced an upheaval of perspective. Samuel French published the libretto in 1972 with a revised edition in 2009.

- The musical theater scene has been notorious for its lack of cultural diversity. One of the memorable works to celebrate the art of African Americans is *Your Arms Too Short to Box with God*, a 1976 musical based on the book of Matthew in the Bible. Alex Bradford wrote the music and lyrics combining gospel, funk, and soul traditions, and Vinnette Carroll wrote the book, adapting the story for modern audiences. The play had a successful 1980 Broadway revival with Patti LaBelle and Al Greene and is frequently presented by community theaters.

irrelevant to the events. The father figure, Mr. Mushnik, is motivated by greed. When he acts as a concerned citizen, threatening to report Seymour's apparent crimes to the police, he dies for acting conscientiously. Punishing a good character would be tragic in a serious play, but in a comedy it is played for laughs.

Mushnik's complexity, as a greedy character with a conscience, is handled with humor. So is the character of Orin Scrivello. Orin is a truly bad person, a violent abuser who gets pleasure from the suffering of others. The only reason he does not bring the musical comedy to a grinding halt is that he is such an exaggerated, ludicrous character. His one redeeming feature is that he dies stupidly.

A terrible character who does not pay for his crimes can work in a dark comedy, representing a laugh at traditionalists who think it is the artist's job to punish evil and reward good. The problem with Orin as a character in comedy does not come from his awful personality—comedies thrive on using bad people effectively as foils for their heroes, who, after all, need someone to triumph over. Venal, craven, nasty, oafish— these characters work fine in comedy. What makes Orin stand out as particularly problematic is that his particular brand of terribleness is rooted in sexual abuse.

Reason dictates that if comedy is based on stretching the envelope and bringing taboo subjects into the open, there still have to be subjects that are legitimately taboo. If there are not, then there is no envelope to stretch, no status quo for the comedy writer to rebel against. If there are inherently unfunny subjects, though, then sexual abuse would certainly fit that category. Orin is funny because, as he shrieks with joy at the pain he inflicts, he inverts standard expectations; he is odd. But he is also a sexual abuser, a rapist, and that makes him problematic for a musical comedy.

Orin is not just a brash character, a boyfriend with a forceful personality or abrasive manner. He does not just overwhelm his girlfriend, Audrey, because she is so comically timid that she is willing to put up with his buffoonery. Audrey has bruises and marks on her wrists from where Orin has handcuffed her, marks that she tries to avoid discussing. Orin insists that she bring handcuffs on their date, so there is clearly something sexual about his use of handcuffs. And though Audrey may see herself

as a willing participant in her relationship with Orin, the philosophical question remains: Can anyone be considered willing who acts against her or his self-interest? If not, the abusive relationship is not really consensual. A sexual relationship that is not consensual is rape.

If Orin were being sold to audiences as a funny rapist, there would be little question of the inappropriateness of this character. There will always be people who complain that it should be acceptable because, this is, after all, just a comedy. Some people will always assert that anything done with humorous intent must be allowable as they moan, "Does everything have to be politically correct?" These arguments are as absolutist as the arguments that they claim to dispute. They are made against the perceived claim that everything must fit rigid social expectations by declaring that nothing should be subject to such rules. It goes without saying that violent sexual abuse is not funny and that a willingness to laugh at it does not make it any funnier or any less repulsive.

The complicating factor is that Ashman has imbued Orin with just enough personality to make him human while making him a flawed human. Audiences are not being asked to laugh about the abuse he inflicts on Audrey; they are asked to laugh at Orin, the misguided man, the deluded fool. He can bully a demure girl like Audrey, but he himself is slave to his obsession—not enough to be pitied, but certainly enough to be mocked. In the song "Dentist!" Orin equates sadism with dentistry—the connection is nonsense, based on an assumption that because going to the dentist can be painful, dentists must enjoy inflicting pain. Being so foolish as to see nothing wrong with his weird obsession makes Orin a comic creation, but somewhat human. Choosing a profession to fit his obsession reduces Orin to the level of cartoon, a caricature of a real person. Although he has human-like complexity, audiences generally know not to take him seriously.

To see how giving Orin complexity helps to contain the gruesomeness of his sexual abuse, the play offers a series of other characters who are bad but more simple and sketchy. Bernstein is a television executive who tries to capitalize on the unusual plant in the window of Mushnik's Skid Row Florists by offering to put quiet, shy Seymour on television. Mrs. Luce is the wife of a magazine publisher who wants to turn the public's interest from the plant and to the boring, semicompetent Seymour. Skip Snip is an agent

The film version, starring Rick Moranis as Seymour, used a large puppet for Audrey II, though some stage productions have an actor in a costume play the part. (© Moviestore collection Ltd | Alamy)

looking to make money by casting Seymour into the limelight. Patrick Martin wants to spread off-shoots of Audrey II across the globe without regard for how this will doom the human race. Each of these characters is onstage for only a few minutes at most. Their sin is greed—much less dangerous than sexual abuse. They are lightweight characters who make little impression, and according to the author's notes, they are all to be played by the actor who plays Orin Scrivello.

If Orin were like them—if he were a walk-on character quickly passing through the play whose one function is to be Audrey's sexually violent boyfriend—he would be even more objectionable. There would be just no way to say that he is funny or that he belongs in a musical comedy. Giving him more time onstage ought to work the other way. It seems as if it would be giving a seal of approval to the play's rapist. Instead, giving Orin more time on stage gives Ashman the space needed to show not only that Orin is as deluded as the worst among us but also that he is that way because he is human.

This play uses a sexually abusive character for laughs. That in itself is a daring prospect, and some in the audience may find it revolting, even more so because the rapist sings and dances as if his role is life affirming. Part of what makes Orin acceptable is context: a dark comedy is supposed to make humor out of awful subjects. Another part is the specificity of the character. *Little Shop of Horrors* cannot be viewed as a comment on sexual abuse in general but can be viewed as a comment on this one exceedingly rare, specific personality that is meant to be extreme. The more the audience knows about this character, the less fearsome his personality is, because he represents nothing but himself.

Source: David Kelly, Critical Essay on *Little Shop of Horrors*, in *Drama for Students*, Gale, Cengage Learning, 2016.

Marc Jensen

In the following excerpt, Jensen examines issues of race and class subtly raised in Little Shop of Horrors.

"AT THIS MOMENT OF INTERACTION, A
FREAKISH TOTAL ECLIPSE OF THE SUN OCCURS,
AND WHEN THE LIGHT RETURNS, SEYMOUR BECOMES
AWARE OF AUDREY II SITTING ON THE TABLE BEHIND
HIM THAT HAD BEEN EMPTY WHEN HE LOOKED
MOMENTS BEFORE."

. . . . Both the stage musical and the 1986 film have a sense of the inescapable, but the staged version is much darker, and the audience is left at the end to digest the unusual spectacle of a monster story in which the monster eats the hero and remains alone onstage at the end to gloat. This ending is unsettling, with Audrey II's presence on stage so physically dominating that Seymour's efforts to fight him throughout the play seem quixotic at best. While the movie-musical was originally intended to follow the plot of the stage musical, this proved untenable in the cinematic context:

> Oz previewed the original ending to a test audience and they were shocked and horrified: "They hated us when the main characters died," Oz said. "In the play, they're eaten by the puppet, but you know they're coming out again for a curtain call. But the power of movies is different. They really believed in those characters and they were angry."

In Oz's altered ending, Seymour and Audrey miraculously defeat Audrey II and escape skid row to live in Andrey's dream house from her song "Somewhere That's Green." As a retelling of Faust, the altered ending of the film makes little sense. Although it can be interpreted as an intentionally improbable, campy horror film resolution, it has often been criticized as pandering to a Hollywood desire for happy endings, compromising the inevitable collapse that is the ultimate point of the story.

As an alternative to the Faust model, Audrey II himself can be interpreted as a manifestation of Seymour's own transgressive desires, a reading that Stephen King would classify as an adaptation of the werewolf story. In a story centered around Seymour's attempt to escape from hopeless poverty, Audrey II's urgings

direct him to do whatever it takes to succeed. Far from being an innocent and heroic character, Seymour emerges as simply weak-willed and unable to resist the temptation to exploit others for personal gain. All of the characters Audrey II eats in the 1986 version of the film stand as obstacles to Seymour's happiness or social mobility, and by giving in to Audrey II's urging, Seymour is actually expressing his own greed. In a sense, this is more obvious in the 1960 version of the film, which presents Audrey II less as an articulate character than as a manifestation of pure unsocialized desire. In the original, Audrey II speaks almost no lines that are not simple commands, such as the ever present "Feed me!" By the end of the original film, Seymour's personality is completely subjugated in service to Audrey II. After finally stating his refusal to kill anymore, he is mysteriously and cheesily hypnotized by Audrey II, henceforth referring to him as "master," and behaving with a mechanical single-mindedness that parallels Audrey II's simple obsession with eating.

The two power dynamics outlined above—an external class struggle balanced against an inner Faustian struggle—form the surface of every version of the story. In terms of the horror movie genre, these conflicts and anxieties are not radical, and in the case of the 1986 movie especially, references to these standard tropes can be seen as self-consciously campy and ironic. Below this surface, however, the mechanism by which Ashman and Menken reformulate this story in its musical adaptation adds another layer of social commentary that was not present in the original film. In the musical and the 1986 film, racial tension and anxiety in the 1950s and 1960s are the unspoken tools used to articulate the problem embodied by Audrey II.

In terms of narrative, the monster that Seymour unleashes on skid row may be his own personal demon, but the mechanism by which this story is delivered is through the personification of the corrupting influence as insidiously African American. Because the issue of race is not conspicuously addressed in the film (as it is, for instance, in *Hairspray* [John Waters, 1988], a contemporaneous musical that is also a retrospective on race relations in the 1960s), its presence here as a subtle tool is provocative and potentially disturbing. As one reviewer of *Little Shop of Horrors* writes: "The problem with this subtle undercurrent of racism is not that it's racist, but that it's subtle."

Little Shop of Horrors's outward basis in class struggle rather than race is pointedly established at the opening of the film, when the first song, "Skid Row," sets the stage by pointedly depicting intermingled African American, white, and Hispanic singers together all sharing this scene of poverty indiscriminately. This opening seems to suggest that although all of the main characters may be white, their race is not really the salient feature of the story. However, contrasted with this all-white lead cast is the one prominent character who is non-white: Audrey II. Although Audrey II is not physically human, he is consistently portrayed as African American.

Levi Stubbs of the *Four Tops* was selected to provide the voice of Audrey II in the movie, and Oz states in one interview that the clear blackness of Stubbs's voice was one of the primary reasons for his selection: "He was exactly what I was looking for . . . [s]omebody who had an edge to him . . . who was real black, real street . . . who had a touch of malevolence but could be real silly and funny at the same time." As though attempting to moderate this statement into something more politically correct, Oz's interviewer continues by explaining that "the 'streetwise' plant envisioned by the screen writers essentially demanded a black voice. 'What is a *white* streetwise voice?' Oz asks. 'I can't imagine it. Actually, if there is such a thing, it's a rip-off of a black voice.'"

While Audrey II's racial identity is rendered clearly enough through the character of his speech alone (accent, use of idiomatic expressions, etc.), he is presented in a physical form that can readily be seen as a caricature of African American physiology: a head that has no features other than a giant pair of exaggerated lips. Oz's response to this criticism of physical caricature comes across as defensive and flat, obviously anticipating that this complaint would arise:

> I tried to make sure when Lionel designed the plant that the lips were toned down as much as possible because I didn't want any comments like that. We weren't trying to make it look black, we were trying to make it look like a plant, but we had to have lips. . . . It certainly wasn't intended, and if people see it that way I'm sorry.

Oz's almost indignant claim that the plant was not intended to look black forms an interesting contrast to his description of selecting Stubbs's voice based specifically on its black, "streetwise" quality.

What does not arise in these interviews, and has not been seriously confronted in existing commentary on the film, is the most important element defining Audrey II's race: the musical style associated with him. A comparison of the musical styles associated with various characters, as well as broader stylistic changes over the course of the film, shows that this is, in fact, the primary medium through which Ashman and Menken express the racial undertones of the film. Although race is never consciously addressed as the issue at hand, Audrey II's "blackness" proves to be the corrupting force that infiltrates and undermines Seymour's universe, both morally and musically.

Apart from these physical and behavioral elements, Audrey II's association with blackness is also suggested by his origin. Unlike the original film, in which Audrey II's origin is inconsistent and ultimately unimportant, his origin in the musical adaptations is of central importance: Audrey II is an invader from outer space, bent on world domination. Racially, Seymour's acquisition of Audrey II is the only point in the film at which Seymour interacts directly with an African American person. While it seems of little significance at the time, its implications become clearer upon examination of the film specifically in terms of race.

Seymour recounts the story of Audrey II's mysterious origins in the song "Da-Doo." While shopping for wholesale flowers, Seymour looks at a vendor's booth and finds nothing of interest. Immediately following this, he walks up to a group of African American men across the street and they all start singing doo-wop harmony together. This interchange is casual, forgettable, but also incongruous within the context of the film, where this kind of interaction with passersby does not otherwise occur. Except for the full-cast opening song "Skid Row," no other songs integrate passersby into the music at all. This interchange is also especially interesting because the act of singing doo-wop harmony on a street corner is in itself a very specific kind of interaction, strongly suggesting African American urban culture of the 1950s.

At this moment of interaction, a freakish total eclipse of the sun occurs, and when the light returns, Seymour becomes aware of Audrey II sitting on the table behind him that had been empty when he looked moments before. In this way, Audrey II enters the story associated with the physical blackness of the eclipse, the otherness of being alien, and also as the product of this provocatively anomalous racial interaction. As a song dealing with the discovery of Audrey II, "Da-Doo" points toward the phenomenon of white Americans becoming aware of African American vocal groups in the 1950s, and toward the fact that these groups emerged as an amateur phenomenon from the streets of New York.

The direct result of Seymour's interaction with the impromptu doo-wop group is his "discovery" of Audrey II, whom he then takes home and nourishes with his own blood. At many levels, the operative factor emphasized in this interchange is clearly the concept of blackness....

Source: Marc Jensen, "'Feed Me!': Power Struggles and the Portrayal of Race in *Little Shop of Horrors*," in *Cinema Journal*, Vol. 48, No. 1, Fall 2008, pp. 53–56.

Elizabeth L. Wollman

In the following excerpt, Wollman places Little Shop of Horrors *in the context of Broadway trends of the 1980s.*

In the early 1980s, as production costs soared and the megamusical took root on Broadway, Off and Off-Off-Broadway reasserted their positions as foci for the adventurous, cutting-edge theater that Broadway was seen to lack. At the end of the 1981–82 season, Otis L. Guernsey Jr., editor of the *Best Plays* series, argued that Broadway was no longer a center for original new productions:

> An alternative seems to lie in evolving Off Broadway into the principal bearer of creative theater, raising the price of the top ticket to more than $20 and pushing the production cost well up into six figures, hoping it will become economically feasible to maintain such a theater in the dozens of auditoriums scattered throughout the city. If this sounds like past Broadway mistakes—raise prices and costs and hope for the best—it should serve as a warning to Off Broadway against playing follow-the-leader over the same cliff. Right now, good plays and willing audiences exist in abundance Off Broadway, even at $14 to $20 a seat. Whether this will enable Off Broadway to establish an economically stable outlet for its creative energies is still very much an ongoing question.

Unfortunately, even as Guernsey was recording his concerns about the future of New York's less commercial theater realms, Off and Off-Off-Broadway were beginning to react to the pressure of rising production costs. Ticket prices Off Broadway, like those on Broadway, rose progressively through the decade, and many productions began to reflect the sheen of increased commercialism traditionally expected of Broadway productions, especially when it came to visual spectacle. The distinctions between "commercial" and "nonprofit" theater, which had begun to blur in the 1970s, continued to do so through the 1980s, as megamusicals attracted the attention of increasingly large entertainment companies, members of which began to take new interest in producing live theater. As the 1980s progressed, and shows on Broadway grew more spectacular, the direction of influence—from Off and Off-Off-Broadway uptown to Broadway—began slowly but surely to reverse itself.

LITTLE SHOP OF HORRORS

A fitting example of an Off Broadway show that reflected this turning of tides is *Little Shop of Horrors*, with book and lyrics by Howard Ashman and music by Alan Menken. Based on the 1960 cult film by B movie king Roger Corman, this rock 'n' roll horror musical was workshopped at the tiny, ninety-eight-seat WPA Theater Off-Off-Broadway in the spring of 1982. While there, it caught the attention of Bernie Jacobs, then the president of the Shubert Organization, and his producing partner, David Geffen, then the president of Geffen Records. *Little Shop* was quickly moved to Off Broadway's Orpheum Theater, where it reopened on July 27, 1982; the film version, also produced by Geffen, would be released four years later.

Set in Mr. Mushnik's flower shop in an unnamed urban ghetto during the Eisenhower era, *Little Shop* recounts the strange and oddly tender tale of the schlemiel Seymour Krelborn, who works for Mr. Mushnik as a salesman. Seymour pines away for his fellow employee, the beautiful but enormously insecure Audrey, who is dating a sadistic, abusive dentist. As the musical begins, Mr. Mushnik is considering closing his shop, since business is horrible and only getting worse (it seems that very few people are in the habit of venturing to skid row to buy flowers). Seymour, however, unveils his new discovery: an exotic little plant that, when placed in the shop window, becomes a tourist attraction that soon gives Mushnik's a much-needed boost in business.

Conflict sets in when Seymour learns that his plant—which he names Audrey II in honor of his secret love—is a carnivore. On occasion, Audrey II will settle for a snack of rare roast beef, but it is much more partial to human blood. At first, Seymour pricks his fingers to keep Audrey II happy, but as the plant grows larger and larger, it begins to demand much more than just a few measly drops. Oddly, it also begins to sing its demands to Seymour in a style strongly reminiscent of the soul singer Otis Redding.

Partway through the musical, Seymour musters up his courage and confronts Audrey's abusive boyfriend, the dentist. As luck would have it, the dentist dies of a laughing gas overdose shortly after Seymour arrives at his office. Seymour decides to feed pieces of the dentist to Audrey II, thereby hiding the evidence and keeping the plant quiet for a few days. What with the dentist out of the way, Audrey realizes her love for Seymour. The new couple enjoys a few brief moments of happiness before Audrey II gets hungry again. In the final act, Audrey II devours Mr. Mushnik, Audrey, and Seymour, before—according to the finale—mutating into hundreds of tiny little plants that move on to consume the rest of the world.

Functioning as a kind of informal Greek chorus in *Little Shop* are three young, black women, all of whom happen to be named after prominent 1960s girl groups: Chiffon, Crystal, and Ronnette. These women, inhabitants of the same rundown neighborhood that is host to Mushnik's flower shop, comment flippantly on the antics of the main characters—all of whom are white—in bouncy, three-part harmony; break into choreographed dances reminiscent of the pony, the twist, and the mashed potato; and provide regular vocal backup for the other characters in the form of countless "bobsha-bops," "sha-la-las," and "chang-da-dos." Once the entire cast has been devoured by the plant, this trio of young women provide the moral of the story: no matter how tempted you may be, don't feed the plants!

Little Shop of Horrors enjoyed strong reviews, and, once it arrived at the Orpheum, a healthy run of 2,209 performances. While this strange little musical's talented cast, cheerful girl-group sound, and macabre plot most certainly had a hand in charming critics and theatergoers alike, there is no question that one of its biggest attractions was essentially a huge, movable prop: Audrey II, the man-eating plant. Designed and operated by the sculptor, actor, and puppeteer Martin P. Robinson (perhaps most famous for playing Mr. Snuffleupagus on "Sesame Street"), the original Audrey II appeared on the *Little Shop* stage in the form of four different puppets—two that were worked by hand, and two that were large enough to be manipulated from within. Initially tiny, the plant grew significantly during the course of the performance, mutating by the end of act II into an enormous, tentacled pod with ferocious jaws that gobbled up the entire cast and snapped at the audience before the final curtain.

The reliance here on "special effects" was not lost on some critics, who voiced concern over the theater's need to imitate, in Walter Kerr's words, "its much younger and less sophisticated brother." Kerr argues that despite a talented cast and some cute, catchy songs, *Little Shop* absent the plant is not a very interesting musical at all. "In the theater," he writes, "special effects can be dandy on an incidental basis. Beware, however, the evening that depends on them for its life's blood." Kerr might, arguably, have been a bit hasty in targeting *Little Shop of Horrors* for criticism; after all, an Off Broadway musical that relied so heavily on spectacle was, at the time, relatively atypical. Yet as the decade continued, Broadway—as well as the mass media that was influencing its musicals—would continue to contribute to changes Off Broadway. . . .

Source: Elizabeth L. Wollman, "Spectacles of the 1980s," in *The Theater Will Rock: A History of the Rock Musical, from "Hair" to "Hedwig"*, University of Michigan Press, 2006, pp. 130–33.

Ed Kaufman

In the following review, Kaufman compares a 2004 production to the original staging.

Attention all Angelenos! After an absence of a couple of decades, Audrey II—that celebrated exotic plant of carnivorous appetites featured in the musical comic book *Little Shop of Horrors*—is back among us. Only bigger and better—and with lots of Broadway glitter and glitz.

With book and lyrics by Howard Ashman (based on Roger Corman's 1960 low-budget horror sci-fi cult classic featuring a young Jack Nicholson) and music by Alan Menken, *Little Shop of Horrors* moved to the tiny Orpheum Theatre in the East Village in 1982, where it literally owned the 1980s with a sort of gritty urban insolence that celebrated B-movie pulpiness and the gutsy, jive-flavored pop of a bygone era.

Onstage at the Ahmanson, *Little Shop* looks clean of bloodstains and benignly picturesque—sort of a campy version of *Grand Guignol*. What seems to be lacking is the grit and grime of the original production in the East Village.

Still, this incarnation of *Little Shop* has lots going for it. The Ashman/Menken score is defoe and droll, Jerry Zaks directs with smooth efficiency, Kathleen Marshall's choreography is first-rate, Scott Pask's skid row set brings back memories of the '80s version, and William Ivey Long's costumes are rich with nostalgia. In short, it's a terrific if somewhat sanitized Broadway show.

Little Shop tells the tale of Seymour (Anthony Rapp), a florist's assistant who befriends an exotic plant he names Audrey II (the silky voice of Michael James Leslie) that grows and thrives only on human flesh and blood. The plant is pretty convincing as it argues its case and offers Seymour everything, including the love of Seymour's fellow floral assistant, Audrey (Tari Kelly). So the intrepid Seymour agrees, much like Dr. Faustus. Only there's a price to pay.

Both Rapp (as nebbish Seymour) and Kelly (as the show's trampy but wide-eyed heroine Audrey) are stage-savvy, convincing and wonderful as they sing "Call Back in the Morning," "Suddenly Seymour" and Audrey's plaintive sendup solo "Somewhere That's Green."

James Moye is first-rate as multiple characters including Orin, Audrey's sadistic, laughing-gas-swilling boyfriend who is Audrey II's first victim, while stage veteran Lenny Wolpe is delightful as Mr. Mushnik, owner of the flower shop. "Mushnik and Son," sung by Wolpe and Rapp, is right out of vaudeville.

All the while, the singing and dancing Urchins (Yasmeen Sulieman, Amina S. Robinson and La-Tonya Holmes) keep up the beat and remind us—like a Greek chorus—that we are in "Downtown (Skid Row)" and in the finale admonish us, "Don't Feed the Plants." We agree.

Source: Ed Kaufman, Review of *Little Shop of Horrors*, in *Hollywood Reporter*, Vol. 385, No. 24, September 1, 2004, p. 12.

Roger Ebert

In the following review, Ebert praises the "off-hand, casual charm" of the 1986 film adaptation.

At a time when so many movies show such cold-blooded calculation, here's one heedless enough to be fun. *Little Shop of Horrors* arrives with enough baggage to make it into a thoroughly timid project—what is less likely to make a fresh movie than a long-running stage hit?—and yet the movie has the offhand charm of something that was concocted over the weekend.

This is not only a musical and a comedy, as we expected, but also a revue of sorts: Comic actors such as Bill Murray, John Candy and James Belushi have walk-ons, and Steve Martin almost steals the show as a sadistic, motorcycle-riding dentist. Yet at the heart of the movie is a basic sweetness, an innocence that extends even to the centerpiece of the story, which is a man-eating plant named Audrey II.

The plant makes its appearance one day in a flower shop window, having arrived from another planet. It immediately begins to grow, to look around itself, to attract attention and to exhibit an appetite for human blood. It also changes the lives of the three people who work in the store: the shop assistant, Seymour (Rick Moranis); the salesclerk, Audrey (Ellen Greene), and their kindly, blustering old boss, Mr. Mushnik (Vincent Gardenia). Suddenly, they have the sort of fame thrust on them that is usually reserved for lottery winners and people who survive freak accidents.

There are all sorts of people with ideas about how to exploit the wonderful plant, and others who wish it no good. The movie uses them as the occasion for gentle satire and broad comedy, and there's the sense that *Little Shop* is amused by just about whatever comes into its mind. There is also a romance; Seymour falls in love with Audrey (I), but must win her away from the evil dentist (Martin), who roars around on a motorcycle and gives her black eyes.

Meanwhile, Audrey (II) inexorably grows, nourishing itself with blood from a nick on

Seymour's finger and developing a taste for human flesh. The progressive growth of the alien plant was, of course, one of the glories of the stage version of *Little Shop*, and the movie's Audrey, designed by Lyle Conway and directed by Frank Oz, is a marvel of technique. The plant actually does seem to have a personality and is remarkably accomplished during its musical numbers.

Moranis also has developed a personality in this movie and, in a way, that's as surprising as Audrey II's achievement. After being typecast as a nerd on SCTV and in such limited and predictable films as *Strange Brew*, he emerges here as a shy, likable leading man in the Woody Allen mode. The movie sometimes makes his work look easy. But he has to carry a lot of the exposition and hold most of the conversations with the plant, and without him the movie might not have been half as confident.

Greene repeats her New York and London role as the human Audrey, and by now the wide-eyed, daffy blond with the pushup bra has become second nature. Her big musical number, "Suddenly Seymour," has the bravado of a Broadway show-stopper even while undermining itself with satire.

The show is punctuated by musical commentary delivered by a Supremes-style trio (Tichina Arnold, Tisha Campbell and Michelle Weeks), that bounces around the flower shop's inner-city neighborhood with a message of hope that seems somewhat optimistic, inspired as it is by a carnivorous plant, but fits right in with the movie's good heart.

All of the wonders of *Little Shop of Horrors* are accomplished with an offhand, casual charm. The movie doesn't labor its jokes or insist on its virtuoso special effects, but devotes its energies to seeming unforced and delightful. The big laughs, when they come, are explosive (such as the payoff of Martin's big musical number), but the quiet romantic moments are allowed to have their coy innocence.

This is the kind of movie that cults are made of, and after *Little Shop* finishes its first run, I wouldn't be at all surprised to see it develop into a successor to *The Rocky Horror Picture Show*, as one of those movies that fans want to include in their lives.

Source: Roger Ebert, Review of *Little Shop of Horrors*, in *RogerEbert.com*, December 19, 1986.

SOURCES

Ashman, Howard, *Little Shop of Horrors*, music by Alan Menken, Samuel French, 1982.

"Bio," Howard Ashman website, 2010, http://howardashman. com/about-bio.html (accessed July 19, 2015).

"Formation of NATO and Warsaw Pact," in *History.com*, 2015, http://www.history.com/topics/cold-war/formation-of-nato-and-warsaw-pact (accessed July 30, 2015).

Gardner, Elysa, "*Shop of Horrors* Never Reaches Full Flower," in *USA Today*, October 2, 2003, http://usatoday30. usatoday.com/life/theater/reviews/2003-10-02-horrors_x. htm (accessed July 23, 2015).

Green, Stanley, *Broadway Musicals: Show by Show*, 2nd ed., Hal Leonard Books, 1987, p. 262.

Gussow, Mel, "Musical: A Cactus Owns *Little Shop of Horrors*," in *New York Times*, May 30, 1982, http:// www.nytimes.com/1982/05/30/theater/musical-a-cactus-owns-little-shop-of-horrors.html?pagewanted = print (accessed July 23, 2015).

Jones, Dan, "Ever a Surprise: Remembering Howard Ashman (Part 1)," in *Geva Journal*, January 14, 2015, https:// gevajournal.wordpress.com/2015/01/14/ever-a-surprise-remembering-howard-ashman-part-1/ (accessed July 19, 2015).

Kenrick, John, "Theatre in NYC: History—Part IV," in *Musicals 101.com: The Cyber Cyplopedia of Musical Theater. Film, and Television*, 2003, http://www.musicals101. com/bwaythhist4.htm (accessed July 30, 2015).

"Little Shop of Horrors," Howard Ashman website, 2010, http://howardashman.com/theatre.html (accessed July 27, 2015).

Shewey, Don, "Little Shop's Big Comeback," in *Advocate*, November 11, 2003, pp. 66–67.

Sunderland, Mitchell, "Beauty and the Plague," in *Vice*, December 26, 2013, http://www.vice.com/read/beauty-and-the-plague (accessed July 19, 2015).

FURTHER READING

Jensen, Marc, "'Feed Me!': Power Struggles and the Portrayal of Race in *Little Shop of Horrors*," in *Cinema Journal*, Fall 2008, pp. 51–67.

    Jensen acknowledges that race is not a main focus in this play but finds that to be all the more reason to discuss the implications of the characters of color who are either on the periphery of the story or, as in the case of the carnivorous plant, menacing.

Meyer, Michael J., *Literature and Musical Adaptation*, Rodopi Perspectives on Modern Literature, 2002.

    Meyer looks at the question of adaptation philosophically and determines that changing a work from one medium to another almost always makes a superior product. Though his examples are from the higher arts, such as opera and literature, Meyer's insights about librettists' finding the inner essence of the original work do apply to the B movie that yielded a Broadway musical.

Nissan, Ephraim, "Deadly Flowers and Lethal Plants: A Theme in Folklore, Fiction and Metaphoric Imagery," in *Fabula*, Vol. 50, Nos. 3–4 2009, pp. 293–311.

This article looks at the ways in which plants have been viewed as dangerous predators in fiction throughout the ages. It includes a section about plants that eat people, specifically discussing *Little Shop of Horrors*.

Tavernier, Bertrand, Bernard Eisenschitz, and Christopher Wicking, "Corman Speaks," in *Roger Corman: Interviews*, edited by Constantine Nasr, University Press of Mississippi, 2011, pp. 5–22.

This interview was conducted in 1967 with some top European filmmakers. Although his autobiography, *How I Made a Hundred Movies in Hollywood and Never Lost a Dime*, emphasizes his showmanship, in this interview Corman discusses the craft and discipline it took to make

popular entertainment on a minuscule budget, which forced him to come up with ideas like the killer plant in *The Little Shop of Horrors*.

SUGGESTED SEARCH TERMS

Little Shop of Horrors AND off-Broadway

Little Shop of Horrors AND puppetry

Howard Ashman AND Alan Menken

Ashman AND Menken AND musicals

Little Shop of Horrors AND adaptation

Little Shop of Horrors AND Ellen Greene

Little Shop of Horrors AND science fiction

Little Shop of Horrors AND Motown

Ashman AND Roger Corman

Ashman AND Menken AND Audrey II

Othello

1995 *Othello* was among the most popular of Shakespeare's plays in his lifetime and remains a perennial favorite, perhaps second only to *Hamlet*. The 1995 adaptation by Oliver Parker is the first professional film to cast a black actor (Laurence Fishburne) in the title role. *Othello* deals with powerful themes of race and sex that are as compelling today as they were in Shakespeare's era. The beauty of the play's language and the perfection of its character studies have rarely been matched.

Othello's title character is a native of North Africa who has led an unusually eventful life, both as a slave and a free man, traveling and fighting around the fringes of the Ottoman Empire. By the time of the play, he has gone through a process that today might be described as defection and become a general in Venice, a leading Christian state. There he plays the role of the *other*, an alien outsider, who on one hand is feared and hated because he is black and, on the other, is valued for his military expertise and deep knowledge of the enemy. When he is appointed to command in Cyprus in the face of an expected Turkish attack, he marries a Venetian noblewoman, Desdemona. Othello's subordinate Iago, who hates the Moor, poisons his mind with jealousy and convinces Othello that his wife has betrayed him. Deceived, Othello murders his wife and then kills himself.

Kenneth Branagh, a well-known veteran of many Shakespeare productions, plays Iago, a man obsessed with conspiracy. (© AF archive | Alamy)

PLOT SUMMARY

Shakespeare begins the play of *Othello* with a scene of Iago reporting to his friend Roderigo how Othello wronged him by refusing to make him his lieutenant, or second in command. Iago plans to revenge himself for this insult by reporting to Senator Brabantio that Othello has carried off his daughter, Desdemona, and married her. The film delays and abbreviates this scene and instead begins with a scene of Othello riding in a gondola. He is accompanied by a woman who, half asleep, is leaning her head on his arm. Contrary to expectation, this is not Desdemona but is probably a prostitute with whom Othello has been celebrating Carnival, which the film takes as its setting. The camera next shows Desdemona coming to Othello in her own gondola and her marriage ceremony with Othello, events Shakespeare had Iago describe.

These scenes are intercut with the meeting in the palace of the Duke (i.e., Doge) of Venice and the senate debate of their reaction to the Turkish attack on Cyprus. They decide to send a relief force under the command of Othello. Iago will serve as Othello's ensign, or third in command, below his rival, Cassio. Iago might have declined, considering the position a snub as Roderigo suggests, but Iago announces his wish to stay near Othello so as to have the opportunity for revenge. In the film, Iago and Roderigo's taunting of Brabantio is delayed to show its relationship to Iago's revenge.

Accompanied by Cassio and Iago, Othello sets out for the Duke's council of war, but they are accosted in the street by Brabantio and his retainers. Swords are drawn, but Brabantio must yield to the Duke's summons of Othello. He claims to the Duke that Othello must have beguiled Desdemona with witchcraft. Othello excuses himself on the ground that he and Desdemona are properly married. Desdemona herself is summoned and confirms she married Othello freely. His appointment to Cyprus is

FILM TECHNIQUE

- Carnival, or Mardi Gras, is traditionally a time of raucous celebration before the Lenten season of fasting. The holiday is best known today through its celebrations in New Orleans and Rio de Janeiro in Brazil but is also an important tradition in Venice. Accordingly, Parker decided to set the beginning of Othello on the night of Mardi Gras. Desdemona is seen running through a square littered with colorful beads. These beads, associated with New Orleans Mardi Gras, were unknown in sixteenth-century Venice but serve as an unmistakable visual cue to a modern American audience, indicating the date. The scene of Othello's wedding is cross-cut with the images of the senate of Venice receiving definite intelligence of the plans of the Ottoman Empire for the year's campaigning season, so Mardi Gras is too early in the year for the true historical date of the sequence. However, Parker is less concerned with establishing definite dates than with following a trend popular in 1980s art house films using the dramatic potential of Venetian Carnival masks, which hid revelers who might be publicly indulging in unseemly acts of pleasure. The simple white masks, usually worn with all-black clothing, produce a striking image and were used in Joseph Losey's *Don Giovanni* (1979), Gérard Corbiau's *The Music Teacher* (1988), and Miloš Forman's *Amadeus* (1984) as a symbol of mystery and death. Many types of masks were worn in Venice during Carnival. The simple white half-mask made iconic in these films was called the *larva* (ghost). A mask commonly worn in Venice was the *Arlecchino* (Harlequin), which combines stereotypical racist depictions of blacks with the traditional appearance of the devil, which also might have had interesting possibilities for Parker, given the racial tensions in the film. Instead, en route to his wedding, Parker's Othello covers his face with a mask of tragedy painted stark white. This symbolically communicates to the audience the pressures on Othello to play a white social role in Venetian society and foreshadows *Othello*'s tragic ending. The device also plays with the tradition of white actors in black face playing Othello.

- In Shakespeare's time, Britain did not yet participate in the Atlantic slave trade, and very few blacks lived in England. A character like Othello would generally be played by an actor wearing dark makeup, called blackface. In later times, blacks were for the most part purposefully excluded from the legitimate stage, especially in the United States. In the very popular minstrel shows that flourished in nineteenth-century America, blacks were the subject of racist satire, and blackface, which was worn by all the actors, both black and white, became a racist caricature. Nevertheless, African American actor Ira Aldridge made a successful career as a dramatic actor in British and European theaters in the mid-nineteenth century and was the first black actor to perform the role of Othello on the stage. Fishburne was the first black actor to portray Othello in a professional film, though an independent film had been made at Howard University in 1980 in which Yaphet Kotto played the title role, and a 1981 stage production with William Marshall was videotaped, though neither was ever released commercially. In his *Othello*, Parker plays with the blackface tradition, particularly in the opening scene in which Fishburne passes a white carnival mask across his face. Later, when Iago says of Desdemona, "So will I turn her virtue into pitch," Parker underlines the statement by having Kenneth Branagh grab a piece of charcoal from the watch fire and smear it over his hands, turning them black.

confirmed, and he sets out, accompanied by Desdemona. Brabantio warns Othello, within Iago's hearing, that Desdemona has deceived her father and so may well deceive her husband.

Roderigo's antipathy for Othello is not purely out of sympathy for Iago. Rather Roderigo is in love with Desdemona. Iago tells him that once her lust for Othello is sated, she is bound to turn away from him, so his friend should go to Cypress and be ready for that moment, while Iago will give him any help he can. In a soliloquy (i.e. speech directly to the camera), Iago reveals he holds Roderigo in contempt and intends to have him supply the money for all his expenses on Cypress. He outlines his plan to deceive Othello into believing that Desdemona is betraying him with Cassio.

The action then moves to Cypress; the change of location is cinematically indicated by having all the women carry parasols. The ship carrying Iago, Desdemona, and her attendant, Emilia, who is also Iago's wife, arrives shortly before Othello's because the fleet has been separated by a storm. When Othello and Desdemona are reunited before a crowd of military officers and aristocrats come to welcome the new governor, the couple's long and passionate kiss—far beyond anything indicated in the stage directions of the play—causes embarrassment among the onlookers. Othello announces that the Turkish fleet has been much worse affected by the storm, so the risk of invasion is over. The film adds a scene that is not in Shakespeare's original script: there is a general celebration, and the Turkish Sultan is burned in effigy. Meanwhile, Iago tells Roderigo that, having traveled with Desdemona, he found out that she is in love with Cassio. He tells Roderigo to advance their plot for revenge, once they are on duty, by finding some excuse to anger Cassio. Parker adopts a different chronological sequence from that of Shakespeare's play and here shows Othello and Desdemona making love, something Shakespeare merely hints at when they leave the stage together somewhat later.

Iago eggs Cassio on to drink more than he should. Cassio makes a fool of himself, flirting with a prostitute named Bianca in front of Montano, the highest-ranking officer in the garrison of Cypress. Iago privately suggests to Montano that Cassio is a serious alcoholic. When Roderigo duly provokes Cassio, Montano, primed to think Cassio is drunker than he is, intervenes, and Cassio, outraged, attacks him.

Othello comes to determine the cause of the commotion. Cassio refuses to speak in his own defense, and Montano is too gravely wounded to talk. Iago reports to Othello just what he saw, being careful to make Cassio seem to be the cause of the trouble. Othello punishes Cassio by expelling him from his service. Cassio laments his lost reputation. He blames his behavior on his own drunkenness, which explains why he made no defense to Othello. Iago advises Cassio that he may restore his position by approaching Desdemona to make her his advocate with her husband.

Iago then has a soliloquy (altered from Shakespeare's original) spoken directly to camera. He asks how anyone can think him a villain when he is only giving Cassio good advice. He replies to himself that the devil can tempt because he seems fair. While Cassio entreats Desdemona, Iago will raise suspicion in Othello. When Desdemona tries to speak in Cassio's favor, Othello will take it as confirmation of her adultery.

Parker now omits several scenes of the play, principally some slapstick between Cassio and a street performer, the first of many scenes with this character that are left out of the film. In the next filmed scene, Cassio, with the help of Emilia, has just gained Desdemona's support for restoring his position. Iago and Othello interrupt the conversation, and Cassio hurries away. Iago pretends not to recognize Cassio and suggests that the man must have been there for some improper purpose because he hastened away to avoid meeting Othello. Yet Othello can see plainly that it was Cassio. This is only the first of many small suggestions of an affair that Iago makes to Othello. Parker abbreviates the scene in which Desdemona obtains Othello's promise to restore Cassio in favor of showing Othello and Iago practicing martial arts.

In the subsequent scene, Iago further implicates Cassio and Desdemona while seeming to wish not to. Parker films the sequence with Iago and Othello working in the fortress armory. It contains some of the most famous of Shakespeare's lines: "Men should be what they seem," "Who steals my purse steals trash," and "Jealousy . . . the green-ey'd monster." Finally, Othello browbeats Iago into *admitting* that he suspects Desdemona and Cassio are having an affair. Othello expresses doubt but orders Iago to have his wife spy on Desdemona. Iago suggests that Othello not reappoint Cassio to his lost position and see whether Desdemona protests.

While Othello is dressing for dinner, Desdemona and Emilia come to get him. His wife perceives he is unwell—he is overcome by intense jealousy, of course, but does not communicate this to Desdemona—and he explains that he has a headache. Desdemona wipes his brow with a handkerchief embroidered with red thread in the shape of strawberries, which she leaves on the bed when they leave the room. Emilia takes the handkerchief and gives it to her husband. Iago had often asked her to steal it, since it was well known as a present from Othello to his wife.

Rather than film the next sequence of the play, Parker takes his cue from the lines, "Not poppy, nor mandragora, / Nor all the drowsy syrups of the world / Shall ever medicine thee to that sweet sleep / Which thou ow'dst yesterday." The film includes a dream sequence in which Othello envisions Cassio and Desdemona making love.

The next day, Othello tells Iago that his condition of doubting and not knowing is intolerable. He orders Iago to find definite evidence of Desdemona's infidelity. Iago says that it is unlikely that he could arrange for Othello to see his wife and Cassio in flagrante delicto but *confesses* the original cause of his suspicion: he heard Cassio mention the infidelity while talking in his sleep. Iago offers further that he has seen Cassio use a handkerchief covered with strawberries, much like the one that was Othello's first gift to Desdemona. Othello goes to Desdemona to demand to see the handkerchief, which, of course she cannot produce because it was stolen by Emilia.

Othello is so overcome with jealousy that he falls into an epileptic fit. In a soliloquy, Iago suggests, metaphorically, that it is the result of the spell he is casting over the Moor. Fishburne's motions on screen are rather like those of a marionette, suggesting another metaphor for Iago's manipulation of Othello. Cassio stumbles onto this scene, and Iago persuades him to hide himself for a moment. Shakespeare then uses a dramatic contrivance where Iago then suggests to Othello that he hide himself so that he may observe his interrogation of Cassio and judge matters for himself. Iago talks to Cassio about his mistress, Bianca, but Othello believes that they are discussing Desdemona. Bianca herself soon appears to return the strawberry handkerchief that Cassio had given her as a gift. He says it mysteriously appeared in his room, but Bianca is jealous because she is convinced he must have gotten it from another woman. Othello can hardly doubt who that is and begins to plan how to kill those who have betrayed him. Iago swears to put himself at Othello's service for the murders; Parker turns it into a blood oath in the film.

While they are in public together, Desdemona speaks up again on Cassio's behalf, and Othello slaps her. When they are alone, Othello makes his wife swear she is faithful to him. When Desdemona leaves, she meets Iago and begs him for advice of how she can restore relations with her husband. Roderigo accosts Iago also, demanding he deliver Desdemona to him as he promised. Iago persuades Roderigo to go and kill Cassio. When Roderigo fights Casio, Iago considers that it would be to his advantage if both men died. They wound each other, and while pretending to help, Iago murders Roderigo.

Passing over another play scene of low comedy in which Emilia and Bianca insult each other's virtue, the film moves to the final scene between Othello and Desdemona. Othello tells her forthrightly he intends to kill her, but he questions her as if he were a prosecutor in a trial. It is impossible for her to satisfy him with her insistence on her innocence, and he proceeds to strangle her, as Iago had suggested. When he is finished, Emilia comes in to report that Cassio has been wounded but is not dead.

In the play, Desdemona revives long enough to assure Emilia that Othello had not killed her, but Othello admits his guilt to her anyway because he thinks his action is justifiable. In the film, Desdemona is simply dead, and Othello is forthright about the murder. Othello explains to Emilia that Iago told him of Desdemona's adultery. Emilia lets out a cry of murder, and Iago and Montano rush into the room. Othello again goes over the evidence against Desdemona, including the handkerchief. Emilia realizes everything when she hears this and briefly explains her own and Iago's part in stealing it. Othello suddenly realizes how Iago has deceived him. Iago kills Emilia and rushes off, but he is soon recaptured. He is brought back to face Othello but refuses to offer any reason for his deception. Cassio is made governor and allows Othello to speak. Othello asks that they consider him "one that lov'd not wisely but too well" and kills himself. In the film, Cassio supplies Othello with a dagger, as an act of mercy to spare him a formal trial, which would have involved torture.

CHARACTERS

Bianca

Bianca, played by Indra Ové, is a black prostitute in Cyprus and Cassio's mistress. Othello sees her give the strawberry-covered handkerchief back to Cassio, jealous over the gift that she is convinced must be a castoff of some other lover of Cassio's. This is the final proof that convinces Othello of Desdemona's infidelity.

Brabantio

Brabantio (Pierre Vaneck) is the father of Desdemona. Judging from his Flemish name, his family must once have come to Venice as foreigners but have become integrated into Venetian society to the extent that he has become a senator. The term has a quite different meaning than in the United States. Venice was ruled by a Duke (the Doge) together with a Great Council of almost five hundred members chosen according to wealth and family. This body elected a senate of sixty members to deal with most business.

Brabantio objected to Roderigo as a suitor for Desdemona, probably on the ground that he was insufficiently connected socially and politically, but he reacts viscerally against Othello because he is black. Indeed, his first suspicion on hearing of the marriage is to take the men of his household and search the city for Othello. When pressed, he claims he intends to imprison Othello until he can be tried, but if Brabantio's mob had found him unprotected, it is difficult to believe they would not have killed him. Brabantio tells the Duke the only the way the marriage could have come about is through witchcraft, though he must accept the Duke's decision on behalf of Othello. Like most of the actors portraying the Venetians, Vaneck speaks with a noticeable foreign accent, as opposed to Fishburne's distinctly American pronunciation and the English accents of Cassio, Roderigo, Iago, and Montano.

Michael Cassio

Cassio, played by Nathaniel Parker, earns Iago's enmity when he is promoted in his place as Othello's lieutenant. Cassio is a Florentine and therefore a foreigner in Venice, but Othello promotes him because of his competence. Iago first contrives to have him removed from Othello's service in disgrace and then makes Othello believes he is Desdemona's lover. When Othello decides to murder his own wife, he deputes revenge against Cassio to Iago, who in turns sends the incompetent Roderigo, so Cassio survives to succeed Othello as governor of Cypress.

Desdemona

Desdemona, played by Irène Jacob, is Othello's wife and, in the tragedy of the play, also his murder victim. Shakespeare represents her as entirely innocent, to heighten the fear and pity the audience feels at the plot that Iago weaves against her and especially when they see Othello driven to kill her, an unusually violent action for the Elizabethan stage. Desdemona is at the prime age for marriage among the Venetian nobility, as shown by not only Othello's but also Roderigo's courting her and even Cassio and Iago's discussing her desirability. This means that she is not likely to be much older than sixteen, compared with Othello, who is probably in his forties. This difference in age would seem more outrageous today than the difference in race, and in the United States their marriage would have been illegal for this reason without Brabantio's consent. The way that Othello captivates her, with his fantastic tales of his travels and exploits, certainly makes more sense for an adolescent than an adult. A. C. Bradley, in his *Shakespearean Tragedy*, excused Desdemona from what he considered the unnatural desire of a white woman for a black man by ascribing to her a childlike innocence, but it would be truer to consider her simply immature. In Parker's film, Jacob was twenty-eight at the time of filming, and Fishburne was thirty-three, avoiding the age problem for the viewing audience. It is worth noting that women were not allowed on stage in Shakespeare's time, because actresses were closely associated in the public's mind with prostitutes. Just as Othello was portrayed by a white man made up to appear black, Desdemona would have been portrayed by a teenage boy dressed as a woman.

The Duke of Venice

The Duke, or Doge (Gabriele Ferzetti), is the political leader of the Venice and heads the senate debate over how to handle the Turkish attack on Cyprus. He appoints Othello as commander of the troops sent to fend off the attack.

Emilia

Emilia (Anna Patrick) is Iago's wife and attendant to Desdemona. She is devoted to her mistress in most matters. However, although she must have some idea of Iago's true character, she obeys him as her husband in the matter of the stolen handkerchief. When she sees that her husband's plotting has resulted in her mistress's death, she confesses everything she knows in front of Othello and the other Venetian officers, causing Iago to openly murder her in retaliation.

Iago

Technically, Iago, played by Kenneth Branagh, is the antagonist of *Othello*, but he has more lines than the title role and is thought by many to be the more interesting character. Many actors, given a choice, want to play Iago rather than Othello. The character Iago, unlike Othello or Cassio, is from an established aristocratic Venetian family and believes he should be given high office and status because of his heritage; he is contemptuous of his two comrades, who earned their superior positions by merit. Iago drives the plot through his scheming, driving Othello to dishonor Cassio; then to doubt and kill his wife, Desdemona; and finally to kill himself.

A perennial question is why. Iago makes the devastatingly simple pronouncement, "I hate the Moor," in a soliloquy, but this is hardly an explanation. Iago mentions two causes of offense Othello has given him. The first is that he suspects Othello has slept with his wife, Emilia (though one has the impression Iago would not mind this if it advanced his career), and the second is that he passed him over for promotion in favor of Cassio. Neither of these seem proportionate to the revenge that Iago takes and particularly not to the horrible, insinuating way he carries it out. Also, once Cassio is disgraced, Iago is, in fact, promoted in his place, which, on a rational calculation, might have brought the matter to a conclusion. In one sense, the answer is that Iago's revenge must be extraordinary, so that Othello's tragedy may be extraordinary and so make a worthy drama. That kind of explanation does little credit to Shakespeare's mastery of character, though it perhaps highlights that he was a greater writer of character than plot.

One approach to the mystery of Iago is psychological. Perhaps he has unspoken, even unconscious, motives for wishing to destroy Othello? One possibility along these lines is to suppose that Iago feels a strong homoerotic attraction to Othello and, considering this feeling unacceptable, replaces it in his consciousness with an extraordinary hatred, a psychological mechanism known as a reaction formation. This would give meaning to Iago's readiness to think that Othello has slept with his wife, even when he admits he has very little reason to believe so; it would be a sort of proxy union between the two men. The same holds true of Iago's offhand comment that he too loves Desdemona. In this case, the elimination of Desdemona would fulfill jealousy felt against a rival. Going a little further, one could support this interpretation in Iago's desire to possess Desdemona's handkerchief.

To take another approach, it is clear that Iago never reveals his true self to anyone he speaks to. Even when he is plotting against Othello with Roderigo and speaks forthrightly about his deviousness and deception, he has another level of falseness in his plots against Roderigo, which Shakespeare immediately reveals through a soliloquy. The effect is quite striking, suggesting there is no limit to Iago's villainous enormity. This means that Iago has two characters: his true self, which may never be revealed fully even to the audience but which drives the violence and deception in the play, and another outward character that he has constructed as a sort of mask to make himself seem as acceptable as possible to those around him: "Honest Iago." This may go some way toward explaining Iago's cryptic statement about himself: "I am not what I am."

Perhaps one can see here the influence of the Roman historian Tacitus, who was a favorite of the Elizabethan dramatists. Tacitus considered his historical writings to be as much as anything an analysis of the psychology of the emperors. For him, figures like Tiberius or Nero were always bloodthirsty tyrants inside but created a false image of virtue necessary to win popular support for their rule. Over time, the mask slips more and more, and the true murderous character is gradually revealed. Iago undergoes the same kind of development in the estimation of those around him, from Othello's implicit trust in him to his wife's final denunciation of him.

Montano

Montano, played by Nicholas Farrell, is the commander of the Venetian garrison stationed in Cypress before Othello's arrival. When he tries to restrain Cassio, who appears drunk, he is wounded, resulting in Cassio's dismissal.

Othello

Othello is played by Laurence Fishburne. He has led a long life filled with incident and adventure and is middle-aged at the time of the play (the character is probably at least ten years older than Fishburne). He was probably born in North Africa and both became enslaved and won his freedom from slavery while traveling in and beyond the Ottoman Empire in Africa. How he came to Venice is not clear, but he must have converted to Christianity at some point and risen from within the ranks of the mercenaries employed by the state. As he rose in rank, he ingratiated himself with Brabantio, a senator, through appealing after-dinner conversation based on his exploits. He noticed, too, that he beguiled Brabantio's daughter, Desdemona.

At the beginning of the play Othello marries Desdemona without gaining her father's consent. When confronted with the angry Brabantio and his mob of armed men, Othello completely masters the situation because he is completely without fear. The same characteristics see him made commander of a Venetian military expedition to Cypress. Carefully assessing the talents of his subordinates, he has made Cassio his chief lieutenant. He has badly misread Iago, however. Because of his confidence in his own judgment, Othello comes to trust Iago implicitly, never realizing his mistake. Iago convinces Othello that Desdemona has betrayed him with Cassio.

The Moor's response is to want to kill both Desdemona and Cassio. This is a proportionate response in an honor-based traditional culture like Renaissance Italy. Othello certainly appears to have been deeply in love with Desdemona, and although he thinks it necessary to kill her with his own hands, he is completely destroyed and overwhelmed by the action. While he might well have escaped punishment for the murder because he was deceived, Othello is almost relived to kill himself once Iago's plot is exposed and he realizes she is innocent.

Roderigo

Roderigo (Michael Maloney) is a Venetian nobleman who has long been in love with Desdemona but was rejected as a suitor by her father. Rather foolishly, Roderigo allows himself to be deceived by Iago and is easily fobbed off whenever he raises objections that Iago is not helping him win Desdemona as he promised. In fact, Iago has been stealing large sums of money from him throughout the play, on the ground that he was buying jewels and sending them to Desdemona on Roderigo's behalf. After Roderigo fails to kill Cassio (who, like Othello, he is convinced is Desdemona's lover), Iago finally kills him.

THEMES

Mystery

Although the audience views the plot from Iago's perspective, from Othello's viewpoint, he is in a detective story. Othello is trying to solve the mystery of whether or not his wife is unfaithful to him. He interrogates Iago as though in a cross-examination, and Iago acts like a hostile witness, so that every fact must be pried out of him. Othello believes that Iago is speaking against his will and against his own interest and also believes Iago considers Cassio his friend; therefore Othello believes everything Iago says. Othello even threatens to beat and kill Iago to get the truth out of him, and one must consider that in the sixteenth century, torture was considered a viable means of criminal investigation and was almost universally used. Even in civil cases, litigants would generally have to submit to thumb screws, as if the pressure assured the validity of their testimony. To use the language of detective stories, Iago is attempting to frame Cassio in order to get revenge against him.

One must admit that the plot is quite fantastic. Although mystery writers stress the verisimilitude of their stories, detectives like Sherlock Holmes or Hercule Poirot have to make leaps of logic to create a satisfyingly intricate rhetorical construct at the end of the story that would be quite impossible in the real world. As Iago plots his revenge, he has to unerringly envisage how Othello, Cassio, and Roderigo will react to each stimulus he provides. Consider, for example, what would have happened if, after the fight with Montano, Cassio had spoken up for himself or Othello had decided to hunt down Roderigo.

READ.
WATCH.
WRITE.

- Rick Yancey's young-adult novel *The Monstrumologist* (2009) draws on the ancient mythology of the Anthropophagi and the Blemmyes (men without heads) but to a quite different purpose from Shakespeare's. They are no longer human but, as animals, stand for threatening nature. Write a paper contrasting Yancey's science-fiction concept with the orientalism of *Othello*.

- *Omkara* (2006), directed by Vishal Bhardwaj, is an Indian film adaptation of *Othello*. It is set in contemporary Indian culture, at the social point where legitimate political parties intersect the criminal underworld. In *Omkara*, the daughter of a member of a provincial legislature marries a crime boss who works for his party. In this regard, class stands in for race. Make a presentation to your class showing comparable scenes from *Omkara* and Parker's *Othello*, commenting on the difference imposed by the transposition to Indian culture.

- Numerous versions of *Othello*, or at least individual scenes of *Othello*, are posted on YouTube. These include clips from professional films and videos made by student groups in high schools and universities who either are involved in student productions of the play or have made the videos to satisfy a class assignment. Select a small group of videos that show different versions of the same scene. Make a presentation to your class based on the videos, commenting on their similarities and differences due to the decisions made by the director of each clip.

- In Shakespeare's time, and even through the late twentieth century, the character of Othello was inevitably played by a white actor in blackface. In Jacobean times, this would have seemed uncontroversial as the orientalist perception of blacks as an exotic other was accepted without reflection by British society. As black identity emerged, especially in the United States, as a reality that highlighted the injustice of socially dominant white attitudes, this kind of portrayal broke down into kitsch and could, as in the case of Laurence Olivier's performance, unintentionally approach satire. The only way forward for Oliver Parker in making an Othello for an American audience was to cast an American black actor in the role. Write a paper considering how this decision affected the racial tensions in the film, compared with those present in the original play.

However, the plot unfolds properly because the narrative allows no one to do anything contrary to Iago's purpose.

Orientalism

Edward Said, in his important essay *Orientalism*, identified the idea of the Orient as a constructed representation of the non-European world that only coincidentally touches on real places like Africa but is created as a useful metaphor or fiction by Europeans for European purposes, namely to make the Orient serve as an *other* that is demonstrably alien and imperfect compared with European culture. (Of course, one can find parallel chauvinism in other cultures; compare the traditional idea in China that the entire world owes the Chinese emperor tribute.) One of the most obvious manifestations of orientalism in literature is when foreign places are represented as fairy tale lands of wonder and marvels. Othello indulges in this kind of fabulation in order to entertain Desdemona when he is courting her in her father's house. He tells her that in his youthful travels, he visited a land populated by "the

Irene Jacob's portrayal of Desdemona received mixed reviews, perhaps because she is not a native English speaker and struggled with Shakespeare's language. (© AF archive | Alamy)

Cannibals that each other eat, / The Anthropophagi, and men whose heads / Do grow beneath their shoulders."

The details of this speech refer to *The Travels of Sir John Mandeville*, a late medieval work (anonymous despite the title) that was remarkably popular in the sixteenth century. The narrator of that work describes strange lands on the edge of the world: "And in another isle towards the south dwell folk of foul stature and of cursed kind that have no heads. And their eyen be in their shoulders." However, the use of the Greek word for "cannibal" (*anthropophagi*) suggests that Shakespeare was directly familiar with *Mandeville*'s own (unacknowledged) source, Herodotus, who tells many such fantastic stories about the edge of the earth, although in his case the cannibals occupy the far northern lands beyond the Black Sea. Shakespeare is confusing the Anthropophagi with the headless men of Roman folklore (known from the natural history of Pliny the Elder). These fantastic creatures were called Blemmyes, which was also the name of a tribe in the Sudan on the border of Roman Egypt.

This double identity emphasizes the inhumanity of the foreign. The headless bodies and murderous habits of these tribes stand as types of the *other*, which is represented also by Othello's black skin. The traditional use of blackface on white actors playing the part of the Moor emphasizes the artificiality of the racial construction of the *other* as well. Othello is well aware of his status as the *other* and exploits it, creating a fictional version of himself through his stories about his youthful travels and the mystical power of the handkerchief, in this way beguiling Brabantio and particularly Desdemona. Contrary to Said's idea of the *other* as a way of depriving a group of power, Othello empowers himself by embracing the only identity that is offered to him.

STYLE

Soliloquy

Soliloquies are one of the most familiar aspects of Shakespeare's drama, particularly through Hamlet's soliloquy beginning "To be or not to be," which is one of the best-known passages in English literature. A soliloquy is a speech in which a character reveals his thoughts to the audience by speaking aloud what would ordinarily be an internal monologue. Although such inner mental activity is easily represented in prose, the use of the soliloquy presents certain problems in drama. Namely, it entails the actor speaking lines that the character would never speak; in fact, soliloquies often expose thoughts that the character most wants to keep hidden, shattering the illusion of reality that the drama depends on. At the same time, the device is necessary to provide psychological insight into character.

In *Othello*, two characters have soliloquies: Iago reveals in soliloquy the details of his evolving plot for revenge, while Othello pours out his emotional turmoil as his mind is turned against his wife. Parker takes several different approaches to the play's various soliloquies. Some are handled simply like spoken dialogue, whereas others, by both characters, are done as narration. When the soliloquy is used as narration, the actor is filmed as if he is lost in the thought represented by the soliloquy, with various emotions represented through his expression and movements, while the text is heard in voice-over. More effective are the soliloquies that Iago speaks directly into the camera, as if the audience were a person present in the drama to whom he is revealing his innermost thoughts. In one case, while reciting the final lines of a soliloquy ("So will I turn her virtue into pitch, / And out of her own goodness make the net / That shall enmesh them all."), Branagh seems to notice that he is being watched and actually ends the scene by putting his hand in front of the lens and blacking out the camera.

Drama

While it might seem needless to emphasize that *Othello* is a drama, since Shakespeare's plays almost define drama in the corpus of English literature, it is worth noting that the play corresponds to classical definitions of tragedy. It takes place in a limited time and in only two locations (although ideally the original Greek dramas played out in the real time of the performance at a single spot represented onstage) and involves the fall of a great man through the revelation of his hidden fault (jealousy in this case).

However, the metaphorical use of drama within the play is more interesting. As an actor and dramatist, Shakespeare naturally loved the theater and depicted its operations onstage when he could. In *Hamlet*, for example, the main character supervises the production of a play, telling the actors how to go about their business, while in the prologue to *Henry V*, the narrator explains to the audience the limits of theatrical production.

Drama also plays its role in *Othello*. When Othello de-escalates what might have become a bloody street brawl between his own armed followers and Brabantio's, he uses a dramatic metaphor: "Were it my cue to fight, I should have known it / Without a prompter." In other words, no fight will take place because the playwright has not put one in the script. The prompter is the person, unseen by the audience but visible to the actors, who follows the production with a written script, reminds a player of dialogue if he forgets it, and gives cues or visual signals for stage actions. More generally, it has often been observed that Iago stands in the place of the playwright or director, guiding the actions and motivations of Othello, the actor.

CULTURAL CONTEXT

Christian-Turkish War

While military matters never take center stage in *Othello*, they form the background within which the plot of the play unfolds. The war with the Ottoman Empire is what Alfred Hitchcock called a MacGuffin, something that is of intense concern to a film's characters and motivates their actions but that does not engage the attention of the audience. Othello is a military officer in Venice, and the plot is set in motion when he snubs Iago for the position of his second in command. Shakespeare is intensely interested in the patronage relationships that governed Italian cities and had Iago note that if Othello had indeed chosen Iago as his lieutenant, he would have woven himself more tightly into the Venetian aristocratic fabric with which Iago is connected, obliging three different noblemen who supported his appointment. Instead, Othello chose Cassio on the ground of merit alone.

More elliptical is the cause of the war itself. Modern audiences are liable to think of war as starting with some specific incident or having some specific cause, but this was not the case in the Mediterranean in the sixteenth century. The sultan of the Ottoman Empire (Turkey) was almost obliged to lead a major military campaign each year by the traditions and internal conditions of his state. If he did not, the perceived loss of dignity could well be a signal for rebellion by the Turkish nobles. Moreover, the military strength of the Ottomans was nearly equal to that of the whole of Western Europe combined (whose inhabitants would have referred to the area as Christendom at the time), so if the Ottomans attacked, it would consume all available strategic resources in resisting them. The states that led this resistance varied according to the Ottoman plans.

The sultan had three general choices of campaign open to him: he could attack Persia to the east (which would spare Europe for the season), invade Hungary, or else conduct a naval expedition in the Mediterranean. In this last case, the burden of defense would fall upon Spain, the papacy (usually supplying some of the enormous amount of money the war would entail), and Venice; this alliance was referred to as the Holy League. If the Turkish blow were to fall against the Mediterranean, there were several possible targets, including the enclave maintained by the Spanish in the city of Tunis; the strategic Island of Malta, which was garrisoned by a powerful crusading order (the Knights of St. John); or Cypress or other colonies that Venice possessed in the eastern Mediterranean.

Accordingly, Western powers strained their considerable intelligence resources each year to discover not if but where the Ottomans intended to campaign. This guessing game is shown in more detail in the play than the film, with each senator mentioning different estimates of the size of the Ottoman fleet based on reports from their own intelligence assets and the conclusion that a Turkish attack on Rhodes is only misdirection meant to deceive the Western powers about the Sultan's true intention to attack Cyprus. Shakespeare understood this process very clearly and reduces weeks of committee meetings and mountains of bureaucratic reports into a single dramatic scene. Parker truncates this further so the rest must be inferred from little more than the Duke's line, "'Tis certain then for Cyprus."

Bride Rape

In the honor-based traditional cultures of the Mediterranean, an aristocratic family's honor was determined in part by the conduct of its female members. The male family members therefore closely controlled the behavior of their female relatives. If a woman acted outside her family's control, for example, if she wanted to marry a man not of her father's choosing, then there would be conflict and dishonor. If she actually ran off with the man she was in love with, her family would be completely shamed. The only way to regain honor would be either to hunt down and kill the newlyweds, their blood erasing the stain to family honor, or else to recognize the marriage, as if the father had approved it all along.

Given human nature, it sometimes happened that young couples gambled with their lives in this way to obtain their desires. Such an action is technically called bride rape, because, it being unthinkable in traditional societies that women could have their own agency, the woman was considered to have been kidnapped (*rape* in this case means "seize"), taken from the legitimate control of one man (her father) to the illegitimate control of another (her new husband). Given the dramatic possibilities of bride rape, the practice is far more common in fiction than in reality and occurs in *Othello*. Desdemona has fallen in love with Othello, a man her father would never accept, so she runs off to marry him.

The taunting that Iago and Roderigo engage in when they inform Brabantio is typical of the dishonor heaped upon the male relatives of shameful women in traditional societies. The idea of a woman's having sexual relations with a man of her own choosing is more shameful than can be borne. Brabantio is reconciled to the marriage only when Othello's increase in status with his new command as governor of Cyprus makes personal revenge impossible. These kinds of concerns about honor gradually vanished in Western culture as society became more heavily institutionalized. In modern culture, if one is outraged, one takes recourse to the courts or the police rather than carrying out a personal act of violent revenge. The concept of individual rights guaranteed by law has supplanted the kind of social control typical of an honor society (just as women and marriage have been removed from patriarchal control). This transformation happened first in northern Europe, and Shakespeare and his Protestant audience are beginning to feel a sense of superiority over the Catholic Mediterranean whose people already begin to seem like exotic orientals, or *others*. The

Reviews of Laurence Fishburne's performance in Othello *are largely favorable.* (© Getty Images / Getty Images)

conflict between modern Western culture and traditional societies has only intensified, and remnants of the honor system, like honor killing, are regularly used to demonize Islamic societies that are viewed as completely alien.

CRITICAL OVERVIEW

Janet Maslin of the *New York Times* wrote a favorable review of Parker's *Othello* on its initial release in 1995. Although Maslin concedes that the play "has been truncated, rearranged and illustrated by its director...in unapologetically high-handed ways," she insists that the film is aided by

> the well-preserved relevance of this play's themes. With Mr. Fishburne as an unusually hotblooded Othello and the first black actor to play the role in a major film, the story's sexual and racial tensions are frankly emphasized.

The casting of Fishburne as Othello has stimulated critical comment. Peter Erickson, in his *Citing Shakespeare*, notes that the casting of black actors such as Paul Robeson or James Earl Jones as Othello onstage or Fishburne on film has not resolved the racial tensions in the play, or rather in the reception of the play. For the audience, the character of Othello can never be black but must be a representation of blackness:

> The substitution of an actual black Othello for the original blacked-up, white Othello fails to overturn the play's deep-seated, intractable racial dynamic. Instead, placing a black actor in the role of Othello reinforces and exacerbates the play's built in limitation: its continuous reenactment of a racial bind.

Through this failure, according to Erickson, "Shakespeare is shown to be part of the problem, not part of the solution." Deborah Cartmell, in *Interpreting Shakespeare on Screen*, points out that Parker's *Othello* was being filmed during the O. J. Simpson trial and suggested that the release and marketing of the film played on similarities between the play and the criminal matter of the trial. Judith Buchanan, in her article "Virgin and Ape, Venetian and Infidel" made the same observation independently. Generally, however, there has not been the critical attention to the film one might have expected. In Sarah Hatchuel and Nathalie Vienne-Guerrin's 2015 volume, *Shakespeare On Screen: Othello*, for instance, Welles's and Olivier's films each receive a chapter, but Parker's does not, though in the introduction the editors do briefly discuss the basic issues of race and sexuality raised by the film, largely echoing Buchanan.

CRITICISM

Rita M. Brown

Brown is an English professor. In the following essay, she addresses the issue of race in Othello, *particularly as Oliver Parker's film places it in its modern American context.*

Because of Shakespeare's prominence in the Western canon, *Othello* has long been a magnet for discussions of race, a factor that has been emphasized in film adaptations of the play, such as those of Lawrence Olivier and Oliver Parker. The divisive role of race in American society is evidence that race is a powerful social construct. At one time, race was legally defined in many US

WHAT DO I SEE NEXT?

- Gioachino Rossini composed an operatic adaptation of *Otello* (note the Italian spelling) in 1816. A recording of the production by the Zürich Opera, conducted by Muhai Tang and staring Cecilia Bartoli and John Osborn was released as a film in 2014 by Decca (rated G). Readers should note that filmed operas are usually recorded from a few simple shots and generally do not use montage and cinematography in the same way films do.

- Giuseppe Verdi adapted *Otello* in 1887, using a libretto by Arrigo Boito (who also may have assisted in some musical matters such as orchestration). Many stage productions of the opera have been filmed, but in 1986 Franco Zeffirelli made a fully produced film (Cannon City Produktie Maatschappij B.V., rated G) based on the opera, with Plácido Domingo and Katia Ricciarelli as the lead singers. The orchestra of La Scala is conducted by Loren Maazel. Verdi supplies dramatic unity to the story by locating the entire opera on Cypress, with characters merely recalling the significant events in Venice.

- Dimitri Buchowetzki directed the first full adaptation of *Othello* in 1922 (Wörner-Filmgesellschaft, rated G), staring Emil Jannings. Parker used this film as a visual resource for certain aspects of his film, for example, Othello's wardrobe.

- Orson Welles's *Othello*, in which he played the title role, was released in 1952. Made effectively as an independent film, with production (which began in 1949) repeatedly suspended so Welles could earn the money necessary to keep the project going by acting in Hollywood historical epics, Welles's *Othello* was one of his greatest achievements.

The film was produced by Mercury Productions and is rated G.

- *All Night Long* (1962), directed by Basil Dearden is a retelling of Othello set among jazz musicians in modern London, staring Patrick McGoohan as Iago. The film was produced by J. Arthur Rank Film and is rated G.

- Stuart Burge directed an *Othello* in 1965, based on the stage production of the National Theatre Company, which was overseen by John Dexter. It starred Laurence Olivier and was the film debut of Derek Jacobi, who plays Cassio. This film also served as a visual reference for many aspects of Parker's version. The film was produced by BHE and is rated G.

- *O*, released in 2001 (Lions Gate, rated R), is a version of the Othello story set in an American high school, directed by Tim Blake Wilson.

- In 2002, Parker directed a version of Oscar Wilde's *The Importance of Being Earnest*. The PG-rated film was produced by Miramax.

- *Stage Beauty* (2004), directed by Richard Eyre and produced by Lions Gate, uses *Othello* to address not race but the social construction of gender roles. It concerns a male actor in Jacobean times who specializes in playing female characters in Shakespeare, particularly Desdemona, because the government prohibits women from appearing onstage on moral grounds. His career is destroyed at a stroke when legislation changes and prohibits men from appearing onstage dressed as women, also on moral grounds. The film is rated R.

---

states by what was known as the one-drop rule, meaning that one drop of black blood made one black. Shakespeare invokes the same idea when

Brabantio, upon discovering Desdemona has indeed gone to marry Othello, shouts out, "O treason of the blood!" Interestingly, the tie

> **SHAKESPEARE IS EXPLOITING THE FEELINGS OF HORROR THAT THE RACIST EXPERIENCES WHEN HE CONTEMPLATES A BLACK MAN MARRYING A WHITE WOMAN."**

between blood and race derives from ancient mythological ideas about inheritance, in which genetic material was thought to be derived from blood. (Parker plays with this idea when he makes Othello and Iago seal their pact of vengeance by mixing their blood.) In any case, the legal specification held that any black ancestry, even if it was a single black ancestor ten generations or one hundred generations in the past, made a person black.

Clearly, this had more to do with contrived ideas of purity and contagion than any reality of human genetics. In fact, by this standard everyone is *black*, because the entire human population is descended from a single population one hundred thousand years ago thought to be genetically similar to the Saan people of southern Africa. One must appeal to mythology, rather than scientific facts, to reach any other conclusion, and science does not support the existence of any human races today, since the genetic diversity within groups and genetic links between groups are both too great to make any such categorization meaningful.

Othello is a Moor. What does that mean? The most general meaning of the term that would have been recognized by Shakespeare's seventeenth-century audience is that he came into the Western, Christian world from the Ottoman Empire. It need not say very much about any racial category. Another, more specific, use of the word would indicate that he came from North Africa, the area today contained in the countries of Morocco, Algeria, or Tunisia. This area has a very diverse population, some of whom would identify themselves as Arabs, whereas others would identify themselves as Berbers. In any ethnicity of the area, however, it would not be difficult to find some individuals whose blue eyes and blond hair would not look out of place in Europe, even northern Europe,

and others whose features suggest Bantu-speaking Africa. The use of the term *black* to describe Othello is not very precise either, since in British, as opposed to American, idiom, it could be used to describe anyone from the Mediterranean or India as well as sub-Saharan Africa. (One cannot make too much out of the epithet "thick-lips," since it is a racist slur uttered by Roderigo.) The racial diversity of Africa simply cannot be made to correspond to the limited, stereotyping terms *Moor* or *black*. These terms are merely ideological constructions of Western culture meant to define an alien inferior, monstrous *other*.

For a long time, speculation about Othello's precise racial background, the exact color of his skin, was a dominant factor in criticism of the play. The romantic poet Samuel Taylor Coleridge, in his *Lectures and Notes on Shakespeare and Other English Poets*, for instance, argued that Othello could not have been really black, because the possibility of Othello's coming from southern Africa rather than being a fairly European-looking Berber was disagreeable. Coleridge's argument relies on the racist idea that it is unpleasant to see a black man and that the audience would have to excuse an excessive, perverted desire on the part of Desdemona. Coleridge explicitly links Othello's blackness with Desdemona's whiteness, which lays bare the heart of the matter. If Othello is too black, Coleridge seems to believe, Iago is right about Desdemona's depravity.

One of the main aims of men in traditional society is to control the women to whom they are attached. Even more than cowardice on the battlefield, the surest way for a man to be shamed was for a female relative to have sex with someone she was not supposed to. Given the status of the black as something entirely *other* and outside one's own society, white women were certainly not supposed to have sex with black men. The reverse was quite acceptable, however. The sexual domination of black women by white men was a legitimate expression of personal and group power. While these factors are, if anything, exacerbated by the history of slavery and discrimination in the United States, they were nevertheless also operative in British culture and are clearly reflected in *Othello*. The idea that a white woman would want a black man is so outlandish that the only explanation for it that Brabantio can think of is that his daughter's mind and will were controlled by witchcraft (black magic). Similarly, Iago explains to Roderigo that Desdemona's desire for Othello can only be because of an excessive passion, a perversion we would say today, and therefore cannot be the foundation of a real relationship. Because of this, he believes, her infatuation and her marriage will both soon end. In contrast, Cassio has a black mistress (who goes by the Italian name *Bianca*, suggesting that a black woman would naturally desire to become white at least in name), a relationship treated as quite ordinary. These racial factors have to condition the reception of the play.

A little over a century ago, A. C. Bradley, in his *Shakespearian Tragedy*, arguing that Othello ought to be played as white as possible, says, "Perhaps if we saw Othello coal-black with the bodily eye, the aversion of our blood, an aversion which comes as near to being merely physical as anything human can, would overpower our imagination." Besides any consideration of the rhetorical and poetic beauty of the play, Shakespeare aims precisely to arouse the racist feelings that Bradley alludes to. He is counting on the audience's sense of outrage to stir them up and produce an emotionally satisfactory anger. Aristotle realized that the purpose of drama was to elicit and thereby discharge the experience of powerful emotions in a controlled, safe way, without the consequences that really experiencing the circumstances that rouse such emotions would bring. He meant the kind of feeling experienced by the audience of Sophocles's *Oedipus Tyrannus* at the idea of a man murdering his own father and marrying his own mother. Shakespeare is exploiting the feelings of horror that the racist experiences when he contemplates a black man marrying a white woman. This, of course, presupposed an audience composed of white racists, but white supremacy was simply the standard assumption in the audiences of the seventeenth century. Bradley surely was not imagining a black man in the audience having a visceral reaction in his blood against seeing a black man on stage. He simply could not conceive of a black audience for *Othello*, and in Shakespeare's time one did not exist. Indeed, Bradley is quick to point out that he rejects as unenlightened a traditional reading of the play, that Desdemona is justly punished for her racial transgression. He considers equally outmoded the interpretation that Othello possesses only a simulated veneer of European manners and slowly exposes his African brutishness in his murder of his wife.

Film adaptations of *Othello* have exploited racism in the same way. In his famous production of the play, filmed in 1965, Laurence Olivier played Othello as a broad black stereotype. He dressed in the flowing gowns that marked African chiefs in Hollywood movies and went barefoot with a great weight of gold ankle bracelets. He boasted of the care he took to study and copy the shuffling, hip-swaying gait of the barefoot black man. Olivier gives an almost fetishistic account of his blackface makeup, quoted by Peter Holland in his article "Rethinking Blackness":

> Black all over my body, Max Factor 2880, then a lighter brown, then Negro Number 2, a stronger brown. Brown on black gives a rich mahogany. Then the great trick: that glorious half yard of chiffon with which I polished myself all over until I shone.... The lips blueberry, the tight curled wig, the white of the eyes, whiter than ever, and the black, black sheen that covered my flesh and bones.

If this cannot be even the image of an African, but only the stereotype of the *other*, Olivier created it to emphasize the sexual transgression with the whiter-than-white Desdemona. Billie Whitelaw, who played Desdemona opposite Olivier (in the stage production), recalls, quoted by Richard Burt in his article "Backstage Pass(ing): Stage Beauty, Othello and the Make-up of Race," "To make my own skin look 'white as alabaster', as the Bard says, I had alabaster makeup all over my body," So Desdemona's whiteness was as much a construct as Othello's blackness. She relates this incident: "Once, as I knelt down beside his feet, I put my hand on his knee. He glared down at me: there was a white mark on his black knee! Some of my white alabaster had come off on his beautiful shiny black makeup." The anecdote stands for the miscegenation, the illicit mixing of black and white, that excites the interest in the play.

Parker's *Othello* certainly moves beyond this unreflective racism. He is very much aware of the racial tensions in the play. Reviews of Parker's film did not hesitate to point out that Fishburne was chosen for the role, as opposed, for example, to an actor like Denzel Washington (who had starred with Branagh in an adaptation of *Much Ado about Nothing* in 1993), because he projected a sexually threatening aura. The *New York Times* review described his performance in phrases like "hotblooded," "dangerous edge," and "smolders." In Bradley's terms, Parker purposefully chose a "coal-black" Othello to maximally disturb the audience. Iago, at least, cannot help but think of sex between the races and an inhuman, animalistic outrage, describing it as the mating between a "white ewe" and a "black ram" and as "the beast with two backs." He calls Othello the devil, and Brabantio shortly calls him a pagan.

Parker is depending on the unease of the audience as much as Shakespeare. He tells his story through Iago's eyes, and the view is filled with hatred, as much against women as against the black man Othello. However, Parker finally expects the audience to have a different final reaction. While Bradley's audience participated in the racism inherent in the play, Parker's is instead supposed to wonder why they are uneasy. Parker shows far more of the intimacy between Othello and Desdemona than Shakespeare did or could have done. Parker is challenging his audience to interrogate the cause of their dis-ease. In their exaggerated kiss, Parker has Fishburne and Jacob demonstrate to the Venetians everything that a racist could find horrible. When the Venetians turn away in disgust, the audience is not supposed to be on their side. Similarly, an American audience can scarcely see the Ottoman Sultan (also a Moor) burned in effigy without realizing that throughout much of American history, Othello would likely have been lynched for his attentions to the white Desdemona. Even for Shakespeare, Othello's fall is after all a tragedy, not a just dessert.

Source: Rita M. Brown, Critical Essay on *Othello*, in *Drama for Students*, Gale, Cengage Learning, 2016.

Desson Howe

In the following review, Howe sees most of the film's actors as "horribly out of place."

Adapting Othello for the screen, as stage director Oliver Parker has discovered, can be troublesome. How do you make credible and galvanize the actions of Othello, the noble Moor (played by Laurence Fishburne) who cruelly sacrifices his dearly beloved Desdemona (Irene Jacob) over innuendo and a strategically placed handkerchief?

How do you bring modern audiences to a finer understanding of Iago (Kenneth Branagh), Othello's conniving lieutenant, whose evil machinations

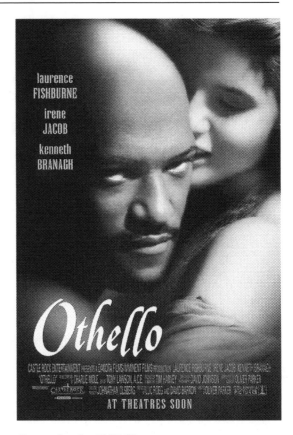

Poster for the 1995 film (© John D. Kisch / Separate Cinema Archive / Getty Images)

irreparably ruin the lives of at least six people—and all this because he was passed over for promotion?

For Shakespeare, solving such dramaturgical problems was simple. He made the richest dramatic poetry in Western civilization flow effortlessly from the mouths of his characters. But in movies, where visual information takes precedence, characters can't just chat beautifully. How they look marks how effective they are.

The screen is also a crudely explicit medium, where motivations lie bare, banal and easily vulnerable to public disapproval. Whether you're Hamlet or Rambo, you go through the same modern wringer. This may explain why one group of twentysomething viewers tittered throughout a recent *Othello* screening.

In the movie, as with the play, Iago becomes jealously disgruntled when military commander Othello takes Cassio as his lieutenant. He hatches an elaborate scheme, in which he needles Othello with the possibility that his new bride, Desdemona, is having an affair with Cassio.

When Othello demands "ocular proof," Iago supplies it, by "discovering" Desdemona's handkerchief on Cassio's person. This false evidence sets a chain of tragic events into motion.

Filmmaker Parker, whose screenplay strips down the original play, merely produces a lackluster essence. What remains is to savor the passing beauty of Shakespeare, no matter who utters it. ("There are many events in the womb of time," says Iago, referring to his nasty scheme, "which shall be delivered.")

Parker's direction is also disappointing. With the exception of Branagh, whose narcissistic, bratty qualities and Shakespearean training inform the role disconcertingly well, the performers seem horribly out of place.

Fishburne, who is an instinctively good, but cold, screen actor, never pulls us into Othello's soul. Trying to portray military bearing, sensuality and innate nobility, he looks unintentionally arrogant in some places, and dramatically outmatched (chiefly by Branagh) in others.

As the object of Othello's grand affections, Irene Jacob (who has starred in films by Polish director Krysztztoff Kieslowski) remains tentative and, frankly, not worth all the fuss. She seems doubly out of place—as a 20th-century movie actress doing Shakespeare, and as a French speaker caught in an English-language picture. Fishburne and Jacob don't look comfortable together; so their affair doesn't look right. In an alarming way, Iago's evil ways almost make sense: This love affair really does have to be stopped.

Source: Desson Howe, Review of *Othello*, in *Washington Post*, December 29, 1995.

SOURCES

Aebischer, Pascale, *Shakespeare's Violated Bodies: Stage and Screen Performance*, Cambridge University Press, 2004, pp. 135–50.

Altman, Joel B., *The Improbability of Othello: Rhetorical Anthropology and Shakespearean Selfhood*, University of Chicago Press, 2010, pp. 1–33, 317–38.

Bradley, A. C., *Shakespearian Tragedy: Lectures on Hamlet, Othello, King Lear, Macbeth*, Macmillan, 2nd ed., 1912, pp. 200–42.

Buchanan, Judith, "Virgin and Ape, Venetian and Infidel: Labelings of Otherness in Oliver Parker's *Othello*," in *Shakespeare, Film, Fin de Siècle*, edited by Mark Thornton Burnett and Ramona Wray, Macmillan, 2000, pp. 179–202.

Burt, Richard, "Backstage Pass(ing): Stage Beauty, Othello and the Make-up of Race," in *Screening Shakespeare in the Twenty-first Century*, edited by Mark Thornton Burnett and Ramona Wray, Edinburgh University Press, 2006, pp. 53–71.

Cartmel, Deborah, *Interpreting Shakespeare on Screen*, Palgrave Macmillan, 2000, pp. 72–77.

Coleridge, Samuel Taylor, *Lectures and Notes on Shakespeare and Other English Poets*, edited by T. Ashe, George Bell & Sons, 1900, pp. 384–94.

Erickson, Peter, *Citing Shakespeare: The Reinterpretation of Race in Contemporary Literature and Art*, Palgrave Macmillan, 2007, pp. 131–42.

Hatchuel, Sarah, and Nathalie Vienne-Guerrin, "Introduction: Ensnared in *Othello* On Screen," in *Shakespeare On Screen: Othello*, edited by idem, Cambridge University Press, 2015, pp. 1–23.

Holland, Peter, "Rethinking Blackness: The Case of Olivier's Othello," in *Shakespeare On Screen: Othello*, edited by Sarah Hatchuel and Nathalie Vienne-Guerrin, Cambridge University Press, 2015, pp. 43–58.

Kolin, Philp C., "Blackness Made Visible: A Survey of *Othello* in Criticism, on Stage, and on Screen," in *Othello: New Critical Essays*, edited by idem, Routledge, 2002, pp. 1–88.

Maslin, Janet, "Fishburne and Branagh Meet Their Fate in Venice," in *New York Times*, December 14, 1995, http://www.nytimes.com/1995/12/14/movies/film-review-fishburne-and-branagh-meet-their-fate-in-venice.html (accessed August 3, 2015).

O'Neill, Stephen, *Shakespeare and YouTube: New Media Forms and the Bard*, Bloomsbury, 2014, pp. 121–60.

Othello, directed by Oliver Parker, Warner Brothers, 1995, DVD.

Parker, Geoffrey, *The Grand Strategy of Philip II*, Yale University Press, 1998, pp. 122–23.

Pit-Rivers, Julian, "Honour and Social Status," in *Honour and Shame: The Values of Mediterranean Society*, edited by Jean G. Peristiany, Weidenfeld and Nicolson, 1965, pp. 167–76.

Said, Edward, *Orientalism*, Vintage, 1979, pp. 1–12.

Shakespeare, William, "The Tragedy of Othello, the Moor of Venice," in *The Riverside Shakespeare*, edited by G. Blakemore Evans, Houghton Mifflin, 1974, pp. 1198–248.

Thompson, Ayanna, "Unmooring the Moor: Researching and Teaching on YouTube," in *Shakespeare Quarterly*, Vol. 61, No. 3, 2010, pp. 337–56.

The Travels of Sir John Mandeville: The Version of the Cotton Manuscript in Modern Spelling, edited by A. W. Pollard, Macmillan, 1900, pp. 133–34.

FURTHER READING

Davidson, Peter, *Othello*, Humanities Press International, 1988.

> Davidson presents an overview of older scholarship on the play.

Hadfield, Andrew, *A Routledge Literary Sourcebook on William Shakespeare's "Othello,"* Routledge, 2003.

> This book is a collection of relevant documents beginning with Geraldi Cinthio's *Gli Hecatommithi*, Shakespeare's source for the story of *Othello*, including reviews of stage and film versions of the play and a selection of modern critical articles.

Hampton-Reeves, Stuart, *The Shakespeare Handbooks: Othello*, Palgrave Macmillan, 2011.

> Hampton-Reeves presents a discursive account of the play's performances on the stage and screen, its intellectual and cultural contexts, and a scene-by-scene commentary.

Raatzsch, Richard, *The Apologetics of Evil: The Case of Iago*, translated by Ladislaus Löb, Princeton University Press, 2010.

> Raatzsch argues that if the play were called *Iago*, the audience would be compelled to see it as a celebration of ruthlessness, but entitling it *Othello* allows for a focus on the complexities of the relationship between the two characters.

SUGGESTED SEARCH TERMS

William Shakespeare

Oliver Parker

Oliver Parker AND Othello

Elizabethan drama

revenge drama

orientalism

blackface

Laurence Fishburne

Kenneth Branagh

Iago

Real Women Have Curves

JOSEFINA LÓPEZ

1992

In her play *Real Women Have Curves*, Josefina López covers a lot of bases. It is a coming-of-age story, an immigrant story, and a family drama—though it also has many comic moments. As the protagonist Ana dreams of college and a writing career, her mother pressures her to slim down and find a man to marry; until that happens, she must work in her sister's sewing factory. As Ana and the other factory workers push to meet a big deadline, they talk about cultural standards of beauty and the changing role of women in society. Although Ana struggles under the pressures of family and tradition, by the end of the play she realizes how much she has learned from the women around her. Dramatic Publishing released an edition of the play in 1996 that is readily available. The dialogue contains frank discussions of sexual matters, making the play more suitable for older students.

AUTHOR BIOGRAPHY

López was born in San Luis Potosí, Mexico, on March 19, 1969. When she was five years old, her family moved to America and settled in Boyle Heights, a neighborhood in East Los Angeles that has a mostly Mexican American, working-class population. For her first thirteen years in the United States, López was undocumented, because the entire family entered the country

Josefina Lopez (© ZUMA Press, Inc. | Alamy)

illegally. In 1987, she was granted amnesty under the Immigration Reform and Control Act. She was naturalized as a US citizen in 1995.

López became interested in the arts as a teenager. She attended Los Angeles County High School for the Arts, majoring in theater, and was a member of the Young Playwrights Lab at the Los Angeles Theatre Center. While she was in high school, López was told by a favorite teacher that she would have to lose weight if she wanted to make it in Hollywood as an actress. After being given an assignment to write a scene depicting a relationship, López continued writing and completed her first play, *Simply Maria, or the American Dream*, at age seventeen. Although paying for school was difficult, López continued her studies after high school, graduating from Columbia College in 1993 and then completing her master of fine arts degree in screenwriting at the School of Theater, Film and Television at the University of California, Los Angeles.

Although she is best known for her play *Real Women Have Curves* and its film adaptation (2002), López's other works include the

plays *Unconquered Spirits* (1995), *Confessions of Women from East L.A.* (1997), *La Pinta* (1998), *Queen of the Rumba* (2000), *Baby Boom* (2005), *Boyle Heights* (2008), *Detained in the Desert* (2008), *The Cleaning Lady* (2009), and *Food for the Dead* (2010). López also wrote the film screenplay for *Detained in the Desert* (released in 2011). In addition to her work as a playwright, López has published the novel *Hungry Woman in Paris* (2009) and also writes poetry and original screenplays.

More than one hundred productions of López's plays have been performed all over the United States. She has been recognized with many honors, including an Imagen Award, a Humanitas Prize, and the Gabriel García Márquez Award. She is an activist and speaks publicly on women's issues, Chicano theater, immigration issues, and minority representation in movies and the arts. To encourage Latino artists, she founded a writing center called the CASA0101 Theater in her childhood neighborhood, Boyle Heights. She also started a sketch comedy troupe that tries to challenge and eliminate stereotypes about Latinas. As of 2015, López continues to teach and write. She still lives in Boyle Heights and has said she is working on a musical version of *Real Women Have Curves* for Broadway. She is married to Emmanuel Deleage, with whom she has two sons, Sebastian and Etienne.

PLOT SUMMARY

López is very specific about the setting of the play: the action occurs in the first week of September in the year 1987 in a small sewing factory in East Los Angeles. Also included is a detailed list of the specific dates and times of day when each scene takes place. Dramatic Publishing's 1996 edition of the play explains that Spanish words and phrases are in bold type and are defined in a glossary at the back of the book.

Act 1

SCENE 1

The play opens at seven o'clock on a Monday morning. Eighteen-year-old Ana is arguing with her mother, Carmen, in the sewing factory about who should fetch bread for breakfast. Carmen nags Ana about her weight, and then Ana gives in and heads out to the bakery.

MEDIA ADAPTATIONS

- López worked with George LaVoo to adapt *Real Women Have Curves* into a screenplay. Patricia Cardoso directed the film adaptation, which debuted at the 2002 Sundance Film Festival, where it won the Audience Award and a Special Jury Prize for Acting for America Ferrera (Ana) and Lupe Ontiveros (Carmen).

Ana writes in her journal, complaining about having to get up early for work, her low wages, and the stresses of being undocumented. She is happy that she will soon get her temporary residence card, which will lead to a green card and permanent resident status.

Carmen makes coffee and wonders why Estela, her other daughter, has not yet arrived at the factory. The other workers appear at the factory. First Pancha arrives and then Rosalí, who reminds the others that she is on a diet and therefore cannot sample the mole that Carmen has brought to share.

Estela appears from under a blanket on the floor, where she slept after working late the night before. Through the window, the women spy Estela's "Tormento," the man who is her "torment" because she is romantically interested in him. She tries to tidy herself up a bit, but he leaves before she can go out to speak to him.

Carmen sees a van outside and panics, afraid that it is "la migra," or immigration officials. All of the workers are frightened for a moment before remembering that they are now legal residents. All were granted amnesty under new legislation that was passed in 1986.

Estela admits that she never sent in her application for amnesty because she has a criminal record. She is being sued because she fell behind in her payments for the factory equipment and cannot appear in court for fear of being deported. If the group can finish a large sewing order by Friday, Estela will get paid a large sum from the customer and be able to catch up on her payments and save the factory.

As the women begin to work on the dresses for the rush order, Carmen and Estela argue about the best way to do the work. Each woman plans to work on one stage of the process, but there are some machines that not everyone knows how to run. Estela shows Ana how to properly iron the dresses once they are finished. The workers are all shocked when Estela explains that their customer pays them thirteen dollars for each dress, which sells in a department store for approximately two hundred dollars.

SCENE 2

Ana takes orders from the others and goes out to a food cart to buy lunch. Carmen shows the others an explicit book she found in the garage. When Ana returns, she kicks open the door because her hands are full. Estela is startled, afraid that it might be la migra. She insists that the door remain closed at all times.

Ana looks at the book the other women were looking at, but her mother believes she is too young to see it. Ana claims to know more about sex than they do. Estela scolds the workers for gossiping and urges them to eat quickly and get back to work.

The women eat the food Ana bought and sample Carmen's mole. Only Rosalí eats nothing. She claims that drinking lots of water prevents her from getting hungry, and then she swallows a pill.

Rosalí sees Andrés, Estela's "Tormento," again, so Estela goes out to speak with him. The women gossip about her after she goes, and Carmen carelessly spills mole sauce on some of the dresses. She hides the dresses from Estela, hoping to clean them later. When Estela returns, she has made a movie date with Andrés. At the urging of the other women, she reads aloud a letter that Andrés wrote to her. She then encourages them to get back to work.

SCENE 3

Rosalí turns on the radio, which plays a talk show about abusive husbands. The radio show sparks a discussion among the women. Ana is the boldest in her opinions, compared with the older women, asserting that women should stand up for themselves. A recent high school graduate, Ana explains that she wants to go to college but must wait a year for financial aid to afford to pay tuition.

Carmen, Pancha, and Rosalí leave at the end of the workday. Ana stays to finish ironing the last few dresses. Estela tells her to leave before Andrés arrives because she does not want Ana to write about it in her journal. Ana writes in her journal, frustrated that the other workers tease her for her modern opinions, while Estela tries to find something to wear for her date.

SCENE 4

Estela is crying, but when the other women ask about her date, she refuses to discuss it. They all begin to work, but Carmen continues to ask about what happened with Andrés, urging Estela to confide in her.

Carmen again sees a van and fears it is la migra. Estela considers going home to work because of her fear of being deported but is too afraid to leave the factory. Ana tricks her into going out by saying she sees Andrés kissing a gringa (a non-Latina woman). When Estela rushes out to see, Ana pushes her out and locks the door. Ana then lets her back in, and Estela decides to stay at the factory. Ana wishes for a fan to fight the heat, but Estela worries a fan would kick up dust onto the dresses.

SCENE 5

Ana writes in her journal. She feels trapped in her low-wage job and sad about having met a friend who is "pregnant, again" and on welfare but does not seem to mind. All of the women are uncomfortable and restless because of the heat. Carmen worries that she may be pregnant. Pancha laments that while Carmen has eight children, she herself has none.

The radio gives the news that twenty undocumented workers at a pillow factory are being arrested. The owner of the factory will be heavily fined for hiring illegal aliens. The news sparks another conversation about Estela's situation. She is afraid to push her customer, the Glitz company, to pay what they owe her because that is the only contract she has. With the others' encouragement, Estela calls and speaks to Mrs. Glitz, who stalls Estela by asking about her proof of employment papers.

Estela discovers that Pancha has accidentally been sewing the skirts of the dresses on backwards, causing a delay because the work must be redone. The heat is bothersome, but

Estela's fear makes her refuse to open the door. Estela finds the stained dresses and becomes furious with her mother. Tempers flare all around, and Pancha tears at the dresses she put together incorrectly, threatening to leave. Rosalí steps between Estela and Pancha and then faints.

Concern for Rosalí makes the others forget their anger. She refuses to go to the hospital, but Pancha decides to take her home. Estela feels guilty but forgets about that when Ana realizes that Rosalí is the only one who knows how to work the overlock machine, which is needed to finish the dress order.

Act 2

SCENE 1

Carmen and Estela are working in the factory. Pancha is late, and they wonder if she will come back at all. Ana arrives with detergent to clean the stained dresses. They see a man in the street and wonder if he is homeless or an immigration officer in disguise. As they watch, Pancha arrives and speaks to him. He tells her that he is a friend of Andrés. Pancha explains that she is late because she stopped to see Rosalí, who is feeling a bit better but will not return to work yet.

The women divide up the work and get started. Estela complains that Ana is working too slowly. Ana explains that she cannot help imagining the wealthy woman who will eventually buy the dress without any thought about how much work went into making it.

Trying to work with the overlock machine, Carmen becomes frustrated. She begins to feel unwell and mentions again that she may be pregnant. Pancha has a brief monologue in which she again mourns the fact that she has no children.

Estela figures out how to fix the overlock machine. Rosalí appears, eager to help, and seems almost disappointed that her knowledge of the machine is not needed. She explains that she fainted because she has not been eating. She does not want Estela to believe it was her fault, because of the heat or the argument. Rosalí admits that she has been taking diet pills. She still refuses to eat but stays to work, wanting to protect Estela from being deported. All of the women get back to work with renewed determination to finish the order in time.

SCENE 2

It is two o'clock in the morning, and the women are still at work. Rosalí's stomach is growling for the first time in a while, and all of the women realize they are hungry. Pancha pulls snacks out of her bag. A catchy song plays on the radio, and the women dance as they eat, trying to wake themselves up.

SCENE 3

Although the workers realize they have only fourteen dresses to finish to complete the order of two hundred, the heat is getting to them. Ana takes off her shirt, intending to work in only her bra, which shocks her mother.

Carmen again worries that she is pregnant. She explains that when she had her last child, she almost died, which Ana never knew. Carmen did not want to have so many children, but she never knew how to say no to her husband.

Ana takes off her pants, leaving her in just her underwear. Carmen mentions her weight, but Ana says she is happy with her appearance. The women debate about whether a woman should try to change her appearance to catch a man.

Estela finally explains what happened with Andrés: she was disappointed that he was interested in her physically when she thought he really liked her as a person. Rosalí admits that she has never had a physical relationship with a man, though she has a steady boyfriend, because she does not want him to touch her when she still feels fat.

All of the women begin to undress, comparing their bodies and what they see as their physical flaws. They are relieved to be out of their clothes in the heat and to be open with one another.

Carmen suggests copying the dress pattern to make some for themselves rather than just for a customer so that they can make more money. She also proposes making the dresses in a wider variety of sizes. Estela imagines someday opening her own shop.

Estela allows the door to be open for relief from the heat, but Carmen again thinks she sees la migra. All of the women rush to put on their clothes. The police, however, are there to arrest Andrés because he is involved in drugs. The man in disguise that Pancha spoke to was actually an undercover cop. Andrés is taken away in the van.

SCENE 4

The women shout, "Surprise!" before they realize that it is Carmen. She has been to the doctor and learned that, rather than being pregnant, she is experiencing the early symptoms of menopause. Estela arrives, and the others again call out "Surprise!" because it is her twenty-fifth birthday.

Estela is pleased that they remembered her birthday. She has delivered the dress order and been paid. After setting up a fan to help combat the heat, she gives each of the workers a check. When they hear how little Estela has left, however, they return the checks, urging her to use the money to clear her debt so that she can keep the factory open.

Estela calls Mrs. Glitz and tells her what she really thinks about her. She does not need to tolerate Mrs. Glitz's bad treatment because she has gotten another contract. The cake is brought out, and the women sing "Happy Birthday" to Estela. The women pose for a picture, holding their green cards.

Ana gives a final speech about what she learned from her time working in the sewing factory. She also explains what happens after the action of the play: she goes to school in New York and becomes a writer, and Estela opens her boutique. The cast comes out dancing, dressed in Estela's beautiful dresses, to take their bows.

CHARACTERS

Andrés

Andrés does not appear onstage, but the women talk about him frequently when they spot him out the factory windows. He is Estela's "Tormento," so called because she is tormented by her interest in him. He pretends to truly care for her, writing a letter listing her many positive qualities, but when he takes her on a date, his interest proves to be only physical. At the close of the play, Andrés is arrested in a drug bust.

Apá

Apá is Carmen's husband and Ana and Estela's father. He also does not appear on stage. Carmen explains that while they were still living in Mexico, he would always make sure that she was pregnant when he left to find work in the United States. She believes he thought being pregnant would make her unattractive to other men while he was gone. He was deported four times but kept trying to make a life in America.

Esperanza

Esperanza is one of the voices on the radio. Her talk show about abusive spouses begins a discussion on the subject among the factory workers.

Ana Garcia

Ana is the central character of the play. López describes her as "plump and pretty." She is eighteen years old and recently graduated from high school. Though she has dreams of going to college and becoming a writer, she must work a low-wage job in her sister Estela's sewing factory until she can afford tuition. As the youngest of the women, Ana plays the part of the forward-thinking, modern feminist. The other women are a little taken aback by her strong opinions and independence. Ana has a difficult relationship with her mother, Carmen, who nags her about her weight.

Carmen Garcia

Carmen is Estela and Ana's mother and a bit of a gossip. She cares about her daughters but often shows her concern by nagging and arguing. She debates with Estela about how best to run the factory, though Estela is the owner. She urges her daughter Ana to lose weight, but she herself is short and very heavy, so overweight that she thinks she could be pregnant without it showing at all in her figure. In addition to Ana and Estela, Carmen has six other children. She fears having any more because she is forty-eight years old and had a difficult time with her last pregnancy.

Estela Garcia

Estela is Carmen's oldest child, Ana's sister, and the owner of the Garcia Sewing Factory. She is twenty-four years old and a little bit plump. López implies that Estela is not as pretty as her sister. Her insecurity about her looks robs her of confidence when it comes to men. She is interested in Andrés and crushed to learn that he is only interested in her physically. However, Estela is brave in trying to keep the factory going. As the owner of the factory, she worries about the customers being late on payments, about broken machinery, and about being sued for money she owes for the equipment. She also has the added worry of being undocumented. She did not apply for amnesty, as the others

did, because she has a criminal record, though her offenses are minor.

Jaime

Jaime is Rosalí's boyfriend. Like the other men mentioned, Jaime does not appear on the stage. Although Rosalí seems to care for him and rely on him, she does not have a physical relationship with him because she feels insecure about her weight.

Pancha

Pancha is one of the workers at the factory. She is thirty-two years old and very overweight. When Carmen complains and worries about possibly being pregnant again, it makes Pancha sad because she herself does not have children. She identifies being a mother as such a vital part of womanhood that she asks God, "Why don't you make me a real woman? If I can't have children, why did you make me a woman?"

Rosalí

Rosalí is another one of the factory workers, the only one who knows how to work the overlock machine. She is twenty-nine years old and has a steady boyfriend, Jaime, though her insecurity about her looks means she has never had a physical relationship with any man. Sweet-tempered and quiet, Rosalí tries to keep the peace; for example, she stands between Estela and Pancha when their argument grows heated. When Rosalí faints, she admits that she has been living on diet pills and endless glasses of water because she always feels fat and unattractive.

THEMES

Immigrant Life

Part of López's motivation for writing *Real Women Have Curves* was to portray her personal experience as an undocumented resident. Threaded throughout the play is the fear of "la migra," or officials of the US Immigration and Naturalization Service, who patrolled the borders and checked for workers' documentation. López shows clearly how the fear of deportation has become so much a part of the women's lives that they sometimes forget that they are now legal residents. They still panic at the sight of a van that might hold immigration officials.

TOPICS FOR FURTHER STUDY

- Read An Na's young-adult novel *Wait for Me* (2006), which tells the story of Mina, a Korean American high school student. Mina's mother has very specific plans for Mina, such as going to Harvard, and puts a lot of pressure on her to conform. Think about the pressures Mina faces and compare them with Ana's situation in *Real Women Have Curves*. Write an essay comparing Ana's experience with Mina's in terms of their heritage, their hopes for the future, and their mothers' expectations.

- Using print and online resources, research immigration legislation from the 1980s to the present. Make a time line that shows the major events. Include information about the number of undocumented immigrants in the United States, where they are from, where they settle, and how population trends have varied throughout the years.

- López captures the tension between the generations in *Real Women Have Curves*. Both Ana and Estela argue with their mother about different issues throughout the play. With a small group of classmates, brainstorm about issues that are common points of dispute between teens and parents today. Chose one of these issues, and work together to write a scene that portrays a conversation between a parent and a child as they present their points of view. The scene can be an argument or a quiet discussion, funny or tragic. Perform your scene with your classmates.

- Using print and online resources, research standards of beauty in different cultures throughout the world, including how they have changed throughout history. Create a PowerPoint presentation that includes images and share it with your class. Then lead a class discussion on how the pressure to conform to such unrealistic standards affects people and relationships.

With Estela, we see how this fear can infect every part of a person's life. Her customers can simply not pay what they owe by threatening to expose her illegal status, as Mrs. Glitz does. Any business owner being sued, as Estela is, must experience a lot stress and worry, but her problem is compounded by the fact that she cannot go to court to defend herself for fear of being arrested. Because she is afraid of being deported, Estela cannot get the money owed to her, which would help her pay her employees and pay her debts, which would resolve the lawsuit. Because of her fear, she could lose her business.

In the 1980s, hiding from immigration officers was part of everyday life for the approximately five million undocumented people living in the United States. As of 2014, that number had almost doubled, with the number of undocumented residents at over eleven million. López hopes that through her writing, people will begin to see illegal residents as individuals rather than as problems. She objects to the term *illegal aliens*, believing that it

> conjures up in our minds the image of extra-terrestrial beings who are not human, who do not bleed when they're cut, who do not cry when they feel pain, who do not have fears, dreams and hopes.

After decades of undocumented people being "used as scapegoats for so many of the problems in the U.S., from drugs and violence, to the economy," López writes in the Playwright's Note, "I hope that someday this country recognizes the very important contribution of undocumented people and remembers that they too came to this country in search of a better life."

Parent-Child Relationships

The relationships that Carmen has with her daughters is an important source of conflict in *Real Women Have Curves*. Though the girls' relationship with their mother is difficult at times, the loyalty of family is clearly important to all of them. They argue about the right way to do things, and they point out each other's flaws with a frankness that is almost rude, but when one of them needs help, the others are willing to do whatever they can.

Carmen wants her daughters to succeed, but her definition of success is a more traditional one: she wants her daughters to get married and have children. She bemoans the fact that she should be a grandmother at her age, and neither Ana nor

The play is set in September 1987 in East Los Angeles. (© IM_photo | Shutterstock.com)

have had any serious adult romantic relationships and therefore has no practical experience in these matters.

In spite of their rocky relationship, Ana obviously cares for her mother. When Carmen admits that her last pregnancy and labor almost killed her, Ana seems shocked to learn about it. Carmen says wistfully, "I was very beautiful," and Ana jumps in immediately to reassure her: "You still are, Amá."

STYLE

Spanish Dialogue

Throughout *Real Women Have Curves*, López sprinkles Spanish words and phrases into her characters' dialogue. Sometimes one or two Spanish words appear in a sentence that is mostly in English. For example, when they fear they see immigration officials, they use the term *la migra*. When Carmen gives Ana money for bread in the opening scene, she says "Ten" instead of "Here" or "Take this." Pancha tacks "Doña" onto Carmen's name, rather than "Mrs.," as a sign of respect. Sometimes a character will utter an entire phrase in Spanish, such as when Estela admits that she owes two thousand dollars on the factory equipment, and Carmen, in shock at the total, says, "Hora si que estamos bien jodidas!" ("Now we're really messed up!") The characters seem to speak in Spanish almost reflexively, as would make sense with one's first language. Incidental words and exclamations pop out in Spanish without much thought. When they are more thoughtful about what they are saying, they tend to speak in English. The inclusion of Spanish words and phrases adds realism to the dialogue because it reflects how López remembers her family, friends, and coworkers speaking.

Storytelling

López was inspired to write *Real Women Have Curves* by hearing the stories of the women in the sewing factory where she worked as a teenager, and that influence is clear in the structure of the play. Because all of the action of the play takes place in the factory, everything that happens outside that room is related in a story, such as Ana's meeting an old friend, the woman on the radio talking about her abusive husband, Estela talking about her date with Andrés, Carmen describing how her husband always left her pregnant when he went north to look for work, and even the

Estela are married. She wants to have a close relationship with both of her daughters, as can be seen in her interest in Estela's relationship with Andrés. However, she does not know how to go about it gracefully. Rather than simply being ready if Estela wants to confide in her, Carmen tries to bully her into talking about her date. Carmen also wants to help Estela's business be a success, but she voices her opinions about how that should be accomplished rather than letting Estela run things her way.

Carmen seems to see the potential in Ana, but rather than offering encouragement, Carmen tends to criticize. She tells Ana that she needs to lose weight or she will never find a man. She does not seem to understand that finding a husband is not a priority for Ana right now. For her part, Ana seems to try to antagonize her mother and the older women with her feminist opinions. She tries to act more worldly than they are and tells them they should stand up to their husbands, though she herself does not seem to

COMPARE & CONTRAST

- **1980s:** President Ronald Reagan signs into law the Immigration Reform and Control Act of 1986. The act allows 2.7 million illegal immigrants to remain in the country without fear of arrest or deportation. Lawmakers hope to keep undocumented workers in the United States to fill vital jobs and to let government immigration workers focus on preventing further illegal immigration at the border.

   Today: On November 20, 2014, President Barack Obama announces a set of executive actions that, when they are implemented, will allow some illegal immigrants to remain temporarily in the United States if they pass a criminal background check and pay taxes. Again, the new legislation is intended to free personnel to more strictly enforce the border and concentrate on deporting felons.

- **1980s:** Approximately 2.7 million of the five million illegal immigrants in the United States are granted permanent resident status under the Immigration Reform and Control Act.

   Today: By the close of the twentieth century, the number of illegal immigrants in the United States again tops five million. That number increases steadily, reaching its peak in 2007 at over twelve million. As of 2014, there are over eleven million illegal immigrants in the United States, of which about half are from Mexico.

- **1980s:** The number of self-employed women in the United States in 1984 is twice what it was in 1977 owing to government programs to help women toward business ownership. Approximately one-quarter of small businesses in the country are owned by women.

   Today: There are almost eight million American businesses owned by women, making up almost 30 percent of all nonfarm businesses. Top industries for women-owned businesses include health care and social assistance, education services, retail, recreation, and entertainment.

women describing the arrest of Andrés in the drug bust as they watch out the window. These events are described by the characters in stories rather than being portrayed on the stage.

Storytelling is important in how people relate to one another around the world. López believes in the particular importance of the oral tradition in Chicano culture. In an interview with Claudia Herrera Hudson, López explains that she "learned to become a writer by listening to my mother's stories and gossip and my grandfather's ghost stories." López continues:

> I think there are so many Latino authors out there who don't know they are writers because they are working in beauty shops telling their stories to other women. If these women simply wrote down their stories and edited them and put them in the acceptable mainstream formats then they could be considered authors instead of "chismosas" ("gossips").

HISTORICAL CONTEXT

Immigration Reform and Control Act of 1986

Ronald Reagan is remembered as a conservative Republican president, so many are surprised by his efforts to extend amnesty to some of the five million illegal aliens living in the United States in the 1980s. The biggest boon to undocumented residents was the provision for anyone who had lived in the United States continuously since January 1, 1982, to apply for temporary residency, which would protect them from being deported. Once granted that legal status, immigrants could apply to be categorized as a permanent resident, which meant receiving a green card. Later, residents could become naturalized US citizens. Approximately 2.7 million illegal aliens were given protection from deportation and then allowed

All of the women, even those with green cards, worry about La Migra, and Estela has the added stress of her business. *(© KieferPix | Shutterstock.com)*

permanent resident status based on this general amnesty legislation.

Some of the motivation of politicians supporting the legislation may have been economic: many of these illegal aliens were migrant workers that American farmers depended on to bring in their vital crops. Because they filled such an important role in the agricultural industry, the legislation was very generous to these undocumented workers, granting legal status to anyone who had worked in agriculture for at least ninety days in the year ending May 1, 1986, even if they had not lived in the country since 1982.

Not all of the support for the amnesty was based on dollars and cents, however. In a television debate with Walter Mondale in the 1984 presidential race, Reagan gave a nobler reason: "I believe in the idea of amnesty for those who have put down roots and lived here, even though sometime back they may have entered illegally." Alan K. Simpson, a former US senator from Wyoming

who helped to draft the legislation and who considered Reagan a personal friend, explained in an interview with NPR that the president "knew that it was not right for people to be abused.... Anybody who's here illegally is going to be abused in some way, either financially [or] physically. They have no rights." López certainly shows this in *Real Women Have Curves*, such as when Estela's customer withheld payment by threatening her with exposure of her illegal status.

The Immigration Reform and Control Act was not enacted just to help undocumented residents. It was also intended to free up personnel and resources to restrict further illegal immigration. It called for tightened security at the US border with Mexico. It also imposed heavy fines on employers who hired undocumented workers; López portrays this in *Real Women Have Curves* when the women hear a report on the radio about arrests at a pillow factory, for which the owner had to pay as much two thousand dollars for each illegal worker. With these goals, however, the Immigration Reform and Control Act largely failed. Some figures show that the amnesty actually increased illegal immigration, because newly legal residents illegally brought their family members to live with them. In 1997, about a decade after the act went into effect, the number of illegal aliens living in the United States was estimated to be five million, basically the same as it had been before the amnesty.

CRITICAL OVERVIEW

Reviews of *Real Women Have Curves* are decidedly mixed. Many critics praise the humor in the play and López's strong message of empowerment and the importance of working together. However, critics such as Stephanie Shaw in *Reader* notice that "Lopez never fully develops the situation or the characters." Shaw feels that

> Actions never seem to have consequences, resentments are aired and dismissed, and the women are far more involved in swapping funny stories than in confronting problems. Any problems that are confronted are usually solved with a one-liner and a hug.

Dennis Schwartz, in a review of the film adaptation for *Ozus' World Movie Reviews*, agrees that the conflict in the play is too thin and that "there's nothing new in these familiar family dilemmas," which are resolved "in a too obvious and predictable way to hold one's interest."

Reactions to the scene near the close of the play in which the women strip down to their underwear show how widely critics' opinions vary. Connie Meng, in a regional theater review for the local public radio station, enjoys the underwear scene and the dialogue when the women compare their cellulite. "This could be touchy," writes Meng, "but it's actually very funny." Shaw agrees that "much of it is very funny" but is uncomfortable noticing that when the heaviest actress on the stage "disrobes one can't help feeling she's being used as a sight gag." Schwartz, however, has a strongly negative view, describing the scene "where the obese factory gals strip down to their undergarments to show that they're proud of their fat" as a "shameless example to show female empowerment."

In spite of the play's problems, most critics see much promise in López's work. Shaw also points out the unique perspective that López brings to theater as a Chicana playwright: "Plays that deal with the lives of Hispanic women in America are not plentiful," Shaw writes. Then she continues:

> It's refreshing to see a play about five women, much less five Latin American women. And Lopez's play has a lot of heart and quite a bit of charm. So much, in fact, that one is tempted to overlook its many flaws.

Shaw encourages the playwright to "keep on reaching," concluding that though López's "skills may need honing, . . . we can't afford to lose her point of view." Meng agrees, explaining that the play has "humor and power," though these qualities may be muffled by a mediocre production: "*Real Women Have Curves* opens a window on both women's roles in Mexican-American culture and on the Latina immigrant experience." If only because the play "expands our knowledge and understanding of a subject and culture most of us have no first-hand knowledge of," continues Meng, it makes a valuable contribution to American drama.

CRITICISM

Kristen Sarlin Greenberg
Greenberg is a freelance writer and editor with a background in literature and philosophy. In the following essay, she traces Ana's path from child-ishness to a more mature understanding in López's Real Women Have Curves.

López begins her play *Real Women Have Curves* establishing a generation gap between her characters by depicting a mother and daughter bickering. The mother-daughter relationship is indeed a significant theme of the play, continuing throughout between Carmen and both of her daughters. The petty argument that opens the first scene, however, does more than just set up the troublesome dynamic between Ana and her mother. It also establishes Ana firmly in the role of a child. Throughout most the first act of the play, Ana is portrayed as self-centered and rebellious, like a sulking teenager, and it is not until the very last scene of act 1 that she begins to show that she is changing.

In Ana's first line, she sounds like a spoiled child. She says, "No. I want to go back to sleep!" To be fair, Carmen is being a little bossy as she sends Ana out to fetch bread for breakfast, but Carmen is looking at the big picture—the

WHAT DO I READ NEXT?

- Whereas Ana feels pressure from her mother to lose weight, in *Staying Fat for Sarah Byrnes* (1993) by young-adult author Chris Crutcher, narrator Eric puts pressure on himself *not* to slim down. Eric's friendship with Sarah started because they both felt like outcasts—Eric because of his obesity and Sarah because of severe burn scars on her hands and face. When Eric joins the swim team and starts to get fit, Sarah stops talking and is put into a mental hospital. Eric is determined to preserve their friendship but uncovers some shocking secrets.

- *Girl in Translation* (2010), by Jean Kwok, centers on Kimberly Chang, whose family moved from Hong Kong to New York in the 1980s. Rather than experiencing the American dream, however, they find themselves living in a rundown apartment and working in a factory in Chinatown. Although the first day of school is daunting, Kimberly eventually excels and earns a scholarship to a prestigious prep school.

- Anzia Yezierska presents a nonfiction immigrant story in her 1950 memoir *Red Ribbon on a White Horse*. Yezierska chronicles her struggles as a Polish Jew living among mostly Gentile neighbors as well as the trials of getting published in the 1920s, when the writing world was dominated by men.

- López's 2010 play *Food for the Dead* satirizes the Mexican traditions of the Day of the Dead, in which families set out food for their deceased loved ones. A family gathers to celebrate the holiday, and many secrets are revealed, leading to over-the-top drama.

- For fifty years, Abraham Cahan was the editor of the *Jewish Daily Forward*, the biggest Yiddish-language newspaper in the United States. In 1917, Cahan published his novel *The Rise of David Levinsky*, which has since become a classic of immigrant literature. Levinsky manages to make himself a material success, but at a cost to his humanity.

- Nigerian author Chimamanda Ngozi Adichie presents a modern novel about immigration in *Americanah* (2013), which tells the tale of Ifemelu, a young woman who has left her politically troubled homeland of Nigeria in search of a better future. She settles in the United States, trying to find satisfying work. She airs her thoughts and observations about race in a blog, entries of which are included in the novel.

---

importance of helping Estela finish a big order—whereas Ana is still thinking selfishly. At first, she refuses to go to the bakery. "I don't want any bread," she says. It does not seem to occur to her to go simply to help her sister, who was up very late the night before, working. When Carmen complains about her arthritis and her failing eyesight, Ana barely listens. The stage directions indicate that she answers "unsympathetically," saying, "Yeah, sure, Amá." One can almost hear the "whatever" that could follow her offhand remark.

Ana does not treat other characters any better than she treats her mother. When Ana is going out to buy lunch, she only begrudgingly lends Estela a dollar so that she can get something to eat. Then, when Estela asks Ana to also pick up some distilled water for the iron, Ana answers flippantly, "Anything else, boss?" When Ana returns to the factory to find the older women looking at an explicit book, they refuse to let her see it. They mean to protect her, but Ana insists, "I'm not a girl. I'm a woman."

She still acts like a child, however. Her behavior is selfish. She teases Estela, rather cruelly given her reasonable fear of "la migra" and deportation. Ana pretends she does not

> ANA HAS GAINED A MATURE OUTLOOK AND LEARNED TO APPRECIATE THE STRENGTH AND WISDOM OF THE OTHER WOMEN, THOUGH THEY MAY MAKE DIFFERENT CHOICES AND THINK DIFFERENTLY THAN SHE DOES."

know it is Estela knocking, refusing to unlock the door and let Estela in. "You think we should open the door?" Ana teases. "What if it's la migra?" Though she obviously knows that it is Estela at the door, Ana forces her to knock the secret code knock before she will let her in.

Ana considers herself to be a budding feminist, and she enjoys making dramatic speeches. "We have to assert ourselves. We have to realize that we have rights!" she says while perched on top of a sewing machine. "We have the right to control our bodies. . . . It all begins when we start saying . . . no more! We should learn how to say no!" Ana cannot tolerate the passivity of the older women. "It just amazes me to hear you talk the way you do," she says. "A women's liberation movement happened 20 years ago, and you act like it hasn't even happened."

She is speaking with a youthful, rebellious spirit, but she does not truly understand what it is like for the older women, who are steeped in traditional roles. Carmen does not even believe that the women's liberation movement has anything to do with her, asserting that "all those gringas shouting about liberation hasn't done a thing for me." She assumes that any progress made will be for Anglo women, not for Latinas. She also points out Ana's lack of experience when it comes to relationships. She tells Ana she would have a different point of view "if you were married."

Another instance of Ana's immature selfishness comes when Estela teaches her how to properly steam the dresses so they are perfect when they go to the customer. Although she has received Estela's careful instructions, Ana does things her own way. When Estela protests, Ana says, "I thought if I did it this way it would be okay and save us time. I can't stand the heat and

the steam." Ana's way of doing things, rushing to avoid the heat, results in the fabric getting singed, so that some of the work has to be redone. Only at the very end of the first act of the play does Ana begin to think about someone other than herself. When Rosalí faints, Ana shows concern, asking Rosalí if she is all right.

In the second act, however, Ana starts to act and speak with a little more maturity. After hearing that Pancha went to see Rosalí before coming to work, Ana asks how she is feeling. When Estela asks Ana to stay late and work in a last push to get the dresses completed on time, Ana agrees after only a moment of hesitation. After much frustration over the broken overlock machine, Estela figures out how to fix it, and Ana is genuinely encouraging and congratulatory. Near the end of the play, though Ana desperately wants a typewriter to help with her dream of becoming a writer, she decides to give Estela half of her check to help save the factory.

Perhaps the clearest moment of the change in Ana's attitude comes when Carmen brings up her phantom pregnancy again. In sharp contrast to the moment early in the play when Carmen talks about her arthritis and Ana brushes her off, barely paying attention, Ana is attentive. She is very concerned and asks, "Amá, do you really want to have it?" Ana is clearly upset to learn that her mother's last pregnancy could have killed her. She is much kinder than in the opening scene. After Carmen has visited the doctor and learns that she is not pregnant but in the early stages of menopause, Ana asks sympathetically, "Then why are you sad?" Ana then reassures Carmen that she is still a "real woman" even if she can no longer bear children.

Realistically, Ana does not become a perfect saint in the second act. She still grumbles about the heat, but so do all of the workers. One gets the feeling that López is just using those bits of dialogue to set up the scene where the women strip down to their underwear, because even Ana's complaints do not have the same petulance as those in the first act. Ana also has another moment of rebellion in the second act, explaining that staying overweight is a kind of defiance, yelling "How dare you try to define me and tell me what I have to be and look like!" Nevertheless, it is clear that Ana is learning to be more sympathetic and to think about someone's feelings other than her own.

The women work long hours to finish a large order on time. (© *Photographee.eu | Shutterstock.com*)

Ana's closing speech clearly shows the shift in her point of view. She recognizes the contempt she feels for her mother and the other workers, believing their work to be "simple and unimportant." Ana thinks herself to be superior to the others, "glad to know that because I was educated, I wasn't going to end up like them." With her grand speeches, she "wanted to show them how much smarter and liberated I was. I was going to teach them about the women's liberation movement...and all the things a so-called educated American woman knows." By the final monologue, however, Ana realizes that "in their subtle ways they taught me about resistance....About the loneliness of being women in a country that looks down on us for being mothers and submissive wives." Ana has gained a mature outlook and learned to appreciate the strength and wisdom of the other women, though they may make different choices and think differently than she does. Most important, she has learned "that women are powerful, especially when working together."

Source: Kristen Sarlin Greenberg, Critical Essay on *Real Women Have Curves*, in *Drama for Students*, Gale, Cengage Learning, 2016.

Yvonne Tasker
In the following excerpt, Tasker provides a feminist reading of the film adaptation, raising many points that relate to the play as well.

... *Girlfight* exploits the connection between gender and genre by positioning a young woman in the boxing movie, reworking sports movie conventions with domestic drama and the teen film. *Real Women Have Curves* suggests different practices and types of generic combination used by independent women filmmakers. Thus *Real Women Have Curves* inflects genres more familiarly associated with women. It is a comedy, a melodrama, and a coming-of-age narrative centered on the character of Ana (America Ferrera), whose developing sense of self brings her into conflict with her mother. Generational conflict is here plainly orchestrated out of the clash between traditional and more modern perspectives on gender and aspiration. Realism is once more central; the film's title points to a desire to evoke real women as against commodified images or media-generated idealizations of women. Such idealized female bodies are present in the film by proxy, evident in the glamorous,

> *REAL WOMEN* MORE GENERALLY ESCHEWS THE CRUDITY OF THE MAKEOVER (A PROMINENT FEATURE OF THE TEEN FILM AND OF MEDIA CULTURE MORE BROADLY), OFFERING INSTEAD A TRANSFORMATION NARRATIVE IN WHICH ANA COMES TO TERMS WITH HER BODY."

small-sized dresses that are assembled in Estela (Ingrid Oliu)'s factory before being sold in Bloomingdales for many times the amount received by the factory workers. In the film's avowedly feminist terms, "real women" are women who must work hard and whose bodies do not conform to the feminine norms posited by these empty dresses. The distance between Hollywood/celebrity bodies and actual women's bodies serves as a sign of other differences to do with working conditions and opportunities for advancement. These "real" women's curves also allude to Latina bodies set against white-defined standards of beauty (Beltrán 2002). While "real" is a synonym for "normal" or "average," Ana is also defined as distinct from the other women in the factory, her capability already evident in having secured a place at a high school in Beverly Hills and (with her teacher's help) a full scholarship to attend Columbia University. As a consequence of her status as both average and exceptional, *Real Women Have Curves* traces Ana's rites of passage in terms of both developing knowledge—of her body and sexuality, of the world of work—and her need to make a choice (should she leave her family to seek a college education?).

A major strand in feminist criticism has long understood narrative cinema as associated with the exclusion of women, defined in terms of a femininity that is persistently denigrated, coded as excessive, in need of control or mastery. Against this context *Real Women* stages a coming-of-age narrative in which its protagonist must come to terms with the limitations and responsibilities of the adult world. It draws on and centralizes not just genre but the pervasive cultural dynamics through which actual women

might come to internalize the thin body as desirable. While *Girlfight* opposes the athletic female body to that emphasized as the feminine ideal, *Real Women* addresses a pervasive cultural opposition between bodies that are appropriately bounded and disciplined in terms of norms of feminine thinness and those that are undisciplined, overweight, and thus require "work." Here the film dialogues primarily with popular media rather than film, not least since Hollywood films aimed at female audiences rarely feature nonnormative bodies.

Ana and her mother Carmen (Lupa Ontiveros) argue about her body throughout the film, a dispute that opens up questions of what it means to be a woman and the rules governing an appropriate performance of femininity. According to Carmen, Ana must lose weight; her jibes and admonishments to that effect punctuate the film, being variously played for comic and emotive effect. Here the film touches on contemporary popular discourses that insist—in contradictory fashion—that women should know themselves and feel confident in their bodies, while also persistently monitoring and disciplining those bodies for signs of excess or physical nonconformity. The prurient tabloid policing of celebrity bodies—particularly female bodies—as either too fat (unattractive, unhealthy) or too thin (dangerous, unhealthy), requiring constant attention, exemplifies this contradictory insistence on a supposedly healthy, self-confident conformity.

An oppressive figure who is played for one-dimensional comedy, Carmen's body too is scrutinized in the film, and marked as in transition. She is entering menopause, as her daughter is becoming a young woman, facing choices to do with sexuality and reproduction. The film scores comic points at Carmen's expense with her misguided reading of the onset of menopause as pregnancy, a "secret" that she confides only to the indifferent Ana. Above all Carmen wants Ana to lose weight in order to perform femininity more effectively, to make herself attractive to men, marry, and have children. In short, she wants Ana to follow in her own path and is both frustrated and uncomprehending at Ana's refusal to see herself in these terms. There are moments of connection between the two—as when Ana glimpses the scar left by her own birth—but ultimately the film cannot reconcile mother and daughter. Indeed, Carmen withholds the blessing that Ana's father and grandfather both bestow when she leaves for university, locking herself into her bedroom with her memories. Carmen's grief at her disappointment is corded less significance and pathos than Ana's choices. Where mainstream films such as *Monster-in-Law* (2005) suggest reconciliation between generations of women, this is almost always centered on the rituals of romance and marriage. *Real Women* certainly encompasses the familiar generic themes of romance (via Ana's developing relationship with classmate Jimmy), but this does not provide the film's narrative resolution.

Generational conflict between women is a prominent feature of the contemporary woman's film. A number of popular examples of the genre, such as *Something's Gotta Give* (2003) or *Monster-in-Law* associate the mother with a restrictive and isolating feminism in contrast to the younger women, who may emphasize freedom through sexuality or celebrate traditional conceptions of marriage and reproduction. In contrast to this mainstream alignment of feminist views with an older generation, *Real Women* has Ana confronting questions as to her own sexuality, how to understand her body in relation to restrictive gender norms, and whether to pursue a college education. The maternal figure of Carmen remains outside, representing an identity that Ana comes into conflict with and must seemingly move beyond as she adopts an adult identity. Rather than accept her mother's understanding of sex as exclusive to the institution of marriage, for instance, Ana initiates a sexual encounter with Jimmy. We see her buying condoms in a local store, suggesting her ability to exercise control over her body. Such scenes suggest a feminist filmmaking that intersects with the more traditional themes of the woman's film, such as the suggestion of personal transformation via costume or the achievement of self-realization through romantic intimacy.

While Ana does not celebrate her physicality, neither does she engage in self-loathing: she expresses her desire to lose weight while reveling in her body's symbolic assertion of her right to take up space in the world. This ambivalence is nicely expressed in the scene in which Ana and the other women at her sister's factory strip to their underwear against the heat, comparing their "real" bodies and celebrating their physicality. The scene is played for both pathos (women's lives are inscribed on our bodies) and

humor, a doubleness evident in Ana's ambiguous assertion, "Who cares what we look like when no one's watching us?" While Carmen routinely expresses her disgust at her daughter's body, the film makes clear that others value Ana's body; Jimmy pronounces her beautiful and Ana insists on keeping the lights on while they have sex, wanting to be seen even as she expresses her insecurity. Ana's sister Estela also expresses implicit approval of her body, designing a beautiful dress for her. Images of Ana holding this dress were widely used in promotional materials; in withholding of an image of Ana wearing it, the film's emphasis falls not on her makeover but on the connection between the sisters. *Real Women* more generally eschews the crudity of the makeover (a prominent feature of the teen film and of media culture more broadly), offering instead a transformation narrative in which Ana comes to terms with her body. This much is conventionally expressed in the final shots of Ana confidently emerging from the subway in New York. Here she is visibly wearing makeup and adopts the stance of an adult woman rather than a slouching teen. Indeed, as some observers have commented, she seems in this parting shot to be following her mother's advice with respect to posture, advice she mocks earlier in the film.

Chris Holmlund describes *Real Women Have Curves* as (largely) a feminist film, consciously differentiating it from postfeminist versions of the woman's film. For Holmlund, the film's emphasis on education and average (rather than media idealized) bodies is crucial in this designation, as is a recognition of women's work (2005, 119). Again it is the realist impulse that defines feminist film for Holmlund, although Ana's personal development through the course of the film is also generic. The tensions in the film are mediated narratively not only through generational conflict between women but in terms of work. Graduating high school, Ana quits her job as a waitress, reluctantly agreeing to work in sister Estela's factory. Ana immediately comes into conflict with her sister and the women who work there; these women's pride in their work is contrasted to Ana's dismissal of the factory as a sweatshop and her labor as dirty work. While she is not wrong about the exploitative conditions in which they labor, the film is at pains to reveal that, through the course of the film, Ana comes to respect her sister's efforts and to understand the harshness of the economy in which she operates. Indeed, she tells her father, "I never realized how hard she works." Estela's aspirations are glimpsed, too—her desire to start her own line and her skill evident in crafting a dress for Ana. In acknowledging the reality of work even as the film triumphantly follows Ana to New York and her new life as a student, *Real Women* simultaneously questions how much choice the majority of women actually have and celebrates Ana as an exceptional young woman who claims a space for herself in a new arena. . . .

Source: Yvonne Tasker, "Bodies and Genres in Transition: *Girlfight* and *Real Women Have Curves*," in *Gender Meets Genre in Postwar Cinemas*, edited by Christine Gledhill, University of Illinois Press, 2012, pp. 91–94.

David Rodney

In the following review, Rodney praises the way the story finds a balance between family and independence.

A delightful coming-of-age comedy-drama about a Mexican-American teen struggling against her environment and the expectations of her overbearing mother as she at tempts to forge her own path in life, *Real Women Have Curves* represents both an empowering entertainment for women and a vindication for all the zaftig girls oppressed by the tyranny of the perfect body. Big-hearted and refreshingly generous toward all of its characters, this winning adaptation of Josefina Lopez's play has drawn one of the more rousing audience responses of any competition feature in Sundance. While HBO broadcast set for later this year reduces the chance of U.S. theatrical exposure, the film has distinct potential to cross beyond Hispanic markets and reach a broader public.

As plump 18-year-old Ana (America Ferrera) prepares to graduate from high school, she faces the choice of pursuing a college degree and a life of her own or remaining bound to her family and taking work in the East L.A. dress factory run by her sister Estela (Ingrid Oliu). Her guilt-inducing mother, Carmen (Lupe Ontiveros), favors the latter course and maps out a traditional path of marriage and family for Ana.

When Estela loses four seamstresses and has trouble meeting deadlines. Ana reluctantly signs on for the summer to help, secretly applying for a college scholarship and putting long-term decisions on hold. Her stint at the factory opens her eyes to the sacrifice, dedication and talent of her older sister, whom she previously undervalued,

and to the injustices of an exploitative marketplace that pays $18 apiece for $600 dresses.

While pitching in to help Estela, Ana shrugs off her mother's constant barbs about her hefty figure and, in an uplifting scene, liberates her co-workers from self-consciousness about their own less-than-perfect bodies. At the same time, Ana finds the strength to take the future firmly into her own hands, even assuming control of her sexual initiation with a schoolmate (Brian Sites).

Two captivatingly drawn women and two truly winning performances help distinguish the material, which is handled with warmth, assurance and genuine affection for the characters and milieu by first-time feature director Patricia Cardoso.

Having frequently sparkled in supporting roles. Ontiveros' superb comic timing is no surprise, humorously lording it over her family while trying to convince herself that her advanced menopause is really a late-in-life pregnancy. The actress strikes an endearing, dignified balance for Carmen as both a manipulative monster and a loving mother.

Relative newcomer Ferrera also is remarkable, her sensitive perf revealing the internally battling forces of strength, resolve, defiance, duty and loyalty that shape and color her character.

Adapted by playwright Lopez and producer George LaVoo, the very satisfying script provides sweet humor, warmly observed relationships, a strongly conveyed sense of the importance of family and community but also of independence and individuality, and a lively sparring match between traditional and emancipated mentalities.

It's a tribute to the writers that while Ana's character frequently rails against attitudes and expectations surrounding Latina women, there's no sense of a laborious feminist agenda behind her dialogue. Simply shot in clean, sharp colors, the piece is successfully opened out for the screen, its stage origins only intermittently evident, most notably in the hilarious set piece in which the factory women learn to love their love handles.

Source: David Rodney, Review of *Real Women Have Curves*, in *Daily Variety*, Vol. 274, No. 38, January 22, 2002, p. 18.

Jenelle Riley

In the following essay, Riley discusses adapting Lopez's play into a film.

When playwright Josefina Lopez sat in the audience for the first screening of *Real Women*

Have Curves at the 2002 Sundance Film Festival, it was the culmination of an 11-year struggle to bring her semi-autobiographical story to the big screen. After 25 productions, an attempted sitcom, and countless rewrites, Lopez's story will finally hit theatres, at least in New York and Los Angeles, on Oct. 18.

The journey began when Lopez was only 19 and decided to write a play based on her experiences working in a sewing factory with her mother and sister. In 1990 she became one of three playwrights selected to spend six weeks in San Francisco developing her script—at the Teatro De La Esperanza as part of its Latino Playwriting Workshop. Hollywood immediately expressed an interest in turning her play into a movie, and she was soon at work on a screenplay. But, Lopez admitted, the material wasn't particularly commercial, and the project stalled. The play continued to be staged throughout the United States, garnering more fans and critical raves, but nobody seemed to want to take a chance on such risky material being translated to the screen. Even television legend Norman Lear, who worked with Lopez on turning the story into a television sitcom, couldn't get the project off the ground. "He was very committed," said Lopez, "but it just couldn't get made."

All changed in 1998, when producer George LaVoo attended a show at the Glaxa Studios in Silverlake. LaVoo and Lopez shared a common bond: their attorney. "[Our] lawyer thought we would have similar sensibilities because George liked doing very specialized films and wasn't afraid of material that wasn't commercial," said Lopez. "She had very good instincts about us clicking, and we did."

Lopez and LaVoo took the project to HBO Films, which had just opened a Latino division. *Real Women Have Curves* was set to be the second film it produced, following the Andy Garcia film *For Love or Country: The Arturo Sandoval Story*. HBO hired Patricia Cardoso, winner of the Student Academy Award for her 1994 film *The Water Carrier* and the former director of the Latino Program at the Sundance Institute, to direct. Cardoso had seen the play in Silverlake and set about reworking the script, which was set entirely in one room, into a feature film. Her first task was to move as many scenes as possible to outdoor locations. "I love Los Angeles as a location," said Cardoso. "I wanted to include it as a character in the movie."

Other major changes were inevitable. While adapting the screenplay, Lopez realized she had been too close to the project for too long. "I couldn't distance myself from it and I couldn't see possibilities because I was so stuck on what really happened," she said. She praised LaVoo as a co-writer, crediting him with making choices that would help the tale work onscreen. Several storylines, including a subplot involving immigration, were cut from the final script. LaVoo and Cardoso worked on writing additional male characters into the story; Cardoso made the father more central to the story. "Usually Latino men are portrayed as these macho types," said Cardoso, "and the ones I know are really nice and sensitive and wonderful."

In casting the project, Lopez felt strongly about one performer. At age 18, Lopez met actor Lupe Ontiveros and promised herself that someday she would write a substantial starring role for the actor. "I wanted her to be a star," said Lopez, "She just has 'it.'" Ontiveros played the role of Carmen in San Diego Rep's 1994 production of *Real Women*, Lopez playing her daughter. "I promised Lupe if the movie ever got made, she would play the role," said Lopez, but Ontiveros remained skeptical. "I think she's been around so long, every Chicano has made her a promise."

Then, when Ontiveros auditioned, there was a concern she might be too well known to play the part. In addition, Cardoso had changed the part of the mother significantly, making her far more verbally abusive and unsupportive. Cardoso worried that Ontiveros would be too attached to the character she had done in the play and would bring that to the movie. But Ontiveros persevered. "She totally understood the difference," said Cardoso. "She didn't get the role just because of who she is and because she'd done the play. I had casting directors see people all over L.A. and Mexico, and Lupe was simply the best by far."

The movie was shot in just 31 days, and Cardoso had only three weeks to complete it before it premiered at the Sundance Film Festival. "I was barely alive the day we got on the plane to go to Sundance," said Cardoso. Lopez and Cardoso found themselves overwhelmed by the strong audience response to the film. "That's the kind of reaction the play gets," said Lopez, "but there's a distancing effect that happens when you put something on-screen, and I wasn't sure how it would play in a movie theatre." When people cheered the film following its first screening, Cardoso found herself moved to tears. Lopez was equally touched. "Eleven years of waiting for this, and this moment is perfect."

Source: Jenelle Riley, "The Women behind *Real Women*: Playwright Josefina Lopez and Director Patricia Cardoso Redefine What's 'Commercial,'" in *Back Stage West*, Vol. 9, No. 42, October 17, 2002, p. 7.

SOURCES

"Author Biography," in *Real Women Have Curves*, Dramatic Publishing, 1996.

"Biography," Josefina Lopez website, http://josefinalopez.co/?page_id=6 (accessed August 6, 2015).

Camarota, Steven A., "New INS Report: 1986 Amnesty Increased Illegal Immigration," Center for Immigration Studies website, October 2000, http://cis.org/articles/2000/ins1986amnesty.html (accessed August 6, 2015).

"Executive Actions on Immigration," US Citizenship and Immigration Services website, http://www.uscis.gov/immigrationaction (accessed August 6, 2015).

Hudson, Claudia Herrera, "Josefina López," My Hero Project website, http://myhero.com/hero.asp?hero=Josefina_Lopez_MAG (accessed August 6, 2015).

Joos, Marion, "Women: The Entrepreneurs of the 1980s," in *Reference Services Review*, Vol. 15, No. 3, 1987, pp. 59–65.

Krogstad, Jens Manuel, and Jeffrey S. Passel, "5 Facts about Illegal Immigration in the U.S.," Pew Research Center website, July 24, 2015, http://www.pewresearch.org/fact-tank/2015/07/24/5-facts-about-illegal-immigration-in-the-u-s/ (accessed August 6, 2015).

López, Josefina, "Playwright's Notes," in *Real Women Have Curves*, Dramatic Publishing, 1996, pp. 5–6.

———, *Real Women Have Curves*, Dramatic Publishing, 1996.

"López, Josefina," Latino Author website, http://thelatinoauthor.com/authors/l/josefinalopez/ (accessed August 6, 2015).

Meng, Connie, "*Real Women Have Curves* at the Depot Theatre," North Country Public Radio website, August 17, 2012, http://www.northcountrypublicradio.org/news/story/20373/20120827/theatre-review-real-women-have-curves-at-the-depot-theatre (accessed August 6, 2015).

Milano, Valerie, "Josefina López to Deliver Commencement Address to 2015 Graduating Class at Columbia College Chicago on Saturday, May 16, 2015 at 10:00 a.m.," in *Hollywood Times*, May 13, 2015, http://thehollywood times.net/2015/05/13/josefina-lopez-to-deliver-commencement-address-to-2015-graduating-class-at-columbia-college-chicago-on-saturday-may-16-2015-at-1000-a-m/ (accessed August 6, 2015).

Pear, Robert, "U.S. Is Expanding Amnesty Program for Illegal Aliens," in *New York Times*, April 6, 1987, http://www.nytimes.com/1987/04/06/us/us-is-expanding-amnesty-program-for-illegal-aliens.html#h&[&] (accessed August 6, 2015).

"A Reagan Legacy: Amnesty for Illegal Immigrants," NPR website, July 4, 2014, http://www.npr.org/templates/story/story.php?storyId=128303672 (accessed August 6, 2015).

"*Real Women Have Curves*," Sundance Institute website, http://history.sundance.org/films/2572/real_women_have_curves (accessed August 6, 2015).

Schwartz, Dennis, Review of *Real Women Have Curves*, in *Ozus' World Movie Reviews*, December 19, 2002, http://www.imdb.com/reviews/336/33613.html (accessed August 6, 2015).

Shaw, Stephanie, Review of *Real Women Have Curves*, in *Reader*, http://www.chicagoreader.com/chicago/real-women-have-curves/Content?oid=883127 (accessed August 6, 2015).

"Women-owned Businesses," National Women's Business Council website, https://www.nwbc.gov/facts/women-owned-businesses (accessed August 6, 2015).

FURTHER READING

Houston, Jeanne D. Wakatsuki, and James D. Houston, *Farewell to Manzanar*, Holt, Rinehart & Winston, 1988.

> Jeanne D. Wakatsuki Houston was seven years old when her family was taken from their home and forced to live in the Manzanar internment camp, which held ten thousand Japanese Americans during World War II. Not all immigrants experience such treatment at the hands of their new country, but Houston's story raises controversial issues about how America welcomes those from other countries.

López, Josefina, *Detained in the Desert*, WPR Publishing, 2011.

> López throws together two very different characters in this play. First there is Sandi, a Latina who is arrested for refusing to show her identification when challenged by a prejudiced police officer, though she was born in the United States. When the bus transporting Sandi to an immigrant detention center crashes, she finds herself alone in the Arizona desert. Then there is Lou, an outspoken radio host whose talk show inspired a racist hate crime. The family of the victim of the crime kidnap Lou, and he ends up in the desert with Sandi. The two must help each other to survive. López adapted *Detained in the Desert* into a screenplay. The film was released in 2013.

Peralta, Dan-el Padilla, *Undocumented: A Dominican Boy's Odyssey from a Homeless Shelter to the Ivy League*, Penguin Press, 2015.

Peralta's family came to the United States from Santo Domingo when he was a child. They struggled to settle in New York, though they entered the country illegally and were undocumented. Peralta's father gave up and returned to the Dominican Republic, but Peralta's mother stayed with her two sons. Determined to get an education, Peralta rose from this difficult background, attending a prestigious private school and then Princeton.

Tan, Amy, *The Joy Luck Club*, Putnam's, 1989.
After her mother's death, Jing-mei Woo gets to know more about her mother's past, both as an immigrant in the United States and as a young woman back in China. As in *Real Women Have Curves*, mother-daughter relationships and the immigrant experience are central themes.

Wolf, Naomi, *The Beauty Myth: How Images of Female Beauty Are Used against Women*, William Morrow, April 1991.

Wolf's best-selling book points out that women have broken out of the traditional role of wife, mother, and homemaker only to be pushed to strive for unrealistic standards of beauty.

SUGGESTED SEARCH TERMS

immigration controversy

coming-of-age literature

cultural standards of beauty

Josefina Lopez AND activist

Josefina Lopez AND Chicano authors

Josefina Lopez AND women's issues

Josefina Lopez AND community programs

Josefina Lopez AND Real Women Have Curves

Six Degrees of Separation

1993

Based on John Guare's screen adaptation of his own Pulitzer Prize–nominated play (1990) and directed by Fred Schepisi, *Six Degrees of Separation* recounts the story of an affluent New York couple, Flan and Ouisa Kittredge (Donald Sutherland and Stockard Channing, respectively) whose lives are infiltrated by a young black man (Will Smith) who is never what he appears to be. As the couple set out on a search to uncover the truth behind the lies, their own lives are laid bare to new levels of self-examination.

The original Broadway production of *Six Degrees of Separation* opened at the Vivian Beaumont Theater on November 8, 1990, ran for 485 performances, and was nominated for the 1991 Tony Award for Best Play. Released on December 8, 1993, and filmed for an estimated budget of twelve million dollars, the screen adaptation is rated R for language and sexual content, specifically scenes of male frontal nudity and men kissing. There are numerous instances of expletives throughout.

PLOT SUMMARY

The film opens with the sound of upbeat symphony music as colors fade in and out of the screen, suggesting a painting of some sort. The scene transitions to a dusk long shot of Central Park in New York City, with the skyline of

FILM TECHNIQUE

- A flashback is a scene or series of scenes inserted into the present time of the film in order to deal with events that have happened in the past (the past tense) of the film. The first forty minutes of *Six Degrees of Separation* essentially make up an extended flashback, with the Kittredges sitting in a country wedding reception recounting the events of the previous evening, when Paul infiltrated their dinner with Geoffrey. While this extended flashback is crucial to creating the backstory of Paul's introduction to this social circle, it also draws attention to the constructedness of the stories that accumulate as the film progresses.

- The film underscores the interconnectedness of stories and characters as well as the claustrophobic nature of Manhattan social circles through the use of aggressive intercuts, which bring together scenes from various locations in such a way that the story appears to progress in a linear fashion even though the various moments are separated across time and place. Time and space are compressed, giving the impression that all parts of the story overlay numerous lives as a unique but shared experience, as Paul moves like a chameleon through the community. Combined with the careful repetition of words, actions, and accessories throughout the film, the technique of intercutting can be seen to add a powerful layer of visual connectivity to the film.

- Panorama shots (or pan shots) emphasize movement of the camera from left to right or right to left around the imaginary vertical axis that runs through the camera. Director Schepisi uses this technique primarily in transition, by way of contrast to the static, tight interior shots that control most of the film. These panning shots serve as a kind of visual emphasis on the six degrees that separate characters within the film, implying visually that however closed off the Kittredges and their friends might think they are (or hope to be), they are connected in powerful ways with the vastness of the city and the multitude of stories contained within it.

- From the opening scene of the film, with its series of tight close-ups on the interior of the Kittredge's Manhattan apartment, *Six Degrees of Separation* is a movie that uses this technique with surgical precision. Linked to the emphasis on interiority and the emotional struggles of so many of the characters, tight close-ups are also thematically connected to the sense of self-imposed isolation and cultural claustrophobia that defines the texture of the story.

Manhattan featured prominently. The camera pans to reveal the interior of a very lavish apartment overlooking the park. Finely decorated, the apartment is full of works of art of various types.

A couple (Flan and Ouisa Kittredge) enter the living area in a state of obvious shock, wondering aloud if anything has been stolen. They become dramatically frantic over a few specific pieces: a Kandinsky painting most specifically. As the man checks out his possessions, his wife muses that they could have had their throats slashed in their sleep. They debate about whether they are in any condition to go to a wedding that day. The phone rings, and while the man runs to answer it, the woman asks him not to.

The scene cuts to a young black man in a relatively bare apartment practicing the word *hello*.

A quick scene change returns to the couple rushing into a small, white country church. As they settle into their seats, they hint to those around them of the amazing story from the night before. The scene shifts back to that night, with the couple showing off the prized

Kandinsky (a double-sided painting representing chaos and control) to an obviously important dinner guest (Geoffrey Miller). A rapid cut takes the viewer back to the wedding reception, where the Kittredges are holding court with friends, recounting the story of the night before.

The film cuts back to the Manhattan apartment, as the trio prepares to go out to dinner for the evening. Another shift back to the wedding allows the couple to explain that Geoffrey's visit was particularly well timed, given that Flan was in need of two million dollars to close a pending art deal. The evening begins with a discussion of apartheid and the global politics of oppression, but as the Kittredges admit to their captive audience at the wedding, their minds are always focused partially on the potential investment of two million dollars.

The scene shifts back to the apartment as Geoffrey and the Kittredges are preparing to leave for dinner. The bell rings, and a well-dressed young black man (Paul) is ushered into the apartment by Ouisa and the doorman. Claiming to be a friend of the couple's children at Harvard, the young man recounts a story of being mugged in Central Park. The couple attend to the young man's wound (because he asks them not to call a doctor) while trying at the same time to keep the attention of Geoffrey. In a series of cuts, the film moves back and forth from wedding to apartment, as Paul spins a story about hearing such wonderful things about the Kittredges from their children at Harvard. Paul reveals that he knows much about the family and the apartment, including the existence of the two-sided Kandinsky. Paul ingratiates himself into the evening's plans with a story about his alleged father, the actor Sidney Poitier. Paul claims that his father is in town directing a film adaptation of the Broadway musical *Cats!*

The film cuts back to Paul's apartment, where he is rehearsing his story about Sidney Poitier, his history, and the relationship (which viewers can sense early is wholly constructed) between father and son. This scene ends with an unknown person applauding Paul's rehearsal of the story that he will eventually unfold in the Manhattan apartment.

Shifting back to the apartment-wedding intercuts, the story continues. Ouisa invites Paul to join them for dinner. Paul offers to cook dinner for the group by way of paying them back for their kindness. As the Kittredges recount the evening to the

wedding guests, they do so with dramatic flair, talking about Paul's wizardry in transforming left-overs into a great meal. During this performance Paul reveals himself to be as well versed in world politics as he has proved to be in art. As the meal is prepared, the conversation turns to race and racism, with Paul suggesting that he does not really even feel black (or American, for that matter), given his global upbringing.

As they move to the rarely used dining room to enjoy the meal, the conversation continues around such topics as food and education. When Paul leaves the room without a word, Flan is nervous, revealing that he is not yet comfortable with the young black man in his apartment. His nerves are appeased when Paul returns from the kitchen with more food for the table. The conversation picks up with Flan asking Paul about his father. Paul regales the group with stories of struggle and the lessons that have been passed down to him. Cutting back to the wedding party, Ouisa states how she feels for Paul and wants to reach out to him. They talk about Paul's Harvard thesis, which focuses on the role of J. D. Salinger's iconic novel *The Catcher in the Rye* (1951) in a number of crimes of anger and hate. What Paul says about the novel is of particular interest: it is about a world in which everyone is a phony. Holden Caulfield, the protagonist, has a single goal—to create a series of lies so comprehensive that everyone in this phony world likes him. In the end, Paul suggests, Holden falls into a kind of paralysis, unable to move forward with his dreams.

Paul continues to hold court about his broader thesis: *The Catcher in the Rye* is about the death of the imagination. He then launches into a far-reaching lecture on the debasement of imagination in the contemporary world. The trio of listeners is transfixed as Paul concludes with the statement that to face the reality of ourselves is the hardest thing of all.

As his lecture ends, Paul gets up to leave, saying that he will walk around the city overnight until his father arrives the next morning. Ouisa insists that he stay the night in the apartment. Paul accepts. As the evening comes to a close, Ouisa offers to help Paul clean up; he declares that he prefers that she watch him work and that he gets a thrill to be looked at. Flan bursts back into the apartment after walking Geoffrey to the elevator, joyous with the news that the South African has agreed to put two million dollars into an investment in a painting by Cezanne. In his celebration, Flan gives Paul fifty dollars for what he calls walking-around money.

Moving to an office within the apartment, Flan explains to Paul how he makes money by acting as a middleman between buyers and sellers of fine art. Walking Paul to one of the children's bedrooms, Flan and Ouisa bid their guest good night. Back in the living room, Flan and Ouisa celebrate their business success, and the audience gets a sense of how fragile their hold on the wealthy lifestyle really is. Burdened by debt, the couple is, in fact, balanced precariously from deal to deal, staying just barely ahead of the banks.

A sweeping exterior shot effects the transition to Ouisa at the wedding, making a joke about how she dreamed about cats, and to Paul, lecturing about how contemporary society has become too focused on the rights of those unborn and those wanting to die. He argues that the focus needs to be resharpened to highlight the eighty years between these two dramatic events. Flan counterbalances Ouisa's remembering of her dream with his remembering of his dream about the wonders of painting and what drew him to his work as an art dealer in the first place:

> This is what I dreamt. I didn't dream, so much as realize this. I feel so close to the paintings. I'm not just selling, like, pieces of meat. I remembered why I loved paintings in the first place, what got me into this. I thought…dreamt…remembered…how easy it is for a painter to lose a painting. He paints and paints, works on a canvas for months, and then, one day, he loses it. Loses the structure, loses the sense of it. You lose the painting. I remembered asking my kids' second-grade teacher: "Why are all your students geniuses? Look at the first grade—blotches of green and black. The third grade—camouflage. But your grade, the second grade, Matisses, every one. You've made my child a Matisse. Let me study with you. Let me into the second grade. What is your secret?" "I don't have any secret. I just know when to take their drawings away from them." I dreamt of colour. I dreamt of our son's pink shirt. I dreamt of pinks and yellows. And the new Van Gogh the Museum of Modern Art got. And the Irises that sold for $53.5 million. And, wishing a Van Gogh was mine, I looked at my English hand-lasted shoes, and thought of Van Gogh's tragic shoes, and remembered me as I was—a painter losing a painting.

As Ouisa sits in the kitchen doing her cross-word puzzle the next morning, she realizes that they forgot to wake Paul for his meeting with his father. Going down the hall to the bedroom, she walks in on Paul engaged in sexual activity with another man, a white prostitute. Flan is appalled that Paul spent his fifty dollars for sex and throws him out. The film loops back to its opening scene, effectively closing an extended flashback that brings viewers to the present moment of the film.

The telephone rings. Geoffrey has called to commit another $250,000 to the purchase of the Cezanne and to share his idea for a black American film festival to be launched in South Africa.

Ouisa and Flan return to the city following the wedding, accompanied by sweeping long shots of the New York cityscape. A brief scene follows that sees the Kittredges meeting friends Kitty and Larkin for lunch, with both couples claiming to have an amazing story to share. A quick cut takes viewers to a police office, where the two couples are beginning to file a report. Another cut back to the restaurant meal, during which both couples come to realize that they have been duped by the same man. Returning to the Kittredge apartment, the couples phone the hotel at which Sidney Poitier is supposedly registered. They try to track down the whereabouts of Poitier in an attempt to make sense of the story.

The scene shifts to the police office, where the couples are still attempting to file the report but are informed by the officer that since no crime has been committed, no report can be filed. At another party, the story continues as both couples bring their children to the Kittredge apartment, where chaos ensues. Family dynamics erupt, undercurrents of family secrets boil to the surface, and arguing abounds. That night Ouisa again dreams about Paul, who comes to her with a message about imagination being her solace in times of trouble.

A call from the police officer who heard the story originally brings a new character into the story: Dr. Fine, who was also a victim of Paul's manipulation. Fine reaches out to his son at Dartmouth, only to realize that he, too, has believed the story told by the young stranger. Fine brings the police to his home, only to find Paul there drinking brandy. There are no grounds for arresting him, so Paul walks away free.

The five victims scour a bookstore for Sidney Poitier's autobiography. Finding it, they come across a picture of the actor with his four daughters. At lunch, the five realize that the only commonality in their lives is that their children attended the same boarding school. The group agree to pursue the mystery to the end regardless of what they find out about their kids.

Heading to Harvard to enlist their children in the detective work, the couples again face the realities of their families as the conversations erode almost immediately into a series of accusations and yelling matches. Despite the blowup, the children go on a hunt through their high-school yearbook and narrow their search to Trent Conway, a former classmate now studying at the Massachusetts Institute of Technology (MIT).

Trent recounts his story of meeting Paul on a rainy night in Boston, working as a street prostitute. Trent agrees to teach Paul how to infiltrate upper-crust society in exchange for his companionship. The goal is to create a new Paul, a young man who is the most sought-after member of the social circles. The creation of Paul takes three months and goes through a full range of linguistic and cultural codes that remake Paul as the product of an upper-crust family. What frustrates the families involved is that Trent can provide no information about Paul's past or his family.

The scene shifts to Ouisa and her daughter, Tess, who are sitting on a bed discussing the idea that gives the film its title—that everyone on the planet is separated from each other by only six people, or six degrees of separation.

Flan and Ouisa visit Rome. They are given the opportunity to be lifted to the ceiling of the Sistine Chapel and witness the ceiling restoration at firsthand. Back in New York, business commences as usual for the Kittredges, though they are asked often about the story of Poitier's son, as Paul has come to be known. The story continues.

Upon returning from Rome, the Kittredges are confronted by their doorman about Flan's illegitimate son, which Paul is now claiming to be. The doorman leads them to Elizabeth, who recounts the story of her and her boyfriend Rick's encounter with Paul. They met in Central Park, where Paul spun a story of Flan's hippie days encounter with a young black woman, who Flan allegedly abandoned when she discovers she is pregnant. Elizabeth and her boyfriend invite Paul to stay with them. He stays with them for two or three weeks and leaves under the pretence of meeting Flan in Maine to collect money that will see him through the coming months. His only problem is that he needs $250 to get to Maine. The young couple debates lending him the money but have so little themselves that they decide not to.

Later that day, when Elizabeth tries to withdraw money from her joint account with Rick, she finds that it has been closed and all funds withdrawn. Returning to her apartment, she waits for her boyfriend, who explains that Paul found some money and took them both out to a very fancy restaurant, the Rainbow Room. The two ate, drank, and, when they took to the dance floor, were escorted out of the restaurant. They leaped into a horse-drawn carriage for a ride around the park, during which two things happen: Rick lent Paul money, and the two young men had sex.

The scene shifts to Kitty and Larkin's recounting another story from the past, this one about an adventure they had at a local roller disco that two clients had opened. As they left the rink, they came across Elizabeth's boyfriend lying in a pool of blood on the sidewalk, having thrown himself out the apartment window above.

At the prompting of the police, the search for Paul begins again. The final chapter is recounted over yet another dinner party. As Ouisa and Flan get dressed for an art auction, Paul telephones, claiming that he had no idea that Rick would kill himself. Ouisa persuades Paul to turn himself in, but the conversation turns to whether Ouisa feels betrayed by his visit, conversations about art, and business. Paul admits to stealing his Salinger speech from a graduation address and his recipes from other people. Paul demands that Ouisa help him start his life, if he agrees to turn himself in. Paul negotiates, wanting Ouisa to deliver him to the police in order to ensure he gets treated fairly.

Ouisa postpones arrival at the auction to pick up Paul and deliver him to the police. The tell each other they love each other, and the phone call ends. Traffic is bad, however, delaying Flan and Ouisa. When they do finally arrive at the meeting place, Paul is already in a police car being whisked away. The next day, Ouisa goes to the precinct to try to find Paul, but she cannot give the name of the man that was arrested. She continues her search but is stymied at each turn because she is not family and does not know Paul's real name.

When a dinner guest asks why this case matters so much to Ouisa, she answers succinctly: he wants to be us. She is angered that Paul has been turned into an anecdote to be told over cocktails and with a punchline that seems trite in the context of the reality of the feelings that Paul's visit spurred in so many people. The film closes with Ouisa running out of an important dinner party, declaring to her husband that they are a terrible match. Ouisa walks away from Flan, heading down a street alone.

CHARACTERS

Trent Conway

Trent Conway (played by Anthony Michael Hall) is a former schoolmate of the Kittredge children and the key player in educating Paul about the ways of Manhattan social circles. A homosexual who fears being judged by his socialite community, he sees in Paul the opportunity to expose the closed minds of Manhattan and allow himself to become more open about his own sexuality. Using his well-stocked address book as his textbook, Trent schools Paul in the language, the subtle coding, and the secrets of the families that he goes on to infiltrate.

Elizabeth

Elizabeth (played by Heather Graham) is Rick's girlfriend and the catalyst for the police to lay charges against Paul following her boyfriend's suicide. A would-be actor from Utah, she is taken in by Paul's story and charm but is very protective of the small savings she has accumulated with Rick and turns down Paul's request for $250. She later goes to the Kittredge's apartment to challenge Flan, based on Paul's story of his being a negligent father.

Dr. Fine

Dr. Fine (played by Richard Masur) is a Manhattan doctor and one of Paul's victims. He is drawn to Paul's story because of his lifelong admiration for his alleged father, Sidney Poitier. Although Dr. Fine is Jewish, he feels an affinity with Poitier as a groundbreaker and challenger of social norms. On the downside, Fine's relationship with his own son is totally

fractured amid charges of abandonment and domestic violence.

John Flanders (Flan) Kittredge

John Flanders (Flan) Kittredge (played by Donald Sutherland) is, as Leonard Klady notes in *Variety*, "the embodiment of the educated, glib and superficial Manhattan social lion that Guare truly loathes." From a Rhode Island family, he is a private art dealer who serves as a middleman between buyers and sellers of rare paintings. Well stocked with facts and trivial details, Flan is, like Paul, a man who uses his charm and storytelling to maintain an illusion. In Flan's care the illusion is one of success (despite the mounting debt), connectedness within the art market (despite the shifting market), and a fine appreciation for art (when all he really thinks about is money).

Flan is at once attracted to Paul's youth, charm, and intelligence, but he disconnects dramatically when Paul claims him as a fictional, but uncaring father. While Flan does thrive on making himself the center of stories, he is much less appreciative of being cast as a primary figure in a story constructed by someone else.

Louisa (Ouisa) Kittredge

Stockard Channing received both an Academy Award and Golden Globe nomination for best actress for the role of Louisa (Oisa) Kittredge. As Jill Gerston suggests in the *New York Times*, Channing creates in Ouisa "a funny, touching heroine rather than some stereotypical social X-ray." Partners with her husband in their art dealership, Ouisa opens the film as another consummate storyteller but evolves after meeting Paul into a woman who begins to feel the world differently and more deeply than those around her. Her concern for Paul's immediate and future well-being is genuine and grows deeper as she learns more. In this sense, Ouisa is the heart of the movie, moving beyond the superficiality that defines the other characters in order to become a more rounded and emotionally connected woman.

Talbot (Tess) Kittredge

Talbot (Tess) Kittredge (played by Catherine Kellner) is one of Flan and Ouisa's two daughters and is the only child to engage directly in the search for Paul. She visits Trent Conway and records his story of educating Paul, which becomes crucial in the development of her mother's feelings. At the same time, she is almost an overly simplistic symbol of the entitlement that comes with privilege, She constantly threatens her parents that she will drop out of Harvard in order to run off to Afghanistan to climb mountains or to get married to someone well below her social status. In her adolescent years, she suffered from anorexia and was hospitalized for the illness for some time.

Woodrow (Woody) Kittredge

Woodrow (Woody) Kittredge (played by Oz Perkins) is Flan and Ouisa's only son and the obvious nonintellectual of the group. Following their unfolding of the story of Paul's infiltration of their lives, he is more concerned that his parents gave Paul a pink shirt he owned than anything else.

Kitty

Kitty (played by Mary Beth Hurt) is the wife of Larkin and one of the parents to vote to continue on the detective mission to track down the truth about Paul regardless of where the path might lead.

Larkin

Larkin (played by Bruce Davison), husband of Kitty, is one half of the couple victimized by Paul the night before his visit to the Kittredges. Notable for his desire to know nothing about the private lives of his wife and children, he is the single parent of the group to vote against pursuing the story of Paul through to the end.

Geoffrey Miller

Geoffrey Miller (played by Ian McKellen) is a South African businessman and friend of the Kittredges, who happens to be at dinner the night of Paul's initial visit. A wealthy gold magnate, he is won over by Paul's charm to the point of proposing to bring a black American film festival to South Africa. To the Kittredges, he represents the potential investment money they need to keep their business afloat despite an almost overwhelming debt. Before departing on his return flight, Geoffrey commits $2.25 million dollars to purchase the Cezanne.

More broadly, he represents the epitome of the pseudo-liberal, paternalistic attitudes toward race that Guare sets out to satirize in his characterizations of the Kittredges and their social circle. He believes that his role in apartheid is to educate black South Africans, even as he exploits their labor in one of his very prosperous gold mines.

Paul

Paul (played by Will Smith) is a "cunning, too-good-to-be-true imposter" who sweeps into the lives of the Kittredges and their Manhattan social circle with his charismatic combination of youth, charm, and eclectic, seemingly mature knowledge of politics, art, and the finer things of life. He claims, initially, to be the ignored son of Sidney Poitier, then later in the film the abandoned son of J. Flanders Kittredge. Schooled in the secrets of this world by Trent Conway, Paul disrupts the complacency of those he comes in contact with, but no one more that Louisa Kittredge, with whom he seems to have a particularly close and almost-honest bond.

More broadly, Paul serves as two prongs within Guare's satire. As a young and preppy black man, he allows the paternalistic attitudes of the Kittredges to be exposed as only shallow platitudes. Nonthreatening, in that he appears to them as an almost idealized version of their own children (polite, smart, respectful, and engaged), Paul is what white, upper-class Americans wish all young black men would be.

Paul is also a master chameleon. A remarkably quick learner and astute observer of his environment, he is also a symbol of the artificiality (or phoniness) of the world that he infiltrates.

Rick

Rick (played by Eric Thal) is Elizabeth's boyfriend. A would-be actor from Utah, he is seduced by Paul's charm, gives him the only savings that he and Elizabeth have, and has sex with Paul during a carriage ride through Central Park. Rick commits suicide by throwing himself from the window of his apartment, just above a roller disco where Larkin and Kitty are out for an evening of fun.

THEMES

Chance

Drawn to the concept that everyone and everything in the world is six (or fewer) steps away from any other person or thing in the world, Ouisa is at once comforted and disturbed by this concept: "I find it extremely comforting that we're so close. I also find it like Chinese water torture, that we're so close because you have to find the right six people to make the right connection...I am bound, you are bound, to everyone on this planet by a trail of six people."

READ.
WATCH.
WRITE.

- In his review for *Variety*, Leonard Klady argues that the seriousness and moralization of Guare's screenplay "won't matter to the sophisticated viewer but poses serious commercial limitations for this classy entertainment." In one sense, Klady's observation seems prophetic given that the film grossed barely over six million dollars in the United States. At the same time, his comments suggest a very clear distinction between what Klady would call sophisticated movies and commercial movies. In a detailed and well-structured essay, discuss whether you agree or disagree with Klady's implied distinction. Can you think of a movie, for instance, that has effectively challenged his distinction by being a sophisticated film that has great commercial success?

- Read J. D. Salinger's iconic novel *The Catcher in the Rye* (1951) and test the novel against Paul's reading of it. Do you agree that it is about the paralysis of imagination? Why or why not? Explain in an oral presentation to your class. Find numerous examples from the text to support the argument that you choose to put forward.

- Consider this truth from the movie: when Paul visits Larkin and Kitty, he accepts twenty-five dollars from this obviously wealthy couple. When he visits Flan and Ouisa, he accepts fifty dollars from another obviously wealthy couple. When he visits Elizabeth and Rick, however, Paul actively cons $250 from one person in a couple that obviously cannot afford that amount of money. Discuss the implications of this important difference in a well-structured and well-written essay. Why would Paul take more money from a couple who is struggling to make their ends meet?

- At the center of *Six Degrees of Separation* is Paul's masterful manipulation of the Kittredges and others within the upper crust of Manhattan social circles. Technically, manipulation occurs when a person tries to change or alter another person's belief system, values, or behaviors through deceptive, scheming, and even abusive strategies. Manipulation is a pathway to controlling or playing upon another person by various means to gain advantage in the end. Supported by the training from one of their own (Trent), Paul clearly looks to talk and charm his way into the lives of those he targets. The question remains, what is the end game of Paul's manipulation? While he succeeds in making his victims reflect upon their own attitudes, politics, and life choices (especially Ouisa), Paul never steals anything of value, and his personal gains are never really clear. Viewers are left to ponder whether Paul is simply a pawn in Trent's game or whether his need to manipulate stems from something deeper. Is his manipulation a means for Paul to feel that he belongs in a community? Or is it the means to fulfill a more common wish to be part of a social class that, in most instances, is beyond reach? Or is it part of Guare's satire on liberal attitudes toward race and inclusivity? Answer this question in a well-structured and well-written essay. Post your essay on a blog and allow your classmates to comment with their thoughts.

What Ouisa understands, too, is that this view of the world situates chance as a very powerful influence in any life. As Janet Maslin explains in her *New York Times* review: "Chance meetings with exactly the right people," she reflects, "can permanently alter unexamined lives." In this world of connectedness, any chance meeting (Trent and Paul on a rainy night in Boston, for instance) can send a ripple of impact through multiple lives. By definition, chance is uncontrollable and unpredictable, which leads Ouisa to see her life as more random than she had previously thought.

Husband-Wife Relationships

Six Degrees of Separation is rarely discussed as a movie about husband-wife relationships, but it does function as an incisive exploration of the dynamics of the various marriages within the movie. The three primary victims of Paul's infiltration reveal different types of relationships, each with its strengths and limitations. Dr. Fine is divorced amid accusations of domestic violence, and his relationship with his ex-wife continues to shape his reactions to the world and his relationship with his son.

Larkin and Kitty are still in a functioning marriage, but Larkin is determined to be at once hypervigilant and in total denial of anything that might challenge his perceptions of his wife or children. His repeated assertion that he does not want to know details becomes a kind of mantra as he tries to negotiate his way through the ebbs and flows of the story.

Flan and Ouisa begin the movie as the best model of a relationship available within this social circle of deeply flawed relationships. Partners in business, life, and storytelling, the couple seem to move and speak in perfect harmony. Their focus on money is shared, and they literally finish sentences for each other as they tell stories at various dinner parties and events. As the movie unfolds and the story of Paul deepens, however, even this seemingly tightly knit couple begin to unravel. As Flan withdraws in indignation and concern for his reputation following Paul's story of a long-past fling that produced a black child, Ouisa finds her feelings (and concern) deepening for the young man. By the end of the film, the couple has fractured completely, with Flan still immersed in his own world of deal making and storytelling while Ouisa literally walks away, unable to accept that the story of Paul will be reduced to an anecdote that is recounted over and over at the parties the couple attends.

Imagination

Of the many topics that Paul speaks about throughout the movie, imagination is one that seems most important to him. As he says to Ouisa:

Poster for the 1993 film (© Everett Collection | Alamy)

I believe the imagination is the passport that we create to help take us into the real world. I believe the imagination is merely another phrase for what is most uniquely us. Jung says, "The greatest sin is to be unconscious."

Psychologists do tell us that the imagination (or the act of imagining) is a fundamental faculty to seeing parts of the world that are not perceived through the usual senses of sight and hearing. Imagination helps convert knowledge (facts and details) to deeper feelings, problem-solving skills, and the ability to integrate learning and experience. A basic training ground for the imagination is storytelling, which, as viewers witness in this movie, is the ability to take facts (the address book) and convert them into compelling stories. While Trent Conway is a holder of facts and secrets, it is Paul who turns them into the stories that allow him to integrate almost seamlessly into the social circles of upper-crust Manhattan.

It is imagination, too, that energizes Ouisa's transition from mere socialite to engaged, questioning woman. Touched deeply by Paul's visit but also by her reflection upon the concept of six degrees of separation as well as her experience touching the hand of God in the Sistine Chapel, Ouisa moves from being a collector of stories to a woman of experience. As she states to a flabbergasted table of Manhattan socialites moments before walking out of the party:

> And we turn him into an anecdote, with no teeth, and a punchline you'll tell for years to come: "Oh, that reminds me of the time the imposter came into our house." "Oh! Tell the one about that boy." And we become these human jukeboxes spitting out these anecdotes to dine out on like we're doing right now. Well I will not turn him into an anecdote, it was an experience. How do we hold onto the experience?

STYLE

Interiority

Six Degrees of Separation is a movie that remains focused on claustrophobic interior scenes. With rare moments of sweeping exteriors (most often used in transition), the characters interact in tightly framed interior spaces: living room, kitchen, police office, doctor's office. Any quick cutaway shots are to and from spaces equally compressed—the apartment in which Paul rehearses his lines, the small country church, or the room within the country club where the reception is being held. Even a ride through Central Park is capturing the sense of worlds that are sealed off from others (the Upper East Side of Manhattan, most obviously) as well as sealed off from any type of self-reflection. These shots underscore the repressive worlds and worldviews that families like the Kittredges tend to celebrate as normal. These are the rooms in which the so-called chattering class gather to talk about art, politics, and the state of the world, despite their desire to remain disconnected from the harsh realities of the world beyond the walls of their apartments, country clubs, or Ivy League school libraries. When the characters do move beyond the walls that define their physical spaces, pent-up emotions tend to explode (as when the families meet in the courtyard at Harvard), or a character begins to sense the vastness of the universe beyond the walls of his or her usual world (as when Ouisa walks the streets at the film's close).

Metafiction

Six Degrees of Separation draws very conscious attention to the mechanisms of storytelling, which is an attribute of metafiction (or storytelling that is, in part, about storytelling). The flashback that opens the film and is repeated later in the film, for instance, underscores the constructedness of the narrative, as the story effectively doubles back on itself in order to fill in gaps and spaces. Viewers see Paul rehearsing his story of origin in front of Trent, getting details correct, as well as tone and accent. His story, the audience learns early in the film, is an artifact built by Paul for a specific audience and purpose. At other times, characters urge listeners within the film as well as the audience outside the film to understand that this is a film very much focused on the mechanics of building and telling stories.

Story and Plot

The basic difference between story and plot, which was pointed out by Aristotle, distinguishes between the structure of a narrative (written, drawn, or filmed) as it appears to the audience. For narrative to be understood as being story-driven, the events of that narrative will be arranged chronologically and as they would appear in the real world. Event A happens, followed by Event B, which is followed in turn by Event C, and so on. Plot-driven narratives are broken apart from chronology and rearranged for a particular artistic impact. Event C might open a narrative, for instance, followed by Event A, and then Event X, and so on.

Six Degrees of Separation focuses, for the most part, on the plotting of the events rather than on the story, which unfolds back and forth across time and space through a series of flashbacks and intercuts. Although the time line of the film is not especially long (months, not decades or centuries), the various threads of the story—Paul's various manipulations, his training with Trent, and the repercussions for Ouisa—form a complex pattern that emphasizes *how* the story is being told rather than *what* story is being told.

CULTURAL CONTEXT

Although *Six Degrees of Separation* was released in 1993, the original play was published in 1990 as a commentary on the culture and morality of the late 1980s. New York City was a barometer for what was going on elsewhere in the country. On the one hand, it was a city and time defined by the egos and empires led by such larger-than-life figures as realtor Donald Trump, Mafia leader John Gotti, and hotelier Leona Helmsley. Wealth and the excesses it allowed were the focal point of a number of books and films, including the original *Wall Street* (1987), with Michael Douglas as the iconic Gordon Gekko, and *Bonfire of the Vanities* (1990), starring Tom Hanks and Bruce Willis. Life imitated art in the world of business as junk bonds (high yield and with very high risk) became a national symbol of unadulterated greed and insider trading stories became routine in the years leading up to the market collapse of October 1987. The decade came to an appropriate end with the indictment of financier Michael Milken on an assortment of fraud and racketeering charges.

On the other hand, social issues continued to illuminate the growing gap between those with excess and those barely able to sustain themselves in one of the richest (and most expensive) cities in the world. Homelessness continued to be a problem, and Central Park, a global symbol of the city that never sleeps, was rife with violence. In late 1986, nineteen-year-old socialite Robert E. Chambers strangled eighteen-year-old Jennifer Dawn Levin as they walked across the park after a night at a local bar. Both had led lives of privilege, defined by private schools, fancy homes, and foreign travel. Three years later, in 1989, a twenty-eight-year-old investment banker, Trisha Ellen Meili, was raped and severely beaten in Central Park. The rape was thought to be one of several random attacks by rampaging gangs of youths that had been terrorizing the park for most of the night of April 19, although the convictions of the supposed attackers were later overturned after another man confessed to the crime.

Racism also continued to rear its head across the city. In 1986, twenty-three-year-old Michael Griffith was killed by a car as he tried to escape the group of white men who had already severely beaten him in a racially motivated attack in Brooklyn. In 1989, the Bensonhurst neighborhood was ground zero for what the *New York Times* labelled "a new generation of racism" when a group of young white men

Many critics were surprised by the skill of Will Smith's performance. (© *MAIDEN MOVIES* | *MGM* | *NEW REGENCY PICTURES* | *Ronald Grant Archive* | *Mary Evans* | *Alamy*)

killed a black teenager who had traveled to the neighborhood to look at a used car but was mistakenly assumed by the gang to be visiting a white girl in the area.

Globally, changes in South Africa's apartheid regime began to take shape. Between 1985 and 1986 the laws prohibiting mixed-race marriage and sex were abolished, as were those controlling where South African blacks could live and work. By 1989 the city of Johannesburg had moved aggressively to eliminate traces of apartheid-era segregation, effectively giving all residents access to swimming pools, recreation centers, and public transport. Despite these gains, acts of racial and political violence continued to capture headlines, from the destruction of a Boeing 747 over Lockerbie, Scotland, in 1988 (over 250 dead) to continuing crackdowns on so-called dissidents across China.

CRITICAL OVERVIEW

With an estimated budget of twelve million dollars and US box office gross revenues of just $6.4 million, *Six Degrees of Separation* does not qualify as a box-office success. Part of the reason for this, suggests Janet Maslin of the *New York Times*, is the fact that although the translation of the story from stage to screen was "bridged very aggressively by the director Fred Schepisi," the film remains "cluttered." Burdened by "so much extra baggage," the "screwball timing takes on a frantic edge." In the end, though, "Mr. Schepisi's directorial vigor wins out over his film's skittishness." Maslin appreciates the performances of all the major players in the film, with the exception of Will Smith, "who plays Paul as a smooth, pleasant interloper without the hints of mockery or desperation that should accompany his deception. Mr. Smith recites his lines plausibly without bringing great passion to the role."

Rita Kempley of the *Washington Post* picks up on this latter point as well, suggesting that Smith's portrayal of Paul "seems far too self-possessed to fall victim to his own creation." More broadly, she concludes that the film suffers because "the relationships feel contrived, less a drama than an exercise in cuteness." She argues that "it's the tail that's wagging this dog. It's too clever by half, an inside joke aimed at the New York gentry."

Writing in *Variety*, Leonard Klady describes the film as "an elaborate mousetrap where getting caught can be delightful fun. But the central scam dissipates into self-analysis and moralization. The more serious it becomes, the more of a pedestrian path it takes, and the tug of war between the rational and the absurd draws no victor." Moreover, he suggests, the film seems unable to define itself, posing variously as farce, thriller, and film of moral introspection. While this shifting ground "provides the material with an edge and uncertainty, the wildly black comic elements evaporate as the script attempts to make sense of the human condition. The thrall of an exciting journey is run aground by rather routine, banal explanations."

Calling the film an "intricate chamber play," Owen Gleiberman of *Entertainment Weekly* is less than enthralled by what he sees as an already dated attempt at strong-armed social commentary. The film

attempts to build a metaphysical bridge between the "haves" and the "have-nots." But if the collapse of the previous decade's [1980s] economic fantasies has taught us anything, it's that this dichotomy is itself a glib, false one; the vast majority of people live somewhere in between.

He concludes:

This is a play about the supposed spiritual emptiness of bourgeois New Yorkers that was essentially written as a cathartic guilt trip for bourgeois New Yorkers.... By the end, most moviegoers are liable to see it as much ado about nothing.

CRITICISM

Klay Dyer

Dyer is a freelance writer specializing in topics relating to literature, popular culture, and the relationship between creativity and technology. In the following essay, he explores Ouisa Kittredge's growing awareness of race and its implications in John Guare's Six Degrees of Separation.

The title of Guare's play and the film of the same name refers to the belief that everyone on the planet is linked to everyone else by a chain of acquaintances no more than six people long. As Ouisa Kittredge comes to understand, however, it is not so much the relatively small number of connections that makes this concept so compelling; it is the realization that chance has such an important role in shaping the six degrees. One connection takes a person down one path, while another leads her in a totally different direction. As Ouisa realizes, late in the film, the collage of connections that has led her to the point that she is—unsatisfied in her marriage, increasingly cynical of the social circles in which she travels—is not one of order and control but "all random."

Ouisa's connection to Paul, stemming from a random meeting on a rainy night in Boston, is one of particular importance, given its emotional and political impact on a woman who has lived so much of her adult life seeing the world through the lens of an East Side Manhattan socialite. Her view of the world has, as the film's opening shot makes clear, always been from a safe distance, far removed from the sirens that punctuate the background sounds of the movie on numerous occasions. Never fully engaged in the ground-level realities of

WHAT DO I SEE NEXT?

- Woody Allen is the master of showcasing the foibles of New York's high society, and of his many films focusing on this theme *Blue Jasmine* (2013) is a strong representation. Tracing one socialite's fall from grace, it presents a dark story of denial, class tensions, and narcissism. This movie is rated PG for language and adult themes.

- *My Fair Lady* (1964) tells the story of a misogynistic and snobbish phonetics professor (Rex Harrison) who bets that he can take a working-class flower girl (Audrey Hepburn) and recreate her as a lady who is accepted into London high society. Based on George Bernard Shaw's play *Pygmalion* (1913), it remains the standard-bearer of films about transcending class through targeted education and training. At one point, Ouisa Kittredge refers to Trent Conway as a modern Henry Higgins, which is a direct reference to this earlier movie. This film is rated PG for very mild profanity.

- From the same lineage as *My Fair Lady*, *Educating Rita* (1983) tells the story of a young wife (Julie Walters) who decides to complete her education. In the process, she meets an eccentric, alcoholic professor (Michael Caine) who teaches her not only how to pass the exams but also to trust her own insights and understanding of the world. This film is rated PG for some profanity.

- Leonardo DiCaprio's portrayal of the real Wall Street huckster Jordan Belfort in *The Wolf of Wall Street* (2013) lifts the curtain on what Flan Kittredge would call the grotty side of big business and the lives of New York's rich and famous. This film is rated R for strong sexual content and language, graphic nudity, and drug use throughout.

- Director Julian Schnabel's *Basquiat* (1996) tells the story of a young street artist, Jean-Michel Basquiat—his meteoric rise to fame within New York art circles and the impact that fame had on his life, his art, and his imagination. This film is rated R for drug use and strong language.

- Ang Lee's 2012 film adaptation of Yann Martel's novel *Life of Pi* is, like *Six Degrees of Separation*, an exploration of the power of storytelling and how stories allow individuals to construct (or survive) realities that might otherwise become incomprehensible. Asked to tell his life story to a local writer, Pi Patel unleashes a tale of survival so incredible that it changes forever the way his listener lives in the world. This film is rated PG for some violence and potentially frightening scenes.

- Fred Schepisi's *Roxanne* (1987) is a modern reimagining of the classic story of Cyrano de Bergerac, a man of beautiful words but with an appearance that he believes will never allow him to capture the heart of the woman he loves. Starring Steve Martin (as C.D. Bales) and Daryl Hannah (as Roxanne, the object of his affection), this is a film, like *Six Degrees of Separation*, that explores the power of words to shape realities in both positive and not-so-positive ways.

---

the city, she has not seen for many years (if ever) the real implications of poverty, sex in the generation of AIDS, and especially race as it plays out in the world around her. As the camera enters the Kittredge's apartment in a luxurious opening shot, it lingers, appropriately, on an overturned table telescope, which symbolizes neatly Ouisa's way of seeing the world: from a point far away from and far above what is actually happening.

> PAUL'S RETORT IS A STATEMENT THAT
> ECHOES ACROSS THE MOVIE FOR BOTH ITS BREVITY
> AND ITS ILLUMINATION OF RACE, WHICH HAS
> REMAINED UNDERSTATED (OR IGNORED) TO THIS
> POINT: 'MRS. LOUISA KITTREDGE,' HE STATES MATTER-
> OF-FACTLY, 'I AM BLACK.'"

Significantly, it is this same telescope that visiting South African gold magnate Geoffrey Miller is looking through moments before Paul first appears in the Kittredge apartment. Paul will offer an undeniable challenge to how Ouisa sees the world and her place in it, and Guare goes out of his way to ensure this connection is understood by the audience. Paul is introduced in the moments after Geoffrey comments on the statue of Balto, a heroic sled dog immortalized by a statue in Central Park, and Paul's mugging, so his story goes, took place in plain view of the Kittredge apartment while he stood in front of the same statue, trying to figure out what a dog that saved lives in Alaska is doing in Central Park. As Jennifer Gillan notes, Paul's very carefully planned (but seemingly random) movement from street level to apartment is a breach of "the safe zone from which the voyeur," observing the world surreptitiously from a distance,

> usually looks without being seen. This movement is signaled by the . . . sirens; in the opening shot, the sirens are just part of the dangerous life in the city that occurs out of the Kittredges's notice, but with the arrival of Paul, the menace invades their protected space and forces itself into their consciousness.

Gillan is only partly correct. While Paul's arrival symbolically brings the street into the apartment, it does not bring the reality of the sirens. In fact, Guare is careful not to allow the full invasion to occur. Paul persuades the Kittredges not to call either police or doctor, and they comply, tending to his wound themselves with the help of a first-aid handbook. It is a distance that is maintained throughout the film, in fact. When the Kittredges do attempt to file a police report, they go to the police station rather than call an officer to their apartment. When charges are eventually filed, they are put in motion not by Ouisa but by Elizabeth, a would-be actress whose knowledge of the realities of streets and sirens is a matter of everyday survival. Struggling to make her ends meet, Elizabeth waits tables in a crowded restaurant and lives in a tenement above a roller disco.

Keeping the sirens at a distance is only part of this opening scene. As Gillan explains, the harsh realities of race, always a simmering undercurrent in American cities, is also kept safely away from Ouisa as the movie begins. Paul's initial appearance to Ouisa, according to Jennifer Gillan, is as "a well-adjusted, articulate, deracialized, and desexualized preppy who espouses a colorblind, anti-affirmative action stance." Carefully trained by Trent Conway to appear as something he is not but also as something comfortably familiar to members of the Kittredge's social circle, Paul provides Ouisa with the opportunity to engage with him both intimately (through his stories to her) and from a telescopic distance that effectively renders her colorblind for most of the film. It is as though she takes in a young black stranger without ever realizing that he is either black or a total stranger. (Ironically, Paul's arrival is juxtaposed neatly in the film with the discussion of the racialist politics of apartheid that has engaged the Kittredges and Miller. Ouisa's response is classic East Side Manhattan, rich with paternalism and superficial pathos. But her conclusion is clear: "You know it doesn't seem right, sitting on the East Side, talking about revolution.")

Paul, of course, perpetuates this colorblindness to his advantage. Educated by Trent in the cultural codes of East Side Manhattan, he talks the talk of whiteness with an eloquence that impresses even Flan, a skilled storyteller himself. He eschews any effects of what he calls the crummy childhood theory and, when asked directly about being black in America, deflects the question masterfully by declaring that he has never felt American and never knew that he was black in the racist sense of the word until he was sixteen. As Gillan astutely notes, even Paul's selection of Poitier films to highlight during his recounting of his fictional father's impressive body of work is designed to underscore black protagonists' winning the admiration of white people through their competence and accomplishments.

This is not to suggest that Paul's race is never seen or realized early in the film. When he disappears from the dining room momentarily during dinner, Flan becomes anxious, shouting "Hello" repeatedly, each time with a growing sense of uncertainty and urgency. He is visibly relieved when Paul returns from the kitchen with more food for the table. What Flan and Miller (and later, Kitty, Larkin, and Dr. Fine) never admit is that the more exceptionally Paul talks about literature, politics, art, and creativity, the more the blinders of race settle into place. Paul is exempt from the normal categories of color not only because of his alleged relationship with Sidney Poitier, the groundbreaking but nonetheless nonthreatening actor, but more immediately because of his ability to sound and look like Manhattan wants him to look. "By adopting upper-class inflections, vocabulary, etiquette, and material signifiers, such as his blue Brooks Brothers blazer," Gillan suggests, Paul performs race with great skill, rendering his skin color more or less irrelevant for much of the film.

Paul's performance is obviously good for business. Geoffrey agrees to contribute more money than Flan has asked for in order to keep a painting of Cezanne out of the hands of Japanese investors, and he even goes so far as to suggest that he is planning a black film festival in South Africa as a way of breaching the racial divide that has existed for generations of violent oppression. Geoffrey further suggests that he will invite Spike Lee and Eddie Murphy, or what he calls representatives of the "new blacks" in America. As Gillan suggests, Paul's role has been not one of challenger or groundbreaker but someone who confirms the self-image of the upper-class liberalism of the Kittredges and, by extension, of their investor/benefactor, Geoffrey. The South African leaves the evening seeing himself "not as an oppressive, imperialist owner of a gold mine but as a benefactor and defender of black self-determination." When asked why a man of his wealth stays in South Africa, Miller responds with only a hint of irony: "One has to stay there. To educate the black workers. And we'll know we've been successful when they kill us." Part of his educational plan is to bring a black American film festival to South Africa in order to highlight the work of Spike Lee, Eddie Murphy, and the great Poitier himself. Whereas the discovery of Paul in bed with a white male prostitute unsettles the sense of complacent safety that has settled over the Kittredge apartment, it is not until the final quarter of the movie

that race factors significantly in Ouisa's worldview in a meaningful way.

Paul is implicated in Rick's suicide, which is triggered by money and sex more than race. Reaching out to Ouisa in a final phone call, Paul pleads with her to help him negotiate the justice system and to promise to serve as his patron once he is released from jail. They banter, negotiate, and share feelings openly until a moment when the reality of Paul's future is tied, finally and determinedly, to the color of his skin. Pleading for the white socialite to deliver him to the police in order to ensure that he is treated with fairness, Paul tries to articulate his fears. "I'll be treated with care if you take me to the police," he explains. "If they don't know you're special," he continues, "they kill you." Ouisa is almost flippant in her response: "Oh, I don't think they kill you." Paul's retort is a statement that echoes across the movie for both its brevity and its illumination of race, which has remained understated (or ignored) to this point: "Mrs. Louisa Kittredge," he states matter-of-factly, "I am black." As though a veil has been lifted from her eyes, Ouisa pauses, changes her plans for the evening, and speaks softly: "I will deliver you to them with kindness and affection."

With these words, Ouisa's world spins into randomness. Blocked by traffic from reaching Paul before the police (who have been called by Flan, not her), she tries desperately to track him down within the bureaucratic maze of the New York City police department. Without a name or direct family affiliation, she is stymied in her attempts. In contrast to Flan, who cares nothing about the fate of the young man and easily turns their encounter into a successful business dinner anecdote, Ouisa is transformed by her encounter with Paul's youth, his intelligence, and his blackness. Open to a new level of self-awareness and reflection, Ouisa sees her life with a sudden and disturbing clarity. Raging at her husband as she storms out of yet another East Side dinner party, she walks away alone, oblivious to his pleadings. As she stops in front of a flower shop, rich with color and texture, Paul's image revisits her with reassuring words that set her off on the next part of her life journey. She is, to borrow Flan's words from early in the film, a woman finally and truly aware of what a burst of color is asked to carry in a world that is lived in rather than viewed from afar.

Stockard Channing received a nomination for an Academy Award for Best Actress for her performance as Ouisa Kittredge. (© AF archive / Alamy)

Source: Klay Dyer, Critical Essay on *Six Degrees of Separation*, in *Drama for Students*, Gale, Cengage Learning, 2016.

Jerry Portwood

In the following review, Portwood looks at Will Smith's performance in the film.

When Will Smith burst into the well-appointed Upper East Side apartment in the opening scene of *Six Degrees of Separation*, the 1993 film adaptation of John Guare's Pulitzer-nominated play, it was only a partial shock. We had no idea that this young African-American man, only 25 at the time, would become one of the most powerful people in Hollywood with eight consecutive blockbusters in the coming years and an eventual entertainment empire and family acting dynasty.

At the time, he was the friendly black guy we had grown familiar with on our TV screens because of *The Fresh Prince of Bel-Air*, on which he played the oddball street-smart kid from Philly who didn't quite match with his bourgie West Coast relatives. The show—and Smith—were the heirs to the Cosby clan, the benign black family that America desired. That he was now portraying Guare's preppy Harvard student Paul Poitier, the fictional gay son of film legend Sidney Poitier, seemed perfectly plausible. Of course rich white folks would let this strange black guy into their living room—hadn't America already done so?

Although he had a couple of prior film credits to his name, this was Smith's big break. In the film, Smith must be smart and charming, warm and articulate as he elegantly manipulates the rich white people with whom he comes into contact—including Donald Sutherland and an Oscar-nominated Stockard Channing. In his first scene, as he explains that his thesis, about the corrupting influence on young men of J.D. Salinger's *Catcher in the Rye*, had been stolen, he commands all white people pay attention and believe him, feeding on their approval in the process. During his monologue, as he explains that "everybody's a phony," he fabulously parrots these privileged white people to get what he wants. "This book is preparing people for bigger moments in their lives than I ever dreamed of," Smith says as Paul, and it seems Smith could be speaking for himself.

The chemistry between Channing (her most successful role since *Grease*) and Smith is palpable. We believe in their platonic romance that straddles maternal care and sexual desire. "You watch, it gives me a thrill to be looked at," he tells her. And Channing devours his youth and vitality.

Now let's talk about the kiss. Smith was supposed to give a big, wet smooch to his co-star Anthony Michael Hall—but he refused (on the advice of Denzel Washington, allegedly). Instead, a series of clunky camera tricks are employed so it appears that Smith kisses him, but it shouldn't be written off as a cowardly move. It's easy to forget now, when gay characters seem to appear in every TV show and plenty of Hollywood films, but this seemed radical at the time. Smith did have a sexy-yet-comedic moment with a white male hustler who jumped out of bed, both of them naked. Smith later seduces handsome Eric Thal, a struggling actor, and his girlfriend (played by an unknown Heather Graham) and has sex with him in the back of a horse-drawn carriage in Central Park—certainly a daring move for an untested actor. And all of it works because, although Smith may not be a great actor, he turned out to be extremely successful at seduction. He makes audiences, everyone near him, believe whatever he's selling—whether it's as an undercover agent that polices aliens or a boxing legend. It's something Smith has done in his career ever since.

Source: Jerry Portwood, "Will Smith in *Six Degrees of Separation*," in *Back Stage*, Vol. 55, No. 6, February 6, 2014, p. 56.

Ryan Gilbey

In the following review, Gilbey writes that there is "nothing about the film that I would change."

John Guare's *Six Degrees of Separation* is about a wealthy Manhattan couple, the Kittredges, who take in for one night a conman posing as the son of Sidney Poitier. He promises them parts in the film version of *Cats* that his "father" is preparing, and they're dazzled; these pampered socialites roll over like dopey puppies. After the fellow's ruse is exposed, they discover that a couple they know were similarly fooled. This leads them to another man in the same boat. They take their collective complaint to the police, who want to know what was stolen. Only he didn't steal anything.

The play is enjoying a revival at the Old Vic in London, and it was thrilling to hear the 71-year-old playwright hungrily picking the text apart with Tom Sutcliffe on Radio 4's *Start the Week*, Tempting though it is to read the work as uniquely pertinent to our tweeting, *Heat*-reading, Brangelina-fixated age, that idea was swiftly rubbished by Guare ("[Celebrity culture] started in the Garden of Eden, I think . . . Cain thought Abel was more famous than he was"). He insisted that it's a play about how our insulated, upholstered cocoons are as fragile as doll's houses. "This young man comes in," he explained, "and brings with him everything [the Kittredges] are trying to keep out of their lives: race, sex, poverty . . ."

I would say that this got me thinking about the 1993 film version, except that I never go very long without thinking about it. I own comparatively few DVDs. My purchasing muscle wasted away a few years ago, around the time I realised that I usually only watch films again when I'm ill; buying them, therefore, became deeply unnecessary, like stockpiling Lemsip. But *Six Degrees of Separation* is one to which I regularly return. When I tell you it's a perfect movie, I do so in the knowledge that this is a ridiculous assertion, and that there is no such thing as perfection. I also do so knowing I am right. There's nothing about the film that I would change. Who among us can say that even of our own families?

Guare wrote the screenplay. He had made only two previous forays into film, both with foreign directors looking askance at America, and both exceptional—Milos Forman's first US film, *Taking Off*, and Louis Malle's *Atlantic City*. The Australian director of *Six Degrees of Separation*, Fred Schepisi (it rhymes with "Pepsi"), fell into the same category. Schepisi brought with him his regular cinematographer, Ian Baker, an expert at finding visual correlatives for that little-people-adrift-in-unfriendly-landscapes theme that had haunted the director since he made his other masterpiece, *The Chant of Jimmie Blacksmith*, in 1978.

The cast is like an ideal dinner party guest-list. Stockard Channing and Donald Sutherland, as the Kittredges, perform a *pas de deux* that is also a balancing act between vulnerability and monstrousness. (A *pas de deux* and a balancing act: can you imagine the flexibility involved? Not to mention the risk of sprained ankles.) As the bogus Poitier Jr, Will Smith is enigmatic, seductive, complex—all the things that superstardom has ironed out of him. And there are gorgeous miniature character studies from Ian McKellen as a South African millionaire (there's a whole complicated lifetime behind the way he says "the blecks"), Bruce Davison, Anthony Michael Hall, Heather Graham and others. Some of these actors get only a handful of scenes, but there's the suspicion, through the harmonious confluence of writing, acting and directing, that every character could easily have merited his or her own movie.

What clinches it all is the narrative structure, the nimble editing (by Peter Honess). I want to liken it to a mosaic because of the accumulation of mysteries and profundities. In fact, it's more fluid than that suggests; it's closer to a word-association game, or a string of sense-memories. This is a kind of film-making that aspires to reproduce consciousness, where our divisions between past, present and future are elided. It's linked closely with Alain Resnais and Nicolas Roeg (you can see it in Takeshi Kitano's *Hanabi*, too), and has come into vogue in the rather academic jigsaw-puzzle structures favoured by Alejandro González Iñárritu and Guillermo Arriaga (*21 Grams, Babel*). Schepisi attempted milder versions in his films *The Russia House* and *Last Orders*. But I don't think another film has integrated this storytelling pattern into mainstream cinema as ambitiously and accessibly as *Six Degrees of Separation*.

Here's Schepisi discussing the method with regard to *The Russia House*:

> [T]here's a point where Sean Connery and Michelle Pfeiffer meet in the tower, and all those beautiful Russian churches are outside. And you think you're just watching them, but actually you're watching five different time zones in the story: you're watching them and the tensions they're going through; you're watching a spy watching them; you're watching the spy's report back to his bosses in the form of a tape, a number of days after the event; and then you're watching two sections of the past, as Michelle Pfeiffer tells a story.

> I think that's how we tell stories. It's how memory operates, how our thoughts operate, because we go on memory, we go on apprehension of the present, and we go on hopes or expectations for the future. When you tell a story, you're throwing other lights on it, which makes the story richer and more interesting. We can't stop saying, "Yeah, but don't forget the time you did such and such . . ."

He's a brilliant director, sorely underrated and rarely discussed. If you can find copies, check out *The Chant of Jimmie Blacksmith*, *The Devil's Playground* (his 1976 debut), *A Cry in the Dark* and *Iceman*. But see *Six Degrees of Separation* first. If it doesn't blow you away, then I'm Sidney Poitier's pride and joy.

Source: Ryan Gilbey, "Gilbey on Film: Is *Six Degrees of Separation* the Perfect Movie?," in *New Statesman*, January 19, 2010.

Gene A. Plunka
In the following excerpt, Plunka traces the theme of alienation in Six Degrees of Separation.

. . . In *Six Degrees of Separation*, alienation and isolation are the norm rather than spiritual connectiveness. Parents do not know their children, heterosexuals are alienated from homosexuals, whites are separated from blacks, and the wealthy do not understand the less fortunate. Guare depicts a bifurcated society in which the emotional and intellectual vitality of individual consciousness is reduced to fragmentation and a neurotic obsession with celebrity status.

> *SIX DEGREES OF SEPARATION*, THEN, REFLECTS THE PINNACLE OF SUCCESS WITH A GENRE THAT LIBERATES THROUGH LAUGHTER YET FORCES THE AUDIENCE TO ENGAGE SERIOUSLY IN AN EXAMINATION OF THEIR OWN HUMANITY IN A GROTESQUE WORLD."

Individuals are divorced from each other, and thus families, classes, and races are also further divided. Of course, the spiritual connection is lost in the modern world; the image of man touching the hand of God in the Sistine Chapel, which Paul longs to see, is, as Ouisa views it, in need of cleaning.

This modern estrangement has allowed us to wear the mask of the con artist to hide our real feelings while taking advantage of others. Paul gains access to houses in order to find the family that he lacks; he is searching for an identity and yearns to be loved, wanted, and appreciated. He seeks contact in a society out of touch with the spiritual and with no passion for individuality. He explains to Ouisa why he sought her advice and comfort:

> No, I only visited you. I didn't like the first people so much. They went out and just left me alone. I didn't like the doctor. He was too eager to please. And he left me alone. But you. You and your husband. We all stayed together.

When Paul is asked what he wanted from the Kittredges, he states, "everlasting friendship." However, Paul, like many of us, is more outwardly interested in rubbing shoulders with the rich and famous, and thus his envy of celebrity forced him to assume the guise of con artist. Similarly, Flan and Ouisa, whose children are alienated from them, reached out to Paul as the ideal son they would love to have as part of their family. On the surface, however, Ouisa and Flan are con artists just like Paul, only their scams involve Cezannes and Kandinskys. Their seduction of Geoffrey is a fine demonstration of the con game fully at work. Like Paul, Flan and Ouisa have learned the art of the deal: figure out what the client wants and then deliver it. Trent Conway fully realizes that the wealthy participate in the con game as well: "Hand to mouth on a higher plateau." The only difference is that people at the bottom of the social stratum have further to go as they aspire to this plateau.

Although Paul is a con man who has borrowed ideas from others, his appearance becomes the catalyst for Ouisa's transformation by the end of the play. Paul the catalyst is similar to the role that Mildred Douglas plays in O'Neill's *The Hairy Ape*. In O'Neill's play, Yank pursues a quest for identity to determine if he "belongs" in the modern world. At first, Yank is in his element as the powerful stoker, at ease in his role as the fire that powers the ship's engines. Even when Paddy mocks Yank's choice to belong to the primitive and animalistic world of the grimy stokehole, Yank, although he internalizes Paddy's remarks, sloughs off any indication that he cannot "connect" with the men and machines around him. However, when Mildred Douglas penetrates the bowels of the ship, appearing to Yank as a ghost in white, he is shocked out of his complacency and pursues a quest to determine his identity. Paul is the Mildred Douglas of *Six Degrees of Separation*. Ouisa and Flan were perfectly content to entertain Geoffrey for the evening in what amounted to just another con game. Paul became the impetus for Ouisa and Flan to become aware of life lived in ignorant bliss.

Paul helps Ouisa understand how estranged modern society has become and how empty her own life is without the vitality of imagination. Paul's first indication of his understanding of the modern *angoisse* is revealed when he mentions his passion for Holden Caulfield, the protagonist in Salinger's *The Catcher in the Rye*. Paul describes Caulfield as a young man suffering from emotional and intellectual paralysis; although Caulfield mocks the phoniness around him, his insight forces him to become divorced from others. To Paul, Salinger's novel reflects the death of the imagination. He tells Flan and Ouisa, "The imagination has moved out of the realm of being our link, our most personal link, with our inner lives and the world outside that world—this world we share." Paul is lamenting the lack of passion in a society where habit, convenience, and style have replaced meaningful human connections. The "world we share" that he speaks of refers to the spiritual commitment necessary to find the "six degrees of communication" that unite humanity. Paul is trying to explain his existence to Flan and Ouisa: he is an effective con man because he is merely mirroring American values and falling prey to the myth of the American Dream as we know it. This type of society, where

human connections are fleeting and imagination is nonexistent, gets what it deserves: hustlers, con men, and impostors. Values are distorted: art is sold mainly for profit in private homes and in public at places like Sotheby's, *Cats* achieves theatrical prominence, and intimate experience is devalued in favor of cocktail-party anecdote. Even Salinger's art is distorted by those who turn the message around to suit their own whims: Mark David Chapman and John Hinckley use the novel as a defense for the shootings of John Lennon and Ronald Reagan, respectively. Paul understands that to connect with others, we must first come to grips with our selves, our imaginations. He states, "I believe the imagination is another phrase for what is most uniquely, *us*." Ouisa begins to understand the need to connect with others by using our imaginations to hold onto a purity of experience that may be alive, vibrant, and poignant rather than to substitute it for disposable anecdotal information. Paul realizes that the imagination is what prevents the American Dream from disintegrating into a nightmare: "It's there to sort out your nightmare, to show you the exit from the maze of your nightmare, to transform the nightmare into dreams that become your bedrock. It we don't listen to that voice, it dies. It shrivels. It vanishes." And during the initial run of *Six Degrees* at Lincoln Center, Guare echoed Paul's comments when he hinted to an interviewer why the play has become significant to a contemporary New York audience: "We're all on top of each other. My concerns are about the imagination and how we live in this city. We can't go on living like this, where the ideals are so high and the opposite of what ideals are, the bedrock, is so weak."

Although the Kittredges are wealthy and seem to have everything to make them feel comfortable, they learn that material things do not suffice when there is no connection with self and others. Again, Guare demonstrates that the lives of the rich and famous are often spiritually hollow at the core—certainly nothing to emulate. Although Flan and Ouisa are appalled that Paul took advantage of them, his presence made the couple suddenly feel alive. They become aware of the artificiality of life devoid of experience where meaningful emotional connections are reduced to constantly changing identities. In this sense, *Six Degrees of Separation* has much in common with director Paul Mazursky's screenplay for *Down and Out in Beverly Hills*. In that film, homeless Jerry Baskin imposes himself on wealthy Dave Whiteman's family in Beverly Hills. Dave rescues Jerry from suicide when the latter attempts to drown in the Whitemans' pool. Dave invites Jerry to stay in his house until he recovers; Jerry, intuitively understanding that he has found a sucker in upper-class white liberals, takes advantage of the situation and "reluctantly" agrees to stay. The Whitemans are attracted to Jerry for various reasons. Dave, who is a successful businessman enamored with Radical Chic, is fascinated by Jerry's devil-may-care attitude, which has enabled him to drop out of the "rat race." Barbara Whiteman, who compensates for her sexless marriage by seeking self-gratification through shopping, aerobics, meditation, and yoga, reaches Nirvana when Jerry gives her a deep massage followed by sex. Jerry also has a profound effect on the Whiteman children: he accepts Max's punk lifestyle and brings Jenny, the snobbish and anorexic Sarah Lawrence student, down to earth. The Whitemans' maid becomes aware of class consciousness through books Jerry lends her, and even Matisse, the canine who is counselled by a dog psychiatrist, is less temperamental around Jerry. Irascible and prickly, Jerry eventually become a nuisance, demanding better quality food and accommodations while making no attempt to leave the mansion. When Jerry does wear out his welcome and returns to the streets, the Whitemans realize that he was not merely an anecdote but instead provided them with meaningful experience, which is priceless. After finding Jerry roaming the streets, the Whitemans bring him back home.

When Ouisa speaks with Paul on the telephone near the end of the play, he declares, "You don't sound happy." Paul realizes that, even with all of their wealth, the Kittredges' lives are empty. Paul provided the Kittredges the chance to connect emotionally with another human being. Paul, like Jerry in *Down and Out in Beverly Hills*, became the catalyst for the release of the imagination, allowing authenticity to replace artificiality. Ouisa tries to get her husband to understand that high culture is not merely wealth and conspicuous consumption but rather a community of lives that connect spiritually despite differences in race, gender, or class. Ouisa realizes that although it only requires six people to connect all humanity, most of us are unable to find the right six people to make the connection, and thus we remain separated. Paul, someone who cared about the Kittredges, provided a meaningful connection for Ouisa. David Román notes, "Moreover, Paul's humanity must be available to her on some level even if he is neither the son of Sidney Poitier nor her children's classmate." In a dehumanizing society where artifice and phoniness are the norm, Paul, despite the fact that he duped the Kittredges, reflected a strong desire to bond with them as family. In a sick society where most people are two-faced like the Kandinsky and contact is bogus and fleeting, reduced primarily to disposable anecdotes, Ouisa desperately wants to hold onto the experience. She explains her feelings to Flan at the end of the play: "But it was an experience. I will not turn him into an anecdote. How do we fit what happened to us into life without turning it into an anecdote with no teeth and a punch line you'll mouth over and over for years to come." As she explores the existential angst troubling her, Ouisa's dilemma concerns the modern identity in a fraudulent society: "But it was an experience. How do we keep the experience?" Through the same sort of redemptive spirit that we witnessed in the tetralogy, Ouisa, willing to forgive Paul for his transgressions, will find the means to locate the right six people in the chain that will lead to an authentic spiritual connection. Guare expects his middle- and upper-class audience of theatergoers to identify with Ouisa and learn from the epiphany she experiences at the end of the play.

Guare's brilliant achievement in *Six Degrees of Separation* is a result of his ability to take black comedy to another level, mixing farce and pathos. As the Kandinsky turns at the beginning of the play, we realize the sarcasm of the duplicity of con artists Flan and Ouisa during their soirée with Geoffrey. Paul's con game develops into farce when he is discovered with a male prostitute. The scene of a naked, aggressive hustler chasing Flan and Ouisa around their apartment is as demonstrative as any sick behavior represented in classical farce from Molière to the Marx Brothers. Moreover, the vision of a young black man who stabs himself to gain access to the apartments of the well-to-do and then charms them with knowledge acquired through others represents the modern neurosis at its best. Guare's black comedy is most effective here as the humorous turns to pain, despair, and horror when the Kittredges discover that they and their colleagues have been duped. As in classical farce or black comedy, the audience laughs but is also disgusted when the comic becomes frighteningly real and thus rather terrifying. As the play moves from the absurdly comic and pathetically disorienting crass materialistic world of the art of the deal to the unexpected pathos of Ouisa's epiphany about the potential of shared humanity, Guare's black comedy comes into its own by depicting modern society as a neurotic circus and simultaneously a vale of tears. *Six Degrees of Separation*, then, reflects the pinnacle of success with a genre that liberates through laughter yet forces the audience to engage seriously in an examination of their own humanity in a grotesque world.

Source: Gene A. Plunka, "*Six Degrees of Separation*," in *The Black Comedy of John Guare*, University of Delaware Press, 2002, pp. 197–202.

SOURCES

Calavita, Marco, "Film Guide: Six Degrees of Separation," in *Cineaste*, Vol. 20, No. 3. 1994, p. 72.

Gerston, Jill, "Stockard Channing Goes West," in *New York Times*, March 6, 1994, http://www.nytimes.com/1994/03/06/movies/film-stockard-channing-goes-west.html (accessed June 8, 2015).

Gillan, Jennifer, "'No One Knows You're Black!': *Six Degrees of Separation* and the Buddy Formula," in *Cinema Journal*, Vol. 40, No. 3, Spring 2001, pp. 47–68.

Gleiberman, Owen, Review of *Six Degrees of Separation*, in *Entertainment Weekly*, December 10, 1993, http://www.ew.com/article/1993/12/10/six-degrees-separation (accessed June 8, 2015).

Grimes, William, ed., *The Times of the Eighties: The Culture, Politics, and Personalities That Shaped the Eighties*, Black Dog & Leventhal, 2013.

Kempley, Rita, Review of *Six Degrees of Separation*, in *Washington Post*, December 22, 1993, http://www.washingtonpost.com/wp-srv/style/longterm/movies/videos/sixdegreesofseparationrkempley_a0a3dd.htm (accessed June 8, 2015).

Klady, Leonard, Review of *Six Degrees of Separation*, in *Variety*, November 30, 1993, http://variety.com/1993/film/reviews/six-degrees-of-separation-3-1200435017/ (accessed June 8, 2015).

Maslin, Janet, Review of *Six Degrees of Separation*, in *New York Times*, December 8, 1993, http://www.nytimes.com/movie/review?res=9F0CE3DE1531F93BA35751C1A965958260&partner=Rotten%2520Tomatoes (accessed June 8, 2015).

Six Degrees of Separation, directed by Fred Schepisi, 1993; Beverly Hills, CA: MGM/UA Home Entertainment, 2000, DVD.

Walzer, Andrew, "Narratives of Contemporary Male Crisis: The (Re)Production of a National Discourse," in *Journal of Men's Studies*, Vol. 10, No. 2, Winter 2002, pp. 209–23.

FURTHER READING

Desmond, Matthew, and Mustafa Emirbayer, *Race in America*, W. W. Norton, 2015.

    Although this is technically an undergraduate textbook, it does provide a comprehensive look at how race and racialist attitudes intersect with gender, class, religion, and preconceptions of creativity and intellect.

Jenkins, Philip, *Decade of Nightmares: The End of the Sixties and the Making of Eighties America*, Oxford University Press, 2006.

    In this well-organized and readable book, Jenkins argues that between 1975 and 1986 (the original setting of Guare's play), Americans set the stage for the rise of the conservative decade of the 1980s. There was, he suggests, a kind of cultural panic that took hold during this period that drove this shift more quickly than many anticipated.

Plunka, Gene A., *The Black Comedy of John Guare*, University of Delaware Press, 2002.

    This valuable and comprehensive book is broad reaching in its exploration of Guare's body of works, with substantial focus on what is considered by many to be his finest achievement, *Six Degrees of Separation*. At the center of Guare's success, Plunka argues, is his ability to manage adeptly the powers of farce, mixing it variously with comedy, satire, and classic pathos (a quality that evokes pity or sadness).

Watts, Duncan J., *Six Degrees: The Science of a Connected Age*, W. W. Norton, 2004.

    In this influential book, Watts sets out to explain the principles and implications of the concept of a planet (and humanity) connected in previously unfathomed ways. Crisis and change, personal and professional relationships are all reimagined into what Watts argues is a new horizon of science.

SUGGESTED SEARCH TERMS

Six Degrees of Separation AND film

Six Degrees of Separation AND play

Will Smith

Donald Sutherland

Stockard Channing

John Guare AND Six Degrees of Separation

Guare AND black comedy

Guare AND race

film AND social satire

film AND imagination

film AND storytelling

Water by the Spoonful

QUIARA ALEGRÍA HUDES

2011

Water by the Spoonful, by Quiara Alegría Hudes, first produced in 2011, is the second in a trilogy of stand-alone plays about the life of Elliot Ortiz, a young Marine whose service in Iraq has left him psychologically and physically damaged. After the death of Mami Ginny Ortiz, the woman who has raised him, Elliot and his cousin Yaz scramble to organize a funeral worthy of the woman who carried their low-income Puerto Rican neighborhood on her back, feeding the hungry, housing the homeless, and mothering those without someone to look after them. Elliot's birth mother, Odessa, gave him up after her addiction to crack cocaine led to the death of her two-year-old daughter. Now in recovery, Odessa lives more comfortably as Haikumom, the founder of recovertogether.com, where she acts as an online sage to other struggling addicts. Those addicts form the play's second leading family: a cynical but loving tribe of misfits for whom each day is a struggle between life and death. Full of humor, darkness, hope, and love, *Water by the Spoonful* is a breathtaking illustration of the power of family.

AUTHOR BIOGRAPHY

Hudes was born in Philadelphia, Pennsylvania, in 1977. Raised in West Philadelphia by her Puerto Rican mother and stepfather, she grew

Quiara Alegría Hudes (© *WENN Ltd* | *Alamy*)

up speaking both English and Spanish. She took piano lessons and developed a love for both music composition and creative writing. After graduating from Central High School, she went on to earn her bachelor's degree in music composition from Yale University and then a master of fine arts degree in playwriting from Brown University. Her first major play, *Yemaya's Belly*, premiered in 2005 at the Portland Stage Company in Portland, Maine. *Elliot, a Soldier's Fugue*, the first of the Elliot plays, premiered at Page 73 Productions, Brooklyn, New York, in 2006. In 2007, the play was a finalist for the Pulitzer Prize for Drama. Hudes wrote the book for the musical *In the Heights*, which went on to win the 2008 Tony Award for Best Musical and was a finalist for the 2009 Pulitzer Prize. Her children's musical, *Barrio Grrrl!* premiered in 2009 at the Family Theater at the Kennedy Center for the Performing Arts. That same year, her play *26 Miles* premiered at

Alliance Theatre in Atlanta. In 2011, *Water by the Spoonful*—the sequel to *Elliot, a Soldier's Fugue*—premiered at Hartford Stage, in Connecticut. The play was awarded the Pulitzer Prize for Drama in 2012. The final installment of Elliot's story, *The Happiest Song Plays Last*, premiered at the Goodman Theatre in Chicago in 2013.

In Chicago, April 27, 2013, was declared Quiara Hudes Day. March 16, 2014, was declared Quiara Alegría Hudes Day in Philadelphia. She was inducted into the Central High School Hall of Fame and serves on the board of Philadelphia Young Playwrights, the group who produced her first play as a high-school sophomore. She has received fellowships from the Goodman Theatre, Eugene O'Neill Theater Center, Hartford Stage, the Cleveland Playhouse, and Sundance Institute Theatre Program and served a residency at New Dramatists. She is married with children and lives New York.

PLOT SUMMARY

Scene 1
Water by the Spoonful takes place in 2009 in two interconnected worlds: the real world and the online world. Elliot Ortiz and his cousin, Yazmin, eat breakfast at Swarthmore College, where Yazmin is an adjunct professor of music. They are waiting on a third person to arrive, but he is late. Elliot is jumpy, his shift at a Subway sandwich shop starts in fifteen minutes. While they wait, Elliot asks Yazmin for help with his mother, Ginny, whose health is declining. In return, Yazmin asks Elliot to be her witness as she signs the papers finalizing her divorce. Elliott argues against it, thinking the decision is too sudden.

Professor Aman arrives. Yazmin introduces Elliot, who asks the professor for a translation of an Arabic phrase he has written down phonetically on a scrap of paper. The professor is curious about how Elliot came across the phrase. Elliot avoids the question, but the dog tags around his neck give him away. He is a veteran of the Iraq war, honorably discharged after a leg injury that causes him to limp. He has been out of the service for a few years, which, Aman points out, is a long time to have a phrase stuck in your head.

After learning Elliot's history, Aman asks him whether he would like to help out a friend who is making a documentary about marines in Iraq, but Elliot says no, even though he is an aspiring actor. Aman assures him he will not be an interview subject but a behind-the-scenes consultant. Elliot takes Aman's business card, considering. Aman says the phrase translates as, "Can I please have my passport back?"

Scene 2

Odessa Ortiz, the founder and site administrator of recovertogether.com, logs on to her website. Her screen name is Haikumom. She writes a haiku about curing restlessness through gardening.

Orangutan logs on for the first time in ninety-one days. Haikumom cannot believe she is back, having given her up as lost. Chutes&Ladders logs on and immediately begins to give Orangutan a hard time about her disappearing act. It is clear that both Haikumom and Chutes&Ladders care a great deal about Orangutan. She tells them she has gone to Japan to teach English. Before leaving, she gave her parents her log-on information for recovertogether.com, letting them read every post she has written. Though they have cut her off financially, reading about her struggles with addiction gives them hope for her future. They have paid for Orangutan's plane ticket to her homeland. Neither of her online companions knew that Orangutan is Japanese. Her birth name is Yoshiko Sakai, but she has changed it.

The three friends talk about the ocean, and Chutes&Ladders reveals that though he was born a few miles from the Pacific Ocean, he has been afraid to swim since being sucked under by a wave at Coronado Beach. He nearly drowned but was saved by a lifeguard. He was addicted to crack at the time of this near-death experience and went to his first narcotics anonymous meeting the very next day, determined to live. The group gives collective thanks for lifeguards. Haikumom tells Chutes&Ladders it is never too late to learn how to swim, promising to send him a pair of water wings.

Scene 3

At Subway, Elliot takes an order over the phone. John Coltrane's album *A Love Supreme* plays in the background. The scene is split to show Yazmin mid class. She stops the music and begins a lecture about dissonance. She begins to play Coltrane's *Ascension*, an album with more difficult, chaotic

music to ingest. At Subway, a ghost appears before Elliot's eyes, repeating the phrase Elliot has asked Aman to translate. Elliot pointedly ignores the ghost. He receives a text message and exits quickly, limping out of Subway.

Yazmin gives the class an assignment: to describe the first time they noticed dissonance in music. She tells the class that she first noticed it during her first piano lesson, which she took after working in a corrugated box factory to save up enough money. She was thirteen years old. The class takes a five-minute break while Yazmin returns Elliot's frantic calls. He tells her that Ginny is still alive but in the hospital. Elliot is furious that rather than calling, his father has texted him the news that his mother is on a breathing machine. To make things worse, his father is not answering the phone. While they are talking, Yazmin receives a message from Elliot's father that says they are waiting for Elliot to arrive before they pull the plug.

Scene 4

A new user arrives and logs on to recovertogether.com. His screen name is Fountainhead. He haltingly tells the story of his addiction to crack. He has a beautiful wife and two sons and a yellow Porsche and has recently been laid off from his job. He has wrecked the Porsche while high on crack and now drives a rental Ford Mustang. He says this is as close to rock bottom as he wants to get. Fountainhead says joining the forum seems like his first day of school with the other recovering addicts as his teachers. He refuses to tell his wife, with whom his seventh wedding anniversary is the next day. He considers the battle ahead to be psychological and asks for any tips to shake his addiction.

At the conclusion of Fountainhead's story, Haikumom becomes emotional as she sits at her computer. Chutes&Ladders finds Fountainhead's arrogance repulsive. Orangutan agrees that he has a long way to go, asking whether he is making a confession or presenting an online dating profile. She thinks he is a fake, infiltrating the site for fun. Chutes&Ladders tells him to cut out the life story and admit his problem directly.

Haikumom breaks up the discussion, introducing herself politely and asking Fountainhead to forgive the behavior of Chutes&Ladders and Orangutan. Haikumom tells him that she also once had a family but that now all she has is six years sober. Orangutan and Chutes&Ladders

start to tease him again. Haikumom scolds them both, saying that just because Fountainhead has not hit absolute rock bottom like them, he is still worthy of a chance. She apologizes to Fountainhead again, but he has been silent since his introductory post. Chutes&Ladders tells him that his ego will keep him from quitting. Until he rids himself of his ego, he has no hope. Fountainhead logs off abruptly.

Scene 5

Yaz and Elliot meet at a flower shop. Yaz asks how he is holding up since his mother's death. Elliot says he has been boxing at the gym to take the stress away. Elliot asks if Odessa (who has so far appeared only online as Haikumom) has called. Yaz says no. Elliot is offended that she has not at least offered to help. Yaz hands him brochures about floral arrangements. Elliot rejects them all because they have carnations, and he considers carnations cheap. He finds an arrangement that resembles Ginny's garden. He feels guilty for telling his mother he was watering her garden in the final weeks of her life. She would ask every day, and he would lie to her. Elliot asks if Yaz will deliver the sermon at the funeral. She agrees, if he will return the favor by calling her ex-husband, William, to ask that he not attend, even though he and Ginny were close. She also wants to travel to Puerto Rico with Elliot to scatter Ginny's ashes. She tells Elliot that she saw his ad for Colgate toothpaste. She asks him to smile for her. He charges her a dollar. They reminisce about their rocky childhood. Their grandmother has died only months before. With Ginny gone, it feels as if their family is disintegrating. Elliot says that once his dad sells the house, he may never set foot in Philadelphia again. He dreams of moving to Los Angeles to pursue his acting career.

Scene 6

Orangutan waits alone online. It is Tuesday at two in the morning in Sapporo, Japan. Chutes&Ladders logs on. It is Monday at one in the afternoon in San Diego, California. Orangutan says she is sitting in a bar. Chutes&Ladders advises her to go home. Orangutan begins to wax poetic about Japan. Chutes&Ladders, sensing her desperation, reminds her that she has been drug-free for ninety-six days and should be proud. She begs him to distract her from her own thoughts. She asks him for little details about his life. He works for the Internal Revenue Service, or IRS. He has a son

from whom he is estranged. She asks if he has any vacation days and if he would like to use them to come to Japan to meet in person.

Chutes&Ladders tells her that he is fifty years old and grossly unattractive with a face like a Corgi dog's. She says in all her thirty-one years she has never met anyone as sarcastic as he is who also believes in God. She begs him to be her knight in shining armor. He says the concept is tempting but that she would be disappointed. He claims to be boring, with no personality. She says they can just watch DVDs and eat popcorn together. She says she wants the challenge of a real human connection. He tells her that working abroad and recovering from addiction should be enough for her.

Haikumom logs on. She tells Chutes&Ladders not to reject Orangutan's offer of companionship, even if she is young and impulsive. She tells him she is sending him a care package at his office.

Fountainhead appears, thanking the group for the brutal welcome he received on his last visit to the site. He admits that after being three days' clean he returned to using again. Orangutan suggests he tell his wife about his problem. He rejects the idea. Chutes&Ladders pushes him to admit that he smokes crack. Fountainhead finally admits it, and Chutes&Ladders backs off teasing him. Haikumom tells Fountainhead that she lives in Philadelphia, too, if he ever needs her in an emergency. The four fall into a more companionable conversation about their favorite slogans to help beat addiction. Meanwhile, the ghost appears before Elliot at the gym, repeating the Arabic phrase. Haikumom, reading the *Daily News*, announces to the group that her sister Ginny is in the paper, only to realize that she has died. The ghost blows on Elliot, knocking him to the floor. He repeats the Arabic phrase, asking for the return of his passport.

Scene 7

Odessa (Haikumom) and John (Fountainhead) sit in a booth at a diner, drinking coffee. John tells her he loves Puerto Rico. She has never been. Her phone rings. She is combative and angry, telling the person that she is busy, to come by in an hour. John is shocked by the difference between her online persona and her demeanor in person. Odessa explains that her sister has just died and that her family always knows how to get under her skin. She offers him information about addiction support groups that cater to the wealthy. He becomes overwhelmed by the openness of their discussion and gets up to leave. She reminds him that he called her for this meeting. He sits back down.

Elliot and Yaz arrive, taking seats at the booth and demanding that Odessa contribute money for Ginny's funeral. Uncomfortable, John introduces himself but is quickly rebuffed by Elliot, who is aware of Odessa's website. Elliot reveals that Odessa is his mother, though Ginny has raised him from a very young age. When Odessa tells Elliot and Yaz she has no money, John offers them two hundred dollars—the full cost for the flowers. Elliot rejects the money, saying he does not accept money from drug addicts.

Elliot tells John a story from his childhood to illustrate his feelings toward Odessa. Elliot and his baby sister caught a stomach virus, but the children's hospital was overrun with similar cases and could not admit them. Instead, Odessa was instructed to feed her children one teaspoon of water every five minutes to keep them from dehydrating. Elliot remembers basking in the one-on-one attention from his mother as she spoon-fed him. Then she disappeared. Six hours later, after the neighbors kicked in the door, Elliot and his sister were found lying on piles of laundry. Elliot had soiled himself. His sister was dead.

John flees the diner, deeply distressed. Yazmin says they can at least say the baby's name: Mary Lou. Odessa hands Elliot the key to her house, telling him to take her computer to the pawn shop and use the money to buy flowers for Ginny's funeral.

Scene 8

Orangutan and Chutes&Ladders talk online. She goads him on as he works up the courage to call his son, Wendell. When Wendell picks up the phone, Chutes&Ladders panics and hangs up. Then he quickly logs off, leaving Orangutan by herself.

Yaz and Elliot enter Odessa's living room. Elliot logs on to recovertogether.com as Haikumom. He begins to insult Orangutan, who realizes immediately that she is talking to an impostor. When she realizes he is Haikumom's son, she compliments his toothpaste ad and asks how his recovery from addiction to pain medication is progressing. Yazmin is shocked by this revelation, especially when Orangutan reveals that Elliot has been hospitalized three times for

overdosing. In a rage, Elliot violently unplugs the computer. He begs Yazmin to leave the subject alone. The ghost appears. Yaz tells him they need to hurry if they are going to make it to the pawnshop on time.

Scene 9

Chutes&Ladders sorts through his mail at the IRS office. Orangutan appears online, ecstatic. She has discovered the address where her birth parents live in Kushiro, Japan, and will board a train within minutes to take her there.

Chutes&Ladders tells Orangutan to abandon her plan immediately. She is three months sober, still too vulnerable to take such an emotional risk. Orangutan argues that she wants to feel something, to form a meaningful relationship with another human. Chutes&Ladders tells her he once visited his son's house only to be asked to leave. Through the front door, he spotted his three grandsons, who did not know him. Though he had been sober for five years, the trauma of that visit led to a relapse.

Orangutan says he is frightened of his own shadow and admits she hoped to impress him. She says she teases him because she adores him, like a little girl who chases a boy on the playground. She logs off, threatening to board the train within five minutes.

Chutes&Ladders throws his calculator, pen cup, and phone, leaving behind a small package on his desk. The package, from Haikumom, contains a single, deflated water wing. He puts it around his arm.

Scene 10

Yaz and Elliot deliver Ginny's eulogy together. Ginny was a pillar in the Philadelphia Puerto Rican American community. She fed the hungry from her own kitchen and turned vacant lots into gardens. She had no biological children yet was the mother to many. As they remember Ginny's life, Odessa sits alone on the floor of her house, slowly spooning water onto the floor until it begins to form a puddle. Meanwhile, Orangutan stands petrified on the platform as her train arrives.

Scene 11

Chutes&Ladders, equipped with a now-inflated water wing, negotiates the sale of his car over the phone.

Scene 12

Yaz and Elliot arrive at Odessa's house to find her collapsed and unconscious. She has over-dosed. She watches passively from the side, as if a ghost, as Yaz and Elliot call an ambulance and move her to the sofa.

In Japan, Orangutan has fallen asleep at the train station. A policeman points his flashlight at her. She wakes up and leaves the station.

A blinding light appears above Odessa. Though Elliot cannot see the light, Yaz can. She urges Odessa toward it, telling her it is okay to leave. At the sound of an ambulance approaching, the light disappears. Yaz tells a bewildered Elliot that he must forgive Odessa.

Scene 13

Orangutan tells Chutes&Ladders that she did not board the train. Chutes&Ladders tells Orangutan that he bought a ticket to Japan. She bubbles over with happiness.

Fountainhead logs on to tell the others in the forum he is at the hospital watching over Haiku-mom. She had listed him as her emergency contact. Orangutan and Chutes&Ladders pelt Fountainhead with questions, making him swear to take care of the woman who has saved their lives. Fountainhead's phone rings. He explains to his wife that he is at the hospital with a friend. She hangs up, suspicious. He texts her instructions to log on to recovertogether.com to view what he has written.

Scene 14

In a hotel room in Puerto Rico, Yaz logs on as Freedom&Noise, introducing herself as the interim site manager while Odessa recovers. She admits she is underqualified but willing to help.

Elliot enters the room, scolding Yaz for her involvement with Odessa's site. Yaz is unfazed. She leaves the room to make a call. Alone, Elliot is confronted by the ghost, who reaches out to touch his face.

Scene 15

At Odessa's house, John carries her to the bathroom, resting her gently in the tub. He uses a sponge to bathe her. Though he is embarrassed at first by such intimacy, he quickly acclimates.

In Japan, Orangutan waits impatiently at the airport for Chutes&Ladders, who is one day and forty-five minutes late. When he arrives, they hug. He introduces himself as Clayton

"Buddy" Wilkie. Her name is Madeleine Mays. Their next hug is much more meaningful, and they exit together.

Yazmin and Elliot prepare to scatter Ginny's ashes over a waterfall in Puerto Rico. Yaz reveals that she has bought Ginny's house. Elliot tells Yaz he is flying to Los Angeles rather than going back to Philadelphia. Together, they throw the ashes.

CHARACTERS

Professor Aman

Professor Aman is a professor at Swarthmore College. A colleague of Yazmin's, he translates an Arabic phrase for Elliot. After learning Elliot was a marine, he asks whether Elliot would help consult on a friend's documentary about marines in Iraq.

Chutes&Ladders

Chutes&Ladders, whose real name is Clayton "Buddy" Wilkie, is a member of recovertogether.com, where his sarcastic sense of humor and cynicism have earned him the love of Orangutan. A fifty-six-year-old African American living in San Diego, Chutes&Ladders works at an IRS office and carefully maintains a boring but nonthreatening existence in order to beat his addiction to crack. Orangutan teases him for his cautiousness, but Chutes&Ladders, after losing his family to his addiction and nearly drowning in the ocean, maintains that a simple life is all he can hope to live. The experience of being rejected from his estranged son's life causes Chutes&Ladders to panic over Orangutan's plan to track down her birth parents for a reunion. In an act of daring spontaneity, he flies to Japan to meet her in person so that they may form a real-world connection.

Fountainhead

Fountainhead (John) is a formerly successful computer programmer, recently laid off from his well-paying salaried job. He has a Porsche, a wife who does not know he is addicted to crack, and two sons. Like the Ortiz family, he lives in Philadelphia, though he is considerably more affluent. Fountainhead's arrival on recovertogether.com is met with contempt from Orangutan and Chutes&Ladders, who find him pretentious, arrogant, and laughably naive. Haikumom is more accepting, and they meet in person at a diner. She coaxes him out of his denial, frightening him with examples from her own life. When she is hospitalized, Fountainhead shares the news with Chutes&Ladders and Orangutan. They charge him with the duty of caring for her.

Fountainhead's Wife

Fountainhead's wife does not know about his addiction. She struggles with her own mental health, causing him to worry about what would happen if she were to learn the truth about her husband. He gives her his recovertogether.com log-on information after Odessa's overdose.

Freedom&Noise

See Yazmin Ortiz

Ghost

The ghost is the image of an Iraqi civilian who haunts Elliot, repeating the phrase "Can I please have my passport back?" He is a symbol of the psychological trauma Elliot suffered as a soldier.

Haikumom

See Odessa Ortiz

John

See Fountainhead

Madeleine Mays

See Orangutan

Orangutan

Orangutan is a thirty-one-year-old recovering crack addict who reappears on recovertogether.com after a ninety-one-day absence. In that time, she has moved to Japan, where she teaches English. Born in Japan, she was raised in the United States. She is energetic, outgoing, spontaneous, and emotionally volatile—a dangerous combination for a recovering addict. She adores Chutes&Ladders, who shares her sarcastic sense of humor and quick wit. Hoping to impress him, she attempts to reunite with her birth family but is talked down from the plan by Chutes&Ladders himself, who worries about what will happen if the reunion goes sour. Afterward, he flies to Japan so they can meet in person, fulfilling a longtime wish of Orangutan's for a real connection. Orangutan's birth name is Yoshiko Sakai, which she has changed to Madeleine Mays.

Elliot Ortiz

Elliot Ortiz is a twenty-four-year-old veteran of the war in Iraq. He works at a Subway sandwich shop but dreams of becoming an actor. He is troubled by an old injury to his leg and by the memory of an Iraqi civilian who appears before him as a ghost asking for the return of his passport. Elliot is Ginny's primary caregiver in her final days. He struggles emotionally after her death, having loved her as a mother. He treats his birth mother, Odessa, with disdain. He cannot forgive her for her role in the death of his sister and looks down on recovertogether.com, though he himself struggles with an addiction to pain medication. He admits at the play's conclusion that by giving him away to Ginny, Odessa saved his life.

Elliot Ortiz's Dad

Elliot's dad has little to do with Elliot, not being his biological father. He notifies Elliot by text that Ginny is in the hospital. After Ginny's death, he sells the house to Yazmin.

Eugenia Ortiz

See Mami Ginny Ortiz

Mami Ginny Ortiz

Mami Ginny, or Ginny, is the woman who raised Elliot when Odessa could no longer care for him. A neighborhood saint, Ginny fed the hungry, turned empty lots into community gardens, and refurbished houses for struggling young couples. She has no children of her own but at the time of her death had twenty-two godchildren. Elliot single-handedly nurses her through a prolonged illness. Her death shakes Elliot, Yazmin, and Odessa, providing the catalyst that brings them together as they plan her funeral.

Mary Lou Ortiz

Mary Lou is Elliot's younger sister. She died when she was two years old, of dehydration after Odessa failed to spoon water into her mouth every five minutes while she was sick with a stomach virus.

Odessa Ortiz

Odessa is Elliot's birth mother, a thirty-nine-year-old woman whose addiction to crack has torn her family apart. Because of her irresponsibility, her two-year-old daughter died of dehydration. Afterward, Elliot lived with Ginny. Odessa finds comfort in the website she founded, recovertogether. com. Writing under the screen name Haikumom,

Odessa spends most of her time on the Internet. She has a job as a janitor and little contact with the Ortiz family until the death of Ginny, her sister. When Elliot and Yaz demand she contribute for the funeral, she refuses until Elliot reminds her of his baby sister. She lets them sell her computer to a pawnshop to pay for Ginny's flowers, but the reminder of her painful past causes her to relapse. She overdoses and has a heart attack. Fountainhead, the newest member of recovertogether.com, with whom she has formed a tenuous connection, takes care of her after her hospitalization.

As Haikumom, the moderator of recovertogether.com, Odessa strives to keep discussion both productive and civil. She writes a daily inspirational haiku, monitors the language and content of posts, and acts as a tough but fair motherly figure for the struggling addicts. Both Orangutan and Chutes&Ladders credit Haikumom for saving their lives and those of countless others.

Yazmin Ortiz
Yazmin is an adjunct professor of music at Swarthmore College. After divorcing her husband, William, Yazmin becomes more involved in the life of her cousin, Elliot, especially after their Aunt Ginny dies. Yazmin is interested in dissonance, especially in the works of the jazz legend John Coltrane. During Odessa's near-death experience, Yazmin witnesses a bright light, finding sympathy and love for her wayward aunt in the process. While Odessa is recovering, Yazmin takes over the role of site manager at recovertogether.com. She buys Ginny's house to provide a sanctuary for the Ortiz family. While planning Ginny's funeral, Yazmin learns of Elliot's emotional and physical pain since returning from Iraq. She encourages him to follow his dream of moving to Los Angeles to be an actor. Freedom&Noise is the screen name Yazmin uses on recovertogether.com when she becomes the interim site manager during Odessa's hospitalization.

Policeman
The policeman wakes Orangutan after she falls asleep at the train station.

Yoshiko Sakai
See Orangutan

Clayton "Buddy" Wilkie
See Chutes&Ladders

Wendell Wilkie
Wendell is Chutes&Ladders's estranged son, now married with three sons. He refuses to let his father into his home, asking him to leave when Chutes&Ladders drops by the house unannounced.

William
William is Yazmin's ex-husband. He had a close bond with both Ginny and Elliot before the divorce.

THEMES

Family
Two families coping with loss make up the cast of *Water by the Spoonful*. The first is the Ortiz family, who have lost their matriarch, Ginny. The second family is the members of recovertogether.com, who have lost themselves to addiction. Both families struggle to right the ship after these blows. For the Ortizes, this takes the form of the scramble to put on a funeral worthy of Ginny's legacy. For Orangutan, Haikumom, and Chutes&Ladders, the crisis comes when a new member of their tightly knit community appears, reminding them all of their past selves—the ones they have left behind as a necessity, along with their addictions. In the Ortiz family, Odessa is the odd woman out, whereas on recovertogether.com, Fountainhead's luxurious lifestyle makes him a target of the others' derision. The meeting of these two black sheep is what brings the two families together: when Yazmin and Elliot crash into the diner booth beside Odessa and Fountainhead, demanding money for Ginny's flowers, they recall with brutal honesty Odessa's darkest moment as a crack addict.

Water by the Spoonful defines a family as a group of people who selflessly take care of one another no matter what. Odessa proves herself to the Ortizes by sacrificing her computer so that her son can buy flowers for the woman he considers his real mother. Fountainhead proves himself an honorable member of recovertogether.com when he obeys to the letter Orangutan and Chutes&Ladders's demands that he take care of Haikumom after her overdose, even if it means he must face his addiction head on. By leaning on each other, Yazmin and Elliot, Orangutan and Chutes&Ladders, and Odessa and Fountainhead grow stronger, and their families become more resilient to life's unexpected plummets.

TOPICS FOR FURTHER STUDY

- Listen to a few selections from each of the two John Coltrane albums Yazmin discusses during class: *A Love Supreme* and *Ascension*. How do these works differ from each other? What similarities do you find between them? How would you describe the mood of each album? How would you relate the dissonant musical style of *Ascension* to *Water by the Spoonful*? Take notes as you listen and have a group discussion. *A Love Supreme* and *Ascension* are available in their entirety on YouTube.

- Read Judith Ortiz Cofer's *An Island like You: Stories of the Barrio* (1995), a short-story collection for young adults. Choose a story from the collection to compare with *Water by the Spoonful*. How is Puerto Rican American life portrayed in each work? What similarities and differences can you find between Cofer's depiction of a New Jersey barrio (Spanish-speaking neighborhood) and the Philadelphia neighborhood where Mami Ginny lived? Compose an essay in which you compare and contrast the two works.

- Create an infographic in which you compare Odessa Ortiz's personality with that of her virtual identity, Haikumom. Feel free to use quotes from the play and your own observations about the character. Along with your infographic, include a short paragraph in which you hypothesize why these differences exist. The website easel.ly has free infographic templates.

- What is the significance of the water wing in *Water by the Spoonful*? What does the object symbolize and to whom is it important? In small groups, trace the water wing from its first mention in scene 2 to its last appearance in scene 15. Come to a consensus on the importance of the object in preparation for a class discussion.

- Write a paragraph summarizing the final moments between the ghost and Elliot, in scene 14. What is different about this appearance of the ghost as opposed to his earlier interactions with Elliot? What do you think leads to Elliot's feeling haunted?

Freedom

Freedom for Elliot means freedom from the ghost, from the memories of war that haunt him. For Orangutan, freedom is holding on to another person, forming a real relationship. For Chutes&Ladders, freedom means a panic attack on a flight to Japan, the courage to take a blind leap. For Fountainhead, freedom is admitting, not only to himself but also to his family, that he is an addict. In her lecture on musical dissonance, Yazmin describes freedom as liable to dissolve into noise, a philosophy reflected in her choice of a pseudonym on recovertogether.com: Freedom&Noise. Freedom and noise, or dissonance and difficulty, are linked in *Water by the Spoonful*. Characters such as the recovering addicts are able to live free of their addictions only by combating the noise of life: unexpected setbacks, sudden emotional blows, risks, family pressures, and urges that must be ignored at all costs. Elliot pays for his freedom with a steady intake of noise—the unwelcome ghost of an Iraqi civilian asking for his passport back, interrupting his attempts to make a peaceful life for himself after years of war. Even Yazmin, the most stable of the characters, experiences the vertigo of freedom as her husband falls out of love with her, without a fight or another woman to blame.

Freedom for Hudes means freedom to experience everything. Not only the good but also the bad flows freely in the lives of the damaged addicts

The characters strive to find personal connections, including in online chat rooms. (© puhhha / Shutterstock.com)

and the struggling Ortiz family, a privilege of belonging to, as Orangutan dubs it, the world of the living. To be free is not to be safe, protected, or unassailable. Yazmin, in her lecture on free jazz, praises the ability to accept ugliness as a component of freedom as important as beauty. To be free is to stand unfettered in the elements, aware that a battering storm can arise, that the earth can split in two between one's feet, or, with luck, that the day may be pleasant and sunny. This is the challenge that Odessa, Elliot, Yazmin, and the members of recovertogether.com rise to meet each morning. Orangutan writes: "I wake up and I think, What's the world got up its sleeve today? And I look forward to the answer."

STYLE

Monologue

A monologue is a speech given by a single character in a drama. Hamlet's "to be or not to be" speech is a famous example of a monologue. In the musically inspired *Water by the Spoonful*, a monologue provides the audience the opportunity to consider the unique qualities of the character speaking, just as an instrumental solo in music envelopes the listener in the instrument's tone. Yazmin's lecture on John Coltrane in scene 3 is an example of a monologue, giving the audience insight into Yazmin's passion for dissonance, rejection of the status quo, the fierce intelligence that has saved her from a life of poverty, and her natural creative flare. Odessa's monologue in scene 12, as she watches Yazmin and Elliot struggle with her unconscious body, mournfully recounts watching a single unclaimed bag circle the carousel at the airport. A metaphor for her own life, the image provides a rare glimpse into Odessa's emotional struggle as the outcast of the Ortiz family. Though she presents a tough front to Elliot, inside her heart remains broken over the loss of her family. Monologues provide an opportunity for deeper insight into a character's inner thoughts and hidden feelings.

Pseudonym

Pseudonyms are names authors use instead of their given names. In *Water by the Spoonful* the screen names of the members of recovertogether.com act as pseudonyms: Orangutan, Chutes&Ladders, Haikumom, Fountainhead, and Freedom&Noise. A necessity for a group of former crack addicts, the pseudonyms also create second identities for the characters. The most striking of the separations between reality and the virtual world is Haikumom, who acts as a pillar of calm strength online but in person is the fractious and defensive Odessa. Orangutan, the hyperactive young teacher, has gone through not one but three names: her birth name (Yoshiko Sakai), her adoptive name (Madeleine Mays), and her online persona (Orangutan, nicknamed Little Monkey by Chutes&Ladders). Chutes & Ladders, a game in which players can quickly lose progress by the roll of the dice, and *The Fountainhead*, a novel by the objectivist Ayn Rand, reveal the personality traits of the men behind the pseudonyms: cautious Clayton and stubborn John. Likewise, Yazmin's chosen screen name Freedom&Noise exemplifies the traits in music she most admires. Hudes imbues her characters' screen names with dramatic significance, creating multiple identities to inhabit their complex worlds.

HISTORICAL CONTEXT

Veterans of the Iraq War

Elliot served multiple tours of duty in Iraq as a marine before his leg injury allowed him to return to civilian life with an honorable discharge. He works at a Subway franchise across town from his neighborhood so that his friends cannot see him serving sandwiches for a living. He has a lingering limp, for which he is prescribed pain medication, and is haunted by the ghost of an Iraqi civilian. He is representative of the veterans of the Iraq War, many of whom have struggled to return to normal life in the United States after their service. The Wounded Warrior Project, a nonprofit organization for the benefit of military personnel wounded in service after 9/11, has found that most of the soldiers wounded in Iraq and Afghanistan have depression, anxiety, post-traumatic stress disorder, and sleep disorders. More than sixty percent experience body pain that interferes with work, more than sixty percent experience emotional problems that interfere with social activity, and more than sixty percent report being unable to escape traumatic memories of their time

overseas. The Elliot plays, of which *Water by the Spoonful* is the second of three, focus on Elliot's journey toward finding peace from his experiences in war. *Water by the Spoonful* highlights the ways in which veterans are often left on their own to deal with overwhelming emotional, physical, and financial burdens upon returning home.

John Coltrane and Free Jazz

John Coltrane (1926–1967) was a legendary jazz saxophonist who helped shape the avant-garde free jazz genre in the final years of his career. Yazmin adores the music of Coltrane, using his albums *A Love Supreme* (1964) and *Ascension* (1965) to teach her college class about the difference between harmony and dissonance. Hudes uses Coltrane's music to shape *Water by the Spoonful*. For example, the ghost appears before Elliot for the first time when Yazmin switches the record from the harmonious *A Love Supreme* to the discordant and chaotic *Ascension*. As *Ascension* plays, Elliot receives the text from his father informing him of Ginny's death. Each of the three Elliot plays utilizes a genre of music. *Elliot, a Soldier's Fugue* is based on classical, *Water by the Spoonful* on jazz, and *The Happiest Song Plays Last* on Puerto Rican folk music.

The jazz of *Water by the Spoonful* is the challenging, unpredictable, and erratic free jazz invented in part by Ornette Coleman and heard on his album *Free Jazz: A Collective Improvisation* (1961). It was further defined through the works of Cecil Taylor and Coltrane. Richard Brody explains the style in "Coltrane's Free Jazz Wasn't Just 'a Lot of Noise,'" for the *New Yorker*: "Lacking beat, harmony, and tonality, free jazz cuts the main connection to show tunes, dance-hall performances, or even background music to which jazz owed much of whatever popularity it enjoyed." Free jazz holds as its philosophical center the ideal of freedom—a significant concept for African American musicians playing during the height of the civil rights movement of the 1960s. With all the conventional rules of musical composition thrown out, free jazz encourages invention, participation, and emotional reaction. The result is a genre so experimental as to be difficult. As Yazmin summarizes for her class: "It was called Free Jazz but freedom is a hard think to express musically without spinning into noise."

Elliot is an Iraq veteran struggling to settle back into life at home. *(© Alexander Smulskiy / Shutterstock.com)*

CRITICAL OVERVIEW

Water by the Spoonful was awarded the 2012 Pulitzer Prize for Drama. Praised by critics for her rendering of the resilience of the human spirit, Hudes was described in the *New Yorker* as going from success to success, winning the Pulitzer Prize soon after receiving the 2008 Tony Award for Best Musical for *In the Heights*.

Charles Isherwood pays tribute to Hudes's writing style in his review, "An Extended Family, Sharing Extended Pain," for the *New York Times*: "Ms. Hudes writes with such empathy and vibrant humor about people helping one another to face down their demons that regeneration and renewal always seem to be just around the corner."

Richard Zoglin, in a review for *Time* titled "*Water by the Spoonful*: The Acclaimed Play Too Good for Broadway," noted that the play was the first since 2003 to win the Pulitzer Prize without a New York premier. At the time of the judges' decision, *Water by the Spoonful* had been staged only in Hartford, Connecticut. Zoglin admires the ties between the seemingly disparate

Ortiz family and the community of recovertoge-ther.com: "They are all part of the same story: the search for human connection in a harsh and destabilizing world." Robert Hurwitt expands on that theme in his review for *SFGate*:

> The virtual is no less engrossing than the "real"...the ways in which the people within those worlds bicker, undermine and support each other are as compelling as the inevitable intersections and intrusions between them.

In her review for the *Washington Post*, Celia Wren appreciates the numerous characters, settings, and plotlines that come together to form a meaningful whole, calling the play "an intimate yet globe-spanning portrait of recovery, lingering hurt, family bonds, and improbable connections with strangers."

CRITICISM

Amy L. Miller

Miller is a graduate of the University of Cincinnati, and she currently resides in New Orleans,

WHAT DO I READ NEXT?

- Cindy Trumbore's *Parrots over Puerto Rico* (2013), the story of the near extinction and successful rehabilitation of the Puerto Rican parrot, won the Américas Award for Children's and Young Adult Literature. The native parrot population of Puerto Rico is tied intimately to the island's history, beginning before humans settled the island to the present day.

- *Billy Lynn's Long Halftime Walk*, by Ben Fountain (2012), explores the American media response to veterans of the Iraq War as Billy Lynn and the other surviving members of the famous Bravo Squad travel the country on a glitzy Victory Tour at odds with their own painful memories and conflicted emotions. The novel takes place at a single stop on the tour at a surreal Thanksgiving Day football game at Texas Stadium in Dallas.

- *The Happiest Song Plays Last*, by Hudes (2014), is the third and final installment of the Elliot plays. Years after the events of *Water by the Spoonful*, Elliot is living on set in the Middle East for his first major role as an actor. Yazmin fills Ginny's role as neighborhood saint for struggling Puerto Rican American families in Philadelphia. The two cousins communicate via cell phone as they navigate their unexpected new lives, providing support and commentary to remind each other where they came from and where they can go.

- Ishmael Reed's 1972 masterpiece *Mumbo Jumbo* traces the violently contagious Jes Grew (jazz) from its first outbreak in New Orleans through its journey across the country to New York City. Those infected show an inability to stop dancing combined with a hilarious irreverence toward authority. Mixing household names with outrageous original characters, Reed satirizes race relations in the United States in this tribute to dissonance in music, society, politics, and language.

- *Latinos and American Popular Culture* (2013), edited by Patricia M. Montilla, provides a history of the Latino population in the United States with a focus on Latino contributions to American pop culture in literature, stage, screen, music, sports, and politics.

- In *The Night of the Gun* (2008), the investigative journalist David Carr investigates his own life, distrusting his memories and relying instead on interviews, official records, and video to uncover the truth of the darkest hours of his addiction.

- In *The House on Mango Street*, by Sandra Cisneros (1991), Esperanza Cordero comes of age amid the poverty and beauty of a Hispanic neighborhood in Chicago. Like Yazmin's, Esperanza's success in school will provide a way out but not before she is taught to never forget those on Mango Street whom she leaves behind.

- Angie Cruz's *Let It Rain Coffee* (2006) tells the story of the Colón family, immigrants to New York City from the Dominican Republic who face the challenges of adapting to life in America with a mixture of humor, desperation, and resilience.

- In *Beautiful Boy: A Father's Journey through His Son's Addiction*, a memoir by David Sheff (2008), a father watches helplessly as his son succumbs to drug addiction. Sheff explores his own emotional struggle and the changes he observes in his son, Nic, in his path through the depths of addiction toward his first steps in recovery.

- *The Yellow Birds*, by Kevin Powers (2013), follows the lives of two young, American soldiers in Iraq who are desperate to survive in an overwhelming situation. As eighteen-year-old Private Murphy becomes increasingly unhinged by the stress of life under constant threat of death, twenty-one-year-old Private Bartle will do anything to see him safely through the war.

**THE CHARACTERS OF *WATER BY THE
SPOONFUL* SEEK BALANCE, NOT OVERABUNDANCE—A
LIFE WITH A MEANING, A REAL HUMAN CONNECTION,
A MOMENT OF REMEMBRANCE."**

*Louisiana. In the following essay, she explores the
motifs of water and music in Hudes's* Water by the
Spoonful.

Two sets of images run through *Water by the
Spoonful*: the disruptive dissonance of free jazz
and the healing touch of water. Like the two
families of the play, this pair of images—one
kinesthetic, one auditory—may seem dissimilar,
but they are inexorably linked in Hudes's vision
of freedom. One family, recovertogether.com, is
wild, unrelated, and ever growing, their voices
crashing together in a cacophony not unlike that
of free jazz. The other family is as simple by
nature as water itself: the Ortizes, linked by
blood whether they like it or not. Yet within
these two families, as within these two images,
there is significant overlap—in Odessa, in the
dysfunction of the Ortiz family, in the ocean-
spanning reach of love in recovertogether.com.
As Yazmin describes in her lecture on the music
of John Coltrane, dissonance is an expression of
freedom, but freedom does not mean convenience. Likewise, one can lose one's life from
lack of water, as Elliot's baby sister does, or
from too much of it, as Chutes&Ladders learns.
The characters of *Water by the Spoonful* seek
balance, not overabundance—a life with a
meaning, a real human connection, a moment
of remembrance. Along the way, they learn, as
Georgia Rowe writes in her review of the play for
the *San Jose Mercury News*, "that change, forgiveness, and reconciliation are never easy. But
neither are they completely out of reach."

Moments of healing, of progress, are far out-
numbered by moments of uncertainty in the play.
Characters find themselves out on a limb more
often than they stand on solid ground. This is
the risk taken in free jazz, as Richard Brody
explains: "playing without a set harmonic structure...without a foot-tapping beat, and sometimes even without the notion of solos, allowing

musicians to join in or lay out as the spirit moves
them." Nowhere is this style more evident than in
the darkest corner of recovertogether.com, where
the former crack addicts congregate to gripe, to
crow, and to sympathize. Haikumom is there, of
course, to censor their expletives, but this censorship comes after the words have been blurted by
an overexcited Orangutan or eye-rolling Chutes-
&Ladders, minimizing its effect. If anything, Haikumom's regular intoning of "Censored," adds a
beat behind the steady noise of the group as the
discussion rolls on.

Not only the words but also the actions of the
bedraggled forum fulfill the meaning of dissonance. Orangutan is loose in Japan but desperately
wants Chutes&Ladders to travel the fifty-five
hundred miles separating them. Haikumom is as
uninspiring in person as she is motivational online.
Chutes&Ladders roasts Fountainhead for not
having sunk low enough to earn his respect while
clinging to his own self-described boring life like a
drowning man. Charles McNulty writes in his
review of the play for the *Los Angeles Times*:
"The characters...earn our empathy not because
of their spotless goodness but because of their
muddling imperfect humanity." They are a mess
of contradictions, emotions, and terrible decisions,
but they are lovable in that they are trying as hard
as they can to do right.

The Ortiz family also struggles with dissonance. For Elliot, dissonance takes the form of
the ghost—an embodiment of the horrors of war
in the form of an innocent civilian whose story
the audience is left to guess. Dissonance for Elliot
is the mother who failed him, the leg that will not
stop hurting, his troubled relationship with his
pain medication, and a job he is embarrassed to
work. When Yazmin's marriage dissolves, she
discovers the depth of her cousin's pain. Distracted by her own successes, she has forgotten
those she has left behind.

A duet, Elliot and Yazmin's bond sets them
on a collision course with the greatest solo act of
the play. Rowe writes, "As Odessa's story emerges,
the drama acquires a devastating edge, illuminating the ways in which the choices of a moment can
bring lifelong consequences." Odessa, pivotal in
the lives of the Ortiz family and the lives of the
recovertogether.com members, is as difficult to
grasp as Coltrane at his most deconstructed.
Brody writes, "His music is like a whirlwind with
an eye of serenity." This could also describe
Odessa. Her frenetic, knee-jerk rejection of Elliot's

request for money when he appears at the diner booth she shares with Fountainhead comes as a shock compared with the demeanor of her online persona—the calming, matronly Haikumom with her too-cheerful good mornings and firm policy of acceptance. According to the casting notes, Odessa "lives one notch above squalor, and she describes herself to John as a "practitioner of the janitorial arts." It is revealed that she gave birth to Elliot when she was fifteen and that she is responsible for the death of her daughter. She is fit to be no one's role model. But that, Haikumom and Odessa agree, is the point. If, as Wren writes, "the concepts of improvisation, soloing, and, most important, dissonance…manifest themselves in the lives of the characters as well as in the shape of the script," then the song swells as Elliot tells the story of Odessa's failure to feed her children their teaspoons of water while she sits across from him, interjecting only to agree. A denial would be preferable, a fight, a challenge, but Odessa is helpless in her absolute guilt: "A teaspoon," she says, and later, "I left."

Odessa links the dissonance of absolute freedom to the intimacy of water. Where there is water in the play, healing can begin. Hurwitt writes, "Water flows seductively throughout—from silvery spoonfuls to rivers, oceans, a rain forest waterfall and a cathartic bath—as a unifying and abidingly resonant metaphor." Chutes&Ladders's near drowning leads to his first day in recovery, and the ocean separating him from Orangutan is crossed with the help of Haikumom's playful gift of a water wing. Odessa drops spoonfuls of water in memoriam onto the empty floor of her home in an act of mourning her lost children. Yazmin and Elliot solidify their bond by jointly throwing Ginny's ashes over the rushing waterfall. Fountainhead faces his own addiction as he slowly bathes Odessa with growing appreciation of the act of caring for a stranger. In all but one of these instances, water is associated with a partnership—a person to lean on in case of troubles, a person on whom to depend.

Water touches each character, and each character is touched by the care of another character. Thus the healing effect spreads through genuine, human contact with the imagery of water as a simple backdrop. Elliot describes the association he made as a child: "Five minutes. Spoon. Five minutes. Spoon. I remember thinking, Wow, this is it. Family time. Quality time. Just the three of us." In the single instance in which water truly is the line between life and death, Odessa's daughter dies

of dehydration, and of abandonment—no contact when contact is needed most. In the absence of the mother, tragedy occurs. The infant's fate could be the fate of Chutes&Ladders or Orangutan, alone and far from home. Odessa would have died too, after her night alone on the floor spilling water, had Yazmin and Elliot not appeared in time to save her, as Chutes&Ladders's lifeguard did for him.

McNulty writes, "Hudes corrals harsh voices and brutal stories into a magnificent whole that is beautiful not because it is lovely but because it is brokenheartedly tender and true." The flawed but resilient characters know better than to expect a miracle, but each pair—Odessa and Fountainhead, Elliot and Yazmin, Chutes&Ladders and Orangutan—make substantial progress toward a more meaningful future. For Odessa, a new dawn breaks, the count of days sober resets, but she now has a friend to help her recover not only her health but also her identity as Odessa Ortiz. Chutes&Ladders and Orangutan begin a relationship in the land of the living. As Yazmin and Elliot give each other permission to pursue their dreams, Yazmin heads back to the neighborhood from which she escaped on academic wings, and Elliot goes to Hollywood to flaunt his perfectly white teeth rather than hide behind a sandwich counter.

By reaching out to one another, the characters help themselves. This is one of the late Mami Ginny's greatest lessons for the world-weary, trampled, and unloved who wash up onto her doorstep. Elliot describes her motherly advice: "Every morning when I left for school, 'Elliot, nobody can make you invisible but you.'" The characters act in their moments of personal crisis to save themselves from disappearing: Orangutan does not step foot on the train that may take her directly to relapse, Chutes&Ladders sells the car he hates to buy a plane ticket he is both determined and terrified to use, and Odessa lists Fountainhead as her emergency contact, saving them both from almost certain doom. Yazmin and Elliot, in gratitude for Ginny's gifts, right the wrongs in their own lives. Above the loud cacophony of a waterfall, they set free the spirit of the Ortiz family.

Source: Amy L. Miller, Critical Essay on *Water by the Spoonful*, in *Drama for Students*, Gale, Cengage Learning, 2016.

Sarah Genton
In the following essay, Genton explains how Water by the Spoonful *is used to reach out to troubled veterans.*

"You train for your job and you do your best to stay alive and keep your brothers alive so you can all go home."—U.S. Marine Elliot Ruiz, the wounded veteran who inspired the play.

By helping stage the Armenian-language premiere in October of the 2012 Pulitzer Prize–winning drama *Water by the Spoonful*, a play about the struggle of an Iraq war veteran to adapt to civilian life, the U.S. Embassy in Yerevan touched on a raw nerve among Armenian audiences. The societal impact of their nation's conflict with Azerbaijan, especially on young men who return from military service with physical and psychological scars, is a live but taboo issue.

More than 20 years after Armenia and Azerbaijan agreed to a cease fire in the Nagorno-Karabakh conflict, tension and occasional border clashes persist. To help promote reconciliation through the arts, the embassy sought the assistance of the American actor who held the lead role in the play's U.S. premiere and the former U.S. Marine on whom the play is based. Embassy Yerevan's public affairs section (PAS) used the play to connect with the public and military recruits, officers and representatives from the Ministry of Defense (MOD).

The performances and events associated with the play generated what some participants called the first public discussion in Armenia of the challenges veterans face and the toll Nagorno-Karabakh has taken on soldiers and their families and friends. The play also helped move Armenian society closer to a clear assessment of the conflict's costs and, hopefully, closer to peace with Azerbaijan.

The play's performances were staged during the HighFest international arts festival, raised issues not generally addressed in Armenia and highlighted problems of post war trauma and disability. As part of the outreach, PAS also leveraged the presence and participation of its two special guests: Armando Riesco, the actor who held the lead role during the U.S. premiere, and U.S. Marine Elliot Ruiz, the wounded veteran who inspired the play. Both engaged with new audiences, including young military recruits, Armenian veterans and policy/planning contacts within the MOD. The performances and collateral programs were viewed as a great success by national media. Certainly, *Water by the Spoonful* brought the best of contemporary American theater to Armenia and helped the embassy broach a sensitive topic among Armenian society: the sense of abandonment felt by Nagorno-Karabakh war vets. To this end, PAS convened a roundtable discussion involving Ruiz, Nagorno-Karabakh veterans, MOD representatives and civil society leaders. Ruiz discussed his combat service, experiences reintegrating into "normal life" as a disabled veteran and the support veterans now receive from the U.S. Department of Defense. The roundtable may have been the first time such disparate segments of Armenian society jointly discussed Armenian veterans' struggles. "We say it's not a problem, but that's not true," observed the nation's former Human Rights Ombudsman, Larissa Alaverdyan.

A leader of the nation's military, Major General Arkady Ter-Tadevosyan, used the roundtable event to note parallels between the plight of American veterans after the Vietnam War and Armenian veterans of NagornoKarabakh, citing what he termed the lack of appreciation demonstrated for veterans' sacrifices.

"War scars people," observed General Ter-Tadevosyan. "Imagine if veterans from a rich, powerful nation like the U.S. have reintegration problems. What can we expect of poor Armenian veterans?"

Following the discussion, MOD representatives asked PAS to cooperate on training for the MOD's Staff College and on re-entry programs for soldiers coming out of combat. The projects, now in their early stages, are likely to influence defense policy and civil society.

On Oct. 3, Ruiz spoke with hundreds of cadets at the Central Military Institute, the Military Aviation Institute and the Military College, which sends its students to both defense institutes. There, he detailed his combat experiences, noting that he enlisted in the Marine Corps at 17, forging his parents' signatures on the enlistment documents, and was sent to Iraq six months into his service—the youngest Marine in his division. The war ended for him in April 2004 when an Iraqi insurgent drove a car through barbed wire at a checkpoint, tearing apart Ruiz's leg.

At each presentation, attendees asked Ruiz to describe his feelings about combat. He stressed that he and his fellow Marines saw combat as a job and experienced a range of emotions. "You train for your job and you do your best to stay alive and keep your brothers alive so you can all go home," he said.

He also noted that a range of re-entry programs helps American combat veterans ease into civilian life. Cadets also asked about the training and preparation of Marines, and pressed him for his views on political topics, such as the current state of American engagement in Iraq. Ruiz used these questions to highlight the apolitical nature of the American military and the fact that the country's service members are all volunteers, a stark contrast with Armenia's mandatory conscription.

Before *Water by the Spoonful* debuted, the cast and crew visited the Marine House at the embassy to talk with our Marines about their experiences in combat and those of their friends. These candid discussions, in which the Marines spoke about the unique ethos of the Marine Corps and the impact of combat on service members and their families, deeply influenced how the actors approached their roles.

Thanks to the work of International Information Programs (IIP) Officer Mike Bandler, actor Armando Riesco was recruited to advise the play's Armenian director and cast. He did so via Skype during the play's initial readings and rehearsals, and then came to Armenia a week before the premiere to finalize the production. Riesco ensured that the play's themes—including drug addiction, disability and Post-Traumatic Stress Disorder, issues rarely discussed or acknowledged in Armenia—shone on the stage; he conducted master classes with actors and students, working with them on their technique and advising them on staging new material.

Coming just two months after the worst violence in the Nagorno-Karabakh conflict in 20 years, the *Water by the Spoonful* program used cultural diplomacy to spark Armenian discussion of how the conflict affects veterans, young soldiers and Armenian society. That, in turn, advanced the mission's objective of encouraging Armenia to take meaningful steps toward reconciliation with Azerbaijan.

The program also led to collaboration between the embassy and MOD to help soldiers reintegrate into civilian life and engaged young military officers (a new PAS audience) in a no-holds-barred conversation about combat's psychological impact.

Source: Sarah Genton, "Veterans Benefit: Play Promotes Healing in Yerevan," in *State*, Vol. 596, January 2015, p. 12.

Marilyn Stasio

In the following review, Stasio asserts that the play "doesn't fully achieve its lofty aspirations."

Although it doesn't fully achieve its lofty aspirations, Quiara Alegria Hudes' 2012 Pulitzer Prize–winning drama *Water by the Spoonful* makes an urgent plea for the human connections that people need to survive in a soulless age of alienation. An extension of the dramatic arc begun in *Elliot: A Soldier's Fugue* (itself a Pulitzer finalist), the play follows the efforts of a wounded vet to return to his old life, and so long as he stays in focus, the play is strong. What gets out of hand are the secondary life stories that, while not unworthy, elbow Elliot off center stage.

Armando Riesco originated the role of Elliot in *A Soldier's Fugue*, then played him again in the original production of *Water by the Spoonful* at Hartford Stage, and as far as this reviewer is concerned, this powerfully committed actor can play him until hell freezes over, because the performance he gives is that intense.

Elliot is doing a drug or two, haunted as he is by the ghosts he brought back with him from Iraq. But his efforts to keep his head together are blown when the beloved aunt who raised him dies. His sympathetic cousin Yaz (Zabryna Guevara, quite nice) is supportive, and there's much tenderness and warmth in the scenes between the cousins.

The person Elliot can't bring himself to face when he returns to his Puerto Rican family in Philadelphia is his mother, Odessa (Liza Colon-Zayas), whose appalling mistreatment of her children when she was a young crack addict seems to have made a psychic cripple of Elliot. Hudes has taken great care with her portrait of this unhappy woman, and Colon-Zayas obliges with a most understanding performance.

The character of Odessa is the linchpin that keeps—or almost keeps—the play's split-focus structure from flying apart. Using the tag of "Haikumom," Odessa established and maintains an Internet chatroom for recovering crack cocaine addicts like herself.

The website exists only in cyberspace, but that doesn't stop Neil Patel (set) and Aaron Rhyne (projections) from designing a gorgeous visual home page for it. Four participants in this sorry collection of misfits keep to their isolated spaces and never speak to one another directly, but the crazy-quilt of colorful icons that pulse and glow on the back wall gives an indication of how many other lost souls are attracted to the site.

The ones Hudes has chosen to represent are all, to some degree, interesting, and all are well-cast by helmer Davis McCallum, who has also done a fine job of respecting their integrity as individual characters.

Bill Heck makes a sad case of Fountainhead, the Philadelphia blueblood who has lost everything, including his pride, to drugs. Sue Jean Kim brings a great deal of invention to Orangutan, a young and adorably manic Japanese-American girl trying to find the courage to look up her birth parents in Tokyo. Broadway veteran Frankie Faison illuminates the sweet soul of Chutes and Ladders, a middle-aged desk jockey who befriends the flaky Orangutan.

While their stories are interesting, these character sketches aren't exactly polished portrait studies. More to the point, they have no connection to Elliot, except through Odessa.

As representatives of the vast world of lost and lonely souls who haunt the chatrooms, Odessa's online friends certainly fit into Hudes' dramatic themes of social isolation and the need for compassionate human connections. But the playwright's disinterest in establishing one last, deep connection—by integrating their life stories with the larger drama of Elliot and his mother—keeps her play from really knocking us out.

Source: Marilyn Stasio, Review of *Water by the Spoonful*, in *Variety*, Vol. 429, No. 9, January 14, 2013, p. 24.

Erik Haagensen

In the following review, Haagensen describes the play's characters as "predictable" but admits the emotional impact of the story.

It will be quite a while before I forget the image of Liza Colon-Zayas as Odessa Ortiz, broken and alone, sitting on the floor of her threadbare Philadelphia home while ladling spoonfuls of water into empty air. At that moment, Quiara Alegria Hudes' *Water by the Spoonful* has all the power expected of a Pulitzer Prize–winning drama. Nevertheless, for much of its duration, this uncontestably warm and generous play is hampered by conventional plotting and engaging but predictable characters.

Act 1 alternates between the story of an Internet chat room for recovering crack addicts that's moderated by the 39-year-old Odessa and the tale of 31-year-old Swarthmore College music professor Yaz and her cousin, wounded Iraq War vet Elliot, who are dealing with the offstage death of their Aunt Ginny, Elliot's saintly surrogate mother. The narratives intersect with the revelation at the Act 1 curtain that Odessa is Elliot's real mother, something that doesn't come as any surprise (and I'm not sure it's meant to). In Act 2 the characters interact and affect each other's lives. Everyone is struggling with a problem, secrets are being kept, and Hudes goes about dealing with all of them open heartedly if tidily.

The denizens of www.recovertogether.com number four. In addition to Odessa, there's 20-something Madeline, Japanese by birth but raised by a white family in Maine; 50ish Clayton, a low-level African-American IRS pencil pusher; and a newcomer, Philadelphia Main Liner John, a highly paid computer programmer and entrepreneur with a young family.

Director Davis McCallum is faced with the uninviting challenge of staging large stretches of Internet conversation and he does what he can to make the exchanges active. There's no typing going on, and we are not subjected to reams of subtitles. Instead, characters simply speak out to the audience, and McCallum even lets them invade one another's space while avoiding eye contact. It helps, but the scenes go on too long, and the lack of subtext (which barely exists on the Web) is a hindrance, flattening the drama.

The show's standout performance comes from Colon-Zayas. Her Odessa is a study in opposites, convincingly magnetic, empathetic, and driven when running her website, then just as palpably unsure, defensive, and self-loathing when roiled by family dynamics. Frankie Faison is a bright but wary Clayton, Sue Jean Kim both bubbles and spits as the hyper Madeline, and Bill Heck infects John's self-congratulatory masculinity with a nasty toxicity, but none of these three skilled actors can quite erase the stereotype that underlies the role.

Zabryna Guevara's Yaz is charmingly earnest as she questions her privilege and relevance, then moving in a sudden epiphany about the need to forgive. Armando Riesco leavens Elliot's anger with a rough grace and flashing intelligence, though his diction is at times indistinct. Ryan Shams plays three small roles effectively, especially the ghost of a young Iraqi.

Spoonful is an admirable attempt to deal with important issues of addiction, repentance,

> I HAVE COME TO TERMS WITH THE FACT
> THAT I WRITE DRAMAS. I WISH I COULD WRITE
> COMEDIES. DEAR GOD! I PLAY THIS GAME WITH
> MYSELF. I'M LIKE: DEAR GOD, HOW DARK CAN IT GET."

and redemption. But I must confess to thinking there were stronger candidates for that Pulitzer.

Source: Erik Haagensen, Review of *Water by the Spoonful*, in *Back Stage*, Vol. 54, No. 2, January 10, 2013, p. 61.

Marcus Gardley and Quiara Alegria Hudes

In the following interview, Hudes discusses her writing process.

Quiara Alegria Hudes writes from the music in her bones. Her work, which delves deeply into notions about family ties, war, love, joy, and despair are all exemplary excavations into the mind of a poet-musician-playwright whose craftsmanship is as profound as her skill for lyricism and whose passion for writing is as infectious as her radiant laughter. For her, writing is as sacred and serious as surgery. She talks about her process with as much clarity as she talks about her product, and one can't help but feel like they are in the presence of a wise teacher and an old friend. Yet it is her love for music that shapes most of her work. She is a musician with a pen.

I sat down with Hudes over brunch in Harlem on a sunny Wednesday afternoon, weeks after she won the prestigious Pulitzer Prize for Drama for her searing, deeply moving play *Water By the Spoonful*. The second part of a familial trilogy, *Water by the Spoonful*, details the life of an Iraq war veteran named Eliot who is struggling with life back home, and the parallel story of four people who connect via an online chatroom for recovering drug addicts. I saw the play at Hartford Stage where it premiered in October of last year and I was so floored by it that I could not get out of my seat long after the actors took their bows and the audience exited the theater. I was exhilarated by how innovative the play was and by how human, fragile, and yet fearless the characters were. I wanted to pick Hudes's brain at brunch. I wanted

to know what her secrets were, how she arrived at such a revelation at the end, and what drives her as a writer. The following are excerpts from that conversation.

MARCUS GARDLEY (RAIL): What was the first play you ever wrote, your first production?

QUIARA ALEGRIA HUDES: My first play was called *My Best Friend Died*. I just wrote it. I didn't even know that I didn't know how to write a play. I wrote it and it was a play. I was writing plays, poems a lot. It was produced in 8th grade and it was about my best friend dying.

RAIL: *What did it feel like for the first time, when you heard your play read aloud? How did that make you feel?*

HUDES: I felt like a genius. [Laughter] Because you're sitting down, and they are saying things much better than you thought possible. And you're thinking: I had no idea what I wrote down was so good. You know, there is chatter about how the Pulitzer committee read the play and didn't see it, and that was a bit controversial, but the cool thing about being a playwright is that you get to be a chameleon. And a play exists in two ways, it exists as a piece of writing and as a performance. And both are valid.

RAIL: *So when did you realize that you were a writer and that you wanted to write plays?*

HUDES: I don't ever remember not writing one thing or another. I wrote as a hobby at first. And then I guess it became a sort of therapy, I wrote to deal with things like loneliness. Then there was a time as an undergrad that I stopped writing—text, that is. Instead I was writing music (scores and lyrics), and I realized that I was missing something. Something was not clicking into place. Then one day my mother said, "Quiara, you miss writing. You wrote every day of your life." I was not self-conscious about it is the thing. It just came natural. It was just something that I did.

RAIL: *Yes, that's fascinating. I find that writing or the profession of being a writer (for many writers) it is something that chooses you. I don't ever remember growing up thinking, "Oh, I'm going to be a writer." It fell in my lap, much like stories do. And speaking of stories that fall into one's lap, how did your play* Water By the Spoonful *come to be? Did you set out knowing that you were going to write a trilogy?*

HUDES: No, not at all. I wrote the first play, *Eliot: A Soldier's Fugue*. Then I wrote *In the*

Heights, followed by *26 Miles*. After writing the last two, the work that felt the most original and exciting to me to write was Eliot. I wanted to live in that writing world a little more. I had a good time writing that piece. It was different. I thought, "I'm the only writer who could have written that." What I found out was that I couldn't go back, couldn't retrace my footsteps. I wanted to do something new. So how do you do that? You can't retread, you must move forward. So I thought about working with music in the same way but using a different type of music so that I would be experiencing the same type of process writing-wise but would be moving forward with a new play. And so I thought about jazz. At the same time my cousin Eliot had some pretty incredible stuff happening in his life. And I thought I wanted to continue with this story and use jazz as a musical background. He has a really neat story. Some of it was too good to be true and at that point I knew I wanted it to be a trilogy and I wanted to use three different musical worlds to place each play in. For Eliot I used western music, which is Bach; and for *Water by the Spoonful* I used jazz; so for the third, which is called *The Happiest Song Plays Last*, I am using global music, which for me is folk music. Puerto Rican folk music and in this case jibaro and guitar and voice.

RAIL: *Does music come naturally to you?*

HUDES: Yes, it does. My first thought is always what kind of music am I going to have in this play. And I base the world, the language of the play, on that type of music. I definitely wanted *Water by the Spoonful* to feel like the language was thick and gnarly because I feel like people online use language that is most surprising. And jazz is surprising; there is improvisation. I feel like the language in *The Happiest Song Plays Last* is definitely straightforward and conversational. And the folk music is akin in that way. It is honest, heartfelt. You know when I studied music at Yale—my instrument is piano—if I was writing something for a string quartet or a jazz band, I know what that feels like, but I don't know how it affects people until I am in the room with them and can feel their heat. It's the same with a play—music and plays operate the same. You don't know what you have until you're playing it before an audience.

RAIL: *It is clear that you think a lot about your plays before you sit down to write. You think about the music of the world, about the set or basic imagery. Do you even start with an outline?*

HUDES: No, never. I end up spending too much money on journals if I write too much about the play beforehand. And I tend to get rid of a journal if there is a page inside that I don't like. So I write on legal pads. My dad made me a writing desk—he is a carpenter. I keep my desk clean. I walk around my room, I pace a lot—that's my process. I only know just enough to get me started, and then I write. I don't know where it's going until I write the first few scenes. After that, I can sit down and write the play. When I wrote *Water by the Spoonful*, I knew that it was going to be about recovery, and that it was going to be about an online chat room and the real world and the online world. I knew it was going to be big and messy. I knew I wanted to have characters from different ethnicities. I knew who some of the characters were but not all. I had no idea that they were going to be throwing ashes at the end. I had no idea that there was going to be a love story between the characters Orangutan and Chutes & Ladders. That was the best. I was so happy because I never wrote a love story, and that was so much fun to write—to watch them fall in love, then lose each other and fight about losing one another. If I write and I start to cry that usually is a good sign. I always have my cup of coffee, my little totem items that are around my desk—and of course music. I always have my music.

RAIL: *What about characters? How much do you think about them beforehand?*

HUDES: It depends; every play is different. For *Water by the Spoonful*, I wrote all these characters from different backgrounds: An African-American, an Asian-American, a Latino, and a white guy—it was thrilling. I never felt more at home than writing this group of people. And I realized again, that I have to do that for *The Happiest Song Plays Last*. I knew I wanted to write from within the Latino community but also outside of it. And so like *Water by the Spoonful*, there are two worlds in this play. There is the world where Eliot is filming his movie, and then there is the world of North Philly. I have come to terms with the fact that I write dramas. I wish I could write comedies. Dear God! I play this game with myself. I'm like: Dear God, how dark can it get. And you know I get sad and miserable, but *The Happiest Song* is a little bit about joy. And the Puerto Rican folk music is a lot about joy. And there is a lot of joy in *The Happiest Song* even though it is quite dark. It was fun to be writing about joy.

RAIL: *It's just a joy to be writing. I remember we talked about that last summer at the O'Neill. Do you think you have to love the art of writing, the every day practice of it? Or would you say it's different for you, perhaps you have a love/hate relationship to writing*

HUDES: No, not at all. I love it. You have to. When I talk to young writers they always want to know how do you make it, how do you know if you are good enough, or how do you become a writer. And I'm like, figure out some way that you can live spending your life writing. And after two years you will know. If you don't like waking up every day and writing, you will know. Writing is an incredible way to spend your day, and if you don't love it, it's not for you. You get to think so much. That's such a pleasure.

RAIL: *And what are you working on now? I know you have two books that are being published by TCG, which is exciting. Do you have a new play that you are writing?*

HUDES: I do. It's called *Daphne's Dive*. And this piece has a live musician. There is a live pianist. I really wanted that. In some ways, I am spoiling myself. I wrote it into the structure of the play. The piano sound comes from a neighbor who is practicing piano at his window. *Daphne's Dive* is the first play that I've written where there is a unit set. It takes place all in one location. It's just the bar. You create a stage with a bar. I wanted to write a play where the set is a character. And music is alive in the world. It is as present as any character. Before music was a part of the background, now it's on stage.

Source: Marcus Gardley and Quiara Alegria Hudes, "Music Is Her Muse: Quiara Alegria Hudes and Her Path to the Pulitzer," in *Brooklyn Rail*, July/August 2012, p. 109.

SOURCES

"Also Notable: *Water by the Spoonful*," in *New Yorker*, http://www.newyorker.com/goings-on-about-town/the-atre/water-by-the-spoonful-2 (accessed June 29, 2015).

"Alumni Survey 2014," Wounded Warrior Project website, http://www.woundedwarriorproject.org/mission/what-our-alumni-say.aspx (accessed July 10, 2015).

"Bio," Quiara Alegría Hudes website, http://www.quiara.com/quiara.com/Bio.html (accessed July 10, 2015).

Brody, Richard, "Coltrane's Free Jazz Wasn't Just 'a Lot of Noise,'" in *New Yorker*, November 10, 2014, http://www.newyorker.com/culture/richard-brody/coltranes-free-jazz-awesome (accessed July 10, 2015).

Haagensen, Erik, "*Water by the Spoonful* is Warm and Generous but Unsurprising," in *BackStage*, January 8, 2013, http://www.backstage.com/review/ny-theater/off-broadway/water-by-the-spoonful-quiara-alegria-hudes-second-stage-theatre-pulitzer-prize/ (accessed June 29, 2015).

Hudes, Quiara Alegría, *Water by the Spoonful*, Theatre Communications Group, 2012.

Hurwitt, Robert, "*Water by the Spoonful* Review: Stories of Real, Online Families," in *SFGate*, August 25, 2014, http://www.sfgate.com/performance/article/A-compelling-Water-by-the-Spoonful-5710776.php (accessed June 29, 2015).

Isherwood, Charles, "An Extended Family, Sharing Extended Pain," in *New York Times*, January 8, 2013, http://www.nytimes.com/2013/01/09/theater/reviews/water-by-the-spoonful-at-the-second-stage-theater.html (accessed June 29, 2015).

Knight, Brian L., "Calculated Dissonance: Avant-Garde Jazz in the 1960s–1970s (Part One)," in *Vermont Review*, http://vermontreview.tripod.com/essays/calculated1.htm (accessed July 10, 2015).

McNulty, Charles, "Review: Bandaging Life's Battle Scars in *Water by the Spoonful*," in *Los Angeles Times*, April 29, 2014, http://www.latimes.com/entertainment/la-et-cm-water-by-the-spoonful-review-20140429-story.html (accessed June 29, 2015).

"Quiara Alegría Hudes," in *NewDramatists.org*, http://newdramatists.org/quiara-alegr%C3%AD-hudes (accessed July 10, 2015).

Rowe, Georgia, "Review: *Water by the Spoonful* Powerful Look at Family in Crisis," in *San Jose Mercury News*, August 25, 2014, http://www.mercurynews.com/entertainment/ci_26402466/review-water-by-spoonful-powerful-look-at-family (accessed June 29, 2015).

Wren, Celia, "Family Bonds, Music Play Together in Quiara Alegria Hudes's *Water by the Spoonful*," in *Washington Post*, February 28, 2014, http://www.washingtonpost.com/entertainment/theater_dance/family-bonds-music-play-together-in-quiara-alegria-hudess-water-by-the-spoonful/2014/02/27/941f00de-9b38-11e3-8112-52fdf646027b_story.html (accessed July 10, 2015).

Zoglin, Richard, "*Water by the Spoonful*: The Acclaimed Play Too Good for Broadway," in *Time*, January 24, 2013, http://entertainment.time.com/2013/01/24/water-by-the-spoonful-the-acclaimed-play-too-good-for-broadway/ (accessed June 29, 2015).

FURTHER READING

Casiano, Catherine, and Elizabeth C. Ramirez, *La Voz Latina: Contemporary Plays and Performance Pieces by Latinas*, University of Illinois Press, 2011.

La Voz Latina collects plays and performance pieces written by Latinas since the 1980s, including works by Diane Rodriguez, Evelina Fernández, Carmen Peláez, Migdalia Cruz, and many others.

Hudes, Quiara Alegría, *Elliot, a Soldier's Fugue*, Theatre Communications Group, 2012.

In the first of Hudes's trilogy of plays about Elliot Ortiz, the nineteen-year-old Elliot prepares for his redeployment to Iraq. The history of the Ortiz family's involvement in Iraq, Korea, and Vietnam is delineated in emotionally evocative scenes tying a history of war abroad with the Philadelphia neighborhood that the Ortiz family calls home.

Klay, Phil, *Redeployment*, Penguin Books, 2012.

The 2014 National Book Award Winner, *Redeployment*, explores the life of American soldiers in Iraq and Afghanistan through a collection of twelve short stories ranging from the surrealism of a corporal caught in military bureaucracy through a chaplain's test of faith to a soldier'sz struggles adapting to life back home.

Lawford, Christopher Kennedy, *Moments of Clarity: Voices from the Front Lines of Addiction and Recovery*, William Morrow, 2009.

In *Moments of Clarity*, Lawford compiles first-hand accounts of a range of celebrities whose battles overcoming their addiction began with a single epiphany. Alec Baldwin, Tom Arnold, Martin Sheen, Jamie Lee Curtis, Anthony Hopkins, and many more share their stories.

SUGGESTED SEARCH TERMS

Water by the Spoonful

Water by the Spoonful AND drama

Water by the Spoonful AND Quiara Alegría Hudes

Water by the Spoonful AND Pulitzer Prize for Drama

Pulitzer Prize for Drama AND 2012

Hudes AND Pulitzer Prize

Water by the Spoonful AND Elliot Ortiz

Water by the Spoonful AND Haikumom

Water by the Spoonful AND Hartford Stage

Water by the Spoonful AND addiction

Glossary of Literary Terms

A

Abstract: Used as a noun, the term refers to a short summary or outline of a longer work. As an adjective applied to writing or literary works, abstract refers to words or phrases that name things not knowable through the five senses. Examples of abstracts include the *Cliffs Notes* summaries of major literary works. Examples of abstract terms or concepts include "idea," "guilt" "honesty," and "loyalty."

Absurd, Theater of the: See *Theater of the Absurd*

Absurdism: See *Theater of the Absurd*

Act: A major section of a play. Acts are divided into varying numbers of shorter scenes. From ancient times to the nineteenth century plays were generally constructed of five acts, but modern works typically consist of one, two, or three acts. Examples of five-act plays include the works of Sophocles and Shakespeare, while the plays of Arthur Miller commonly have a three-act structure.

Acto: A one-act Chicano theater piece developed out of collective improvisation. *Actos* were performed by members of Luis Valdez's Teatro Campesino in California during the mid-1960s.

Aestheticism: A literary and artistic movement of the nineteenth century. Followers of the movement believed that art should not be mixed with social, political, or moral teaching.

The statement "art for art's sake" is a good summary of aestheticism. The movement had its roots in France, but it gained widespread importance in England in the last half of the nineteenth century, where it helped change the Victorian practice of including moral lessons in literature. Oscar Wilde is one of the best-known "aesthetes" of the late nineteenth century.

Age of Johnson: The period in English literature between 1750 and 1798, named after the most prominent literary figure of the age, Samuel Johnson. Works written during this time are noted for their emphasis on "sensibility," or emotional quality. These works formed a transition between the rational works of the Age of Reason, or Neoclassical period, and the emphasis on individual feelings and responses of the Romantic period. Significant writers during the Age of Johnson included the novelists Ann Radcliffe and Henry Mackenzie, dramatists Richard Sheridan and Oliver Goldsmith, and poets William Collins and Thomas Gray. Also known as Age of Sensibility

Age of Reason: See *Neoclassicism*

Age of Sensibility: See *Age of Johnson*

Alexandrine Meter: See *Meter*

Allegory: A narrative technique in which characters representing things or abstract ideas are used to convey a message or teach a lesson.

Allegory is typically used to teach moral, ethical, or religious lessons but is sometimes used for satiric or political purposes. Examples of allegorical works include Edmund Spenser's *The Faerie Queene* and John Bunyan's *The Pilgrim's Progress.*

Allusion: A reference to a familiar literary or historical person or event, used to make an idea more easily understood. For example, describing someone as a "Romeo" makes an allusion to William Shakespeare's famous young lover in *Romeo and Juliet.*

Amerind Literature: The writing and oral traditions of Native Americans. Native American literature was originally passed on by word of mouth, so it consisted largely of stories and events that were easily memorized. Amerind prose is often rhythmic like poetry because it was recited to the beat of a ceremonial drum. Examples of Amerind literature include the autobiographical *Black Elk Speaks,* the works of N. Scott Momaday, James Welch, and Craig Lee Strete, and the poetry of Luci Tapahonso.

Analogy: A comparison of two things made to explain something unfamiliar through its similarities to something familiar, or to prove one point based on the acceptedness of another. Similes and metaphors are types of analogies. Analogies often take the form of an extended simile, as in William Blake's aphorism: "As the caterpillar chooses the fairest leaves to lay her eggs on, so the priest lays his curse on the fairest joys."

Angry Young Men: A group of British writers of the 1950s whose work expressed bitterness and disillusionment with society. Common to their work is an anti-hero who rebels against a corrupt social order and strives for personal integrity. The term has been used to describe Kingsley Amis, John Osborne, Colin Wilson, John Wain, and others.

Antagonist: The major character in a narrative or drama who works against the hero or protagonist. An example of an evil antagonist is Richard Lovelace in Samuel Richardson's *Clarissa,* while a virtuous antagonist is Macduff in William Shakespeare's *Macbeth.*

Anthropomorphism: The presentation of animals or objects in human shape or with human characteristics. The term is derived from the Greek word for "human form." The fables of Aesop, the animated films of Walt Disney, and Richard Adams's *Watership Down* feature anthropomorphic characters.

Anti-hero: A central character in a work of literature who lacks traditional heroic qualities such as courage, physical prowess, and fortitude. Anti-heros typically distrust conventional values and are unable to commit themselves to any ideals. They generally feel helpless in a world over which they have no control. Anti-heroes usually accept, and often celebrate, their positions as social outcasts. A well-known anti-hero is Yossarian in Joseph Heller's novel *Catch-22.*

Antimasque: See *Masque*

Antithesis: The antithesis of something is its direct opposite. In literature, the use of antithesis as a figure of speech results in two statements that show a contrast through the balancing of two opposite ideas. Technically, it is the second portion of the statement that is defined as the "antithesis"; the first portion is the "thesis." An example of antithesis is found in the following portion of Abraham Lincoln's "Gettysburg Address"; notice the opposition between the verbs "remember" and "forget" and the phrases "what we say" and "what they did": "The world will little note nor long remember what we say here, but it can never forget what they did here."

Apocrypha: Writings tentatively attributed to an author but not proven or universally accepted to be their works. The term was originally applied to certain books of the Bible that were not considered inspired and so were not included in the "sacred canon." Geoffrey Chaucer, William Shakespeare, Thomas Kyd, Thomas Middleton, and John Marston all have apocrypha. Apocryphal books of the Bible include the Old Testament's Book of Enoch and New Testament's Gospel of Peter.

Apollonian and Dionysian: The two impulses believed to guide authors of dramatic tragedy. The Apollonian impulse is named after Apollo, the Greek god of light and beauty and the symbol of intellectual order. The Dionysian impulse is named after Dionysus, the Greek god of wine and the symbol of the unrestrained forces of nature. The Apollonian impulse is to create a rational, harmonious world, while the Dionysian is to express the irrational forces of personality.

Friedrich Nietzche uses these terms in *The Birth of Tragedy* to designate contrasting elements in Greek tragedy.

Apostrophe: A statement, question, or request addressed to an inanimate object or concept or to a nonexistent or absent person. Requests for inspiration from the muses in poetry are examples of apostrophe, as is Marc Antony's address to Caesar's corpse in William Shakespeare's *Julius Caesar*: "O, pardon me, thou bleeding piece of earth, That I am meek and gentle with these butchers!...Woe to the hand that shed this costly blood!..."

Archetype: The word archetype is commonly used to describe an original pattern or model from which all other things of the same kind are made. This term was introduced to literary criticism from the psychology of Carl Jung. It expresses Jung's theory that behind every person's "unconscious," or repressed memories of the past, lies the "collective unconscious" of the human race: memories of the countless typical experiences of our ancestors. These memories are said to prompt illogical associations that trigger powerful emotions in the reader. Often, the emotional process is primitive, even primordial. Archetypes are the literary images that grow out of the "collective unconscious." They appear in literature as incidents and plots that repeat basic patterns of life. They may also appear as stereotyped characters. Examples of literary archetypes include themes such as birth and death and characters such as the Earth Mother.

Argument: The argument of a work is the author's subject matter or principal idea. Examples of defined "argument" portions of works include John Milton's *Arguments* to each of the books of *Paradise Lost* and the "Argument" to Robert Herrick's *Hesperides*.

Aristotelian Criticism: Specifically, the method of evaluating and analyzing tragedy formulated by the Greek philosopher Aristotle in his *Poetics*. More generally, the term indicates any form of criticism that follows Aristotle's views. Aristotelian criticism focuses on the form and logical structure of a work, apart from its historical or social context, in contrast to "Platonic Criticism," which stresses the usefulness of art. Adherents of New Criticism including John Crowe Ransom and Cleanth Brooks utilize and value the basic ideas of Aristotelian criticism for textual analysis.

Art for Art's Sake: See *Aestheticism*

Aside: A comment made by a stage performer that is intended to be heard by the audience but supposedly not by other characters. Eugene O'Neill's *Strange Interlude* is an extended use of the aside in modern theater.

Audience: The people for whom a piece of literature is written. Authors usually write with a certain audience in mind, for example, children, members of a religious or ethnic group, or colleagues in a professional field. The term "audience" also applies to the people who gather to see or hear any performance, including plays, poetry readings, speeches, and concerts. Jane Austen's parody of the gothic novel, *Northanger Abbey,* was originally intended for (and also pokes fun at) an audience of young and avid female gothic novel readers.

Avant-garde: A French term meaning "vanguard." It is used in literary criticism to describe new writing that rejects traditional approaches to literature in favor of innovations in style or content. Twentieth-century examples of the literary *avant-garde* include the Black Mountain School of poets, the Bloomsbury Group, and the Beat Movement.

B

Ballad: A short poem that tells a simple story and has a repeated refrain. Ballads were originally intended to be sung. Early ballads, known as folk ballads, were passed down through generations, so their authors are often unknown. Later ballads composed by known authors are called literary ballads. An example of an anonymous folk ballad is "Edward," which dates from the Middle Ages. Samuel Taylor Coleridge's "The Rime of the Ancient Mariner" and John Keats's "La Belle Dame sans Merci" are examples of literary ballads.

Baroque: A term used in literary criticism to describe literature that is complex or ornate in style or diction. Baroque works typically express tension, anxiety, and violent emotion. The term "Baroque Age" designates a period in Western European literature beginning in the late sixteenth century and ending about one hundred years later. Works of this period often mirror the qualities of works more generally associated with the label "baroque" and sometimes feature elaborate conceits. Examples of Baroque works include John Lyly's *Euphues: The Anatomy of Wit,* Luis de Gongora's *Soledads,* and William Shakespeare's *As You Like It.*

Baroque Age: See *Baroque*

Baroque Period: See *Baroque*

Beat Generation: See *Beat Movement*

Beat Movement: A period featuring a group of American poets and novelists of the 1950s and 1960s—including Jack Kerouac, Allen Ginsberg, Gregory Corso, William S. Burroughs, and Lawrence Ferlinghetti—who rejected established social and literary values. Using such techniques as stream of consciousness writing and jazz-influenced free verse and focusing on unusual or abnormal states of mind—generated by religious ecstasy or the use of drugs—the Beat writers aimed to create works that were unconventional in both form and subject matter. Kerouac's *On the Road* is perhaps the best-known example of a Beat Generation novel, and Ginsberg's *Howl* is a famous collection of Beat poetry.

Black Aesthetic Movement: A period of artistic and literary development among African Americans in the 1960s and early 1970s. This was the first major African-American artistic movement since the Harlem Renaissance and was closely paralleled by the civil rights and black power movements. The black aesthetic writers attempted to produce works of art that would be meaningful to the black masses. Key figures in black aesthetics included one of its founders, poet and playwright Amiri Baraka, formerly known as LeRoi Jones; poet and essayist Haki R. Madhubuti, formerly Don L. Lee; poet and playwright Sonia Sanchez; and dramatist Ed Bullins. Works representative of the Black Aesthetic Movement include Amiri Baraka's play *Dutchman,* a 1964 Obie award-winner; *Black Fire: An Anthology of Afro-American Writing,* edited by Baraka and playwright Larry Neal and published in 1968; and Sonia Sanchez's poetry collection *We a BaddDDD People,* published in 1970. Also known as Black Arts Movement.

Black Arts Movement: See *Black Aesthetic Movement*

Black Comedy: See *Black Humor*

Black Humor: Writing that places grotesque elements side by side with humorous ones in an attempt to shock the reader, forcing him or her to laugh at the horrifying reality of a disordered world. Joseph Heller's novel *Catch-22* is considered a superb example of the use of black humor. Other well-known authors who use black humor include Kurt Vonnegut, Edward Albee, Eugene Ionesco, and Harold Pinter. Also known as Black Comedy.

Blank Verse: Loosely, any unrhymed poetry, but more generally, unrhymed iambic pentameter verse (composed of lines of five two-syllable feet with the first syllable accented, the second unaccented). Blank verse has been used by poets since the Renaissance for its flexibility and its graceful, dignified tone. John Milton's *Paradise Lost* is in blank verse, as are most of William Shakespeare's plays.

Bloomsbury Group: A group of English writers, artists, and intellectuals who held informal artistic and philosophical discussions in Bloomsbury, a district of London, from around 1907 to the early 1930s. The Bloomsbury Group held no uniform philosophical beliefs but did commonly express an aversion to moral prudery and a desire for greater social tolerance. At various times the circle included Virginia Woolf, E. M. Forster, Clive Bell, Lytton Strachey, and John Maynard Keynes.

Bon Mot: A French term meaning "good word." A *bon mot* is a witty remark or clever observation. Charles Lamb and Oscar Wilde are celebrated for their witty *bon mots.* Two examples by Oscar Wilde stand out: (1) "All women become their mothers. That is their tragedy. No man does. That's his." (2) "A man cannot be too careful in the choice of his enemies."

Breath Verse: See *Projective Verse*

Burlesque: Any literary work that uses exaggeration to make its subject appear ridiculous, either by treating a trivial subject with profound seriousness or by treating a dignified subject frivolously. The word "burlesque" may also be used as an adjective, as in "burlesque show," to mean "striptease act." Examples of literary burlesque include the comedies of Aristophanes, Miguel de Cervantes's *Don*

Quixote, Samuel Butler's poem "Hudibras," and John Gay's play *The Beggar's Opera*.

C

Cadence: The natural rhythm of language caused by the alternation of accented and unaccented syllables. Much modern poetry—notably free verse—deliberately manipulates cadence to create complex rhythmic effects. James Macpherson's "Ossian poems" are richly cadenced, as is the poetry of the Symbolists, Walt Whitman, and Amy Lowell.

Caesura: A pause in a line of poetry, usually occurring near the middle. It typically corresponds to a break in the natural rhythm or sense of the line but is sometimes shifted to create special meanings or rhythmic effects. The opening line of Edgar Allan Poe's "The Raven" contains a caesura following "dreary": "Once upon a midnight dreary, while I pondered weak and weary...."

Canzone: A short Italian or Provencal lyric poem, commonly about love and often set to music. The *canzone* has no set form but typically contains five or six stanzas made up of seven to twenty lines of eleven syllables each. A shorter, five- to ten-line "envoy," or concluding stanza, completes the poem. Masters of the *canzone* form include Petrarch, Dante Alighieri, Torquato Tasso, and Guido Cavalcanti.

Carpe Diem: A Latin term meaning "seize the day." This is a traditional theme of poetry, especially lyrics. A *carpe diem* poem advises the reader or the person it addresses to live for today and enjoy the pleasures of the moment. Two celebrated *carpe diem* poems are Andrew Marvell's "To His Coy Mistress" and Robert Herrick's poem beginning "Gather ye rosebuds while ye may...."

Catharsis: The release or purging of unwanted emotions—specifically fear and pity—brought about by exposure to art. The term was first used by the Greek philosopher Aristotle in his *Poetics* to refer to the desired effect of tragedy on spectators. A famous example of catharsis is realized in Sophocles's *Oedipus Rex,* when Oedipus discovers that his wife, Jacosta, is his own mother and that the stranger he killed on the road was his own father.

Celtic Renaissance: A period of Irish literary and cultural history at the end of the nineteenth century. Followers of the movement aimed to create a romantic vision of Celtic myth and legend. The most significant works of the Celtic Renaissance typically present a dreamy, unreal world, usually in reaction against the reality of contemporary problems. William Butler Yeats's *The Wanderings of Oisin* is among the most significant works of the Celtic Renaissance. Also known as Celtic Twilight.

Celtic Twilight: See *Celtic Renaissance*

Character: Broadly speaking, a person in a literary work. The actions of characters are what constitute the plot of a story, novel, or poem. There are numerous types of characters, ranging from simple, stereotypical figures to intricate, multifaceted ones. In the techniques of anthropomorphism and personification, animals—and even places or things—can assume aspects of character. "Characterization" is the process by which an author creates vivid, believable characters in a work of art. This may be done in a variety of ways, including (1) direct description of the character by the narrator; (2) the direct presentation of the speech, thoughts, or actions of the character; and (3) the responses of other characters to the character. The term "character" also refers to a form originated by the ancient Greek writer Theophrastus that later became popular in the seventeenth and eighteenth centuries. It is a short essay or sketch of a person who prominently displays a specific attribute or quality, such as miserliness or ambition. Notable characters in literature include Oedipus Rex, Don Quixote de la Mancha, Macbeth, Candide, Hester Prynne, Ebenezer Scrooge, Huckleberry Finn, Jay Gatsby, Scarlett O'Hara, James Bond, and Kunta Kinte.

Characterization: See *Character*

Chorus: In ancient Greek drama, a group of actors who commented on and interpreted the unfolding action on the stage. Initially the chorus was a major component of the presentation, but over time it became less significant, with its numbers reduced and its role eventually limited to commentary between acts. By the sixteenth century the chorus—if employed at all—was typically a single person who provided a prologue and an epilogue and occasionally appeared between acts to introduce or underscore an important event. The chorus in William Shakespeare's *Henry V* functions in this way. Modern dramas rarely feature a chorus, but T. S. Eliot's *Murder in the Cathedral* and Arthur Miller's *A View from the Bridge* are notable exceptions. The Stage Manager in Thornton Wilder's *Our Town* performs a role similar to that of the chorus.

Chronicle: A record of events presented in chronological order. Although the scope and level of detail provided varies greatly among the chronicles surviving from ancient times, some, such as the *Anglo-Saxon Chronicle,* feature vivid descriptions and a lively recounting of events. During the Elizabethan Age, many dramas—appropriately called "chronicle plays"—were based on material from chronicles. Many of William Shakespeare's dramas of English history as well as Christopher Marlowe's *Edward II* are based in part on Raphael Holinshead's *Chronicles of England, Scotland, and Ireland.*

Classical: In its strictest definition in literary criticism, classicism refers to works of ancient Greek or Roman literature. The term may also be used to describe a literary work of recognized importance (a "classic") from any time period or literature that exhibits the traits of classicism. Classical authors from ancient Greek and Roman times include Juvenal and Homer. Examples of later works and authors now described as classical include French literature of the seventeenth century, Western novels of the nineteenth century, and American fiction of the mid-nineteenth century such as that written by James Fenimore Cooper and Mark Twain.

Classicism: A term used in literary criticism to describe critical doctrines that have their roots in ancient Greek and Roman literature, philosophy, and art. Works associated with classicism typically exhibit restraint on the part of the author, unity of design and purpose, clarity, simplicity, logical organization, and respect for tradition. Examples of literary classicism include Cicero's prose, the dramas of Pierre Corneille and Jean Racine, the poetry of John Dryden and Alexander Pope, and the writings of J. W. von Goethe, G. E. Lessing, and T. S. Eliot.

Climax: The turning point in a narrative, the moment when the conflict is at its most intense. Typically, the structure of stories, novels, and plays is one of rising action, in which tension builds to the climax, followed by falling action, in which tension lessens as the story moves to its conclusion. The climax in James Fenimore Cooper's *The Last of the Mohicans* occurs when Magua and his captive Cora are pursued to the edge of a cliff by Uncas. Magua kills Uncas but is subsequently killed by Hawkeye.

Colloquialism: A word, phrase, or form of pronunciation that is acceptable in casual conversation but not in formal, written communication. It is considered more acceptable than slang. An example of colloquialism can be found in Rudyard Kipling's *Barrack-room Ballads:* When 'Omer smote 'is bloomin' lyre He'd 'eard men sing by land and sea; An' what he thought 'e might require 'E went an' took—the same as me!

Comedy: One of two major types of drama, the other being tragedy. Its aim is to amuse, and it typically ends happily. Comedy assumes many forms, such as farce and burlesque, and uses a variety of techniques, from parody to satire. In a restricted sense the term comedy refers only to dramatic presentations, but in general usage it is commonly applied to non-dramatic works as well. Examples of comedies range from the plays of Aristophanes, Terrence, and Plautus, Dante Alighieri's *The Divine Comedy,* Francois Rabelais's *Pantagruel* and *Gargantua,* and some of Geoffrey Chaucer's tales and William Shakespeare's plays to Noel Coward's play *Private Lives* and James Thurber's short story "The Secret Life of Walter Mitty."

Comedy of Manners: A play about the manners and conventions of an aristocratic, highly sophisticated society. The characters are usually types rather than individualized personalities, and plot is less important than atmosphere. Such plays were an important aspect of late seventeenth-century English comedy. The comedy of manners was revived in the eighteenth century by Oliver Goldsmith and Richard Brinsley Sheridan, enjoyed a second revival in the late nineteenth century, and has endured into the twentieth century. Examples of comedies of manners include William Congreve's *The Way of the World* in the late seventeenth century, Oliver Goldsmith's *She Stoops to Conquer* and Richard

Brinsley Sheridan's *The School for Scandal* in the eighteenth century, Oscar Wilde's *The Importance of Being Earnest* in the nineteenth century, and W. Somerset Maugham's *The Circle* in the twentieth century.

Comic Relief: The use of humor to lighten the mood of a serious or tragic story, especially in plays. The technique is very common in Elizabethan works, and can be an integral part of the plot or simply a brief event designed to break the tension of the scene. The Gravediggers' scene in William Shakespeare's *Hamlet* is a frequently cited example of comic relief.

Commedia dell'arte: An Italian term meaning "the comedy of guilds" or "the comedy of professional actors." This form of dramatic comedy was popular in Italy during the sixteenth century. Actors were assigned stock roles (such as Pulcinella, the stupid servant, or Pantalone, the old merchant) and given a basic plot to follow, but all dialogue was improvised. The roles were rigidly typed and the plots were formulaic, usually revolving around young lovers who thwarted their elders and attained wealth and happiness. A rigid convention of the *commedia dell'arte* is the periodic intrusion of Harlequin, who interrupts the play with low buffoonery. Peppino de Filippo's *Metamorphoses of a Wandering Minstrel* gave modern audiences an idea of what *commedia dell'arte* may have been like. Various scenarios for *commedia dell'arte* were compiled in Petraccone's *La commedia dell'arte, storia, technica, scenari,* published in 1927.

Complaint: A lyric poem, popular in the Renaissance, in which the speaker expresses sorrow about his or her condition. Typically, the speaker's sadness is caused by an unresponsive lover, but some complaints cite other sources of unhappiness, such as poverty or fate. A commonly cited example is "A Complaint by Night of the Lover Not Beloved" by Henry Howard, Earl of Surrey. Thomas Sackville's "Complaint of Henry, Duke of Buckingham" traces the duke's unhappiness to his ruthless ambition.

Conceit: A clever and fanciful metaphor, usually expressed through elaborate and extended comparison, that presents a striking parallel between two seemingly dissimilar things— for example, elaborately comparing a beautiful woman to an object like a garden or the sun. The conceit was a popular device throughout the Elizabethan Age and Baroque Age and was the principal technique of the seventeenth-century English metaphysical poets. This usage of the word conceit is unrelated to the best-known definition of conceit as an arrogant attitude or behavior. The conceit figures prominently in the works of John Donne, Emily Dickinson, and T. S. Eliot.

Concrete: Concrete is the opposite of abstract, and refers to a thing that actually exists or a description that allows the reader to experience an object or concept with the senses. Henry David Thoreau's *Walden* contains much concrete description of nature and wildlife.

Concrete Poetry: Poetry in which visual elements play a large part in the poetic effect. Punctuation marks, letters, or words are arranged on a page to form a visual design: a cross, for example, or a bumblebee. Max Bill and Eugene Gomringer were among the early practitioners of concrete poetry; Haroldo de Campos and Augusto de Campos are among contemporary authors of concrete poetry.

Confessional Poetry: A form of poetry in which the poet reveals very personal, intimate, sometimes shocking information about himself or herself. Anne Sexton, Sylvia Plath, Robert Lowell, and John Berryman wrote poetry in the confessional vein.

Conflict: The conflict in a work of fiction is the issue to be resolved in the story. It usually occurs between two characters, the protagonist and the antagonist, or between the protagonist and society or the protagonist and himself or herself. Conflict in Theodore Dreiser's novel *Sister Carrie* comes as a result of urban society, while Jack London's short story "To Build a Fire" concerns the protagonist's battle against the cold and himself.

Connotation: The impression that a word gives beyond its defined meaning. Connotations may be universally understood or may be significant only to a certain group. Both "horse" and "steed" denote the same animal, but "steed" has a different connotation, deriving from the chivalrous or romantic narratives in which the word was once often used.

Consonance: Consonance occurs in poetry when words appearing at the ends of two or more verses have similar final consonant sounds but have final vowel sounds that differ, as with "stuff" and "off." Consonance is found in "The curfew tolls the knells of parting day" from Thomas Grey's "An Elegy Written in a Country Church Yard." Also known as Half Rhyme or Slant Rhyme.

Convention: Any widely accepted literary device, style, or form. A soliloquy, in which a character reveals to the audience his or her private thoughts, is an example of a dramatic convention.

Corrido: A Mexican ballad. Examples of *corridos* include "Muerte del afamado Bilito," "La voz de mi conciencia," "Lucio Perez," "La juida," and "Los presos."

Couplet: Two lines of poetry with the same rhyme and meter, often expressing a complete and self-contained thought. The following couplet is from Alexander Pope's "Elegy to the Memory of an Unfortunate Lady": 'Tis Use alone that sanctifies Expense, And Splendour borrows all her rays from Sense.

Criticism: The systematic study and evaluation of literary works, usually based on a specific method or set of principles. An important part of literary studies since ancient times, the practice of criticism has given rise to numerous theories, methods, and "schools," sometimes producing conflicting, even contradictory, interpretations of literature in general as well as of individual works. Even such basic issues as what constitutes a poem or a novel have been the subject of much criticism over the centuries. Seminal texts of literary criticism include Plato's *Republic,* Aristotle's *Poetics,* Sir Philip Sidney's *The Defence of Poesie,* John Dryden's *Of Dramatic Poesie,* and William Wordsworth's "Preface" to the second edition of his *Lyrical Ballads.* Contemporary schools of criticism include deconstruction, feminist, psychoanalytic, poststructuralist, new historicist, postcolonialist, and reader- response.

D

Dactyl: See *Foot*

Dadaism: A protest movement in art and literature founded by Tristan Tzara in 1916. Followers of the movement expressed their outrage at the destruction brought about by World War I by revolting against numerous forms of social convention. The Dadaists presented works marked by calculated madness and flamboyant nonsense. They stressed total freedom of expression, commonly through primitive displays of emotion and illogical, often senseless, poetry. The movement ended shortly after the war, when it was replaced by surrealism. Proponents of Dadaism include Andre Breton, Louis Aragon, Philippe Soupault, and Paul Eluard.

Decadent: See *Decadents*

Decadents: The followers of a nineteenth-century literary movement that had its beginnings in French aestheticism. Decadent literature displays a fascination with perverse and morbid states; a search for novelty and sensation—the "new thrill"; a preoccupation with mysticism; and a belief in the senselessness of human existence. The movement is closely associated with the doctrine Art for Art's Sake. The term "decadence" is sometimes used to denote a decline in the quality of art or literature following a period of greatness. Major French decadents are Charles Baudelaire and Arthur Rimbaud. English decadents include Oscar Wilde, Ernest Dowson, and Frank Harris.

Deconstruction: A method of literary criticism developed by Jacques Derrida and characterized by multiple conflicting interpretations of a given work. Deconstructionists consider the impact of the language of a work and suggest that the true meaning of the work is not necessarily the meaning that the author intended. Jacques Derrida's *De la grammatologie* is the seminal text on deconstructive strategies; among American practitioners of this method of criticism are Paul de Man and J. Hillis Miller.

Deduction: The process of reaching a conclusion through reasoning from general premises to a specific premise. An example of deduction is present in the following syllogism: Premise: All mammals are animals. Premise: All whales are mammals. Conclusion: Therefore, all whales are animals.

Denotation: The definition of a word, apart from the impressions or feelings it creates in the reader. The word "apartheid" denotes a political and economic policy of segregation by race, but its connotations—oppression, slavery, inequality—are numerous.

Denouement: A French word meaning "the unknotting." In literary criticism, it denotes the resolution of conflict in fiction or drama. The *denouement* follows the climax and provides an outcome to the primary plot situation as well as an explanation of secondary plot complications. The *denouement* often involves a character's recognition of his or her state of mind or moral condition. A well-known example of *denouement* is the last scene of the play *As You Like It* by William Shakespeare, in which couples are married, an evildoer repents, the identities of two disguised characters are revealed, and a ruler is restored to power. Also known as Falling Action.

Description: Descriptive writing is intended to allow a reader to picture the scene or setting in which the action of a story takes place. The form this description takes often evokes an intended emotional response—a dark, spooky graveyard will evoke fear, and a peaceful, sunny meadow will evoke calmness. An example of a descriptive story is Edgar Allan Poe's *Landor's Cottage,* which offers a detailed depiction of a New York country estate.

Detective Story: A narrative about the solution of a mystery or the identification of a criminal. The conventions of the detective story include the detective's scrupulous use of logic in solving the mystery; incompetent or ineffectual police; a suspect who appears guilty at first but is later proved innocent; and the detective's friend or confidant—often the narrator—whose slowness in interpreting clues emphasizes by contrast the detective's brilliance. Edgar Allan Poe's "Murders in the Rue Morgue" is commonly regarded as the earliest example of this type of story. With this work, Poe established many of the conventions of the detective story genre, which are still in practice. Other practitioners of this vast and extremely popular genre include Arthur Conan Doyle, Dashiell Hammett, and Agatha Christie.

Deus ex machina: A Latin term meaning "god out of a machine." In Greek drama, a god was often lowered onto the stage by a mechanism of some kind to rescue the hero or untangle the plot. By extension, the term refers to any artificial device or coincidence used to bring about a convenient and simple solution to a plot. This is a common device in melodramas and includes such fortunate circumstances as the sudden receipt of a legacy to save the family farm or a last-minute stay of execution. The *deus ex machina* invariably rewards the virtuous and punishes evildoers. Examples of *deus ex machina* include King Louis XIV in Jean-Baptiste Moliere's *Tartuffe* and Queen Victoria in *The Pirates of Penzance* by William Gilbert and Arthur Sullivan. Bertolt Brecht parodies the abuse of such devices in the conclusion of his *Threepenny Opera.*

Dialogue: In its widest sense, dialogue is simply conversation between people in a literary work; in its most restricted sense, it refers specifically to the speech of characters in a drama. As a specific literary genre, a "dialogue" is a composition in which characters debate an issue or idea. The Greek philosopher Plato frequently expounded his theories in the form of dialogues.

Diction: The selection and arrangement of words in a literary work. Either or both may vary depending on the desired effect. There are four general types of diction: "formal," used in scholarly or lofty writing; "informal," used in relaxed but educated conversation; "colloquial," used in everyday speech; and "slang," containing newly coined words and other terms not accepted in formal usage.

Didactic: A term used to describe works of literature that aim to teach some moral, religious, political, or practical lesson. Although didactic elements are often found in artistically pleasing works, the term "didactic" usually refers to literature in which the message is more important than the form. The term may also be used to criticize a work that the critic finds "overly didactic," that is, heavy-handed in its delivery of a lesson. Examples of didactic literature include John Bunyan's *Pilgrim's Progress,* Alexander Pope's *Essay on Criticism,* Jean-Jacques Rousseau's *Emile,* and Elizabeth Inchbald's *Simple Story.*

Dimeter: See *Meter*

Dionysian: See *Apollonian and Dionysian*

Discordia concours: A Latin phrase meaning "discord in harmony." The term was coined by the eighteenth-century English writer Samuel Johnson to describe "a combination of dissimilar images or discovery of occult resemblances in things apparently unlike." Johnson created the expression by reversing a phrase by the Latin poet Horace. The metaphysical poetry of John Donne, Richard Crashaw, Abraham Cowley, George Herbert, and Edward Taylor among others, contains many examples of *discordia concours*. In Donne's "A Valediction: Forbidding Mourning," the poet compares the union of himself with his lover to a draftsman's compass: If they be two, they are two so, As stiff twin compasses are two: Thy soul, the fixed foot, makes no show To move, but doth, if the other do; And though it in the center sit, Yet when the other far doth roam, It leans, and hearkens after it, And grows erect, as that comes home.

Dissonance: A combination of harsh or jarring sounds, especially in poetry. Although such combinations may be accidental, poets sometimes intentionally make them to achieve particular effects. Dissonance is also sometimes used to refer to close but not identical rhymes. When this is the case, the word functions as a synonym for consonance. Robert Browning, Gerard Manley Hopkins, and many other poets have made deliberate use of dissonance.

Doppelganger: A literary technique by which a character is duplicated (usually in the form of an alter ego, though sometimes as a ghostly counterpart) or divided into two distinct, usually opposite personalities. The use of this character device is widespread in nine-teenth- and twentieth- century literature, and indicates a growing awareness among authors that the "self" is really a composite of many "selves." A well-known story containing a *doppelganger* character is Robert Louis Stevenson's *Dr. Jekyll and Mr. Hyde,* which dramatizes an internal struggle between good and evil. Also known as The Double.

Double Entendre: A corruption of a French phrase meaning "double meaning." The term is used to indicate a word or phrase that is deliberately ambiguous, especially when one of the meanings is risque or improper. An example of a *double entendre* is the Elizabethan usage of the verb "die," which refers both to death and to orgasm.

Double, The: See *Doppelganger*

Draft: Any preliminary version of a written work. An author may write dozens of drafts which are revised to form the final work, or he or she may write only one, with few or no revisions. Dorothy Parker's observation that "I can't write five words but that I change seven" humorously indicates the purpose of the draft.

Drama: In its widest sense, a drama is any work designed to be presented by actors on a stage. Similarly, "drama" denotes a broad literary genre that includes a variety of forms, from pageant and spectacle to tragedy and comedy, as well as countless types and sub-types. More commonly in modern usage, however, a drama is a work that treats ser-ious subjects and themes but does not aim at the grandeur of tragedy. This use of the term originated with the eighteenth-century French writer Denis Diderot, who used the word *drame* to designate his plays about middle- class life; thus "drama" typically fea-tures characters of a less exalted stature than those of tragedy. Examples of classical dra-mas include Menander's comedy *Dyscolus* and Sophocles' tragedy *Oedipus Rex.* Con-temporary dramas include Eugene O'Neill's *The Iceman Cometh,* Lillian Hellman's *Little Foxes,* and August Wilson's *Ma Rainey's Black Bottom.*

Dramatic Irony: Occurs when the audience of a play or the reader of a work of literature knows something that a character in the work itself does not know. The irony is in the contrast between the intended meaning of the statements or actions of a character and the additional information understood by the audience. A celebrated example of dramatic irony is in Act V of William Sha-kespeare's *Romeo and Juliet,* where two young lovers meet their end as a result of a tragic misunderstanding. Here, the audience has full knowledge that Juliet's apparent "death" is merely temporary; she will regain her senses when the mysterious "sleeping potion" she has taken wears off. But Romeo, mistaking Juliet's drug-induced trance for true death, kills himself in grief. Upon awakening, Juliet discovers Romeo's corpse and, in despair, slays herself.

Dramatic Monologue: See *Monologue*

Dramatic Poetry: Any lyric work that employs elements of drama such as dialogue, conflict, or characterization, but excluding works that are intended for stage presentation. A mono-logue is a form of dramatic poetry.

Dramatis Personae: The characters in a work of literature, particularly a drama. The list of characters printed before the main text of a play or in the program is the *dramatis personae.*

Dream Allegory: See *Dream Vision*

Dream Vision: A literary convention, chiefly of the Middle Ages. In a dream vision a story is presented as a literal dream of the narrator. This device was commonly used to teach moral and religious lessons. Important works of this type are *The Divine Comedy* by Dante Alighieri, *Piers Plowman* by William Langland, and *The Pilgrim's Progress* by John Bunyan. Also known as Dream Allegory.

Dystopia: An imaginary place in a work of fiction where the characters lead dehumanized, fearful lives. Jack London's *The Iron Heel,* Yevgeny Zamyatin's *My,* Aldous Huxley's *Brave New World,* George Orwell's *Nineteen Eighty-four,* and Margaret Atwood's *Handmaid's Tale* portray versions of dystopia.

E

Eclogue: In classical literature, a poem featuring rural themes and structured as a dialogue among shepherds. Eclogues often took specific poetic forms, such as elegies or love poems. Some were written as the soliloquy of a shepherd. In later centuries, "eclogue" came to refer to any poem that was in the pastoral tradition or that had a dialogue or monologue structure. A classical example of an eclogue is Virgil's *Eclogues,* also known as *Bucolics.* Giovanni Boccaccio, Edmund Spenser, Andrew Marvell, Jonathan Swift, and Louis MacNeice also wrote eclogues.

Edwardian: Describes cultural conventions identified with the period of the reign of Edward VII of England (1901-1910). Writers of the Edwardian Age typically displayed a strong reaction against the propriety and conservatism of the Victorian Age. Their work often exhibits distrust of authority in religion, politics, and art and expresses strong doubts about the soundness of conventional values. Writers of this era include George Bernard Shaw, H. G. Wells, and Joseph Conrad.

Edwardian Age: See *Edwardian*

Electra Complex: A daughter's amorous obsession with her father. The term Electra complex comes from the plays of Euripides and Sophocles entitled *Electra,* in which the character Electra drives her brother Orestes to kill their mother and her lover in revenge for the murder of their father.

Elegy: A lyric poem that laments the death of a person or the eventual death of all people. In a conventional elegy, set in a classical world, the poet and subject are spoken of as shepherds. In modern criticism, the word elegy is often used to refer to a poem that is melancholy or mournfully contemplative. John Milton's "Lycidas" and Percy Bysshe Shelley's "Adonais" are two examples of this form.

Elizabethan Age: A period of great economic growth, religious controversy, and nationalism closely associated with the reign of Elizabeth I of England (1558-1603). The Elizabethan Age is considered a part of the general renaissance—that is, the flowering of arts and literature—that took place in Europe during the fourteenth through sixteenth centuries. The era is considered the golden age of English literature. The most important dramas in English and a great deal of lyric poetry were produced during this period, and modern English criticism began around this time. The notable authors of the period—Philip Sidney, Edmund Spenser, Christopher Marlowe, William Shakespeare, Ben Jonson, Francis Bacon, and John Donne—are among the best in all of English literature.

Elizabethan Drama: English comic and tragic plays produced during the Renaissance, or more narrowly, those plays written during the last years of and few years after Queen Elizabeth's reign. William Shakespeare is considered an Elizabethan dramatist in the broader sense, although most of his work was produced during the reign of James I. Examples of Elizabethan comedies include John Lyly's *The Woman in the Moone,* Thomas Dekker's *The Roaring Girl, or, Moll Cut Purse,* and William Shakespeare's *Twelfth Night.* Examples of Elizabethan tragedies include William Shakespeare's *Antony and Cleopatra,* Thomas Kyd's *The Spanish Tragedy,* and John Webster's *The Tragedy of the Duchess of Malfi.*

Empathy: A sense of shared experience, including emotional and physical feelings, with someone or something other than oneself. Empathy is often used to describe the response of a reader to a literary character. An example of an empathic passage is

William Shakespeare's description in his narrative poem *Venus and Adonis* of: the snail, whose tender horns being hit, Shrinks backward in his shelly cave with pain. Readers of Gerard Manley Hopkins's *The Windhover* may experience some of the physical sensations evoked in the description of the movement of the falcon.

English Sonnet: See *Sonnet*

Enjambment: The running over of the sense and structure of a line of verse or a couplet into the following verse or couplet. Andrew Marvell's "To His Coy Mistress" is structured as a series of enjambments, as in lines 11-12: "My vegetable love should grow/Vaster than empires and more slow."

Enlightenment, The: An eighteenth-century philosophical movement. It began in France but had a wide impact throughout Europe and America. Thinkers of the Enlightenment valued reason and believed that both the individual and society could achieve a state of perfection. Corresponding to this essentially humanist vision was a resistance to religious authority. Important figures of the Enlightenment were Denis Diderot and Voltaire in France, Edward Gibbon and David Hume in England, and Thomas Paine and Thomas Jefferson in the United States.

Epic: A long narrative poem about the adventures of a hero of great historic or legendary importance. The setting is vast and the action is often given cosmic significance through the intervention of supernatural forces such as gods, angels, or demons. Epics are typically written in a classical style of grand simplicity with elaborate metaphors and allusions that enhance the symbolic importance of a hero's adventures. Some well-known epics are Homer's *Iliad* and *Odyssey,* Virgil's *Aeneid,* and John Milton's *Paradise Lost.*

Epic Simile: See *Homeric Simile*

Epic Theater: A theory of theatrical presentation developed by twentieth-century German playwright Bertolt Brecht. Brecht created a type of drama that the audience could view with complete detachment. He used what he termed "alienation effects" to create an emotional distance between the audience and the action on stage. Among these effects are: short, self-contained scenes that keep the play from building to a cathartic climax; songs that comment on the action; and techniques of acting that prevent the actor from developing an emotional identity with his role. Besides the plays of Bertolt Brecht, other plays that utilize epic theater conventions include those of Georg Buchner, Frank Wedekind, Erwin Piscator, and Leopold Jessner.

Epigram: A saying that makes the speaker's point quickly and concisely. Samuel Taylor Coleridge wrote an epigram that neatly sums up the form: What is an Epigram? A Dwarfish whole, Its body brevity, and wit its soul.

Epilogue: A concluding statement or section of a literary work. In dramas, particularly those of the seventeenth and eighteenth centuries, the epilogue is a closing speech, often in verse, delivered by an actor at the end of a play and spoken directly to the audience. A famous epilogue is Puck's speech at the end of William Shakespeare's *A Midsummer Night's Dream.*

Epiphany: A sudden revelation of truth inspired by a seemingly trivial incident. The term was widely used by James Joyce in his critical writings, and the stories in Joyce's *Dubliners* are commonly called "epiphanies."

Episode: An incident that forms part of a story and is significantly related to it. Episodes may be either self-contained narratives or events that depend on a larger context for their sense and importance. Examples of episodes include the founding of Wilmington, Delaware in Charles Reade's *The Disinherited Heir* and the individual events comprising the picaresque novels and medieval romances.

Episodic Plot: See *Plot*

Epitaph: An inscription on a tomb or tombstone, or a verse written on the occasion of a person's death. Epitaphs may be serious or humorous. Dorothy Parker's epitaph reads, "I told you I was sick."

Epithalamion: A song or poem written to honor and commemorate a marriage ceremony. Famous examples include Edmund Spenser's "Epithalamion" and e. e. cummings's "Epithalamion." Also spelled Epithalamium.

Epithalamium: See *Epithalamion*

Epithet: A word or phrase, often disparaging or abusive, that expresses a character trait of someone or something. "The Napoleon of crime" is an epithet applied to Professor

Moriarty, arch-rival of Sherlock Holmes in Arthur Conan Doyle's series of detective stories.

Exempla: See *Exemplum*

Exemplum: A tale with a moral message. This form of literary sermonizing flourished during the Middle Ages, when *exempla* appeared in collections known as "example-books." The works of Geoffrey Chaucer are full of *exempla.*

Existentialism: A predominantly twentieth-century philosophy concerned with the nature and perception of human existence. There are two major strains of existentialist thought: atheistic and Christian. Followers of atheistic existentialism believe that the individual is alone in a godless universe and that the basic human condition is one of suffering and loneliness. Nevertheless, because there are no fixed values, individuals can create their own characters—indeed, they can shape themselves—through the exercise of free will. The atheistic strain culminates in and is popularly associated with the works of Jean-Paul Sartre. The Christian existentialists, on the other hand, believe that only in God may people find freedom from life's anguish. The two strains hold certain beliefs in common: that existence cannot be fully understood or described through empirical effort; that anguish is a universal element of life; that individuals must bear responsibility for their actions; and that there is no common standard of behavior or perception for religious and ethical matters. Existentialist thought figures prominently in the works of such authors as Eugene Ionesco, Franz Kafka, Fyodor Dostoyevsky, Simone de Beauvoir, Samuel Beckett, and Albert Camus.

Expatriates: See *Expatriatism*

Expatriatism: The practice of leaving one's country to live for an extended period in another country. Literary expatriates include English poets Percy Bysshe Shelley and John Keats in Italy, Polish novelist Joseph Conrad in England, American writers Richard Wright, James Baldwin, Gertrude Stein, and Ernest Hemingway in France, and Trinidadian author Neil Bissondath in Canada.

Exposition: Writing intended to explain the nature of an idea, thing, or theme. Expository writing is often combined with description, narration, or argument. In dramatic writing, the exposition is the introductory material which presents the characters, setting, and tone of the play. An example of dramatic exposition occurs in many nineteenth-century drawing-room comedies in which the butler and the maid open the play with relevant talk about their master and mistress; in composition, exposition relays factual information, as in encyclopedia entries.

Expressionism: An indistinct literary term, originally used to describe an early twentieth-century school of German painting. The term applies to almost any mode of unconventional, highly subjective writing that distorts reality in some way. Advocates of Expressionism include dramatists George Kaiser, Ernst Toller, Luigi Pirandello, Federico Garcia Lorca, Eugene O'Neill, and Elmer Rice; poets George Heym, Ernst Stadler, August Stramm, Gottfried Benn, and Georg Trakl; and novelists Franz Kafka and James Joyce.

Extended Monologue: See *Monologue*

F

Fable: A prose or verse narrative intended to convey a moral. Animals or inanimate objects with human characteristics often serve as characters in fables. A famous fable is Aesop's "The Tortoise and the Hare."

Fairy Tales: Short narratives featuring mythical beings such as fairies, elves, and sprites. These tales originally belonged to the folklore of a particular nation or region, such as those collected in Germany by Jacob and Wilhelm Grimm. Two other celebrated writers of fairy tales are Hans Christian Andersen and Rudyard Kipling.

Falling Action: See *Denouement*

Fantasy: A literary form related to mythology and folklore. Fantasy literature is typically set in non-existent realms and features supernatural beings. Notable examples of fantasy literature are *The Lord of the Rings* by J. R. R. Tolkien and the Gormenghast trilogy by Mervyn Peake.

Farce: A type of comedy characterized by broad humor, outlandish incidents, and often vulgar subject matter. Much of the "comedy" in film and television could more accurately be described as farce.

Feet: See *Foot*

Feminine Rhyme: See *Rhyme*

Femme fatale: A French phrase with the literal translation "fatal woman." A *femme fatale* is a sensuous, alluring woman who often leads men into danger or trouble. A classic example of the *femme fatale* is the nameless character in Billy Wilder's *The Seven Year Itch,* portrayed by Marilyn Monroe in the film adaptation.

Fiction: Any story that is the product of imagination rather than a documentation of fact. characters and events in such narratives may be based in real life but their ultimate form and configuration is a creation of the author. Geoffrey Chaucer's *The Canterbury Tales,* Laurence Sterne's *Tristram Shandy,* and Margaret Mitchell's *Gone with the Wind* are examples of fiction.

Figurative Language: A technique in writing in which the author temporarily interrupts the order, construction, or meaning of the writing for a particular effect. This interruption takes the form of one or more figures of speech such as hyperbole, irony, or simile. Figurative language is the opposite of literal language, in which every word is truthful, accurate, and free of exaggeration or embellishment. Examples of figurative language are tropes such as metaphor and rhetorical figures such as apostrophe.

Figures of Speech: Writing that differs from customary conventions for construction, meaning, order, or significance for the purpose of a special meaning or effect. There are two major types of figures of speech: rhetorical figures, which do not make changes in the meaning of the words, and tropes, which do. Types of figures of speech include simile, hyperbole, alliteration, and pun, among many others.

Fin de siecle: A French term meaning "end of the century." The term is used to denote the last decade of the nineteenth century, a transition period when writers and other artists abandoned old conventions and looked for new techniques and objectives. Two writers commonly associated with the *fin de siecle* mindset are Oscar Wilde and George Bernard Shaw.

First Person: See *Point of View*

Flashback: A device used in literature to present action that occurred before the beginning of the story. Flashbacks are often introduced as the dreams or recollections of one or more characters. Flashback techniques are often used in films, where they are typically set off by a gradual changing of one picture to another.

Foil: A character in a work of literature whose physical or psychological qualities contrast strongly with, and therefore highlight, the corresponding qualities of another character. In his Sherlock Holmes stories, Arthur Conan Doyle portrayed Dr. Watson as a man of normal habits and intelligence, making him a foil for the eccentric and wonderfully perceptive Sherlock Holmes.

Folk Ballad: See *Ballad*

Folklore: Traditions and myths preserved in a culture or group of people. Typically, these are passed on by word of mouth in various forms—such as legends, songs, and proverbs—or preserved in customs and ceremonies. This term was first used by W. J. Thoms in 1846. Sir James Frazer's *The Golden Bough* is the record of English folklore; myths about the frontier and the Old South exemplify American folklore.

Folktale: A story originating in oral tradition. Folktales fall into a variety of categories, including legends, ghost stories, fairy tales, fables, and anecdotes based on historical figures and events. Examples of folktales include Giambattista Basile's *The Pentamerone,* which contains the tales of Puss in Boots, Rapunzel, Cinderella, and Beauty and the Beast, and Joel Chandler Harris's Uncle Remus stories, which represent transplanted African folktales and American tales about the characters Mike Fink, Johnny Appleseed, Paul Bunyan, and Pecos Bill.

Foot: The smallest unit of rhythm in a line of poetry. In English-language poetry, a foot is typically one accented syllable combined with one or two unaccented syllables. There are many different types of feet. When the accent is on the second syllable of a two syllable word (con-*tort*), the foot is an "iamb"; the reverse accentual pattern (*tor* -ture) is a "trochee." Other feet that commonly occur in poetry in English are "anapest," two unaccented syllables followed by an accented syllable as in in-ter-*cept*, and "dactyl," an accented syllable followed by two unaccented syllables as in *su*-i-cide.

Foreshadowing: A device used in literature to create expectation or to set up an explanation of later developments. In Charles Dickens's *Great Expectations,* the graveyard encounter at the beginning of the novel between Pip and the escaped convict Magwitch foreshadows the baleful atmosphere and events that comprise much of the narrative.

Form: The pattern or construction of a work which identifies its genre and distinguishes it from other genres. Examples of forms include the different genres, such as the lyric form or the short story form, and various patterns for poetry, such as the verse form or the stanza form.

Formalism: In literary criticism, the belief that literature should follow prescribed rules of construction, such as those that govern the sonnet form. Examples of formalism are found in the work of the New Critics and structuralists.

Fourteener Meter: See *Meter*

Free Verse: Poetry that lacks regular metrical and rhyme patterns but that tries to capture the cadences of everyday speech. The form allows a poet to exploit a variety of rhythmical effects within a single poem. Free-verse techniques have been widely used in the twentieth century by such writers as Ezra Pound, T. S. Eliot, Carl Sandburg, and William Carlos Williams. Also known as *Vers libre.*

Futurism: A flamboyant literary and artistic movement that developed in France, Italy, and Russia from 1908 through the 1920s. Futurist theater and poetry abandoned traditional literary forms. In their place, followers of the movement attempted to achieve total freedom of expression through bizarre imagery and deformed or newly invented words. The Futurists were self-consciously modern artists who attempted to incorporate the appearances and sounds of modern life into their work. Futurist writers include Filippo Tommaso Marinetti, Wyndham Lewis, Guillaume Apollinaire, Velimir Khlebnikov, and Vladimir Mayakovsky.

G

Genre: A category of literary work. In critical theory, genre may refer to both the content of a given work—tragedy, comedy, pastoral—and to its form, such as poetry, novel, or drama. This term also refers to types of popular literature, as in the genres of science fiction or the detective story.

Genteel Tradition: A term coined by critic George Santayana to describe the literary practice of certain late nineteenth-century American writers, especially New Englanders. Followers of the Genteel Tradition emphasized conventionality in social, religious, moral, and literary standards. Some of the best-known writers of the Genteel Tradition are R. H. Stoddard and Bayard Taylor.

Gilded Age: A period in American history during the 1870s characterized by political corruption and materialism. A number of important novels of social and political criticism were written during this time. Examples of Gilded Age literature include Henry Adams's *Democracy* and F. Marion Crawford's *An American Politician.*

Gothic: See *Gothicism*

Gothicism: In literary criticism, works characterized by a taste for the medieval or morbidly attractive. A gothic novel prominently features elements of horror, the supernatural, gloom, and violence: clanking chains, terror, charnel houses, ghosts, medieval castles, and mysteriously slamming doors. The term "gothic novel" is also applied to novels that lack elements of the traditional Gothic setting but that create a similar atmosphere of terror or dread. Mary Shelley's *Frankenstein* is perhaps the best-known English work of this kind.

Gothic Novel: See *Gothicism*

Great Chain of Being: The belief that all things and creatures in nature are organized in a hierarchy from inanimate objects at the bottom to God at the top. This system of belief was popular in the seventeenth and eighteenth centuries. A summary of the concept of the great chain of being can be found in the first epistle of Alexander Pope's *An Essay on Man,* and more recently in Arthur O. Lovejoy's *The Great Chain of Being: A Study of the History of an Idea.*

Grotesque: In literary criticism, the subject matter of a work or a style of expression characterized by exaggeration, deformity, freakishness, and disorder. The grotesque often includes an element of comic absurdity. Early examples of literary grotesque include Francois Rabelais's *Pantagruel* and *Gargantua* and Thomas Nashe's *The Unfortunate Traveller,* while more recent examples can be found in the works of Edgar Allan Poe, Evelyn Waugh, Eudora Welty, Flannery O'Connor, Eugene Ionesco, Gunter Grass, Thomas Mann, Mervyn Peake, and Joseph Heller, among many others.

H

Haiku: The shortest form of Japanese poetry, constructed in three lines of five, seven, and five syllables respectively. The message of a *haiku* poem usually centers on some aspect of spirituality and provokes an emotional response in the reader. Early masters of *haiku* include Basho, Buson, Kobayashi Issa, and Masaoka Shiki. English writers of *haiku* include the Imagists, notably Ezra Pound, H. D., Amy Lowell, Carl Sandburg, and William Carlos Williams. Also known as *Hokku*.

Half Rhyme: See *Consonance*

Hamartia: In tragedy, the event or act that leads to the hero's or heroine's downfall. This term is often incorrectly used as a synonym for tragic flaw. In Richard Wright's *Native Son,* the act that seals Bigger Thomas's fate is his first impulsive murder.

Harlem Renaissance: The Harlem Renaissance of the 1920s is generally considered the first significant movement of black writers and artists in the United States. During this period, new and established black writers published more fiction and poetry than ever before, the first influential black literary journals were established, and black authors and artists received their first widespread recognition and serious critical appraisal. Among the major writers associated with this period are Claude McKay, Jean Toomer, Countee Cullen, Langston Hughes, Arna Bontemps, Nella Larsen, and Zora Neale Hurston. Works representative of the Harlem Renaissance include Arna Bontemps's poems "The Return" and "Golgotha Is a Mountain," Claude McKay's novel *Home to Harlem,* Nella Larsen's novel *Passing,* Langston Hughes's poem "The Negro Speaks of Rivers," and the journals *Crisis* and *Opportunity,* both founded during this period. Also known as Negro Renaissance and New Negro Movement.

Harlequin: A stock character of the *commedia dell'arte* who occasionally interrupted the action with silly antics. Harlequin first appeared on the English stage in John Day's *The Travailes of the Three English Brothers.* The San Francisco Mime Troupe is one of the few modern groups to adapt Harlequin to the needs of contemporary satire.

Hellenism: Imitation of ancient Greek thought or styles. Also, an approach to life that focuses on the growth and development of the intellect. "Hellenism" is sometimes used to refer to the belief that reason can be applied to examine all human experience. A cogent discussion of Hellenism can be found in Matthew Arnold's *Culture and Anarchy.*

Heptameter: See *Meter*

Hero/Heroine: The principal sympathetic character (male or female) in a literary work. Heroes and heroines typically exhibit admirable traits: idealism, courage, and integrity, for example. Famous heroes and heroines include Pip in Charles Dickens's *Great Expectations,* the anonymous narrator in Ralph Ellison's *Invisible Man,* and Sethe in Toni Morrison's *Beloved.*

Heroic Couplet: A rhyming couplet written in iambic pentameter (a verse with five iambic feet). The following lines by Alexander Pope are an example: "Truth guards the Poet, sanctifies the line,/ And makes Immortal, Verse as mean as mine."

Heroic Line: The meter and length of a line of verse in epic or heroic poetry. This varies by language and time period. For example, in English poetry, the heroic line is iambic pentameter (a verse with five iambic feet); in French, the alexandrine (a verse with six iambic feet); in classical literature, dactylic hexameter (a verse with six dactylic feet).

Heroine: See *Hero/Heroine*

Hexameter: See *Meter*

Historical Criticism: The study of a work based on its impact on the world of the time period in which it was written. Examples of postmodern historical criticism can be found in the work of Michel Foucault, Hayden White, Stephen Greenblatt, and Jonathan Goldberg.

Hokku: See *Haiku*

Holocaust: See *Holocaust Literature*

Holocaust Literature: Literature influenced by or written about the Holocaust of World War II. Such literature includes true stories of survival in concentration camps, escape, and life after the war, as well as fictional works and poetry. Representative works of Holocaust literature include Saul Bellow's *Mr. Sammler's Planet,* Anne Frank's *The Diary of a Young Girl,* Jerzy Kosinski's *The Painted Bird,* Arthur Miller's *Incident at Vichy,* Czeslaw Milosz's *Collected Poems,* William Styron's *Sophie's Choice,* and Art Spiegelman's *Maus.*

Homeric Simile: An elaborate, detailed comparison written as a simile many lines in length. An example of an epic simile from John Milton's *Paradise Lost* follows: Angel Forms, who lay entranced Thick as autumnal leaves that strow the brooks In Vallombrosa, where the Etrurian shades High over-arched embower; or scattered sedge Afloat, when with fierce winds Orion armed Hath vexed the Red-Sea coast, whose waves o'erthrew Busiris and his Memphian chivalry, While with perfidious hatred they pursued The sojourners of Goshen, who beheld From the safe shore their floating carcasses And broken chariot-wheels. Also known as Epic Simile.

Horatian Satire: See *Satire*

Humanism: A philosophy that places faith in the dignity of humankind and rejects the medieval perception of the individual as a weak, fallen creature. "Humanists" typically believe in the perfectibility of human nature and view reason and education as the means to that end. Humanist thought is represented in the works of Marsilio Ficino, Ludovico Castelvetro, Edmund Spenser, John Milton, Dean John Colet, Desiderius Erasmus, John Dryden, Alexander Pope, Matthew Arnold, and Irving Babbitt.

Humors: Mentions of the humors refer to the ancient Greek theory that a person's health and personality were determined by the balance of four basic fluids in the body: blood, phlegm, yellow bile, and black bile. A dominance of any fluid would cause extremes in behavior. An excess of blood created a sanguine person who was joyful, aggressive, and passionate; a phlegmatic person was shy, fearful, and sluggish; too much yellow bile led to a choleric temperament characterized by impatience, anger, bitterness, and stubbornness; and excessive black bile created melancholy, a state of laziness, gluttony, and lack of motivation. Literary treatment of the humors is exemplified by several characters in Ben Jonson's plays *Every Man in His Humour* and *Every Man out of His Humour.* Also spelled Humours.

Humours: See *Humors*

Hyperbole: In literary criticism, deliberate exaggeration used to achieve an effect. In William Shakespeare's *Macbeth,* Lady Macbeth hyperbolizes when she says, "All the perfumes of Arabia could not sweeten this little hand."

I

Iamb: See *Foot*

Idiom: A word construction or verbal expression closely associated with a given language. For example, in colloquial English the construction "how come" can be used instead of "why" to introduce a question. Similarly, "a piece of cake" is sometimes used to describe a task that is easily done.

Image: A concrete representation of an object or sensory experience. Typically, such a representation helps evoke the feelings associated with the object or experience itself. Images are either "literal" or "figurative." Literal images are especially concrete and involve little or no extension of the obvious meaning of the words used to express them. Figurative images do not follow the literal meaning of the words exactly. Images in literature are usually visual, but the term "image" can also refer to the representation of any sensory experience. In his poem "The Shepherd's Hour," Paul Verlaine presents the following image: "The Moon is red through horizon's fog;/ In a dancing mist the hazy meadow sleeps." The first line is broadly literal, while the second line involves turns of meaning associated with dancing and sleeping.

Imagery: The array of images in a literary work. Also, figurative language. William Butler Yeats's "The Second Coming" offers a powerful image of encroaching anarchy: Turning and turning in the widening gyre The falcon cannot hear the falconer; Things fall apart....

Imagism: An English and American poetry movement that flourished between 1908 and 1917.

The Imagists used precise, clearly presented images in their works. They also used common, everyday speech and aimed for conciseness, concrete imagery, and the creation of new rhythms. Participants in the Imagist movement included Ezra Pound, H. D. (Hilda Doolittle), and Amy Lowell, among others.

In medias res: A Latin term meaning "in the middle of things." It refers to the technique of beginning a story at its midpoint and then using various flashback devices to reveal previous action. This technique originated in such epics as Virgil's *Aeneid*.

Induction: The process of reaching a conclusion by reasoning from specific premises to form a general premise. Also, an introductory portion of a work of literature, especially a play. Geoffrey Chaucer's "Prologue" to the *Canterbury Tales,* Thomas Sackville's "Induction" to *The Mirror of Magistrates,* and the opening scene in William Shakespeare's *The Taming of the Shrew* are examples of inductions to literary works.

Intentional Fallacy: The belief that judgments of a literary work based solely on an author's stated or implied intentions are false and misleading. Critics who believe in the concept of the intentional fallacy typically argue that the work itself is sufficient matter for interpretation, even though they may concede that an author's statement of purpose can be useful. Analysis of William Wordsworth's *Lyrical Ballads* based on the observations about poetry he makes in his "Preface" to the second edition of that work is an example of the intentional fallacy.

Interior Monologue: A narrative technique in which characters' thoughts are revealed in a way that appears to be uncontrolled by the author. The interior monologue typically aims to reveal the inner self of a character. It portrays emotional experiences as they occur at both a conscious and unconscious level. images are often used to represent sensations or emotions. One of the best-known interior monologues in English is the Molly Bloom section at the close of James Joyce's *Ulysses.* The interior monologue is also common in the works of Virginia Woolf.

Internal Rhyme: Rhyme that occurs within a single line of verse. An example is in the opening line of Edgar Allan Poe's "The Raven": "Once upon a midnight dreary, while I pondered weak and weary." Here, "dreary" and "weary" make an internal rhyme.

Irish Literary Renaissance: A late nineteenth- and early twentieth-century movement in Irish literature. Members of the movement aimed to reduce the influence of British culture in Ireland and create an Irish national literature. William Butler Yeats, George Moore, and Sean O'Casey are three of the best-known figures of the movement.

Irony: In literary criticism, the effect of language in which the intended meaning is the opposite of what is stated. The title of Jonathan Swift's "A Modest Proposal" is ironic because what Swift proposes in this essay is cannibalism—hardly "modest."

Italian Sonnet: See *Sonnet*

J

Jacobean Age: The period of the reign of James I of England (1603-1625). The early literature of this period reflected the worldview of the Elizabethan Age, but a darker, more cynical attitude steadily grew in the art and literature of the Jacobean Age. This was an important time for English drama and poetry. Milestones include William Shakespeare's tragedies, tragi-comedies, and sonnets; Ben Jonson's various dramas; and John Donne's metaphysical poetry.

Jargon: Language that is used or understood only by a select group of people. Jargon may refer to terminology used in a certain profession, such as computer jargon, or it may refer to any nonsensical language that is not understood by most people. Literary examples of jargon are Francois Villon's *Ballades en jargon,* which is composed in the secret language of the *coquillards,* and Anthony Burgess's *A Clockwork Orange,* narrated in the fictional characters' language of "Nadsat."

Juvenalian Satire: See *Satire*

K

Knickerbocker Group: A somewhat indistinct group of New York writers of the first half of the nineteenth century. Members of the group were linked only by location and a common theme: New York life. Two famous members of the Knickerbocker Group were Washington Irving and William Cullen

Bryant. The group's name derives from Irving's *Knickerbocker's History of New York*.

L

Lais: See *Lay*

Lay: A song or simple narrative poem. The form originated in medieval France. Early French *lais* were often based on the Celtic legends and other tales sung by Breton minstrels—thus the name of the "Breton lay." In fourteenth-century England, the term "lay" was used to describe short narratives written in imitation of the Breton lays. The most notable of these is Geoffrey Chaucer's "The Minstrel's Tale."

Leitmotiv: See *Motif*

Literal Language: An author uses literal language when he or she writes without exaggerating or embellishing the subject matter and without any tools of figurative language. To say "He ran very quickly down the street" is to use literal language, whereas to say "He ran like a hare down the street" would be using figurative language.

Literary Ballad: See *Ballad*

Literature: Literature is broadly defined as any written or spoken material, but the term most often refers to creative works. Literature includes poetry, drama, fiction, and many kinds of nonfiction writing, as well as oral, dramatic, and broadcast compositions not necessarily preserved in a written format, such as films and television programs.

Lost Generation: A term first used by Gertrude Stein to describe the post-World War I generation of American writers: men and women haunted by a sense of betrayal and emptiness brought about by the destructiveness of the war. The term is commonly applied to Hart Crane, Ernest Hemingway, F. Scott Fitzgerald, and others.

Lyric Poetry: A poem expressing the subjective feelings and personal emotions of the poet. Such poetry is melodic, since it was originally accompanied by a lyre in recitals. Most Western poetry in the twentieth century may be classified as lyrical. Examples of lyric poetry include A. E. Housman's elegy "To an Athlete Dying Young," the odes of Pindar and Horace, Thomas Gray and William Collins, the sonnets of Sir Thomas Wyatt and Sir Philip Sidney, Elizabeth Barrett

Browning and Rainer Maria Rilke, and a host of other forms in the poetry of William Blake and Christina Rossetti, among many others.

M

Mannerism: Exaggerated, artificial adherence to a literary manner or style. Also, a popular style of the visual arts of late sixteenth-century Europe that was marked by elongation of the human form and by intentional spatial distortion. Literary works that are self-consciously high-toned and artistic are often said to be "mannered." Authors of such works include Henry James and Gertrude Stein.

Masculine Rhyme: See *Rhyme*

Masque: A lavish and elaborate form of entertainment, often performed in royal courts, that emphasizes song, dance, and costumery. The Renaissance form of the masque grew out of the spectacles of masked figures common in medieval England and Europe. The masque reached its peak of popularity and development in seventeenth-century England, during the reigns of James I and, especially, of Charles I. Ben Jonson, the most significant masque writer, also created the "antimasque," which incorporates elements of humor and the grotesque into the traditional masque and achieved greater dramatic quality. Masque-like interludes appear in Edmund Spenser's *The Faerie Queene* and in William Shakespeare's *The Tempest*. One of the best-known English masques is John Milton's *Comus*.

Measure: The foot, verse, or time sequence used in a literary work, especially a poem. Measure is often used somewhat incorrectly as a synonym for meter.

Melodrama: A play in which the typical plot is a conflict between characters who personify extreme good and evil. Melodramas usually end happily and emphasize sensationalism. Other literary forms that use the same techniques are often labeled "melodramatic." The term was formerly used to describe a combination of drama and music; as such, it was synonymous with "opera." Augustin Daly's *Under the Gaslight* and Dion Boucicault's *The Octoroon, The Colleen Bawn,* and *The Poor of New York* are examples of melodramas. The most popular media for twentieth-century melodramas are motion pictures and television.

Metaphor: A figure of speech that expresses an idea through the image of another object. Metaphors suggest the essence of the first object by identifying it with certain qualities of the second object. An example is "But soft, what light through yonder window breaks?/ It is the east, and Juliet is the sun" in William Shakespeare's *Romeo and Juliet*. Here, Juliet, the first object, is identified with qualities of the second object, the sun.

Metaphysical Conceit: See *Conceit*

Metaphysical Poetry: The body of poetry produced by a group of seventeenth-century English writers called the "Metaphysical Poets." The group includes John Donne and Andrew Marvell. The Metaphysical Poets made use of everyday speech, intellectual analysis, and unique imagery. They aimed to portray the ordinary conflicts and contradictions of life. Their poems often took the form of an argument, and many of them emphasize physical and religious love as well as the fleeting nature of life. Elaborate conceits are typical in metaphysical poetry. Marvell's "To His Coy Mistress" is a well-known example of a metaphysical poem.

Metaphysical Poets: See *Metaphysical Poetry*

Meter: In literary criticism, the repetition of sound patterns that creates a rhythm in poetry. The patterns are based on the number of syllables and the presence and absence of accents. The unit of rhythm in a line is called a foot. Types of meter are classified according to the number of feet in a line. These are the standard English lines: Monometer, one foot; Dimeter, two feet; Trimeter, three feet; Tetrameter, four feet; Pentameter, five feet; Hexameter, six feet (also called the Alexandrine); Heptameter, seven feet (also called the "Fourteener" when the feet are iambic). The most common English meter is the iambic pentameter, in which each line contains ten syllables, or five iambic feet, which individually are composed of an unstressed syllable followed by an accented syllable. Both of the following lines from Alfred, Lord Tennyson's "Ulysses" are written in iambic pentameter: Made weak by time and fate, but strong in will To strive, to seek, to find, and not to yield.

Mise en scene: The costumes, scenery, and other properties of a drama. Herbert Beerbohm Tree was renowned for the elaborate *mises en scene* of his lavish Shakespearean productions at His Majesty's Theatre between 1897 and 1915.

Modernism: Modern literary practices. Also, the principles of a literary school that lasted from roughly the beginning of the twentieth century until the end of World War II. Modernism is defined by its rejection of the literary conventions of the nineteenth century and by its opposition to conventional morality, taste, traditions, and economic values. Many writers are associated with the concepts of Modernism, including Albert Camus, Marcel Proust, D. H. Lawrence, W. H. Auden, Ernest Hemingway, William Faulkner, William Butler Yeats, Thomas Mann, Tennessee Williams, Eugene O'Neill, and James Joyce.

Monologue: A composition, written or oral, by a single individual. More specifically, a speech given by a single individual in a drama or other public entertainment. It has no set length, although it is usually several or more lines long. An example of an "extended monologue"—that is, a monologue of great length and seriousness—occurs in the one-act, one-character play *The Stronger* by August Strindberg.

Monometer: See *Meter*

Mood: The prevailing emotions of a work or of the author in his or her creation of the work. The mood of a work is not always what might be expected based on its subject matter. The poem "Dover Beach" by Matthew Arnold offers examples of two different moods originating from the same experience: watching the ocean at night. The mood of the first three lines—The sea is calm tonight The tide is full, the moon lies fair Upon the straights . . . . is in sharp contrast to the mood of the last three lines— And we are here as on a darkling plain Swept with confused alarms of struggle and flight, Where ignorant armies clash by night.

Motif: A theme, character type, image, metaphor, or other verbal element that recurs throughout a single work of literature or occurs in a number of different works over a period of time. For example, the various manifestations of the color white in Herman Melville's *Moby Dick* is a "specific" *motif,* while the trials of star-crossed lovers is a "conventional" *motif* from the literature of all periods. Also known as *Motiv* or *Leitmotiv*.

Motiv: See *Motif*

Muckrakers: An early twentieth-century group of American writers. Typically, their works exposed the wrongdoings of big business and government in the United States. Upton Sinclair's *The Jungle* exemplifies the muckraking novel.

Muses: Nine Greek mythological goddesses, the daughters of Zeus and Mnemosyne (Memory). Each muse patronized a specific area of the liberal arts and sciences. Calliope presided over epic poetry, Clio over history, Erato over love poetry, Euterpe over music or lyric poetry, Melpomene over tragedy, Polyhymnia over hymns to the gods, Terpsichore over dance, Thalia over comedy, and Urania over astronomy. Poets and writers traditionally made appeals to the Muses for inspiration in their work. John Milton invokes the aid of a muse at the beginning of the first book of his *Paradise Lost:* Of Man's First disobedience, and the Fruit of the Forbidden Tree, whose mortal taste Brought Death into the World, and all our woe, With loss of Eden, till one greater Man Restore us, and regain the blissful Seat, Sing Heav'nly Muse, that on the secret top of Oreb, or of Sinai, didst inspire That Shepherd, who first taught the chosen Seed, In the Beginning how the Heav'ns and Earth Rose out of Chaos . . . .

Mystery: See *Suspense*

Myth: An anonymous tale emerging from the traditional beliefs of a culture or social unit. Myths use supernatural explanations for natural phenomena. They may also explain cosmic issues like creation and death. Collections of myths, known as mythologies, are common to all cultures and nations, but the best-known myths belong to the Norse, Roman, and Greek mythologies. A famous myth is the story of Arachne, an arrogant young girl who challenged a goddess, Athena, to a weaving contest; when the girl won, Athena was enraged and turned Arachne into a spider, thus explaining the existence of spiders.

N

Narration: The telling of a series of events, real or invented. A narration may be either a simple narrative, in which the events are recounted chronologically, or a narrative with a plot, in which the account is given in a style reflecting the author's artistic concept of the story. Narration is sometimes used as a synonym for "storyline." The recounting of scary stories around a campfire is a form of narration.

Narrative: A verse or prose accounting of an event or sequence of events, real or invented. The term is also used as an adjective in the sense "method of narration." For example, in literary criticism, the expression "narrative technique" usually refers to the way the author structures and presents his or her story. Narratives range from the shortest accounts of events, as in Julius Caesar's remark, "I came, I saw, I conquered," to the longest historical or biographical works, as in Edward Gibbon's *The Decline and Fall of the Roman Empire,* as well as diaries, travelogues, novels, ballads, epics, short stories, and other fictional forms.

Narrative Poetry: A nondramatic poem in which the author tells a story. Such poems may be of any length or level of complexity. Epics such as *Beowulf* and ballads are forms of narrative poetry.

Narrator: The teller of a story. The narrator may be the author or a character in the story through whom the author speaks. Huckleberry Finn is the narrator of Mark Twain's *The Adventures of Huckleberry Finn.*

Naturalism: A literary movement of the late nineteenth and early twentieth centuries. The movement's major theorist, French novelist Emile Zola, envisioned a type of fiction that would examine human life with the objectivity of scientific inquiry. The Naturalists typically viewed human beings as either the products of "biological determinism," ruled by hereditary instincts and engaged in an endless struggle for survival, or as the products of "socioeconomic determinism," ruled by social and economic forces beyond their control. In their works, the Naturalists generally ignored the highest levels of society and focused on degradation: poverty, alcoholism, prostitution, insanity, and disease. Naturalism influenced authors throughout the world, including Henrik Ibsen and Thomas Hardy. In the United States, in particular, Naturalism had a profound impact. Among the authors who embraced its principles are Theodore Dreiser, Eugene O'Neill, Stephen Crane, Jack London, and Frank Norris.

Negritude: A literary movement based on the concept of a shared cultural bond on the part of black Africans, wherever they may be in the world. It traces its origins to the former French colonies of Africa and the Caribbean. Negritude poets, novelists, and essayists generally stress four points in their writings: One, black alienation from traditional African culture can lead to feelings of inferiority. Two, European colonialism and Western education should be resisted. Three, black Africans should seek to affirm and define their own identity. Four, African culture can and should be reclaimed. Many Negritude writers also claim that blacks can make unique contributions to the world, based on a heightened appreciation of nature, rhythm, and human emotions—aspects of life they say are not so highly valued in the materialistic and rationalistic West. Examples of Negritude literature include the poetry of both Senegalese Leopold Senghor in *Hosties noires* and Martiniquais Aime-Fernand Cesaire in *Return to My Native Land*.

Negro Renaissance: See *Harlem Renaissance*

Neoclassical Period: See *Neoclassicism*

Neoclassicism: In literary criticism, this term refers to the revival of the attitudes and styles of expression of classical literature. It is generally used to describe a period in European history beginning in the late seventeenth century and lasting until about 1800. In its purest form, Neoclassicism marked a return to order, proportion, restraint, logic, accuracy, and decorum. In England, where Neoclassicism perhaps was most popular, it reflected the influence of seventeenth- century French writers, especially dramatists. Neoclassical writers typically reacted against the intensity and enthusiasm of the Renaissance period. They wrote works that appealed to the intellect, using elevated language and classical literary forms such as satire and the ode. Neoclassical works were often governed by the classical goal of instruction. English neoclassicists included Alexander Pope, Jonathan Swift, Joseph Addison, Sir Richard Steele, John Gay, and Matthew Prior; French neoclassicists included Pierre Corneille and Jean-Baptiste Moliere. Also known as Age of Reason.

Neoclassicists: See *Neoclassicism*

New Criticism: A movement in literary criticism, dating from the late 1920s, that stressed close textual analysis in the interpretation of works of literature. The New Critics saw little merit in historical and biographical analysis. Rather, they aimed to examine the text alone, free from the question of how external events—biographical or otherwise—may have helped shape it. This predominantly American school was named "New Criticism" by one of its practitioners, John Crowe Ransom. Other important New Critics included Allen Tate, R. P. Blackmur, Robert Penn Warren, and Cleanth Brooks.

New Negro Movement: See *Harlem Renaissance*

Noble Savage: The idea that primitive man is noble and good but becomes evil and corrupted as he becomes civilized. The concept of the noble savage originated in the Renaissance period but is more closely identified with such later writers as Jean-Jacques Rousseau and Aphra Behn. First described in John Dryden's play *The Conquest of Granada*, the noble savage is portrayed by the various Native Americans in James Fenimore Cooper's "Leatherstocking Tales," by Queequeg, Daggoo, and Tashtego in Herman Melville's *Moby Dick*, and by John the Savage in Aldous Huxley's *Brave New World*.

O

Objective Correlative: An outward set of objects, a situation, or a chain of events corresponding to an inward experience and evoking this experience in the reader. The term frequently appears in modern criticism in discussions of authors' intended effects on the emotional responses of readers. This term was originally used by T. S. Eliot in his 1919 essay "Hamlet."

Objectivity: A quality in writing characterized by the absence of the author's opinion or feeling about the subject matter. Objectivity is an important factor in criticism. The novels of Henry James and, to a certain extent, the poems of John Larkin demonstrate objectivity, and it is central to John Keats's concept of "negative capability." Critical and journalistic writing usually are or attempt to be objective.

Occasional Verse: poetry written on the occasion of a significant historical or personal event. *Vers de societe* is sometimes called occasional verse although it is of a less serious nature. Famous examples of occasional verse include Andrew Marvell's "Horatian Ode upon Cromwell's Return from England," Walt Whitman's "When Lilacs Last in the Dooryard Bloom'd"—written upon the death of Abraham Lincoln—and Edmund Spenser's commemoration of his wedding, "Epithalamion."

Octave: A poem or stanza composed of eight lines. The term octave most often represents the first eight lines of a Petrarchan sonnet. An example of an octave is taken from a translation of a Petrarchan sonnet by Sir Thomas Wyatt: The pillar perisht is whereto I leant, The strongest stay of mine unquiet mind; The like of it no man again can find, From East to West Still seeking though he went. To mind unhap! for hap away hath rent Of all my joy the very bark and rind; And I, alas, by chance am thus assigned Daily to mourn till death do it relent.

Ode: Name given to an extended lyric poem characterized by exalted emotion and dignified style. An ode usually concerns a single, serious theme. Most odes, but not all, are addressed to an object or individual. Odes are distinguished from other lyric poetic forms by their complex rhythmic and stanzaic patterns. An example of this form is John Keats's "Ode to a Nightingale."

Oedipus Complex: A son's amorous obsession with his mother. The phrase is derived from the story of the ancient Theban hero Oedipus, who unknowingly killed his father and married his mother. Literary occurrences of the Oedipus complex include Andre Gide's *Oedipe* and Jean Cocteau's *La Machine infernale,* as well as the most famous, Sophocles' *Oedipus Rex.*

Omniscience: See *Point of View*

Onomatopoeia: The use of words whose sounds express or suggest their meaning. In its simplest sense, onomatopoeia may be represented by words that mimic the sounds they denote such as "hiss" or "meow." At a more subtle level, the pattern and rhythm of

sounds and rhymes of a line or poem may be onomatopoeic. A celebrated example of onomatopoeia is the repetition of the word "bells" in Edgar Allan Poe's poem "The Bells."

Opera: A type of stage performance, usually a drama, in which the dialogue is sung. Classic examples of opera include Giuseppi Verdi's *La traviata,* Giacomo Puccini's *La Boheme,* and Richard Wagner's *Tristan und Isolde.* Major twentieth-century contributors to the form include Richard Strauss and Alban Berg.

Operetta: A usually romantic comic opera. John Gay's *The Beggar's Opera,* Richard Sheridan's *The Duenna,* and numerous works by William Gilbert and Arthur Sullivan are examples of operettas.

Oral Tradition: See *Oral Transmission*

Oral Transmission: A process by which songs, ballads, folklore, and other material are transmitted by word of mouth. The tradition of oral transmission predates the written record systems of literate society. Oral transmission preserves material sometimes over generations, although often with variations. Memory plays a large part in the recitation and preservation of orally transmitted material. Breton lays, French *fabliaux,* national epics (including the Anglo-Saxon *Beowulf,* the Spanish *El Cid,* and the Finnish *Kalevala*), Native American myths and legends, and African folktales told by plantation slaves are examples of orally transmitted literature.

Oration: Formal speaking intended to motivate the listeners to some action or feeling. Such public speaking was much more common before the development of timely printed communication such as newspapers. Famous examples of oration include Abraham Lincoln's "Gettysburg Address" and Dr. Martin Luther King Jr.'s "I Have a Dream" speech.

Ottava Rima: An eight-line stanza of poetry composed in iambic pentameter (a five-foot line in which each foot consists of an unaccented syllable followed by an accented syllable), following the abababcc rhyme scheme. This form has been prominently used by such important English writers as Lord Byron, Henry Wadsworth Longfellow, and W. B. Yeats.

Oxymoron: A phrase combining two contradictory terms. Oxymorons may be intentional or unintentional. The following speech from William Shakespeare's *Romeo and Juliet* uses several oxymorons: Why, then, O brawling love! O loving hate! O anything, of nothing first create! O heavy lightness! serious vanity! Mis-shapen chaos of well-seeming forms! Feather of lead, bright smoke, cold fire, sick health! This love feel I, that feel no love in this.

P

Pantheism: The idea that all things are both a manifestation or revelation of God and a part of God at the same time. Pantheism was a common attitude in the early societies of Egypt, India, and Greece—the term derives from the Greek *pan* meaning "all" and *theos* meaning "deity." It later became a significant part of the Christian faith. William Wordsworth and Ralph Waldo Emerson are among the many writers who have expressed the pantheistic attitude in their works.

Parable: A story intended to teach a moral lesson or answer an ethical question. In the West, the best examples of parables are those of Jesus Christ in the New Testament, notably "The Prodigal Son," but parables also are used in Sufism, rabbinic literature, Hasidism, and Zen Buddhism.

Paradox: A statement that appears illogical or contradictory at first, but may actually point to an underlying truth. "Less is more" is an example of a paradox. Literary examples include Francis Bacon's statement, "The most corrected copies are commonly the least correct," and "All animals are equal, but some animals are more equal than others" from George Orwell's *Animal Farm*.

Parallelism: A method of comparison of two ideas in which each is developed in the same grammatical structure. Ralph Waldo Emerson's "Civilization" contains this example of parallelism: Raphael paints wisdom; Handel sings it, Phidias carves it, Shakespeare writes it, Wren builds it, Columbus sails it, Luther preaches it, Washington arms it, Watt mechanizes it.

Parnassianism: A mid nineteenth-century movement in French literature. Followers of the movement stressed adherence to well-defined artistic forms as a reaction against the often chaotic expression of the artist's ego that dominated the work of the Romantics. The Parnassians also rejected the moral, ethical, and social themes exhibited in the works of French Romantics such as Victor Hugo. The aesthetic doctrines of the Parnassians strongly influenced the later symbolist and decadent movements. Members of the Parnassian school include Leconte de Lisle, Sully Prudhomme, Albert Glatigny, Francois Coppee, and Theodore de Banville.

Parody: In literary criticism, this term refers to an imitation of a serious literary work or the signature style of a particular author in a ridiculous manner. A typical parody adopts the style of the original and applies it to an inappropriate subject for humorous effect. Parody is a form of satire and could be considered the literary equivalent of a caricature or cartoon. Henry Fielding's *Shamela* is a parody of Samuel Richardson's *Pamela*.

Pastoral: A term derived from the Latin word "pastor," meaning shepherd. A pastoral is a literary composition on a rural theme. The conventions of the pastoral were originated by the third-century Greek poet Theocritus, who wrote about the experiences, love affairs, and pastimes of Sicilian shepherds. In a pastoral, characters and language of a courtly nature are often placed in a simple setting. The term pastoral is also used to classify dramas, elegies, and lyrics that exhibit the use of country settings and shepherd characters. Percy Bysshe Shelley's "Adonais" and John Milton's "Lycidas" are two famous examples of pastorals.

Pastorela: The Spanish name for the shepherds play, a folk drama reenacted during the Christmas season. Examples of *pastorelas* include Gomez Manrique's *Representacion del nacimiento* and the dramas of Lucas Fernandez and Juan del Encina.

Pathetic Fallacy: A term coined by English critic John Ruskin to identify writing that falsely endows nonhuman things with human intentions and feelings, such as "angry clouds" and "sad trees." The pathetic fallacy is a required convention in the classical poetic form of the pastoral elegy, and it is used in the modern poetry of T. S. Eliot, Ezra

Pound, and the Imagists. Also known as Poetic Fallacy.

Pelado: Literally the "skinned one" or shirtless one, he was the stock underdog, sharp-witted picaresque character of Mexican vaudeville and tent shows. The *pelado* is found in such works as Don Catarino's *Los effectos de la crisis* and *Regreso a mi tierra.*

Pen Name: See *Pseudonym*

Pentameter: See *Meter*

Persona: A Latin term meaning "mask." *Personae* are the characters in a fictional work of literature. The *persona* generally functions as a mask through which the author tells a story in a voice other than his or her own. A *persona* is usually either a character in a story who acts as a narrator or an "implied author," a voice created by the author to act as the narrator for himself or herself. *Personae* include the narrator of Geoffrey Chaucer's *Canterbury Tales* and Marlow in Joseph Conrad's *Heart of Darkness.*

Personae: See *Persona*

Personal Point of View: See *Point of View*

Personification: A figure of speech that gives human qualities to abstract ideas, animals, and inanimate objects. William Shakespeare used personification in *Romeo and Juliet* in the lines "Arise, fair sun, and kill the envious moon,/ Who is already sick and pale with grief." Here, the moon is portrayed as being envious, sick, and pale with grief—all markedly human qualities. Also known as *Prosopopoeia.*

Petrarchan Sonnet: See *Sonnet*

Phenomenology: A method of literary criticism based on the belief that things have no existence outside of human consciousness or awareness. Proponents of this theory believe that art is a process that takes place in the mind of the observer as he or she contemplates an object rather than a quality of the object itself. Among phenomenological critics are Edmund Husserl, George Poulet, Marcel Raymond, and Roman Ingarden.

Picaresque Novel: Episodic fiction depicting the adventures of a roguish central character ("picaro" is Spanish for "rogue"). The picaresque hero is commonly a low-born but clever individual who wanders into and out of various affairs of love, danger, and farcical intrigue. These involvements may take place at all social levels and typically present a humorous and wide-ranging satire of a given society. Prominent examples of the picaresque novel are *Don Quixote* by Miguel de Cervantes, *Tom Jones* by Henry Fielding, and *Moll Flanders* by Daniel Defoe.

Plagiarism: Claiming another person's written material as one's own. Plagiarism can take the form of direct, word-for-word copying or the theft of the substance or idea of the work. A student who copies an encyclopedia entry and turns it in as a report for school is guilty of plagiarism.

Platonic Criticism: A form of criticism that stresses an artistic work's usefulness as an agent of social engineering rather than any quality or value of the work itself. Platonic criticism takes as its starting point the ancient Greek philosopher Plato's comments on art in his *Republic.*

Platonism: The embracing of the doctrines of the philosopher Plato, popular among the poets of the Renaissance and the Romantic period. Platonism is more flexible than Aristotelian Criticism and places more emphasis on the supernatural and unknown aspects of life. Platonism is expressed in the love poetry of the Renaissance, the fourth book of Baldassare Castiglione's *The Book of the Courtier,* and the poetry of William Blake, William Wordsworth, Percy Bysshe Shelley, Friedrich Holderlin, William Butler Yeats, and Wallace Stevens.

Play: See *Drama*

Plot: In literary criticism, this term refers to the pattern of events in a narrative or drama. In its simplest sense, the plot guides the author in composing the work and helps the reader follow the work. Typically, plots exhibit causality and unity and have a beginning, a middle, and an end. Sometimes, however, a plot may consist of a series of disconnected events, in which case it is known as an "episodic plot." In his *Aspects of the Novel,* E. M. Forster distinguishes between a story, defined as a "narrative of events arranged in their time- sequence," and plot, which organizes the events to a "sense of causality." This definition closely mirrors Aristotle's discussion of plot in his *Poetics.*

Poem: In its broadest sense, a composition utilizing rhyme, meter, concrete detail, and expressive language to create a literary experience with emotional and aesthetic appeal. Typical poems include sonnets, odes, elegies, *haiku,* ballads, and free verse.

Poet: An author who writes poetry or verse. The term is also used to refer to an artist or writer who has an exceptional gift for expression, imagination, and energy in the making of art in any form. Well-known poets include Horace, Basho, Sir Philip Sidney, Sir Edmund Spenser, John Donne, Andrew Marvell, Alexander Pope, Jonathan Swift, George Gordon, Lord Byron, John Keats, Christina Rossetti, W. H. Auden, Stevie Smith, and Sylvia Plath.

Poetic Fallacy: See *Pathetic Fallacy*

Poetic Justice: An outcome in a literary work, not necessarily a poem, in which the good are rewarded and the evil are punished, especially in ways that particularly fit their virtues or crimes. For example, a murderer may himself be murdered, or a thief will find himself penniless.

Poetic License: Distortions of fact and literary convention made by a writer—not always a poet—for the sake of the effect gained. Poetic license is closely related to the concept of "artistic freedom." An author exercises poetic license by saying that a pile of money "reaches as high as a mountain" when the pile is actually only a foot or two high.

Poetics: This term has two closely related meanings. It denotes (1) an aesthetic theory in literary criticism about the essence of poetry or (2) rules prescribing the proper methods, content, style, or diction of poetry. The term poetics may also refer to theories about literature in general, not just poetry.

Poetry: In its broadest sense, writing that aims to present ideas and evoke an emotional experience in the reader through the use of meter, imagery, connotative and concrete words, and a carefully constructed structure based on rhythmic patterns. Poetry typically relies on words and expressions that have several layers of meaning. It also makes use of the effects of regular rhythm on the ear and may make a strong appeal to the senses through the use of imagery. Edgar Allan Poe's

"Annabel Lee" and Walt Whitman's *Leaves of Grass* are famous examples of poetry.

Point of View: The narrative perspective from which a literary work is presented to the reader. There are four traditional points of view. The "third person omniscient" gives the reader a "godlike" perspective, unrestricted by time or place, from which to see actions and look into the minds of characters. This allows the author to comment openly on characters and events in the work. The "third person" point of view presents the events of the story from outside of any single character's perception, much like the omniscient point of view, but the reader must understand the action as it takes place and without any special insight into characters' minds or motivations. The "first person" or "personal" point of view relates events as they are perceived by a single character. The main character "tells" the story and may offer opinions about the action and characters which differ from those of the author. Much less common than omniscient, third person, and first person is the "second person" point of view, wherein the author tells the story as if it is happening to the reader. James Thurber employs the omniscient point of view in his short story "The Secret Life of Walter Mitty." Ernest Hemingway's "A Clean, Well-Lighted Place" is a short story told from the third person point of view. Mark Twain's novel *Huck Finn* is presented from the first person viewpoint. Jay McInerney's *Bright Lights, Big City* is an example of a novel which uses the second person point of view.

Polemic: A work in which the author takes a stand on a controversial subject, such as abortion or religion. Such works are often extremely argumentative or provocative. Classic examples of polemics include John Milton's *Aeropagitica* and Thomas Paine's *The American Crisis*.

Pornography: Writing intended to provoke feelings of lust in the reader. Such works are often condemned by critics and teachers, but those which can be shown to have literary value are viewed less harshly. Literary works that have been described as pornographic include Ovid's *The Art of Love,* Margaret of Angouleme's *Heptameron,* John Cleland's *Memoirs of a Woman of Pleasure; or, the Life of Fanny Hill,* the anonymous

My Secret Life, D. H. Lawrence's *Lady Chatterley's Lover,* and Vladimir Nabokov's *Lolita.*

Post-Aesthetic Movement: An artistic response made by African Americans to the black aesthetic movement of the 1960s and early '70s. Writers since that time have adopted a somewhat different tone in their work, with less emphasis placed on the disparity between black and white in the United States. In the words of post-aesthetic authors such as Toni Morrison, John Edgar Wideman, and Kristin Hunter, African Americans are portrayed as looking inward for answers to their own questions, rather than always looking to the outside world. Two well-known examples of works produced as part of the post-aesthetic movement are the Pulitzer Prize-winning novels *The Color Purple* by Alice Walker and *Beloved* by Toni Morrison.

Postmodernism: Writing from the 1960s forward characterized by experimentation and continuing to apply some of the fundamentals of modernism, which included existentialism and alienation. Postmodernists have gone a step further in the rejection of tradition begun with the modernists by also rejecting traditional forms, preferring the anti-novel over the novel and the anti-hero over the hero. Postmodern writers include Alain Robbe-Grillet, Thomas Pynchon, Margaret Drabble, John Fowles, Adolfo Bioy-Casares, and Gabriel Garcia Marquez.

Pre-Raphaelites: A circle of writers and artists in mid nineteenth-century England. Valuing the pre-Renaissance artistic qualities of religious symbolism, lavish pictorialism, and natural sensuousness, the Pre-Raphaelites cultivated a sense of mystery and melancholy that influenced later writers associated with the Symbolist and Decadent movements. The major members of the group include Dante Gabriel Rossetti, Christina Rossetti, Algernon Swinburne, and Walter Pater.

Primitivism: The belief that primitive peoples were nobler and less flawed than civilized peoples because they had not been subjected to the tainting influence of society. Examples of literature espousing primitivism include Aphra Behn's *Oroonoko: Or, The History of the Royal Slave,* Jean-Jacques Rousseau's *Julie ou la Nouvelle Heloise,* Oliver Goldsmith's

The Deserted Village, the poems of Robert Burns, Herman Melville's stories *Typee, Omoo,* and *Mardi,* many poems of William Butler Yeats and Robert Frost, and William Golding's novel *Lord of the Flies.*

Projective Verse: A form of free verse in which the poet's breathing pattern determines the lines of the poem. Poets who advocate projective verse are against all formal structures in writing, including meter and form. Besides its creators, Robert Creeley, Robert Duncan, and Charles Olson, two other well-known projective verse poets are Denise Levertov and LeRoi Jones (Amiri Baraka). Also known as Breath Verse.

Prologue: An introductory section of a literary work. It often contains information establishing the situation of the characters or presents information about the setting, time period, or action. In drama, the prologue is spoken by a chorus or by one of the principal characters. In the "General Prologue" of *The Canterbury Tales,* Geoffrey Chaucer describes the main characters and establishes the setting and purpose of the work.

Prose: A literary medium that attempts to mirror the language of everyday speech. It is distinguished from poetry by its use of unmetered, unrhymed language consisting of logically related sentences. Prose is usually grouped into paragraphs that form a cohesive whole such as an essay or a novel. Recognized masters of English prose writing include Sir Thomas Malory, William Caxton, Raphael Holinshed, Joseph Addison, Mark Twain, and Ernest Hemingway.

Prosopopoeia: See *Personification*

Protagonist: The central character of a story who serves as a focus for its themes and incidents and as the principal rationale for its development. The protagonist is sometimes referred to in discussions of modern literature as the hero or anti-hero. Well-known protagonists are Hamlet in William Shakespeare's *Hamlet* and Jay Gatsby in F. Scott Fitzgerald's *The Great Gatsby.*

Protest Fiction: Protest fiction has as its primary purpose the protesting of some social injustice, such as racism or discrimination. One example of protest fiction is a series of five novels by Chester Himes, beginning in 1945 with *If He Hollers Let Him Go* and ending in

1955 with *The Primitive*. These works depict the destructive effects of race and gender stereotyping in the context of interracial relationships. Another African American author whose works often revolve around themes of social protest is John Oliver Killens. James Baldwin's essay "Everybody's Protest Novel" generated controversy by attacking the authors of protest fiction.

Proverb: A brief, sage saying that expresses a truth about life in a striking manner. "They are not all cooks who carry long knives" is an example of a proverb.

Pseudonym: A name assumed by a writer, most often intended to prevent his or her identification as the author of a work. Two or more authors may work together under one pseudonym, or an author may use a different name for each genre he or she publishes in. Some publishing companies maintain "house pseudonyms," under which any number of authors may write installations in a series. Some authors also choose a pseudonym over their real names the way an actor may use a stage name. Examples of pseudonyms (with the author's real name in parentheses) include Voltaire (Francois-Marie Arouet), Novalis (Friedrich von Hardenberg), Currer Bell (Charlotte Bronte), Ellis Bell (Emily Bronte), George Eliot (Maryann Evans), Honorio Bustos Donmecq (Adolfo Bioy-Casares and Jorge Luis Borges), and Richard Bachman (Stephen King).

Pun: A play on words that have similar sounds but different meanings. A serious example of the pun is from John Donne's "A Hymne to God the Father": Sweare by thyself, that at my death thy sonne Shall shine as he shines now, and hereto fore; And, having done that, Thou haste done; I fear no more.

Pure Poetry: poetry written without instructional intent or moral purpose that aims only to please a reader by its imagery or musical flow. The term pure poetry is used as the antonym of the term "didacticism." The poetry of Edgar Allan Poe, Stephane Mallarme, Paul Verlaine, Paul Valery, Juan Ramoz Jimenez, and Jorge Guillen offer examples of pure poetry.

Q

Quatrain: A four-line stanza of a poem or an entire poem consisting of four lines. The following quatrain is from Robert Herrick's "To Live Merrily, and to Trust to Good Verses": Round, round, the root do's run; And being ravisht thus, Come, I will drink a Tun To my *Propertius*.

R

Raisonneur: A character in a drama who functions as a spokesperson for the dramatist's views. The *raisonneur* typically observes the play without becoming central to its action. *Raisonneurs* were very common in plays of the nineteenth century.

Realism: A nineteenth-century European literary movement that sought to portray familiar characters, situations, and settings in a realistic manner. This was done primarily by using an objective narrative point of view and through the buildup of accurate detail. The standard for success of any realistic work depends on how faithfully it transfers common experience into fictional forms. The realistic method may be altered or extended, as in stream of consciousness writing, to record highly subjective experience. Seminal authors in the tradition of Realism include Honore de Balzac, Gustave Flaubert, and Henry James.

Refrain: A phrase repeated at intervals throughout a poem. A refrain may appear at the end of each stanza or at less regular intervals. It may be altered slightly at each appearance. Some refrains are nonsense expressions—as with "Nevermore" in Edgar Allan Poe's "The Raven"—that seem to take on a different significance with each use.

Renaissance: The period in European history that marked the end of the Middle Ages. It began in Italy in the late fourteenth century. In broad terms, it is usually seen as spanning the fourteenth, fifteenth, and sixteenth centuries, although it did not reach Great Britain, for example, until the 1480s or so. The Renaissance saw an awakening in almost every sphere of human activity, especially science, philosophy, and the arts. The period is best defined by the emergence of a general philosophy that emphasized the importance of the intellect, the individual, and world affairs. It contrasts strongly with the medieval worldview, characterized by the dominant concerns of faith, the social collective, and spiritual salvation. Prominent writers during the Renaissance include Niccolo Machiavelli and Baldassare Castiglione in Italy, Miguel de Cervantes and Lope de Vega in Spain, Jean Froissart and Francois Rabelais in France, Sir Thomas More and Sir Philip Sidney in England, and Desiderius Erasmus in Holland.

Repartee: Conversation featuring snappy retorts and witticisms. Masters of *repartee* include Sydney Smith, Charles Lamb, and Oscar Wilde. An example is recorded in the meeting of "Beau" Nash and John Wesley: Nash said, "I never make way for a fool," to which Wesley responded, "Don't you? I always do," and stepped aside.

Resolution: The portion of a story following the climax, in which the conflict is resolved. The resolution of Jane Austen's *Northanger Abbey* is neatly summed up in the following sentence: "Henry and Catherine were married, the bells rang and every body smiled."

Restoration: See *Restoration Age*

Restoration Age: A period in English literature beginning with the crowning of Charles II in 1660 and running to about 1700. The era, which was characterized by a reaction against Puritanism, was the first great age of the comedy of manners. The finest literature of the era is typically witty and urbane, and often lewd. Prominent Restoration Age writers include William Congreve, Samuel Pepys, John Dryden, and John Milton.

Revenge Tragedy: A dramatic form popular during the Elizabethan Age, in which the protagonist, directed by the ghost of his murdered father or son, inflicts retaliation upon a powerful villain. Notable features of the revenge tragedy include violence, bizarre criminal acts, intrigue, insanity, a hesitant protagonist, and the use of soliloquy. Thomas Kyd's *Spanish Tragedy* is the first example of revenge tragedy in English, and William Shakespeare's *Hamlet* is perhaps the best. Extreme examples of revenge tragedy, such as John Webster's *The Duchess of Malfi,* are labeled "tragedies of blood." Also known as Tragedy of Blood.

Revista: The Spanish term for a vaudeville musical revue. Examples of *revistas* include Antonio Guzman Aguilera's *Mexico para los mexicanos,* Daniel Vanegas's *Maldito jazz,* and Don

Catarino's *Whiskey, morfina y marihuana* and *El desterrado.*

Rhetoric: In literary criticism, this term denotes the art of ethical persuasion. In its strictest sense, rhetoric adheres to various principles developed since classical times for arranging facts and ideas in a clear, persuasive, appealing manner. The term is also used to refer to effective prose in general and theories of or methods for composing effective prose. Classical examples of rhetorics include *The Rhetoric of Aristotle,* Quintillian's *Institutio Oratoria,* and Cicero's *Ad Herennium.*

Rhetorical Question: A question intended to provoke thought, but not an expressed answer, in the reader. It is most commonly used in oratory and other persuasive genres. The following lines from Thomas Gray's "Elegy Written in a Country Churchyard" ask rhetorical questions: Can storied urn or animated bust Back to its mansion call the fleeting breath? Can Honour's voice provoke the silent dust, Or Flattery soothe the dull cold ear of Death?

Rhyme: When used as a noun in literary criticism, this term generally refers to a poem in which words sound identical or very similar and appear in parallel positions in two or more lines. Rhymes are classified into different types according to where they fall in a line or stanza or according to the degree of similarity they exhibit in their spellings and sounds. Some major types of rhyme are "masculine" rhyme, "feminine" rhyme, and "triple" rhyme. In a masculine rhyme, the rhyming sound falls in a single accented syllable, as with "heat" and "eat." Feminine rhyme is a rhyme of two syllables, one stressed and one unstressed, as with "merry" and "tarry." Triple rhyme matches the sound of the accented syllable and the two unaccented syllables that follow: "narrative" and "declarative." Robert Browning alternates feminine and masculine rhymes in his "Soliloquy of the Spanish Cloister": Gr-r-r—there go, my heart's abhorrence! Water your damned flower-pots, do! If hate killed men, Brother Lawrence, God's blood, would not mine kill you! What? Your myrtle-bush wants trimming? Oh, that rose has prior claims— Needs its leaden vase filled brimming? Hell dry you up with flames! Triple rhymes can be found in Thomas Hood's "Bridge of

Sighs," George Gordon Byron's satirical verse, and Ogden Nash's comic poems.

Rhyme Royal: A stanza of seven lines composed in iambic pentameter and rhymed *ababbcc*. The name is said to be a tribute to King James I of Scotland, who made much use of the form in his poetry. Examples of rhyme royal include Geoffrey Chaucer's *The Parlement of Foules,* William Shakespeare's *The Rape of Lucrece,* William Morris's *The Early Paradise,* and John Masefield's *The Widow in the Bye Street.*

Rhyme Scheme: See *Rhyme*

Rhythm: A regular pattern of sound, time intervals, or events occurring in writing, most often and most discernably in poetry. Regular, reliable rhythm is known to be soothing to humans, while interrupted, unpredictable, or rapidly changing rhythm is disturbing. These effects are known to authors, who use them to produce a desired reaction in the reader. An example of a form of irregular rhythm is sprung rhythm poetry; quantitative verse, on the other hand, is very regular in its rhythm.

Rising Action: The part of a drama where the plot becomes increasingly complicated. Rising action leads up to the climax, or turning point, of a drama. The final "chase scene" of an action film is generally the rising action which culminates in the film's climax.

Rococo: A style of European architecture that flourished in the eighteenth century, especially in France. The most notable features of *rococo* are its extensive use of ornamentation and its themes of lightness, gaiety, and intimacy. In literary criticism, the term is often used disparagingly to refer to a decadent or over-ornamental style. Alexander Pope's "The Rape of the Lock" is an example of literary *rococo.*

Roman à clef: A French phrase meaning "novel with a key." It refers to a narrative in which real persons are portrayed under fictitious names. Jack Kerouac, for example, portrayed various real-life beat generation figures under fictitious names in his *On the Road.*

Romance: A broad term, usually denoting a narrative with exotic, exaggerated, often idealized characters, scenes, and themes. Nathaniel Hawthorne called his *The House of the Seven Gables* and *The Marble Faun* romances in order to distinguish them from clearly realistic works.

Romantic Age: See *Romanticism*

Romanticism: This term has two widely accepted meanings. In historical criticism, it refers to a European intellectual and artistic movement of the late eighteenth and early nineteenth centuries that sought greater freedom of personal expression than that allowed by the strict rules of literary form and logic of the eighteenth-century neoclassicists. The Romantics preferred emotional and imaginative expression to rational analysis. They considered the individual to be at the center of all experience and so placed him or her at the center of their art. The Romantics believed that the creative imagination reveals nobler truths—unique feelings and attitudes—than those that could be discovered by logic or by scientific examination. Both the natural world and the state of childhood were important sources for revelations of "eternal truths." "Romanticism" is also used as a general term to refer to a type of sensibility found in all periods of literary history and usually considered to be in opposition to the principles of classicism. In this sense, Romanticism signifies any work or philosophy in which the exotic or dreamlike figure strongly, or that is devoted to individualistic expression, self-analysis, or a pursuit of a higher realm of knowledge than can be discovered by human reason. Prominent Romantics include Jean-Jacques Rousseau, William Wordsworth, John Keats, Lord Byron, and Johann Wolfgang von Goethe.

Romantics: See *Romanticism*

Russian Symbolism: A Russian poetic movement, derived from French symbolism, that flourished between 1894 and 1910. While some Russian Symbolists continued in the French tradition, stressing aestheticism and the importance of suggestion above didactic intent, others saw their craft as a form of mystical worship, and themselves as mediators between the supernatural and the mundane. Russian symbolists include Aleksandr Blok, Vyacheslav Ivanovich Ivanov, Fyodor Sologub, Andrey Bely, Nikolay Gumilyov, and Vladimir Sergeyevich Solovyov.

S

Satire: A work that uses ridicule, humor, and wit to criticize and provoke change in human nature and institutions. There are two major types of satire: "formal" or "direct" satire speaks directly to the reader or to a character in the work; "indirect" satire relies upon the ridiculous behavior of its characters to make its point. Formal satire is further divided into two manners: the "Horatian," which ridicules gently, and the "Juvenalian," which derides its subjects harshly and bitterly. Voltaire's novella *Candide* is an indirect satire. Jonathan Swift's essay "A Modest Proposal" is a Juvenalian satire.

Scansion: The analysis or "scanning" of a poem to determine its meter and often its rhyme scheme. The most common system of scansion uses accents (slanted lines drawn above syllables) to show stressed syllables, breves (curved lines drawn above syllables) to show unstressed syllables, and vertical lines to separate each foot. In the first line of John Keats's *Endymion,* "A thing of beauty is a joy forever:" the word "thing," the first syllable of "beauty," the word "joy," and the second syllable of "forever" are stressed, while the words "A" and "of," the second syllable of "beauty," the word "a," and the first and third syllables of "forever" are unstressed. In the second line: "Its loveliness increases; it will never" a pair of vertical lines separate the foot ending with "increases" and the one beginning with "it."

Scene: A subdivision of an act of a drama, consisting of continuous action taking place at a single time and in a single location. The beginnings and endings of scenes may be indicated by clearing the stage of actors and props or by the entrances and exits of important characters. The first act of William Shakespeare's *Winter's Tale* is comprised of two scenes.

Science Fiction: A type of narrative about or based upon real or imagined scientific theories and technology. Science fiction is often peopled with alien creatures and set on other planets or in different dimensions. Karel Capek's *R.U.R.* is a major work of science fiction.

Second Person: See *Point of View*

Semiotics: The study of how literary forms and conventions affect the meaning of language. Semioticians include Ferdinand de Saussure, Charles Sanders Pierce, Claude Levi-Strauss, Jacques Lacan, Michel Foucault, Jacques Derrida, Roland Barthes, and Julia Kristeva.

Sestet: Any six-line poem or stanza. Examples of the sestet include the last six lines of the Petrarchan sonnet form, the stanza form of Robert Burns's "A Poet's Welcome to his love-begotten Daughter," and the sestina form in W. H. Auden's "Paysage Moralise."

Setting: The time, place, and culture in which the action of a narrative takes place. The elements of setting may include geographic location, characters' physical and mental environments, prevailing cultural attitudes, or the historical time in which the action takes place. Examples of settings include the romanticized Scotland in Sir Walter Scott's "Waverley" novels, the French provincial setting in Gustave Flaubert's *Madame Bovary,* the fictional Wessex country of Thomas Hardy's novels, and the small towns of southern Ontario in Alice Munro's short stories.

Shakespearean Sonnet: See *Sonnet*

Signifying Monkey: A popular trickster figure in black folklore, with hundreds of tales about this character documented since the 19th century. Henry Louis Gates Jr. examines the history of the signifying monkey in *The Signifying Monkey: Towards a Theory of Afro-American Literary Criticism,* published in 1988.

Simile: A comparison, usually using "like" or "as," of two essentially dissimilar things, as in "coffee as cold as ice" or "He sounded like a broken record." The title of Ernest Hemingway's "Hills Like White Elephants" contains a simile.

Slang: A type of informal verbal communication that is generally unacceptable for formal writing. Slang words and phrases are often colorful exaggerations used to emphasize the speaker's point; they may also be shortened versions of an often-used word or phrase. Examples of American slang from the 1990s include "yuppie" (an acronym for Young Urban Professional), "awesome" (for "excellent"), wired (for "nervous" or "excited"), and "chill out" (for relax).

Slant Rhyme: See *Consonance*

Slave Narrative: Autobiographical accounts of American slave life as told by escaped slaves. These works first appeared during the abolition movement of the 1830s through the 1850s. Olaudah Equiano's *The Interesting Narrative of Olaudah Equiano, or Gustavus Vassa, The African* and Harriet Ann Jacobs's *Incidents in the Life of a Slave Girl* are examples of the slave narrative.

Social Realism: See *Socialist Realism*

Socialist Realism: The Socialist Realism school of literary theory was proposed by Maxim Gorky and established as a dogma by the first Soviet Congress of Writers. It demanded adherence to a communist worldview in works of literature. Its doctrines required an objective viewpoint comprehensible to the working classes and themes of social struggle featuring strong proletarian heroes. A successful work of socialist realism is Nikolay Ostrovsky's *Kak zakalyalas stal* (*How the Steel Was Tempered*). Also known as Social Realism.

Soliloquy: A monologue in a drama used to give the audience information and to develop the speaker's character. It is typically a projection of the speaker's innermost thoughts. Usually delivered while the speaker is alone on stage, a soliloquy is intended to present an illusion of unspoken reflection. A celebrated soliloquy is Hamlet's "To be or not to be" speech in William Shakespeare's *Hamlet.*

Sonnet: A fourteen-line poem, usually composed in iambic pentameter, employing one of several rhyme schemes. There are three major types of sonnets, upon which all other variations of the form are based: the "Petrarchan" or "Italian" sonnet, the "Shakespearean" or "English" sonnet, and the "Spenserian" sonnet. A Petrarchan sonnet consists of an octave rhymed *abbaabba* and a "sestet" rhymed either *cdecde, cdccdc,* or *cdedce.* The octave poses a question or problem, relates a narrative, or puts forth a proposition; the sestet presents a solution to the problem, comments upon the narrative, or applies the proposition put forth in the octave. The Shakespearean sonnet is divided into three quatrains and a couplet rhymed *abab cdcd efef gg.* The couplet provides an epigrammatic comment on the narrative or problem put forth in the quatrains. The Spenserian sonnet uses three quatrains and a couplet like the Shakespearean, but links their three rhyme schemes in this way: *abab bcbc cdcd ee.* The Spenserian sonnet develops its theme in two parts like the Petrarchan, its final six lines resolving a problem, analyzing a narrative, or applying a proposition put forth in its first eight lines. Examples of sonnets can be found in Petrarch's *Canzoniere,* Edmund Spenser's *Amoretti,* Elizabeth Barrett Browning's *Sonnets from the Portuguese,* Rainer Maria Rilke's *Sonnets to Orpheus,* and Adrienne Rich's poem "The Insusceptibles."

Spenserian Sonnet: See *Sonnet*

Spenserian Stanza: A nine-line stanza having eight verses in iambic pentameter, its ninth verse in iambic hexameter, and the rhyme scheme ababbcbcc. This stanza form was first used by Edmund Spenser in his allegorical poem *The Faerie Queene.*

Spondee: In poetry meter, a foot consisting of two long or stressed syllables occurring together. This form is quite rare in English verse, and is usually composed of two monosyllabic words. The first foot in the following line from Robert Burns's "Green Grow the Rashes" is an example of a spondee: Green grow the rashes, O.

Sprung Rhythm: Versification using a specific number of accented syllables per line but disregarding the number of unaccented syllables that fall in each line, producing an irregular rhythm in the poem. Gerard Manley Hopkins, who coined the term "sprung rhythm," is the most notable practitioner of this technique.

Stanza: A subdivision of a poem consisting of lines grouped together, often in recurring patterns of rhyme, line length, and meter. Stanzas may also serve as units of thought in a poem much like paragraphs in prose. Examples of stanza forms include the quatrain, *terza rima, ottava rima,* Spenserian, and the so-called *In Memoriam* stanza from Alfred, Lord Tennyson's poem by that title. The following is an example of the latter form: Love is and was my lord and king, And in his presence I attend To hear the tidings of my friend, Which every hour his couriers bring.

Stereotype: A stereotype was originally the name for a duplication made during the printing process; this led to its modern definition as a person or thing that is (or is assumed to be) the same as all others of its type. Common stereotypical characters include the absent-minded professor, the nagging wife, the troublemaking teenager, and the kind-hearted grandmother.

Stream of Consciousness: A narrative technique for rendering the inward experience of a character. This technique is designed to give the impression of an ever-changing series of thoughts, emotions, images, and memories in the spontaneous and seemingly illogical order that they occur in life. The textbook example of stream of consciousness is the last section of James Joyce's *Ulysses*.

Structuralism: A twentieth-century movement in literary criticism that examines how literary texts arrive at their meanings, rather than the meanings themselves. There are two major types of structuralist analysis: one examines the way patterns of linguistic structures unify a specific text and emphasize certain elements of that text, and the other interprets the way literary forms and conventions affect the meaning of language itself. Prominent structuralists include Michel Foucault, Roman Jakobson, and Roland Barthes.

Structure: The form taken by a piece of literature. The structure may be made obvious for ease of understanding, as in nonfiction works, or may obscured for artistic purposes, as in some poetry or seemingly "unstructured" prose. Examples of common literary structures include the plot of a narrative, the acts and scenes of a drama, and such poetic forms as the Shakespearean sonnet and the Pindaric ode.

Sturm und Drang: A German term meaning "storm and stress." It refers to a German literary movement of the 1770s and 1780s that reacted against the order and rationalism of the enlightenment, focusing instead on the intense experience of extraordinary individuals. Highly romantic, works of this movement, such as Johann Wolfgang von Goethe's *Gotz von Berlichingen,* are typified by realism, rebelliousness, and intense emotionalism.

Style: A writer's distinctive manner of arranging words to suit his or her ideas and purpose in writing. The unique imprint of the author's personality upon his or her writing, style is the product of an author's way of arranging ideas and his or her use of diction, different sentence structures, rhythm, figures of speech, rhetorical principles, and other elements of composition. Styles may be classified according to period (Metaphysical, Augustan, Georgian), individual authors (Chaucerian, Miltonic, Jamesian), level (grand, middle, low, plain), or language (scientific, expository, poetic, journalistic).

Subject: The person, event, or theme at the center of a work of literature. A work may have one or more subjects of each type, with shorter works tending to have fewer and longer works tending to have more. The subjects of James Baldwin's novel *Go Tell It on the Mountain* include the themes of father-son relationships, religious conversion, black life, and sexuality. The subjects of Anne Frank's *Diary of a Young Girl* include Anne and her family members as well as World War II, the Holocaust, and the themes of war, isolation, injustice, and racism.

Subjectivity: Writing that expresses the author's personal feelings about his subject, and which may or may not include factual information about the subject. Subjectivity is demonstrated in James Joyce's *Portrait of the Artist as a Young Man,* Samuel Butler's *The Way of All Flesh,* and Thomas Wolfe's *Look Homeward, Angel.*

Subplot: A secondary story in a narrative. A subplot may serve as a motivating or complicating force for the main plot of the work, or it may provide emphasis for, or relief from, the main plot. The conflict between the Capulets and the Montagues in William Shakespeare's *Romeo and Juliet* is an example of a subplot.

Surrealism: A term introduced to criticism by Guillaume Apollinaire and later adopted by Andre Breton. It refers to a French literary and artistic movement founded in the 1920s. The Surrealists sought to express unconscious thoughts and feelings in their works. The best-known technique used for achieving this aim was automatic writing— transcriptions of spontaneous outpourings from the unconscious. The Surrealists proposed to unify the contrary levels of conscious and unconscious, dream and reality, objectivity and subjectivity into a new level of "super-realism." Surrealism can be found in the poetry of Paul Eluard, Pierre Reverdy, and Louis Aragon, among others.

Suspense: A literary device in which the author maintains the audience's attention through the buildup of events, the outcome of which will soon be revealed. Suspense in William Shakespeare's *Hamlet* is sustained throughout by the question of whether or not the Prince will achieve what he has been instructed to do and of what he intends to do.

Syllogism: A method of presenting a logical argument. In its most basic form, the syllogism consists of a major premise, a minor premise, and a conclusion. An example of a syllogism is: Major premise: When it snows, the streets get wet. Minor premise: It is snowing. Conclusion: The streets are wet.

Symbol: Something that suggests or stands for something else without losing its original identity. In literature, symbols combine their literal meaning with the suggestion of an abstract concept. Literary symbols are of two types: those that carry complex associations of meaning no matter what their contexts, and those that derive their suggestive meaning from their functions in specific literary works. Examples of symbols are sunshine suggesting happiness, rain suggesting sorrow, and storm clouds suggesting despair.

Symbolism: This term has two widely accepted meanings. In historical criticism, it denotes an early modernist literary movement initiated in France during the nineteenth century that reacted against the prevailing standards of realism. Writers in this movement aimed to evoke, indirectly and symbolically, an order of being beyond the material world of the five senses. Poetic expression of personal emotion figured strongly in the movement, typically by means of a private set of symbols uniquely identifiable with the individual poet. The principal aim of the Symbolists was to express in words the highly complex feelings that grew out of everyday contact with the world. In a broader sense, the term "symbolism" refers to the use of one object to represent another. Early members of the Symbolist movement included the French authors Charles Baudelaire and Arthur Rimbaud; William Butler Yeats, James Joyce, and T. S. Eliot were influenced as the movement moved to Ireland, England, and the United States. Examples of the concept of symbolism include a flag that stands for a nation or movement, or an empty cupboard used to suggest hopelessness, poverty, and despair.

Symbolist: See *Symbolism*

Symbolist Movement: See *Symbolism*

Sympathetic Fallacy: See *Affective Fallacy*

T

Tale: A story told by a narrator with a simple plot and little character development. Tales are usually relatively short and often carry a simple message. Examples of tales can be found in the work of Rudyard Kipling, Somerset Maugham, Saki, Anton Chekhov, Guy de Maupassant, and Armistead Maupin.

Tall Tale: A humorous tale told in a straightforward, credible tone but relating absolutely impossible events or feats of the characters. Such tales were commonly told of frontier adventures during the settlement of the west in the United States. Tall tales have been spun around such legendary heroes as Mike Fink, Paul Bunyan, Davy Crockett, Johnny Appleseed, and Captain Stormalong as well as the real-life William F. Cody and Annie Oakley. Literary use of tall tales can be found in Washington Irving's *History of New York,* Mark Twain's *Life on the Mississippi,* and in the German R. F. Raspe's *Baron Munchausen's Narratives of His Marvellous Travels and Campaigns in Russia.*

Tanka: A form of Japanese poetry similar to *haiku.* A *tanka* is five lines long, with the lines containing five, seven, five, seven, and seven syllables respectively. Skilled *tanka* authors include Ishikawa Takuboku, Masaoka Shiki, Amy Lowell, and Adelaide Crapsey.

Teatro Grottesco: See *Theater of the Grotesque*

Terza Rima: A three-line stanza form in poetry in which the rhymes are made on the last word of each line in the following manner: the first and third lines of the first stanza, then the second line of the first stanza and the first and third lines of the second stanza, and so on with the middle line of any stanza rhyming with the first and third lines of the following stanza. An example of *terza rima* is Percy Bysshe Shelley's "The Triumph of Love": As in that trance of wondrous thought I lay This was the tenour of my waking dream. Methought I sate beside a public way Thick strewn with summer dust, and a great stream Of people there was hurrying to and fro Numerous as gnats upon the evening gleam, . . .

Tetrameter: See *Meter*

Textual Criticism: A branch of literary criticism that seeks to establish the authoritative text of a literary work. Textual critics typically compare all known manuscripts or printings of a single work in order to assess the meanings of differences and revisions. This procedure allows them to arrive at a definitive version that (supposedly) corresponds to the author's original intention. Textual criticism was applied during the Renaissance to salvage the classical texts of Greece and Rome, and modern works have been studied, for instance, to undo deliberate correction or censorship, as in the case of novels by Stephen Crane and Theodore Dreiser.

Theater of Cruelty: Term used to denote a group of theatrical techniques designed to eliminate the psychological and emotional distance between actors and audience. This concept, introduced in the 1930s in France, was intended to inspire a more intense theatrical experience than conventional theater allowed. The "cruelty" of this dramatic theory signified not sadism but heightened actor/audience involvement in the dramatic event. The theater of cruelty was theorized by Antonin Artaud in his *Le Theatre et son double* (*The Theatre and Its Double*), and also appears in the work of Jerzy Grotowski, Jean Genet, Jean Vilar, and Arthur Adamov, among others.

Theater of the Absurd: A post-World War II dramatic trend characterized by radical theatrical innovations. In works influenced by the Theater of the Absurd, nontraditional, sometimes grotesque characterizations, plots, and stage sets reveal a meaningless universe in which human values are irrelevant. Existentialist themes of estrangement, absurdity, and futility link many of the works of this movement. The principal writers of the Theater of the Absurd are Samuel Beckett, Eugene Ionesco, Jean Genet, and Harold Pinter.

Theater of the Grotesque: An Italian theatrical movement characterized by plays written around the ironic and macabre aspects of daily life in the World War I era. Theater of the Grotesque was named after the play

The Mask and the Face by Luigi Chiarelli, which was described as "a grotesque in three acts." The movement influenced the work of Italian dramatist Luigi Pirandello, author of *Right You Are, If You Think You Are*. Also known as *Teatro Grottesco*.

Theme: The main point of a work of literature. The term is used interchangeably with thesis. The theme of William Shakespeare's *Othello*—jealousy—is a common one.

Thesis: A thesis is both an essay and the point argued in the essay. Thesis novels and thesis plays share the quality of containing a thesis which is supported through the action of the story. A master's thesis and a doctoral dissertation are two theses required of graduate students.

Thesis Play: See *Thesis*

Three Unities: See *Unities*

Tone: The author's attitude toward his or her audience may be deduced from the tone of the work. A formal tone may create distance or convey politeness, while an informal tone may encourage a friendly, intimate, or intrusive feeling in the reader. The author's attitude toward his or her subject matter may also be deduced from the tone of the words he or she uses in discussing it. The tone of John F. Kennedy's speech which included the appeal to "ask not what your country can do for you" was intended to instill feelings of camaraderie and national pride in listeners.

Tragedy: A drama in prose or poetry about a noble, courageous hero of excellent character who, because of some tragic character flaw or *hamartia*, brings ruin upon him- or herself. Tragedy treats its subjects in a dignified and serious manner, using poetic language to help evoke pity and fear and bring about catharsis, a purging of these emotions. The tragic form was practiced extensively by the ancient Greeks. In the Middle Ages, when classical works were virtually unknown, tragedy came to denote any works about the fall of persons from exalted to low conditions due to any reason: fate, vice, weakness, etc. According to the classical definition of tragedy, such works present the "pathetic"—that which evokes pity—rather than the tragic. The classical form of tragedy was revived in the sixteenth century;

it flourished especially on the Elizabethan stage. In modern times, dramatists have attempted to adapt the form to the needs of modern society by drawing their heroes from the ranks of ordinary men and women and defining the nobility of these heroes in terms of spirit rather than exalted social standing. The greatest classical example of tragedy is Sophocles' *Oedipus Rex*. The "pathetic" derivation is exemplified in "The Monk's Tale" in Geoffrey Chaucer's *Canterbury Tales*. Notable works produced during the sixteenth century revival include William Shakespeare's *Hamlet, Othello,* and *King Lear*. Modern dramatists working in the tragic tradition include Henrik Ibsen, Arthur Miller, and Eugene O'Neill.

Tragedy of Blood: See *Revenge Tragedy*

Tragic Flaw: In a tragedy, the quality within the hero or heroine which leads to his or her downfall. Examples of the tragic flaw include Othello's jealousy and Hamlet's indecisiveness, although most great tragedies defy such simple interpretation.

Transcendentalism: An American philosophical and religious movement, based in New England from around 1835 until the Civil War. Transcendentalism was a form of American romanticism that had its roots abroad in the works of Thomas Carlyle, Samuel Coleridge, and Johann Wolfgang von Goethe. The Transcendentalists stressed the importance of intuition and subjective experience in communication with God. They rejected religious dogma and texts in favor of mysticism and scientific naturalism. They pursued truths that lie beyond the "colorless" realms perceived by reason and the senses and were active social reformers in public education, women's rights, and the abolition of slavery. Prominent members of the group include Ralph Waldo Emerson and Henry David Thoreau.

Trickster: A character or figure common in Native American and African literature who uses his ingenuity to defeat enemies and escape difficult situations. Tricksters are most often animals, such as the spider, hare, or coyote, although they may take the form of humans as well. Examples of trickster tales include Thomas King's *A Coyote Columbus Story*, Ashley F. Bryan's *The Dancing Granny* and Ishmael Reed's *The Last Days of Louisiana Red*.

Trimeter: See *Meter*

Triple Rhyme: See *Rhyme*

Trochee: See *Foot*

U

Understatement: See *Irony*

Unities: Strict rules of dramatic structure, formulated by Italian and French critics of the Renaissance and based loosely on the principles of drama discussed by Aristotle in his *Poetics*. Foremost among these rules were the three unities of action, time, and place that compelled a dramatist to: (1) construct a single plot with a beginning, middle, and end that details the causal relationships of action and character; (2) restrict the action to the events of a single day; and (3) limit the scene to a single place or city. The unities were observed faithfully by continental European writers until the Romantic Age, but they were never regularly observed in English drama. Modern dramatists are typically more concerned with a unity of impression or emotional effect than with any of the classical unities. The unities are observed in Pierre Corneille's tragedy *Polyeuctes* and Jean-Baptiste Racine's *Phedre*. Also known as Three Unities.

Urban Realism: A branch of realist writing that attempts to accurately reflect the often harsh facts of modern urban existence. Some works by Stephen Crane, Theodore Dreiser, Charles Dickens, Fyodor Dostoyevsky, Emile Zola, Abraham Cahan, and Henry Fuller feature urban realism. Modern examples include Claude Brown's *Manchild in the Promised Land* and Ron Milner's *What the Wine Sellers Buy*.

Utopia: A fictional perfect place, such as "paradise" or "heaven." Early literary utopias were included in Plato's *Republic* and Sir Thomas More's *Utopia*, while more modern utopias can be found in Samuel Butler's *Erewhon*, Theodor Herzka's *A Visit to Freeland*, and H. G. Wells' *A Modern Utopia*.

Utopian: See *Utopia*

Utopianism: See *Utopia*

V

Verisimilitude: Literally, the appearance of truth. In literary criticism, the term refers to aspects of a work of literature that seem true to the reader. Verisimilitude is achieved in the work of Honore de Balzac, Gustave Flaubert, and Henry James, among other late nineteenth-century realist writers.

Vers de societe: See *Occasional Verse*

Vers libre: See *Free Verse*

Verse: A line of metered language, a line of a poem, or any work written in verse. The following line of verse is from the epic poem *Don Juan* by Lord Byron: "My way is to begin with the beginning."

Versification: The writing of verse. Versification may also refer to the meter, rhyme, and other mechanical components of a poem. Composition of a "Roses are red, violets are blue" poem to suit an occasion is a common form of versification practiced by students.

Victorian: Refers broadly to the reign of Queen Victoria of England (1837-1901) and to anything with qualities typical of that era. For example, the qualities of smug narrowmindedness, bourgeois materialism, faith in social progress, and priggish morality are often considered Victorian. This stereotype is contradicted by such dramatic intellectual developments as the theories of Charles Darwin, Karl Marx, and Sigmund Freud (which stirred strong debates in England) and the critical attitudes of serious Victorian writers like Charles Dickens and George Eliot. In literature, the Victorian Period was the great age of the English novel, and the latter part of the era saw the rise of movements such as decadence and symbolism. Works of Victorian literature include the poetry of Robert Browning and Alfred, Lord Tennyson, the criticism of Matthew Arnold and John Ruskin, and the novels of Emily Bronte, William Makepeace Thackeray, and Thomas Hardy. Also known as Victorian Age and Victorian Period.

Victorian Age: See *Victorian*

Victorian Period: See *Victorian*

W

Weltanschauung: A German term referring to a person's worldview or philosophy. Examples of *weltanschauung* include Thomas Hardy's view of the human being as the victim of fate, destiny, or impersonal forces and circumstances, and the disillusioned and laconic cynicism expressed by such poets of the 1930s as W. H. Auden, Sir Stephen Spender, and Sir William Empson.

Weltschmerz: A German term meaning "world pain." It describes a sense of anguish about the nature of existence, usually associated with a melancholy, pessimistic attitude. *Weltschmerz* was expressed in England by George Gordon, Lord Byron in his *Manfred* and *Childe Harold's Pilgrimage,* in France by Viscount de Chateaubriand, Alfred de Vigny, and Alfred de Musset, in Russia by Aleksandr Pushkin and Mikhail Lermontov, in Poland by Juliusz Slowacki, and in America by Nathaniel Hawthorne.

Z

Zarzuela: A type of Spanish operetta. Writers of *zarzuelas* include Lope de Vega and Pedro Calderon.

Zeitgeist: A German term meaning "spirit of the time." It refers to the moral and intellectual trends of a given era. Examples of *zeitgeist* include the preoccupation with the more morbid aspects of dying and death in some Jacobean literature, especially in the works of dramatists Cyril Tourneur and John Webster, and the decadence of the French Symbolists.

Cumulative
Author/Title Index

Cumulative Nationality/Ethnicity Index

Subject/Theme Index